Lawrence Nicodemus's

Coeur d'Alene Dictionary

in Root Format

Lawrence Nicodemus, circa 2000, courtesy of Sacred Heart Mission, DeSmet, ID.

Lawrence Nicodemus, 1930. Gonzaga High School Senior portrait, scanned from *The Luigian*. Courtesy Jennifer Doolittle, Gonzaga Preparatory School, Spokane, WA.

UM

OCCASIONAL PAPERS IN LINGUISTICS NO. 20, 2007

LAWRENCE NICODEMUS'S

COEUR D'ALENE DICTIONARY

IN ROOT FORMAT

Edited by

JOHN LYON AND REBECCA GREENE-WOOD

With a Biographical Note by
RAYMOND BRINKMAN

First Published October 2007

UMOPL — A series dedicated to the study
of the Native languages of the Northwest.

SERIES EDITORS
Anthony Mattina, University of Montana (anthony.mattina@umontana.edu)
Timothy Montler, University of North Texas (montler@unt.edu)

Address all correspondence to:
    UMOPL — Linguistics Laboratory
    The University of Montana
    Missoula, MT 59812
    USA

Library of Congress Cataloging-in-Publication Data

Nicodemus, Lawrence G., 1909-

Lawrence Nicodemus's Coeur d'Alene dictionary in root format / edited by John Lyon
and Rebecca Greene-Wood ; with a biographical note by Raymond Brinkman.
p. cm. -- (University of Montana occasional papers in linguistics; no. 20)
Rev. ed. of: Snchitsu'umshtsn.
Includes bibliographical references.

ISBN 978-1-879763-20-3 (pbk. : alk. paper)

1. Coeur d'Alene language--Dictionaries--English. 2. English language--Dictionaries--
Coeur d'Alene. 3. Coeur d'Alene language--Grammar. I. Lyon, John, 1975- II. Greene-
Wood, Rebecca, 1981- III. Nicodemus, Lawrence G., 1909- Snchitsu'umshtsn. IV. Title.

PM916.Z5N53 2007

497'.943--dc22

2007027195

TABLE OF CONTENTS

ACKNOWLEDGMENTS

First and foremost, we would like to thank Anthony Mattina for his great knowledge of Colville-Okanagan and the Salish language family, his suggestions for the content and organization of this work, his patience in helping us develop our technical writing skills, and for always taking time from his many other projects to help with this dictionary.

Secondly, we wish to thank Raymond Brinkman, director of the Coeur d'Alene Language Program, for his enthusiastic support of this project, and for his insights into the problematic entries of Chapter III.

We also wish to thank Nancy Mattina, director of the University of Montana Writing Center, for her editorial recommendations as well as her dedication to Salish language dictionary work.

In addition, we would like to express our gratitude to Mizuki Miyashita and Tully Thibeau of the University of Montana Linguistics Program for their recognizing the importance of linguistic diversity and their dedication to the science of linguistics.

Lastly, we would like to express our gratitude toward the Salish Research Foundation and its president, Mrs. M. Terry Thompson, for its financial contribution to our work. Their publication subsidy helped to defray some of the printing costs in order to make this work available to the public.

LIST OF SYMBOLS

√	Lexical Root
+	Boundary of derivational affix
-	Boundary of inflectional affix
=	Boundary of lexical affix
'	Glottalization
‿	Tie under (following proclitic set of intransitive pronouns čn, kʷ, č, kʷp)
†	Intransitive entries
‡	Transitive entries
//	Complex entries
§	Compound entries
[ ]	Brackets for editorial emendations within the dictionary and for special symbols in Chapter II.
< >	Brackets that enclose Nicodemus's transcriptions
/ /	Brackets that enclose phonemic data

LIST OF ABBREVIATIONS

adj	adjective		neg	negative
adv	adverb		onom	onomatopoeic
conj	conjunction		orig	originally
dim	diminutive		pl	plural
etym	etymology		pref	prefix
excl	exclamation		prep	preposition
gr	greeting		pro(n)	pronoun
h/h	his, her		qu	question
h/h/i	him, her, it		ref	referring to
h/s/i	he, she, it		sg	singular
imp	imperative		suf(f)	suffix
interj	interjection		v	verb
lit	literally		vi	verb intransitive
l.w.	loan word (lexical borrowing)		vt	verb transitive
metaph	metaphor(ically)		w/c	which
N	Nicodemus		xref	cross-reference
n	noun			

Coeur d'Alene Consonant Phoneme Chart

	labial	alveo-lar	alveo-palatal	lateral	palatal	labio-velar	uvular	labio-uvular	pharyn geal	labio-pharyn geal	glottal
Voiceless Stops and Affricates	p	t	c		č	kʷ	q	qʷ			ʔ
Glottalized Voiceless Stops and Affricates	p'	t'	c'		č'	k'ʷ	q'	q'ʷ			
Voiced Stops and Affricates	b	d			ǰ	gʷ					
Voiceless Fricatives		s		ł	š	xʷ	x̌	x̌ʷ			h
Plain Resonants	m	n	r	l	y	w			ʕ	ʕʷ	
Glottalized Resonants	m'	n'	r'	l'	y'	w'			ʕ'	ʕ'ʷ	

BIOGRAPHICAL NOTE

Lawrence Nicodemus (1909-2004)

Julia Antelope Nicodemus wanted her son Lawrence to go to Gonzaga High School in Spokane, WA. He had entered the Jesuit boarding school in DeSmet, ID in 1918 at the age of nine, subsequently been a good student, and had successfully completed the eighth grade, as far as he could go at the Boys' School, then. Entering as a native speaker of *Coeur d'Alene*, only, he succeeded through tutoring in mastering English and his classes.

However, Father Post did not think that Lawrence was yet prepared for the academic rigors of the Jesuit high school, so convinced Julia to keep Lawrence in DeSmet to take an additional year of Latin and Greek.

Lawrence did not, in later years, ever mention that he had applied what he learned about grammatical analysis from his Classics studies to his native *Coeur d'Alene* before 1929, but when he met Gladys Reichard during her fieldwork in Idaho, everything fell into place. She had already met and worked with his paternal grandmother at her home east of the Mission. Dorothy Nicodemus was the widow of James Teit's chief consultant in 1904 for the Coeur d'Alene ethnography (Teit 1930). In 1929 Gladys Reichard was working with Julia on transcriptions and translations of the old woman's stories. Lawrence did recount the moment when Reichard asked Julia a grammar-related question about *Coeur d'Alene*, and Lawrence volunteered the answer from an adjoining room. They were working in his mother's house in the Moctelme Valley and Lawrence was home for the summer.

Gladys Reichard was in her second season of summer fieldwork at the request of Franz Boas, investigating *Coeur d'Alene*. Meeting Dorothy had been fortuitous. Reichard's goal had been *Coeur d'Alene*, but the lack of success finding speakers two years earlier had almost convinced her to work with *Spokan* speakers instead. However, the one resident native speaker who seemed most likely to offer her assistance in understanding the grammar of *Spokan* was unreliable. She instead found that Julia was more than a competent translator of Dorothy. Julia also assisted Reichard's understanding of *Coeur d'Alene* grammar.

Lawrence had another set of talents, including acquisition of those skills necessary to write the language. Not only was he fluent in *Coeur d'Alene*, like the other members of his mother's and father's families, and fluent in English after his boarding school training, he had several years of study in Reichard's undergraduate major, Latin.

Lawrence graduated from Gonzaga High School in 1930. As Reichard notes in the foreword to her grammar (1938), he stayed in New York during the 1935-36 school year at Columbia University while they collaborated on her publications about the language.

Had the avenue been open to him, Lawrence might have become a scholar. For several years as an adolescent and young adult he considered the priesthood as a vocation. The Depression forced him to abandon his studies at Gonzaga University, though in the subsequent decades an income from his family's farm leases allowed him to pursue independent studies and contributions to his tribe.

When World War II broke out, Lawrence edited and published a newsletter mailed to tribal men and women serving in the armed forces. The *Morning Star* not only reported on Reservation life for tribal members abroad, it reported the war for the Idaho community. Letters home to Lawrence became, essentially, dispatches from the European and Pacific theaters. The newsletter also became a repository for tribal lore and accounts of customs from elder contributors, through Lawrence's interviews.

After the war Lawrence Nicodemus served as the Coeur d'Alene Tribal Judge. His experience motivated him to complete a law degree by correspondence through LaSalle College in Chicago. His final exam for his degree was proctored locally by Lawrence's godson, the Spokane civil rights attorney Carl Maxey, who himself had been raised at the DeSmet Mission. Lawrence used his training as an advocate for tribal legal rights, and served on the Coeur d'Alene Tribal Council in the 1950s.

Following his mother's death in 1969, Lawrence returned to college and received a bachelor's degree in music from Eastern Washington State College (now, University) in Cheney, WA., at the age of sixty-four.

In the mid 1970s Lawrence Nicodemus's talents as a linguist came to the fore again and the last thirty years of his life were marked by scholarly contribution. The community of linguists and anthropologists working on Salish family languages grew after 1960. Lawrence's legendary contributions a generation earlier led graduate students to seek him out. He remained the expert and primary consultant to five Ph.D. dissertations and a number of scholarly articles in the subsequent decades. In 1975 the Coeur d'Alene Tribe published his self-study course in the tribal language. The primer, two-volume dictionary, and audio cassette package were delivered to every Reservation family, and remain an invaluable record of the language.

In the mid 1980s Lawrence was a co-author of two publications funded by the Idaho Humanities Council. One is a record of tribal family and historical names in *Coeur d'Alene*; the other is an ethnogeography of *Coeur d'Alene* place names for the aboriginal territory. Several tribal elders contributed significantly to both works, but Lawrence was the primary source of technical expertise on the *Coeur d'Alene* terms.

Even if there were decades between Lawrence's own output in materials in *Coeur d'Alene*, those skills came in mighty handy in the latter part of his life when he was sought after by students, assisted the Tribe, and became the living authority for the tribe's heritage language revitalization efforts. It was unfortunate that only he remained to consult on grammatical matters. It was extraordinarily fortunate that he could do so brilliantly.

In the 1990s there was an efflorescence of Coeur d'Alene Tribe-sponsored activities to revitalize the heritage language. The Tribe procured grants and used its gaming revenues to create a Tribal Language Program, develop a curriculum for *Coeur d'Alene* instruction at Lakeside High School in Plummer, ID, and support a college course in the language. Lawrence Nicodemus, then in his late eighties, was a tireless contributor to each of those activities.

He was forced to retire in the Fall 2003 in declining health after breaking his hip, yet remained a cheerful advisor to employees who worked with him until his final days. In July of that same year, on his ninety-fourth birthday, he spent the afternoon at the Language Center working on *Coeur d'Alene*. He was cared for in his home the last few years by descendents of his mother's family.

* * *

The Root Dictionary project renews my appreciation for the dictionary Lawrence authored among materials he produced for the Coeur d'Alene people in 1975. He called his primer "A Modern Course" for self-study, hoping, I think, that the basic introduction to making *Coeur d'Alene* sentences would encourage and motivate students of the language from among the tribal membership. More than twenty years later he was the indispensable consultant to the creation of a high school curriculum at Lakeside High School in Plummer, ID, attending classes nearly five days per week for two school terms annually, for six years. At the same time he was a regular attendee and consultant for college classes in introductory *Coeur d'Alene*, and a part-time employee and consultant for the Coeur d'Alene Tribe's Language Program.

But in 1975 the dictionary was not intended for regular classes, nor did it offer more than a cursory mention of grammatical features. I suspect that its genesis was the stem-list Reichard published in 1939, distilled from Dorothy's texts and Reichard's work with Lawrence and his mother. I believe that secondarily the mid 1970s work began from a model English language dictionary and translated entries from it into *Coeur d'Alene*.

It was Lawrence's joy and practice to both derive roots from longer *Coeur d'Alene* forms and phrases, and to work in the other direction; he answered multiple requests for *Coeur d'Alene* expressions; in classes, from the public and the tribal membership, and from the governmental offices of the Tribe. He had an unmatched sense for how to do that. Lawrence's dictionary, too, is primarily a collection of texts he never uttered, sentences coined for the purposes of demonstrating the range of the language. Therein lies all of the paradigms he first recognized in the collaboration with Reichard, fleshed out according to how he intuited grammaticality in *Coeur d'Alene*. In some sections of the dictionary he piled on the inflections and the derivations.

Rebecca Greene and John Lyon have taken the content of the two volumes and sorted it in such a way that Lawrence's information is consolidated, and organized. The Root Dictionary routinely points us toward entries we've never noticed in the dictionary, making connections among entries that are otherwise separated across pages (or volumes). It also points out some of the ambiguities. Reichard made mistakes. Lawrence didn't resolve all of them, and was capable of mistakes, or at least changed his mind, sometimes, in his later years. There are plenty of editing mistakes that didn't get corrected before the Nicodemus dictionary went to print, but there are also instances when Lawrence couldn't decide in favor of a post-velar, or not, or a glottalized stop, or not. Reichard struggled with some of that. Those of us who work in the Language Program struggle with it, and our remaining consultants do, too. The Root Dictionary pulls together some of those contradictions and shows us that we're in good company.

It's not just that John and Becky have compiled or sorted entries, however. Their morphological analyses offer the reader insight into Lawrence's often impossibly long forms. They show how the language works in ways not otherwise transparent to casual students or tribal members curious about *Coeur d'Alene*. The analyses are also instructive for those serious students trying to internalize grammar lessons and coin new sentences. This is a place where Lawrence's word play comes to the fore.

It's astonishing how much Lawrence accomplished, given that he was the only contributor to the original dictionary entries. Note how full some of the entries are in the Root Dictionary. Today we might not organize a dictionary according to phrases that mean 'not,' but look at how many ways Lawrence showed us how to say something in *Coeur d'Alene* by stating its obverse. Or at the semantic field for 'sweetness': éclairs, huckleberries, Waverly, WA ('it has sweetness'), cookies, brown sugar, diabetes, among many, many other examples. We just don't have any other evidence that another *Coeur d'Alene* speaker had the vocabulary that Lawrence did.

In his later years, beginning in 1993, we in the Tribal program created opportunities for him to challenge the range of his knowledge of *Coeur d'Alene*. We had regular Wednesday lunch meetings with the remaining native speakers and the discussions helped jog memories and sharpen recall. Lawrence often had something to say during those discussions, about phonetic detail or grammaticality that entered into our records, and into what was instructed to classes.

This was the kind of work he *loved* doing, even as he aged and his health declined. In his last few months before retirement, he could still be found answering, as always, the same kinds of questions about stem composition, phonetic detail, and nuances in meaning.

He would be thrilled at the Root Dictionary. He would dearly appreciate how John and Becky have preserved his own way of doing things, utilizing his practical orthography in the contents of each of the entries, especially as they've completed the morphological analyses for us. It's the information he wanted to convey, how affixation created sound and music and humor and insight in *Coeur d'Alene*, and allowed his family, his friends, and his tribe to say everything they possibly wanted to say about their culture.

He thought every one of those entries through. He'd have been delighted that these two students of *Coeur d'Alene* have come along and done the same, have learned enough of the grammar to understand what he's tried to demonstrate about the language, and then pulled together all of his information. We could convince him, easily, that the use of a phonetic alphabet in the root entries allow students to compare the *Coeur d'Alene* stems across the language family, according to the ways that the Spokanes, the Flatheads, the Colvilles and others are teaching their students. That was one of his stated goals in the introductory material in his dictionary.

He wasn't given to more than a passing interest in technologies; he'd know that it wasn't a computer program that created this volume. He of all people would appreciate how much work went into this; the delight in recognizing underlying forms, the puzzle in settling among competing, reasonable explanations, the juxtapositions among expressions born of the same roots.

For the serious tribal students of the language, especially those building up their vocabularies as a function of their greater grasp of the grammar, there's insight and value to be found in the Root Dictionary. There is otherwise no one to ask, no place to look, for information about the semantic range of these roots; it's become near impossible to surmise which would necessarily be most appropriate in a desired circumstance. No one living has quite the felicity with the language to coin expressions.

Lawrence did. He tried to tell everyone that it was still possible to learn how to do so, with as many examples as he could muster. He sat through hundreds of high school and college classes, letting someone else offer the explanations of how *Coeur d'Alene* grammar works, so that he could serve as the expert consultant when the time came to try it out on a native speaker.

This volume is one place where we can reasonably say, "This is everything Lawrence had to say about making *Coeur d'Alene* words and sentences," now in a way that is student-friendly. It is a terrific way to honor and perpetuate Lawrence's singular efforts.

Raymond Brinkman, Director
hnqwa'qwe'eln
[Coeur d'Alene Language Center]
Coeur d'Alene Tribe
Plummer, ID

INTRODUCTION

This introductory chapter provides a brief description of the Coeur d'Alene language, the linguistic work of Gladys Reichard and Lawrence Nicodemus, as well as a description of the *Snchitsu'umshtsn*[1] dictionary and factors which motivated the editors to undertake this project. In Chapter II, we explain the methodology that we have used in reworking the original data into a new edition. Chapter III provides an exhaustive account of our editorial emendations.

1.1 Language Background

The Coeur d'Alene language is a member of the Interior Branch of the Salish family, which consists of seven languages spoken from central British Columbia, through Washington, Idaho and western Montana. These languages are Lillooet, Shuswap, Thompson, Moses-Columbian, Okanagan, Spokane-Kalispel-Flathead, and Coeur d'Alene. The last four are closely related and comprise the southern subset of the Interior Salish group.

Linguistic research on Coeur d'Alene began in 1927 with Gladys Reichard, who over the next several years produced a grammar and numerous field notes. Lawrence Nicodemus, a native Coeur d'Alene, worked with Reichard both as she was doing research in Idaho, and later at Columbia University. Nicodemus compiled a two volume Coeur d'Alene dictionary (*Snchitsu'umshtsn*) in the 1970's. Understanding the close ties between language and cultural identity, Nicodemus had hoped that this dictionary, as well as a language learning manual with cassettes, would help younger members of the Coeur d'Alene community learn the language which he had grown up speaking.

Lawrence Nicodemus passed away during the summer of 2004. Members of the community have expressed regret at his passing, and his memory is held in high esteem. He asks a question, in regard to saving the language, in the preface to the original edition: "Is it too late to do something about it?". Today, there are only three semi-fluent speakers left, a fact which greatly increases the relative importance of written records.

1.2 The Motivation for a New Edition

Snchitsu'umshtsn is a two volume bilingual dictionary printed by University Press, Spokane, in 1975. Volume I is Coeur d'Alene-English, with approximately 8,000 entries arranged in alphabetical order, beginning with the Coeur d'Alene and followed by grammatical notations and the English translation, as seen in the following examples:

---

[1] The indigenous name for the Coeur d'Alene language, literally *language of the discovered people*.

1

(1.) a.   na'qhiɫ etspiyichtmistkwlsh, v. Maybe you (pl.) delight them.

  b.   na'qhiɫ etspiyichtmistmekhw, v. Maybe you (sg.) delight me.

  c.   na'qhiɫ etspiyichtmistmelp, v. Maybe you (pl.) delight me.

  d.   peypiyt, adj. delightful.

  e.   piy, adj. happy.

Volume II is English-Coeur d'Alene, and provides an additional 9,035 entries on 360 pages. These entries are arranged alphabetically by English translation, grammatical notation and Coeur d'Alene transcription, as seen in the following examples:

(2.) a.   *comrade*, n. s'laqht.

  b.   *friend*, n. laqh (stem).

  c.   *friend*, n. s'laqht.

  d.   *sociable*, adj. aa'laqht'm'nshesh (lit. H/s usually makes friends).

The two volumes overlap by 78%, but there is nevertheless additional information in each volume which is not present in the other.

Two factors motivate the reworking of this dictionary: organization and orthography. As seen in examples (1a-c), the entries are listed alphabetically by the first word <na'qhiɫ> which translates as *maybe*. <na'qhiɫ> is followed by longer morphological material containing the recurring segment <piy>. Next, by looking at the entries <peypiyt> or <piy> in examples (1d-e), it becomes clear that the recurring form <piy> is common to all entries in example (1). <piy> is a lexical root which translates as *happy* or *delight*. Lexical roots are recurring forms, with the usual shape CVC(C), that we have identified after parsing words into inflectional and derivational components. In the alphabetical English listings of volume II, some related entries, such as those pertaining to *friend* (see example (2)), do occur consecutively; however, many other entries which are based on the lexical root <laqh>, such as words that translate as *comrade* or *sociable*, do not. Although the form <laqh> is clearly present in the entry translated as *sociable*, the researcher who is using Nicodemus's volume II is compelled to search the dictionary for words that share this lexical root; a task which this dictionary will render unnecessary. In reworking *Snchitsu'umshtsn*, we use lexical roots, such as <piy> and <laqh>, as common denominators for organizing all entries. In order to help the researcher look up data, we also arrange these lexical roots by their root consonant skeleta. A root consonant skeleton consists of the consonants that comprise a lexical root, minus the vowel[2]. For example, the root consonant skeleton for <piy> is indicated by √py.

Nicodemus's practical orthography presents the Coeur d'Alene language in a "more popular, less scientific form for the benefit of the layman who wishes to master the language." (Nicodemus I, iv.). Unfortunately, this orthography (similar in some ways to the orthography used by Reichard), necessarily complicates the task of the researcher who wants to identify cognates, as well as grasp the derivational and inflectional systems of the language. By reworking Nicodemus's data using a standard Salish orthography generally accepted in contemporary linguistic circles, we hope to simplify the task of the

---

[2] See section 2.3.1 for our rationale behind this method of organization.

linguistic researcher. We also hope that the Native community may find the organization and orthography of this project useful for their language program.

During the course of this project, we have consulted the grammars of Reichard (1938) and Doak (1997), which have been extremely helpful. We discuss the aspects of Coeur d'Alene grammar relevant to this dictionary in Chapters II and III, and the appendices.

The Coeur d'Alene people prefer Nicodemus's orthography, perhaps in deference to an esteemed member of the community. Learners who are literate in English and who wish to learn Coeur d'Alene can rely on their native knowledge of English to "sound out" a word in Coeur d'Alene, with notable exceptions[3]. If continuing efforts on the reservation using Nicodemus's orthography can stimulate interest in the language and a viable language environment for Coeur d'Alene, while linguists using a standard Salish orthography gain a greater understanding of the language family and individual languages, then a common goal of interest in, respect for, and utilization of the language will have been reached.

---

[3] The exceptions are: pharyngeals, written as parentheses; /ł/; and glottal stop, written as an apostrophe.

METHODS

Snchitsu'umshtsn volume I (Coeur d'Alene-English) was edited by Rebecca Greene-Wood as an MA thesis at the University of Montana in 2004. It seemed appropriate that volume II (English-Coeur d'Alene) should be reworked in a similar manner, and so *Snchitsu'umshtsn* volume II (English-Coeur d'Alene) was edited by John Lyon as an MA thesis at the University of Montana in 2005.

The reworking of the two volumes consisted of essentially the same process, which we outline in this chapter. We will discuss the following stages of the project and give examples that show the progress of our work through these stages: scanning and proofreading (2.1), root identification and morphemic analysis (2.2), and the collapsing of root entries under a single root header (2.3).

2.1 Scanning of Original Data

First, we scanned all pages containing lexical entries into ten Word files, each containing an average of 2.6 alphabetical sections under which they were originally grouped[4]. The scanner did not recognize non-English characters such as /ł/, which we manually inserted during proofreading. We reorganized the material by aligning the scanned lexical entries, italicizing Nicodemus's English translation, then proofreading and correcting mis-scanned characters. This process took approximately one month for volume II, during which time we became aware of other errors, such as duplicate entries and entries with no Coeur d'Alene form. Some entries were duplicate, with the exception of an underlined vowel, meant to indicate stress[5]:

(1.)   a.   *hoof*, n. sts'u̲'shn.
       b.   *hoof*, n. sts'u'shn.

Other times, glottalization marks (apostrophes) or consonants were underlined. We analyze these occurrences as typographical errors, which must nevertheless be dealt with on a case-by-case basis. We catalog all such errors in Chapter III.

Nicodemus organized the lexical entries of volume II as follows: the English word, followed by grammatical notations, the Coeur d'Alene form, and optional additional information in English which is usually a literal interpretation of the entry. Here are a few examples of scanned and proofed entries:

---

[4] Over half of volume II covers the first four letters of the alphabet, with the remaining 22 letters occupying less than half of the dictionary.

[5] All examples in this chapter are taken from volume II.

(2.) a. fried (I...the meat), vt. ts'aqhn.

     b. friend, n. laqh (stem).

     c. friend, n. s'laqht.

     d. friend (intimate...), n. sdumtsn.

     e. friendly, adj. aa'laqht'm'nshesh (lit. H/s usually makes friends).

Some entries contain additional information after the initial English word, as seen in (2a).

After we scanned and proofread the entries, we transliterated the Coeur d'Alene and replaced Nicodemus's orthography with standard Salish characters using macro commands[6]. The result is shown in the following example:

(3.) *Circling Raven*, n. Shlltshłmnachalqs → šlltšłmnačalqs

The above example shows that we represent <sh> as /š/ and <ch> as /č/. Although we had to check the macro-generated transcriptions in all cases, this macro saved countless hours during which we otherwise would have devoted to manually re-transliterating each lexical entry. The macro also moved the new transliteration, written with a custom Coeur d'Alene font, to the head of the entry. Nicodemus's original material follows, as seen in (4):

(4.) **lut smiyesčínt.** *commoner*, n. lut smiyeschint (lit. He is not a nobleman).

The aim of the new transliterations is a phonemic representation of each word. The following chart lists the characters which Nicodemus uses, and the modern Salish transliteration using Americanist characters:

(5.)

	Nicodemus	Standard Salishan		Nicodemus	Standard Salishan
1	'(w	ʕ'ʷ	17	sh	š
2	q'w	q'ʷ	18	t'	t'
3	qhw	x̌ʷ	19	p'	p'
4	k'w	k'ʷ	20	ts	c
5	khw	xʷ	21	'w	w'
6	ch'	č'	22	'y	y'
7	ts'	c'	23	'l	l'
8	(w	ʕʷ	24	'r	r'
9	'(	ʕ'	25	'n	n'
10	qw	qʷ	26	'm	m'
11	q'	q'	27	i	í
12	qh	x̌	28	e	é
13	kh	x	29	a	á
14	kw	kʷ	30	o	ó
15	gw	gʷ	31	u	ú
16	ch	č	32	j	ǰ

---

[6] Macros for this dictionary were written by Anthony Mattina using Microsoft Word.

After we identified the roots and parsed the entries into morphemes, we used additional macros to change Nicodemus's original data to Times New Roman font and move Nicodemus's grammatical notations to the end of the entry. We employed a final macro to collapse entries with common roots into a single root header[7].

2.2 Root Identification and Morphemic Analysis

The next phase of the reorganization was the parsing of forms into lexical root(s) and affixes (derivational, inflectional, and lexical). [+] marks a derivational affix boundary, [-] an inflectional affix boundary, and [=] a lexical affix boundary.

We then added the consonant skeleton of the lexical root to the left of the entry, as seen in (6). Later, a sorting of all paragraphs would bring together the forms having the same root. At this point, we were still unsure about the analysis of many entries, so we included notes in red type next to these entries, to check against cognates at a later time. We rearranged entries by root skeleton and the transliterated Coeur d'Alene, followed by Nicodemus's English translation, grammatical notations, and additional information:

(6.) √č'ʕʷ t+č'éʕʷ=ple?-nt-s *dedicate.* (tch'e̱(wple'nts (lit. He prayed for its special use), v.)

2.2.1 Typographical Corrections

In the following subsections, we discuss various editorial changes that we have made, including typographical corrections, analysis of ambiguous glottalization and laryngealization, superscript rounding of consonants which precede rounded vowels, vowels which are probably schwa, and the transliteration of long vowels.

Where we thought a character was missing from Nicodemus's original, we have inserted it in square brackets [ ]. We give three examples of typographical errors in the original data in this section. The examples also show the effects of a macro, which places Nicodemus's original material and other grammatical notations in parenthesis. Example (7) shows where we interpret <q> as /g/, (8) shows where we interpret <qh> as /q/, and (9) where we have inserted an extra character, interpreting <t> as <ts>.

(7.) √gʷrp gʷɬ s+[g]ʷ+gʷar'p+m' *corsage.* (guɬ squgwa'rpm' (lit. little flowers), n.)

In example (7), Nicodemus writes the reduplicated morpheme with a <qu>, instead of the expected reduplicated /gʷ/. There are a few instances where <q> is mistakenly typed for /g/, and vice versa. Similar errors occur with <t> and /ł/, presumably because the characters looked similar to the typist. In (8), the mistake is not quite so obvious:

(8.) √ǰy' √qxʷ ǰiy'+ǰiy'+áɬ+[q]ixʷ *smells (it...bad).* (ji'yji'ya̱ɫqhikhw, vi.)

Because the root is √qxʷ *smell*, one would expect to find this root in the entry that translates *it smells bad*. Nicodemus's transcription <qhikhw> would be transliterated as /x̌ixʷ/. The vowelless root skeleton √x̌xʷ, however, is not attested in Coeur d'Alene. We

---

[7] We use the term "root header" to refer to the head of a paragraph under which all related roots are grouped. See 2.3.5 for further explanation and examples.

have instead ignored the <h>, interpreting the form as <qikhw> which transliterates as √qxʷ, which is an attested root. There are a few similar cases of spurious /h/ in the sequences <qh> or <kh>, and we have identified them as /q/ and /k/ respectively. As (8) also shows, many entries contain more than one root. Such compound entries are cross-referenced under each of the roots.

We illustrate a third type of correction in example (9). For the entry that is translated as *brunch*, the expected final affricate of the root is <ts>, which we write as /c/. The root itself, translated as *early*, is √kʷc, not √kʷt. Thus we interpret <kwet> as <kwets>.

(9.)   √kʷc s+n+kʷe[c]=mš=cín *brunch*. (snkwetmshtsi̲n (lit. eating very early), n.)

We have resolved most of these discrepancies after alphabetical sorting and before the collapsing stage, when we combine adjacent and nearly identical entries. The majority rules approach most often yields the correct form because adjacent, duplicate entries most likely will not contain the same typographical errors.

2.2.2 Ambiguous Glottalization

Nicodemus indicates laryngealized resonants with an apostrophe before the resonant, and glottalized stops with an apostrophe after the stop. He also marks a glottal stop with an apostrophe, so some knowledge of skeletal root structure and morphology is necessary to distinguish which of the above three possibilities an apostrophe actually represents. Some forms were ambiguous because of these practices, for example:

(10.)   √p'lč' p'elč'+m-stu-s *overturn*. (p'elch'mstus, v.)

In (10), the second glottalization mark may be construed as belonging to the /č/ or to the /m/. After comparing this entry to other, less ambiguous entries with the same root, we conclude that it belongs with the /č/, because derivational affixes such as <+m> are not usually glottalized. We analyze apostrophes which occur inter-vocalically as glottal stops, and apostrophes which occur before resonants on a case-by-case basis as either a glottal stop or a glottalized resonant. In this edition of the dictionary, we place the glottalization mark after all consonants.

2.2.3 Laryngealization of Resonants

Laryngealization of resonants sometimes marks diminutive, but there are also cases of unexplained laryngealization of resonants. We write laryngealized resonants in the root header only when the great majority of the contained entries exhibit the laryngealized resonant. When this is not the case, we do not mark laryngealization in the root header. The entry *gʷɬ s+[g]ʷ+gʷar'p+m'* does have /r'/[8], however we identify the root header as √gʷrp because all other entries relating to *flower* are written with a plain, non-laryngealized /r/. Conversely, forms with the root √ǰr' *firm, strong, sturdy*, consistently show a laryngealization of the resonant, so we write the root header as √ǰr'.

---

[8] See Example 7 in section 2.2.1.

2.2.4 Superscript Rounding of Consonants Before Rounded Vowels

In the original, <u>, <o> and <w> following /k, g, x, q, x̌, ʕ/ mark rounding of the preceding consonants. We have added the superscript [ʷ] to these symbols to give these complex symbols: /kʷ, gʷ, xʷ, qʷ, x̌ʷ, ʕʷ/. We interpreted root-internal unstressed rounded vowels as rounding of the preceding consonant, which we mark with a superscript [ʷ], to reflect this rounding. We have kept stressed rounded vowels.

(11.)   √x̌ʷs s+x̌ʷús+m *foam berries*. (sqhu̱sm, n.)

2.2.5 Schwa

We think that Nicodemus's <e> sometimes represents schwa, and sometimes /e/. In (12), the stressed rounded vowel in the root √kʼʷúlʼ remains in the new transliteration, and we add rounding to /kʼ/. The final <uʼl> is the result of C_2 reduplication (the suffixal copying of the second consonant of the root).[9] We take the unstressed final vowel <u> to be a schwa, and so omit it from the new transliteration:

(12.)   √kʼʷlʼ xʷe ciʔ+ɬ+kʼʷúlʼ+lʼ *birthplace*. (khwe tsiʼɬkʼu̱ʼluʼl (lit. Where he was born), n.)

2.2.6 Long Vowels

Nicodemus writes long vowels as repeat vowels, for example:

(13.)   √šɬ u·+šíɬ-stu-s *befit*. (uushi̱ɬstus (lit. It is suitable or appropriate for him), vt.)

In this case, we changed *uu+šíɬ-stu-s* to *u·+šíl-stu-s*, with the long vowel marked by [·]. We mark lengthened consonants in a similar manner.

2.3 Collapsing

At the end of the parsing stage, we sorted the entries by root header. We used the sort function in Microsoft Word to roughly organize the entries into alphabetical order, but because Word does not recognize non-English characters, we had to manually reorganize the file to conform to the Coeur d'Alene alphabet. We used a final macro to collapse entries of the same root under 1,384 different lexical root headers.

We discuss the benefits of grouping by root skeleton in the next subsection, which is followed, in turn, by discussions of problems we encountered while collapsing the entries.

2.3.1 The Rationale Behind Root Skeleton Sub-grouping

All instances of the same root skeleton do not necessarily represent a single root. For example, √cgʷ is the root skeleton for both √cegʷ which includes entries relating to

---

[9] See Reichard § 607-612 or Doak 2.2.4.2. for functions of C_2 reduplication.

personality or *behavior*, and √cug^w which means *feathered*. Where Coeur d'Alene has two separate roots with identical consonants but different vowels, we keep them separate with subscripts. Thus, √cg^w₁ contains all entries relating to *personality* or *behavior*, and √cg^w₂ contains all entries relating to *feathered*. At a glance, the researcher can distinguish homophonous root skeleta. We have arranged subscripted root headers in alphabetical order of their vowels, thus √ceg^w precedes √cug^w.

Not all roots can be distinguished by their vowels, however. For instance √mlq'^w, which means *spherical* or *rounded*, occurs as *malq'^w* in stem form, but *m'l'mel'q'^w* as the diminutive *little spheres* or *bullets*. In cases like these, we have kept the forms together, because the alternation in surface form vowels can interfere with the researcher looking up the form.

There are several instances of root headers with segments, or glottalization, in parentheses. Rather than use separate, cross-referenced root headers, our level of confidence is such that we have used parentheses as an abbreviation to indicate that there are two forms of the same lexical root:

(14.)   √c'r(') † c'aʔar *ache, hurt, ill.* (ts'a'ar (stem). to be hurt, ache, adj.); s+c'áʔar *ache (to...), pain (to feel...), illness.* (sts__a'ar, vi, n.); s+c'aʔar *illness, sickness.* (sts'a'ar, n.); hn+c'ar'+n *ailment, disease, sickness.* (hnts'a'rn, n.)[10]

2.3.2 Collapsing Identical Entries

We collapsed Coeur d'Alene entries with near synonymous English glosses into the same entry, for example:

(15.)   a.   √ctx^w cétx^w *dwelling.* (ts__etkhw, n.)
         b.   √ctx^w cétx^w *home.* (ts__etkhw, n.)
         c.   √ctx^w cetx^w *house.* (tsetkhw, n.)
         d.   √ctx^w cétx^w *house.* (ts__etkhw, n.)
         e.   √ctx^w cétx^w *residence.* (ts__etkhw, n.)

The Coeur d'Alene transcriptions are identical, with the exception of (15c), which lacks a stress mark on the vowel. We have collapsed all five entries into a single entry:

(16.)   √ctx^w cétx^w *dwelling, home, house, residence.* (ts__etkhw, n.)

2.3.3 Stress Anomalies

In some cases, it is probable that a missing stress is simply a typographical omission, especially when all other forms and annotations are identical as in the previous example. Example 17 shows two nearly identical forms, which Nicodemus analyzes as belonging to different word classes: intransitive verb and noun.

---

[10] Brinkman points out that the entry *hn+c'ar'+n* may actually be *hn+c'aʔr+n*, identical to the lexical root *c'aʔar* except for the second vowel.

(17.)   a.   √**c'r** s+c'á?ar *ache (to...), pain (to feel...).* (sts'a̲'ar, vi.)

       b.   √**c'r** s+c'a?ar *illness, sickness.* (sts'a'ar, n.)

Because there is most likely no grammatical contrast between the two entries, we have retained only the entry which marks stress, but include English glosses and grammatical notations from both stressed and non-stressed entries.

2.3.4 Nicodemus's Grammatical Notations

The following two entries seem identical, with the exception of the English glosses and the grammatical notations assigned to these glosses.

(18.)   a.   √**cw'** cuw'=íčt+m *boxing (he feinted in...).* (tsu'wi̲chtm, n.)

       b.   √**cw'** cuw'=íčt+m *feinted (he...in boxing).* (tsu'wi̲chtm, vi.)

In cases like these, we have combined the two translations into a single entry, and retained all glosses and annotations:

(19.)   √**cw'** cuw'=íčt+m *boxing (he feinted in...), feinted (he...in boxing).* (tsu'wi̲chtm, n, vi.)

We have moved Nicodemus's grammatical notations to the end of the entry. For example, if there are four separate entries that Nicodemus identifies as a noun, two adjectives, and one adverb, and which are identical in other respects and therefore warrant collapse into a single entry, we have retained the grammatical notations in the series: (n, adj, adv.). The following two entries are also identical except for the English glosses and grammatical notations:

(20.)   a.   √**ps(t')** cen+pís=cn *have (They...big necks).* (tsenpi̲stsn, vt.)

       b.   √**ps(t')** cen+pís=cn *necks (They have big...).* (tsenpi̲stsn, n.)

In these cases, where the main English gloss is *have* or *is* and all other lexical information is present in a duplicate entry, we delete the gloss *have* or *is*, and retain the other lexical annotations. We have so amended 16 entries with *have* and 43 entries with *is* (h/s is...).

2.3.5 Samples of Complete Root Headers

Within a root header, we organize entries beginning with the least complex and move towards more complex forms. Each entry is separated by a semi-colon. Nicodemus sometimes identifies the simplest forms as *(stem)*, but not in all cases. In (21), the entry *st'm'a*, translated as *buffalo, cow*, although not identified by Nicodemus as (stem), is the simplest and therefore the first entry under the root header √t'm. Intransitive and simple nominalized forms directly follow, then reduplicated forms, complex forms (those with lexical suffixes), and finally transitive forms and compounds. We use the following symbols to separate the different types of entries: intransitive (†), transitive (‡), complex (//), and compound (§) entries. There are no transitive entries in the following example.

(21.) √t'm † s+t'm'a *buffalo, cow*. (st"m<u>a</u>, sg.n.); ha s+t'má *mammal (bovine...)*.
(hast'm<u>a</u>, n.); čn⏝ʔp+s+t'má *cattle (I have...)*. (ch'npst'm<u>a</u>, n.); čn⏝ʔp+s+t'ma
cattle (to own). (ch'npst'ma (lit. I have cattle), vt.); ∥ s+t'm'=ált=mš *cattle (herd*
of), *bison (herd of)*. (st"m<u>a</u>ltmsh. buffalo, n.); s+t'+t'm=alt=mš *buffalo (herd of)*.
(st"tmaltmsh. bison, cow, n.); ʔap+s+t'm=ált=mš *buffalo country*. (apst'm<u>a</u>ltmsh
(lit. It has a herd, bison), n.); ya+s+t'm=ált=mš *buffalo (He killed the...)*.
(yast'm<u>a</u>ltmsh, n.); § u+x̌ʷal'á+ s+t'm'=ált=mš *bovine*. (uqhwa'l<u>a</u> st"m<u>a</u>ltmsh (lit.
It resembles a cow), n.); t'uk'ʷ=ilt+m x̌ʷa s+t'm'a *calve*. (t'uk'wiltm khwa st"m<u>a</u>
(lit. the cow gave birth to a calf), n.); s+n+laqʷ=ús+s ha s+t'm'=ált=mš *cud*.
(snlaqu<u>s</u>s ha st"m<u>a</u>ltmsh (lit. a cow's chewing gum), n.)

The entry translated as *bovine* in (21) is also cross referenced under √x̌ʷl' *resembling*.
Similarly, the entry translated as *calve* is cross referenced under √t'k'ʷ *drop*.

Several roots such as √py, which includes entries similar to *delight*, have a nearly
complete transitive paradigm, with 1st, 2nd, and 3rd person singular and plural in both
subject and object positions (e.g. I delight h/h, etc.). There are also paradigms inflected
for future and past, and in compound forms with √nx̌l, translated as *maybe* (e.g. Maybe I
will delight h/h, etc.). In these cases, we have retained all of Nicodemus's original data.
Here is another example of a complete root header, √ctxʷ *house*, seen previously in (15)
and (16):

(22.) √ctxʷ † cétxʷ *dwelling, home, house, residence*. (ts<u>e</u>tkhw, n.); c+cétxʷ
bungalow. (tsts<u>e</u>tkhw (lit. small cottage), n.); c+cetxʷ *cabin, cottage, shack*.
(tstsetkhw (lit. little house), n.); e+gʷeł+cetxʷ *home (to go...)*. (egwełtsetkhw (lit.
He went toward home), vi.); § cétxʷ+s x̌ʷa ma'?+ma?+ám=al'qs *convent*.
(ts<u>e</u>tkhws khwa ma'ma'<u>a</u>ma'lqs (lit. their house those who wear women's clothes
(nuns)), n.); ul mac'p he cétxʷ+s *apiary*. (ul mats'p he ts<u>e</u>tkhws (lit. belonging
to a bee's house), n.); nuk'ʷ+ł+cétxʷ *caste*. (nuk'włtsetkhw (lit. one house), n.);
či?c=?egʷeł+cétxʷ=mš *bound*. (chi'ts'egwełts<u>e</u>tkhumsh (lit. I am headed for
home), adj.)

2.3.6 Combining the Two Volumes

In the year following the reworking of volume II as an MA thesis, we began the process
of consolidating both MA theses into one comprehensive root dictionary. For the reader's
perspective, while the new edition of volume II is 134 pages, the new combined
dictionary is 170 pages. We compared each root header in volume II with the
corresponding root header in volume I. All entries from volume I which were not present
in identical form in volume II were copied directly into volume II in the appropriate
place. By comparing identical entries across volume I and II, we were able to better
achieve consistency in our analyses.

Once the two volumes were consolidated into a single root dictionary, the editors
worked jointly to review the entries for consistency. This involved checking volume I
entries against volume II entries to ensure the same analysis was provided for each

similar morpheme. We marked problematic and inconsistent entries, however scarce, for further evaluation and made the appropriate adjustments to the analysis.

2.4 Primary Resources

We have contacted the Coeur d'Alene Tribal Language Program in Idaho to verify that the corrections that we have made are warranted. Raymond Brinkman, a student of Lawrence Nicodemus, and current director of the Language Program, meets regularly with elders who have some knowledge of the language.

2.5 Appendices

While parsing and identifying roots, we created four appendices to complete this edition: a list of prefixes, a list of lexical suffixes, a list of other miscellaneous grammatical and lexical elements, and a list of lexical borrowings. We have removed entries which Nicodemus identifies as being inflectional prefixes and lexical suffixes from the main body of the dictionary. In this edition, the dictionary contains only lexical roots. Lexical borrowings, however, are listed both in the main body of the dictionary, as well as in a separate appendix.

Editorial Emendations and Reinterpretations

The goal of this chapter is to account for all editorial changes that we have made to *Snchitsu'umshtsn*. Where duplicate entries do not solve questions concerning possible errors, Kuipers' *Salish Etymological Dictionary* is useful because cognates suggest what corrections may be appropriate. In sections 3.1 and 3.2, we catalog the inconsistencies we found within the original work. In sections 3.3 through 3.11, we explain the corrections or reinterpretations that we have made to the original data using materials other than the *Snchitsu'umshtsn* volumes.

3.1 Entries with No Coeur d'Alene Transcription

In volume II, several entries have English glosses with no corresponding Coeur d'Alene form. We have removed these from this version of the dictionary:

aver vt. assert affirm (lit. He said what is true).

bait n. (for fishing or trapping).

beeline n. (lit. that which is put on a fast straight course).

beer n. (lit. Foaming water).

body n.

born (be...) vi.

chattel n. (lit. a useful thing).

-contra suf. lit. eye of other half.

devotee n. (lit. One who has vowed to do a specific duty).

exhausted (I am...) vi. (lit. I became worn out).

face cream n. (lit. means of oiling one's face).

fasting n. (lit. becoming hungry).

Independence Day (celebration of) n.

priest n. (lit. One dressed in black).

quit excl. (lit. Let's quit!).

tile n. this word is Coeur d'Alene for maternal grandfather[11].

stripe vt. (stem).

---

[11] Brinkman says the word *tile* is a typo for *sile*, the Coeur d'Alene word for maternal grandfather.

3.2 Stress Emendations

3.2.1 Underlined Glottalization Marks

There are several examples with underlined apostrophes, which we suspect indicate a missing vowel:

√šl' u+š+šl'. *shapely*, adj. ushsh'l. It is very fine, nicely formed.

√pl' u+p+p'l. *whisky*, n. upp'l (lit. little flat thing (refers to bottle)).

√p'č' u·+p'č'. *burnish*, vi. uup'ch' (lit. It is shiny (as by rubbing).

√p'č' u·+p'č'. *shiny*, adj. uup'ch'. chrome.

In three examples with roots √dn and √qxʷ, we interpret the underline as belonging to the adjacent vowel.

√dn u·+dún'. *moved (it suddenly...)*, vi. uudu'n.

√qxʷ s+qí?xʷ. *smell*, n. sqi'khw. scent, odor.

√qxʷ s+qí?xʷ. *scent*, n. sqi'khw. odor, smell.

Nicodemus writes one entry with a hyphen, which we think is meant to be an apostrophe:

√lq'ʷ laq'ʷ-en. *able (to do)*, vt. laq-wen (lit. I can do it).

3.2.2 Multiple Characters Underlined

Some entries have two underlined vowels. In such cases, we have marked stress on both vowels:

√qp hn+qép=íčn'+n. *saddle pad*, n. hnqepich'nn.

√x̌c s+n+x̌éc+t=ús. *ally*, n. snqhetstus.

More often, the underline extends to a consonant. We have ignored this part of the underline. All such occurences of underlined consonants from volume II are listed here:

√c'r hn+c'ór=kʷe?-nt-s. *salted (he...it)*, vt. hnts'orkwe'nts.

√c'? čs+c'u?+mín-t-s. *bewail*, vt. chst'su'mints (lit. He expressed sorrow or regret over it).

√č'p'xʷ č'ép'xʷ. *clip*, vt. ch'ep'khw (stem).

√č'p'xʷ č'ép'xʷ-n. *clip*, vt. ch'ep'khwn (lit. I clipped it (paper, etc).

√ml mel+mel=cn+mí+ncut. *babble*, vi. melmeltsnmintsut (lit. He played himself with his mouth).

√ml mel+mel=cn+mí+ncut. *chatter*, vi. melmeltsnmintsut (lit. He played himself with his mouth).

√mys √qʷ? ac+miyás+n+qʷi?. *cavern*, n. atsmiyasnqwi' (lit. A hollow that is larger than usual).

14

√**pčs** píč(=)us. *peaches*, n. pi<u>c</u>hus.

√**pčs** píč(=)us. *peach-face*, n. pi<u>c</u>hus.

√**qʷn** t+qʷn=sq'it. *blue (...sky)*, n. tqw<u>n</u>sq'it.

√**q'ʷl** q'ʷl+x̌ʷí?. *Burnt Mountain*, n. Q'wlqh<u>wi</u>'.

√**šr** a+t+šár. *appendage*, vi. atsh<u>ar</u> (lit. It is appended).

√**šrš** an+šari·š+íɫ. *upstream*, adv. anshariishi<u>ɫ</u>.

√**tm** en+tém+tm=ens. *cavity (teeth)*, n. ent<u>em</u>tmens, vt. (lit. To have decayed teeth).

√**t'qʷ** an+t'oqʷ+m=íw'es. *join together*, vi. ant'oqmi'wes, vi. (lit. They are joined together).

√**t'qʷ** an+t'oqʷ+m=íw'es. *united (to be...)*, vi. ant'oqmi'wes, vi. (lit. They are united).

√**t'qʷ** an+t'oqʷ+m=íw'es. *conjoin*, vi. ant'oqmi'wes, vi. (lit. They are joined together).

√**t'qʷ** an+t'oqʷ+m=íw'es. *conjunct*, vi. ant'oqmi'wes, vi. (lit. They are joined together).

√**?ɫn** √**ql** ec+?iɫ+s+qil=tč. *carnivorous*, vi. ets'iɫsqit<u>l</u>ch (lit. He eats flesh).

?pɫ- čn‿?pɫ. *have (I...)*, vt. c<u>h</u>'npɫ.

One entry has an underlined /t/. We have assumed that it was meant for the adjacent vowel:

√**č't'** t+č't'=élxʷ. *brown*, adj. tch'<u>t</u>'elkhw (lit. A horse with brown fur (hide)).

3.2.3 Underlined [w]

We have analyzed the <w> after /k, q, g, x, x̌/ as rounding of the preceding consonant, and transcribe the <w> as superscript [ʷ]. The following six entries have <w> between two consonants. We have interpreted the <w> to represent rounding of the preceding consonant, and have not inserted any vowels[12]. Incidentally, all these entries have to do with colors.

√**kʷl** u·kʷ<u>l</u>. *crimson*, adj. uuk<u>wl</u>.

√**kʷl** u·+kʷl. *red (it is...)*, adj. uuk<u>wl</u>.

√**kʷl** t+kʷl=qn. *redhead*, n. tk<u>wl</u>qn (lit. red on the head).

√**qʷn** u·+qʷn. *blue*, adj. uuq<u>wn</u>. It is green.

√**qʷn** u·+qʷn. *green*, adj. uuq<u>wn</u>. It is blue.

√**qʷn** u·+qʷn-lš. *green (They are...)*, adj. uuq<u>wn</u>lsh.

Unlike the previous examples where vowels are missing in the roots, it is not clear in the following examples whether vowels are missing in the root, or if stress falls elsewhere:

√**kʷl** hn+kʷl=kʷe?. *wine*, n. hnk<u>wl</u>kwe'. claret. (lit. red water).

√**qʷn** u·+qʷn=ul'umxʷ. *ground (The...is green)*, n. uuq<u>wn</u>u'lumkhw.

√**q'ʷd** q'ʷ+q'ʷd. *horse (little black)*, n. q'wq'<u>wd</u>.

---

[12] Because the vowels in these roots are not /u/, one cannot automatically assume the underlined [w] is a stressed /u/.

3.2.4 Duplicate Entries (One with Stress, One without)

Nicodemus writes the following pairs of entries from volume II consecutively. He writes one entry with an underlined vowel, and the other entry without. In this dictionary, we retain only the entry with the stress.

√**ctxʷ** cetxʷ. *house*, n. tsetkhw.

√**ctxʷ** cétxʷ. *house*, n. tsetkhw.

√**c'r** s+c'aʔar. *illness*, n. sts'a'ar.

√**c'r** s+c'áʔar. *illness*, n. sts'a'ar.

√**c'ʔ** s+c'uʔ=šn. *hoof*, n. sts'u'shn.

√**c'ʔ** s+c'úʔ=šn. *hoof*, n. sts'u'shn.

√**ps** p+pus. *kitten*, n. ppus.

√**ps** p+pús. *kitten*, n. ppus.

√**px̌** s+pax̌+pax̌+t. *intelligence*, n. spaqhpaqht.

√**px̌** s+páx̌+pax̌+t. *intelligence*, n. spaqhpaqht.

√**px̌ʷ** hn+t+pex̌ʷ+n. *spittoon*, n. hntpeqhwn.

√**px̌ʷ** hn+t+péx̌ʷ+n. *spittoon*, n. hntpeqhwn.

√**pʔ** s+piʔ+peʔ+t. *liberality*, n. spi'pe't.

√**pʔ** s+píʔ+peʔ+t. *liberality*, n. spi'pe't.

√**q'l** čat+q'eleʔ. *lake*, n. chatq'ele'.

√**q'l** čat+q'éleʔ. *lake*, n. chatq'ele'.

√**tɫ** teʔ+teʔɫi·ʔ+útm. *airplane*, n. te'te'ɫii'utm (lit. that which flies by itself).

√**tɫ** teʔ+teʔɫi·ʔ+útm. *airplane*, n. te'te'ɫii'utm (lit. that which flies by itself).

√**t'k'ʷ** hn+t'ék'ʷ-nt-s. *deposit*, v. hnt'ek'wnts (lit. He put it in a bank).

√**t'k'ʷ** hn+t'ek'ʷ-nt-s. *deposit*, v. hnt'ek'wnts (lit. He put it in a bank).

√**t'q'** hn+t'aq'+n. *Hayden Lake*, n. Hnt'aq'n.

√**t'q'** hn+t'áq'+n. *Hayden Lake*, n. hnt'aq'n.

√**t'x̌** hn+t'ax̌=cn. *loud*, adj. hnt'aqhtsn (lit. He is loud).

√**t'x̌** hn+t'áx̌=cn. *loud*, adj. hnt'aqhtsn (lit. He is loud).

√**x̌ʷl** hn+x̌ʷel+x̌ʷl+n. *lifestyle*, n. hnkhwelkhwln.

√**x̌ʷl** hn+x̌ʷél+x̌ʷl+n. *lifestyle*, n. hnkhwelkhwln.

√**ʔns** ʔenis. *depart*, vi. enis.

√**ʔns** ʔenís. *depart*, vi. en_i_s.

√**ʔns** ʔenis. *go away*, vi. enis.

√**ʔns** ʔenís. *go away*, vi. en_i_s.

√**ʔpł** ʔepł. *have*, vt. epł.

√**ʔpł** ʔepł. *have*, vt. epł.

√**ʔx̌l** √**nkʷ** ʔax̌el+ł+č+nékʷeʔ. *each*, adj. aqhelłchn_e_kwe' (lit. every person of a number).

√**ʔx̌l** √**nkʷ** ʔax̌el+ł+č+nkʷeʔ. *each*, adj. aqhelłchnekwe' (lit. every person of a number).

In some cases, Nicodemus provides additional semantic information in one of the entries. In these cases, we retain the entry with the stress and additional semantic information, and collapse both entries into one.

√**bm** s+t+bem+bm. *hummingbird*, n. stbembm.

√**bm** s+t+bém+bm. *hummingbird*, n. stb_e_mbm. bumblebee.

√**c'p'q** t+c'áp'q. *adhere*, vi. tts'_a_p'q (lit. It stuck fast as if glued to something; he became firmly attached).

√**c'p'q** t+c'ap'q. *adhere*, vt. tts'ap'q.

√**c'p'q'** ča+c'p'q'=iłx̌ʷ+n. *asphalt*, n. chats'p'q'iłkhwn.

√**c'p'q'** ča+c'p'q'=iłx̌ʷ+n. *asphalt*, n. chats'p'q'iłkhwn. black-top. (lit. means of paving roads).

√**c'p'q'** ča+c'p'q'=iłx̌ʷ+n. *asphalt*, n. chats'p'q'iłkhwn. pitch.

√**č'm'** č'im'+n. *horn*, n. ch'i'mn (antler).

√**č'm'** č'ím'+n. *horn*, n. ch'_i_'mn.

√**č'x̌ʷ** č'ux̌ʷ+x̌ʷáʔ. *almost*, adj. ch'ukhukhw_a_'. approximate. (lit. slightly short of, not quite, just so much).

√**č'x̌ʷ** č'ux̌ʷ+x̌ʷaʔ. *almost*, adv. ch'ukhukhwa'.

√**d** du·+du. *insect*, n. duudu (a child's word).

√**d** du·+dú. *insect*, n. duud_u_.

√**dx̌ʷ** hn+dex̌ʷ+x̌ʷ+n. *jealousy*, n. hndekhukhwn (lit. means of envying).

√**dx̌ʷ** hn+déx̌ʷ+x̌ʷ+n. *jealousy*, n. hnd_e_khukhwn.

√**jpn** ǰe·pni. *Japanese*, n. jeepni (l.w. from Engl.).

17

√jpn ǰeˑpní. *Japanese*, n. Jeepni.

√lč' hn+lč'+min+n. *jail*, n. hnlch'minn.

√lč' hn+lč'+mín+n. *jail*, n. hnlch'minn. prison, calaboose, clink.

√lmn laˑmna. *honey*, n. laamna.

√lmn laˑmná. *honey*, n. laamna. syrup.

√łxʷ łuxʷ+mín+n. *needle*, n. łukhwminn (lit. a means of sewing).

√łxʷ łúxʷ+min+n. *needle*, n. łukhwminn.

√ł? č+łí?+i?. *saturday*, n. chłi'i' (lit. it came next to the wall).

√ł? č+łi?+i?. *Saturday*, n. chłi'i' (lit. What comes next to Sunday).

√mrm marim+ncut+n. *medicine*, n. marimntsutn (orig. old medicinal herb cures).

√mrm marím+ncut+n. *medicine*, n. marimntsutn.

√mšl mšel. *Michael*, n. Mshel (l.w. from French).

√mšl mšél. *Michael*, n. Mshel.

√p?s hn+pú?s+n. *imagination*, n. hnpu'sn (lit. the means of thinking, that which is thought of).

√p?s hn+pu?s+n. *imagination*, n. hnpu'sn.

√qʷn uˑ+qʷn. *green*, adj. uuqwn (Blue or green).

√qʷn uˑ+qʷn. *green*, adj. uuqwn. It is blue.

√q'c' at+q'ec. *basket*, n. atq'ets.

√q'c' at+q'ec'. *basket*, n. atq'ets' (lit. That which is interwoven).

√št' t+št'=íw'es. *kettle*, n. tsht'i'wes (lit. spout jutting from another object).

√št' t+št'=iw'es. *kettle*, n. tsht'iw'es.

√tł eˑ+ti?+te?ł. *airplane*, n. eeti'te'ł (flying machine).

√tł eˑ+ti?+te?ł. *airplane*, n. eeti'te'ł.

√t'd? s+t'ede?. *hay*, n. st'ede'.

√t'd? s+t'éde?. *hay*, n. st'ede'. grass, alfalfa, clover.

√t'x̌ hn+t'ax̌=cn. *loud-mouthed*, adj. hnt'aqhtsn (lit. He is loud).

√t'x̌ hn+t'áx̌=cn. *loud-mouthed*, adj. hnt'aqhtsn (lit. He is loud-mouthed).

√tpłq s+tapałqi. *Liberty Butte (near Tensed and DeSmet)*, n. Stapałqi.

√tpłq s+tapałqí. *Liberty Butte*, n. Stapałqi (about three miles SW of Tensed, Idaho).

√**x̌y'** x̌ay'+x̌iʔ+t. *large*, adj. qha'yqhi't.

√**x̌y'** x̌áy'+x̌iʔ+t. *large*, adj. qha̱'yqhi't. It is big, huge, ample, bulky.

√**ʔtš** n+ʔitš+n. *inn*, n. 'nitshn (lit. a place for sleeping).

√**ʔtš** n+ʔítš+n. *inn*, n. 'ni̱tshn. bedroom, bedchamber, hotel, cubicle, caravansary.

The following examples from volume II are duplicates in all ways, with the exception of additional information provided after the original Coeur d'Alene transcription:

√**čnt** s+čint. *human being*, n. schint.

√**čnt** s+čint. *human being*, n. Schint. Indian.

√**č's** č'es+t. *mean*, adj. ch'est (lit. He is...).

√**č's** č'es+t. *mean*, adj. ch'est.

√**dkʷ** ee+díkʷ+s+m. *ebb*, vi. eedi̱k'wsm (lit. It ebbs).

√**dkʷ** ee+díkʷ+s+m. *ebb*, vi. eedi̱k'wsm (lit. It ebbs).

√**łqʷ** łoqʷ. *and*, conj. łoqw.

√**łqʷ** łoqʷ. *and*, conj. łoqw. also.

√**mkʷ** s+mikʷ+n. *January*, n. smik'wn (lit. month of snows).

√**mkʷ** s+mikʷ+n. *January*, n. Smik'wn.

The first of the next pair of entries has etymological information:

√**ml** ml=qn=úps. *eagle*, n. mlqnu̱ps (etym. mlqn-dark, ups-tail).

√**ml** ml=qn=úps. *eagle*, n. mlqnu̱ps.

Lastly, we have treated the following examples as duplicates, and have ignored the extra apostrophe in the second and fourth forms:

√**łp'** łp'+łp'+m'in'+n'. *pen*, n. łp'łp'm'in'n' (lit. a small line marker).

√**łp'** łp'+łp'+m'in'+n'. *pen*, n. łp'łp"mi'n'n.

√**łp'** łp'+łp'+m'in'+n'. *pencil*, n. łp'łp'm'in'n' (lit. a small line marker).

√**łp'** łp'+łp'+m'in'+n'. *pencil*, n. łp'łp"mi'n'n.

3.3 Character Change and Replacement

We have decided to make many of the following changes based on comparisons between the two volumes. We have made changes to approximately a dozen entries based on comparisons to Okanagan cognates[13].

---

[13] We have discussed problematic entries with Anthony Mattina, and he has offered several Okanagan cognates as possible solutions.

3.3.1 Assimilation of Root Consonant into Adjacent Morpheme

In a few cases we have proposed a morphophonemic transcription that shows the underlying forms of morphemes. For example, the first sound of affricate /c/, written as <ts> by Nicodemus, belongs with the root √čnt, but also forms the initial sound in the borrowed root √cc, which means *George*. We have parsed all occurences of this root in the following manner:

√cc s+čn[t]+coc *Canada, British.* (Schntsots. Canada (lit. Indian (or people) of George), adj.)

Here are two other examples of this type of correction:

√gʷnt hn+gʷní[t]=cn *cadge.* (hngwniṯsn (lit. He begged for food), vi.)

√k'ʷd tel' s+en+k'ʷde?=ú[s]=šn *derivative.* (te'l senk'wde'uṣhn (lit. from the source), n.)

3.3.2 Missing Characters

Where it is probable that a character was omitted by Nicodemus, we have inserted the expected character. In the following example, the root √bm is reduplicated, but C₂ of the second consecutive root is not written in Nicodemus's transcription, so we insert it here:

√bm₃ is+bém+b[m]+iš *whirr.* (lit. It is...), (isbẹmbish, vi.)

When a consonant is not rounded in the original data, but we think that it should be rounded by comparison with similar entries, we add a superscript [ʷ] to show our changes:

√cqʷ t+coq[ʷ]+cɑ́q[ʷ]=us *blood-shot (He has...eyes).* (ttsoqtsẹqus, adj.)

√lskʷ lés·k[ʷ] *cripple, lame.* (lame (lit. He became lame), lcṣsk. vt.)

√mqʷ moq[ʷ] *aggressive, forward.* (moq (stem), adj.)

√mʕʷ ac+meʕ[ʷ] *to be broken.* (atsmẹ(, vi.)

√plms pláms=alq[ʷ] *plum tree, prunes.* (plạmsalq, n.)

√px̌ʷ₂ čat+péx̌[ʷ]+pex̌[ʷ]+m' *H/S spat on this and that, or here and there).* (chatpẹqhwpeqh'm, vi.)

√slkʷ hn+séluk[ʷ] *a place on the Coeur d'Alene river where canoes mysteriously stop and many were killed, a place of superstition.* (Hnsẹluk, n.)

√x̌ʷq'ʷ₂ i s+x̌[ʷ]óq'[ʷ]+x̌ʷoq[']ʷ+iš *He was grunting.* (isqhọq'qhoqwish, vi.)

√y'qʷ hn+y'óq[ʷ]+p=al'qs *He told a false story.* (hn'yọqpa'lqs, vt.)

√?sqʷ [?]asq[ʷ]+qʷ=ése? *small boy, chiquito, boy (lit. Little blurred son).* (asqqwẹse', n.)

√?x̌ʷ in+?ax̌[ʷ]+tíɫ *catadromous.* (i'naqhtị̄ɫ) (lit. The fish is going back to the sea to spawn), adj.)

There are a few examples where Nicodemus writes half of a digraph that stands for an affricate. We write the expected affricate in brackets. In the first example, C_1C_2 reduplication (the copying of the first two consonants of the root) [14] should copy the root √c'q^w with C_1 /c/, not <t> as written in the original.

√c'q^w$_2$ † c'uq^w+[c']uq^w+čs+n'cút *acclaim.* (ts'uqwt'uqwchs'ntsu̱t (lit. clapping one's hands), n.)

In two roots, we have inserted the expected vowel in brackets:

√bm$_2$ b[e]m *roar (...of motor or engine).* (bm (stem), vi.)

√p'č' p'[e]č' *glitter.* (p'ch' (stem), vi.); u· p'[e]č' *burnish, shiny, chrome.* (uup'ch' (lit. It is shiny (as by rubbing), vi, adj, n.)

Here, we list all other changes:

√c'ʔ$_1$ č‿y'c+[c']úʔu=mš *weeping (I am...).* (chi'tssu̱'umsh, vi.)

√čnt n+[ʔ]ił+sčín+n *cannibalism.* (niłsch̲i̱nn, n.)

√dx̌$_1$ a· dé[x̌]+t-lš *walk.* (aade̱q'tlsh (lit. They walk), vi.)

√čʔ$_3$ √g^{w}nt g^{w}n[it]+el'+s+či+če? *H/s summoned h/h livestock.* (gwne'lsch̲i̱che', vt.)

√g^{w}l$_1$ √tl' te[l]' s+g^{w}el+p *igneous.* (te' sgwelp, adj.)

√ł?$_1$ hn+łá[ʔ]p=alqs he s+yux^{w}m=ús+m=ul'umx^w *North Pole.* (hnła̱palqs he syukhwmu̱smu'lumkhw. (lit. the most cold land), n.)

√ms t'uʔ čn‿mus+e·l [ʔ]úpan *Well, I am forty.* (t'u'chn mus ee lu̱pan, v.)

√my$_4$ sye+mi[y]+p=ng^{w}íln *collegian.* (syemipngwi̱ln (lit. a learner), n.)

√my' k^{w}u[p]‿n+máy'+ay'=qn+m *You (pl) dined.* (kunma̱'ya'yqnm, vi.)

√nk'^{w} √p?s s+nuk'^{w}+e+?łiy+c+pú?[s] *concordance.* ((lit. having one heart), n, (snuk'we'łiytspu̱'.)

√py iʔ c+piy=íčt+m[n]+m-s *H/s is delighting h/h.* (i'tspiyi̱chtmms, vt.)

√p'x̌^{w} h[n]+p'ax̌^{w}iʔ+t *cough.* (hp'aqhwi't (lit. He expelled air from the lungs suddenly and noisily), vt.)

√ql$_2$ √?łn sye+?ił+s+qíl=[t]č *carnivore (lit. One who eats meat).* (sye'iłsqi̱lch, n.)

√q^{w}l na+?x̌íł q^{w}á?+q^{w}e?e[l]-stu-s-lš *speak (They may...to h/h).* (na'qhi̱ł qwa̱'qwe'estuslsh, vi.)

√q'c' s+n+q'e?c'=ít[k]^{w}e? *aquatic flora.* (snq'e'ts'i̱twe' (lit. grass or weeds in the water), n.)

√q'x^w ac+q'ex^w+x[^{w}]-emis *desire.* (atsq'ekhukhemis. (stem), vt.); hn-iʔ‿c+q'ex^w+x^w+[m]ín+m-lš *I am desiring to have them.* (hi'tsq'ekhukhwi̱nmlsh, vt.)

√sc$_2$ síc=i[t]k^w *winter.* (si̱tsikw, n.)

√šn k'^{w}ne[ʔ]+č+šén+n *We are going to work.* (k'wnechshe̱nn, v.)

---

[14] See Reichard § 592-602 or Doak 2.2.4.4. for discussion of augmentative reduplication.

√t'p₁ h[n]+t'ap-n't-w'eš+n' *field (battle...)*. ((lit. place of battle), ht'ap'nt'wesh', n.)

√t'xʷl t'ixʷx[ʷ]l+m *different, alienated (He became different or alienated)*. (t'i̱khukhlm, adj.)

√xʷl xʷél+[x]ʷl+s-n *conserve, preserve, save*. (khwe̱lkwlsn. (lit. I preserved (saved) his life), vt.)

√x̌ˤ x̌a[ˤ] *fan (to...)*. (qha (stem), vt.)

√yl'xʷ č+yél'+ye[l]'xʷ=al'q=šn *chaps*. (chye̱'lye'khwa'lqshn. (lit. covering for the legs), n.); s+cen+y'+y'l'[x]ʷ=íl'gʷes *bibs*. (stsen'y'y'lkwi̱'lgwes, n.)

√ʔkʷn hiy+n+[ʔ]ekʷún+mn *desire*. (hiyneku̱nmn (lit. Means of willing, n.)

√ʔkʷs ʔekʷús-t-[u]lm-n *I told you (pl.)*. (eku̱stlmn, vt.)

√ʔgʷ [ʔ]igʷ- *set out for*. (igw-)

√ʔsl [ʔ]as(=)ásq'it *day (two...)*. (asa̱sq'it, n.); uł [ʔ]as=ásq'it *Tuesday*. (Uła̱sasq'it, n.)

√ʔsqʷ p+[ʔ]asqʷ+qʷése? *small boys*. (pasquqwe̱se', n.)

3.3.3 Incorrect Characters

Some relatively common typographical errors are the confusion of /g/ and /q/, /ł/ and /t/, /ł/ and /l/, /m/ and /n/, and /č/ and /š/. The confusion is probably attributable to handwriting, to their visual similarities as characters, or to their proximity on the keyboard. Based on analogy with other entries with the same root, comparing entries in volume II with those in volume I and occasionally with Okanagan cognates, we have changed bracketed consonants in the following examples:

√cqʷ₂ céqʷ+[q]ʷ=alqʷ *dogwood, elderberry bush. Redwood*. (tseqwgwalqw, n.)

√cx̌ʷ₂ s+céx̌ʷ=[t]kʷe? *Spokane Falls, Spokane, Wash*. (stse̱qhwłkwe', n.)

√c'l₂ s+t+c'ál=[q]n *cowlick*. (stts'a̱lwn, n.)

√c'm'₁, √x̌m x̌amá+[c]'am' *heavy-boned*. (qhama̱st'a'm (lit. He is heavy as to the bone), adj.)

√c'm'₂ ⱡ c'o[m]' *suck (on a solid object)*. (ts'o'n (stem), vt.)

√č?₃ kʷ'u[ł][]+s+čí+če? *H/S loaned a horse*. (k'ut'lschiche', vt.)

√č?₃ √dlm dele[m]+l'e+s+čí+če? *cause*. (delen'leschi̱che' (lit. He caused his horse to gallop), vt.)

√čłs s+čłí[s]+m'šeš *opposition*. (schłi̱sh'mshesh (lit. putting side by side with something else), n.);

√č's [č]'es+t *bad (it is...)*. (q'est, vi.) [xref √q's]; s+ni?+[č]'és+č's+s+m=enč *constipation*. (sni'sh'esch'ssmench (lit. something going wrong with the bowels), n.)

√dxʷ s+n+doxʷ+m=qí[n] *cataclinal*. (sndokhmqi̱m (lit. going down headlong descending with the dip, as a valley), adj.)

√gʷc' in+gʷíc'=e[ns]=mš *teeth (tooth) (H/s is picking h/h...), picking (H/s is...h/h teeth (tooth))*. (ingwits'emshmsh, n, vt.)

√gʷp e+ni?+gʷáp+[g]ʷp=i?qs *hairy (nostrils)*. (eni'gwa̱pqupi'qs, vt. (lit. He has hair in his nostrils), adj.)

√gʷrp gʷł s+[g]ʷ+gʷar'p+m' *corsage*. (guł squgwa'rpm' (lit. little flowers), n.);

√ǰy' √qxʷ ǰiy'+ǰiy'+áł+[q]ixʷ *smells (it...bad)*. (ji'yji'ya̱łqhikhw, vi.)

√kʷm'₂ kʷim'+[t] *immediately.* (kwi'mł, adv.)

√k'ʷl ul s+k'ʷul'+[c]n+cút *culinary.* (ul sk'u'lsntsut (lit. pertaining to cooking), adj.); et+k'ʷul' he+y[l]éxʷ *brocade.* (etk'u'l heyłekhw (lit. A woven thing of design), n.)

√k'ʷnš e· [k]'ʷinš *want.* (eed'winsh? (lit. How many (much) do you want?), vt.)[15]

√lǰ √łq' [ł]aq'+t he lǰ+mín+n *broad-sword.* (łaq't he lǰminn (lit. It is broad which is a sword), n.)

√lqʷ √ʔłn s+[n]+yałn+laqʷ=ús *gum (extra...).* (smyałnlaqus, n.)

√łk'ʷ₂ h[n]+łuk'ʷ+łuk'ʷ=el'gʷes+ncút+n' *diary, memorandum.* (hułuk'włuk'we'lgwesntsutn'. (lit. means of reminding oneself), n.)

√łxʷ ni s+[ł]uxʷ=čt-s *Is it his glove?* (ni stukhwchts? (qu.).)

√mʔt hn+mey't+eʔw+ał+[x̌]élexʷ *bucktooth (lit. middle tooth).* (hnme'yte'wałkhelekhw, n.)

√pq péq=a[s]gʷel *halibut.* (peqsagwel, n.)

√p'lk'ʷ a t+p'[l]k'ʷ=ax̌n *his arm is wrapped around.* (atp'łk'waqhn, vi.)

√p'm₁ hn+p'ó[m]=qn *smoked (hides).* (hnp'onqn, vt.) [see v. 1]

√ql ec+ʔił+s+qil+[t]č *carnivorous.* (ets'iłsqitlch (lit. He eats flesh), vi.)

√q'pqʷ q'e[p]qʷ *snare.* (q'ewqw (stem), vt.) [see v.1]

√q'x̌ʷʔ q'+q'í[x]ʷeʔ *few.* (q'q'ikwe', adj.) [see vol. 1]

√q'ʔ₂ sya+n+q'eʔ+eʔ=íl[g]ʷes *committee.* (syanq'e'e'ilqwes, n.)

√qʷc [q]ʷic+t *warm.* (gwitst, adj.)

√qʷh u· [q]ʷíh *upper class, wealthy, well-to-do.* (uuqhih. He is wealthy, rich, upper class, adj.)

√qʷʕʷ qʷeʕʷ=cn+mí+[n]cut *blather.* (qwe(wtsnmimtsut (lit. He spoke foolishly or nonsensically), vi.)

√q'ʷl₂ s+q'ʷl=ál[q]ʷ=astq *fruit.* (sq'wlalgwastq (lit. ripened crops), n.)

√q'ʷs hn+q'ʷ+q'ʷs+m'=íčn'+š[n]=kʷʔ *walrus, seal.* (hnq'oq'os'mich'nshtkwe' (lit. water dog), n.)

√q'ʷy'₁ čn‿q'ʷéy'+m+nc[u]t *danced (I...).* (chnq'we'ymntsnt, vi.); č‿y'c+q'ʷé[y]'+m+ncut *dancing (I am...), dancing (we are...).* (chi'tsq'we'umntsut, vi.)

√słq sła[q] *sarvice berry.* (słag, n.)

√sʔq' t+séʔ+seʔq'+m-stu-[s] *H/S punned on it.* (t-se'se'q"mstun, vi.)

√st'q ac+sé[t]=q'it *date, day, time.* (atsseq'it (lit. day), n.)

√šp₅ čs+[š]íp-nt-ses *chase.* (chschipntses (lit. He chased me), vt.)

√št'₃ hi+[š]t'=ílt *apprentice.* (hischt'ilt (lit. He is (my) child under my charge), n.)

√št'₄ š+[š]t'+út *calculus.* (shst'ut (lit. small rock), n.)

√sx̌ʷ₂ // sáx̌ʷ=[t]kʷeʔ *aorta, arteries, blood vessels, veins.* (saqhwłkwe', n)

√sy₂ k'ʷnéʔ+čn‿siy+m-s[c]út *best (I am going to do my...).* (k'wne'chnsiymstut, n.)

√šʔ(t) hn+šiʔt+s+n[c]út+n *ancestor.* (hnshi'tsnsutn. (lit. one who goes before oneself), n.); sye+c+ší[ʔ]t *bell-wether.* (sye'tsshit (lit. One who acts as leader), n.)

√tl'q sya+č+tl'+t[l]'q=íčn' *cyclist.* (syacht'lt'qich'n, n.)

√tmx̌ʷ₂ ul li·béč he tmíx̌ʷ=ul'm[x̌ʷ] *diocese.* (ul liibech he tmikhu'lms (lit. It is a land or district in which a bishop has authority), n.);

---

[15] Brinkman offers the possible transcription *tkʷinš* meaning *how many people?*, assuming the typist accidentally wrote a /d/ instead of a /t/.

√tq [t]áq+[t=č]t+m *waved*. (ɫaqɫshtm (lit. He put his hand in a touching attitude), vi.)

√tq₂ [t]a+tq *hang (strips of smoked fat)*. (ɫatq (stem), vt.) [see vol. 1]

√t?ɫ ti?[ɫ] *fly*. (ti'l (stem), vi.)

√t'c'₁ sye·+t'íc'+t[']ec'=[š]n *boot-black*. (syeet'i'tste'tschn, n.)

√t'k'ʷ₁ h[n]+t'ák'ʷ+k'ʷ=alqs *brunt*. (hmt'ak'uk'walqs (lit. He fell in the middle of the road), n.)

√wy' √x̌m čn‿x̌e[m]=čt s+wi?+núm+t=mš *aesthete*. (chnqhencht swi'numtmsh (lit. I love beautiful persons), n.)

√xʷl √x̌ɫ can+x̌i[ɫ]+ɫ+xʷél+xʷl+t *condone*. (tsanqhilɫkhwelkhwlt (lit. He abandoned another's debt to himself), vt.)

√xʷc s+can+[x]ʷ+xʷic=cn' *bob*. (stsanqhukhwitsts'n (a short haircut on a woman or child), n.)

√x̌ɫ hn+x̌áɫ+x̌a[ɫ]+n' *deterrent*. (hnqhaɫqhal'n (lit. means of discouraging by fear), n.); s+x̌i[ɫ]+n *abandonment*. (sqhiln, n.); § can+x̌i[ɫ]+ɫ+xʷél+xʷl+t *condone*. (tsanqhilɫkhwelkhwlt (lit. He abandoned another's debt to himself), vt.)

√x̌m₂ čn'‿in+[x̌]em=ínč *love*. (chn'ingheminch. (lit. you (sg.) love me), vt.)

√x̌t x̌at+x̌at=[a]pqn-t-s *clubbed (He...several persons)*. (qhatqhatpqnts, vt.)

√x̌y'₁ x̌ay'+x̌í=q[n]' *He has a big head*. (qha'yqhiq'm, vi.)

√x̌ʷd s+x̌ʷad+x̌ʷa[d]+m'+scut *comedy*. (sqhwadqhwas'mstsut, n.)

√x̌ʷt' s+[x̌]ʷt'i? *billy goat*. (sqwt'i', n.) [see Ok cognate sx̌ʷƛ'i? for possible cognacy]

√ʕc'₁ ʕe[c]' *exhausted, worn out*. ((eɫs' (stem), adj.)

√?ɫn čet+?i[ɫ]n+n *table*. (chet'itnn, n.); n+[?]iɫ+s+čín+n *cannibalism*. (niɫschinn, n.)

√?ngʷt čn‿[?]ingʷe *say*. ((lit. What did I say?), chningwe, vt.)

3.3.4 Extra Characters

There are a few instances where we have deleted a consonant from the original, indicated here by empty square brackets. In the first example, the lexical suffix refers to "head" which is =qn rather than the uvular voiceless fricative =x̌n. Comparing the second example from volume II with the corresponding form in volume I, we discovered that there is no rounding in the entry in volume I, and similar entries also do not have rounding; therefore we delete the <w>. In the third example, the entry should end with the expected object/subject transitive morphemes. The word-final <w> in the original is most likely a typographical error. In the final example, /t/ has been deleted.

√čn₃ kʷu‿y'‿n ha?+čána=q[]n *Where do you intend to go? (lit. Where is your head going?)*. (ku'yn ha'chanaqhn, qu.)

√č? √x̌y s+x̌[]ey+l'+s+či+če? *horse (worn out...), plug*. (sqhwey'lschiche'. old horse, n.)

√py na+?x̌íɫ ec+piy=íčt-mi-st-me-s[] *delights (Maybe h/s...me)*. (na'qhiɫ etspiyichtmistmesw, vt.); ec+piy=íč-st-mi-s[]-xʷ *You (sg.) delight h/h*. (etspiyichstmistkhw, vt.)

√šč'₂ cen+šé[]č'-n *I waited for him*. (tsenshetch'n, vi.)

Nicodemus occasionally uses repeat consonants for alliterative purposes, as seen in the following example. Repeat consonants are designated in the same manner as long vowels:

√gʷɫ † uˑgʷɫˑ *twinkling (continuously), glitter.* (uugwɫɫɫ, adj, n.)

3.4 Missing Glottalization and Laryngealization

Many of the bracketed corrections involve entries with omitted apostrophes, which mark glottalization of stops, laryngealization of resonants, or a glottal stop. We have made editorial changes in laryngealization only rarely, because they are always suspect. More often, we mark discrepancies in the laryngealization of a given root by *[also recorded as...]*[16]. We have made many of these changes based on the majority rules approach, as well as by comparing the two volumes because the apostrophes may be written in one volume but not in the other.

3.4.1 Glottalization of Stops

√c'l₂ c'él[']+l' *arrive.* (ts'e̲l'l (lit. He reached his destination), vi.)
√c'l₁ kʷl'+ɫ+c[']íl'+c'el'+t *delineate.* (k'u'lɫtsi̲'lts'e'lt (lit. He formed a shadow), vt.)
√c'p ye+c[']óp *to tighten (suddenly).* (yetso̲p)
√c'w s+n+c[']aw'+ɫ+qap=íɫc'eʔ *dish washing.* (sntsa'w'ɫqapi̲ɫts'e', n.)
√c'x̌ʷ₂ s+t+miy+iy=ipeleʔ+s x̌ʷe s+t+c[']éx̌ʷ+ncut *astronomy.* (stmiyiyipele's khwe sttse̲qhwntsut, n.)
√c'ʔ kʷp‿hiʔ+čs+c[']uʔ+mí-n-m *weeping (I am...for you (pl)).* (kuphi'chstsu'mi̲nm, vi.)
√č'm'₁ † č'am' *left (...over ,...out).* (ch'a'm, adj.); č[']am' *left, remaining.* (cha'm, vi.)
√č'p' č'ip[']+m+ncut *dawdles, loiters.* (ch'ipmntsut (lit. he pinched himself), adj.)
√č's č[']és+m+ncut *delinquent.* (che̲smntsut (lit. He made himself a delinquent), n.); s+č's+č[']s=níx̌ʷ *abhorred.* (sch'schsni̲khw, v.)
√č't'₃ is+č'át'+č'at[']+iš *chirrup.* (isch'a̲t'ch'atish (lit. The bird is uttering a series of chirps), vi.)
√č'ˁʷ t+č[']eˁʷ=peleʔ-nt-s *bless, pray over.* (tche(wpele'nts, vt.)
√k'ʷl s+k[']ʷl'-nt-m-lš *bridal, wedding.* (sku'lntmlsh (lit. their being made (husband and wife)), n.); s+cen+k[']ʷúl'+l'+s x̌ʷe tmíx̌ʷ=l'umx̌ʷ *map.* (stsenku̲'l'ls khwe tmi̲khw'lumkhw (lit. means of making a description of land), n.)
√ɫp'₂ † ɫep['] *distasteful.* (ɫep (stem), adj.); ɫép[']+ɫp'+t *disappointing (He is very...).* (ɫe̲pɫp't, adj.)
√ɫt'₁ ɫet[']+p *to jump.* (ɫetp')
√mlq'ʷ s+can+ml'q[']ʷ=áp=qn' *chignon.* (stsanm'lqwa̲pq'n (lit. A lump (of hair) at the back of the head), n.)
√p'c'₂ teˑ+p'íc[']-nt-s *counteract.* (teep'i̲tsnts (lit. He counteracted him by pushing him back), v.)
√p'č' p'eč['] *shine.* (p'e'ch (stem), vi.)
√p'm' ec+p[']em'=íw'es *compact, compressed.* (etspe'mi̲'wes, vi. (lit. It is closely and

---

25

firmly packed), adj.)

√**p'r** p[']er+t *flooded (It...).* (pert, vi.)

√**p'x̌ʷ₁** p'ex̌ʷ+p[']ux̌ʷ *camas (bulbs).* (p'ekhwpukhw, n.)

√**p'x̌ʷ₂** p[']íx̌ʷ+m-stu-s *brighten.* (pi̱khumstus (lit. He made it bright), vt.); §
elu+s+p[']í?x̌ʷ *aphotic, dark.* (eluspi̱'khw (lit. It has no light), adj.)

√**q'c'** s+can+q[']íc'=šn *undergrowth.* (stsanq)i̱"tsshn, n.)

√**q'y'** t+q[']ey'+mín+n *blackboard.* (tqe'yminn (lit. that on which one writes), n.);
s+q[']ey'-šít-ew'eš *communication (by letter), correspondence.* (sqe'yshi̱te'wesh, n.);
kʷen+ł+q[']ey'+mín+n *H/s took a book along.* (kwenłqe'yminn, v.)

√**q'ʷp'** q'ʷup[']+t *rained.* (q'upt, vi.); s+q'ʷup'+t *rain.* (sq'up't, n.); ic+q'ʷup[']+t
raining (It is...). (itsq'upt, v.)

√**sp'y'** sip'ey' *buckskin.* (sip'e'y (stem), n.); sip[']ay' *leather.* (sipa'y, n.)

√**sq'₂** čeł‿čin‿séq[']=mš *deviate (I am going to...).* (cheł chinse̱qmsh, vi.);
čeł‿čis+n+séq[']=mš *astray (I am going...).* (cheł chisnse̱qmsh, vi.)[17]

√**šc'₁** šec[']+šc'+t *solid (It is...).* (shet'ssh'tst, vi.); s+šéc'+šc'+t *firmness, solidity.*
(sshe̱ts'shts't, n.)

√**št'₂** č+šet[']=íw'es *kettle.* (chshe'ti̱'wes (lit. vessel with a projection from the body), n.)

√**št'₃** s+č+šet[']+m *custody.* (schshe'tm (lit. act of guarding), n.)

√**t'c'₁** sye·+t'íc'+t[']ec'=[š]n *boot-black.* (syeet'i̱'tste'tschn, n.)

√**t'k'ʷ** x̌ʷey+t[']ék'ʷ *appointee.* (khweyte̱k'w (lit. one who put down (set)), n.); t[']ék'ʷ-
nt-s *deposit.* (te̱k'wnts (lit. He put it down), v.)

√**t'k'ʷ₂** s+t'ek[']+lš+scút *conjuration.* (st'e'kwlshstsu̱t. sorcery (lit. the practice of
magic), n.); s+t'ek[']ʷ+lš+scút *sorcery.* (st'e'kwlshstsu̱t. conjuration (lit. the practice of
magic), n.)

√**yc'** yec[']+óp *tighten (to...suddenly).* (yetso̱p (stem), vt.)

√**?lk'ʷ** y+?ílk[']ʷ+emn *heirloom.* ('yi̱lkwemn, n.)

√**?sqʷ** [?]asq[ʷ]+qʷ=ése? *small boy, chiquito, boy (lit. Little blurred son).* (asqqwe̱se',
n.)

3.4.2 Laryngealization of Resonants

√**čm'₁** čim['] *grab some.* (ch'im (stem), vt.)

√**tm'** √**łqʷ** łoqʷ+s+tim['] *what else.* (łoqwstim, adv.)

√**tn'** √**k'ʷl'** s+ten[']+k'ʷl'+ł *structure.* (stenk'u'lu'l (lit. a model formed under), n.)

√**t'm'₁** s+n+t'ám[']=cn *kiss.* (snt'a̱mtsn, n.)

√**q'y'** sya+q'éy[']+m *author, clerk, secretary.* (syaq'e̱ym, n.); can+q'éy[']-nt-s
circumscribe. (tsanq'e̱ynts (lit. He drew a line around it), vt.)

3.5 For Expected

We have used this comment sparingly. If there is only one entry which corresponds
closely to a group of entries in a root header, and the single entry is not a typographical
error, we have simply said *[for expected...]* so that the reader can readily identify the

---

[17] čeł, a proclitic in Coeur d'Alene, is presumed to be cognate with Ok kł–, a prefix.

expected form of the root. The following examples show changes we made when internal evidence suggests that uvulars should be velars (and vice versa):

√cx̌ʷ₃ † s+cex̌ʷ+n *condolence, caressing.* (stseqhwn, n.) [for expected √cxʷ]

√px̌ʷ₂ † hn+t+péx̌ʷ+n *cuspidor, spittoon.* (hntpeqhwn, n.); [for expected √pxʷ]

√qʷr † qʷ+qʷár'e?+t *gold.* (qoqwa're't, n.); ∥ t+qʷar+éq=qn *blonde.* (tqwareqqn (lit. one with pale or yellowish hair), n.) [for expected √kʷr]

√x̌ʷl † s+x̌ʷu?ul *awl, bodkin.* (sqhu'ul, n.) [for expected √xʷl]

Here, the aberrant entry diverges from the expected form in glottalization:

√gʷč' u+t+gʷč'+gʷéč'=us *eyesight (H/s has clear...).* (utgwch'gwech'us, n.) [for expected √gʷč]

√t'kʷ₃ † t'ikʷ *old.* (t'ikw (stem), adj.) [for expected √t'k'ʷ₃]

The next entry shows a probable misinterpretation of /ɬ/ for /t/:

√p't [for expected p'ɬ] p'it *to sit (e.g. persons).* (p'it)

We have no explanation for the following example, except that it may be borrowed from another Salish language. There is only one entry with this root:

√q's₂ † q'es+t *bad (it is...).* (q'est, vi.) [for expected √č's]

3.6 Cross-Referencing

We cross-reference (abbreviated as *xref*) entries or roots when the two roots seem related. The *[see also...]* means that there are only very few entries are in the cross referenced root, which implies that the cross-referenced root is either well-attested with many entries, or if not, at least as well-attested as its cross-referenced pair. It is a milder, less confident suggestion of relatedness than the normal *[xref]*. We have based our decision to cross-reference roots on several factors which are discussed in this section. We have illustrated only one or two example entries under each root.

3.6.1 Semantic Similarity

The following example shows that the root √cɬxʷ could possibly be √ctxʷ, which contains all the other entries related to *house*. Volumes I and II both show the first form as <tseɬkhw>, so we have chosen not to interpret /ɬ/ as /t/.

√cɬxʷ † c(=)eɬxʷ *house.* (tseɬkhw (stem), n.) [xref ctxʷ]

√ctxʷ † cétxʷ *dwelling, home, house, residence.* (tsetkhw, n.) [see also √cɬxʷ]

3.6.2 Miscellaneous Discrepancies in Place of Articulation

Some entries, such as the following pair which differ only in place of articulation of C_2, show considerable overlap in their semantics, as well as similar root consonants. For these reasons we have cross-referenced them.

√cs † ces *fine, long, slender.* (tses (stem). long, fine, adj.); ∥ s+cas=alqs *mosquito.* (stsasalqs, n.) [xref √cš]

√cš † ciš *heated, hot, long, tall.* (tsish (stem), adj.); [xref √cs]

The following list shows cross-referenced roots differing in place of articulation of one consonant:

√g^{w}s$_2$ √g^{w}š$_2$

√šc'$_2$ √šč'$_2$

3.6.3 Discrepancies in Glottalization and Laryngealization

Roots with glottalized consonants are cross-referenced with otherwise identical roots with non-glottalized consonants. The different vowels in the following four roots, and a different C_1 in the fourth root, support keeping the root headers separate, but also cross-referencing them, as they are all related to *pinching*.

√c'p † u+y+c'óp *grasp, hold (H/i suddenly gets a very tight hold or grasp), suddenly (it...became tightened).* (uyts'op, adv, n.); ∥ s+n+c'ip=s+m *cat nap.* (snts'ipsm (lit. an eye pinching), n.) [xref √c'p']

√c'p'$_1$ † c'ep' *airtight, lightproof.* (ts'ep' (stem), adj.); ‡ c'ep+m-st-m *caulk.* (ts'epmstm (lit. It (canoe) was made watertight by packing seams with pitch), vt.) [xref √c'p]

√c'p'$_2$ † c'ip' *pinch.* (ts'ip (stem), v.); ‡ c'+c'íp'-n't-s *chuck.* (ts'ts'íp"nts (lit. He pinched her slightly (playfully), vt.) [xref √c'p, √č'p']

√č'p' č'ip[']+m+ncut *dawdles, loiters.* (ch'ipmntsut (lit. he pinched himself), adj.) [xref √c'p']

Two similar sets of examples, whose root headers differ in glottalization, also exhibit a uvular/velar match:

√ɫx^{w}p k^{w}l=u?s+ɫux^{w}p+ú *Red Lasso.* (Kwlu'sɫukhwpu, n.) [xref √ɫx̌^{w}p]

√ɫx̌^{w}p ɫáx̌^{w}p tel' hn+lč'+mín+n *prison (He escaped from...).* (ɫaqhwp te'l hnlch'minn, n.); [xref √ɫx^{w}p, √ɫx̌^{w}p']

√ɫx̌^{w}p' ɫax̌^{w}p' *rush (to...out).* (ɫaqhwp' (stem), vi.); hn+ɫáx̌^{w}p'+m *rush, dart, dash.* (hnɫaqhop'm. (lit. He rushed in), vt.) [xref √ɫx̌^{w}p]

√x^{w}t$_1$ x^{w}et *depleted.* (khwet (stem), adj.); ac+x^{w}t=áx̌n *amputee.* (ats khwtaqhn (lit. He is amputated as to the arm), n.); [xref √x^{w}t'$_2$ and √x̌^{w}t]

√x̌^{w}t hn+x̌^{w}t=ús-nt-m *behead.* (hnqhwtusntm (lit. He was beheaded), vi.); [xref √x^{w}t'$_2$ and x^{w}t$_1$]

√xʷt'₂ s+teč+s+xʷét'+p+n *counterattack.* (stechskhwet'pn (lit. counterattack by

One last example of cross-referencing involves roots which seem to be connected, but which we have kept separate because of discrepancies in glottalization or laryngealization. There is not enough evidence in these cases to make bracketed corrections:

√k'ʷn? k'ʷne? *going to.* (k'wne', vi.); k'ʷné? *future.* (k'wne̱', n.); [xref √k'ʷn']
√k'ʷn' úw'e k'ʷ+k'ʷn=iy'e? *awhile.* (u̱'we k'uk'w'ni̱'ye' (lit. for a short time only), adv.) [xref √k'ʷn?]

√y'd y'id=čt *avenge.* ('yidcht, vt.); y'id=cn *antonym, comeback, retort.* ('yidtsn. antonym, comeback (lit. presenting a counter-argument, using words of a sense opposite to that of other words), n.) [xref √?d]
√?d † n+?id *exchange.* ('nid (stem), stem.); [see also √y'd]

The following list shows all roots which we have cross-referenced because of differences in stop glottalization where the evidence has not been strong enough to make bracketed corrections:

√cxʷ₂	√c'xʷ	
√čl?	√č'l	
√čw'	√č'w'	
√łp₁	√łp'	
√kʷs₁	√k'ʷs₁	
√nkʷ	√nk'ʷ	
√py'	√p'y'	
√p'k	√p'q	√pq
√qʷł₁	√q'ʷł	
√q'ʷt	√q'ʷt'₂	
√tm₅	√t'm'₃	
√t'qʷ₂	√t'q'ʷ	

We have cross-referenced the following roots because of the laryngealization of a resonant:

√kʷn	√kʷn'
√lx̌	√l'x̌₂
√my	√m'y'
√tr₁	√tr'

3.6.4 Confusion of Uvular and Velar Consonants

Nicodemus sometimes writes uvular stops and fricatives when velar stops and fricatives are expected, or vice versa. When the connection is clear, but there is not enough evidence to make a bracketed correction, we have cross referenced the two roots. There are more forms with √gʷl than with √qʷl'.[18]

√gʷl, te[l]' s+gʷel+p *igneous.* (te' sgwelp, adj.) [xref √qʷl']

√qʷl', † qʷel' *kindle, light.* (qwe'l (stem), vt.); // hn+t+qʷil'=kʷp+n *oven, stove.* (hntqwi̱'lkupn (lit. place for kindling), n.) [xref √gʷl]

The following is a list of all roots which we have cross-referenced based on an apparent match between uvular and velar consonants:

√kp	√qp	
√k'ʷˤ	√q'ʷˤ	
√lp'xʷ	√lp'x̌ʷ	
√mk'ʷ	√mx̌ʷ₁	
√mlk'ʷ₁,₂	√mlq'ʷ	
√p'k	√p'q	√pq
√pr'kʷ	√pr'qʷ	
√p'rk'ʷ	√p'rq'	
√q'x	√q'x̌	
√wxʷ	√wx̌ʷ	
√xʷc	√x̌ʷc	
√xʷdnt	√x̌ʷdnt	
√xʷk'ʷ	√x̌ʷk'ʷ	
√xʷny'	√x̌ʷny'	
√xʷɬ₂	√x̌ʷɬ₂	

In the next example, there is only one entry written with a velar stop. We have cross-referenced it with the expected uvular root. Within the expected root header √qʷˤʷ, we have again listed the entry after *[also written as √kʷˤʷ]*. While we suspect that the two roots are the same, we have left them separate and cross-referenced them. Because Nicodemus consistently writes some forms with <k> and others with <q>, we have not made bracketed corrections.

√kʷˤʷ s+kʷéʔˤʷ+kʷeˤʷ+ʔˤʷ *insanity.* (skwe̱'(wkwe(u'(,n.) [xref √qʷˤʷ]

√qʷˤʷ [also written as √kʷˤʷ] ic+kʷeʔˤʷ+kʷeʔˤʷ+ʔˤʷ *demented.* (itskwe'(wkwe'('(w (lit. He is going crazy), adj.)

Our degree of confidence is somewhat lower in the following example. Only one entry has the root √kp, and we believe it is related (or identical) to √qp, but have left it up to the researcher to make their own decision, by marking it as *[see also...]*.[19]

---

[18] Brinkman notes that these are two separate roots with some sort of semantic overlap.

√kp s+n+ká+kap=qn' *cap.* (snkakapq'n, n.) [see also √qp]

√qp s+n+caw'+ł+qap=íłc'eʔ *dish washing.* (sntsa'w'łqapiłts'e', n.) [see also √kp]

The following pairs show one form with a stop, and one with a fricative, and may be related. Reichard lists both stems:

√qgʷ † s+qígʷ+t+s *water potatoes.* (sqigwts, n.); qegʷ+gʷ+n+útm *smellable.* (qegugwnutm. (lit. It was capable of being smelled), adj.); [xref √qxʷ₁]

√qxʷ₁ † qiʔxʷ *smell, stink.* (qi'khw (stem), vi.); [see also √qgʷ]

√skʷ₂ ul s(=)ikʷeʔ ha soltes *blue-jacket.* (ul sikwe'ha soltes (lit. soldier of the sea), n.); [xref √sxʷ₁]

√sxʷ₁ sixʷ-nt-xʷ *spill.* (sikhwntkhw (lit. you(s) poured it out), v.); č+síxʷ+ł+p-nt-s *decant.* (chsikhwłpnts (lit. He poured (the water) out of doors outside; he poured it forth), vt.); [xref √skʷ₂]

√dkʲʷ eˑ+dikʲʷ+s+m *go, recede, return.* (eedik'wsm (lit. H/s/i recedes/goes back/returns), vi.) [xref √dxʷ]

√dxʷ₁ † dexʷ *descend, dismount, dropped (it was...), lower.* (dekhw (stem), vi.); [see also √dkʲʷ]

3.6.5 Confusion of <ł> and <t>

The following example shows nearly identical sets of entries, except for C₂ in both roots. Although <ł> can be mistaken for /t/ and vice versa, it cannot be mistaken for /l/. We have left these roots separate:

√kʷl'₂ // s+t+kʷel'+tem+n=elwís *visiting (He is going about...people).* (stkwe'ltemnelwis, vt.); s+t+kʷel'+čs+xʷy+s+čínt *people (He is going about visiting...), gathering (He is going about...people).* (stkwe'lchskhuyschint, n, vt.) [xref √kʷł₁]

√kʷł₁ § t+kʷeł+tem+n=elwís *visiting (He went about...people, treating them sociably), went (He...about visiting people, treating them sociably).* (tkwełtemnelwis, vt, vi.); t+kʷeł+xʷy=elwís *circulate.* (tkwełkhuyelwis (lit. He moved around from place to place), vi.) [xref √kʷl'₂]

A similar example is:

√ʔǎl   √ʔǎł

---

[19] While Brinkman suggests that *kap* is borrowed from English *cap*, Mattina questions this because English [æ] is not borrowed as [a], (see [epls] apples). See also Okanagan *n+qap=qn* to support the indigenous origin of the word.

3.6.6 Inversion

There are very few roots that we have cross-referenced based on apparent inversion[20] of C_1 and C_2. Consider these two pairs of cross-referenced roots[21]:

√lxʷ₂ léxʷ-n *bore, drill.* (lekhwn (lit. I made a hole in or through it), vt.); [xref √xʷl] [see also √łxʷ]

√xʷl en+xʷúl=ul'mxʷ *burrow, cave.* (enkhulu'lmkhw (lit. a hold dug in the ground), n.); [xref √lxʷ]

√qʷs₁ as+qʷ+qʷés+eʔ *boy, chiquito.* (asqqwese' (lit. Little blurred son), n.); s+qʷás+qʷs+eʔ *child.* (sqwasqwse', n.); [xref √ʔsqʷ]

√ʔsqʷ p+[ʔ]asqʷ+qʷése? *small boys.* (pasquqwese', n.); [xref √qʷs]

In addition, there was only one entry in which the characters in the lexical suffix were inverted.

√kʷr hn-k'ʷax̌=qín'=čt *It is my fingernail.* (hnk'waqhqi'ntch.)

3.6.7 Ablaut

We have kept roots with identical consonant skeleta and different vowels separate. Despite obvious connections involving vowel ablaut[22], we err on the side of caution in separating the two:

√pxʷ₁ † pexʷ *wind-blown.* (pekhw (stem), adj.); s+pexʷ+n *chaff.* (spekhwn (grain husks separated from), n.); péxʷ+t+n' *snow drift.* (pekhwt'n, n.); [xref √pxʷ₂]

√pxʷ₂ † puxʷ *blow (with mouth).* (pukhw (stem), vt.); t+póxʷ=qn-t-m *was (H/h head...blown on).* (tpokhwqntm (ref. to curing technique), vi.); [xref √pxʷ₁]

Similarly:

√t'ł₁ t'eł-nt-s *daub.* (t'ełnts (lit. He smeared it), v.); t'eł-nt-m *besmirch.* (t'ełntm, v.); [xref √t'ł₂]

√t'ł₂ č+t'ół=c'eʔ-nt-m *besmeared (it was body...).* (cht'ołts'e'ntm, vi.); [xref √t'ł₁]

√my₃ x̌e+ec+méy+stm *celebrated, famous, well-known, celebrity, star.* (qhe etsmeystm. celebrated, well-known, celebrity, star, adj, n.) [xref √my₂,₄, √mys]

√my₄ mi· *discover, learn.* (mii (stem), vt.); s+miy+scút *awareness, consciousness, self-knowledge.* (smiystsut, n.); [xref √my₂,₃]

We cannot explain the different vowel in the final entry of √p'm₁ translated as *smoked (h/s...it)*:[23]

---

[20] See Kuipers and Noonan for a discussion of inversion in Salish roots.

[21] Brinkman notes that √lxʷ means *to pierce,* and √xʷl can mean *to spin or twist.* The roots may therefore not be related.

[22] See Reichard § 198-250 or Doak 2.2.1.2 for discussion of vowel ablaut and other vocalic processes.

√p'm₁ † p'em *mouse-colored*. (p'em (stem), adj.); ∥ s+n+p'óm=qn *hides (smoking...)*. (snp'o̲mqn, n.); hn+p'ó[m]=qn *smoked (hides)*. (hnp'o̲nqn, vt.)[see v. 1]; ‡ p'um-nt-s *smoked (h/s...it)*. (p'umnts (lit. h/s made it mouse-color), v.)

3.6.8 Relation Between 2 and 3 Consonant Roots

There seem to be relationships between several 2-consonant roots and 3-consonant roots, which we have cross-referenced:

√čgʷ čigʷ *extend*. (chigw (stem). (lit. extend across), vt.); čet+čigʷ+iš *course*. (chetchigwish, vt.); e+čet+čígʷ+iš *traverse*. (echetchi̲gwish (lit. H/s crossed/traversed the plain), vt.) [see also √čhgʷ]

√čhgʷ čet+čihgʷ *area, field, plain*. (chetchihgw, n.) [xref √čgʷ]

Similarly:

√t'č'₂ t'ič' *provide (food for travel), stock up (as food for travel)*. (t'ich' (stem), vt, vi.); t'ič'+t+m *took (He...along provisions)*. (t'ich'tm, vt.); [xref √t'č'l]

√t'č'l s+t'íč'l *provisions (travelling...)*. (st'i̲ch'l, pl.n.); t'ič'l+m *provisions (He took along...)*. (t'ich'lm, n.) [xref √t'č']

Other examples include:

√dl'₂	√dlm
√my₅	√mys
√mʔm	√mʔym
√tm₂	√tmn₂,₃
√ʔm₂	√ʔmt

3.6.9 Relation Between Pharyngeals and Other Consonants

There are possible, sporadic correspondences between pharyngeals and other consonants which have also been cross-referenced:

√č'rw s+t+č'érw+um *pray, prayer*. (stch'e̲rwum, vi, n.) [xref √č'ʕʷ]

√č'ʕʷ č'eʕʷ *pray*. (ch'e(w (stem), vi.) [see also √č'rw] [24]

√hy' húy'-nt-s *cajole, coax, wheedle*. (hu̲'ynts, vt.) [xref √ʕʷy]

√ʕʷy ʕʷuy *cajole, coax, urge, waste*. ((uy (stem), vt.); ʕʷuy=čt *mistreat (the old or helpless)*. ((uycht (stem), vt.) [xref √hy']

√lw líw+m-st-m *chime, ding, rung*. (li̲wmstm. bell toll, vi.); [xref √lʕʷ]

---

[23] Brinkman has the form *p'um* for the entry translated as *mouse-colored*. Faucal lowering would then explain the different vowels.

[24] Brinkman notes that although /ʕ/ sometimes sounds like /r/, Nicodemus used only /ʕ/ and anything else used in these cases is an error attributable to somone other than Nicodemus.

√lʕ^w₃ u· léʕ^w *crash.* (uule̱(w (lit. It made the loud noise of glass crashing), vi.) [xref √lw]

√yl'x^w † yél'x^w *cover (to...with cloth).* (ye̱'lkhw (stem), vt.) [see also √ʕl'x^w]

√ʕl'x^w ∥ ʕal'x^w=alqs+n *coverall.* ((a'lkhwalqsn (lit. a covering for clothes), n.) [xref √yl'x^w]

√yr₂ ul a·yár hay+ne+ʔk^wún+am-is *will (it is the...of all).* (ulaaya̱r hayne' ku̱namis, n.) [see also √yʕ₁]

√yʕ₁ yaʕ *assemble, crowd, gather.* (ya((stem), vi.) [see also √yr₂]

3.6.10 Other Discrepancies in Glottalization

We have kept a few roots separate where one consonant skeleton is glottalized, and one is plain. Incidentally, where the glottalization mark is analyzed as a glottal stop, the form may be inchoative:

√mc' mc'=us+n *balm.* (mt'susn (lit. means of oiling one's face), n.); [xref √mʔc]

√mʔc † meʔc *grease.* (me'ts (stem), n.) [xref √mc']

√dk'^w † dik'^w *turn about in going (cross face).* (dik'w, vi.) [xref √dʔk'^w]

√dʔk'^w † diʔk'^w *cross.* (di'k'w (stem), vt.) [xref √dʔk'^w]

The following case illustrates only a probable connection, and it has been noted as such:

√wx̌₂ † wex̌ *chapped.* (weqh (stem), adj.) [see also √wʔx̌]

√wʔx̌ † waʔx̌ *sting, smart (to...).* (wa'qh (stem), vi.) [probable inchoative of √wx̌₂]

If there are only one or two examples of the inchoative form, and the evidence for the connection is strong, the inchoative form is not listed as a separate root, but is instead included with the other non-inchoative forms and marked with *[also recorded as...]*.

√cg^w ceg^w *behave, character (to have...).* (tsegw (stem), n.); [also recorded as √cʔg^w] x̌es+eł+cʔég^w+t *courtly, refined.* (qhesełts'e̱gwt. He has nice manners, he is courtly, adj.)

3.6.11 Cross-Referencing of Roots with Slim Phonological Similarity

The following pairs are semantically similar, but have slim phonological similarity in their root skeleta. The connections are therefore tenuous:

√q'^wh † q'^wih *black (ref. to a person).* (q'wih (stem), adj.); ∥ s+t+q'^wíh=šn=mš *Blackfoot.* (Stq'wi̱hshnmsh (lit. one of the Blackfoot Tribe), n.) [xref √q'^wy₄]

√q'^wy₄ ∥ q'^wiy=ós *Negro.* (qwiyo̱s, n.) [xref √q'^wh]

√tm'₂ † tim' *use.* (ti'm (stem), vt.); s+tim' *device.* (sti'm. appliance, tool (lit. something that is used), n.); [xref √tʔ]

√tʔ₂ † s+tiʔ *article, belonging, possession (personal).* (sti', n.); hi+s+tiʔ *mine (It is...).*

(histi', vi.) [xref √tm']

3.7 Also Recorded As

Those roots which are well-attested usually have a consistent form which is easily identifiable. At times, however, one or two entries are written as having a different form than the rest of the entries. When there is no evidence that these aberrant forms are separate roots, and no strong evidence to make bracketed corrections, we have grouped these forms with the rest of the consistent forms under the same root header, but with a preceding note *[also recorded as...]* to alert the reader to possible connections. Common examples include confusion of velars and uvulars, laryngealized and unlaryngealized resonants, unexplained vowels, and variations of /y'/ and /i?/. We were comfortable proposing emendations based on internal evidence, but nevertheless give an account of what we have done.

√cqʷ₂ [also recorded with low vowel] s+cáqʷ+m *arbutus, strawberry (wild...).* (stsaqum, n.)

√cw'₂ cuw' *punch.* (tsu'w (stem), vt.); [also recorded as √c?] cú?+um *hit (he...something with the fist).* (tsu'um, vt.)

√c'm'₂ [also recorded as √cm'] s+cóm'+m *sucking.* (stso'mm, n.);

√c'p'q' † [also recorded as √c'p'q] c'ap'q *adhere, stick to (as glue).* (ts'ap'q' (stem). adhere, vi.)

√c'x̌ʷ₂ [also recorded as √c'xʷ] č+súxʷ=me?+n ha s+t+c'exʷ+ncut *astrology.* (chsukhwme'n ha stts'ekhwntsut (lit. self illuminating body that is guide), n.)

√č?₁ [also recorded as √čy'] e+čs+n+číy'=ep *open.* (echsnchi'yep (lit. The door, gate is open), adj.)

√č'np' [also recorded as √čnp'] čynp'=íc'e? *barrel.* (chynp'its'e'. (lit. a wooden container held together by hoops), n.)

√ǰly [also recorded as *tsooray*] ǰu·lay *July.* (Juulay, n.)

√ǰy' [also recorded as √ǰ?] s+ǰi?+ǰi?+t=il'š *corruption, debauchery.* (sji'ji'ti'lsh, n.)

√kʷr [also recorded as √qʷr] qʷar+éq *yellow (it is...).* (qwareq, vt.);

√kʷn₂ [recorded once as √kʷs] ec+kʷís+t=us *carry.* (etskwistus (He is carrying it), vi.)

√k'ʷn' [also recorded as √k'ʷn] ni?+k'ʷín-n *cull.* (ni'k'winn (lit. I picked it out from others), vt.);

√k'ʷt' [also recorded as √k'ʷt] u· k'ʷt+út *vivid (It is...), plain (It is...).* (uuk'wtut, adj.); u k'ʷt+ut *clear (It is...).* (uuk'wtut, adj.);

√lʕʷ₂ [also recorded as √l'ʕ'ʷ] kʷan+ɫ+č+l'ʕ'ʷ+l'ʕ'ʷ+p=al'qʷ *pocket knife (h/s took a...).* (kwanɫch'l'(w'l'(wpa'lqw, n.)

√l'x̌₁ [stem recorded as √lx̌] † lax̌ *friend.* (laqh (stem), n.); s+l'ax̌+t *buddy, comrade, friend.* (s'laqht, n.)

√ɫx̌ʷ [also recorded as √lx̌ʷ] láx̌ʷ+lux̌ʷ *wild cherries, wild cherry.* (laqhwluqhw. cherry, choke cherry, n, pl n.)

√ɫʔ [also recorded as √ɫw'n] teč+ɫuw' *there (over there).* (techɫu'w, adv.)

√my₄ [also recorded as √mʔ] s+t+mi?=s+m *attention (paying...).* (stmi'sm, n.); s+t+mi?=s+mn *concentration.* (stmi'smn, n.);

√p'c [also recorded as √p'c'] † p'oc' *smash.* (p'ots' (stem), vi.);

√p't'₄ [also recorded as √p't and √pt'] † p'u?t *greasy (It got...).* (p'u't, vi.); pu?t' *greasy, oily.* (pu't (stem), adj.);

√q'ʷʔ ∥ [one entry recorded as √qʷʔ] an+qʷa?+qʷa?=ep=e?s+t *castrate, geld.* (anqwa'qwa'epe'st (lit. He, e.g. bull, is castrated), vt, n.)

√skʷ₂ [also recorded as √sqʷ] s+s(=)áqʷa?=qn *lake (little crater...).* (ssa̲qwa'qn (lit. water on the head (mountain), n.)

√šlč [also recorded as √šlč'] † šelč' *circle.* (shelch' (stem), vt.); šelč *circled (h/i...).* (shelch (lit. He went around, in a circle), vi.)

√tk'ʷ₂ † tí?+k'ʷt *Tekoa.* (ti̲'k'ut, n.); [also recorded as √tkʷ] s+tikʷ=mš *Tekoa people.* (Stikwmsh, n.)

√tʔɫ [also recorded as √tɫ] e·+ti+teɫ *machine.* (eetiteɫ (flying machine, airplane), n.)

√t'x̌ † [also recorded as √tx̌] tax̌ *swift.* (taqh (stem), adj.); s+t'áx̌+m *accelerate.* (st'a̲qhm (lit. speeding a thing up), vt.)

√xʷy [also recorded as √x̌ʷy] sye·+x̌ʷúy *ambassador, consul.* (syeeqhu̲y (lit. One who goes to a place for another or others), n.)

√x̌t'₂ [also recorded as √x̌t] † x̌it *corrugated.* (qhit (stem). marked, adj.); x̌it' *marked.* (qhit' (stem). corrugated, adj.)

√x̌ʷy [also recorded as √xʷy] t+xʷéy=ep *peninsula.* (tkhwe̲yep, n.)

√yxʷm [also recorded as √ykʷm] teč+n+peste?=us ha yukʷk'ʷm=ús+m= ul'umxʷ *antarctic.* (technpeste'us ha yukkwmu̲smu'lumkhw, n.)

√ʕʷʔ [also recorded as √ʕ'ʷʔ] s+t+ʕ'ʷe?=ɫc'e?=ip *pocket (hip).* (st'(we'ɫts'e'ip, n.)

√ʔcč [also recorded as √ʔc'č] y+ʔíc'eč+č+n *diversion, pastime, recreation.* ('yi̲ts'echchn. (lit. playing of several people), n.)

√ʔkʷ [also recorded as √ʔk'ʷ] ec+ʔe+ʔúk'ʷ+ukʷ+t *bug.* (ets'e'u̲k'ukwt (lit. Little creature that crawls about), n.)

√ʔtx̌ʷ [also recorded as √ʔtxʷ] ʔapɬ+ʔétxʷeʔ *camas (a sweet, edible bulb).* (apł'e̲tkhwe'. baked, n.)

3.8 See Also

See also serves two functions: Firstly, we have written it with well-attested roots to cross-reference to related roots with only one or two entries. Secondly, it serves as an alternate way of cross-referencing, when we have a lower level of confidence about the relatedness of the two roots:

√cxʷ céxʷ-nt-s-es *condole.* (tse̲khwntses (lit. She expressed sympathy to me by caressing me̲), vi.) [see also √cx̌ʷ]

√čš₁ † češ *accompany.* (chesh, vt.); češ+n *accompanied (he...).* (cheshn, vt.); s+čéš+n *concurrence, consent.* (sche̲shn (lit. going along), n.) [see also √č'š]

√č's [č']es+t *bad (it is...).* (q'est, vi.) [see also √q's]

√č'š ‡ č'éš-nt-eli-s *conform.* (ch'e̲shntelis (lit. He went along with us. He conformed his behavior with ours), vt.) [see also √čš]

√č'ʕʷ t+č[']eʕʷ=peleʔ-nt-s *bless, pray over.* (tche(wpele'nts, vt.) [see also √č'rw]

√ds₁ † des *camp.* (des (stem), n.) [see also √sds]

√dxʷ s+čic+en+déxʷ+xʷ+t+m *come (...down).* (schitsende̲khukhtm (lit. a decline this way in status), vi.) [see also √dk'ʷ]

√lq'₂ † laq' *pare, peel.* (laq' (stem), vt.) [see also √ɬq'ʼʷ]

√lxʷ₂ léxʷ-n *bore, drill.* (le̲khwn (lit. I made a hole in or through it), vt.) [xref √xʷl] [see also √ɬxʷ]

√lʕʷ₂ lʕʷ+lʕʷ+útm *dale.* (l(wl(u̲tm (lit. It is a long passage in which something can be inserted), n.) [see also √lʔ];

√lʔ₃ † loʔ+loʔ+ótm *valley.* (lo'lo'o̲tm (a Spokane word), n.) [see also √lʕʷ]

√l'x̌₂ sye·+k'ʼʷul' a s+l'+l'áx̌+m' *electrician.* (syeek'u'l a s'l'la̲qh'm (lit. One who produces (works) with electricity), n.) [see also √lx̌]

√ɬkʷ₁ † ɬi+ɬikʷ *speckled, spotted.* (ɬiɬikw (stem), adj.) [see also √ɬkʷ₂]

√ɬkʷ₂ † ɬukʷ *bloodstained.* (ɬukw (stem), adj.); ɬuʔkʷ *bled.* (ɬu'kw, vi.); u· ɬúkʷ *bloody (it is...).* (uuɬu̲kw, adj.) [see also √ɬkʷ₁]

√ɬt'₂ † ɬit' *sprinkle (ceremonially).* (ɬit' (stem), vt.); ‡ ɬit'-nt-s *besprinkle.* (ɬit'nts, vt.) [see also √ɬt'q'ʼʷ]

√ɬt'q'ʼʷ † ɬet'q'ʼʷ *splash.* (ɬet'q'w (stem), vi.); ∥ hn+ɬát'+ɬt'q'ʼʷ=cn *brusque.* (hnɬa̲t'ɬt'q'wtsn (lit. He is discourteously blunt), adj.) [see also √ɬt'₂]

√łx̌ʷ₁ sya·+q'éy'+n t+gʷl' č+ł+łx̌ʷ=álqʷ *composer*. (syaaq'e̲'yn tgwe'l chłłqhwa̲lqw (lit. writer for the flute, piano, etc.), n.) [see also √lxʷ]

√płₐ s+pił=elgʷes *belongings (scattering one's...)*, *scattering (...one's belongings)*. (spiłelgwes, n, v.); [see also √pt]

√pl'₁ ∥ s+pál'=aqł *yesterday*. (aspa̲'laqł, adv.) [see Ok √pn' *time* for possible cognacy] [see also √pn]

√pn ∥ pin=tč *always*. (pintch, adv.); [see also √pl'₁]

√qʷy₃ l+qʷe·y=úl'mxʷ+n *bonanza*. (lqweeyu̲'lmkhwn. (lit. means of becoming wealthy), vi.) [see also √qʷh]

√sds † sídis+t *during (...the night)*. (si̲dist, adv.) [see also √ds]

√šr₁ hn+šár+šar=cn *bull-headed, headstrong*. (hnsha̲rshartsn. bull-headed. (lit. he is steep (difficult) for the mouth (of the speaker)), adj.) [see also √šrč]

√šrč † šarč *troublesome*. (sharch (stem), adj.) [see also √šr]

√tqw' † taqáw' *deaf-mute, dumb (He is a...(mute) person)*. (taqa̲'w, n, adj.) [see also √tq]

√xʷk'ʷ t+xʷék'ʷ-nt-s *efface, delete*. (tkhwe̲k'wnts (lit. He cleaned it off, he erased it), v.) [see also √x̌ʷk'ʷ]

√x̌ʷł₁ † x̌ʷał *dart*. (qhwał (stem), n.); x̌ʷił *hurry (at something)*. (qhwił (stem), vi.); [see also √x̌ʷt'] x̌ʷł+x̌ʷáł *billy goat*. (qhwłqhwa̲ł, n.);

√yr₁ [see also √yrp, √yrp']

√yrp [see also √yr, √yrp']

√yrp' [see also √yr, √yrp]

√yʕ a·+yaʔʕ+ec+k'ʷl'-stu-s *almighty, omnipotent*. (aaya')etsk'u'lstus (lit. one who makes all things), adj.); [see also √yr]

√ʕhm † t+ʕehím *warhoop, yell*. (t(ehi̲m (stem), vi.) [see also √ʕʷh]

√ʕʷh † t+ʕʷeh+ím *shout*. (t(wehi̲m (lit. He uttered a loud and sudden cry), vi.); s+t+ʕʷeh+ím *clamor*. (st(wehi̲m (lit. shouting), n.); [see also √ʕhm]

√ʔkʷs ʔekʷʔs-tul-m-n *tell*. (eku'stulmn, vt.) [see also √ʔkʷn]

3.9 Typographical Errors in English Forms

This short list consists of changes we have made to spellings in Nicodemus's English forms. Although minor, sometimes they interfere with the correct interpretation of an entry. We have bracketed the corrections:

√č'c₃ č'ec' *gull[i]ble*. (ch'ets', adj.);

√č'w₂ č'uw+č'uw=úl'umxʷ *eeri[e], weird.* (ch'uwch'uwu̱'lumkhw. (lit. It is a territory that is usually without people, a lonely, weird, mysterious place), adj.);

√č'x̌ č'+č'ax̌+ax̌+m' *[b]udge.* (ch'ch'aqhaqh'm, vi.);

√gʷš₁ gʷš=úl'mxʷ+n *harrow.* (gwshu̱'lmkhwn (lit. means of com[b]ing the ground), vt.);

√k'ʷl s+k'ʷúl'=cn+cut *cookery, cu[i]sine.* (sku̱'ltsntsut (lit. cooking), n.);

√łq s+łaq+ła·q'=ic'e *[q]uilt.* (słaqłaaq'its'e, n.) [xref łq']

√txʷ his+ti?xʷa+s+l'áx̌+t *acqua[i]ntance.* (histi'khwas'la̱qht (lit. He is one who became a friend), n.)

√tx̌ s+t+ta+téx̌=el'č *[d]olly.* (sttate̱qhe'lch (lit. a little doll), n.)

√wx̌₁ † wax̌ *murm[u]r (e.g. a brook).* (waqh (stem), v.);

√ym' s+yím'+m+šeš *con[j]uncture.* (syi̱'mmshesh (lit. critical time), n.)

3.10 Additional Information Added in Brackets

There are two entries where we have added additional information in brackets in order to clarify the meanings of entries under a root header. For example, the root √p't' means *to dream,* but also means *mushy stuff.* [25] Although several entries towards the end of this particular root header have to do with the latter meaning, Nicodemus lists the root only as *to dream,* and so we are compelled to include the related meaning with the simplest entries:

√p't'₁ † p'at' *dream, [mushy stuff (see below)].* (p'at' (stem), vi.); s+n+p't'+p't'=os+ncót *daydream, dream.* (snp't'p't'osntso̱t (lit. putting mushy stuff in one's own eyes), n.)

In this example, the English gloss *cause* defines the transitive morphology more than the root. To remedy this, we have bracketed *[run]* to better describe the meaning of the root:

√xʷt'₂ ‡ xʷét'+p+m-stu-s *[run] cause.* (khwe̱t'pmstus (lit. He caused it to run, as a car), vt.)

3.11 Possible Connections

3.11.1 List of Entries with Tenuous Analyses

The most problematic entries in the dictionary have a bracketed question mark following the entry, or else a bracketed note explaining the reason that we question the analysis. The majority of the entries in this section are the only ones under a given root header.

√čc₁ ‡ čec-nt-m *electrocute.* (chetsntm (lit. he was struck by lightning), vt.) [?]
√d? dí?+de?+t *demure.* (di̱'de't (lit. is saddening), adj.) [?]
√d?t de?ét *surprisingly.* (de'e̱t. (stem), adv.) [?]
√k'ʷs₂ k'ʷus *splittable.* (k'us (stem). easily split, adj.); [possible connection]
s+k'ʷus+t *cedar.* (sk'ust, n.)

---

[25] Brinkman recalls a Spokan story where a magpie defecates in the eyes of a sleeping boy through a tepee opening. Nicodemus also connected the act of dropping stuff in the eyes with dreaming.

√k'ʷt' k'ʷet' *evident, exposed, plain.* (k'wet' (stem), adj.); [possible connection] s+k'ʷét'=elt *fawn.* (sk'wet'elt, n.); s+k'ʷt'=ílt *fawn.* (sk'wt'ilt, n.);

√ɬʔ₃ ɬuʔ+uʔ+um+n=us=us *fell (he...forward).* (ɬu'u'umnusus, vi.) [?]

√mnt † mntú+wil'š *punctual.* (mntuwi'lsh (stem), adj.) [see vol. 1 for stress]

√qʷl qʷá?+qʷeʔel-eč *You (sg.) speak to h/h (imper.). address.* (qwa'qwe'lech, vt.) [-ech is possible imperative marker]

√q'n q'an-t-siš *struggle (for one's life, as in a fire).* (q'antsish (stem), vi.) [?]

√q'y₂ q'a+q'ay'+q'ey'=íl'xʷ *perch.* (q'aq'a'yq'e'yi'lkhw, n.) [?]

√sls † sils+us *blow down (e.g. houses).* (silsus (stem), vt.) [?]

√šrš s+n+šár+iš *going upstream.* (snsharish, n.); ∥ an+šar+i·šíɬ *upstream.* (anshariishiɬ, adv.); [?]

√tp₁ s+tp=čín *tin.* (stpchin, n.) [?]

√tʕl sya+tʕél=qn *barber.* (syat(elqn (lit. One who trims another head), n.) [?]

√t'l e+čs+t'lú·-stu-s *bystander (to be a...).* (echst'luuustus, vi.) [see vol. 1 for stress] [?]

√t'qʷ₄ s+n+t'uqʷ+úmn *sheath (for arrows), quiver.* (snt'uqumn, n.) [v. 1 has √t'gʷ, analysis unclear]

√wʔp s+w'iʔp+ɬ+t'áq=ney' *flour sack.* (s'wi'pɬt'aqne'y, n.) [related to √wyp, lit. *white man's sack*]

√ʕʷ aʕʷ *abundant, ample, many, much.* (a(w- (pref.), adj.); aʕʷ+eɬ+wl+wlím *rich, well-to-do, wealthy (to be...).* (a(weɬwlwlim (lit. H/s has much money), adj, vi.); ʕʷa+ʕʷ+s+c'ám' *bony.* ((a(wsts'a'm (lit. it has many bones), adj.) [analysis unclear, possibly a prefix]

√ʔkʷn ul a·yár hay+ne+ʔkʷún+am-is *will (it is the...of all).* (ulaayar hayne' kunamis, n.) [possibly related to √ʔk'ʷn, see also √ʔkʷs]

√ʔk'ʷn cen+ʔuk'ʷ+k'ʷún'+em'n' *temptation.* (tse'nuk'uku'ne'm'n (lit. undermining verbally), n.); ‡ cen+ʔuk'ʷ+k'ʷún-t-s *tempt.* (tse'nuk'uku'nts (lit. He allured h/h), vt.) [possibly related to √ʔkʷn]

√ʔʕʷ s+t+ʔáʕʷ+ʔaʕʷ+p=us *teardrops.* (st'a(w'a(wpus, pl.n.) [?]

3.11.2 Specific Examples of Tenuous Analyses

This subsection lists examples of roots whose entries presented specific problems with analysis, and explanations.

a. We have listed the entry for *catbird* under the same root √c's as *collect, salvage* because of the familiar nature of the catbird's feeding habits:

√c's c'es *collect (by picking), salvage.* (ts'es (stem), vt.); [probably same root] c's+c's=qín'+n' *catbird.* (ts'sts'sqi'n'n, n.)

b. We have listed this entry with √gʷq, which contains entries having to do with *roomy* or *spacy*. It seems probable that the entry should be listed with √gʷq', meaning *divided*, giving the literal meaning *divided feet*, which accurately describes the cloven nature of the pig's feet. There is not enough information to warrant a bracketed correction, however.

√gʷq gʷáq=šn *feet (pig's...)*. (gwaqshn, n.) [possibly *gʷáqʼ=šn* "divided feet"]

c. We have listed the next example under √łtʼ, which includes entries with the meaning *jump*. The literal translation *trip* seems to be related to *jump*, although it is not clear how the segment /čʼ/ is related to the root √łtʼ.

√łtʼ₁ √nkʷ [see vol. 1 for stress] nukʷ+ł+łtʼ+čʼ=ús+m-n-n *coincide*. (nukwłłtʼchʼusmnn (lit. We tripped simultaneously), vi.) [?]

d. Vowels are normally predictably lowered by following faucal consonants, however the low vowel in the entry for *apart* can not be explained in this way.

√pkʷ₂ † pekʷ *lay*. (pekw (stem), vt.); s+pekʷ *crumbs*. (spekw, n.); s+pekʷ+kʷ *fragments*. (spekukw, n.); [low vowel unexplained] ac+pákʷ+m *apart*. (atspakum, vi. (lit. It is put apart; scattered), adj.)

e. The next two entries are examples which should most likely be cross-referenced with similar roots, however the evidence is not strong enough:

√kʷd? ∥ s+kʷede?=cín+p=ene? *chin*. (skwedeʼtsinpeneʼ, n.) [xref? √kʼʷd]
√qʼʷlʼ † qʼʷulʼ *produce*. (qʼuʼl (stem), vt.) [xref? √kʼʷlʼ]

f. This root may represent a confusion of √pt for √pł, but the evidence is not strong enough to make bracketed corrections:

√pt † pet+pet+mʼ+ulʼ *moves (He habitually...around)*. (petpetʼmuʼl, v.); ‡ pít+m-st-m *diffuse*. (pitmstm (lit. It was spread (out)), adj.) [possibly √pł]

g. The initial segment of the form glossed as *pepper shaker* is not clear. This is the only instance in the dictionary of a reduplicated root entry beginning with /x/. The expected initial segment would be /s/. The entries in √tx̌₂ are most likely related to √tx̌₁, which contains entries having to do with *bitterness*. *Bowel, colon, intestine* could be literally interpreted as *bitter insides*, however we have not taken this liberty and have instead left the two roots with √tx̌ as separate skeleta.

√tx̌₁ x+tax̌+tax̌+n *pepper shaker*. (khtaqhtaqhn, n.) [?]
√tx̌₂ s+táx̌=enč *bowel, colon, intestine*. (staqhench, n.); ni?+s+táx̌+tax̌=enč *intestines*. (niʼstaqhtaqhench, pl.n.); § ul pus ha s+táx̌=anč+s *catgut*. (ul pus ha staqhanchs (lit. of cat his gut), n.); [probably the same as √tx̌₁]

h. There are only two examples in the dictionary of the lexical suffix *=isčʼeyʼt*. It occurs in the expected form in the entry for *long-winded*. For *deathbed*, however, the /č/ is not written with glottalization, however given the literal translation of *near his last breath*, the suffix is most likely *=isč'ey't*. The meaning of the analyzed root √hl remains unclear.

√hl₃ is+hel'=íščey't *deathbed.* (ishe'lishche'yt (lit. He is near his last breath), n.) [lexical suffix maybe =isč'ey't, meaning pharynx]
√t'x̌ t'ax̌=ísč'ey't *long-winded (He is ...).* (t'aqhisch'e'yt (lit. He has fast breath), adj.)

i. The second, reduplicated entry with the gloss *left over*, does not occur in volume I. Despite the different vowels, and the inconsistent rounding of pharyngeals, we have placed all of these entries together under √pʕ.

√pʕ₂ † paʕ *excess.* (pa((stem). left over, n.); peʕ+peʕʷ *left over.* (pe(pe(w (stem). excess, adj.); hi-s+péʕʷ+ʕʷ *surplus (it is my...).* (hispe(wu(w (lit. It is what I have left over), n.) [pharyngeal sometimes rounded]

j. The entry which is translated as *squirrel* has /č/ in volume 2, but /č'/ in volume I. Because there is no further supporting evidence, we have simply referenced volume I.

√sč₁ † sič *squirrel.* (sich, n.) [v. 1 has √sč']

√a † a *hello*. (a, gr.); a *so*. (lit. Is that so?), (a? adv.); a· *cut out, knock off!, quit, stop*. (lit. Cut it out!, Knock it off, quit it, Stop it!), (aaaa...! imper.); aye *aye*. (hey, adv.)

√bc † buc *boots*. (buts, n.); // ec+búc+buc=šn *boots (to be wearing...)*. (etsbutsbutsshn (lit. He is wearing boots), n.); s+búc+buc=šn *boot*. (sbutsbutsshn (lit. a borrowed root), n.); s+búc+buc=šn+mš *rubber boots (putting on...)*. (sbutsbutsshnmsh, vt, pl.n.)

√bl † bu·lí *bull*. (buuli, n.)

√bm₁ † bam *go (...fast and far), speeded (be...), be versatile, intoxicated*. (bam (stem), vi.); bám+bm+t *speedy (H/s is...)*. (bambmt, adj.); bam+p *speeded (He...), tipsy (He became...)*. (bamp, vi.); s+bam+p *speeding*. (sbamp, v.); ic+bam+p *intoxicated (H/s is being...)*. (itsbamp (lit. H/s is speeding), vt.); // ni?+b[a]m+p=aw'es *orgy*. (ni'bmpa'wes (lit. there is speeding or intoxication among them), n.)

√bm₂ † bem *buzz*. (bem (stem), vi.); b[e]m *roar (...of motor or engine)*. (bm (stem), vi.); is+bém+b[m]+iš *whirr*. (lit. It is...), (isbembish, vi.); is+bem+bm+iš *buzz*. (isbembmish (lit. It is...), vi.); is+bém+bm+iš *hum, humming*. (isbembmish (lit. H/s is making humming sounds/purring), vi, vt.); s+bém+bm+iš *humming, any humming sound*. (sbembmish, n.); s+t+bém+bm *bumblebee, hummingbird*. (stbembm, n.); u+b[e]m+m+m *humming (continuous...)*. (ubmmm, n.)

√bn † benéne *banana*. (benene, n.)

√bns † bins *bean*. (bins (l.w. from Engl.), n.)

√bnwh // s+bi·nwáh=ulumxʷ *Benewah County*. (Sbiinwahulumkhw (lit. Benewah land, named after a Coeur d'Alene), n.)

√bs † s+t+bi·só *dragonfly*. (stbiiso, n.)

√btlym † be·tlyém *Bethlehem*. (beetlyem, n.)

√cc § s+čn[t]+coc *Canada, British*. (Schntsots. Canada (lit. Indian (or people) of George), adj.); gʷɫ s+čin[t]+cóc *Angles*. (guł schintsots (lit. King George men, n.); ul s+čin[t]+cóc *Anglican*. (ul schintsots (lit. pertaining to King George's men)., n.); ul s+čen[t]+cóc ha s+qʷ'ʷenp' *sunset (Canadian...)*. (ul schentsots ha sq'wenp', n.); elu+s+x̌em=ínč e s+čin[t]+coc *Anglophobe, (lit. One who does not love England)*. (elusqheminch e Schntsots, n.)

√cč † ceč *thunder*. (tsech (stem), vi.)

√cč' ceč' *lightening striking*. (tsech').

√cgʷ₁ † cegʷ *behave, character (to have...)*. (tsegw (stem), n.); cegʷ+t *character, custom, nature, structure (the moral or ethical...of a person or group)*. (tsegwt, n.); cegʷ+t-s *nature (his...)*. (tsegwts (lit. the way he was born), n.); // cugʷ=ílt+m *begat*. (tsugwiltm (lit. H/s begat children), vt.); i+cugʷ=ílt+mš *breed*. (itsugwiltmsh (lit. He is producing offspring), vt.); s+cugʷ=ílt+m *begetting offspring*. (stsugwiltm, vi.); s+n+cugʷ+cugʷ=íčt *burlesque*. (sntsugwtsugwicht (lit. imitation), n.); sye+n+cugʷ+cugʷ=íčt *copycat, imitator*. (syentsugwtsugwicht, n.);

s+n+cegʷ=elt-núnt *concupiscence.* (sntsegweltnu̱nt (lit. desire to beget children (morally), n.); s+n+cugʷ= elt-númt *aphrodisiac.* (sntsugweltnu̱mt (lit. desire for be-getting offspring, progeny, young), n.); ‡ cugʷ+cugʷ=ús-n't-s *demonstrate.* (tsugwtsugu̱s'nts (lit. He gave him a example), vt.); hn+cugʷ+cugʷ= íč+s-nt-s *copy, emulate, imitate.* (hntsugwtsugwi̱chsnts (lit. He imitated him), vt.); § s+cegʷ+es+čínt *animal magnetism, archetype, model (example for a person).* (stsegweschi̱nt (lit. animal example, model; model for a human being; talisman, anything that has a magical effect), n.); s+cugʷ+cugʷ+s+čín't *demonstration.* (stsugwtsuguschi̱nt (lit. teaching a person by one's own example), n.); gʷl+gʷl+ł+cégʷ+t *weird.* (gwlgwlłtsegwt (lit. He does queer things), adj.); ti?xʷ+eł+cégʷ+t *acquire (to...).* (ti'khwełtsegwt (lit. He acquired a way (habit), vt.); e+t'ixʷl+m+ł+cégʷ+t *eccentric, odd, queer, strange.* (et'ikhwlmłtse̱gwt, vi. (lit. H/s has different ways), adj.); s+t'ixʷl+m+ł+cégʷ+t *eccentricity, idiosyncrasy, peculiarity.* (st'ikhwlmłtse̱gwt. eccentricity, idiosyncrasy, peculiarity (lit. differences of a person's ways), n.); t'ixʷl+m+ł+cégʷ-nt-m *denature.* (t'ikhwlmłtse̱gwntm (lit. He was changed as to his nature), v.); sul+sul+ł+cégʷ+t *bleak.* (sulsulłtse̱gwt (lit. He has a somber and gloomy manner (nature)), n.); č's+eł+cégʷ+t *cad, churl.* (ch'sełtse̱gwt (lit. He has bad manners-an ungentlemanly man), n.); sl'+sl'+eł+cégʷ+t *block-head, chump.* (s'ls'lełtse̱gwt (lit. A person who is uncertain in his ways), n.); č's+eł+cégʷ+t he s+mi?y+em

cotquean. (ch'sełtsegwt he smi̱'yem (lit. woman of bad manners), n.); ec+me?+m+ł+cégʷ+t *effeminate.* (etsme'młtse̱gwt (lit. He is delicate or unmanly), adj); pinč+cegʷ+t *customary, usual.* (pinchtsegwt, adj.); ł+č'is+eł+cegʷ+t *boor.* (łech'isełtsegwt. (lit. one who has bad manners), n.); pos+pos+ł+cégʷ+t *He has comical ways.* (posposłtsegwt, vi.); qʷy'+qʷi+ł+cegʷ+t *He has a poor personality. (lit. He is poor as to his nature).* (qwu'yqwiłtsegwt, vi.); [also recorded as √c?gʷ] x̌es+eł+c?égʷ+t *courtly, refined.* (qhesełts'egwt. He has nice manners, he is courtly, adj.)

√cgʷ₂ † cugʷ *feathered.* (tsugw (stem), adj.); ∥ s+t+cugʷ+cugʷ=í?sn *feather(s).* (sttsugwtsugwi̱'sn, n.)

√ch₁ † cehé *an example, a specified instance, a case* (tsehe̱ (lit. See!), n.); ‡ ceh+t=cín+m-nt-s *allude.* (tsehttsi̱nmnts (lit. He mentioned it, He alluded to it), vi.)

√ch₂ ∥ s+t+ceh=íp=tč *thumb.* (sttsehi̱ptch, n.); t+ceh=íčn' *ridge (He went along the...).* (ttsehi̱ch'n, n, vi.)

√ch₃ † cih *to reach.* (tsih)

√ckʷ₁ † cekʷ *pull, drag.* (tsekw (stem), vt.); cékʷ+kʷ *to be drawn, attracted.* (tse̱kukw, vi.); s+cekʷ+kʷ *attraction (lit. state of being pulled).* (stse̱kukw, n.); t+cékʷ+kʷ+m *attract.* (ttse̱kukum (lit. He was drawn), vi.); s+t+cékʷ+kʷ+m *attraction.* (sttse̱kukum (lit. state of being pulled), n.); t+cukʷ+kʷ+útm *attractive.* (ttsukuku̱tm (lit. capable of drawing (something), adj.); c+cukʷ+m'ín'+n' *bob-sled.* (tstsukw'mi̱'n'n (lit. means of dragging, pulling), n.); ‡ či+cen+cékʷ-n *educe (lit. I drew it out (this way).* (chitsentse̱kwn, vt.); hn+cukʷ=úlmxʷ-nt-s *he pulled it out of the ground.* (hntsukwu̱lmkhwnts, vt.); hn+cukʷ=úl'mxʷ-nt-xʷ *You dug it* *up*. (hntsukwu'lmkhwntkhw, vt.); t+cékʷ-nt-s *detract*. (ttsekwnts (lit. He drew it off), vt.); t+cukʷ=šn= íw'es-nt-m *banish, debunk*. (ttsukwshni'wesntm (lit. He was snatched away by the feet), vt.); t+cukʷ=šn=íw'es-nt-s *drag away, carry off*. (ttsukwshni'wesnts (lit. He carried h/h off), vt, v.)

√ckʷ₂ † cikʷ *cranium, stupidity*. (tsikw (stem). (a cover for the brain, ref. to stupidity), n.)

√cl ∥ cil=čt *five*. (tsilcht (lit. 5 fingers), n.); cél=č=sq'it *Friday*. (Tselchsq'it (lit. five days), n.); s+ni?+cl=áw'as= qn *quill (porcupine...over head)*. (sni'tsla'wasqn, n.); § ?upen uł cil *fifteen*. (upen uł tsil, n.); cil+čl+?úpen *fifty*. (tsilch'lupen (lit. 5 times 10), n.)

√cl' § s+cil'+eł+x̌élexʷ *denture*. (stsi'lełqhelekhw (lit. substitute for teeth), n.); s+cil'+eł+s+t'š=ástq *blueberry (lit. a huckleberry substitute)*. (stsi'lełst'shastq, n.)

√cł † s+cúł+m *bull, steer*. (stsułm, n.); s+c+cúł+m' *bull (young...), bullock, steer (young)*. (ststsuł'm, n.); ∥ c+cół+m'=qn *Little Bull Head*. (Tstsoł'mq'n (name of a Flathead Indian), n.)

√cłxʷ † c(=)ełxʷ *house*. (tsełkhw (stem), n.) [xref ctxʷ]; c(=)iłxʷ *house*. (tsiłkhw); čet+čm'+cíłxʷ *porch, eaves, awning*. (chetch'mtsiłkhw, n.)

√cm † cum+t *prompt*. (tsumt. (H/s arrived just on time), adj.)

√cm'₁ † ci+cem'e? *small, they are small*. (tsitse'me' (stem), adj.); ∥ s+c+cm'=íl't *children, offspring*. (ststs'mi'lt, n.); c+cm'=íc'e? *midgets, pygmies*. (tsts'mits'e', n.); t+c+cm'e?= ús *beads*. (ttsts'me'us (lit. little eyes), n.); hn+c+cám'=al'qs+n' *roads (small...), vegetables*. (hntstsa'ma'lqsn', n.); § elu+s+c+cm'=íl't *barren,*

sterile. (eluststs'mi'lt (lit. H/s has no children), adj.)

√cm'₂ ∥ s+cóm'=łxʷ *longhouse*. (stso'młkhw (lit. house of mats), n.)

√cn₁ † cun *indicate, point, show*. (tsun (stem), vt.); ∥ cún=čt+m *pointed (he...with index finger), seven*. (tsunchtm, vt, n.); § ?upen uł cun= čt+m *seventeen*. (upen uł tsunchtm, n.); cun=čt+m+e·l+?úpen *seventy*. (tsunchtmee'lupen (lit. 7 times 10), n.)

√cn₂ ∥ hi·y+cún=me? *student, disciple*. (hiiytsunme' (lit. H/S is the one I taught or am teaching), n.); hn+cun= me?+n *conservatory, school*. (hntsunme'n, n.); hn+cun+cún'= m'e?+n' *college*. (hntsuntsu'n'me'n' (lit. school), n.); ul hn+cun'+cun'= m'a?+n' *academic*. (ul hntsu'ntsu'n'ma'n' (lit. belonging to a school), adj.); i·+cún=me? *directory*. (iitsunme' (lit. It is guiding), n); s+cún=me?+m *declaration, documentation, instruction, directive*. (stsunme'm, n.); sye·+cún=me?+n *director*. (syeetsunme'n (lit. One who guides or shows), n.); cun= me?+ncút+n *He is a means of teaching oneself (said only of a high qualified teacher)*. (tsunme'ntsutn, v.); s+cun'+cun'=m'e?+ncút *curriculum*. (stsu'ntsu'n'me'ntsut (lit. teaching oneself repeatedly), n.); č‿y'c+cun= me?+ncút *We are teaching ourselves*. (chi'tsunme'ntsut, vt.); ‡ cún= me?-nt-s-n. *taught (I...you (sg.))*. (tsunme'ntsn, vt.); cún=me?-n *taught (I...h/h)*. (tsunme'n, vt.); cún=me?+ł-n *showed (I...it to him)*. (tsunme'łn, vt.); cún=me?-nt-ul[t]-n *taught (I...you (pl.))*. (tsunme'ntulmn, vt.); cún= me?-n-lš *taught (I...them)*. (tsunme'nlsh, vt.); cún=me?-nt-se-xʷ *You (sg.) taught me*. (tsunme'ntsekhw, vt.); cún=me?-nt-s *declare*. (tsunme'nts (lit. He pointed it out to

h/h; he taught h/h), vt.); cún=
me?-nt-se-s *He taught me.*
(tsu̱nme'ntses, vt.); cún=me?-nt-sel-p
You (pl.) taught me. (tsu̱nme'ntselp,
vt.); cun+un=me?+útm-lš *docile.*
(tsu̱nunme'u̱tmlsh (lit. They are easy to
teach), adj.); § cun=me?+s+čínt
*taught (he...Indians, human beings,
people).* (tsu̱nme'schi̱nt, vt.);
sye+cun=me?+s+čínt *teacher (of
human beings).* (syetsu̱nme'schi̱nt, n.);
c̱ún=me?-n xʷa hi+s+l'áx̌+t *taught
(I...him who is my friend).* (tsu̱nme'n
khwa his'la̱qht, vt.); hn+cun'+cún'=
m'e?+n ł n+?ítš+n *boarding school.*
(hntsu'ntsu̱'n'me'n ł 'ni̱tshn (lit. place
for teaching and sleeping), n.);
x̌áy'+x̌i?+t he n+cún=me?+n *school
(It is a big...).* (qha̱'yqhi't hentsu̱nme'n,
n.)

√cnl † cénel *he, she (It is he or she).*
(tse̱nel, n.); ul+cénel *belong.* (ultse̱nel
(lit. It belongs to him), vi.);
cenel+mí+ncut *egocentric.*
(tse̱nelmi̱ntsut (lit. H/S is by h/h self;
regarding self as the center of all
things), adj.); e+cenel+mí+ncut
asocial, egotistic, self-centered.
(etse̱nelmi̱ntsut, vi. (lit. He is usually
by himself), adj.); ‡ cníl-ilš *they (It
is...).* (tsni̱lilsh, n.); ul cníl-lš *theirs (It
is...).* (ul tsni̱llsh, adj.)

√cnmn † cánmn *chinese.* (Tsa̱nmn, n.)

√cp // u· cáp=us *blink.* (uutsa̱pus (lit.
His eye blinked), vi.)

√cq † caq *bowl, bucket, plate (to put
down a bowl,...,bucket).* (tsaq, n.);
s+caq+m *upright (placing a vessel...).*
(stsaqm, adj.); s+cáq+aq=n *depot,
railway station.* (stsa̱qaqn (lit. a
stopping place), n.); s+cán+caq
casserole. (stsa̱ntsaq (lit. putting under
a receptacle with upper side up), n.);
can+c+caq+m'ín'+n' *saucer.*
(tsa̱ntstsaq'mi̱'n'n (lit. concave object),
n.); // caq=cn *phonograph (lit. that

which is put by the mouth with concave
side up (refers to megaphone).*
(tsaqtsn, n.); t+caq=cn *phonograph.*
(ttsaqtsn (lit. that which is put by the
mouth with concave side up (refers to
megaphone), n.); s+caq+aq=cín=
kʷe?+n *dock.* (stsaqaqtsi̱nkwe'n, n.);
caq=í?łc'e? *broil.* (tsaqi̱'łts'e' (lit. He
cooked by direct radiant heat), vi.);
s+caq=íłc'e? *smoking process.*
(stsaqi̱łts'e', n.); s+caq=í?łc'e? *Indian
barbecue.* (stsaqi̱'łts'e', n.); hn+caq=
íłce?+n *broiler.* (hntsaqi̱łtse'n, n.);
t+caq=ene?+utm *audible.*
(ttsaqene'utm (lit. capable of being
heard), n.); hn+t+caq=íne?+n
acoustics. (hnttsaqi̱ne'n (lit. means of
hearing sounds), n.); caq=ip *follow.*
(tsaqip (stem), vt.); a+caq=e·p=íw'es
consecutive. (atsaqeepi'wes (lit. They
follow one another), n.);
caq+caq+aq=l'íp+m *backwards (He
fell...), fell (He...backwards).*
(tsaqtsaqaq'li̱pm, adv, vi.); ‡ caq-nt-s
*park (...a car), put down or place a
cup, bowl, vessel.* (tsaqnts (lit. He
placed a vessel upright), vt.); caq=
íp-nt-s *followed (He...).* (tsaqi̱pnts,
vi.); t=caq=íne?+m-nt-s *heeded,
heard, obeyed (He...him).*
(ttsaqi̱ne'mnts, vt.);

√cqʷ₁ † caqʷ *insert (a long object in a
tube), long object slips into hollow
object.* (tsaqw (stem), vt.); cáqʷ+m
stuck (He...a long object in something).
(tsaqwm, vt.); ‡ cáqʷ-nt-s *stuck
(He...it in lengthwise).* (tsa̱qwnts, vt.)

√cqʷ₂ † ceqʷ *pink (color of tamarack
wood).* (tseqw (stem), adj.); u· céqʷ
scarlet. (uutse̱qw, adj.); céqʷ+lš *larch,
tammarack.* (tse̱qwlsh, n.); [also
recorded with low vowel]
s+cáqʷ+m *arbutus, strawberry
(wild...).* (stsa̱qum, n.); // céqʷ+[q]ʷ=
alqʷ *dogwood, elderberry bush.
Redwood.* (tse̱qwgwalqw, n.);

t+coq[ʷ]+céqʷ=us *blood-shot (He has...eyes).* (ttsoqtsequs, adj.)

√cry † co·ray *July.* (tsooray, n.) [see also √ǰly]

√cs₁ † ces *fine, long, slender.* (tses (stem), adj.); ∥ s+cas=alqs *mosquito.* (stsasalqs, n.) [xref √cš]

√cs₂ † cus *to rattle (e.g. snake).* (tsus); cus+cú·s *jingle jingle.* (tsustsuuus!, excl.)

√csp ni kʷu⏜cósep *Are you Joseph?* (ni ku Tsosep? (qu.).) [xref √jssp]

√cš † ciš *heated, hot, long, tall.* (tsish (stem), adj.); ciš+t *long (it is...).* (tsisht, adj.); ∥ céš=alqʷ *tall (he is...).* (tseshalqw, adj.); t+céš+ceš=qn *comet.* (ttseshtseshqn (lit. It (star) is long-hair), n.); § s+cen+cíš+tis=čn=šn *high top shoes.* (stsentsishtischnshn, n.) [xref √cs]

√ct₁ † cut *although.* (tsut, conj.); cut ci? *although.* (tsut tsi', conj.)

√ct₂ † cut *self.* (tsut, n.)

√ctxʷ † cétxʷ *dwelling, home, house, residence.* (tsetkhw, n.); c+cétxʷ *bungalow, cabin, cottage, shack.* (tstsetkhw (lit. small cottage, little house), n.); e+gʷeł+cetxʷ *home (to go...).* (egwełtsetkhw (lit. He went toward home), vi.); č⏜y'c+?egʷeł+cétxʷ+mš *bound.* (chi'ts'egwełtsetkhumsh (lit. I am headed for home), adj.); § cétxʷ+s xʷa ma?+ma?ám=al'qs *convent.* (tsetkhws khwa ma'ma'ama'lqs (lit. their house those who wear women's clothes (nuns)), n.); ul mac'p he cétxʷ+s *apiary.* (ul mats'p he tsetkhws (lit. belonging to a bee's house), n.); nuk'ʷ+ł+cétxʷ *caste.* (nuk'włtsetkhw (lit. one house), n.); aˤʷ+eł+cetxʷ *H/s has many houses.* (a(wełtsetkhw, vt.); [see also √cłxʷ]

√cw'₁ † ciw' *child (youngest).* (tsi'w (stem), n.); ∥ s+cíw'+t'=mš *child (youngest...).* (stsi'wt'msh, n.);

s+c+cíw'+t'=mš *baby (...of the family).* (ststsi'wt'msh, n.); s+c+céw'+t=m'š=qn'=čt *finger (little or fourth...).* (ststse'wt'mshq'ncht (lit. youngest finger), n.)

√cw'₂ † cuw' *punch.* (tsu'w (stem), vt.); [also recorded as √c?] cú?+um *hit (he...something with the fist).* (tsu'um, vt.); s+cú?+u? *blow.* (stsu'u' (lit. a sudden hard stroke, as of the fist), n.); s+cuw'-n't-w'íš *boxing.* (stsu'w'nt'wish (lit. hitting one another with the fist), vt.); sye+cuw'-n't-w'íš *boxer.* (syetsu'w'nt'wish (lit. One of two who hit each other with the fist), n.); ∥ cuw'=íčt+m *boxing (he feinted in...), feinted (he...in boxing).* (tsu'wichtm, n, vi.); s+cuw'=íłc'e? *clout.* (stsu'wiłts'e' (lit. hitting a person with the fist), vt.); ‡ cúw'-nt-s *hit (he...him with the fist).* (tsu'wnts, vt.); cú?+cuw'-nt-s *hit (he...him repeatedly), repeatedly (he hit him...).* (tsu'tsu'wnts, adv, vt.); t+co?=qin-t-m *clobber (slang).* (ttso'qintm (lit. He was batted with fists as to the head), v.); § ul sye+cuw'-n't-wíš he s+łúxʷ=čt *glove (boxing...).* (ul syetsu'w'ntwish he słukhwcht (lit. glove of a boxer), n.)

√cxʷ₁ † cexʷ *caress, fondle.* (tsekhw (stem), vt.); ‡ céxʷ-nt-s *caress.* (tsekhwnts (lit. He touched or treated him in an affectionate or loving manner), vt.); céxʷ-nt-se-s *condole.* (tsekhwntses (lit. She expressed sympathy to me by caressing me), vi.) [see also √cx̌ʷ]

√cxʷ₂ † hn+c+cxʷ+út *creek, rivulet.* (hntstskhut, n.) [xref √c'x̌ʷ]

√cx̌ʷ₁ † cax̌ʷ *accumulate.* (tsaqhw (stem), vt.)

√cx̌ʷ₂ ∥ s+céx̌ʷ=[t]kʷe? *Spokane Falls, Spokane, Wash.* (stseqhwłkwe', n.)

√cx̌ʷ₃ † s+cex̌ʷ+n *condolence, caressing*. (stseqhwn, n.) [for expected √cxʷ]

√cy' † cuy' *chilling*. (tsu'y (stem), adj.); u· cúy' *chilly (it is...).* (uutsu'y, adj.); cúy'+cuy'+t *clammy.* (tsu'ytsu'yt (lit. It is disagreeably moist and cold; it causes chills), adj.); s+cúy'+y' *chill.* (stsu'y'y (lit. becoming chilled), n.); ∥ cen+c'úy'+c'uy'=čt *chills.* (tsents'u'yts'u'ycht (lit. He causes chills (by being scantly clad) in cold weather), n.)

√cy'ʔ † c+cíy'eʔ *sister (a woman's younger...).* (tstsi'ye', n.)

√cˁ † caˁ *scream, shriek.* (tsa((stem), vi.)

√cˁʷ † caˁʷ *fringe.* (tsa(w (stem), n.); a· cáˁʷ *fringed.* (aatsa(w (lit. It is fringed), adj.); ∥ s+can+cuˁʷ=íc'eʔ *shawl.* (stsantsu(wits'e', n.)

√cʔ † ciʔ *concede, near (a second person there).* (tsi' (lit. that which is away from me but near you; all right), n, adv.); e n+cíʔ *there (near you).* (entsi', adv.); t'iʔ+ciʔ *adequate, sufficient.* (t'i'tsi' (lit. That is enough), adj.); teč+ciʔ *there (over there).* (techtsi', adv.); mel'+ciʔ *by that.* (me'ltsi', adv.); cut ciʔ *although.* (tsut tsi', conj.); teč+ciʔ-š *begone!, get (...away!), go ((You)...in that direction!).* (techtsi'sh, vi.)

√cʔt † coʔot *sob, weep.* (tso'ot (stem), vi.); coʔót *bawl, blubber, wailed (h/s...).* (tso'ot (lit. He cried out loudly), vi.); s+cóʔot *wailing, weeping.* (stso'ot, vi.); ∥ coʔo·t=álumxʷ *brownie, elf.* (tso'ootalumkhw (lit. one who weeps, wails about on the land), n.)

√c'č₁ ∥ hn+c'áč'=qn *log (...on the head).* (hnts'ach'qn, n.); hn+c'ač=qn *mountain northeast of Plummer.* (hnts'achqn, n.)

√c'č₂ † c'eč *count, number.* (ts'ech (stem), vt.); s+c'éč+č *amount, numbers.* (sts'echch, n.); s+c'éč+m *computation.* (sts'echm (lit. counting), n.); s+cen+c'éč+m *auction.* (stsents'echm (lit. counting from under), n.); sye·+c'éč+m *counter.* (syeets'echm (lit. One who counts), n.); sye·+c'éč+n *computer.* (syeets'echn (lit. One who counts), n.); ∥ hn+c'éč= us *accounted, calculate, ciphered, compute, computed, count, counted, figure.* (hnts'echus, v, vi.); hn+c'č= ús+n *calculator, calculation.* (hnts'chusn (lit. keyboard machine for the automatic performance of arithmetic operations), n.); s+n+c'éč= us *algebra, arithmetic, calculation, figuring.* (snts'echus (lit. counting heads (faces)), n.); sye+n+c'éč=us *bookeeper.* (syents'echus (lit. One who counts heads), n.); s+c'č=ásq'it *almanac, calendar.* (sts'chasq'it (lit. means of counting days or skies), n.); t+c'áč=alqs *Tekoa Mountain.* (Tts'achalqs (lit. numbered point), n.); ‡ cen+c'éč-nt-s *evaluate, to appraise.* (tsents'echnts (lit. He counted it from under), vt.)

√c'č₃ † c'ič *prickly, rough.* (ts'ich (stem), adj.)

√c'kʷ † c'ékʷ+kʷ *alder shrub, bearberries, elderberries.* (ts'ekukw, n.); ∥ c'ákʷ+kʷ=alqʷ *elderberry bush.* (ts'akukwalqw, n.)

√c'kʷʔ † c'ikʷeʔ *left-handed.* (ts'ikwe' (stem), adj.); et+c'íkʷeʔ *left-handed.* (etts'ikwe' (lit. He is...), adj.); s+t+c'iʔkʷeʔ *hand (left...).* (stts'i'kwe, n.); s+t+c'íkʷeʔ *left hand.* (stts'ikwe', n.); čn'⌣t+c'íkʷeʔ *(lit. I am left-handed).* (ch'ntts'ikwe', vt.); § tač s+t+c'íkʷeʔ *apart.* (tach stts'ikwe' (lit. toward the left hand), n.); teč+s+t+c'íkʷeʔ *apart (lit. toward the left hand).* (tech stts'ikwe', n.)

√c'kʷn † s+c'ukʷín+m *running (of a human being)*. (st'sukwinm, n.); c'ukʷkʷín+m *balance (he ran to regain...), ran (he...to regain balance)*. (ts'ukukwinm, n, vi.); c'ukʷ+c'ukʷín'+m' *practiced (he...running), running (he practiced...)*. (ts'ukwts'ukwi'n'm, vt, n.); čn‿cukʷín+m *ran*. (chntsukwinm (lit. I ran), vt.); § čn‿t+c'ukʷen+ł+niw' *(lit. I ran by the side of, i.e., moving car)*. (chntts'ukwenłni'w, vt.)

√c'kʷ' † c'ekʷ' *poke*. (ts'ek'w (stem), vt.); c'ekʷ' *stiff (ref. to body), to be stiff (as bones)*. (ts'ek'w (stem), adj.); c'ukʷ'+mín+n *cue*. (ts'uk'wminn (lit. means of thrusting; the tapering rod used in billiards, pool), n.); cen+c'ukʷ'+mín+n *column, buttress, support*. (tsents'uk'wminn (lit. a prop), n.); e cen+c'ékʷ' *braced, bracketed, supported (to be...)*. (etsents'ek'w (lit. It is propped up), vi.); ∥ c'ukʷ'=íčs+n *cane*. (ts'uk'wichsn (lit. walking stick), n.); hn+c'okʷ'+c'okʷ'=áx̌n *crutches*. (hnts'ok'wts'ok'waqhn (lit. means of supporting the armpits), n.); § li·béč he c'ukʷ'=íčs+is *crosier*. (liibech he ts'uk'wichsis (lit. a bishop's staff (cane), n.)

√c'l₁ ∥ ča·+c'ál=alqs. *Tensed, Idaho*. (Chaats'alalqs (lit. Grove on a spur), n.)

√c'l₂ † c'el *stand (ref. to a person)*. (ts'el (stem), vi.); c'el'+l' *arrive, stop (come to a...)*. (ts'e'l'l, vi.); c'él[']+l' *arrive*. (ts'el'l (lit. He reached his destination), vi.); s+c'él'+l' *arrival (of one person)*. (sts'e'l'l., n.); c'él+iš *arise, rise, stand, arose (He...), came (He...to a standstill), got (He...up from a chair), stood (He...up)*. (ts'elish, vi.); s+či·+c'él+iš *moon (new...)*. (schiits'elis, n.); e·+c'él+m+ncut *budge, move*. (eets'elmntsut (lit. It moves itself), vi.); i·+c'él+m+ncut *astir, bestir*. (iits'elmntsut. (lit. He is moving himself), vt.); ∥ c'el=álqʷ *to play with the stick game (lit. setting up sticks against a board)*. (ts'elalqw, v.); s+t+c'ál=[q]n *cowlick*. (stts'alwn, n.); c'l+l+íš=ul'umxʷ *alight*. (ts'llishu'lumkhw (lit. The bird came to a stand after a flight), vi.); c'l=qín+n *bonnet, war-bonnet*. (ts'lqinn (means of putting juttings up from the head), n.); s+c'l=qín *headdress*. (sts'lqin, n.)

√c'l₃ ∥ c'l=íčt+m *bungle*. (ts'lichtm (lit. He acted ineptly or inefficiently), vi.)

√c'ls † c'alus *kingfish, kingfisher (bird)*. (ts'alus, n.)

√c'lx̌ʷ † c'alx̌ʷ *claw*. (ts'alqhw (stem). scratch with claws, vt.); c'lx̌ʷ+mín+n *claw*. (ts'lqhuminn (lit. means of scratching), n.); ‡ c'álx̌ʷ-nt-s *fingernails (he scratched it with his...), scratched (he...it with his fingernails)*. (ts'alqhwnts, n, vt.); c'álx̌ʷ-nt-se-s *claw*. (ts'alqhwntses (lit. He (cat) clawed me), vt.)

√c'l'₁ † c'il' *outline, shadow*. (ts'i'l (stem), n.); s+c'íl'+c'el'+t *contour, shadow*. (sts'i'lts'e'lt, n.); § kʷ'l'+ł+c[']íl'+c'el'+t *delineate*. (k'u'łtsi'lts'e'lt (lit. He formed a shadow), vt.)

√c'l'₂ † c'ul' *news (bad...), tidings (ill...)*. (ts'u'l (stem), n.); c'el+ł *to fear a fierce one*. (ts'ell); c'él'+c'l'+t *frightening (It is...), is (one who...horrible, fierce)*. (ts'e'lts"lt, vi.); c'él'+p *He became frightened*. (ts'e'lp, adj, v.); čn‿c'él'+p *horrified*. (chnts'e'lp. (lit. I was horrified), vt.); c'él'+s+c'l'+t *fierce, horrible (one who is horrible or fierce)*. (ts'e'lsts"lt, adj.); s+c'él'+c'l+t *fright*. (sts'e'lts'lt. confuse, n.)

√c'ł † c'ił *cool (weather)*. (ts'ił (stem), adj.); c'íʔł *cooled (it...off)*. (ts'i'ł, vi.); u· c'ił *cool*. (uuts'ił, adj.); u c'u+c'eʔłí· *cool (It remains...)*. (uts'uts'e'łiii, adj.)

√c'm † c'am *pointed (almost..., as a football).* (ts'am (stem), adj.); ∥ c'ám+c'm=alqs *pears.* (ts'amts'malqs (lit. pointed at the ends), n.)

√c'm', † s+c'am' *bone.* (sts'a'm, n.); u s+c'ám' *bone (It is all...).* (usts'a'm, n.); ∥ s+c'ám'=qn *brain, cerebellum, cerebrum.* (sts'a'mqn, n.); ul s+c'ám'= qn *cerebral.* (ul sts'a'mqn (lit. of or pertaining to the brain), adj.); hn+c'+c'm=ál'n *arrowhead.* (hnts'ts'ma'ln (lit. piece of bone on end of an arrow), n.); § ac+p'n+p'n'+as+c'am' *H/h bones are in a lying position.* (atsp'np'nasts'a'm, vi.); ˤaˤʷ+s+c'ám' *bony.* ((aˤwsts'a'm (lit. it has many bones), adj.); u+x̌ʷal'+á s+c'am' *bony.* (uqhwa'la sts'a'm (lit. It is like a bone), adj.); x̌amá+[c]'am' *heavy-boned.* (qhamast'a'm (lit. He is heavy as to the bone), adj.); x̌am+a+s+c'am' ł dol+dólq'ʷ+t *burly, husky.* (qhamats'a'm ł doldolq'wt. (lit. He is heavy-boned and strong), adj.)

√c'm', † c'o[m]' *suck (on a solid object).* (ts'o'n (stem), vt.); [also recorded as √cm'] s+cóm'+m *sucking.* (stso'mm, n.); s+c'úm'+m *making the sound of sucking.* (sts'u'mm, vt.); i s+c'úm'+c'm'+iš *H/S is making the sound of sucking; h/s is making the sound of a mouse.* (ists'u'mts'u'mish, vt.); ‡ c'óm'-nt-s *sucked (H/s...on it), sucked (he...it).* (ts'o'mnts, vi, vt.)

√c'm'ł † s+c'óm'+c'om'ł+t *abscess, boil, carbuncle.* (sts'o'mts'o'młt, n.) [see also √mc'łt]

√c'p † u+y+c'óp *grasp, hold (H/i suddenly gets a very tight hold or grasp), suddenly (it...became tightened).* (uyts'op, adv, n.); ya+c'p *clam up (lit. It became tightened up).* (yats'p, vt.); ye+c[']óp *to tighten (suddenly).* (yetsop); ∥ s+y+c'p=a'wes *connection, tightening together.* (syts'pa'wes, n.); s+n+c'ip=s+m *cat nap.* (snts'ipsm (lit. an eye pinching), n.) [xref √c'p']

√c'p', † c'ep' *airtight, lightproof.* (ts'ep' (stem), adj.); ‡ c'ep'+m-st-m *caulk.* (ts'epmstm (lit. It (canoe) was made watertight by packing seams with pitch), vt.) [xref √c'p]

√c'p', † c'ip' *pinch.* (ts'ip (stem), v.); hn+c'ap'-s *She "snapped" her eyes (a sign of contempt).* (hnts'ap's, v.); ‡ c'+c'íp'-n't-s *chuck.* (ts'ts'ip"nts (lit. He pinched her slightly (playfully), vt.) [xref √c'p, √č'p',]

√c'p'l § s+c'ip'al+yóh+m *dole.* (sts'ip'alyohm (lit. dealing out something sparingly), vt.)

√c'p'q' † [also recorded as √c'p'q] c'ap'q *adhere, stick to (as glue).* (ts'ap'q' (stem), vi.); t+c'áp'q *adhere, stick to.* (tts'ap'q (lit. It stuck fast as if glued to something; he became firmly attached), vi, vt.); c'p'q'+mín+n *glue, agglutinin.* (ts'p'q'minn, n.); ∥ ča[t]+c'p'q'=iłx̌ʷ+n *asphalt, glue for the roof.* (chats'p'q'iłkhwn. black-top, pitch. (lit. means of paving roads), n.); s+c'p'q'=íw'es *cohesion.* (sts'p'q'i'wes (lit. sticking together), n.); ‡ c'p'q'= íw'es-nt-s *agglutinate.* (ts'p'q'i'wesnts (lit. He stuck two or more things together), vt.); c'p'q'=íw'es-n *compose.* (ts'p'q'i'wesn (lit. I stuck it together), vt.); t+c'áp'q'-n *annex.* (tts'ap'q'n (lit. I glued it to something else), v.)

√c'p'x̌ʷ † c'+c'p'x̌ʷ=íl'=us *hole (tiny...).* (Ts'ts'p'qhwi'lus (lit. little spring north of Old Daniel place, west of De Smet, Idaho), n.)

√c'q' † c'aq' *batch, bunched, clumped, cluster.* (ts'aq', n.); a·+c'áq' *clump, cluster, system (root or nerve).* (aats'aq' (lit. A cluster or clump of bushes), n.); ∥ c'aq'=álx̌ *battery.*

(ts'aq'<u>a</u>lqh, n.); c'aq'=álx *brain, brainpower*. (ts'aq'<u>a</u>lkh, n.); ul c'aq'= álx̌ *cerebro-spinal*. (ul ts'aq'<u>a</u>lqh (lit. pertaining to the brain and spinal cord), adj.); c'áq'=ałp *fir*. (ts'<u>a</u>q'ałp, n.); c'áq'=ełp *fir*. (ts'<u>a</u>q'ełp, n.)

√c'qʷ₁ † c'eqʷ *butcher*. (ts'eqw (stem), n.)

√c'qʷ₂ † c'uqʷ+[c]'uqʷ+čs+n'cút *acclaim*. (ts'uqwt'uqwchs'nts<u>u</u>t (lit. clapping one's hands), n.)

√c'qʷ' c'+c'óq'ʷ=ops *nit, young of lice*. (ts'ts'<u>o</u>q'ops (larvae of lice), n.); c'+c'óq'ʷ+l'=ípeʔ *red nit*. (ts'ts'<u>o</u>q"l<u>i</u>pe', n.)

√c'qʷ'n † c'uq'ʷn *pronounce*. (ts'uq'un (stem), vt.); c'uq'ʷn+cút *name (H/s pronounced h/h own...)*. (ts'uq'wnts<u>u</u>t, n.); s+c'aq'ʷ+c'úq'ʷn' *catechism*. (sts'aq'wts'<u>u</u>q'w'n (lit. that which is pronounced repeatedly (ref. to catechetic (al) instruction), n.); c'uq'ʷ+c'uq'ʷún'+m' *chattered, read aloud, recited*. (ts'uq'wts'uq'<u>u</u>'n'm. (lit. H/s pronounced one thing after another), vi.); hn+c'oq'ʷ+coq'ʷún'+em'n' *classroom*. (hnts'oq'wtsoq'<u>u</u>'ne'mn' (lit. a room for reading), n.); i+c'uq'ʷ+c'uq'ʷún'+m'š *articulate, reading, reciting, school (going to...)*. (its'uq'wts'uq'<u>u</u>'n'msh (lit. He is uttering (speech sounds), vi.); ‡ c'uq'ʷún-t-s *designate, named (he...), pronounced (he...it)*. (ts'uq'<u>u</u>nts, vt.); c'uq'ʷún-šit-s *bequeath*. (ts'uq'<u>u</u>nshits (lit. He gave or left something to him by will), vt.); § s+mel'+c'uq'ʷún+m *connotation*. (sme'lts'uq<u>u</u>nm (lit. mentioning (or inferring) something with what is said), n.); s+nukʷ+c'uq'ʷ+c'uqʷún'+m' *classmate (lit. fellow reader)*. (snukwts'uq'wts'uq<u>u</u>'n'm, n.)

√c'r₁ † c'ar *cold (to the touch)*. (ts'ar (stem), adj.); c'ar+t *bleak, cold (It*

is...). (ts'art, n.); hn+c'ár+t *water (cold...)*. (hnts'<u>a</u>rt, n.); § pinč c'ar+t *remains (It...cold or chilly)*. (pinch ts'art, vi.)

√c'r₂ † s+c'ér=us *currants*. (sts'<u>e</u>rus, n.)

√c'r₃ † c'or *salt, sour*. (ts'or (stem), n, adj.); u· c'ór *brackisk, salty, sour (it is...)*. (uuts'<u>o</u>r, adj.); c'ór+emn *salt shaker*. (ts'<u>o</u>remn, n.); hn+c'óʔor *sour (it became...)*. (hnts'<u>o</u>'or, vi.); // a+n+c'ór=kʷeʔ *salt water*. (ants'<u>o</u>rkwe', n.); hn+c'or=kʷeʔ *brine*. (hnts'orkwe' (lit. salt water), n.); hn+c'or+c[']ór'=kʷeʔ *soda-pop*. (hnts'orts<u>o</u>r'kwe' (lit. sour water), n.); hn+c'+c'ór=us *eyes wincing because of extremely sour sensation (ie. lemon)*. (hnts't's<u>o</u>rus, vt.); hn+c'ór= s+m *winked (he...)*. (hnts'<u>o</u>rsm, vi.); s+n+c'ór=s+m *winking*. (snts'<u>o</u>rsm, vi.) ‡ hn+c'ór=kʷeʔ-nt-s *salted (he...it)*. (hnts'<u>o</u>rkwe'nts, vt.); hn+c'ór= s+m-nt-s *winked (he...at him)*. (hnts'<u>o</u>rsmnts, vi.)

√c'r(') † c'aʔar *ache, hurt, ill*. (ts'a'ar (stem). to be hurt, adj.); s+c'áʔar *ache (to...), pain (to feel...), illness, sickness*. (sts'a'ar, vi, n.); hn+c'ar'+n *ailment, disease, sickness*. (hnts'a'rn, n.); č⌣y'c+c'aʔar *ill, sick*. (chi'ts'a'ar (lit. I am sick), adj.); // i·+c'áʔar=qn *crapulous*. (iits'<u>a</u>'arqn (lit. He is having an ache as to his head), adj.); s+c'aʔar=qn *headache*. (sts'a'arqn, n.); s+c'aʔar=qín *headache*. (sts'a'arq<u>i</u>n, n.); s+c'aʔar=qín=šn' *arthritis*. (sts'a'arq<u>i</u>nsh'n (lit. feeling pain in the knee), n.); s+t+c'ar'=ilgʷes *ailing, ill (lit. feeling pain physically at heart)*. (stts'a'rilgwes, vt, n.); hn+t+c'ar'= ílgʷes+n *clinic, hospital*. (hntts'a'r<u>i</u>lgwesn. (lit. place for the sick), n.); ul hn+t+c'ar'=ílgʷes+n *clinical*. (ul hntts'a'r<u>i</u>lgwesn, adj.); s+niʔ+c'áʔ+c'ar'=enč *pains (intestinal...)*. (sni'ts'<u>a</u>'ts'a'rench, n.);

s+n+c'ar'=ínč+n' *backache.* (snts'a'ri̲nch'n (lit. suffering pain in the back), n.); s+n+c'ar'=íne? *earache.* (snts'a'ri̲ne' (lit. having pain in the ear), n.); s+t+c'á?ar=gʷl *bellyache, colic, stomach ache.* (stts'a̲'argul, n.)

√c's † c'es *collect (by picking), salvage.* (ts'es (stem), vt.); c'es+p *annihilate, consume, destroy.* (ts'esp (stem), vt.); c'es+p *gone (It is all...).* (ts'esp (lit. It went away piece by piece), adj.); ∥ [probably same root] c's+c's=qín'+n' *catbird.* (ts'sts'sqi'n'n, n.); ‡ hn+c's+p+nún-t-s *deplete.* (hnts'spnu̲nts (lit. He succeeded in emptying it), vt.); hn+c's+p+núm-t-m *empty.* (hnts'spnu̲mtm (lit. It (ie. bag) was emptied), vi.); hn+c's+p=úl'mxʷ-st-m *devastate.* (hnts'spu̲'lmkhwstm (lit. The land was deprived of inhabitants), vi.)

√c'sl † s+c'sl'=úse? *hail.* (sts's'lu̲se', n.)

√c'št † s+c'išt *brother-in-law.* (sts'isht, n.)

√c'wn † s+c'uwe·ní *giant.* (sts'uweeni̲ (lit. big-foot), n.); § s+c'uwe·ní he t+t'míxʷ *dinosaur.* (sts'uweeni̲ he tt'mi̲khw (lit. It is a giant one who is an animal), n.)

√c'w' † c'aw' *boring, dry, soaked, washed out.* (ts'a'w (stem), adj.); c'á?aw' *dilute, thin out.* (ts'a̲'a'w (lit. It was washed), v.); c'áw'+c'aw'+t *insipid, stale (It is stale...).* (ts'a̲'wts'a'wt, adj.); c'áw'+emn *detergent.* (ts'a̲'wemn (lit. a cleansing liquid), n.); ∥ c'áw'=s+m *washed (He...his face).* (ts'a̲'wsm, vt.); c'áw'+c'aw'=s+m *washed (They...their faces).* (ts'a̲'wts'a'wsm, vt, n.); c'áw'=s+n *soap.* (ts'a̲'wsn (lit. means of washing face), n.); hn+c'á?=us+n *basin, washbowl.* (hnts'a̲'usn (lit. means of washing the face), n.); hn+c'áw'+c'aw'=cn *cliche.* (hnts'a̲'wts'a'wtsn (lit. He speaks word that are washed up, insipid), n.); i t+c'áw'=qn+mš *He is washing his hair (lit. He is shampooing).* (itts'a̲'wqnmsh, vt.); a+can+c'áw'+c'aw'=qs+t+m *bureau, chest (of drawers), dresser.* (atsants'a̲'wts'a'wqstm, n.); § s+n+c['] aw'+ɬ+qap=íɬc'e? *dish washing.* (sntsa'w'ɬqapiɬts'e', n.)

√c'w'q † c'aw'q *extract, pull out (a solid object).* (ts'a'wq (stem). to extract a solid object (as nail out of board), vt.); ∥ c'ow'q=ín+n *corkscrew.* (ts'o'wqi̲nn (lit. spiral shaped device for drawing corks from bottles), n.); ‡ c'áw'q-nt-s *nail (He pulled out the...), pulled (He...out the nail).* (ts'a̲'wqnts, n, vt.); hn+c'ow'+c'ow'q=íns-nt-n *teeth (his...were extracted).* (hnts'o'wts'o'wqi̲nsntn, n.)

√c'xʷ₁ † hn+c'éxʷ+t *channel, creek, stream.* (hnts'ekhut, n.) [xref √cxʷ]

√c'xʷ₂ † c'ixʷ *to prepare chips by peeling and tying.* (ts'ikhw)

√c'x̌₁ † c'ax̌ *fry.* (ts'aqh (stem), vt.); s+c'ax̌ *meat (fried...), steak.* (sts'aqh, n.); ‡ c'áx̌-n *fried (I...the meat).* (ts'aqhn, vt, n.)

√c'x̌₂ s+c'+c'x̌=í?st *gravel.* (sts'ts'qhi̲'st, n.)

√c'x̌ʷ₁ † c'ax̌ʷ *acquiesce, choose, guilty, voluntarily (to do...).* (ts'aqhw (stem). responsible, vi, vt, adj, adv.); c'áx̌ʷ+m *betroth, devoted.* (ts'a̲qhum (lit. He promised solemnly, H/s vowed, h/s promised marriage), vt, vi.); s+c'ax̌ʷ+m *betrothal, bond, commitment, obligation, promising.* (sts'aqhum, n.); c'áx̌ʷ+c'ux̌ʷ+n *admonish, advise, counsel.* (ts'aqhwts'uqhwn (lit. Give good counsel), vt.); s+c'á·x̌ʷ+c'ux̌ʷ+n *counsel.* (sts'a̲aqhwts'uqhwn (lit. giving advice or guidance), n.); s+c'áx̌ʷ+c'ux̌ʷ+m *advice.* (sts'a̲qhwts'uqhum, n.); sya·+c'áx̌ʷ+m devotee (lit. One who has vowed to do a specific duty). (syaats'a̲qhum, n.); sya·+c'áx̌ʷ+c'ux̌ʷ+n counselor. (syaats'a̲qhwts'uqhwn (lit. One who gives advice), n.); i-y+t+c'áx̌ʷ You did it willingly, on purpose. (iytts'a̲qhw, v.); hiy+t+c'áx̌ʷ deliberate. (hiytts'a̲qhw (lit. It was done deliberately), vt.); s+c'ux̌ʷ-n't-w'íš compromise. (sts'uqhw'nt'wish (lit. promising mutually), vi.); ⫽ hn+c'ux̌ʷ= íl+m devaluation. (hnts'uqhwi̲lm (lit. teaching (promising) that is handed down to offspring forebearers), n.); t+c'ux̌ʷ=ípele? decide, judged (He...). (tts'uqhwi̲pele', v.); s+t+c'ux̌ʷ=ípele? arbitrament, judgement. (stt'suqhwi̲pele', n.); s+t+c'ox̌ʷ=ipele? decision. (stts'oqhwipele', n.); hn+t+c'ux̌ʷ=ípele?+n bar, bench, canon, chancery, judgement, law (the...), law. (hntts'uqhwi̲pele'n, n.); hn+t+c'ux̌ʷ=íple?+n edict, equity, law. (hntts'uqhwiple'n (lit. promise made by one for others, public announcement having the force of a law, means of judging), n.); sya+t+c'ux̌ʷ=iple? arbiter. (syatts'uqhwiple', n.); sya+t+c'ux̌ʷ= ipele? judge. (syatts'uqhwipele', n.); siya+t+c'ux̌ʷ=ípele? judge, chancellor. (siyatts'uqhwipele', n.); § ul s+čint hen+t+c'ux̌ʷ=ípele?-is democracy. (ul schint hentts'uqhwipele'is (lit. government of the people), n.); miy+miyał+sya+t+c'ux̌ʷ=ipele? judge (competent and critical), connoisseur. (miymiyałsyatts'uqhwipele', n.); s+meˤʷ+ł+s+c'áx̌ʷ+m promise (a...broken, breach of...). (sme(wlsts'a̲qhum, n.); hi+s+nukʷ+meˤʷ+ł+nt+c'ux̌ʷ= íple?+n complicity. (hisnukwme(włntts'uqhwiple'n (lit. He

is my partner in violating the law), n.); elu+ł+n+t+c'ux̌ʷ=ípele?+n anarchic, lawless. (elułntts'uqhwipele'n (lit. H/s/i has no law), adj.)

√c'x̌ʷ₂ † c'ex̌ʷ spark. (ts'e̲qhw (stem), n.); c'éx̌ʷ+c'ex̌ʷ+t ember, coal, spark spark. (ts'e̲qhwts'eqhwt, n.); s+t+c'ex̌ʷ+ncut asteroid, stars, self-illuminating body. (stts'e̲qhwntsut, n.); § ul [u+x̌ʷel'+e] s+c'éx̌ʷ+ncut astral. (ul sts'e̲qhwntsut or uqhwe'le̲ (lit. It is like a star), adj.); sye+č+súx̌ʷ=ene? tel' s+t+c'éx̌ʷ+ncut astrologer, one who understands the stars. (syechsu̲khwene' te'l stts'e̲qhwntsut, n.); [also recorded as √c'xʷ] č+súx̌ʷ=me?+n ha s+t+c'ex̌ʷ+ncut astrology. (chsu̲khwme'n ha stts'ekhwntsut (lit. self illuminating body that is a guide), n.); s+t+miy+iy= ipele?+s x̌ʷe s+t+c[']éx̌ʷ+ncut astronomy. (stmiyiyipele's khwe sttse̲qhwntsut, n.)

√c'yx̌ʷ † hn+c'oy'+cóy'x̌ʷ+m Spangle, Washington. (Hnts'o'ytso̲'yqhwm (lit. town in Washington, n.)

√c'ˤn ⫽ c'aˤ'+c'in'=šn' character (name of...in a parable). (ts'a')ts'i'nsh'n, n.)

√c'?₁ † c'ú?u+m cry, weep, wept (h/s...). (ts'u'um (stem), vi.); e· c'ú?u+m weep, cry. (eets'u̲'um (lit. H/s weeps), vi.); c'ú?+c'u?+m+ul cry!, weep!. (ts'u̲'ts'u'mul, v.); eč+s+c'u?+m+ís weep. (echsts'u'mi̲s..., vi.); s+c'ú?u+mš mourning. (sts'u̲'umsh, vi.); čn'‿c'ú?u+m weep, wept. (ch'nts'u̲'um (lit. I, customarily, weep/I wept), vt.); č‿y'c+[c']ú?u+mš weeping (I am...). (chi'tssu̲'umsh, vi.); čeł‿č‿y'c+c'ú?u+mš weep. (chełchists'u̲'umsh (lit. I will weep), vi.); kʷ'ne? čn‿c'ú?u+m weep (I am going to...). (k'wne'chnts'u̲'um, vi.);

kʷu‿iʔ-čs+c'uʔu+m+mín+m *I am weeping for you (sg.).* (kwi'chsts'u'mi̱nm, vi.); hiʔ-čs+c'uʔ+mín+m *weeping (I am...for h/h).* (hi'chsts'u'mi̱nm, vi.); kʷup‿hiʔ-čs+c'uʔ+mín+m *I am weeping for you (pl).* (kuphi'chstsu'mi̱nm, vi.); kʷp‿hiʔ-čs+c[']uʔ+mín+m *weeping (I am...for you (pl)).* (kuphi'chstsu'mi̱nm, vi.)); hiʔ-čs+c'uʔ+mín+m-lš *weeping (I am...for them).* (hi'chsts'u'mi̱nmlsh, vi.); kʷʔ‿c'úʔu+m *weep (you (sg.)...).* (ku'ts'u̱'um, vi.); kʷu‿c'úʔu+m *You (sg) wept, weep.* (kuuts'u̱'um, vi.); kʷʷneʔ kʷu·‿c'úʔu+m *You (sg.) are going to weep.* (kwne'kuuts'u̱'um, vi.); kʷu‿y'‿c'úʔu+mš *You (sg) are weeping.* (ku'yts'u̱'umsh, vi.); čeł‿kʷu‿s+c'uʔu+mš *(lit. you (sg.) will weep).* (chełkusts'u'umsh, vt.); čn‿iʔ+čs+c'uʔ+mín+m-p *weeping.* (chni'chsts'u'mi̱nmp. (lit. you(s) are weeping for me), vt.); i-čs+c'uʔ+mín+m *You (sg.) are weeping for h/h. sobbing, crying.* (ichsts'u'mi̱nm, vi.); e·c'úʔ+c'uʔ+m-lš *weep, cry (lit. H/s weeps (pl.))* (eets'u̱'ts'u'mlsh, v.); i·+c'úʔu+mš *H/s is weeping, crying, sobbing.* (iits'u̱'umsh, vi.); čes‿cuʔ+uʔ+mš *he/she will weep.* (chestsu'u'msh, vi.); kʷʷneʔ c'úʔu+m *H/s is going to weep.* (k'wne'ts'u̱'um, vi.); č‿y'c+čs+cuʔ+mín+m-s *lit. h/s is weeping for me.* (chi'chstsu'mi̱nms, vt.); kʷu‿y'‿čs+c'uʔu+m+mín+m-s *H/S is weeping for you (sg).* (ku'ychsts'u'mi̱nms, vi.); č‿c'úʔ+c'uʔu+m *wept (we...).* (chts'u̱'ts'u'um, vi.); č'e·‿c'úʔ+cuʔu+m *weep (we...).* (ch'eets'u̱'tsu'um, vi.); č‿ʔi·+c'úʔ+c'uʔu+mš *lit. we are weeping.* (ch'iits'u̱'ts'u'umsh, vt.); čeł‿č‿s+c'ú+c'uʔ+mš *weep (lit. we will weep).* (chełchsts'u̱'ts'u'umsh, vi.); k'ʷneʔ č‿c'ú?+c'uʔ+m *We are going to weep.* (k'wne'chts'u̱'ts'u'um, vi.); kʷup‿c'ú?+c'uʔu+m *You (pl.) wept.* (kupts'u̱'ts'u'um, vi.); kʷup‿ʔe·‿c'ú+c'uʔu+m *You (pl) weep.* (kup'eets'u̱'ts'u'um, vt.); kʷup‿ʔi·‿c'ú+c'uʔu+mš *You (pl) are weeping.* (kup'iits'u̱'tsu'umsh, vi.); k'ʷ neʔ kʷup‿c'ú+c'uʔu+m *You (pl.) are going to weep.* (k'wne'kupt'su'tsu'um, vi.); čeł‿kʷup‿s+c'uʔ+c'uʔu+mš *(lit. you (pl) will weep).* (chełkupsts'u̱'ts'u'umsh, vi.); čn‿ʔi+ʔ+čs+c'uʔ+mín+m-p *you (pl.) are weeping for me.* (chn'i'chsts'u'mi̱nmp, vt.); i-čs+c'uʔ+mín+m-lš *You (pl.) are weeping for them. sobbing, crying.* (ichsts'u'mi̱nmlsh, vi.); c'úʔ+c'uʔ+m-lš *wept (they...).* (ts'u̱'ts'u'mlsh, vi.); i· c'ú+c'uʔ+m-lš *They are weeping, sobbing, crying.* (iits'u̱'tsu'mlsh, vi.); čes‿c'uʔ+cuʔ+mš *weep.* (chests'u'tsu'um. (lit. they will weep), vi.); k'ʷneʔ c'ú+c'uʔu+m *They are going to weep.* (k'wne'ts'u̱'tsu'um, vi.); č‿y'c+čs+cuʔ+mín+m-s-lš *lit. they are weeping for me.* (chi'chstsu'mi̱nmslsh, vt.); kʷup‿ʔi‿čs+c'uʔ+mín+m-s-lš *They are weeping for you (pl.).* (kup'ichsts'u'mi̱nmslsh, vi.); ‡ čs+c'uʔ+mí-nt-s *bewail.* (chst'su'mi̱nts (lit. He expressed sorrow or regret over it), vt.); e čs+c'uʔ+mí-st-m-n *I (cust.) weep for you (sg.).* (echsts'u'mi̱stmn, vi.); e čs+c'uʔ+mí-s-n *I weep for h/h.* (echsts'u'mi̱sn, vi.); e čs+c'uʔ+mí-s-n-lš *I weep for them.* (echsts'u'mi̱snlsh, vi.); e čs+c'uʔ+mí-st-ulm-n *I weep for you (pl.)*. (echsts'u'mistulmn, v.); e čs+c'uʔ+mí-st-me-xʷ *You (sg.) weep for me.* (echsts'u'mistmekhw, vi.); e čs+c'uʔ+mí-st-xʷ *You (sg.) weep for h/h.* (echsts'u'mistkhw, vi.); e čs+c'uʔ+mí-st-me-s *H/s weeps for me.* (echsts'u'mistmes, vi.); e čs+c'uʔ+mí-st-mi-s *H/s weeps for you.* (echsts'u'mistmis, vi.); e čs+c'uʔ+mí-st-me-lp *You (pl.) weep for me.* (echsts'u'mistmelp, vi.); e čs+c'uʔ+mí-st-xʷ-lš *You (pl.) weep for them.* (echsts'u'mistkhwlsh, vi.); e čs+c'uʔ+mí-st-me-s-lš *They weep for me.* (echsts'u'mistmeslsh, vi.); e čs+c'uʔ+mí-st-mi-s-lš *They weep for you (pl.).* (echsts'u'mistmislsh, vi.)

√c'ʔ₂ † c'iʔ *deer, venison.* (ts'i', n.); ye·+c'íʔ *deer (He killed the...), killed (He...the deer).* (yeets'i', n, vt.); ∥ c'íʔy=elxʷ *buckskin, deer hide.* (ts'i'yelkhw, n.); § ul s+yuxʷm=ús+m=ul'mxʷ he c'iʔ *caribou.* (ul syukhmusmu'lmkhw he ts'i' (lit. deer of a cold country), n.); čn‿xʷuy hiɫ čn‿gʷič e c'iʔ *lit. I went over there and I saw a deer.* (chnkhuy hiɫ chngwich e ts'i', vt.)

√c'ʔ₃ ∥ s+c'íʔ+c'eʔ=ečt *hands.* (sts'i'ts'e'echt, n.)

√c'ʔ₄ ∥ s+c'úʔ=šn *foot, hoof.* (sts'u'shn, n.); s+c'úʔ+c'uʔ=šn *feet.* (sts'u'ts'u'shn, n.)

√čc₁ ‡ čec-nt-m *electrocute.* (chetsntm (lit. he was struck by lightning), vt.) [?]

√čc₂ † čic *arrive, discover.* (chits (stem), vi, vt.); s+čic *discovery.* (schits, n.); s+číc+c *company, visitors.* (schitsts, n.); hi-s+číc *discovery (it is my...).* (hischits, n.); sye·+číc *detective.* (syeechits (lit. One who discovers things), n.); ∥ s+čícuʔu=mš *Tribe (the discovered), Coeur d'Alene.* (Schitsu'umsh (lit. discovered people),

n.); s+n+čícuʔu=mš=cn. *Coeur d'Alene.* (snchitsu'umshtsn, (to speak...).); ‡ číc-n *discovered (I...it), discern.* (chitsn, vt.); číc-nt-s *chance on, detect.* (chitsnts (lit. He found it or met it accidently), vt.); číc-nt-eli-t *visited (we are...).* (chitsntelit (lit. we have an unusual visitor), vt.)

√čdl † čdel+n *guard, protect, shield.* (chdeln, vt.); čdél+ncut *assert ones rights, (lit. he defended himself)* (chdelntsut, vt.); kʷ‿iʔ-čdél+m *I am defending you (sg.).* (kwi'chdelm, vt.); čeɫ‿kʷ‿is+čdél+m *defend.* (cheɫkwischdelm. (lit. I will defend you (sg.)), vt.); hiʔ-čdél+m *defending (I am...h/h).* (hi'chdelm, vt.); čeɫ‿hi-s+čdel+m *defend.* (cheɫhischdelm (lit. I will defend h/h), vt.); kʷp‿hiʔ-čdél+m *defending (I am...you (pl)).* (kuphi'chdelm, vt.); čeɫ‿kʷp‿hi-s+čdel+m *defend, protect.* (cheɫkuphischdelm (lit. I will defend you (pl)), vt.); hiʔ-čdél+m-lš *defending (I am...them).* (hi'chdelmlsh, vt.); čeɫ‿hi-s+čdél+m-lš *I will defend them.* (cheɫhischdelmlsh, vt.); čn‿ʔiʔ+čdél+m *you (sg.) are defending me.* (chn'i'chdelm, vt.); čn‿ʔiʔ+čdél+m-p *defending.* (chn'i'chdelmp. (lit. you (sg.) are defending me), vt.); čeɫ‿čn‿ʔi-s+čdél+m *you (s) will defend me, you (sg.) are to defend me.* (cheɫchn'ischdelm, vt.); iʔ-čdél+m *You (sg.) are defending h/h.* (i'chdelm, vt.); čeɫ‿ʔi-s+čdél+m *you (s) will defend h/h.* (cheɫ'ischdelm, vt.); iʔ-čdél+m-lš *You [sg.] are defending them.* (i'chdelmlsh, vt.); č‿y'c+čdél+m-s *h/s is defending me.* (chi'chdelms, vt.); čeɫ‿či‿s+čdél+m-s *h/s will defend me.* (cheɫchischdelms, vt.); čeɫ‿kʷu‿s+čdél+m-s *(lit. h/s will defend you (s)).* (cheɫkuschdelms, vt.);

kʷu‿y'‿čdél+m-s *H/S is defending you (sg).* (ku'ychdelms, vt.);
čn‿ʔiʔ+čdél+m-p *defending (you (pl) are...me).* (chn'ichdelmp, vt.);
čeł‿či‿s+čdél+m-p *you (pl) will defend me.* (chełchischdelmp, vt.);
čeł‿ʔi-s+čdél+m-lš *you (pl) will defend them.* (cheł'ischdelmlsh, vt.);
č‿y'c+čdél+m-s-lš *lit. they are defending me.* (chi'chdelmslsh, vt.);
čeł‿či‿s+čdél+m-lš *they will defend me.* (chełchischdelmlsh, vt.);
kʷup‿ʔi‿čdél+m-s-lš *They are defending you (pl.).* (kup'ichdelmslsh, vt.); čeł‿kʷup‿s+čdél+m-lš *(lit. they will defend you (pl)).* (chełkupschdelmlsh, vt.); ∥ s+čdel=łc'eʔ *apologetic.* (schdelłts'e' (lit. defending another person), adj.); s+čdl=ílt *offspring (defending one's...), defending (...one's offspring).* (schdlilt, n, vt.); ‡ čdél-nt-s-n *I defended you (s).* (chdelntsn, vt.); e čdél-st-m-n *I defend you (sg.).* (echdelstmn, vt.); kʷneʔ čdél-nt-s-n *I am going to defend you (sg.).* (k'wne'chdelntsn, vt.); čdél-n *defend, guard, shield, protect. (lit. I defended him/her).* (chdeln, vt.); e+čdél+s-n *defend, intercede, behalf (speak on one's).* (echdelsn. (lit. I defend h/h/i.), vt.); k'ʷ neʔ čdél-n *I am going to defend h/h.* (k'wne'chdeln, vt.); čdél-nt-ulm-n *I defended you (pl).* (chdelntulmn, vt.); e čdél-st-ulm-n *I defend you (pl.).* (echdelstulmn, vt.); k'ʷ neʔ čdél-nt-ulm-n *I am going to defend you (pl.).* (k'wne'chdelntulmn, vt.); čdél-n-lš *defend (lit. I defended them).* (chdelnlsh, vt.); e čdél-s-n-lš *I defend them.* (echdelsnlsh); k'ʷ neʔ čdél-n-lš *I am going to defend them.* (k'wne'chdelnlsh, vt.); čdél-nt-se-xʷ *You (s) defended me.* (chdelntsekhw, vt.); e čdél-st-xʷ *You defend h/h/i.* (echdelstkhw, vt.); e čdél-st-me-xʷ *You (sg.) defend me.* (echdelstmekhw, vt.); k'ʷ neʔ čdél-nt-se-xʷ *You (sg.) are going to defend me.* (k'wne'chdelntsekhw, vt.); čdél-nt *You defend him/her.* (chdelnt, vt. (imper.)); čdél-nt-xʷ *you (s) defended him/her.* (chdelntkhw, vt.); k'ʷ neʔ čdél-nt-xʷ *You (sg.) are going to defend h/h.* (k'wne'chdelntkhw, vt.); čdél-nt-m *He was defended.* (chdelntm, vt.); čdél-nt-se-s *He/she defended me.* (chdelntses, vt.); e čdél-st-me-s *H/s defends me.* (echdelstmes, vt.); k'ʷ neʔ čdél-nt-s-es *H/s is going to defend me.* (k'wne'chdelntses, vt.); čdél-nt-si-s *he/she defended you (s).* (chdelntsis, vt.); e čdél-st-mi-s *H/s defends you (sg.).* (echdelstmis, vt.); k'ʷ neʔ čdél-nt-si-s *H/s is going to defend you (sg.).* (k'wne'chdelntsis, vt.); čdél-nt-sel-p *You (pl) defended me.* (chdelntselp, vt.); e čdél-st-me-lp *You (pl.) defend me.* (echdelstmelp, vt.); k'ʷ neʔ čdél-nt-sel-p *You (pl.) are going to defend me.* (k'wne'chdelntselp, vt.); čdél-nt-ul *you (pl) defended him/her (imperative).* (chdelntul, vt.); čdél-nt-xʷ-lš *you (pl) defended them.* (chdelntkhwlsh, vt.); e čdél-st-xʷ-lš *You (pl.) defend them.* (echdelstkhwlsh, vt.); k'ʷ neʔ čdél-nt-xʷ-lš *You (pl..) are going to defend them.* (k'wne'chdelntkhwlsh, vt.); čdél-nt-se-s-lš *They defended me.* (chdelntseslsh, vt.); e čdél-st-me-s-lš *They defend me.* (echdelstmeslsh, vt.); k'ʷ neʔ čdél-nt-s-es-lš *They are going to defend me.* (k'wne'chdelntseslsh, vt.); čdél-nt-si-s-lš *they defended you (pl).* (chdelntsislsh, vt.); e čdél-st-mi-s-elš *They defend you (pl.).* (echdelstmiselsh, vt.); k'ʷ neʔ čdél-nt-ulmi-s *They are going to*

defend you (pl.).(k'wne'chdelntulmis, vt.)

√čgʷ † čigʷ *extend.* (chigw (stem). (lit. extend across), vt.); čigʷ+š *(lit. go out on the prairie)* (chigwsh, vt.); čet+čigʷ+iš *he went across, course.* (chetchigwish, vt.); e+čet+čígʷ+iš *cross, traverse.* (echetchigwish (lit. H/s crossed/traversed the plain), vt.); s+čet+čígʷ+iš *setting out (...across a plain), Big Bend country (going into the...), plain (setting out across a...), prairie (going into the...).* (schetchigwish, n, vi.); čn'‿čet+čigʷ+iš *traverse.* (ch'nchetchigwish (lit. I traversed the plain), vi.); kʷʔ‿čet+čígʷ+iš *traverse (you (sg.)...).* (ku'chetchigwish, vt.); č‿ʔe+čet+čígʷ+iš *We traverse the plain.* (ch'echetchigwish, vt.); kʷp'‿e+čet+čígʷ+iš *traverse (you (pl.)...the plain).* (kup'echetchigwish, vt.); **∥** s+čugʷ=áx̌n *arm, limb (body).* (schugwaqhn (lit. that which extends into space from the body), n.); ul s+čogʷ=ax̌n *brachial.* (ul schogwaqhn (lit. of the arm), adj.) [see also √čhgʷ]

√čhgʷ † čet+čihgʷ *area, field, plain.* (chetchihgw, n.) [xref √čgʷ]

√čl₁ † čel *await (...eagerly, anxiously).* (chel (stem), vt.)

√čl₂ † hn+či+člí *little lake near Benewah Lake.* (Hnchichli, n.)

√člš ∥ s+n+čélš=elps *hardtack.* (snchelshelps. (lit. hard food) ("story" word), n.)

√člxʷ † čélexʷ *muskrat.* (chelekhw, n.); č+čl'ixʷ *muskrat, small muskrat.* (chch'likhw, dim n.)

√člʔ † čeleʔ *bark, cradle board.*(chele', n.) [xref √č'l]

√čl' † čel' *cough up.* (che'l (stem), vi.); čil' *nauseated, throw up, vomit.* (chi'l, v, vt.)

√čł₁ † čeł *divorce, part, separate.* (cheł (stem), vi, vt.); e·čeł+m *alone, independent, isolated.* (eechełm (lit. H/s is separated from other people), adj.); ec+t+čéł+m *unique.* (etstchełm (lit. It is separated from others), adj.); čeł+m+ncut *anchorite.* (chełmntsut (lit. he set himself aside/apart), n.); s+cén+čeł+ł+m *break away.* (stsenchełłm, vi.); ∥ s+čł+čł=íw'es *division.* (schłchłi'wes (lit. The act or state of being separated into parts), n.); ‡ čeł+m-s-n *compart.* (chełmsn (lit. I divided it, I separated it), vt.); čéł+m-st-m *asunder.* (chełmstm (lit. He put apart in position or direction), adv.); čéł+čł+m-st-m *bracket.* (chełchłmstm (lit. They were classified or grouped together), vt.); čł=iwes-nt-m *disjointed, disconnect.* (chłiwesntm. (lit. It was disjointed), vi.); čł=iw'es-nt-m-lš *detribalize, disorganized.* (chłi'wesntmlsh, vi.)

√čł₂ † čił *give.* (chił, vt.); číł+šeš *conduce.* (chiłshesh (lit. He gave to others), vi.); s+čił+šeš *concession, consignment, present.* (schiłshesh (lit. giving one something), n.); s+číł+ł+šeš *datum.* (schiłłshesh (lit. something given), n.); sye+číł+šeš *bartender.* (syechiłshesh (lit. One who gives (sells) liquors), n.); číł+šeš+mn *delivery.* (chiłsheshmn, n.); s+číł+šeš+mn *delivery (lit. giving something away).* (schiłsheshmn, n.); čeł+šeš+mi+ncut *surrender, betray.* (chełsheshmintsut (lit. He gave himself away; h/s submitted/gave up), vi, vt.); čeł‿kʷp‿hi-s+čił+t+m *give, present.* (chełkuphischiłtm (lit. I am going to give it to you), vt.); čeł‿č‿s+číł+t+m-s *give (lit. he is going to give it to us).* (chełchschiłtms, vt.); ∥ s+n+číł=us *compensation.* (snchiłus, n.); uł n+číł=us *reimbursed (He...).* (ułnchiłus, vt.); ‡ čił-n *I gave it* *to him or her.* (chiḻn, vt.); čił-n-lš *I gave it to them.* (chiḻnlsh, vt.); čił-t-s-n *I gave it to you (sg.).* (chiḻtsn, vt.); číł-t-ulm-n *I gave it to you (pl.).* (chiḻtulmn, vt.); číł+šeš+mn-n *consign.* (chiḻsheshmnn (lit. I gave it away), vt.); číł-t-sel-em *I was given it.* (chiḻtselem, vt.); číł-t-se-xʷ *You (sg.) gave it to me.* (chiḻtsekhw, vt.); číł-t-si-t *You (sg.) were given it.* (chiḻtsit, vt.); číł-t-se-s *H/s gave it to me.* (chiḻtses, vt.); čił+t+m *He was given it, bestow.* (chiḻtm, vt.); číł+šeš+m-nt-s *deliver, H/s sold it.* (chiḻsheshmnts (lit. He gave it away), vt.); číł-t-sel-p *You (pl.) gave it to me.* (chiḻtselp, vt.); číł-t-ulmi-t *You (pl.) were given it.* (chiḻtulmit, vt.); číł-t-se-s-lš *They gave it to me.* (chiḻtseslsh, vt.);

√čłp₁ † čłip *hunted.* (chłip (lit. he hunted game), vi.); čł+čłip *they hunted game.* (chłchłip, vt.); s+čłíp *hunt, hunting, to hunt.* (schłip, v.); ‡ in+čełep-núm-t *hunt (He wants to...game), game (He wants to hunt...).* (inchełepnumt, n, vt.)

√čłp₂ čłp+m=ew'es+i·ʔú *horse trapping with long fringes over buttocks.* (chłp'me'wesii'u, n.)

√čłs † s+čłís+is+m *analogue.* (schłisism, n.); s+čłis+m+šeš *analogy, metaphor, comparison.* (schłismshesh, n.); s+čłí[s]+m'šeš *opposition.* (schłish'mshesh (lit. putting side by side with something else), n.); ul s+čłís+m+šeš *comparative.* (ul schłismshesh (lit. involving comparison), adj.); čłis+s+útm *comparable.* (chłissutm (lit. It's worthy of comparison), adj.); ‡ čłís+m-stu-s *compare, coordinate.* (chłismstus (lit. He measured (compared) it with something else), vi.); § ʔep+s+čłís+s+mn *analogous.* (epschłissmn. vi. (lit. It has similarity),

adj.); elu+s+čłís+is+m *asymmetric, unequal.* (eluschłisism (lit. It has no comparison), adj.)

√čm ∥ čm=iw'es *Chatcolet (Lake).* (chmi'wes (lit. midsection), n.); hn+čem=cn *confluence, St. Maries, Idaho.* (Hnchemtsn, n.)

√čmn † č+čmin *fling, hurl, toss.* (chchmin (lit. throw one object), vi.); č+čmí *throw.* ((lit. throw one object), chchmi, vt.); ‡ č+čmin-t-s *cast, discard, throw away.* (chchmints, vt.); tč+čmín+p=łxʷ-nt-m *degrade, eject.* (tchchminpłkhwntm (lit. He was thrown out of the house, He was deprived of dignity, He was ousted), vi.)

√čm'₁ † čem' *grab, grasp.* (che'm (lit. take hold of objects (stem)), vt.); čim['] *grab some.* (ch'im (stem), vt.); t+čém'+m *detract.* (tche'mm (lit. He plucked (berries, etc.), v.); s+t+čem'+m *taking hold of them (berries) on tree, plant.* (stche'mm, vt.); čet+čem'+čm' *Emida, Idaho. Emida.* (Chetche'mch'm (lit. gathering objects on the meadow), n.); ∥ t+čm'=cín+m *He took them (berries) off bush to eat.* (tch'mtsinm, v.); s+čm'=íčn' *armament.* (sch'mich'n (lit. weapons taken along), n.); či·‿čím[']=čt+m *h/s took a handful this way.* (chiich'imchtm, vt.); hn+čm'=íłxʷ *burglarize, robbed.* (hnch'miłkhw (lit. One who takes from a house), vi.); sye+n+čm'=íłxʷ *bandit, brigand, burglar, buccaneer.* (syench'miłkhw (lit. One who takes from a house), n.); ‡ čem'-nt-s *grasp.* (che'mnts, vi.); tep+cen+čém'-nt-s *deduct.* (teptsenche'mnts (lit. He took to be left several things), v.); hn+čm'=íłxʷ-nt-s *rob (lit. he robbed him).* (hnch'miłkhwnts, vi.); čm'=íčn'-t-sel-em *disarm.* (ch'mich'ntselem (lit. I was deprived of weapons), vi, vt.);

hn+čm'=iłx̌ʷ-nt-sel-m *despoil, burglarized.* (hnch'miłkhwntselm (lit. My house was burglarized), vi.); **§** čam'+ʔelu+ł+x̌al+x̌elex̌ʷ *toothless.* (cha'm'elułqhalqhelekhw (lit. he no longer has his teeth), adj.)

√čm'₂ čim' *disdain.* (chi'm (stem), vt.)

√čn₁ † čn‿ *I.* (chn, interrogative.); čnʔe *I, me, ego.* (chn'e, pro.); čn+ʔeng̣ʷet *I.* (chn'engwet (lit. it is I, I am I), pro.); u čnʔé? *alone (I..).* (uchn'e, adj.); **§** t'uʔ u+čn‿x̌é·s *am (Well, I...fine.* (t'u' uchnqheees, , vi.); čn‿x̌es+e·y+ʔitš *slept.* (chnqhesee'yitsh (lit. I slept well), vt.);

√čn₂ † čen+t *smell (strong), strong (to smell...).* (chent, vi.); **//** čen+čen+t=ičt *alligator, crocodile, lizard.* (chenchenticht, n.)

√čn₃ † e+čín+m *happen.* (echinm? (lit. what happened to h/h?, *What did h/s do?*), vi.); kʷu‿y'‿c+ʔi+čín+mš *What are you doing?* (ku'yts'ichinmsh, qu.); čin+mš *What in the world are you doing (here)?* (chinmsh?, qu.); kʷu‿ʔe+čín+m *What did you (sg.) do?* (ku'echinm, qu.); kʷu‿ʔc+čín+m *How are you (sg.)?* (ku'tschinm?, vi.); kʷu‿y'‿n ha?+čána=q[]n *Where do you intend to go? (lit. Where is your head going?).* (ku'yn ha'chanaqhn, qu.)

√čn₄ † u· čn· *is rumbling (It...).* (uuchnnn, vi.); hn+cén+čn=cn *clamor, din.* (hnchenchntsn. (lit. It (engine) makes a deep and violent noise), n.)

√čnkʷ en+čnúkʷ=cn *Chinook (to speak...).* (enchnukwtsn, n.)

√čnl † čníl+emn *deadly, baneful, venomous, poison.* (chnilemn, adj, n.); s+čníl+n *contagion.* (schniln (lit. poisoning another), n.); **§** ul šiw't he čníl+emn *rat poison.* (ul shi'wt he chnilemn, n.); hn+péste?=us+s x̌ʷe čníl+emn *antidote.* (hnpeste'uss khwe chnilemn (lit. the opposite side of poison, something that counteracts poison, injury or contagion), n.)

√čnt † s+čint *human being, Indian.* (Schint, n.); ʔep+s+čínt *there are people/Indians.* (epschint, vi.); **§** s+cegʷ+es+čínt *animal magnetism, archetype, model (example for a person).* (stsegweschint (lit. animal example, model; model for a human being; talisman, anything that has a magical effect), n.); s+cugʷ+cugʷ+s+čín't *demonstration.* (stsugwtsuguschi'nt (lit. teaching a person by one's own example), n.); s+miyes+čínt *aristocracy, aristocrat, baron, dignitary, bigwig, blue blood, noble descent, nobleman.* (smiyeschint (lit. more than ordinary human beings), n.); lut s+miy+es+čínt *commoner.* (lut smiyeschint (lit. He is not a nobleman), n.); s+m'+m'iy'es+čín't *bourgeois.* (sm"mi'yeschi'nt (lit. little nobleman), n.); miyes+čint+m-st-m *elevate, dignify, ennoble.* (miyeschintmstm (lit. h/s was made noble), vi.); ul s+čint hen+t+c'ux̌ʷ=ípele?-is *democracy.* (ul schint hentts'uqhwipele'is (lit. government of the people), n.); s+lem+t+me+s+čínt *charm.* (slemtmeschint (lit. The power or quality of pleasing people), n.); e+tem+n+es+čínt *kind.* (etemneschint, vt. (lit. He treats others sociably), adj.); s+tem+n+es+čint *entertain, host.* (stemneschint, vt.); ul+s+qʷic=ul'mx̌ʷ-s he s+čint *Apache (lit. Indian of a warm country).* (ul sqwitsu'lmkhws he schint, n.); s+čint+eł+yilmix̌ʷ+m *agency, agent (Indian), superintendent.* (schintełyilmikhm (lit. Indian chief), n.); s+čint+eł+ylmíx̌ʷ+m *bureaucrat, chief (indian...).* (schintełylmikhum, n.); s+ʕem+ʕem+s+čínt *animosity, animus, hate, hostility.* (s(em(emschint. (lit. feeling hostility

toward a human being), n.);
s+can+q'ey'+iy'+s xʷe s+čint
demography. (stsanq'e'yi'ys khwe
schint (lit. writing concerning people),
n.); cun=meʔ+s+čínt *taught
(he...Indians, human beings, people).*
(tsunme'schint, vt.); sye+cun=
meʔ+s+čínt *teacher (of human
beings).* (syetsunme'schint, n.);
a+c+pon'eʔ+mi+s+čént *opportunist.*
(atspo'ne"mischent (lit. One who takes
advantage of others), n.); suxʷ+s+čínt
recognized (He...a human being).
(sukhwschint, vt.); e+tem+n+es=čínt
convivial. (etemneschint, vt. (lit. He
treats others sociably), adj.);
elu+s+temn+es+čínt *cantankerous,
perverse (disposition), unfriendly,
unsociable.* (elustemneschint (lit. One
who is not sociable), adj.);
s+t+kʷel'+čs+xʷy+s+čínt *people (He
is going about visiting...), gathering
(He is going about...people).*
(stkwe'lchskhuyschint, n, vt.);
s+gʷič+s+čínt *seeing people.*
(sgwichschint, n.); gʷn+es+čínt
convoke, summoned. (gwneschint (lit.
H/s called people together), vt.);
s+lč'+me+s+čínt *coercion.*
(slch'meschint (lit. compelling people
to do things), n.); s+puteʔ+s+čínt
curtsy, bow. (spute'schint (lit. showing
respect for a person), n.); s+čn[t]+coc
Canada, British. (Schntsots. Canada
(lit. Indian (or people) of George),
adj.); gʷł s+čin[t]+cóc *Angles.* (guł
schintsots (lit. King George men, n.);
ul s+čin[t]+cóc *Anglican.* (ul
schintsots (lit. pertaining to King
George's men)., n.); ul s+čen[t]+cóc
ha s+q'ʷenp' *sunset (Canadian...).* (ul
schentsots ha sq'wenp', n.);
elu+s+x̌em=ínč e s+čin[t]+coc
Anglophobe. (elusqheminch e
Schntsots, n.); n+[ʔ]ił+sčín+n
cannibalism. (niłschinn, n.); x̌em=

enč+es+čínt *Indian-lover.*
(qhemencheschint (lit. one who loves
Indians), n.); s+taq+aq+nu+s+čínt
chicanery, deception. (staqaqnuschint.
(lit. deceiving people), n.);
s+myes+taq+aq+nu+s+čínt *coup,
deception (extraordinary...).*
(smyestaqaqnuschint, n.);
n+ʔukʷ+s+čín+n *cab, bus, coach,
taxicab.* ('nukwschinn. (lit. vehicle for
carrying passengers), n.)

√čn'₁ † čen' *take hold of large object.*
(che'n, vt.); čen'+m *grasp.* (che'nm,
vi.); čen'+n *held, pinned.* (che'nn, vi.);
čen'+šeš *aid, assistant, assist, boost,
help.* (che'nshesh (lit. take hold for
someone), v, vi.); s+čen'+šeš *aid,
assistance, help.* (sche'nshesh, n.);
s+t+čén'+čn'+m *dependence.*
(stche'nch'nm (lit. holding on), n.);
čn'+ši·+cútn *accompanist, aide de
camp, aide, assistant.* (ch'nshiitsutn,
(lit. m.o. helping oneself), n.);
s+t+čn'+n'+útm *dependability.*
(stch'n'nutm (lit. state of being worthy
of holding on to), n.); t+čén'+čn'+m
cling. (tche'nch'nm (lit. He held fast to
something physically or emotionally),
vi.); uʔ+t+čén'+čn'+m' *depend.*
(u'tche'nch'n'm (lit. He just holds on to
him, He habitually depends upon him),
vi.); sye·+čén'+šeš *aide, butler.*
(syeeche'nshesh, n.); s+čn'-šít-ew'es
alliance, confederacy, league, union.
(sch'nshite'wes. confederation. (lit.
upholding one another), n.); ∥
s+t+čn'=qín' *holding the steering
wheel.* (stch'nqi'n, vt.); s+t+čn'=
ápalaʔ=qn *steering (a horse).*
(stch'napala'qn, vt.); sya+čs+čn'=qín
chauffeur, coachman. (syachsch'nqin
(lit. One who holds the head (tip) of
the tail (steering wheel), n.); s+t+čn'=
ípeleʔ+n *broomstick.* (stch'nipele'n
(lit. handle), n.); ‡ čn'-šit *help.*
(ch'nshit (lit. Help h/h !), imp.); čen'-n

held, pinned (lit. I held it, I pinned him). (che'nn, vi.); čn'-šít-n *helped (I...him).* (ch'nshitn (lit. I held something for him), vt.); čn'-šít-ulm-n *I helped you (pl.).* (ch'nshitulmn, vt.); čn'-šít-n-lš *helped (I...them).* (ch'nshitnlsh, vt.); čn'-šít-s-n *helped (I...you (sg.)).* (ch'nshitsn, vt.); ne?+čn'-šít-se-xʷ *help (Please...me).* (ne'ch'nshitsekhw (lit. You (sg.) are to help me), v.); čen'-nt-s *pinned.* (che'nnts (lit. he pinned him), vi.); čn'-šít-s *aided (he...him), assist (to...).* (ch'nshits (lit. he helped for him), vi.); čn'-šít-se-s *He (sg.) helped me.* (ch'nshitses, vt.); § mel'+čen'-nt-s *comprise.* (me'lche'nnts, vt.); hn+čn'+n'+m+eł+i·c+pú?s *come.* (hnch'n'nmełiitspu's. (lit. his heart came back to its own position), vt.)

√čn'₂ † čen'+u?š *wish.* (che'nu'sh, vt.); čen'+u?š+čn‿šén+n *I desire work.* (che'nu'shchnshenn, vt.); čen'+u?š+č‿šén+n *we desire work.* (che'nu'shchshenn, vt.); čen'+u?š+kʷu·‿šén+n *you (s) desire work.* (che'nu'shkuushenn, vt.); čen'+u?š+kʷup‿šén+n *you (pl) desire work.* (che'nu'shkupshenn, vt.); čen'+u?š+šén+n *h/s desire works.* (che'nu'shshenn, vt.); čen'+u?š+šen+n-lš *they desire work.* (che'nu'shshennlsh, vt.)

√čn'xʷ † čen'xʷ *contact (come in contact with), touched.* (che'nkhw (lit. to be touched), vi.); // et+čn'xʷ=íw'es *contiguous, touching.* (etch'nkhwi'wes (lit. They have common boundary), adj.); s+čn'xʷ=íw'es *contact.* (sch'nkhwi'wes (lit. a touching together), n.)

√čp † čip *soften.* (chip (stem), vi.); č+čip *satin-like.* (chchip (lit. soft and smooth), adj.); u č+čí·p *nice (it is...and soft), be unexpectedly soft.* (uchchiiip!, adj.); s+č+čí·p *is (it...nice and soft).* (schchiiip!, vi.); čip+emn *cushion, pillow.* (chipemn (lit. softener), n.); // čp=qín+n *fur, hair.* (chpqinn (lit. head cushion, head softener), n.); hn+č+čí·p=cn' *blarney.* (hnchchiiiptsn'. (lit. He spoke softly, smoothly), n.); s+n+č+číp=cn' *diplomacy.* (snchchipts'n (lit. smoothness of talk), n.); u+n+č+číp=cn' *affable, diplomatic.* (unchchipts'n (lit. He is soft (courteous) in speech), adj.); § u+xʷal'+á čp=qín+n *capillary.* (uqhwa'la chpqinn (lit. It resembles hair), n.); s+kʷ'l'+ł+čp=qín+n *wig.* (sk'u'łchpqinn (lit. artificial hair), n.)

√čpxʷ † čépxʷ *Snap (body) with finger.* (chepkhw, vt.)

√čs₁ † čis *cheese.* (chis, n.); § u· péq he čis *cottage cheese.* (uupeq he chis (lit. white cheese), n.)

√čs₂ † e+čís+t+m *bawl out, berate, rebuke.* (echistm. (lit. He was rebuked harshly), vt.) // čis=cn *He spoke a long time.* (chistsn, vi.)

√čstq † č(=)astq *dig (roots, camas).* (chastq, vi.); i· čá(=)stq *She is digging roots.* (iichastq, vt.); s+ča(=)stq *to die roots, digging.* (schastq, n.); s+t+čá(=)stq+n *time of year for digging camas.* (stchastqn, adv.); § yuqʷ+e?+s+čá(=)stq *She pretended (to go) digging roots.* (yuqwe'schastq, v.)

√čš₁ † češ *accompany.* (chesh, vt.); češ+n *accompanied (he...).* (cheshn, vt.); s+čéš+n *concurrence, consent.* (scheshn (lit. going along), n.) [see also √č'š]

√čš₂ † s+čiš+t *dimension, length.* (schisht, n.)

√čt ‡ čet-nt-s *leaned (lit. he stood up by a person loose - someone to lean on).* (chetnts, vi.)

√čtm † čtím+n *blame, blamed.* (chtimn, v, vt.); s+čtim+m *blame, blaming.* (schtimm, n, vt.) ; s+čtím+n

blame, criticism, default. (schtimn, n.);
ul s+čtím+n critical. (ul schtimn (lit.
belonging to criticism), adj.);
čtim+un+útm blameworthy (it is...),
culpable. (chtimnutm, adj.);
čtem+tem+n-úl captious (he is...).
(chtemtemnul (lit. He is marked by a
disposition to find fault), vi.); ‡
č+tím-n accuse. (chtimn (lit. I accused
him), vt.); čtím-nt-s criminate,
criticize. (chtimnts (lit. He accused
him of a crime/He found fault with
him), vt.); § elu+s+čtím+m to be
blameless, innocent. (eluschtimm, adj.)

√čt' † s+či·t'=í?čn east. (schiit'i'chn,
n.); s+či·t'=í?č sunrise. (schiit'i'ch (lit.
coming from the east), n.); § teč
s+či·t'=í?čn Eastern. (tech schiit'i'chn
(lit. situated toward the part of the
earth which is toward the sunrise
(rising this way), adj.)

√čw' † čew'+t circumference. (che'wt
(lit. it is big in circumference), n.); ∥
kʷu‿n+čáw'=qn You (sg.) have a
deep voice. (kunchaʼwqn, vt.);
kʷup‿gʷt+n+čáw'=qn You (pl.) have
deep voices. (kupgutnchaʼwqn, vt.);
gʷɬ+n+čáw'=qn voices (They have
deep...). (guɬnchaʼwqn, n.); § čaw'n'+š
a·c+?aǎal amen (lit. would that it be
so). (cha'w'nsh aats'aqhal, interj.) [xref
√č'w']

√čy † čay enduring, firm, solid. (chay
(lit. one is enduring), adj, vi.); u· čáy
firm (It is very...). (uuchay, adj.);
čay+p hard (to be...). (chay(-p), vi.);
čay+p dryness, hard (to become),
hard, hardened (be...). (chayp (stem).
(lit. It became hard by dryness). adj,
vi.); s+čay+p bone-dry. (schayp (lit.
that which is hard from dryness), adj.);
s+či+čáy'+p meat (dried...).
(schicha'yp, n.); s+č+čáy'+p dried
meat, chipped beef. (schcha'yp, n.); ∥
t+čáy+p=cn agape. (tchayptsn (lit. His
mouth became hard), adj.); ut+čáy=

c'e? crusty. (utchayts'e (lit. It is hard
on the surface), adj.); § s+č+čáy'+p
he s+mɬíč dried salmon. (schcha'yp
he smɬich, n.)

√čy? † č+čey'e? grandmother
(maternal)

√čʕ † če+čaʕ cylindrical, slender.
(checha(, adj.); č+čaʕ+t cylindrical,
slender, hair-like. (chcha(t (lit. it is
slender and cylindrical, e.g. a stem/
fine and slender), vi, adj.); ∥ če+čaʕ=
al'qʷ thin (lit. he is thin).
(checha(a'lqw, adj.); č+čaʕ=al'qʷ lean,
skinny, slender, trim (to be thin).
(chcha(a'lqw, ripple. adj, vi.);
hn+č+čaʕ=iɬc'e? tube, narrow.
(hnchcha(iɬ'se'. (lit. It has a very small
internal diameter), adj.)

√č?₁ † či? open, uncover, unveil. (chi'
(lit. to open), adj.); ∥ [also recorded
as √čy'] e+čs+n+číy'=ep open.
(echsnchi'yep (lit. The door, gate is
open), adj.); en+čí?=us open (to be...).
(enchi'us (referring to window), adj.);
‡ čet+če?=in?-nt-s reveal, disclose,
uncover. (chetche'in'nts, vi.); e
čet+če?=íne?-stu-s uncover, unveil,
divulge. (echetche'ine'stus (lit. H/s
uncovers it), vt.)

√č?₂ † hi+če? where?. (hiche', inter.);
čeɬ‿kʷu s+te·čí+če? (lit. Where
are you(s) going?).
(cheɬkusteechiche'?, vt.)

√č?₃ † es+čí+če? livestock, horse,
mount. (eschiche', n.); n'+s+čí+če?+n
barn. ('nschiche'n (lit. building for
horses), n.); § kʷu[ɬ][]+s+čí+če? H/S
loaned a horse. (k'ut'lschiche', vt.);
?esel'+s+čí+če? H/s has two horses.
(ese'lschiche', vt.); n+?ed=us=
el'+s+čí+če? H/S traded horses with
another person (sg.).
('neduse'lschiche', vt.);
gʷn[it]+el'+s+či+če? H/s summoned
h/h livestock. (gwne'lschiche', vt.);
s+t+č+?umút=ew'es+n cow pony.

(stch'um<u>u</u>te'wesn. saddle pony, n.);
ʕec+el'+s+čí+če?+n *rope.*
((etse'lschi<u>c</u>he'n (lit. the means of
lassoing a horse), n.);
hn+ʕac+ʕac+el'+s+čí+če?+n *corral.*
(hn(ats(atse'lschi<u>c</u>he'n. (lit. enclosure
for lassoing horses), n.);
hn+ʕec+el'+s+čí+če?+n *hitching
post.* (hn(etse'lschi<u>c</u>he"n, n.);
s+q'ey'+al'+s+čí+če? *brand.*
(sq'e'ya'lschi<u>c</u>he' (lit. act of marking
animals), n.); sya+daх̣+él'+s+či+če?
cattle herder. (syadaqh<u>e</u>'lschiche', n.);
sye+č+št'+el'+s+čí+če? *cowboy.*
(syechsht'e'lschi<u>c</u>he' (lit. One who
tends horses, (livestock, or cattle) for
another), n.); ul
sye+č+št'+el'+s+čí+če? *bucolic.* (ul
syechsht'e'lschi<u>c</u>he' (lit. belonging to a
cattle herder), adj.); s+t+gʷiš=
elxʷe?+l+s+čí+če? *curry.*
(stgwishelkhwe'lschi<u>c</u>he' (lit. rubbing
down and cleaning a horse), vt.);
?em+n+el'+s+čí+če? *feed.*
(emne'lschi<u>c</u>he' livestock, vt.);
s+х̣[]ey+l'+s+čí+če? *horse (worn
out...), plug.* (sqhwey'lschi<u>c</u>he'. old
horse, n.); dele[m]+l'e+s+čí+če?
cause. (delen'leschi<u>c</u>he' (lit. He caused
his horse to gallop), vt.); wl+wlím ha
ʕec+el'+s+čí+če?+n *cable.* (wlwl<u>i</u>m
ha (etse'lschi<u>c</u>he'n (lit. metal what is a
rope), n.); pulut+l'+s+čí+če? *He
slaughtered livestock.* (pulut'lschi<u>c</u>he',
vt.); t'm'+m+čí·? *caravan.* (t'm'mch<u>iii</u>!
(lit. There goes a single file of many
vehicles or pack animals), n.)

√č?łs † čí?łes *three.* (chi'łes, n.); **∥**
t+če?łís=elps *bears (three grizzly...),
pigs (three...).* (tche'łiselps, n.); **§**
t+čí?łes parsón *Blessed Trinity.*
(Tchi'łes Pars<u>o</u>n (lit. three persons),
n.); če?łe·l+?úpen *thirty.*
(che'łee'l<u>u</u>pen, n.); če?łe·l+?upn
thirty. (che'łee'lupn (lit. three times

ten), n.); ?upen uł čí?łes *thirteen.*
(upen uł chi'łes, n.)

√č'c'₁ † e·+č'éc' *log, pole, rod, stick.*
(eech'<u>e</u>ts' (lit. The log/pole/rod/stick
lies there), n.); e+č'c'+útm
Monumental Peak. (Ech'ts'<u>u</u>tm. A
ridge in the Clearwater Mountains in
the St. Joe Forest east of Clarkia,
Idaho, n.); **∥** č'ec'+t=ene?st *mountain
north of DeSmet (lit. log on rock cliff).*
(Ch'ets'tene'st, n.); č'c'=us=e?st *brink,
cliff, bluff, precipice (lit. edge of a 90°
angle, rocky cliff).* (ch'ts'use'st, n.);
s+č'c'=us=e?st *precipice.*
(sch'ts'use'st, n.)

√č'c'₂ † č'ec' *gull[i]ble.* (ch'ets', adj.); **∥**
s+č'éc'=elt *gullible, cat's paw,
credulous, dupe.* (sch'<u>e</u>ts'elt. (lit. son or
daughter easily deceived), n.)

√č'd † č'ed *shady (be...).* (ch'ed (stem),
vi.); č'id *shade.* (ch'id, n.); u·+č'íd
dim. (uuch'<u>i</u>d (lit. It is something dark),
adj.); č'ed+p *winter (...set in).* (ch'edp,
vi.); u+n+č'id *shady.* (unch'id (lit. It is
shady), adj.); s+č'ed+p *late autumn,
fall.* (sch'edp, n.); s+č'e?d *verge of
winter.* (sch'<u>e</u>'d, n.); s+č'í?d *winter
(verge of...).* (sch'<u>i</u>'d, n.); s+can+č'íd
shade. (stsanch'<u>i</u>d, n.); s+cen+č'íd
shade. (stsench'<u>i</u>d, n.)

√č'gʷl † t+č'ígʷl *clamber.* (tch'igul (lit.
He climbed), vt.); t+č'ígʷl+n *step
ladder.* (tch'iguln, n.); s+t+č'ígʷl+n
ladder, stair. (stch'iguln. (lit. means of
climbing), n.); sye+t+č'ígʷl *climber.*
(syetch'igul (lit. One who climbs), n.)

√č'h † č'ih *approach, near.* (ch'ih (lit.
get near), vi.); **∥** e t+č'íh=etč *to be
right-handed.* (etch'ihetch, vi.);
s+t+č'íh=ečt *dextro(o)-, right hand,
right-handed (to be...).* (stch'ihecht, n,
vi.); čn'‿t+č'íh=ečt *(lit. I am
right-handed).* (ch'ntch'<u>i</u>hecht, vt.)

√č'hy † s+t+č'i·háy=us *buttercups.*
(stch'iih<u>a</u>yus, pl.n.)

√č'l † č'él+eʔ *cradleboard, bark (of a tree).* (ch'e̱le', n.) [xref √člʔ?]

√č'lxʷ † č'elxʷ *(lit. be receptacle with concave surface down).* (ch'e̱lkhw, n.); e· č'élxʷ *concave.* (eech'e̱lkhw (lit. It is laid with the vaulted side down), adj.); ∥ hn+č'+č'el'xʷ=ičn' *roof (a car...).* (hnch'ch'e'lkhwichn' (lit. concave form as one's back), n.); s+č'+č'l'xʷ=íłxʷ *tent.* (sch'ch''lkhwi̱łkhw (lit. House turned upside down), n.); s+can+č'lxʷ=áp=qn *canope.* (stsanch'lkhwa̱pqn (lit. vault covering with the concave side over the head), n.); t+č'lxʷ=íc'eʔ+n *eggshell.* (tch'lkhwits'e'n (lit. the hard (but brittle) outside covering (as on an egg), n.); t+č'lxʷ=íp=łxʷ *annex.* (tch'lkhwipłkhw (lit. A building added on to another building), n.); e čet+č'lxʷ=ín'eʔ *wagon (covered).* (echetch'lkhwi̱ne' (lit. a wagon with an arched cover, tent over it), n.); ‡ č'elxʷ-nt-s *(lit. he lay down something (cup, bowl) upside down).* (ch'elkhwnts, vt.); § t+č'lxʷ=íc'eʔ+is xʷa s+p'árkʷ=alqs *crust.* (tch'lkhwi̱ts'e'is khwa sp'a̱rk'walqs (lit. covering (crust of turtle), n.)

√č'lx̌ † hn+č'elax̌+emn *canyon, Colfax, Washington.* (Hnch'elaqhemn, n.)

√č'l'₁ † hn+č'el'eʔ *coyote.* (hnch'e'le'. (Kalispel), n.); hn+č'+č'a·l'í *Little Coyote, a medicine man.* (Hnch'ch'aa'li̱, n.)

√č'l'₂ † t+č'l'+el=íneʔ *hearing (He has sharp...).* (tch'l'eli̱ne' (lit. He is alert as to the ears), n.)

√č'm₁ ∥ hn+č'm=ip *bottom.* (hnch'mip, n.); s+č'm=íp=ens *chin.* (sch'mipens, n.); s+čet+č'ém=cn *upper lip.* (schetch'e̱mtsn, n.); hn+č'em=up *buttocks.* (hnch'emup, n.); s+čet+č'ém+č'm=up+s *buttocks.* (schetch'e̱mch'mups, n.); s+čet+č'm=

íčn'=us *brow, brae.* (schetch'mi̱ch'nus (lit. side of the head). temple, n.); s+čet+č'm=íl'=us *forehead.* (schetch'mi̱'lus, n.); s+can+č'm'=ap= qn' *head (back of...).* (stsanch''mapq'n, n.); s+niʔ+č'm=áw'as=qn *chest.* (sni'ch'ma̱wasqn (lit. The top of the head), n.); s+cen+č'em=cn *neck.* (stsench'emtsn, n.); s+cen+č'ém=us *cheek.* (stsench'e̱mus, n.); s+cen+č'ém+č'm=us *cheeks.* (stsench'e̱mch'mus, n.); s+cen+č'm= cín=čt *carpus, wrist.* (stsench'mtsi̱ncht, n.); s+cen+č'm+p'= cín=čt *bracelet.* (stsench'mp'tsi̱ncht, n.); ul s+cen+č'm=cín=čt *carpal.* (ul stsench'mtsincht (anat.), adj.); s+niʔ+č'ám=iʔqs *nose (surface of the).* (sni'ch'a̱mi̱qs, n.); s+niʔ+č'm= ús=šn *clitoris.* (sni'ch'mu̱sshn (lit. surface (covering) of "small hill" at upper end of vulva), n.); s+n+č'ám= alq=šn *crotch.* (snch'a̱malqshn (lit. the surface of fork formed by the junction of legs, n.); s+n+č'ám=qn *apex.* (snch'a̱mqn (lit. top of the head), n..); s+n+č'ám+č'm=qn *apices.* (snch'a̱mch'mqn (lit. tops of heads), pl.n.); hn+č'm=qín=kʷeʔ *Coeur d'Alene, Idaho.* (hnch'mqinkwe' (lit. waterhead), n.); s+n+č'm=íčn' *back, derriere.* (snch'mich'n (lit. surface of the back), n.); s+n+č'm=íčn'+s *carapace.* (snch'mich'ns (lit. the back of a turtle), n.); s+s+čet+č'em=up+s *buttocks, breech, hind end.* (sschetch'emups, n.); s+t+č'ám=alq= šn *calf.* (stch'a̱malqshn (lit. surface of the leg), n.); s+t+č'ám+č'm=alq=šn *legs.* (stch'a̱mch'malqshn, pl.n.); s+t+č'em=cis *beak, bill.* (stch'emtsis. (his mouth), n.); s+t+č'ém=cn *beak, bill, mouth.* (stch'emtsn, n.); s+t+č'ém=gʷl *abdomen, belly.* (stch'emgul, n.); ul s+t+č'ém=gʷl *celiac.* (ul stch'e̱mgul (of or relating to

the abdomen), adj.); s+č'm=áx̌n *edge.*
(sch'maqhn (lit. extreme border; outer
side of arm), n.); s+can+č'm=áx̌n
armpit. (stsanch'maqhn (lit. surface of
under the arm), n.); s+t+č'om=os=áx̌n
shoulder. (stch'omosaqhn, n.);
s+t+č'm+č'm=ós=ax̌n *shoulders.*
(stch'mch'mosaqhn, pl.n.);
s+cen+č'm=cín=šn *ankle.*
(stsench'mtsinshn, n.);
s+cen+č'm+č'm=cín=šn *ankles.*
(stsench'mch'mtsinshn, n.); § s+č'm=
álpqʷ+s he t+tm'íxʷ *craw.*
(sch'malpqws he tt'mikhw (lit.
esophagus of a bird), n.)
√č'm₂ † čet+č'm+c=iɫxʷ *awning, porch,
eaves.* (chetch'mtsiɫkhw, n.);
s+čet+č'm+c=iɫxʷ *balcony.*
(schetch'mtsiɫkhw (lit. surface
extending from wall or roof), n.);
čs+n+č'ém=ep *door, doorway.*
(chsnch'emep, n.); t+č'm=íp=ɫxʷ *earth
(surface of the...), ecology.*
(tch'mipɫkwh (lit. outside of a house,
surroundings of a house), n.);
a+t+č'm=íp=ɫxʷ *outdoors, outside.*
(atch'mipɫkhw, adv.); hn+č'ám=qn
brim. (hnch'amqn. (lit. surface of head
(of a cup)), n.); hn+č'ém=enč *wall.*
(hnch'emench. (lit. the surface of the
inside), n.); t+č'm=ásq'it *atmosphere,
heaven, firmamanet, sky.* (tch'masq'it,
(lit. vault of the sky), n.); ul č'm=
ásq'it *celestial.* (ul ch'masq'it (lit.
pertaining to the sky or the heavens),
adj.); ul+t+č'm=ásq'it *celestial (lit.
pertaining to the sky or the heavens).*
(ult ch'masq'it, adj.); § s+t+miy+iy=
ípele?+s xʷe t+č'm=ásq'it twe
tmíxʷ=ulmxʷ *cosmography, science of
what is in the sky and earth.*
(stmiyiyipele's khwe tch'masq'it twe
tmikhulmkhw, n.)
√č'ml † č'imul *pine needle.* (ch'imul,
n.)

√č'm'₁ † č'am' *left (...over ,...out).*
(ch'a'm, adj.); č[']am' *left, remaining.*
(cha'm, vi.)
√č'm'₂ † č'em' *dark, dark (to be...), e.g.
night.* (ch'e'm, vi.); u· č'ém' *dark (It
is...).* (uuch'em, adj.)
√č'm'₃ † č'ím'+n *antler, horn.* (ch'i'mn,
n.); § ul s+x̌ʷt'+í? he č'ím'-is
Capricornus. (ul sqhwt'i'he ch'i'mis
(lit. a horn that belongs to the goat), n.)
√č'm'₄ † s+č'ím' *marmot, woodchuck.*
(sch'i'm, n.)
√č'm'c? † hn+č'm'cí? *Clark's Fork,
Idaho.* (Hnch"mtsi, n.)
√č'n † č'in *dangerous (be...).* (ch'in,
vi.); č'ín+č'in+t *breakneck, danger,
dangerous, hazardous (It is...).*
(ch'inch'int, adj, n, vi.);
i+č'in+č'in+m+scút *desperate.*
(ich'inch'inmstsut (lit. He is putting
himself in a very dangerous situation),
adj.); s+č'n+č'n+m+scút *adventure.*
(sch'nch'nmstsut (lit. endangering
oneself), n.)
√č'np' † č'enp' *clasp, encircle.* (ch'enp',
vt.); ∥ [also recorded as √čnp']
čynp'=íc'e? *barrel.* (chynp'its'e'. (lit. a
wooden container held together by
hoops), n.); č'np'=qín'=čt *annulus,
curio.* (ch'np'qi'ncht, n.); cen+č'np'=
cín=šn *bangle.* (tsench'np'tsinshn (lit.
anklet), n.); s+č'np'=áx̌n *armlet,
bracelet.* (sch'np'aqhn, n.);
s+can+č'n'+č'np'=áx̌n' *vest, corset.*
(stsanch"nch"npaqh'n, n.); ‡
č'enp'-nt-s *cuddle, fondle, hug.*
(ch'enp'nts. (lit. he fondled her, hugged
her), vi.); cen+č'np'=cín-t-s *clasp.*
(sench'np'tsints (lit. He embraced her
around the neck), vt.); § u+x̌ʷal'+a
č'n'p'=qín'=čt *annular.* (uqhwa'la
ch"np'qi'ncht (lit. It is like a ring), n.)
√č'n'₁ † č'+č'en'e? *diminutive, small,
bit, a small piece or amount.*
(ch'ch'e'ne', adj.); ∥ č'n'+n'=úl'umxʷ
Don George's ancestor.

(Ch"n'nu̱'lumkhw, n.); č'+č'n'e?=ilš
decrease, grow small. (ch'ch"ne'ilsh
(lit. it became small or smaller), v.);
č'n'+č'ne?=cin'+m'n' *belittle.*
(ch'n'ch'ne'tsi'n'm'n (lit. Make small by
word of mouth), v.); hn+č'+č'án'+a?=
al'qs *cheap, inexpensive.*
(hnch'ch'a̱'na'a'lqs. (lit. the road is
small (narrow)), adj.); ‡ č'+č'n'e?=
il'š-s-n *diminish.* (ch'ch"ne'i'lshsn, vt.);
č'+č'n'e?=il'š-t-m' *attenuate.*
(ch'ch"ne'i'lsht'm, vt.); č'+č'n'e?=
il'š-t-m *slender.* (ch'ch"ne'i'lshtm (lit.
he was made smaller), n.);
č'+č'n'+č'n'e?=cin'+m'-n't-s
disparage. (ch'ch"nch"ne'tsi'n'm'nt,
vt.); č'+č'n'+č'n'e?=cin'+m'-n't-s
*belittle (lit. he spoke of him as small or
unimportant).* (ch'ch"nch"ne'tsi'n'm'nts,
vt.); § č'+č'en'e? he wl+wlim *chicken
feed (lit. small money, trifling amount
of money).* (ch'ch'e'ne' he wlwli̱m, n.);
č'n'+č'n'e?=cin'+m'e?+tn-se-s *decry.*
(ch"nch"ne'tsi'n'me'tnses, vi.)

√č'n'₂ † č'en' *one round object lies.*
(ch'e'n, vt.); č'en'+n' *it (ball) fell on
the ground.* (ch'e'n'n, vt.); ∥ s+č'n'=
álpqʷ *cowbell.* (sch"nalpqw (lit. that
(ball that strikes a bell) which is hung
to the (anterior portion of the) neck),
n.); s+n+č'n'=íčn *ammunition,
cartridge.* (snch'ni̱chn (lit. ball on the
back), n.); t+č'én'=gʷl *person (...with
bulging stomach), stomach (person
with bulging...).* (tch'e̱'ngul, n.);
at+č'án'=qn *Afro (hairdo), bouffant.*
(atch'a̱'nqn, vi. (lit. H/h hair is puffed
out), adj.); čs+n+č'en'=ípn *padlocks,
deadlock.* (chsnch'e'nipn, n); §
n+?ilk'ʸʷ=elgʷes+n a sn+č'n'=íčn?
caisson. ('nilk'welgwesn a snch'n'i̱chn'
(lit. storage (box) for ammunition), n.)

√č'pxʷ † č'epxʷ *trap, He (mouse) was
trapped.* (ch'epkhw (lit. it was
trapped), vt.)

√č'p' † č'ip' *pinch.* (ch'ip' (stem), vt.);
č'ip'+č'ep'+t *dawdles, dilatory.*
(ch'ip'ch'ep't (lit. he is slow), adj.);
č'ip[']+m+ncut *dawdles, loiters.*
(ch'ipmntsut (lit. he pinched himself),
adj.) [xref √c'p']

√č'p'xʷ † č'ép'xʷ *click, clip.* (ch'ep'khw
(stem), vt.); č'p'uxʷ *click.* (ch'p'ukhw!
(lit. It went click), n.); č'p'xʷ+mín+n
clip, pliers, pinchers. (ch'p'khumi̱nn
(lit. a device for fastening), n.);
č'p'+č'p'xʷ+m'ín'+n' *clippers,
scissors.* (ch'p'ch'p'khu'mi̱'n'n (lit.
instrument for clipping), n.);
t+č'p'xʷ+mín+n *clothespin.*
(tch'p'khumi̱nn (lit. a clip for fastening
clothes on a line), n.); ‡ č'ép'xʷ-n *clip.*
(ch'ep'khwn (lit. I clipped it (paper,
etc), vt.); č'ép'xʷ-nt-s *clip, trim (off),
clipped (he...it).* (ch'ep'khwnts, vt.)

√č'r₁ † č'ar *swim.* (ch'ar (referring to an
animal), vi.); č'ar+p *animal swims, to
swim (referring to an animal).* (ch'arp,
vi.); hn+č'ar+p *He (animal) swam.*
(hnch'arp, vi.); s+n+č'ar+p *to swim.
(animal).* (snch'arp, v.)

√č'r₂ † č'ar *cut.* (ch'ar (light or flimsey
objects with shears), vt.); a n+č'ar=
úl'mxʷ *trench, channel, dike, furrow,
groove.* (anch'aru̱'lmkhw, n.); hn-
n+č'ar=úl'umxʷ *ditch, trench.*
(hnnch'aru̱'lumkhw. (lit. It is my trench
cut in the earth), n.); § ni?č'+č'ar'=
ál'qʷ *Sanders, Idaho.* (Ni'ch'ch'a'ra̱'lqw
(lit. a cut in the woods), n.)

√č'rp' ∥ č'ar'p'=qin'=čt *ring (for the
finger).* (ch'a'rp'qi'ncht, n.);
s+can+č'arp'=áx̌n *corona.*
(stsanch'arp'a̱qhn (lit. ring around the
armpits or ring around the planet, star,
or moon), n.)

√č'rw † s+t+č'érw+um *pray, prayer.*
(stch'e̱rwum, vi, n.) [xref √č'ʕʷ]

√č's † č'es *bad (be...).* (ch'es (stem),
vi.); č'es+t *bad, brutal, contemptuous,
cruel, despicable, evil, mean,*

overbearing, scornful, (lit. He is...).
(ch'est, adj.); [č']es+t *bad (it is...).*
(q'est, vi.) [see also √q's]; s+č'es+t
brutality, cruelty. (sch'est, n.);
hn+č'és+n *depravity, sin,*
wrongdoing. (hnch'esn, condition of
being bad, evil, n.); č[']és+m+ncut
delinquent. (chesmntsut (lit. He made
himself a delinquent), n.);
s+č'és+m+ncut *delinquency.*
(sch'esmntsut (lit. making oneself bad),
n.); s+n+č'es+č's+t+m+ncút *to be*
sorry, to feel remorse.
(snch'esch'stmntsut, v.);
s+č's+t+mín+šeš *contempt, disdain,*
scorn. (sch'stminshesh (lit. treating as
bad), n.); // s+č's=cín *abuse*
(foul-mouthed...), billingsgate, curse.
(sch'stsin, n.); č's=ci·n'+útm
abominable, accursed, outrageous.
(ch'stsii'nutm (lit. it is accursed), adj.);
č's+č's=ci·n'=íye? *dispute.*
(ch'sch'stsii'niye' (lit. He exchanged
mean words with another), n.);
s+č's+č's=ci·n'=íy'e? *argue, bicker,*
brawl, quarrel, debate.
(sch'sch'stsii'ni'ye' (lit. exchanging
mean/angry words), vi.); č's+č's=
ci·n'=iy'e?-l'š *debate.*
(ch'sch'stsii'ni'ye''lsh (lit. they
quarreled), vi.); s+č's+e·č=iye? *rock*
lichen. (sch'seechiye'. skunk cabbage,
n.); č's=ul'mxʷ *badlands.*
(ch'su'lmkhw, n.); hn+č's=ílgʷes
bad-tempered, brutal, unkind.
(hnch'silgwes. (lit. He is mean as to the
heart.), adj.); s+n+č's+s+m=ílgʷes
antipathy. (snch'ssmilgwes (lit. feeling
aversion at the heart), n.); hn+č's=
ítkʷe? *stagnant.* (hnch'sitkwe'. (lit. bad
water, bitter water), adj.); s+č'és=ep
skunk. (sch'esep (lit. bad bottom), n.);
s+č's=íčt+m+n *abuse.* (sch'sichtmn
(lit. treating wrongly with the hand),
n.); s+č's+t=íl'š *demoralization.*
(sch'sti'lsh (lit. becoming spoiled), n.);

s+č's+t=íl'š+m *depravation.*
(sch'sti'lshm (lit. making
someone/something bad), n.);
s+č's+č[']s=níxʷ *abhor (to...),*
abhorred. (sch'schsnikhw, v, vt.);
či+s+č's+č's=č=nixʷ-s *disdain,*
despise. (chisch'sch'schnikhws (lit. h/s
loathes me), n.); čis+č's+č's=čs=
nixʷ-s *despises.*
(chisch'sch'schsnikhws, n.);
čis+s+č's+č's=čs=nixʷ *detest.*
(chissch'sch'schsnikhw (lit. I am
customarily hated), vt.); č's=qin+m
h/s threw off (waste matter) from the
body. (ch'sqinm, vt.); s+č'[e]s=qín+m
defecation. (sch'sqinm (lit. excretion
through the intestines), n.);
s+ni?+č'és+č's+s+m=enč
constipation, upset stomach.
(sni'ch'esch'ssmench (lit. something
going wrong with the bowels), n.); ‡
č's=íčt+me-nt-s *botch.* (ch'sichtments
(lit. He repaired it clumsily), vt.); č's=
cín+m-nt-s *assail, curse, damn, (lit.*
he spoke evil words to him).
(ch'stsinmnts, vi.); č's+t=íl'š-st-m
deprave, spoiled (h/s was...).
(ch'sti'lshstm (lit. He was caused to
become bad), vt.); č's+t=íl'š-stu-s
corrupt, deprave. (ch'sti'lshstus (lit. He
made it bad), vi.); č's+t+mí-nt-s *hated*
(He...him), resented (H/s...it very
much). (ch'stmints, vt.); § č's=
cin+m-nt-s xʷa xes+t *blasphemy,*
profanity. (ch'stsinmnts khwa qhest,
n.); hn+łá?p=alqs č'es+t *evil.*
(hnła'palqs ch'est. (lit. He is extremely
evil), adj.); hn+łáp=alqs č'es+t
atrocious. (hnłapalqs ch'est. (lit. He is
extremely evil), adj.); č's+eł+cégʷ+t
cad, churl. (ch'sełtsegwt (lit. He has
bad manners-an ungentlemanly man),
n.); č's+eł+cégʷ+t he s+mi?yem
cotquean. (ch'sełtsegwt he smi'yem
(lit. woman of bad manners), n.);
s+č's=cín+m+n łen+gʷís+t

blasphemy. (sch'stsinmn łengwist (lit. speaking evil of the One on High), n.); tel' ci' č'es+t+íl'š-st-m *degenerate*. (te'l tsi' ch'estilshstm (lit. He was made worse), v.); č's+č's+t+men+ł le·swíp *anti-Semite*. (ch'sch'stmenł leeswip, n.); lut č'es+t *amoral*. (lut ch'est (lit. It is not bad), adj.); łe+č'is+eł+ceg^w+t *boor*. (łech'isełtsegwt. (lit. one who has bad manners), n.)

√č'š ‡ č'éš-nt-eli-s *conform*. (ch'eshntelis (lit. He went along with us. He conformed his behavior with ours), vt.) [see also √čš]

√č't † č'et *beat, tick*. (ch'et. nod. (stem), vt.); u·+č't+č't+č't *chuckle*. (uuch'tch'tch't (lit. He laughed quietly by nodding repeatedly), vi.)

√č't? † č'íte? *near (be...)*. (ch'ite' (stem), vi.); č'+č'ite? *close, near*. (ch'ch'ite', adj.); ‡ t+č'íte?+m-nt-s *to approach*. (tch'ite'mnts (lit. He came close to him), v.)

√č't'₁ † č'et' *chop (off), cut (off completely), separate, sever*. (ch'et', vi, vt.); ‡ hn+č't'=ús-nt-m *decapitated*. (hnch't'usntm. (lit. He was decapitated), adj.)

√č't'₂ † č't['] *brown*. (ch't. horse, n.); t+č't'=élx^w *brown*. (tch't'elkhw (lit. A horse with brown fur (hide)), adj.)

√č't'₃ † čet'+č'et' *blackbird*. (chet'ch'et', n.) [see also √t'č'₁]; is+č'át'+č'at[']+iš *chirrup*. (isch'at'ch'atish (lit. The bird is uttering a series of chirps), vi.)

√č'w₁ † č'ew *nostalgic*. (ch'ew. (stem), adj.)

√č'w₂ † č'u *absent, away, gone, missing*. (ch'u, adj.); č'uw *absent (he is...)*. (ch'uw!, vi.); č'u· *blank, empty, nothing there*. (ch'uu!, adj.); s+č'uw *abscence*. (sch'uw (lit. being gone away), n.); č'uw+ín'š *barely, hardly*. (ch'uwi'nsh, adv.); // hn+č'uw+p=ílg^wes *lit. He was lonely*.

(hnch'uwpilgwes, adj.); č'uw+č'uw=úl'umx^w *eeri[e], weird*. (ch'uwch'uwu'lumkhw. (lit. It is a territory that is usually without people, a lonely, weird, mysterious place), adj.)

√č'w? † č'íwe? *father (...of deceased mother)*. (ch'iwe', n.)

√č'w' † č'ew' *cylinder*. (ch'e'w. (lit. to be large, cylinder shaped), adj.); // t+č'éw'=ečt *bough, limb*. (tch'e'wecht (lit. a large arm (hand), n.); č'uw'=íl'k^we? *comber, billow*. (ch'u'wi'lkwe' (lit. a large wave), n.); hn+č'áw'=qn *bass, basso*. (hnch'a'wqn. (lit. He has a wide girth at the head, he has a deep (low) voice), n.); hn+č'+č'áw'=qn *baritone*. (hnch'ch'a'wqn. (lit. little deep voice), n.); čn‿hn+č'aw'=qn *voice (to have a deep voice)*. (chn(h)nch'a'wqn, vi.); čn‿n+č'áw'=qn *voice (I have a deep...)*. (chnnch'a'wqn, n.); čn‿(h)n+č'aw'=qn *deep (voice)*. (chn(h)nch'a'wqn, vi. (lit. I have a deep voice)., adj.); č‿g^wuł+n+č'áw'=qn *lit. we have deep voices*. (chgułnch'a'wqn, vt.) [xref √čw']

√č'x^w₁ † č'ax^w *clack, clang, clop*. (ch'akhw! (lit. sound of hard object striking another), vi.); u· č'áx^w *clack*. (uuch'akhw (lit. It went "clack"), vi.)

√č'x^w₂ † č'ix^w *lean against*. (ch'ikhw, vi.); č'áx^w=qn *bolt, cushion, pillow*. (ch'akhwqn. (lit. bolsterer of the head, that on which the head is laid), n.); č'íx^w *lean (...against), lean*. (ch'ikhw (stem), vi.); e·+č'íx^w+p=ens *chin, lean*. (eech'ikhwpens (lit. He is leaning on his chin), vi.); hn+č'ux^w+č'ux^w=áp=en'e?+m *retired, slept*. (hnch'ukhwch'ukhwape'ne"m. (lit. H/s laid his head against (something)), vt.); ‡ č'íx^w-nt-s *He opened it; he removed or lifted it (ie. lid)*. (ch'ikhwnts, vt.); t+č'íx^w-nt-s *lean*. (tch'ikhwnts, vi.)

√č'xʷ₃ † č'uxʷ+xʷá? *approximate, almost*. (ch'ukhukhwa̲'. (lit. slightly short of, not quite, just so much), adj, adv.)

√č'xʷ₄ † s+č'éxʷ+xʷ *asthma, comsumption*. (sch'e̲khukhw. tuberculosis, n.); i·+č'éxʷ+xʷ *consumptive*. (iich'e̲khukhw (lit. He is consumptive), adj.)

√č'x̌₁ † č'ax̌ *push, shove*. (ch'aqh. (lit. move to one side), vi.); č'ax̌+ax̌+m *move*. (ch'aqhaqhm (lit. it moved), vt.); č'+č'ax̌+ax̌+m' *[b]udge, it was budged*. (ch'ch'aqhaqh'm, vi.); ∥ č'ax̌+ax̌=íp=ep *he moved along on his buttocks*. (ch'aqhaqhipep, vi.); ‡ č'ax̌+m-st-m *remove (he was removed)*. (ch'aqhmstm, vt.); č'ax̌+m-stu-s *remove*. (ch'aqhmstus (lit. he removed it), vt.)

√č'x̌₂ † č'ex̌ *rub (against)*. (ch'eqh, vt.); ∥ č'ex̌=qn' *helldiver, loon*. (ch'eqhq'n, n.)

√č'ʕʷ † č'eʕʷ *pray*. (ch'e(w (stem), vi.); s+t+č'éʕʷ+m *congregation, fellowship, prayer, to pray*. (stch'e̲(um. (lit. praying (together)), n.); hn+t+č'eʕʷ+emn *altar, church (Christian), place for praying, worship (place of...)*. (hntch'e(wemn, n.); s+n+t+č'éʕʷ+emn *chapel, church*. (sntch'e̲(wemn (lit. A meeting place for prayer), n.); ul+s+n+t+č'éʕʷ+emn *ecclesiastical*. (ulsntch'e̲(wemn, adj.); ∥ s+t+č'éʕʷ=pele? *benediction, benison, blessing, consecration, dedication*. (stch'e̲(wpele'. (lit. praying for the origin of one), n.); at+č'éʕʷ=pele? *blessed, consecrated*. (atch'e̲(wpele', vi. (lit. Divine favor was invoked upon h/h/i), adj.); ‡ t+č'éʕʷ=ple?-nt-s *dedicate*. (tch'e̲(wple'nts (lit. He prayed for its special use), v.); t+č'[']eʕʷ=pele?-nt-s *bless, pray over*. (tche(wpele'nts, vt.) [see also √č'rw]

√č'?₁ ∥ s+č'a?=qin'=šn' *knee cap, knee joint, knee*. (sch'a'qi'nsh'n, n.);

√č'?₂ † č'e?+š *condescend*. (ch'e'sh (stem), vi.); ‡ č'e?+č'e?=šn+mí-nt-se-xʷ *condescend*. (ch'e'ch'e'shnmi̲ntsekhw (lit. You (a noble) humbled yourself before a humble person (me), vi.)

√č'?t † č‿y'c+č'i?t(=)ci·níɫ *the sound of talking is coming nearer*. (chi'ch'ittsiiniɫ, vt.)

√dkʷ † dikʷ *turn about in going (cross face)*. (dik'w, vi.); e·+díkʷ+s+m *go, recede, return, ebbs*. (eedi̲k'wsm (lit. H/s/i recedes/goes back/returns), vi.) [xref √dxʷ, √d?kʷ]

√dl₁ † del *sit (...up like animal)*. (del (stem), vi.); e·+dél+ut *haunches, seated*. (eede̲lut (lit. The dog is seated), n, adj.); e·+dél+dl+ut *seated*. (eede̲ldlut (lit. The dogs are seated), adj.)

√dl₂ † dul *sing (...warsong)*. (dul, vi.)

√dl₃ † sí+dl=emš *Indians (Jocko Valley...of Montana)*. (Si̲dlemsh, n.)

√dlkʷ † delkʷ *cover entirely with cloth*. (delk'w, vt.)

√dlm † delím *galloped*. (delim (lit. He went riding a galloping horse), vi.); č+dlam=alqʷ *railway, train*. (chdlamalqw (lit. he galloped on the log, rail, etc.), n.); č+dl+dlám=alqʷ *trains*. (chdldla̲malqw, n.); hn+dlám=alqs *lit. He galloped along the road*. (hndla̲malqs, vt.); § dele[m]+l'e+s+čí+če? *cause*. (delen'leschiche' (lit. He caused his horse to gallop), vt.) [xref √dl']

√dlqʷ † dolqʷ *person (...is strong)*. (dolq'w (stem), n.); dól+dolqʷ+t *almighty, athletic, omnipotent, powerful (he is...), strong, virtuous*. (doldolq'wt, adj.); s+dól+dolqʷ+t *brawn, power (muscular...), strength, virtue*. (sdo̲ldolq'wt, n.); ∥ hn+dol+dolqʷ+t=íl'š+n *confirmation (sacrament of).* (hndoldolq'wti̱'lshn. (lit. means of becoming strong), n.); ‡ dol+dolq'ʷ+t=íl'š-st-m *enable, confirm.* (doldolq'wti̱'lshstm. (lit. he was strengthened), vt.); § x̌am+a+s+c'am' ł dol+dólq'ʷ+t *burly, husky.* (qhamats'a'm ł doldo̱lq'wt. (lit. He is heavy-boned and strong), adj.); ti?xʷ+eł+n+dol+dolq'ʷ+t=íl'š+n *confirmed.* (ti'khwełndoldolq'wti̱'lshn (lit. He gained strength, he received the rite of confirmation), vi.)

√dl? † s+dílu? *switch, whip.* (sdi̱lu, n.)

√dl', † e·+del' *bush, plant, shrub, a low branching woody plant.* (eede'l, n.)

√dl'₂ † dul' *run (...away).* (du'l, vi.); č+dúl'+m+ncut *elope, run away.* (chdu̱'lmntsut (lit. we ran away), vi.) [xref √dlm]

√dl'p † č+del'p+dil'p *bat (mammal).* (chde'lpdi'lp. vampire, n.)

√dł † dił *rustle, shake.* (dił (stem), vt.); duł+duł+p *poplar tree.* (dułdułp, n.); § dar+eł+dúł+duł+p *poplars (with small round leaves).* (darełdu̱łdułp, n.); s+dar+eł+dúł+duł+p *poplar (species of...).* (sdarełdu̱łdułp (lit. small round leaves that rustle-white bark with spots and stripes), n.); s+miyeł+díł+m+šeš *concussion.* (smiyełdi̱łmshesh (lit. more than ordinary jarring), n.)

√dm₁ † a·dám *Adam.* (Aadam, n.)

√dm₂ ∥ dm=íne? *birdhouse, nest.* (dmi̱ne', n.); hn+č+dm=íne?=kʷe? *Moctelme Creek.* (Hnchdmi̱ne'kwe'. (lit. nest creek), n.)

√dm₃ † dem *be very old.* (dem, vi.); dém+m *decrepit.* (de̱mm (lit. H/s grew old), adj.) ; i·+dém+m *effete.* (iide̱mm (lit. He is wearing out as a result of age), adj.); s+dém+m *age (decrepid...), old age.* (sde̱mm, n.)

√dm₄ ∥ s+dúm=cn *bosom friend, chum, friend (intimate...).* (sdu̱mtsn, n.); s+dum=cn=íw'es *chum.*

(sdumtsni̱'wes (lit. They are good friends), vi.)

√dn₁ † de·n+yél *Daniel.* (Deenyel, n.); den *Dan* (Den, proper name.); di·ní *Denny.* (Diini̱, n.)

√dn₂ † u·+dún' *moved (it suddenly...).* (uudu̱n, vi.)

√dpt † da·pít *David.* (Daapi̱t, n.)

√dq' † daq' *peer (...through cracks).* (daq', vi.)

√dq'ʷ † doq'ʷ *wood (...is rotten).* (doq'w (stem), n.)

√dr † dar *curved objects stand with concave surface up.* (dar, vi.); ča+dar+mín+n *table (for pots, pans, pails).* (chadarminn, n.); ∥ ?ał+dár=enč *moon, sun.* (ałda̱rench, n.); ?ał+d+dar'=ín'č *clock, sundial, timepiece, watch, chronometer, little sun.* (ałdda'ri̱'nc, n.); ?apł+?ał+dar=en[č] *clear, sunny (to be...).* (apł'ałdarensh (lit. It has sun), vi.); ‡ dáre-nt-s *He set the table (lit. He set vessels upright).* (da̱rents, vt.); § s+t'uk'ʷ+k'ʷ=ip+ms ha?ł+dar=enč *calends, the first day of the month (lit. its beginning what is a moon).* (st'uk'uk'wipms ha'łdarench, n.); s+can+q'ʷenp'+eł+?ał+dár=enč *eclipse.* (stsanq'wenp'eł'ałda̱rench (lit. sun/moon going behind something), n.); ?ax̌el+ł ?esel ha?+ł+dár=enč *bimonthly.* (aqhełł esel ha'łdarench (lit. happening every two months), adj.); dar+eł+dúł+duł+p *poplar, species of (lit. small, round leaves that rustle-white bark with spots and stripes).* (darełdu̱łdułp, n.); s+dar+eł+dúł+duł+p *poplar (species of...), poplars (with small round leaves).* (sdarełdu̱łdułp (lit. small round leaves that rustle-white bark with spots and stripes), n.)

√ds₁ † des *camp.* (des (stem), n.); des+t *camped (he...), encamp.* (dest, vi.); s+des+t *camp (to...), camping.*

(sdest, vt, n.); hn+dés+n *camp, campground.* (hndęsn. (lit. place where people camp), n.) [see also √sds]

√ds₂ † dis *appear.* (dis (stem), vi.)

√dš † déš+š+i? *decreased, diminished, lessened (the number...).* (dęshshi', vi.); deš+š+i? *diminish, lessen, smaller (to grow...).* (deshshi' (lit. It grew smaller; it diminished), vi.)

√dščqʷ † déščeqʷe *husband's brother, sister's husband.* (dęshcheqwe, n.)

√dw † a·+dwa *Edward.* (Aadwa. A Coear d'Alene chief in the 1800's, n.); pan' a·dwá *She is Mrs. Edward.* (pa'n Aadwą, vi.)

√dxʷ₁ † dexʷ *descend, dismount, dropped (it was...), lower.* (dekhw (stem), vi.); dexʷ+t *dropped (he...), fell (he...down), fell (it...(off)).* (dekhwt, vt.); hn+déx̱ʷ+xʷ+n *envy, jealousy.* (hndękhukhwn (lit. means of envying), n.); déx̱ʷ+m+ncut *descend.* (dekhwmntsut (lit. he went down), v.); s+déx̱ʷ+m+ncut *catabasis.* (sdękhwmntsut (lit. putting oneself down), n.); dux̱ʷ+m+ncút+n *chute.* (dukhwmntsutn (lit. m.o. lowering oneself-an inclined trough or passage down which things can pass), n.); s+čic+en+déx̱ʷ+x̱ʷ+t+m *come (...down).* (schitsendękhukhtm (lit. a decline this way in status), vi.); ∥ an+doxʷ+m=qín+m *dip, headfirst, slope.* (andokhumqinm (lit. That which goes down headfirst, a downward slope), n.); hn+duxʷ+m=qín+m *cascade, descend.* (hndukhomqinm. (lit. He came down (from the mountain) (headlong)), vt.); hn+duxʷ+x̱ʷ=elgʷes+mí+ncut *begrudge, envious.* (hndukhukhwelgwesmįntsut. (lit. He felt his heart drop, become lower), vt, adj.); s+duxʷ+t=íl'kʷe? *cascade, waterfall.* (sdukhwti'lkwe', n.); s+n+doxʷ+m=qí[n]+[m] *cataclinal.*

(sndokhmqįm (lit. going down head-long descending with the dip, as a valley), adj.); hn+duxʷ+p=ílgʷes *despond, discourage, dishearten.* (hndukhwpilgwes. (lit. He was lowered in heart. He became sorrowful), vt.); s+n+duxʷ+p=ílgʷes *dolor, grief, sorrow.* (sndukhwpilgwes (lit. lowering of the heart), n.); ‡ dexʷ+m-st-m *cheapen.* (dekhwmstm (lit. it was lowered), vt.); cen+déxʷ+t+m-stu-s *depreciate.* (tsendekhwtmstus (lit. He lowered the value or rate of it), vi.); cen+déxʷ+xʷ+m-st-m *discount.* (tsendekhukhwmstm (lit. He dropped from a higher to a lower state), vt.); cen+déxʷ+xʷ-t-m *depreciate.* (tsendekhukhwtm (lit. It became lower (in value), vt.); [see also √dk'ʷ]

√dxʷ₂ ∥ ec+?e+dxʷ=íw'es *cross, crucifix.* (ets'edkhwi'wes, n.); ‡ e+dxʷ=iw'es-nt-en *crisscross.* (edkhwiw'esnten, adj.); e dxʷ=ílgʷes-nt-em *to be blessed, made holy (lit. A sign of the cross was made over h/h).* (edkhwilgwesntem, v.)

√dx̌₁ † dax̌ *go, depart, travel.* (daqh (stem). drive, vi.); dex̌ *depart.* (deqh (stem), vi.); déx̌+t+ul *walk (You...).* (deqhtul, imper.); t+ča·+déx̌+n *catwalk.* (tchaadęqhn (lit. space for walking on), n.); č'a· dex̌+t *walk.* (ch'aadeqht (lit. we walk), vi.); čat+čs+déx̌+t *walk.* (chatchsdęqht (lit. we will walk), vi.); č+dex̌+t *walk, (lit. we walked).* (chdeqht, vi.); č ?i·+déx̌+t *lit. we are walking.* (ch'iideqht, vt.); č' in+déx̌+t *advancement, progressing.* (ch'indeqht (lit. we are walking on the road, *We are walking on the trail. We are travelling on the path of life.*), n, vt.); k'ʷ ne? č+déx̌+t *We are going to walk.* (k'wne'chdeqht, vi.); k̓ʷp déx̌+t *departed (you (pl.)...).* (kupdeqht, vi.);

kʷp‿ʔa·+déǩ+t *walk (you (pl.)...).* (kup'aadeqht, vi.); déǩ+t+ul *You (pl.) walk.* (deqhtul, imper.); čeł‿kʷup‿s+déǩ+t *you (pl) will walk.* (chełkupsdeqht, vi.); kʷup‿ʔi·‿déǩ+t *You (pl) are walking, departing.* (kup'iideqht, vi.); k'ʷ neʔ kʷup‿deǩ+t *You (pl.) are going to walk.* (k'wne'kupdeqht, vi.); déǩ+t-lš *walked (they...).* (deqhtlsh, vt.); a· dé[ǩ]+t-lš *walk.* (aadeq'tlsh (lit. They walk), vi.); i· déǩ+t-lš *They are walking.* (iideqhtlsh, vi.); k'ʷ naʔ déǩ+t-lš *They are going to walk.* (k'wna'deqhtlsh, vi.); **//** č+d+deǩ+deǩ+t=al'qʷ *bum.* (chddeqhdeqhta'lqw. (lit. those who walk on log, RR), n.)

√dǩ₂ † daǩ *round-up, drive (cattle, etc.).* (daqh (stem), n.); i·+dáǩ+m *driven (The herd is being...), herd (The...is being driven).* (iidaqhm, vt, n.); ‡ daǩ-nt-s *he drove it (cow/cattle).* (daqhnts, vt.); § sya+daǩ+él'+s+či+čeʔ *cattle herder.* (syadaqhe'lschiche', n.)

√dʕʷ † dáʕʷ+p+mncut *h/s exerted h/h self (lit. h/s used h/h self with an effort).* (da(wpmntsut, vt.); s+dáʕʷ+p+m+ncut *contest, exerting (oneself).* (sda(wpmntsut (lit. putting oneself in strenuous effort), n, vt.)

√dʔ † díʔ+deʔ+t *demure.* (di'de't (lit. is saddening), adj.) [?]; **//** deʔ=us+m *He put on a sad face.* (de'usm, vt.)

√dʔkʷ † duʔkʷ *stingy (be...about something).* (du'kw, adj.); duʔ+duʔkʷ+úl *avaricious, cheap-skate, close-fisted, stingy.* (du'du'kul. (lit. he is a miserly person), adj.)

√dʔk'ʷ † diʔk'ʷ *cross.* (di'k'w (stem), vt.); č+diʔk'ʷ *Monday.* (chdi'k'w, n.); čn‿n+diʔk'ʷ *crossed.* (chnndi'k'w (lit. I crossed the stream, river.), vi.); s+n+díʔk'ʷ+n *crossing.* (sndi'k'wn.

(lit. the place at which a river or other obstacle can be crossed), n.); **//** čn‿n+deʔk'ʷ+s=iw'es *cross.* (chnnde'k'uwsi'wes (lit. I crossed the street, valley, etc.), vt.); hn+deʔk'ʷ= us=íw'es+n *crosswalk.* (hnde'k'uusi'wesn. (lit. a street crossing marked for pedestrians), n.); hn+daʔk'ʷ=qn *lit. He went overhead.* (hnda'k'wqn, vi.); hn+d+daʔk'ʷ=qín' *afternoon, midday.* (hndda'k'wqi'n. (lit. that which goes over the middle of the head, (the sun) passed overhead), n.) [xref √dk'ʷ]

√dʔł † deʔł *exceptionally.* (de'ł, adv.); heʔ+deʔł *of course.* (he'de'ł, adv.)

√dʔt † deʔét *surprisingly.* (de'et. (stem), adv.) [?]

√gʷc' **//** hn+gʷíc'=ens+n *toothpick.* (hngwits'ensn (lit. means of picking the teeth), n.); hn+gʷíc'+gʷec'=cn *elicit.* (hngwits'gwets'tsn (lit. H/s is skilled in picking things out of another person's mouth, he is an argumentative person), vt.); in+gʷíc'=e[ns]+mš *picking (H/s is...h/h teeth (tooth)).* (ingwits'emshmsh, n, vt.)

√gʷč † gʷič *He saw.* (gwich, vt.); gʷič+t *see.* (gwicht (stem), vt.); s+gʷíč+č *complexion.* (sgwichch (lit. general character or appearance), n.); čn‿ʔc+gʷíč *see.* (ch'ntsgwich. (lit. I, usually see, things, of that nature), vt.); cen+gʷič+mí+ncut *to anticipate.* (tsengwichmintsut (lit. He foresaw something concerning himself), vt.); is-cen+gʷíč+mí+ncut *divination.* (istsengwichmintsut (lit. It is your means of seeing forward for yourself), n.); gʷíč+ič+út+m *It is capable of being seen.* (gwichichutm, vi.); s+gʷíč+t-ew'eš *seeing (wholly, entirely or exclusively) (...each other).* (sgwichte'wesh, n.); **//** gʷeč=stq *He found or saw a wild crop.* (gwechstq, vt.); gʷeč=alqʷ+ncút *cocky.*

(gwechalqwntsut (lit. He saw his own height; he became conceited), adj.); gʷeč=qan=áʔst *Wenatchee.* (gwechqanaʼst (lit. he saw over a rock, cliff, precipice), n.); čn‿n+gʷíč=kʷeʔ *I saw in the water. I saw something therein.* (chnngwichkweʼ, vt.); u t+gʷčʼ+gʷéčʼ=us *H/s has clear eyesight.* (utgwchʼgwechʼus, vi.); ‡ gʷíč-n *saw (I...i/h/h).* (gwichn, vt.); gʷič-t-m *H/s was seen.* (gwichtm, vt.); ec+gʷíč-s-n *I customarily see h/h/i physically or mentally.* (etsgwichsn, vi.); hn-gʷíč+ečʼ-nt-se-s *H/s saw my back.* (hngwichechʼntses, vt.); gʷeč=álqʷ-nt-s *He saw another person's stature.* (gwechalqwnts, vt.); gʷič=ús-n *saw (I...his face).* (gwichusn, vt.); can+gʷéč+p=qnʼ-nʼ *saw (I...the back of h/h head).* (tsangwechpqʼnʼn, n, vt.); cen+gʷíč=šn-t-s *saw (H/s...h/h tracks), tracks (H/s saw h/h...).* (tsengwichshnts, vt, n.); § s+gʷíč+s+čínt *seeing people.* (sgwichschint, n.); ec+gʷíč+s+čínt *h/s sees people.* (etsgwichschint, vt.); čn‿gʷíč e siwʼs *groundhog.* (chngwich e siʼws, n.); čn‿gʷič e· siwʼs *groundhog.* (chngwich ee siʼws (lit. I saw a groundhog), n.); neʔ t+gʷíč+gʷič=us-nt-s xʷa s+lʼax̌+t-s *He will see the eyes of one who is his friend.* (neʼtgwichgwichusnts khwa sʼlaqhts, v.); čn‿xʷuy hiɬ čn‿gʷič e cʼiʔ *lit. I went over there and I saw a deer.* (chnkhuy hiɬ chngwich e tsʼiʼ, vt.)

√gʷčʼ † gʷičʼ *ignite, kindle, light.* (gwichʼ, vt.); ∥ u+t+gʷčʼ+gʷéčʼ=us *eyesight (H/s has clear...).* (utgwchʼgwechʼus, n.) [for expected √gʷč]; gʷíčʼ+s=kʷp+n *kindling.* (gwichʼskupn, n.); čeɬ‿gʷíčʼ+s=kʷup+n *H/s went after kindling.* (cheɬgwichʼskupn, vt.); hn-gʷíčʼ+s=kʷup+n *It is my kindling.* (hngwichʼskupn, vi.); ‡ gʷíčʼ+s=

kʷup+m-nt-s *H/s used it for kindling.* (gwichʼskupmnts, vt.)

√gʷčʔ ‡ gʷíčeʔ-nt-se-s *H/s brought me ill luck.* (gwicheʼntses, vt.)

√gʷgʷ ∥ gʷigʷ=ep *step (...back).* (gwigwep (stem), vi.); hn+gʷígʷ=ep+m *back up, cringe, retreat, reverse (go in).* (hngwigwepm (lit. H/s stepped back), vi.); s+n+gʷígʷ=ep+m *retreating, reverse (going in...).* (sngwigwepm, n.)

√gʷl₁ † gʷel *blaze (stem), burn, light (kindle).* (gwel (stem), vt.); gʷel+p *blaze, burn (catch fire), burnt, flamed (it...).* (gwelp, v, vi.); s+gʷel+p *combustion, fire.* (sgwelp, n.); ec+gʷel+p *hell, inferno.* (etsgwelp, n.); gʷl+p+útm *burnable, flammable, combustible.* (gwlputm. (lit. It is capable of burning), adj.); ic+gʷél+p *ablaze, it is blazing.* (itsgwelp, adj.); s+gʷél+gʷl+m *bonfire.* (sgwelgwlm, n.); s+gʷl+p+níʔ+m+ut *blaze.* (sgwlpniʼmut (lit. a destructive fire, especially one that spreads rapidly), n.); ∥ t+gʷál+p=alqʷ *burned (The log...), log (The...burned).* (tgwalpalqw, vt, n.); niʔ+gʷal+p=alqʷ *burned (The forest was...), forest (the...was burned).* (niʼgwalpalqw, v, n.); gʷl+p=ax̌n *His arm was burned.* (gwlpaqhn, vi.); gʷil+p=íɬxʷ *H/s house burned down.* (gwilpiɬkhw, vi.); s+gʷl=íɬxʷ *arson.* (sgwliɬkhw (lit. burning a house), n.); ‡ gʷl=íɬcʼeʔ-nt-m *cremate.* (gwliɬtseʼntm (lit. His corpse was burn, vt.); § s+miyes+gʷél+p *conflagration.* (smiyesgwelp (lit. extraordinary fire), n.); te[l]ʼ s+gʷel+p *igneous.* (teʼ sgwelp, adj.) [xref √qʷlʼ]

√gʷl₂ † gʷil *trust.* (gwil (stem), vt.)

√gʷlʼ † gʷelʼ *slant, tilt.* (gwelʼ (stem), vt.); gʷélʼ+lʼ+m *It was tilted.* (gweʼlʼlm, vi.); ec+gʷélʼ+m *tilted (to be), beveled.* (etsgweʼlm (lit. It is inclined upward and downward), vi.);

// gʷl'+l'=íɫxʷ *h/h house became tilted.* (gw'l'lmiɫkhw, vt.); gʷl'+l'+m=íɫc'eʔ *h/h body was tilted.* (gw'l'lmiɫt'se', vt.); gʷl'+l'+m=íw'es *converge, unite.* (gw'l'lmi'wes (lit. They inclined together), vi.); s+gʷl'+l'+m=íw'es *convergence.* (sgw'l'lmi'wes (lit. inclining together), n.)

√gʷɫ † u· gʷɫ· *twinkling (continuously), glitter.* (uugwɫɫ, adj, n.)

√gʷm † gʷum *crumble, disintegrate.* (gum (stem), vi.); gʷum+t *It became crumbled.* (gumt, vi.); s+gʷum+t *crumbling.* (sgumt, vi.); gʷ+gʷm'+gʷúm' *crackers.* (gugu'mgu'm (lit. that which crumbles and crumbles), n.); // s+gʷóm=aqs *name of the wife of Ignace Timothy, (both of whom died long ago) (lit. crumbling of one's chest).* (Sgomaqs, n.)

√gʷn † gʷen *below (be...), deep (be...), low (be...).* (gwen (stem), vi.); hn+gʷen+t *deep.* (hngwent (lit. It is a deep (hole)), adj.); cen+gʷén+t *basement, basic, under, (lit. substructure of a building).* (etsengwent (lit. In a lower place), n, adj, adv.); cen+gʷen+t *beneath, under.* (tsengwent, prep.); ul cen+gʷén+t *basal, basic.* (ul tsengwent (lit. belonging to what is under), adj.); e cen+gʷén+t *beneath, under.* (etsengwent (lit. In a lower place), adv.); // can+gʷán+t=al'qs *chemise.* (tsangwanta'lqs (lit. a loose, shirtlike garment), n.); hn+gʷén=ep *bottom, base.* (hngwenep (lit. the lowest or deepest part of anything), n.); s+n+gʷén=ep *bottom (...of a container).* (sngwenep, n.); hn+gʷn= itkʷeʔ *the bottom of the water, river, etc. It is deep water.* (hngwnitkwe', n.); gʷn=úl'umxʷ *lowland.* (gwnu'lumkhw, n.); hn+gʷn=úl'umxʷ *chasm.* (hngwnu'lumkhw (lit. The hole in the

ground is deep), n.); hn+gʷn+t= úl'umxʷ *low land (He went by..., perhaps through a valley, gulch, etc.).* (hngwntu'lumkhw, vi.); t+gʷén+t= us+t *path, road (H/s went by a low...).* (tgwentust, n.); § hn+gʷen+t eɫ+s+n+kʷ'deʔ=ús=šn *deep-rooted.* (hngwent eɫsnk'wde'usshn, adj.); elu+ɫ+cen+gʷén+t *baseless, foundation (without...), groundless. metaph. H/s has no underwear.* (eluɫtsengwent, n, adj.); ul s+mi?yem ha can+gʷán+ts=al'qs *camisole.* (ul smi'yem ha tsangwanta'lqs (lit. belonging to woman an undergarment), n.)

√gʷnt † gʷnít *call, summon.* (gwnit (stem), vt.); gʷnit+m *ask, beg (for), entreat.* (gwnitm, vt.); // hn+gʷni[t]= cn *beg, entreat.* (hngwnitsn (lit. Beckon with the mouth), v.); hn+gʷní[t]=cn *cadge.* (hngwnitsn (lit. He begged for food), vi.); s+n+gʷní[t]=cn *beg (to...).* (sngwnitsn (lit. asking for food), v.); hn+gʷn'+gʷn'e[t]=cn'+úl' *beggar.* (hngw'ngw'nets'nu'l (He habitually begs), n.); gʷn=íčt+m *H/s beckoned (with h/h hand).* (gwnichtm, vt.); gʷnit=elt *She (hen) summons her chicks. H/s summons h/h child.* (gwnitelt, vt.); gʷn+gʷnít=elt *H/s summoned h/h children.* (gwngwnitelt, vt.); ‡ gʷnít-n-lš *called (I...them).* (gwnitnlsh, vt.); gʷnít-s *defy.* (gwnits (lit. He called him out-he challenged him), vt.); gʷnít=čs-n [possibly *I beckoned him*] *He beckoned him.* (gwnitchsn, vt.); § gʷn+es+čínt *convoke, summoned.* (gwneschint (lit. H/s called people together), vt.); gʷn[it]+el'+s+či+čeʔ *H/s summoned h/h livestock.* (gwne'lschiche', vt.)

√gʷnxʷ † gʷníxʷ *acknowledgable, actual, authentic, believable, bona fide, credible, de facto, genuine, true* *(be...).* (gwni̲khw (lit. It is true, I admit it is true, it exists in reality), adj, vt.); s+gʷníxʷ *certitude, It is the truth.* (sgwni̲khw (lit. truth, complete assurance), n.); ne^{ʔ}+gʷníxʷ *maybe, perhaps.* (ne'gwni̲khw. it's true, adv.); łe s+gʷníxʷ+s *truth, that which is true, it's truth.* (łe sgwni̲khws, n, vi.); hn+gʷnnixʷe^{ʔ}+utm *persuasive, cogent.* (hngwnnikhwe'utm. believable. adj.); // gʷníxʷ=cn *assert, aver, affirm.* (gwni̲khwtsn. (lit. He said what is true), vt.); i c+gʷníxʷ=cn *H/s is telling the truth.* (itsgwni̲khwtsn, vt.); hn+gʷnnixʷ=ene^{ʔ} *believe.* (hngwnnikhwene' (lit. Hold as true with the ear), v.); hn+gʷnníxʷ=ene^{ʔ}+n *belief, creed, faith.* (hngwnni̲khwene'n (lit. It is a means of believing), n.); s+n+gʷnnixʷ=ene^{ʔ} *believe, trust, to have faith, confidence, (lit. becoming true to the ear).* (sngwnnikhwene', vi.); ‡ hn+gʷnníxʷ=ene^{ʔ}+m-nt-s *He believed him, He gave him credit.* (hngwnnikhwene'mnts, vt.); hn+gʷnníxʷ=ene^{ʔ}+m-nt-se-s *believed (H/s...me).* (hngwnnikhwene'mntses, vt.); § s+hoy+ł+n+gʷnníxʷ=ene^{ʔ}+n *apostasy.* (s-hoyłngwnni̲khwene'n (lit. abandoning one's acceptance of the truth through the hearing), n.); lut+gʷníxʷ *deceptive, spurious.* (lutgwni̲khw (lit. It is untrue), adj.)

√gʷp † gʷep *grassy (be...), hairy (be...).* (gwep (stem), vi.); gʷep+t *It (the grass) is tall and thick.* (gwept, vi.); ni^{ʔ}+gʷép+t *bushiness.* (ni'gwe̲pt (lit. The forest is bushy within), n.); // s+gʷép=cn *beard, mustache, whiskers.* (sgwe̲ptsn, n.); ^{ʔ}ep+s+gʷép=cn *beard (to have a...), whiskers (to have...).* (epsgwe̲ptsn, n.); t+gʷép=elxʷ *He (bear, etc.) is hairy on the body.* (tgwe̲pelkhw, vi.);

s+t+gʷp+gʷp=íčn'=us *eyebrows.* (stgupgupich'nus, pl.n.); en+gʷup=iłce^{ʔ} *to have thick hair inside, e.g., a coat.* (engupi̲łtse', vt.); s+t+gʷp+gʷp=iłc'e^{ʔ}=us *eyelashes.* (stgupgupiłts'e'us, pl.n.); s+t+gʷp+t=ós+m=al'qs *fur coat.* (stgupto̲sma'lqs, n.); t+gʷáp=qn *hair (H/s has thick...).* (tgwa̲pqn, n.); t+gʷép+gʷp=šn *ankles, feet. (The horse has hairy...).* (tgwe̲pgupshn, n.); a+t+gʷáp+gʷp=alq=šn *hairy-legged.* (atgwa̲p gupalqshn (lit. H/s has hairy-legged), adj.); e+ni^{ʔ}+gʷáp+[g]ʷp=i^{ʔ}qs *hairy (nostrils).* (eni'gwa̲pqupi'qs, vt. (lit. He has hair in his nostrils), adj.); gʷp=úl'mxʷ *It (ground) is covered with much grass.* (gupu'lmkhw, vt.); § elu+s+gʷép=cn *bare-faced, beardless.* (elusgwe̲ptsn (lit. He is w/o a beard on his face), adj.); t+gʷép=elxʷ ha s+x̌ʷet'+i^{ʔ} *Angora.* (tgwe̲pelkhw ha sqhwet'i' (lit. He (the goat) has long hair), n.); gʷp=ci^{ʔ}+ka·+ká^{ʕ} *brother (young boy's name of older...),(lit. a bearded brother).* (guptsi'kaaka̲(, n.)

√gʷq₁ † gʷaq *roomy (be...), space (have...).* (gwaq (stem), adj, vt.); u· gʷáq *empty, roomy, spacious.* (uugwa̲q. (as a room), adj.); ac+gʷaq *It (space) is empty.* (atsgwaq, vi.); // gʷáq=šn *feet (pig's...).* (gwa̲qshn, n.) [possibly gʷáq'=šn "divided feet"]; u+n+gʷáq=łc'e^{ʔ} *empty, spacious (it (room) is empty,...).* (ungwa̲qłts'e', adj.)

√gʷq₂ † gʷoq *make way through crowd.* (gwoq, vt.)

√gʷq'₁ † gʷaq' *spread apart as to part hair, remove layers.* (gwaq', vt.); ac+gʷáq' *divided, parted, cracked.* (atsgwa̲q', vi.); // a+ni^{ʔ}+gʷáq'=us *parted (hair).* (ani'gwa̲q'us, vi. (lit. H/h hair is parted in the middle from the front), adj.); s+gʷáq'+m=ep *anus, butt.* (sgwa̲q'mep (lit. opening at the bottom (door, gate)), n.); ‡ gʷaq'-nt-s h/s removed layer from it. (gwaq'nts, vt.)

√gʷq'₂ † gʷá?+gʷaq'+t *mustang*. (gwa'gwaq't. bronco (lit. wild horse), n.); gʷáq'+gʷaq'+t *bronco*. (gwaq'gwaq't. mustang (lit. wild horse), n.); ic+gʷá?q' *is acting (He...wild)*. (itsgwa'q', vi.)

√gʷq'm s+gʷaq'ím' *full moon, moonlight*. (sgwaq'i'm, n.)

√gʷr † gʷar *scrape*. (gwar (stem), vt.); s+gʷár+gʷar+t *Mica Peak, Washington (near Spokane)*. (Sgwargwart, n.); hn+gʷar+min+n *hoe, scraper*. (hngwarminn (lit. means of scraping inside a cow barn, etc.), n.); ∥ hn+gʷár=alqs+n *grader*. (hngwaralqsn, n.); ‡ gʷar-n *I scraped it with a hard tool (snow, etc.)*. (gwarn, vt.); gʷár-nt-s *grated, scraped*. (gwarnts, vt.); § x̌áy'+x̌i?+t ha gʷar=úl'mxʷ+n *bulldozer*. (qha'yqhi't ha gwaru'lmkhwn (lit. big ground scraper), n.)

√gʷrp † gʷarp+m *bloom, blossom*. (gwarpm (lit. it bloomed), v.); s+gʷárp+m *bloom, blossom, flower*. (sgwarpm, n.); gʷł s+[g]ʷ+gʷar'p+m' *corsage*. (guł squgwa'rpm' (lit. little flowers), n.); s+gʷár+gʷarp+m *bouquet*. (sgwargwarpm (lit. flowers), n.); § x̌al s+gʷarp+m *dandelion*. (qhal sgwarpm, n.); x̌al+hn+nak'ʷá?=al·'qs ha s+gʷárp+m *daisy*. (qhalhnnak'wa'al'lqs ha sgwarpm, n.); hn+nák'ʷa?=alqs ha s+gʷárp+m *daffodil*. (hnnak'wa'alqs ha sgwarpm, n.)

√gʷr'₁ ∥ s+n+gʷár'=us *breeding, descendant, descent, offspring*. (sngwa'rus, n.); § s+n+gʷár'=us xʷe·tíł+teł=l'mxʷ *boysenberry*. (sngwa'rus khwee tiłteł'lmkhw (lit. descendant of blackberry vine), n.)

√gʷr'₂ † gʷar' *metal, shiny, silvery (be...)*. (gwar' (stem), n, adj.); u· gʷár'

clear, shiny. (uugwa'r. like silver, adj.); ∥ un+gʷár'=kʷe? *clear, crystal (The water is....)*. (ungwa'rkwe', adj, n.); ut+gʷár'=c'e? *shiny*. (utgwa'rts'e'. It is silvery on the outside, as a silver plate, adj.); u n+gʷár'=łc'e? *shiny, silvery*. (ungwa'rłts'e'. It is shiny, silvery inside, as a silver cup, adj.); u+t+gʷár'=sq'it *sky (The...is clear)*. (utgwa'rsq'it, n.); u+t+gʷár'=us *eye (H/s has a clear...)*. (utgwa'rus, n.); u t+gʷar'+gʷár'=us *H/s has clear eyes*. (utgwa'rgwa'rus, vi.)

√gʷs₁ † gʷes *spin, thread, twist*. (gwes (stem), vt.); gʷés+mn *canvas, gunnysack*. (gwesmn. hemp for rope, n.); ‡ gʷes-nt-s *h/s spinned it (thread, etc.)*. (gwesnts, vt.)

√gʷs₂ † gʷis *high (be...)*. (gwis (stem), vi.); hn+gʷí?s *late morning*. (hngwi's (lit. The sun rose up high), n.); če?t+n+gʷi?s *oversleep, (lit. it became high (sun) on h/h)*. (che'tngwi's, vt.); hn+gʷís+t *elevated, eminence, high (It is...), upstairs, heaven*. (hngwist, adj, n, vi, adv.); s+n+gʷís+t *altitude, depth, elevation*. (sngwist. height, n.); s+ni?+n+gʷís+t *acme*. (sni'ngwist (lit. the highest point), n.); ∥ gʷs=qn=é?st *The cliff is high*. (gwsqne'st, vt.); gʷł gʷés=alqʷ *They are tall trees*. (guł gwesalqw, vi); t+gʷés=i?qs *nose (H/s has a high...), Pat Swan (name of the late...), Father of the Swans*. (Tgwesi'qs, n.); § tel' hn+gʷis+t *high (from on...)*. (te'l hngwist, adv.); tel' n+gʷis+t *above (from...)*. (te'l ngwist, adv.); teč+n+gʷís+t *above, aloft, overhead, upstairs, in heaven, into a high place, toward the sky*. (techngwist, adv.); s+č's=cín+m+n łe n+gʷís+t *blasphemy*. (sch'stsinmn łengwist (lit. speaking evil of the One on High), n.); ylmixʷ+m a+n+gʷís+t *the chief who*

dwells on high. (ylmikhumangwi̱st, n.);
[xref √gʷš₂]

√gʷš₁ † gʷeš *comb.* (gwesh (stem), vt.);
∥ gʷš=úl'mxʷ *harrowed.*
(gwshu̱'lmkhw (lit. He combed the
ground), vt.); gʷš=úl'mxʷ+n *harrow.*
(gwshu̱'lmkhwn (lit. means of
com[b]ing the ground), vt.); gʷš=
qin+n *comb, hairbrush, (lit. a means
of combing).* (gwshqinn, n.);
čn'‿c+gʷš=qín+m *comb.*
(ch'ntsgwshqi̱nm. (lit. I, customarily,
comb my hair), vt.); ‡ gʷéš-nt-s
combed (he...it). (gwe̱shnts, vt.);
čs+gʷeš-nt-s *H/S combed his
(horse's) tail.* (chsgwe̱shnts, vt.);
t+gʷš=ílxʷ-nt-s *combed (H/s...the
horse's hide or hair).* (tgwshi̱lkhwnts,
vt.); § s+t+gʷiš=elxʷe?+l+s+čí+če?
curry. (stgwishelkhwe'lschi̱che' (lit.
rubbing down and cleaning a horse),
vt.)

√gʷš₂ † gʷiš *rise.* (gwish (stem), vi.);
hn+gʷíš+iš *arise, ascend (to...), H/s
went up into the air, sky.* (hngwi̱shish
(lit. He moved upward), vi.);
hn+gʷíš+gʷeš+iš *bounce.*
(hngwi̱shgweshish (lit. It went up and
down repeatedly), vi.);
hn+gʷíš+iš+emn *crane, elevator,
jack, lifter.* (hngwi̱shishemn (lit. That
which raises up or exalts), n.);
s+n+gʷíš+iš *going up (...into the air).*
(sngwi̱shish, n.); ‡ e+n+gʷíš+š-st-xʷ
elevate, raise. (engwishshtkhw (lit.
You raise it up), vt.);
hn+gʷíš+iš-stu-s *caused (H/s...it to
rise), lifted (H/s...it).* (hngwi̱shishstus,
vi, vt.) [xref gʷš₂]

√gʷt † gʷt *twinkle (stem).* (gwt (stem),
vi.)

√gʷt' † gʷt'+gʷt' *sound (chewing...).*
(gut' gut', n.); is+gʷút'+gʷt'+iš *chomp,
crunch.* (isgu̱t'-gut'-ish (lit. He is
making repeatedly the chewing sound),
vi.)

√gʷt'č' † gʷét'č' *gore, prong.* (gwet'ch'
(stem), vt, n.); gʷt'č'+mín-is *horn.*
(gwt'ch'mi̱nis (lit. It is his (bull's)
means of goring), n.); ∥
ec+gʷt'+gʷt'č'=íɫce? *gore.*
(etsgwt'gwt'ch'i̱ɫtse' (lit. He. e.g. bull,
gores people), vt.); ‡ gʷét'č'-nt-m
gored (he was...). (gwe̱t'ch'ntm, vt.);
gʷét'č'-nt-s *gored (he...him).*
(gwe̱t'ch'nts, vt.);
gʷét'+gʷt'č'+m-nt-m-lš *They were
gored (by bull).* (gwe̱t'gwt'ch'mntmlsh,
vt.); § [na?]x̌iɫ en+gʷt'č'=íčn'-st-mi-t
You (s) might get gored on the back.
(qhiɫne'engwt'ch'ich'nstmit, v.)

√gʷt's † gʷit's *pick out with stick.*
(gwit's, vt.)

√gʷw' † gʷiw' *shreads (wear in...),
seams.* (gwi'w (stem), vi.); gʷíw'+ew' *I
became worn into shreads.* (gwi̱'we'w,
vi.); čn‿gʷíw'+ew' *I am exhausted
(lit. I became worn out).* (chngwi̱'we'w,
vi.); ∥ i c+gʷá?+gʷu?w=alqs *H/h
clothing is becoming worn out (in
shreds).* (itsgwa̱'gwu'walqs, vi.);
gʷíw'+ew'=šn *H/h shoe became worn
out.* (gwi̱'we'wshn, vi.);
gʷíw'+gʷew'+w'=šn *His moccasins or
shoes wore out.* (gwi̱'wgwe'wu'wshn,
vi.); gʷíw'+gʷew'+w'=ečt *H/h gloves
became worn out.*
(gwi̱'wgwe'wu'wecht, vi.);
čn‿gʷíw'+ew'=ečt *became (my hand
(glove)...worn out.* (chngwi̱'we'wecht,
vi.)

√gʷxʷ † gʷéxʷ *objects (...hang).*
(gwe̱khw (stem), vi.); e+t+gʷéxʷ
hanging (to be...). (etgwe̱khw (lit.
They are in a hanging state, e.g., meats
to dry), vi.); t+gʷxʷ+mín+n *hanger.*
(tgukhwmi̱nn. means of hanging
things, n.); ∥ e t+gʷéxʷ+gʷxʷ=ečt *He
had things hanging on his hands.*
(etgwe̱khwgukhwecht, vi.); e
t+gʷexʷ+gʷxʷ=šn *H/h legs are
hanging from sitting on high object.*

(etgwe̱khwgukhwshn, vi.); ‡
t+g^wéx^w-n *hung (I...them up).*
(tgwe̱khwn, vt.); t+g^wéx^w-nt *hang (You
(sg.)...them up).* (tgwe̱khwnt (imper.),
vt.)

√g^wx̌ † g^wax̌ *young (be...).* (gwaqh
(stem), adj.); ∥ g^wax̌+t=els+cút *h/s
acted young.* (gwaqhtelstsu̱t, vt.);
g^wáx̌+t=elt *a young offspring, a young
person.* (gwaqhtelt, n.); g^w+g^wax̌+t=il't
baby. (gugwaqhti'lt, n.); g^w+g^wax̌i+t=
íl't *cradleboard (for doll).*
(gugwaqhti̱ti'lt, n.); g^w+g^wax̌+t=íl'ey'
doll, cradleboard (for doll).
(gugwaqhti̱'le'y, n.); § ux^wal'a·
g^wáx̌+t=elt *childlike, humble, innocent
(he is...).* (uqhwa'laagwa̱qhtelt, adj.);
s+nuk^w+g^wáx̌+t=elt *one of the same
young age.* (snukwgwa̱qhtelt, n.)

√g^wy' † g^wey' *finish.* (gwe'y (stem), vt.);
∥ g^wéy'=cn *to finish eating (lit. He
finished eating).* (gwe̱'ytsn, v.);
s+g^wey'=cn *finishing a repast.*
(sgwe̱'ytsn, vt.); hn+g^wáy'=qn *mature
(physically), finished growing.*
(hngwa̱'yqn, vt.); in+g^wáy'=qn
growing up (He is...). (ingwa̱'yqn (lit.
He is finishing at the head), vt.);
s+n+g^way'=qn *maturity.* (sngwa'yqn,
n.); s+n+g^wiy'=qín+m+šeš *education
(lit. causing a person to mature).*
(sngwi'yqi̱nmshesh, n.); ‡ g^wéy'-stu-s
finished (he...it). (gwe̱'ystus, vt.);
hn+g^wiy'=qín+m-st-x^w *educate (lit.
You caused h/h to mature).*
(hngwi'yqi̱nmstkhw, vt.); §
g^wiy'+a+s+x̌át=qn *harvest (after...).*
(gwi'yasqha̱tqn, n.);
hi+s+nuk^w+n+g^wáy'=qn
concrescence. (hisnukwngwa̱'yqn (lit.
He is my fellow in growing up), n.)

√h † he *right (that is...).* (he, vi.); ha
laugh (...loudly). (ha (stem), vi.);
hú+he *okay!.* (hu̱he, interj.); hu+he
swell. (huhe, interj.); is+há+ha+h+iš

chortle. (is-ha̱hahish (lit. He is making
the sounds "ha ha"), vi.)

√hl₁ † hn+hala·=cé? *raspberry.*
(hnhalaatse̱', n.)

√hl₂ † hel+t *bruised (it was...).* (helt,
vi.)

√hl₃ ∥ is+hel'=íščey't *deathbed.*
(ishe'li̱shche'yt (lit. He is near his last
breath), n.) [lexical suffix may be
=isč'ey't *pharynx*]

√hm † ham· *What a big crowd
swarming!* (hammm!, (excl.)); ∥ ham=
áłt=mš *fly.* (hama̱łtmsh (lit. swarming
tribe), n.)

√hm? † heme? *Frenchman.* (heme',
n.); ∥ e+n+heme?=cn *French (to
speak...).* (enheme'tsn, vt.)

√hn₁ † hen *grayish (be...).* (hen (stem),
vi.); ∥ t+hán=qn *brunette.* (thanqn (lit.
one who has brown hair), n.); § u· hén
he t'iš *brown sugar.* (uuhe̱n he t'ish
(lit. sugar that is more or less tan), n.)

√hn₂ † čat+hn+na *Clarkia, Idaho.*
(Chat(h)nna, n.)

√hp † hep *gobble.* (hep (stem), vi.)

√hq † haq *have space.* (haq, vt.)

√hr † har *snore.* (har (stem), vi.); ∥
s+har-í?qc-mǒ *snore (to...).*
(s-hari̱'qsmsh, vi.)

√hw₁ † hú+hwe *okay! swell!* (hu̱hwe,
interj.)

√hw₂ † u· héw· *buzz.* (uuhe̱www (lit.
They (bees) kept buzzing), vt.)

√hy₁ † hey *yes.* (hey, adv.);

√hy₂ † hoy *don't do it, stop it.* (hoy!,
excl.); hoy *befall, come about,
happen.* (hoy (lit. It happened by
chance), vi.); ci?ł hoy *that's all.* (tsi'ł
hoy!, excl.); s+hóy+emn *abandoned
(one who is...), derelict, deposed.*
(s-ho̱yemn, adj, vi, vt.); s+hóy+m
annulment. (s-ho̱ym, n.); ∥ ul s+hóy=
cn *conclusive.* (ul sho̱ytsn (lit.
pertaining to a decisive end), adj.); ‡
hóy-st-m *annulled, deposed,
discontinued, excommunicated, jilted,*

√hy

stopped. (hoystm, vt.); hóy-stu-s
abdicate, cease, depose, desist,
dilapidate, discontinue. (hoystus. (lit.
He discontinued it), vt.); hoy
s+hoy-met *(lit. Let's quit!).* (hoy
shoymet! excl.); § ti?i?xʷ+as+hoy+s
afterwards, later. (ti'i'khwashoys,
adv.); lut'+hay'p+s+hóy+oy+s
ageless, eternal, incessant, continual,
continuous. (lut'ha'yps-hoyoys (lit. It is
ageless, it is existing forever, it does
not cease, it has no end), adj.); hoy ɫe
pecčl+es *defoliate.* (hoyɫe petschles
(lit. Its leaves were no more), vi.);
s+hoy+ɫ+n+gʷnníxʷ=ene?+n
apostasy. (s-hoyɫngwnnikhwene'n (lit.
abandoning one's acceptance of the
truth through the hearing), n.)

√hy₃ † huy *all right, O.K., go ahead, I*
dare you!, permission (granted),
welcome, please (if you please). (huy
(lit. you're welcome to it), excl, adv,
imp, vi.); § ?ekʷú-stu-s hoy *allow*
(lit. say all right). (ekustus "huy", v.)

√hy₄ † háy(=)aqs *pearl.* (hayaqs, n.)

√hy' † huy *a cajoling phrase.* (huy,
interj.); ‡ húy'-nt-s *cajole, coax,*
wheedle. (hu'ynts, vt.) [xref √Sʷy]

√hSʷ † heSʷ *growl (...like bear).* (he(w
(stem), vi.)

√h?n' † he?ín' *eight.* (he'i'n (stem), n.);
he?ín'+m *eight.* (he'i'nm, n.);
t+he?ín'+m *eight persons.* (the'i'nm,
n.); § he?en'+m+e·l+?úpen *eighty.*
(he'e'nmee'lupen (lit. eight times ten),
n.); ?upen uɫ ha?ín'+m *eighteen.*
(upen uɫ ha'i'nm, n.)

√jly † ǰu·lay *July.* (Juulay, n.); [also
recorded as *tsooray*] ǰso·ráy *July.*
(Jsooray, n.); i ǰuláy+[m]š
Independence Day (celebration of).
(Ijulaynsh, n.); s+ǰu·lay+mš *Fourth of*
July, Independence Day. (sjuulaymsh,
n.)

√jm₁ † ǰem *brace, pin.* (jem (stem), n.);
s+t+ǰm+ín+n *pincushion.* (stjminn,

n.); ∥ ǰm=ílčs+n *brooch.* (jmilchsn (lit.
safety pin), n.); ‡ ǰém-nt-s *pinned*
(she...it). (jemnts, vt.); t+ǰém-nt-s
pinned (She...it on something).
(tjemnts, vt.); ǰem=íw'es-nt-s *She*
pinned it (them) together. (jemi'wesnts,
vt.)

√jm₂ † mi ǰim *Jim (I am...).* (mi Jim,
n.); ni?+kʷu‿ǰim *Are you Jim?* (ni ku
Jim?(qu.))

√jn ∥ t+ǰín=šn *an old person who walks*
briskly. (tjinshn, n.)

√jpn † ǰe·pní *Japanese.* (jeepni (l.w.
from Engl.), n.); ǰ+ǰe·pn'í *little*
Japanese. (Jjeep'ni, n.)

√jr' † ǰar' *firm, strong, sturdy.* (ja'r
(stem), adj.); u· ǰár' *firm, strong,*
sturdy. (uuja'r, adj.); u+ǰ+ǰár' *sturdy*
(He (little one) is...). (ujja'r, adj.);
ǰar'+ǰar'+t *He is solid, sturdy.* (ja'rja'rt,
vi.); s+ǰár'+ǰar'+t *consistency.*
(sja'rja'rt (lit. sturdiness), n.); ∥
hn+ǰár'+ǰar'=us *die-hard.* (hnja'rja'rus
(lit. He is stiff-necked), n.);
s+ǰar'+ǰar'+t=íl'š *becoming (...solid or*
sturdy), consolidate. (sja'rja'rti'lsh, vt.);
‡ ǰar'+ǰar'+t=íl'š-stu-s *consolidate.*
(ja'rja'rti'lshstus (lit. He made it solid,
sturdy), vt.)

√js † ǰi·sú *Jesus.* (Jiisu, n.); ul+ǰiso·+krí
Christian (lit. pertaining to Christ). (ul
Jisoo Kri, n.); § ?ew+t=us+s xʷa
ǰisukrí *antichrist.* (ewtuss khwa jisukri
(lit. opponent of Jesus Christ), n.)

√jssp † ǰsúsep *Joseph.* (Jsusep (lit.
Chief of Nez Perce). Suusep, n.)

√jx̌ † ǰex̌ *itch, scratch.* (jeqh (stem), vt.);
čn‿ǰex̌+ex̌ *scratched (to get).*
(chnjeqheqh (lit. I became marked by
scratching), vi.); ‡ ǰéx̌-nt-s *scraped*
(he...it). (jeqhnts (lit. striped it by
scraping), vt.); ǰéx̌=us-nt-s *H/S*
marked h/h face by scratching.
(jeqhusnts, vt.)

√jy' † ǰey'+ǰiy' *homely, ugly, unsightly.*
(je'yji'y (stem), adj.); ǰéy'+ǰi'+t *H/S/I is*

ugly. (je'yji't, vi.); gʷł ǰey+ǰiy'+t *They are ugly*. (guł jeyjit, vi.); ǰéy'+iy'+m *deform*. (je'yi'ym (lit. It became ugly), vt.) ; s+ǰey'+iy+m *deformation, ugliness*. (sje'yiym, n.); ǰiy'+ǰiy'+m'+scút *adulterate*. (ji'yji'y'mstsut (lit. H/S made h/h self corrupt, h/s commited adultery), vt.); ∥ ǰáy'+ǰiy'=alqs *H/S has ugly clothes*. (ja'yji'yalqs, vt.); ǰiy'+ǰiy'=ełc'e=gʷt (note glott) *H/S has bad, ugly, offensive manners or nature*. (ji'ji'yełtsegwt, vt.); hn+ǰiy'+ǰiy'=ítkʷe? *It is bad water*. (hnji'yji'yitkwe', vi.); hn+ǰáy'+ǰiy'=qn *blatant*. (hnja'yji'yqn (lit. He has an unpleasant voice), adj.); ǰéy'+ǰey'=us *H/S has an ugly face*. (je'yji'yus, vt.); [also recorded as √ǰ?] s+ǰi?+ǰi?+t=il'š *corruption, debauchery*. (sji'ji'ti'lsh, n.); ǰiy'+ǰiy'+t=íl'š *H/S/I became ugly, bad*. (ji'yji'yti'lsh, vi.); ‡ ǰiy'+ǰiy'+t=íl'š-st-m *debauch, disfigure, deflower, defile*. (ji'yji'yti'lshstm (lit. He was corrupted in moral principles), vt.); ǰiy'+ǰiy'+t+íl'š-stu-s *deface*. (ji'yji'yti'lshstus (lit. He made it bad, he injured its beauty), vt.); ǰiy'+p+mí·nt-s *despise*. (ji'ypmints (lit. He looked upon him as bad (ugly), vt.); ǰey'=íčt+m-nt-s *He treated it in an ugly manner; he made it wrong*. (je'yichtmnts, vt.); § ǰiy'+ǰiy'+áł+[q]ixʷ *smells (it...bad)*. (ji'yji'yałqhikhw, vi.); s+nukʷ+ǰéy'+m+ncut *correspondent*. (snukwje'ymntsut (lit. fellow evildoer), n.)

√klts § káltes pa·láč *bonus (Chinook jargon)*. (kaltes paałach, n.) [also written as √šlts] šáltes pa·lač *bonus (Chinook jargon)*. (shaltes paalach, n.)

√kml † ke·mél *camel*. (keemel, n.)

√kp ∥ s+n+ká+kap=qn' *cap*. (snkakapq'n, n.) [xref √qp]

√kr † kri *Christ*. (Kri, n.); § ul ǰiso· krí *Christian*. (ul Jisoo Kri (lit. pertaining to Christ), n.)

√kˤ § gʷp+ci?+ka·+káˤ *brother (young boy's name of older...)*. (guptsi'kaaka(, n.)

√kʷc † kʷi?c *dusk, evening, nightfall*. (kwi'ts (stem), n.); kʷic+t+m *forenoon (in the...), morning (in the...)*. (kwitstm, adv.); u· kʷíc+t+m *early*. (uukwitstm (lit. early in the morning), adv.); s+n+kʷí?c *becoming night, getting inside*. (snkwi'ts, n.); e+s+n+kʷí?c *night (last...)*. (esnkwi'ts, adv.); hn+kʷí?c *nightfall*. (hnkwi'ts, n.); hn+kʷíc+t *interior*. (hnkwitst. (lit. far inside), n.); ∥ hn+kʷác=qn *dawn*. (hnkwatsqn. (lit. time when morning star rises), n.); s+n+kʷec+t+mš=cín *breakfast, brunch*. (snkwetstmshtsin (lit. eating very early), n.)

√kʷd? ∥ s+kʷede?=cín+p=ene? *chin*. (skwede'tsinpene', n.) [xref? √k'ʷd]

√kʷgʷ † kʷigʷ *see (faintly)*. (kwigw (stem), vt.); cu·+kʷigʷ *unclear, dim, indistinct*. (tsuukwigw (stem), adj.)

√kʷkʷ₁ † is+kʷákʷ+akʷ+iš *cluck*. (iskwakwakwish (lit. The hen making a cluckcluck sound), vi.) [also written as √k'ʷk'ʷ] i s+k'ʷákʷ+akʷ+iš *cluck* (lit. The hen is making a cluck-cluck sound). (isk'wakwakwish, vi.)

√kʷkʷ₂ † kʷu+kʷúkʷ *in the other room*. (kukukw, adv.)

√kʷl₁ † kʷl *red*. (kwl (stem), adj.); kʷil *red (to become...)*. (kwil (stem), adj.); u· kʷl *carmine, cardinal, crimson, red (it is...)*. (uukwl, adj.); ∥ hn+kʷl=kʷe? *wine, claret*. (hnkwlkwe'. (lit. red water), n.); t+kʷl'+kʷl'=íl'xʷ *calf*. (tkw'lkw'li'lkhw (lit. red red hide), n.); t+kʷl=qn *redhead, the name of the late Ignace Timothy, father of Josephine Perry. Ignace got this name because he dyed his hair red)*. (tkwlqn (lit. red on the head), n.); § kʷl=uʔs+łuxʷp+ú *Red Lasso.* (Kwlu'słukhwpu, n.)

√kʷl₂ † kʷl=sét-s *help (ask for...), ask me for or seek assistance.* (kulsets (stem), n.); s+kʷúl=st *asking one to do an errand.* (skulset, v.); hi-s+kʷúl=set *H/S is one I asked to do an errand for me.* (hiskulset, n.); kʷúl=set-n't-w'eš *They asked one another to do errands for one another.* (kulset'nt'wesh, vt.); ‡ kʷúl=set-n *I asked h/h to do an errand for me.* (kulsetn, vt.); kʷúl=set+t-se-s *H/S asked me to an errand for h/h.* (kulsettses, vt.)

√kʷlw † kʷléw *dog (pet name for a...).* (kwlew, n.)

√kʷl'₁ † kʷel' *hot, sunny, warm.* (kwe'l (stem), adj.); kʷel'+l' *sunshine.* (kwe'l'l (lit. the sun shown), n.); s+kʷel'+l' *heat, sunlight, sunshine, warmth.* (skwe'l'l (lit. having hot weather, being hot), n.); kʷel'+t *hot (it is...).* (kwe'lt, adj.); s+kʷel'+t *heat.* (skwe'lt, n.); t+kʷél'+t *hot (It is...on the surface).* (tkwe'lt, adj.); hn+kʷel'+t *the liquid is hot.* (hnkwe'lt, vi.); s+čs+kʷél'+t *sweating, cold sweat, perspire.* (schskwe'lt, v.); čet+kʷel'+kʷl' *Chatcolet meadow before the lake was formed by a dam (lit. sunshine on...).* (chetkwe'lkw'l, n.); či?‿čs+kʷel'+t *perspiring, sweating, I am sweating, perspiring.* (chi'chskwe'lt, vi.); čn‿čs+kʷel'+t *perspire, sweat, I was sweating, perspire, to sweat.* (chnchskwe'lt, vi.); ∥ čet+kʷel'=kʷe? *Chatcolet.* (chetkwe'lkwe, n.); čn‿kʷ+kʷel'=ín'č+m' *bask, sunbathe.* (chnkukw'li'nch'm. (lit. I sunbathed my entrails, belly, etc.), vi.); ic+kʷ+kʷl'=ín'č+m'š *sunbath, sunbathe.* (itskukw'li'nch'msh. (lit. (He is taking a) sunbath), n, vi.); s+t+kʷl'+l'=ic'e? *aura, (lit. light on the body).* (stkw'l'lits'e', n.); t+kʷl'+l'=íc'e? *aura (a person with a visible...), sunshine*

(...on the body, name of a Coeur d'Alene). (Tkw'l'lits'e', n.)

√kʷl'₂ § s+t+kʷel'+tem+n=elwís *visiting (He is going about...people).* (stkwe'ltemnelwis, vt.); s+t+kʷel'+čs+xʷy+s+čínt *people (He is going about visiting...), gathering (He is going about...people).* (stkwe'lchskhuyschint, n, vt.) [xref √kʷł₁]

√kʷl'₃ † s+kʷul' *avocation, work.* (sku'l, n.) [xref √k'ʷl']

√kʷł₁ § t+kʷeł+tem+n=elwís *visiting (He went about...people, treating them sociably), went (He...about visiting people, treating them sociably).* (tkwełtemnelwis, vt, vi.); t+kʷeł+xʷy=elwís *circulate.* (tkwełkhuyelwis (lit. He moved around from place to place), vi.) [xref √kʷl'₂]

√kʷł₂ † kʷuł *borrow, lend.* (kuł (stem). to borrow, vt.); kʷuł+n *borrow.* (kułn, vt.); s+kʷúł+n *borrowing, lending.* (skułn, vt.); hiyc+kʷúł *borrow.* (hiytskuł (lit. something I borrowed), vt.); hi-s+kʷúł+n *It is something lent to me; it is something I borrowed.* (hiskułn, n.); kʷúł=gʷl *H/S borrowed a car, etc.* (kułgul, vt.); ‡ kʷúł-nt-se-s *H/S loaned me.* (kułntses, vt.); kʷáł=qn-t-se-s exp *H/S borrowed my hat, etc.* (kałqntses, vt.)

√kʷm † s+kʷm+kʷm=íw+t=šn *rainbow.* (skumkumiwtshn, n.)

√kʷm'₁ † kʷum' *and.* (ku'm, conj.); kʷm'+ey'níł *of course, you betcha!* (ku'me'ynił, adv.)

√kʷm'₂ † kʷim'+[t] *immediately.* (kwi'mł, adv.); u+yu+kʷím'+t *abruptly (he left...).* (uyukwi'mt, adv.)

√kʷn₁ † kʷin *sing.* (kwin (stem), vt.); hn+kʷín+m *chanted, sang.* (hnkwinm. (lit. He sang, he chanted), vi.); s+n+kʷín+m *sing (to...), singing.* (snkwinm, vi.); s+n+kʷín+mš *chant.* (snkwinmsh, vi.); hn+kʷen+en+útm *cantabile*. (hnkwenenutm (lit. It is singable), adj.); sye+n+kʷín+m *bard, cantor, chorister*. (syenkwinm (lit. one who sings songs, the official soloist or chief singer of the liturgy in a church), n.); gʷɫ sye+n+kʷín+m *choir, chorale*. (guɫ syenkwinm (lit. singers), n.); n.); ul gʷɫ sye+n+kʷín+m *choral*. (ul guɫ syenkwinm (lit. of or for a chorus or choir), adj.); § tč+n+kʷín+pele? *carol*. (tchnkwinpele' (lit. He celebrated or praised in song), v.)

√kʷn₂ † kʷin *grasp (a small object), hold (a small object)*. (kwin (stem), vt.); s+kʷin+m *taking, to accept*. (skwinm, v.); kʷín+t+m *captured (he was...)*. (kwintm, vi.); sye·+kʷín+m *bobby, constable, policeman (or woman)*. (syeekwinm (lit. One who takes one), n.); s+kʷín'+t-ew'eš *Taking one another, as a couple in marriage*. (skwi̱nte'wesh, vt.); ∥ s+kʷán=axn *bondage, captive, hostage, prisoner*. (skwa̱naqhn (lit. taking the arm of a person), n.); sya·+kʷán=axn *captor*. (syaakwa̱naqhn (lit. One who takes (another) by the arm), n.); kʷin=čt+ncút+n *depend, someone to depend on (lit. you are my means of taking care of myself)*. (kwintshtntsu̱tn, vi.); [recorded once as √kʷs] ec+kʷís+t=us *carry*. (etskwi̱stus (He is carrying it), vi.); ‡ kʷín-t-s *accept, apprehend, capture, carry, he carried it, catch, he took it away*. (kwints, vt.); kʷen+en-nun-t-s *caught*. (kwenennunts (lit. he succeeded in taking it, he caught it), vt.); § kʷen+ɫ=y'íɫn *food (h/s took...), took (h/s...food)*. (kwenɫ'yi̱ɫn, n, vt.); kʷen+ɫ+píce? *She took a root digger*. (kwenɫpi̱tse', v.); kʷen+ɫ+ɫp'+ɫp'+m'ín'+n' *took (H/s...a pencil, a pen)*. (kwenɫɫp'ɫp''mi̱'n'n, vt.); kʷan+ɫ+xec+núm'+n *took (h/s...along*

clothes). (kwanɫqhetsnu̱'mn, n, vt.); s+kʷan+s+p'án'+p'an'x *baggage*. (skwansp'a̱np'a'nqh (lit. bags carried while travelling), n.); kʷan+ɫ+s+p'án'x *took (she...a bag)*. (kwanɫsp'a̱nqh, n, vt.); kʷan+ɫ+lebu·tém *bottle (h/s took a...)*. (kwanɫlebuute̱m, n.); kʷen+ɫ+w'l'+w'l'ím' *took (h/s....a knife)*. (kwenɫ'w'l'w'li̱'m, n, vt.); kʷen+ɫ+wl+wlím *took (h/s...some money)*. (kwenɫwlwli̱m, n, vt.); kʷan+ɫ+č+l'ˤ'ʷ+l'ˤ'ʷ+p=al'qʷ *pocket knife (h/s took a...)*. (kwanɫch'l'(w'l'(wpa'lqw, n.); kʷen+ɫ+s+míl'xʷ *took (H/s...tobacco along)*. (kwenɫsmi̱'lkhw, vt.); kʷan+ɫ+pn'+pn'=aqs *par flesche*. (kwanɫp'np'naqs (h/s took along a case of dried hide bent up), n.); kʷen+ɫ+q[']ey'+mín+n *took (H/s...a book along)*. (kwenɫqe'ymi̱nn, vt.); kʷan+ɫ+čat+qal=tč=al'qs *overcoat (h/s took along a...), coat (h/s took along a...)*. (kwanɫchatqaltcha'lqs, n.); s+tep+kʷín+m *detention*. (stepkwi̱nm (lit. withholding something from things taken away), n.); kʷan+ɫ+ɫčíp *H/s took a bucket*. (kwanɫɫchi̱p, v.); kʷan+ɫ+s+ɫáqʷ=qn *H/s took along a bark basket (lit. that which is pulled off a cedar tree)*. (kwanɫsɫa̱q'wqn, v.); čn‿kʷán+ɫq'ʷe?=ep *I took a bark basket(s) along*. (chnkwa̱nlq'we'ep, vt.); s+kʷán+ɫqʷe?=ep *Bark basket taken along*. (skwa̱nɫqwe'ep, vi.) [Cf Spokane √ɫq'ʷ]; kʷan+ɫ+sc+šár=čt *H/S took (along) a valise, lantern, etc*. (kwanɫstsha̱rcht, vt.); kʷan+ɫ+l'+l'pot *cup (h/s took a...)*. (kwanɫ'l'lpot, n.) [xref √kʷn']

√kʷnxʷ ∥ cen+kʷínxʷ=cn *answer, reply, respond*. (tsenkwi̱nkhwtsn (lit. He received the question of another by replying), v, vt.); s+cen+kʷínxʷ=cn *answer, response*. (stsenkwi̱nkhwtsn,

n.); ‡ cen+kʷínxʷ=cn-n *answered
(I...him)*. (tsenkwinkhwtsnn (lit. I
understood that which came out of his
mouth and replied), vt.); cen+kʷínxʷ=
cn-t-s *answered (he...h/h)*.
(tsenkwinkhwtsnts, vt.); cen+kʷínxʷ=
cn-t-se-s *answered (he...me)*.
(tsenkwinkhwtsntses, vt.);
cen+kʷínxʷ=cn-t-si-s *answered
(he...you (sg.))*. (tsenkwinkhwtsntsis,
vt.)

√kʷn' // t+kʷen'+kʷen'+m'=íw'es
*confluence (...of streams, original
name of Tekoa, Wash., confluent),
confluent (original name of Tekoa,
Wash....)*. (Tkwe'nkwe'n'mi'wes (lit.
taking one another at the mid-section),
n.) [xref √kʷn₂]

√kʷp // s+t+kʷúp=šn+mš *assault,
attack*. (stkupshnmsh. (lit. attacking on
foot by many), vt.)

√kʷr † kʷar *yellow*. (kwar (stem), adj.);
kʷar+eq *It is yellow*. (kwareq, vt.)
[also recorded as √qʷr] qʷar+éq
yellow (it is...). (qwareq, vt.); u
kʷar+éq *yellow (It is...)*. (ukwareq,
adj.); u kʷar+kʷar+éq *yellow (They
are...)*. (ukwarkwareq, adj.);
kʷ+kʷár'e?+t' *bullion, gold*.
(kukwa're't' (lit. $20.00 in gold), n.);
t+kʷar'+m'+kʷár'+m' *canary*.
(tkwa'r'mkwa'r'm (lit. yellow, yellow
on surface), n.); a+t+kʷári?+t
Harrison, Idaho. (Atkwari't, n.); //
hn+kʷár=kʷe? *yellow water*.
(hnkwarkwe', n.); s+kʷar=šn *yellow
foot, crane*. (skwarshn, n.);
hn+kʷar+ar'=?ós=alpqʷ *cock, capon,
chanticleer, rooster*.
(hnkwarar'osalpqw (lit. He became
yellow in the mouth by opening it
when crowed), n.); t+kʷar+kʷar+éq=
e?st *orange*. (tkwarkwareqe'st (lit.
yellow yellow on the outside), adj.)
[also recorded as √xʷr]
t+xʷar+xʷar+éq=e?st *orange (lit.*

yellow yellow on the outside).
(tkhwarkwareqe'st, adj.); [see also
√qʷr]; t+kʷar+éq=qn *blonde (lit. one
with pale or yellowish hair)*.
(tqwareqqn, n.); §
hn+kʷar+ar+?óh+m *crow (to...)*.
(hnkwarar'ohm, vi.); u+kʷar+éq ha
s+máy=qn *clay*. (ukwareq ha smayqn
(lit. mud that it yellow), n.)

√kʷs₁ † u· kʷé·s *weather (mild...)*.
(uukweees (lit. almost like spring), n.)
[xref √kʷs₁]

√kʷs₂ † s+kʷés+kʷs *chicken*.
(skweskws (lit. pheasant), n.);
s+kʷ+kʷés+kʷs *chick*. (skukweskws
(lit. little (young) pheasant), n.);
hn+kʷés+kʷs+n *coop*. (hnkweskwsn.
chicken coop, n.)

√kʷs₃ † kʷis *name*. (kwis (stem), vt.);
s+kʷis+t *brand, name, noun*. (skwist,
n.); s+kʷís+kʷes+t *catalogue*.
(skwiskwest (lit. names or list of
names), n.); § elu+s+kʷís+t
anonymous, nameless. (eluskwist (lit.
H/s/i has no name), adj.);
s+nukʷ+s+kʷís+t *a name two persons
have in common*. (snukwskwist, n.);
s+nuk'ʷ+s+kʷís+t *alias, one (another)
name*. (snuk'wskwist, n.);
tuxʷ+ł+s+kʷís-nt-s *named (He...him)*.
(tukhwłskwisnts, vt.); p'oy-n xʷe
hi+s+kʷís+t *scribbled*. (p'oyn khwe
hiskwist (lit. I scribbled my name),
vt.); ?epł+ˤep+s+kʷís+t *anonymous,
nameless*. (epł(epskwist, v. (lit. He has
a hidden name), adj.); sti?m xʷe
s+kʷes+t=ílumxʷ-s *What is the name
of the place?* (sti'm khwe
skwestilumkhws? (qu.).);
ul+n+?esl+s+kʷís+t *exp It belongs to
him who has 2 names*. (ul 'nselskwist,
v.)

√kʷs₄ † kʷus *frisky, shy, skittish, timid,
curly, It became curly, or horse
became skittish*. (kus (stem), adj.);
kʷus+s *curly, It became curly, or*

horse became skittish. (kuss, adv.);
ec+kʷús *corrugated, crimped, curled.*
(etsk<u>u</u>s, vi.); et+kʷús *corduroy, crepe.*
(etkus, vi. (lit. it is crisp or curly on the
surface, e.g. cloth), adj.); kʷus+kʷus+t
He is a frisky (scarey) horse. (k<u>u</u>skust,
vi.); ∥ a+t+kʷos=qn *curly (...haired).*
(atkosqn, adj.); s+t+kʷos=qi(n)-s *It's
h/h curly headedness.* (stk<u>o</u>sqis, vi.)

√kʷt ∥ kʷút=gʷl *eel.* (k<u>u</u>tgul, n.)

√kʷt'n' † kʷít'en' *mouse, shrew.*
(kw<u>i</u>t'en, n.)

√kʷʕ̱ʷ † i c+kʷéʕ'ʷ+kʷeʕ'ʷ+ʕ'ʷ
demented (lit. He is going crazy).
(itskw<u>e</u>'(wkwe'('(w, adj.);
s+kʷéʕ'ʷ+kʷeʕ'ʷ+ʕ'ʷ *insanity.*
(skw<u>e</u>'(wkwe(u'(, n.) [xref √qʕ'ʷ]

√kʷl' † kʷ'ʷul' *do, fix, make, to produce.*
(k'u'l (stem), vt.); kʷ'ʷul'+l' *born, made
(to be...).* (k'u'lu'l (lit. H/s was born),
vi.); kʷ'ʷúl+l' *become.* (k'<u>u</u>lu'l, vi.);
s+kʷ'ʷúl+l' *birth.* (sk'<u>u</u>'lu'l (lit.
becoming made), n.); s+kʷ'ʷul'+ł *fake,
false, artificial.* (sk'u'lł, n.);
hn+kʷ'ʷúl'+n *ceremony.* (hnk'<u>u</u>'ln (lit.
way of acting), n.); kʷ'ʷúl'+emn
contraption. (k'<u>u</u>'lemn (lit. means of
making), n.); hn+kʷ'ʷúl'+emn
convention. (hnk'<u>u</u>'lemn (lit. way of
doing things, general usage or custom),
n.); ul'+n+kʷ'ʷúl'+emn *conventional.*
(u'lnk'<u>u</u>'lemn (lit. pertaining to general
way of doing things), adj.); s+t+kʷ'ʷúl'
adornment, ornament. (stk'<u>u</u>'l, n.);
s+t+kʷ'ʷúl'+m *decoration, ornament.*
(stk'<u>u</u>'lm. decoration, n.); s+t+kʷ'ʷúl'+l'
decor. (stk'<u>u</u>'lu'l (lit. a decorative

style), n.); e+t+kʷ'ʷúl' *attached (...to),
beaded-work, something attached to.*
(etk'<u>u</u>'l, n.); s+cen+kʷ'ʷúl'+l' *form,
statue, configuration, copy, effigy,
diagram, structure.* (stsenk'u'lu'l (lit. a
model formed under), n.);
kʷ'ʷl'+ncút+n *deity, God.* (K'u'lntsutn
(lit. the means of making oneself), n.);
s+kʷ'ʷl'+ncút+n *divine will, divinity.*
(sk'u'lntsutn, n.); s+kʷ'ʷl'+ncút+m+n
*deification, exaltation (...to divine
rank).* (sk'u'lntsutmn, n.);
twe+kʷ'ʷul'+ncút+n *enthusiasm.*
(twek'u'lntsutn (lit. means of making
oneself in company with God), n.); ul
kʷ'ʷl'+ncút+n *divine, belonging to God.*
(ul k'u'lntsutn, adj.); s+kʷ'ʷúl'+šeš
duty, employment, service. (sk'<u>u</u>'lshesh,
n.); sye·+kʷ'ʷúl' *agent, creator, dean,
intermediary, originator, servant.*
(syeek'<u>u</u>'l (lit. One who produces), n.);
kʷ'ʷl'+ul'+útm *contingent.* (k'u'lu'l<u>u</u>tm
(lit. It is capable of being done), adj.);
s+kʷ'ʷl'+l'+útm *contingency.*
(sk'u'lu'l<u>u</u>tm (lit. possibility of being
made (done); a fortuitous or possible
event), n.); xʷe ci?+ł+kʷ'ʷl'+l'
birthplace. (khwe tsi'łk'<u>u</u>'lu'l (lit.
Where he was born), n.); t+kʷ'ʷl'+l'+n
birthday. (tk'u'lu'ln, n.);
čeł‿?i·c+kʷ'ʷúl *calling.* (cheł'iitsk'<u>u</u>l
(lit. It is to be your work (calling), n.);
hiy+s+kʷ'ʷúl' *deed.* (hiysk'<u>u</u>'l (lit. that
which is done), n.); hiyc+kʷ'ʷúl' *deed
(lit. that which is done).* (hiytsk'<u>u</u>'l, n.);
čey+c+kʷ'ʷl' *career, chore, affair,
routine, agenda.* (cheytsk'u'l (lit. that
which is to be done), n.);
kʷ'ʷul+ul'+nún+n *He succeeded in
doing something.* (k'u'lu'ln<u>u</u>nn);
s+kʷ'ʷl'+l'+nún *effect, result.*
(sk'u'lu'ln<u>u</u>n (lit. that which is
accomplished), n.); s+kʷ'ʷ?l'+nún+m
achievement. (sk'u''ln<u>u</u>nm (lit. success
in making (something), n.);
s+kʷ'ʷl'+l'+nún+m *execution.*

(sku'lnunm (lit. success in doing something), n.); ‖ s+k'ʷúl=łxʷ *architecture.* (sk'ułtkhw (lit. making buildings), n.); sye·+k'ʷúl=łxʷ *architect, carpenter.* (syeek'u'łtkhw (lit. One who builds a house), n.); k'ʷol'=stq *colonize.* (k'o'lstq (lit. He farmed or settled), vt.); s+k'ʷl'=stq *agriculture, farming, garden, produce.* (sk'ol'stq (lit. crop-making), n.); hn+k'ʷól'=stq+n *colony, grain field, farm, garden, settlement.* (hnk'o'lstqn, n.); sya·+k'ʷl'=stq *settler, colonist.* (syaak'o'lstq (lit. a crop raiser), n.); ul+n+k'ʷól'=stq+n *colonial.* (ulnk'o'lstqn (of or pertaining to a farm), adj.); in+k'ʷúl'=us *compensate.* (ink'u'lus (lit. He is making up for or offsetting), vt.); s+n+k'ʷúl'=us *atonement, punishment.* (snk'u'lus (lit. making amends on a head), n.); k'ʷul'=cn+cút *He prepared food for himself.* (k'u'ltsntsut, vt.); k'ʷl'=cn+cút at+čm=íp=łxʷ *cookout.* (k'u'ltsntsut atchmipłkhw (lit. She cooked a meal outdoors), n.); hn+k'ʷúl'=cn+cút+m *cookstove.* (hnk'u'ltsntsutm (lit. means of preparing something for one's mouth), n.); s+k'ʷúl'=cn+cut *cookery, cu[i]sine.* (sku'ltsntsut (lit. cooking), n.); ul s+k'ʷul'=[c]n+cút *culinary.* (ul sk'u'lsntsut (lit. pertaining to cooking), adj.); sya+k'ʷl'=cn+cút *chef, cook.* (syak'u'ltsntsut (lit. One whose business is to prepare something for the mouth), n.); s+n+k'ʷúl'+ul'=łc'e? *pregnancy.* (snk'u'lu'łts'e', n.); s+k'ʷl'+l'=ngʷíln *accomplish.* (sk'u'lu'lngwiln (lit. successful in making something), n.); e+c+k'ʷul'+l'=ngʷíln *effective.* (etsk'u'lu'lngwiln (lit. It is capable of producing results), vi.); ‡ k'ʷúl'-nt-s *do, make, perform.* (k'u'lnts (lit. He made it), vt.); k'ʷúl'-nt-eli-t *create, do.* (k'u'lntelit (lit. We were produced by God, vt.);

k'ʷúl'-nt-m-lš *marriage (They are made, united in...).* (k'u'lntmlsh, n.); s+k[']ʷl'-nt-m-lš *bridal, wedding.* (sku'lntmlsh (lit. their being made (husband and wife)), n.); k'ʷul'+l'+nún-t-s *achieve.* (k'u'l'lnunts (lit. He succeeded in making it, *h/s carried it out, executed it*), vi.); k'ʷl'+l'+nún-t-p *do.* (k'u'l'lnuntp (lit. You (pl.) carried it out/You (pl.) achieved it), vt.); k'ʷúl'=cn-n *prepared (I...food for h/h).* (k'u'ltsnn, vt.); hn+k'ʷúl'+l'=łc'e+m'-nt-m *conceive, pregnant.* (hnk'u'lu'łts'e'mntm (lit. Someone was created within her), vi, adj.); k'ʷl'+ncút+m-nt-s *deify.* (k'u'lntsutmnts, vt.); t+k'ʷúl'-nt-m *bedeck.* (tk'u'lntm (lit. It was adorned), vt.); t+k'ʷúl'-nt-s *adorn, decorate.* (tk'u'lnts (lit. He put beads on it), vt.); § a·+yaʕ'+ec+k'ʷul'-stu-s *almighty, omnipotent.* (aaya')etsk'u'lstus (lit. one who makes all things), adj.); u+x̌ʷel'+e k'ʷ‿k'ʷl'+ncút+n *divine.* (uqhwe'le kuk'u'lntsutn (lit. You (sg.) are godlike), adj.); s+nukʷ+k'ʷúl' *associate, fellow worker, partner.* (snukwk'u'l. colleague, n.); s+nukʷ+k'ʷúl'+l' *spouse, component, mate, consort.* (snukwk'u'lu'l, n.); tč+ʔsél+kʷ s+nukʷ+k'ʷúl'+l' *two spouses.* (tch'selkw snukk'u'lu'l, n.); tč+ʔséł s+nukʷ+k'ʷl'+l' *bigamy.* (tch'seł snukk'u'lu'l, n.); s+cen+k[']ʷúl'+l'+s x̌ʷe tmíxʷ=l'umxʷ *map.* (stsenku'l'ls khwe tmikhw'lumkhw (lit. means of making a description of land), n.); k'ʷl'+ł+cíl'+c'el'+t *delineate.* (k'u'łtsi'lts'e'lt (lit. He formed a shadow), vt.); elu+ł+k'ʷl'+ncút+n *unbeliever, agnostic, atheist.* (elułk'u'lntsutn (lit. One who has no God), n.); tel' s+k'ʷ+k'ʷúl'+l' *congenital.* (te'l sk'uk'u'lu'l (lit. It exists from birth), adj.); s+ten[']+k'ʷl'+l' *structure.* (stenk'u'lu'l (lit. a model formed under), n.); s+k'ʷul'+ɬ ʔasqʷ *to adopt.* (sk'u'lɬ asqw (lit. making one a son), vt.); sye·+k'ʷul' a s+l'+l'áx̌+m' *electrician.* (syeek'u'l a s'l'laqh'm (lit. One who produces (works) with electricity), n.); sye+k'ʷul'+ɬ+q'ey'+mín+n *bookie, bookmaker.* (syek'u'ɬq'e'yminn (lit. One who accepts and pays off bets/One who makes paper (books)), n.); his+k'ʷl'+ɬ+x̌ést *deign.* (hisku'ɬqhest (lit. I deem it worthy), vt.); s+k'ʷul'+ɬ x̌es+t *deem.* (sk'u'lɬ qhest (lit. It is something considered good), n.); et+k'ʷul' hey+ɬéx̌ʷ *brocade.* (etk'u'l heyɬekhw (lit. A woven thing of design), n.); s+k'ʷul'+ɬ wl+wlím *coinage.* (sk'u'lɬ wlwlim (lit. making money), n.); s+k'ʷl'+ɬ+čp=qín+n *coiffure, wig.* (sk'u'ɬchpqinn (lit. artificial hair), n.); yoqʷe?+s+k'ʷúl' *counterfeit, fake, pretend.* (yoqwe'sk'u'l, (lit. He pretended to work), vt.)

√k'ʷl'₂ † s+k'ʷ+k'ʷél' *porcupine.* (sk'k'we'l, n.)

√k'ʷɬ † k'ʷeɬ *tickle.* (k'weɬ (stem), vt.)

√k'ʷɬš † k'ʷeɬš *startle, surprise, he was startled.* (k'weɬsh (stem), vt.); k'ʷeɬš+m+ncut *brisk.* (k'weɬshmntsut (lit. he acted as though he startled himself), adj.); **//** k'ʷɬš=íčt+m *abrupt, curt.* (k'wɬshichtm. (lit. He did an abrupt act/thing), adj.)

√k'ʷm // ul k'ʷóm=qn *cephalic.* (ul k'omqn (lit. in, on, or relating to the head or skull), adj.)

√k'ʷm' † k'ʷim' *presently, right now.* (k'wi'm, v.)

√k'ʷnš † k'ʷinš *How many? How much? (inter.).* (k'winsh, qu.); e·+k'ʷínš *many, much.* (eek'winsh? (lit. How many do you want?), adj.); e· [k]'ʷinš *want.* (eed'winsh? (lit. How many (much) do you want?), vt.);

t+k'ʷinš *how many?.* (tk'winsh, qu.); **§** k'ʷu‿s+k'ʷinš+es+pín=tč *How old are you?* (k'usk'winshespintch?, vi.)

√k'ʷn? † k'ʷné? *future, going to.* (k'wne', n, vi.); **§** k'ʷné?+čn‿siy+m+scút *best (I am going to do my...), do (I am going to...my best).* (k'wne'chnsiymstsut, vt.); k'ʷna?+čn‿qʷa?+qʷe?el *speak.* (k'wna'chnqwa'qwe'el (lit. I am going to speak), vi.); [xref √k'ʷn']

√k'ʷn'₁ // k'ʷ+k'ʷn'=iy'e? *by and by, minute (in a...), moment (in a...), soon (very...), in a short while...* (k'uk'w'ni'ye', adv.); u+k'ʷ+k'ʷn'=íy'e *anon, elapse, soon.* (uk'uk'w'ni'ye' (lit. It slipped or glided away in a short time), vi, adv.); e s+k'ʷ+k'ʷn=iy'e? *a while ago.* (esk'ukw'ni'ye', adv.); **§** úw'e k'ʷ+k'ʷn=iy'e? *awhile.* (u'we k'uk'w'ni'ye' (lit. for a short time only), adv.) [xref √k'ʷn?]

√k'ʷn'₂ † k'ʷin' *choose, consider, try.* (k'wi'n (stem), vt.); s+k'ʷín'+m *assay, examination.* (sk'wi'nm (lit. testing, test of knowledge or fitness), n.); s+ni?+k'ʷín'+m *alternative, choice.* (sni'k'wi'n (lit. something chosen from among several/that which is chosen from two or more possibilities), n.); s+ni?+k'ʷín'+m *election.* (sni'k'wi'nm (lit. the act of choosing someone), n.); ni?+k'ʷen'+en'+útm *eligible.* (ni'k'we'ne'nutm (lit. H/s is capable of being, or fit to be, chosen), adj.); ɬey+ní?+k'ʷin' *elect, chosen.* (ɬeyni'k'wi'n. (lit. one of the elect, the elect collectively), n.); hiy+ni?+k'ʷín' *eclectic.* (hiyni'k'wi'n (lit. that which is picked out), adj.); **‡** k'ʷín'-n *tested, tried (I...it).* (k'wi'nn, vt.); k'ʷín'-nt-s *tested (He...it), tried (He...it).* (k'wi'nnts, vt.); [also recorded as √k'ʷn] ni?+k'ʷín-n *cull.* (ni'k'winn (lit. I picked it out from others), vt.); k'ʷín'-nt-s *trial.* (k'wi'nnts (lit. H/S

scrutinized or investigated it carefully),
n.); ni?+k'ʷín'-nt-m *elect*.
(ni'k'wi̲'nntm (lit. H/s was chosen),
vt.); ni?+k'ʷín'-nt-s *appoint, choose,
name, select*. (ni'k'wi̲'nnts. (lit. he
picked it out after testing it from
among), vt.); § hi?c+miyes+k'ʷin'+m
collate. (hi'tsmiyesk'wi'nm (lit. I am
testing, taking it very carefully), vt..)

√k'ʷp † k'ʷep+t *backbone, core, spine,
vertebra*. (k'wept, n.)

√k'ʷr † is+k'ʷár+k'ʷar+iš *burr*.
(isk'wa̲rk'warish (lit. He made whirring
sounds). ice breaking(sound), vi.)

√k'ʷr' † s+k'ʷar'=íne? *bivalve, clam,
oyster*. (sk'wa'ri̲ne' (lit. cracked on the
ears), n.)

√k'ʷs₁ † u· k'ʷé·s *mild weather (lit.
almost like spring)*. (uuk'wee̲es, n.); //
s+k'ʷés=us *February*. (sk'we̲sus, n.)
[xref √kʷs₁]

√k'ʷs₂ † k'ʷus *splittable*. (k'us (stem).
easily split, adj.); [possible
connection] s+k'ʷus+t *cedar*. (sk'ust,
n.)

√k'ʷs₃ // k'ʷus=če? *haunted, spook,
ghost*. (k'usche' (stem). adj. n.);
s+k'ʷus+ús=če? *apparition, ghost*.
(sk'usu̲sche', n.); s+k'ʷs+k'ʷs=če?=cín'
haunted house, place.
(sk'usk'usche'tsi̲'n. haunted, n.); ‡
k'ʷús=če?-nt-s *ghosted (he...him)*.
(k'u̲sche'nts., vt.)

√k'ʷt' † k'ʷet' *evident, exposed, plain,
take off (clothes), to divest*. (k'wet'
(stem), adj.); k'ʷit' *divest, take off
(clothes)*. (k'wit' (stem), vt.); k'ʷet'+t'
appear, appeared (he...), show (up).
(k'wet't', vi.); ul s+k'ʷét'+t' *chromatic*.
(ul sk'we̲t't' (lit. pertaining to
appearance (color or colors), adj.);
[also recorded as √k'ʷt] u· k'ʷt+út
clear, vivid, plain (It is...). (uuk'wtu̲t,
adj.); u k'ʷt'+ú·t *apparent (It is...),
visible (It is clearly...), bare, chiffon,
exposed (...to view), sheer (It (fabric)*

is...). (uuk'wt'u̲uut, (lit. It is readily
seen), n, adj, vi.); hn+k'ʷét'+p+ncut
disarray. (hnk'wet'pntsut. (lit. He
undressed himself), vt.);
s+k'ʷt'+út+mš *clearance*.
(sk'wt'u̲tmsh (lit. making clear), n.); //
k'ʷít'=šn *barefoot*. (k'wit'shn, adv.);
u+n+k'ʷt'+ú·t=cn *aloud*.
(unk'wt'u̲uutsn (lit. He speaks audibly),
adv.); [possible connection]
s+k'ʷét'=elt *fawn*. (sk'wet'elt, n.);
s+k'ʷt'=ílt *fawn*. (sk'wt'i̲lt, n.);
a+t+k'ʷet'=á?st=qn *bare-headed*. ((lit.
His head is uncovered), adj.
atk'wet'a̲'stqn, vi.); a+t+k'ʷét'=alq=šn
bare-legged. (atk'wet'alqshn, vi. (lit.
His legs are uncovered), adj.);
ec+k'ʷít'+k'ʷet'=čt *bare-handed*.
(etskwi̲t'k'wet'cht, vi. (lit. His hands
are uncovered), adj.)

√k'ʷx̌ † k'ʷax̌ *claw, fingernail*. (k'waqh
(stem), n.); // k'ʷax̌=qín'=čt *fingernail*.
(k'waqhqi'ncht, n.); k'ʷax̌=qin'=šn' *toe
nail*. (k'waqhqi'nsh'n, n.); k'ʷax̌+k'ʷax̌=
qin'=šn' *toe nails*.
(k'waqhk'waqhqi'nsh'n, n.); hn-k'ʷax̌=
qín'=čt *It is my fingernail*.
(hnk'waqhqi'ntch.); in-k'ʷax̌=qín=čt *It
is your fingernail*. (ink'waqhqi'ncht,);
k'ʷax̌=qin'=čt-s *fingernail (It is h/h...)*.
(k'waqhqi'nchts, n.); k'ʷax̌=qin'=čt-et
fingernail(s) (It is our...).
(k'waqhqi'nchtet, n.); k'ʷax̌=qín=
čt-m'p *fingernail (It is your (pl)...)*.
(k'waqhqi̲ncht'mp, n.) k'ʷax̌=qin'=
čt-s-lš *fingernail (it is their...)*.
(k'waqhqi'nchtslsh, n.)

√k'ʷy₁ § k'ʷay'+q'es+p *past, long-ago*.
(k'wayq'esp, adj.); ul k'ʷay+q'és+p
archaic, antique. (ul k'wa'yq'e̲sp (lit.
belonging to ancient time), adj.); łe
k'ʷey' teč+ci? *before*. (łe k'we'y
techtsi̲'. in former days, adv.);
k'ʷey'+lút *not yet*. (k'we'ylut, adv.)

√k'ʷy₂ † k'ʷiy' *quiet, still*. (k'wi'y (stem),
adj.); // ec+k'ʷ+k'ʷiy=cín *croon*.

(etsk'uk'wiyts<u>i</u>n (lit. He sings or speaks softly). whisper, vi.)

√k'ʷy's // k'ʷay's=alqʷ *cedar (tree)*. (k'wa'ysalqw, n.); s+t+k'ʷéy's=ečt *cedar branch*. (stk'w<u>e</u>'ysecht, n.)

√k'ʷʕ † k'ʷaʕ *skid, slide, slip*. (k'wa((stem), vi.); // k'ʷaʕ+aʕ+p+l=iyeʔ *coasted (he...)*. (k'wa(a(pliye', vi.) [xref √q'ʷʕ]

√k'ʷʔ₁ † k'ʷeʔ+min+n *pipe wrench, wrench (pipe)*. (k'we'minn, n.); k'ʷ+k'ʷeʔ+mí?n *pliers*. (k'uk'we'mi'n' (lit. little wrench), n.)

√k'ʷʔ₂ † k'ʷiʔ *bite*. (k'wi' (stem), vt.); k'ʷiʔ+m *bite*. (k'wi'm, vt.); k'ʷíʔ+k'ʷeʔ+m *chew*. (k'wi'k'we'm (lit. He ground something with the teeth), vi.); // k'ʷeʔ+k'ʷeʔ=iɬc'eʔ *bedbug, flea*. (k'we'k'we'iɬts'e' (lit. That which bites and bites the flesh), n.); ‡ k'ʷíʔ-nt-m *bitten (He was...)*. (k'w<u>i</u>'ntm, vi.); k'ʷíʔ+k'ʷeʔ-nt-s *munched (He...it)*. (k'wi'k'we'nts, vt.); §
k'ʷaʔ+k'ʷaʔ+a+s+n+laqʷ=ús *chewed (he...gum), gum (he chewed...)*. (k'wa'k'wa'asnlaqus, v, n.);

√lbč † li·bḗč *bishop*. (liib<u>e</u>ch (l.w. from French), n.); § li·béč he c'uk'ʷ=íčs+i̱s *crosier*. (liib<u>e</u>ch he ts'uk'wichsis (lit. a bishop's staff (cane), n.); ul li·béč he tmíxʷ=ul'ms *diocese*. (ul liibech he tm<u>i</u>khu'lms (lit. It is a land or district in which a bishop has authority), n.)

√lbtm₁ † lebe·tém+m *baptize, (he...)*. (lebeet<u>e</u>mm (l.w. from French), v.); s+lebe·tém+n *christening*. (slebeetemn (lit. The Christian sacrament of baptism), n.); ‡ lebe·tém-nt-m *baptize, christen, he was baptized*. (lebeetemntm, vt.)

√lbtm₂ † lebu·tem *bottle, can, flask*. (lebuutem (from French, le bouteille), n.); leb+lebu·tém *bottles*. (leblebuut<u>e</u>m, pl.n.); §
k'ʷan+ɬ+lebu·tém *bottle (h/s took a...)*. (kwanɬlebuut<u>e</u>m, n.)

√lčm † lče·mí *corn, corncob, maize*. (lcheem<u>i</u>. Indian corn, n.)

√lč' † leč' *aggressive, bind, domineering*. (lech' (stem). adj, vt.); leč'+m *arrest*. (lech'm (lit. tie up), vt.); e· leč' *tied, bound, handcuffed, jailed, manacled*. (eelech' (lit. He is in jail, bound), adj.); e+cen+léč' *bundle, fascicle, package*. (etsenl<u>e</u>ch' (lit. That which is tied together), n.); léč'+lč'+t *aggressive, arrogant, audacious, bold, bossy, despotic, overbearing*. (l<u>e</u>ch'lch't. (lit. He is habitually tied (committed) to be bold), adj.); s+léč'+lč'+t *arrogance*. (sl<u>e</u>ch'lch't, n.); lč'+mín+n *band, binding*. (lch'm<u>i</u>nn. (lit. means of binding together), n.); hn+lč'+mín+n *calaboose, clink, jail, prison, stockade (lit. a place where one is tied up)*. (hnlch'm<u>i</u>nn. n.); léč'+m+ncut *arrogate*. (l<u>e</u>ch'mntsut (lit. He acted arrogantly), vi.); s+léč'+m+ncut *aggression, compulsion, despotism*. (sle'chmntsut (lit. tying (committing) oneself to be bold, n.) ; i·+leč'+m+ncút *compulsive, compulsory*. (iilech'mntsut (lit. He is exercising compulsion), adj.); s+léč'+m+šeš *constraint, compulsion*. (sl<u>e</u>ch'mshesh, n.); // hn+lč'=íw'es+n *belt, sash*. (hnlch'i'wesn. (means of tying midsection), n.); lč'=qín+n *bandana, headband, kerchief, scarf*. (lch'qinn. (lit. means of binding the head), n.); č+leč'+m=ípeleʔ *commandeer*. (chle-chm<u>i</u>pele (lit. he seized arbitrarily), v.); ‡ léč'-n *arrested, apprehended, tied up*. (l<u>e</u>ch'n. arrested, apprehended (lit. I tied him up), vt.); léč'-nt-m *arrested, apprehended, tied up (lit. I tied him up)*. (lech'ntm, vt.); léč'-nt-s *He arrested him. apprehended, tied up*. (lech'nts, vt.); léč'+m-st-m *blackmail, coerce, compel, constrain, extort, force*. (l<u>e</u>ch'mstm (lit. He was forced against his will). vt, *extortion*, Cf. extort, n.); léč'+m-st-m *arrogate (lit. He acted arrogantly).* (lech'mntsut, vi.); § s+lč'+me+s+čínt *coercion.* (slch'meschint (lit. compelling people to do things), n.); s+pig^w+l'č' *belt, cincture.* (spigw'lch', n.); miyeł+leč'+lč'+t *belligerent.* (miyełlech'lch't (lit. he is too (very) aggressive), n.); łáx̌^wp tel' hn+lč'+mín+n *prison (He escaped from...).* (łaqhwp te'l hnlch'minn, n.)

√lg^w † lig^w *entrap, snare.* (ligw (stem), vt.)

√lǰ † leǰ *stab, sting.* (lej (stem), vt.); s+le[d]ǰ+m *to sting.* (sledjm, v.); léǰ+p *shot (He was...).* (lejp, vt.); lǰ+mín+n *bayonet, sword.* (ljminn (lit. a means of piercing), n.); ∥ s+n+lǰ=úps *coitus.* (snljups, n.); hn+lǰ=oʔp=stq *copulate.* (hnljo'pstq. (lit. He engaged in coitus), vi.); lǰ=ísg^wel *harpoon, spear.* (ljisgwel (lit. He speared fish, usually salmon), n, vt.); ‡ leǰ-nt-s *He stabbed him.* (lejnts, vt.); § [ł]aq'+t he lǰ+mín+n *broad-sword.* (laq't he ljminn (lit. It is broad which is a sword), n.)

√lkp † lka·pí *coffee.* (lkaapi (l.w. from French), n.); hn+lka·pí+hn *coffeepot.* (hnlkaapihn. (lit. a pot for brewing or serving coffee), n.)

√lk^w † lek^w *far.* (lekw (stem), adj.); lék^w+t *far (It is...away).* (lekut, adv.); lék^w+k^w-š *begone!, go away!.* (lekuksh!, excl.); en+luk^w+k^w+útm *dilatory, lagging.* (enlukukutm (lit. He customarily goes far behind), adj, vi.); hn+luk^w+k^w+útm *behind.* (hnlukukutm (lit. He fell behind), adv.); s+n+luk^w+útm *arrears.* (snlukutm (lit. falling behind), n.); s+n+luk^w+k^w+út+m *arrears (lit. falling behind).* (snlukukutm, n.); č+lék^w+t *aloof.* (chlekut, adv.); č+luk^w+ú·t *There he is at a distance.* (chlukuuut!, excl.); u+č+luk^w+ú·t *avoids (he...).* (uchlukuuut! (lit. He remains aloof), excl.); s+niʔ+lék^w+t *apogee.* (sni'lekut (lit. the farthest point), n.); § tel' lék^w+t *afar (from...).* (te'l lekut, adv.)

√lk^ws † lok^wo·só *pig.* (lokooso (l.w. from French), n.); luk^wo·só *bristle.* (lukooso (lit. hair of a pig), n.); § qel'+tmx^w+lok^wo·so *boar.* (qe'ltmxhwlokooso. (lit. male pig), n.)

√lk'^w₁ † luk'^w *pick off (fuzz, lint, etc.).* (luk'w (stem), vt.)

√lk'^w₂ ∥ e·+luk'^w=us *disguised, masked.* (eeluk'us (lit. H/s is masked), adj.)

√lm † lim *appreciative, glad, pleased, thankful.* (lim (stem), adj.); s+lim+t *allelula, joy, rejoicing.* (slimt, n.); čn‿lím+t *glad (I was...), glad (to be), rejoice, rejoiced (I...).* (chnlimt, vi.); lím+lem+t-[š] *Thank you!.* (limlemtsch! (lit. It is gratifying), excl.); lím+lem+t-š *thank you, gratifying.* (limlemtsh, n.); ∥ lam+m=ástq *He made another person happy.* (lammastq, vt.); hn+lím+lem=elg^wes *bonny.* (hnlimlemelgwes (lit. He rejoices and rejoices in heart), adj.); s+n+lím=elg^wes *cheer, heartiness, rejoicing.* (snlimelgwes, n.); un+lím=elg^wes *cheerful, thankful.* (unlimelgwes (lit. He is in good spirits), adj.); § lim-t-š ma·rí *Ave Maria, Hail Mary!.* (Limtsh Maari! (lit. Rejoice, Mary!), excl.); s+lem+t+me+s+čínt *charm.* (slemtmeschint (lit. The power or quality of pleasing people), n.); s+nuk^w+lím+t *congratulation, felicitation, (lit. rejoicing with).* (snukwlimt, n.); nuk^w+lím+t+m-n-n. (nukwlimtmnn (lit. I rejoiced with, or expressed sympathetic pleasure to, him), vt.)

√lmn † la·mná *honey, syrup.* (laamna, n.)

√lp † lup *dry (be...), thirsty.* (lup, vi.); lu?p *It became dry.* (lu'p, vi.); e· lup *dehydrated, dried.* (eelup (lit. That w/c has been dried), adj.); u l'+l'up'í *arid.* (ul"lu'pi (lit. It is dry), adj.); s+lúp+m *fish, meat (drying...).* (slupm, n.); čs+n+lu?+lu?p+úl *One who is in the habit of becoming thirsty.* (chsnlu'lu'pul, n.); čn‿čs+n+lu?p *thirsty (to get...), (lit. I became thirsty).* (chnchsnlu'p, vi, adj.); i čs+n+lu?p *He is thirsty.* (ichsnlu'p, adj.); // can+lop+lóp= ax̌n *It is dry in the armpits, No rain by the moon.* (tsanloplopaqhn, v.); ‡ lúp-n *dehydrate.* (lupn (lit. I dried the meat or berries), vt.); lúp-nt-s *desiccate.* (lupnts (lit. He preserved it by taking the moisture from it), vt.)

√lpl † li·púl *hen, chicken.* (liipul (l.w. from French, l.w. from Kalispel, used mostly by the Kalispel), n.)

√lpp † ul la pap *apostolic.* (ul la Pap (lit. belonging to the Pope), adj.)

√lpst † kʷup‿lípust *You are they.* (kuplipust,); kʷup‿?ul+lípust *It is yours (pl.).* (kup'ullipust, vi.); ul č‿lipust *ours (it is...).* (ul chlipust, adj.)

√lpt † l'+l'pót *chalice, cup, dipper, glass.* (l'l'pot, n.); // č'+l'+l'pót=c'e? *pickled, preserved, canned.* (ch'l'l'potts'e' (lit. It is preserved in a container (jar, bottle, can).), adj.); č+l'+l'pót=c'e? *amphora, can, jar.* (ch'l'lpotts'e', n.); č+l'+l'pót=ce?+e? *jar.* (ch'l'lpottse'e', n.); hn+č+l'+l'pót= c'e?+n *cannery.* (hnch'l'lpotts'e'n. (lit. cupping around; place where food is canned), n.); hn+l'+l'póte?+n *cupboard.* (hn'l'lpoten'. (lit. a closet for holding cups), n.); § kʷanɬ+l'+l'pot *cup (h/s took a...).* (kwanł'l'lpot, n.); nukʷ+ɬ+l'+l'pót *cupful.* (nuk'włl'lpot (lit. just one cup (of content)), n.)

√lpw † li·pwé *pea(s).* (liipwe (l.w. from French), n.)

√lp'xʷ // lup'xʷ=ús=šn *slang for making fun of a person* (lup'khusshn (lit. a hole resulted in front of his feet), vt.); hn+lép'xʷ=ep *punctured.* (hnlep'khwep. (lit. it (bucket) was punctured on the bottom), adj.) [xref √lp'x̌ʷ]

√lp'x̌ʷ † lep'x̌ʷ *fit into.* (lep'qhw (stem), vi.); lép'x̌ʷ+emn *tack.* (lep'qhwemn, n.); // hn+lp'x̌ʷ=íne? *earful.* (hnlp'qhwine'. (lit. H/s got an earful), n.) [xref √lp'xʷ]

√lq † laq *pull (out plants), weed.* (laq (stem), vt.); // laq=cín+m *pluck (one's whiskers), plucked (He...his whiskers with tweezers), tweezers (He plucked his whiskers with...).* (laqtsinm, vt, pl.n.); laq=cón+m *whiskers (He plucked his...with tweezers).* (laqtsonm, pl.n.)

√lq'₁ † laq' *search.* (laq' (stem), vi.); // i·+laq'=álpqʷ *looked, search, food (He looked for...).* (iilaq'alpqw. vt, n.); ‡ lá?q-nt-s *He looked for it.* (la'qnts, vt.)

√lq'₂ † laq' *pare, peel.* (laq' (stem), vt.) [see also √łq'ʷ]

√lq'₃ † leq' *bury.* (leq' (stem), vt.); leq'+m *baked (She...(camas) in the ground).* (leq'm, vt.); hn+léq'+ncut+n *sweathouse.* (hnleq'ntsutn, n.); ‡ ča·+léq'-nt-m *buried (He was...).* (chaaleq'ntm, vi.)

√lqʷ s+n+láqʷ *tallow.* (snlaqw, n.); s+n+la?qʷ *tallow.* (snla'qw, n.); // s+n+laqʷ=ús *chicle, gum (bubble...).* (snlaqus, n.); § kʷa?+kʷa?+a+s+n+laqʷ=ús *gum (he chewed...).* (k'wa'k'wa'asnlaqus, n.); s+n+laqʷ=ús+s ha s+t'm'=ált=mš *cud.* (snlaquss ha st"maltmsh (lit. a cow's chewing gum), n.); s+myaɬ+n+laqʷ=ús *bubble gum.* (smyałnlaqus, n.); s+[n]+yaɬn+laqʷ= ús *gum (extra...).* (smyałnlaqus, n.)

√lq'ʷ₁ † laq'ʷ *able*. (laq'w (stem), adj.); ‡ laq[']ʷ-en *able (to do)*. (laq-wen (lit. I can do it), vt.); láq'ʷ-n *can (I...do it)*. (laq'wn, vi.); láq'ʷ-nt-s *He can do it.* (laq'wnts, vi.); § lut láq'ʷ-nt-s *be unable*. (lut laq'wnts (lit. He cannot do it), vi.)

√lq'ʷ₂ ∥ hn+loq'ʷ=íw'es *divorced, split*. (hnloq'wi'wes, vt.); s+n+luʔq'ʷ=íw'es *breach*. (snlu'q'wi'wes (lit. splitting up), n.)

√lskʷ † leskʷ *limp*. (leskw (stem). to become crippled, walk with a limp, vi.); lés·k[ʷ] *cripple, lame*. (lessk (lit. He became lame), vt.); les·kʷ *crippled, lame*. (lesskw (stem). to become crippled, walk with a limp, adj.); les·kʷ+ncut *to become crippled, lame, to walk with a limp*. (lesskwnsut, vi.)

√lswp † le·swíp *Jew, French Le Juif*. (Leeswip, n.); § č's+č's+t+men+ł le·swíp *anti-Semite*. (ch'sch'stmenł leeswip, n.)

√lš † liš *bump, lump*. (lish, n.); liš *mountainous*. (lish (stem), adj.); s+liš+š *clump*. (slishsh (lit. something put together in a single bunch), n.); e·+liš *lump, mound, mountain*. (eelish, n.); e·+liš+liš *lump, mound, mountain*. (eelishlish, pl.); e+l'+l'íš *clod, a small hill*. (e'l'ish, n.); § u+x̌ʷel'+e+l'íš *mountain (it is like a...)*. (uqhwe'le'lish, n.); kʷup‿x̌ʷuy teč+e·líš *You went to the mountain*. (kupkhuy tech eelish, vi.)

√lt₁ † lut *mischievous, negative, no, not*. (lut (stem)(sometimes lu), adj, adv, neg.); lút+m *deny*. (lutm (lit. He failed in his project), vt.); s+lut+m *declination, decline, denial, failure, refusal*. (slutm, n.); lúst+m *black-ball, ban, debar*. (lustm, vt.); lu·t+útm *degenerate*. (luututm (lit. He is worthy of rejection), adj.); l'+l'u·t+útm' *cur, base, bastard*. ('l'luutut'm. baseborn (lit. He is worthy of naught), n, adj.);

s+lút+emn *boycott, contraband*. (slutemn (lit. something not wanted), n.); gʷł s+lút+emn *black list*. (guł slutemn (lit. Those who are unwanted), n.); ∥ hn+lút=cn *coarse, cynical*. (hnlutsn (lit. He uses words lacking in delicacy or refinement), adj.); hn+luteʔ+s=cín *animadvert, contradict, dispute*. (hnlute'stsin (lit. He commented critically, usually with disapproval), vt, vi.); s+n+lú(t)=cn *cynicism, negative in thoughts: statements*. (snlutsn, n.); ul+n+lú(t)+s=cn *cynical*. (ulnlutsn (lit. belonging to a cynic), adj.); s+n+luteʔ=s=cín *contradiction, protest, defiance*. (snlute'stsin, n.); s+n+luteʔ=s=cin'-t-ew'eš *discord*. (snlute'stsi'nte'wesh (lit. disagreement with one another), n.); s+n+lút=elgʷes *discontent*. (snlutelgwes (lit. dissatisfaction as to the heart), n.); cen+t+lu·t=íl'š *bereaved, orphaned*. (tsentluuti'lsh (lit. He became an orphan), vt.); ‡ lú-stu-s *deny, decline, disapprove*. (lustus (lit. He rejected it, he refused it), vt.); e·+lu-stu-s *criticise, deprecate, disagree*. (eelustus (lit. He disapproves strongly of it), v.); lut láq'ʷ-nt-s *be unable*. (lut laq'wnts (lit. He cannot do it), vi.); hn+lut+eʔs=cín-t-s *disobey, contradict, controvert*. (hnlute'stsints (lit. He said "no" to what he said), vt.); lut he s+n+luteʔ-st-sí-s *acquiesce*. (lut he snlute'stsis (lit. He did not say no), vi.); l'+l'u·t+útm'-st-m' *bastardize*. ('l'luutut'mst'm (lit. He was made of low birth), vt.); § lut hey'p+súxʷ=meʔ+is *anesthesia*. (lut he'ypsukhwme'is (lit. He has no feeling), n.); lut hey'+suxʷ=meʔ+m+s *analgesia*. (lut he'ysukhwme'ms (lit. He does not feel), n.); k'ʷey'+lút *not yet*. (k'we'ylut, adv.); lut+u·+míh *ambiguous*. (lutuumih (lit. It is not certain), adj.); elu+s+n+łú+łus+mn *bold, brash, reckless, daring, daredevil.* (elusnłułusmn (lit. He has no inner eyes), adj.); elu+ł+mít'č'= ede? *bloodless.* (elułmit'ch'ede' (lit. It has no blood), adj.); elu+s+tčíy'+m *anuresis.* (elustchi'ym (lit. It does not urinate), n.); lut hey'+n+tččiy'= ngʷílis *urinate (unable to...).* (lut he'yntchchi'yngwilis, vi.); elu+ł+s(=)íkʷe? *waterless, parched, anhydrous.* (elułsikwe' (lit. It has no water), adj.); elu+s+č+tém'+p *clear (sky), cloudless.* (eluschte'mp (lit. It has no cloud), adj.); čam'+?elu+ł+xal+xelexʷ *toothless.* (cha'm'elułqhalqhelekhw (lit. he no longer has his teeth), adj.); č'am' a+lut xál+xalexʷ *toothless, he no longer has his teeth.* (ch'a'm alut qhalqhalekhw, adj.); elu+s+n+qʷéy'+t *cold-blooded, ruthless, merciless.* (elusnqwe'yt (lit. He has no mercy), adj.); elu+s+c+c'm=íl't *barren, sterile.* (eluststs'mi'lt (lit. H/s has no children), adj.); elu+s+čtím+m *blameless, innocent.* (eluschtimm, adj.); elu+ł+n+muq'ʷ=íčn'+n *bareback.* (elułnmuq'wich'nn (lit. It, e.g. horse, is w/o a saddle), adj.); miyeł+lút *extravagant, unreasonable.* (miyełlut, adj.); elu+s+temn+es+čínt *cantankerous, perverse (disposition), unfriendly, unsociable.* (elustemneschint (lit. One who is not sociable), adj.); elu+s+čłís+is+m *asymmetric, unequal.* (eluschłisism (lit. It has no comparison), adj.); elu+s+n+xep=íw'es *dead, dead (to be...).* (elusnqhepi'wes (lit. It has no second self, soul), adj.); elu+s+p'í?xʷ *to be w/o light, aphotic, dark.* (eluspi'khw (lit. It has no light), adj.); elu+s+gʷép=cn *bare-faced, beardless.* (elusgweptsn (lit. He is w/o a beard on his face), adj.); elu+ł+n+t+c'uxʷ= ípele?+n *anarchic, lawless.*

(elułntts'uqhwipele'n (lit. H/s/i has no law), adj.); e+lu+ł+cen+gʷén+t *foundation (without...), groundless, baseless, metaph. H/s has no underwear.* (elułtsengwent, n, adj.); lut+gʷníxʷ *deceptive, spurious.* (lutgwnikhw (lit. It is untrue), adj.); lut+xes+t *amoral, immoral.* (lutqhest (lit. It is not good), adj.); lut ha s-xes+t-s *It is not good.* (lut ha sqhests, vi.); lut č'es+t *amoral.* (lut ch'est (lit. It is not bad), adj.); elu+ł+kʷl'+ncút+n *unbeliever, agnostic, atheist.* (elułk'u'lntsutn (lit. One who has no God), n.); e+lu+ł+t'íkʷ+t *bastard, illegitimate.* (elułt'ik'ut (lit. H/s is w/o legitimate elders), n, adj.); elu+s+kʷís+t *anonymous, nameless.* (eluskwist (lit. H/s/i has no name), adj.); elu+ł+n+mús=elgʷes+n *despair.* (elułnmuselgwesn (lit. H/s is w/o hope), n.); lut s+tim' *cipher, nothing, zero.* (lut sti'm, n.); lut'+hay'p+s+hóy+oy+s *ageless.* (lut'ha'yps-hoyoys (lit. It is ageless, it is existing forever, it does not cease), adj.); lut+hay'p+s+hóy+oy+s *continual, continuous, eternal, incessant.* (lutha'yps-hoyoys (lit. It is ageless, it is existing forever, it does not cease, it has no end), adj.); lut hay'p+s+n+xił-s *to be brave, courageous, fearless (lit. He has no fear).* (lut ha'ypsnqhiłs, vi.); elu+s+łe?+p=ús=šn *boundless, limitless.* (elusłe'pusshn (lit. It is w/o limit), adj.); lut'+hey'p+s+łe?+p=ús= ši-s *infinity.* (lut'he'ypsłe'pusshis (lit. It has no limit), n.); e+lus+ce·n+?íd+ed *enduring, lasting.* (elustsee'nided, adj.); e+lus+ce·n+?íd+et *changeless, durable.* (elustsee'nidet, adj.); lut hay'+n+xił+s *bravery.* (lut ha'ynqhiłs (lit. He has no fear), n.); elu+s+n+xíł *brave, daring, dauntless, courageous.*

(elusnqhiɫ (lit. He has no fear), adj.);
lut hey'+s+n+x̌iɫ+s *courage.* (lut
he'ysnqhiɫs (lit. He has no fear), n.);
lut ul wášn *apolitical.* (lut ul W<u>a</u>shn
(lit. not belonging to Wash., D.C.),
adj.); lut hey's+p'út'+m+s *abyss.* (lut
he'ysp'ut'ms (lit. It has no bottom, It
has no end.), n.); lut hey'+c+méy+s
casual, unsorted. (lut he'ytsmeys (lit. It
is uncertain, without design or
premeditation), adj.); lut
s+miyes+čínt *commoner.* (lut
smiyeschint (lit. He is not a
nobleman), n.); elu+s+x̌em=ínč e
s+čint+soc *Anglophobe, (lit. One who
does not love England).* (elusqhem<u>i</u>nch
e Schnts<u>o</u>ts, n.); lut un+míy=elgʷes
capricious, fickle. (lut unm<u>i</u>yelgwes
(lit. He has no definite thoughts), adj.);
lut+u·+míy *chancy, conditional.*
(lutuum<u>i</u>y (lit. It is uncertain), adj.); lut
ši?+še?+t *cheeky.* (lut sh<u>i</u>'she't (lit. He
is disrespectful), adj.); miyeɫ+lut
degenerate, person of low morals.
(miyeɫlut, n.); lut soltes *civilian.* (lut
soltes (lit. He is not a soldier);
soltes=l.w. from English), n.); lut
as+paˤ+aˤ+út+m-s *colorfast.*
(lutaspa(a(<u>u</u>tms (lit. It is incapable of
fading), adj.); lut es+peˤ+eˤ+út+m-s
colorfast (lit. It is incapable of fading).
(lutespe(e(<u>u</u>tms, adj.); elu+s+pá?q
unbleachable. (eluspa̱'q (lit. It does not
whiten e.g. by exposure to the sun),
vi.); lut+as+p'á?x̌+s *wound (the...did
not heal).* (lutasp'<u>a</u>'qhs, n.); lut
hey'p+s+p'ugʷ=ílumx̌ʷ+s *anechoic.*
(lut he'ypsp'ugw<u>i</u>lumkhws (lit. It has
no echoes), adj.); lut t'é+t'd+t'
effortless. (lut t'<u>e</u>t'dt' (lit. It is not too
difficult), adj.); s+lus+x̌áq'+n
decompensation. (slusqh<u>a</u>q'n (lit.
reversal of recompense), n.);
ni?+sel+m-st-m e lut šiɫ *adulterate.*
(ni'selmstm e lut shiɫ (lit. It was mixed
with something not just right, it was

made impure by mixing in a foreign or
poorer substance), vt.); lut he·
y+?el+mncut+s *H/S did not move h/h
self, h/s did not go anywhere.*
(luthee'yelmnts<u>u</u>ts, vt.)

√lt₂ † li·tí *tea.* (liit<u>i</u> (l.w. from French),
n.); hn+li·tíh+n *caddy.* (hnliit<u>i</u>hn (lit. a
small box-like container for tea), n.)

√ltkʷ † ltkʷú *otter.* (ltk<u>u</u>, n.)

√lw † liw *chime, chink, sound of a bell,
a short metallic sound.* (liw!, n.); u·
lí·w *chink.* (uul<u>i</u>iiw (lit. It made a
matallic sound), n.); líw+liw+iš *bell.*
(l<u>i</u>wliwish (lit. that which tolls time
and again), n.); ‡ líw+m-st-m *chime,
ding, rung, it (bell) was rung.*
(l<u>i</u>wmstm. bell toll, vi.) [xref √lˤʷ]

√lw' ∥ s+le·w'=íneč *cricket.*
(slee'w<u>i</u>nech. locust, n.)

√lxʷ₁ † lexʷ *hurt.* (lekhw (stem), vt.);
s+lexʷ+p *casualty, detriment.*
(slekhwp (lit. an unfortunate chance or
accident, especially one involving
bodily injury, n.); čn‿léxʷ+p *hurt (I
got...).* (chnl<u>e</u>kh'wp, vi.); čn‿lexʷ+p
hurt (to get). (chnlekhwp, vi.);
s+luxʷ+p+nu+ncút *boomerang.*
(slukhwpnunts<u>u</u>t (lit. One who makes
an action that rebounds detrimentally).
hurting oneself, n.); ‡ luxʷ+p+nún-t-s
*H/S succeed in excruciating (causing
great pain to) h/h.* (lukhwpn<u>u</u>nts, vt.)

√lxʷ₂ † e·+lexʷ *aperture, hole, opening.*
(eelekhw (lit. There is an opening), n.);
en+léxʷ *cavity, atrium, auricle, hole.*
(enl<u>e</u>khw, n.); ∥ ni?+loxʷ=alqʷ
*opening in the woods slightly SW of
Tensed.* (Ni'lokhw<u>a</u>lqw, n.); luxʷ=
l'úmxʷ *cave.* (lukhu'l<u>u</u>mkhw, n.);
luxʷ=úl'umxʷ *cave.* (lukh<u>u</u>'lumkhw,
n.); en+luxʷ=úl'umxʷ *cave, cavern,
hole (in the ground), posthole.*
(enlukh<u>u</u>'lumkhw, n.); hn+luxʷ=
úl'mxʷ *burrow.* (hnlukh<u>u</u>'lmkhw (lit.
The mole dug a hole in the ground),
vt.); hn+láxʷ=qn *bunghole.*

(hnlakhwqn. (lit. the hole in a cask, keg or barrel through which liquid is poured in or drained out), n.); luxʷ+íl'=kʷeʔ *dug (he...a well).* (lukhwi'lkwe', vt.); luxʷ+il'=kʷeʔ *well (to dig a...).* (lukhwil'kwe' lit. He dug in the ground for water), n.); s+lúxʷ=il'kʷeʔ *artesian well (lit. A hole dug for water).* (slukhwi'lkwe', n.); l'+l'xʷ=íl=uʔs *spring on north side of DeSmet Mission Hill (lit. little hole on the forehead of the hill).* ('1'lkhwi'lus, n.); ‡ léxʷ-n *bore, drill.* (lekhwn (lit. I made a hole in or through it), vt.) [xref √xʷl] [see also √łxʷ]

√lx̌ † lax̌ *lightening.* (laqh (stem), n.) [xref √l'x̌]

√lx̌ʷ † lax̌ʷ *lie (round objects).* (laqhw (stem), vi.)

√ly' ‡ láy'+m-st-m *clatter, rattle.* (la'ymstm. (lit. It was caused to make a rattling sound), vi.)

√lʕʷ₁ ‡ hn+láʕʷ-nt-m *arraign, cite.* (hnla(wntm. (lit. He was arraigned, cited, summoned before a court of law, inserted into a sheath), vt.)

√lʕʷ₂ † leʕʷ *adjust, fit.* (le(w (stem), vt.); ul'+l'eʕʷ *convenient.* (ul''le(w (lit. it is loose, relaxing), adj.); léʕʷ+ʕʷ+m *decompress.* (le(u(m (lit. It became loosened), vt.); s+léʕʷ+m+n *convenience.* (sle(wmn (lit. that which increases comfort or makes work easier), n.); luʕʷ+luʕʷ+útm *valley, dell.* (lu(wlu(utm, n.); lʕʷ+lʕʷ+útm *dale, valley.* (l(wl(utm (lit. It is a long passage in which something can be inserted), n.) [see also √lʔ]; leʕʷ+m+ncut *loose, relax, He relaxed. (lit. he loosened himself).* (le(wmntsut, vi.); léʕʷ+s+m+ncut *relaxed.* (le(smntsut, vt.); s+leʕʷ+m+ncút *detents, ease, relaxation, turning oneself loose, vacation.* (sle(wmntsut, n.); s+léʕʷ+m+ncut *ease.* (sle(wmntsut, n.); ∥ č+léʕʷ=gʷl+um *humorous way of speaking of relaxing (in general) (lit. h/s relaxed h/h stomach or abdomen).* (chle(wgulum, vt.); s+č+léʕʷ=gʷl+umš *loosening (...one's stomach).* (schle(wgulumsh, vt.); § [also recorded as √lʕ'ʷ] kʷan+ł+č+l'ʕ'ʷ+l'ʕ'ʷ+p=al'qʷ *pocket knife (h/s took a...).* (kwanłch'l'(w'l'(wpa'lqw, n.)

√lʕʷ₃ † u· léʕʷ *crash.* (uule(w (lit. It made the loud noise of glass crashing), vi.) [xref √lw]

√lʔ₁ ∥ hn+leʔ=úl'mxʷ+n *dibble.* (hnle'u'lmkhwn. (lit. hole in the ground poker or piercer), n.)

√lʔ₂ † li?+leʔ+t *soar, fly, to fly, they soared.* (li'le't (stem), vi.); e·+li+l'eʔ+t *birds, fly.* (eeli'le't (lit. flying creatures), n.,v.); e+l'+l'i+l'eʔ+t *bird (small).* (e'li'le't, n.); e·+l'+l'i?+l'eʔ+t *fly.* (ee'l'li''le't. (lit. flying creatures, dim, e.g., flies, bugs, bees.), v.); eč+lí?+leʔ *lightly, scantily.* (echli'le'. (lit. He is scantily dressed, e.g. in winter.), adv.)

√lʔ₃ † lo?+lo?+ótm *valley, especially Spokane Valley.* (lo'lo'otm (a Spokane word), n.) [see also √lʕʷ]

√lʔ₄ † lu? *thump (on ground).* (lu'!, excl.); u· lú? *made (it...a thumping sound), sound (it made a thumping...).* (uulu', vt, n.)

√lʔx̌ʷ † lá?x̌ʷ *dawned, daytime, morning, tomorrow.* (la'qhw (stem), (lit. It became today/the day which is to come next), vi, n, adv.); t'u?+lá?x̌ʷ *tomorrow (Well,...I am coming).* (t'u'la'qhw, vi, adv.)

√l'c † ul'c *anew.* (u'lts, adj.)

√l'č † l'+l'ič *thin (like cloth).* ('l'lich (stem), adj.); u+l'+l'íč *thin (It is...).* (ul''lich, adj.)

√l'q'ʷ l'é+l'q'ʷ+l'+š *ripples.* ('le'lq'w'lsh, n.)

√l'w' l'aá+l'ew'eʔ *lout, bumpkin, slouch.* ('laa'le'we', n.); l'a+l'éw'e *messy (He is...and untidy), untidy (He is messy and...).* ('la'l<u>e</u>'we, adj.)

√l'x̌₁ [stem recorded as √lx̌] † lax̌ *friend.* (laqh (stem), n.); s+l'ax̌+t *buddy, comrade, friend.* (s'laqht, n.); s+l'ax̌+l'áx̌+t *friends.* (s'laqh'l<u>a</u>qht, n.); his+ti?x̌ʷa+s+l'áx̌+t *acquantance.* (histi'khwas'l<u>a</u>qht (lit. He is one who became a friend), n.); a·+l'ax̌+t'+m+n'+šeš *friendly, sociable.* (aa'laqht'm'nshesh (lit. H/s usually makes friends), adj.); ∥ s+l'ax̌+t=iw'es *camaraderie, comradely good.* (s'laqhti'wes (lit. friends between), n.); gʷł l'ax̌+t=íw'es *coterie.* (guł 'laqhti'wes (lit. They are mutual friends), n.); ‡ l'ax̌+t+m'-n't-s *befriend.* (l'aqhtm'n'ts (lit. He acted as a friend to him), vt.); l'ax̌+t+m'-nt-s *befriend.* ('laqht'mnts (lit. He acted as a friend to him, treated him as a friend), vt.); § t+tw'ít ha s+l'ax̌+t *boyfriend.* (tt'w<u>i</u>t ha sl'aqht, n.); cún=me?-n x̌ʷa hi+s+l'áx̌+t *taught (I...him who is my friend).* (ts<u>u</u>nme'n khwa his'laqht, vt.); ne? gʷíč+gʷíč=us-nt-s x̌ʷa s+l'áx̌+t-s *He will see the eyes of one who is his friend.* (ne'tgwichgwichusnts khwa s'laqhts, v.)

√l'x̌₂ † l'+l'ax̌ *lighten.* (l'laqh (stem), vt.); s+l'+l'áx̌+m' *electricity, lightening.* (s'l'laqh'm, n.); § sye·+k'ʷul' a s+l'+l'áx̌+m' *electrician.* (syeek'u'l a s'l'l<u>a</u>qh'm (lit. One who produces (works) with electricity), n.) [see also √lx̌]

√ł † ł (a connective) *no meaning.* (ł); łe *one who is.* (łe, n.)

√łc₁ † łac *a drop falls.* (łats)

√łc₂ † łec *side-by-side (flat objects).* (łets (stem), adv.); ∥ č+łec+łec=w'es+cútn' *boutonniere.* (chłetsłets'wests<u>u</u>tn (lit. buttons), n.)

√łc' † łuc' *break (sticklike objects).* (łuts' (stem), vt.); łu?c *to break sticklike objects.* (łu'ts)

√łč † łe?č *break (string).* (łe'ch (stem), v.)

√łčp † łčíp *bucket, pail.* (łch<u>i</u>p, n.); § kʷan+ł+łčíp *H/s took a bucket.* (kwanłłch<u>i</u>p, v.)

√łkʷ₁ † łi+łikʷ *speckled, spotted.* (łiłikw (stem), adj.) [see also √łkʷ₂]

√łkʷ₂ † łukʷ *bloodstained.* (łukw (stem), adj.); łu?kʷ *bled.* (łu'kw, vi.); u· łúkʷ *bloody (it is...).* (uul<u>u</u>kw, adj.) [see also √łkʷ₁]

√łk'ʷ₁ † łek'ʷ *break (a hairlike object).* (łek'w (stem), vt.)

√łk'ʷ₂ † łek'ʷ *barb, fork, needle, spike.* (łek'w (stem), n.); łek'ʷ+łuk'ʷ+t *cactus, thistle, sticker.* (łekw'lukw't, n.); s+č+łek'ʷ *meat (broiled...), spit.* (schłek'w, n.); ‡ č+łék'ʷ-nt-s *broiled (he...it (salmon)).* (chłek'wnts, vt.); § č+łuk'ʷ+łuk'ʷ+p+sín'+n *fork.* (chłuk'włuk'wpsi'nn., n.)

√łk'ʷ₃ † łuk'ʷ *recall, remember.* (łuk'w (stem), vt.); e·+łek'ʷ *rosary, beads.* (eełek'w (lit. That w/c is linked together), n.); ∥ hn+łuk'ʷ+łuk'ʷ=ílgʷes *He has a good memory.* (hnłuk'włuk'wilgwes, n.); hn+łuk'ʷ+łuk'ʷ=el'gʷes+ncút *bethink, remind, brushed up.* (hnłuk'włuk'we'lgwesntsut. (lit. He reminded (himself)), vt.); h[n]+łuk'ʷ+łuk'ʷ=el'gʷes+ncút+n' *diary, memorandum.* (hułuk'włuk'we'lgwesntsutn'. (lit. means of reminding oneself), n.)

√łl † łel *sprinkle.* (łel (stem), vt.); łil *to sprinkle.* (łil); ‡ łél-nt-s *dabble, spatter, splash, splatter.* (ł<u>e</u>lnts. (lit. He splashed or spattered it, as with liquid), vt.)

√łm₁ † łom+en' *scold* [probably *I scolded him*] (łome'n (stem), vt.); hn+łóm+emn *trachea, windpipe.* (hnł<u>o</u>memn. (lit. instrument of scolding (shouting)), n.); ‡ łome-n't-s *chide, scold, scolded.* (łome'nts (lit. H/s scolded h/h), vt.)

√łm₂ † s+č+łem+t *dew.* (schłemt, n.); ‡ č+łem-nt-m *bedew.* (chłemntm (lit. It became wet with dew), vt.)

√łm' † łem' *apologize.* (łe'm (stem), vi.)

√łn † łén+łn+t *bumptious, chit, insistent, pushy.* (łenłnt. (lit. He is cruelly forward and self-assertive in behavior/a girl who is pert), adj, n.); łen+p *H/S insisted on going along.* (łenp, vi.); ‡ čs+łén+p-nt-s *desire.* (chsłenpnts (lit. He desired it)., v.)

√łn' † łen' *opposite (on the...side).* (łe'n (stem), adj.); łun' *opposed, opposite.* (łu'n (stem), adj.); ∥ hn+łen'=ítkʷe? *Europe, overseas, the Continent.* (hnłe'nitkwe'. (lit. on the other side of the water), n.); hn+łen'=u·s=iw'es *across.* (hnłe'nuusi'wes, prep.)

√łp † łe?p *stripe, welt (make a...).* (łe'p (stem), vt, n.) [xref √łp']

√łpx̌ † łapx̌ *bruise, skin.* (łapqh (stem), vt.)

√łp'₁ † łip' *to stripe.* (łip'); łep' *to strip, mark, make a welt.* (łe'p); łp'+min+n *crayon, marker (a line...).* (łp'minn. E.g to mark a line with a stick, stone, crayon, n.); łp'+łp'+m'in'+n' (dim form) *pen, pencil.* (łp'łp'm'in'n' (lit. a small line marker), n.); ∥ łp'=ul'umxʷ+n *border, frontier.* (łp'u'lumkhwn (lit. a means of marking the line of land), n.); łup'=úl'umxʷ+n *border (lit. means of marking the boundary of land).* (łup'u'lumkhwn, n.); s+cen+łp'=ełníw' *definition. (lit. circumstances, limiting).* (stsenłp'ełni'w, n.); ‡ łep'-nt-s *line (He marked it with a...), marked (He...it with a line).* (łep'nts, n, vt.); łp'+úl'mxʷ-nt-s *demarcate.* (łp'u'lmkhwnts (lit. he drew a line on the ground), vt.); cen+łp'=ełníw'-n *define.* (tsenłp'ełni'wn (lit. I circumscribed it; I fixed its limits),

vt.); § u+n+málqʷ'=qn he łp'+łp'+mín'+n' *pen (ball-point...).* (unmalq'wqn he łp'łp'mi'n'n, n.); kʷen+ł+łp'+łp'+m'ín'+n' *took (H/s...a pencil, a pen).* (kwenłłp'łp'mi'n'n, vt.) [xref √łp]

√łp'₂ † łep['] *disappoint, distasteful.* (łep (stem), adj.); łép[']+łp'+t *disappointing (He is very...).* (łepłp't, adj.)

√łp'č' ‡ łáp'č'-nt-s *bolt, devour, gulp, consume.* (łap'ch'nts. (lit. He ate it hurriedly), vt.)

√łq † łaq *mend, patch.* (łaq (stem), vt.); ∥ s+łaq+ła·q'=ic'e *[q]uilt.* (słaqłaaq'its'e, n.) [xref łq']

√łq? † łaqi? *drop.* (łaqi' (stem). they, vt.)

√łq'₁ † łaq' *broad, wide.* (łaq' (stem), adj.); łaq' *crouch, lie (on one's stomach).* (łaq' (stem), prone, vi.); łaq'+t *broad, capricious, wide.* (łaq't, adj.); s+łaq'+t *breadth, width.* (słaq't, n.); łáq+łaq'+t *bass (fish).* (łaqłaq't (lit. wide wide), n.); ∥ ł+łq'=ín'č *brisling, sardine.* (łłq'i'nch. (lit. little wide intestine), n.); hn+łaq'=íłc'e? *ample, capacious, commodious, roomy, spacious.* (hnłaq'iłt'se'. (lit. It is wide inside), adj.); s+łáq'=gʷl *barge.* (słaq'gul (lit. wide flat boat), n.); s+ł+łaq'=gʷíl' *bateau.* (słłaq'gwi'l (lit. small, wide boat), n.); č+łaq'+łaq'=íne? *ears (he has big...).* (chłaq'łaq'ine', n.); s+łaq'=ítkʷe? *Atlantic Ocean, large lake, ocean, sea, wide water.* (słaq'itkwe', n.); ‡ łaq'+p+m-stu-s *broaden, widen.* (łaq'pmstus (lit. H/s made it broader), vt.); łaq'+t=íl'š-stu-s *widen.* (łaq'ti'lshstus (lit. He widened it), vt.); § [ł]aq'+t he lj+mín+n *broad-sword.* (laq't he ljminn (lit. It is broad which is a sword), n.)

√łq'₂ † łaq' *corral, round up.* (łaq' (stem), vt.)

√łqᵂ₁ † łaqᵂ *band, belt, hang.* (łaqw (stem). to hang as in a sack or on a line, band, belt, n, vt.); ∥ hn+łoqᵂ=ílgᵂes+n *cabinet, closet.* (hnłoqwilgwesn. (lit. place for hanging (storing) things), n.)

√łqᵂ₂ † łoqᵂ *also, and, besides, likewise.* (łoqw, conj, adv.); § łoqᵂ+s+tim *what else.* (łoqwstim, adv.)

√łq'ᵂ † łaq'ᵂ *peel, skin.* (łaq'w (stem), vt.); łoq'ᵂ *bald, bare (head), hairless.* (łoq'w (stem), adj.); ∥ č+łaq'ᵂ=álqᵂ *He stripped bark off a tree.* (chłaq'walqw, vt.); niʔ+łóq'ᵂ=aw'as=qn *bald.* (ni'łoq'wa'wasqn (lit. one lacking hair on the top of the head), adj.); ‡ č+łáq'ᵂ-nt-s *peeled (he...it off).* (chłaq'wnts, vt.); čs+łóq'ᵂ-nt-s *depilate.* (chsłoq'wnts (lit. He removed hair from his (dog's) tail), v.); § kᵂan+ł+s+łáq'ᵂ=qn *H/s took along a bark basket (lit. that which is pulled off a cedar tree).* (kwanłsłaq'wqn, v.); s+kᵂán+łq'ᵂeʔ=ep *Bark basket taken along.* (skwanłqwe'ep, vi.); čn‿kᵂán+łq'ᵂeʔ=ep *I took a bark basket(s) along.* (chnkwanłqwe'ep, vt.)

√łs₁ † łis *measure, weigh.* (łis (stem), vt.); łis+emn *caliper, measure.* (łisemn, n.); łs+łs+n'cút *calisthenics (to do...).* (łsłs'ntsut (lit. He measured himself repeatedly), n.); sye·+łís+m *critic.* (syeełism (lit. One who measures standards), n.); č+łis+cút+m *comparable (lit. It's worthy of comparison).* (chłissutm, adj.); ∥ łs+łs=m'eʔ+n'cút *exercise, exercising, do calisthenics.* (łsłs'me"ntsut (lit. He measured himself repeatedly), vi, vt.); łs+łs=m'eʔ+ncut+n' *barbell, (lit. means of measuring oneself repeatedly).* (łsłs'me'ntsut'n, n.); i+łs+łs=m'eʔ+n'cút *exercising (He is...).* (iłsłs'me"ntsut (lit. He is measuring

over and over), vt.); s+łis+łis=m'eʔ+ncút *calisthenics.* (słisłis'me'ntsut (lit. measuring, measuring one's own strength), n.); ‡ łis-nt-s *measure, he measured it, root of measure.* (łisnts, vt.); č+łís+m-stu-s *compare, coordinate (lit. He measured (compared) it with something else).* (chłismstus, vi.); łis=meʔ-nt-s *budget, calculated, calibrated, figured, measure, (lit. he measures it out).* (łisme'nts, vt.)

√łs₂ † s+łus+mn *countenance, face.* (słusmn, n.); s+n+łús+mn *eye (mental...), mind's eye.* (snłusmn, n.); s+č+łús+mn *eye.* (schłusmn, n.); s+č+łu+łús+mn *eyes.* (schłułusmn, n.); s+n+łú+łus+mn *vision (mental...), eyes (inner...), insight, penetration.* (snłułusmn, n.); § elu+s+n+łú+łus+mn *bold, brash, reckless, daring, daredevil.* (elusnłułusmn (lit. He has no inner eyes), adj.)

√łtkᵂ † łitkᵂ *jerk, twitch.* (łitk'w (stem), vi.)

√łt'₁ † łet' *jump, to splash.* (łet' (stem), vi.); łit' *jump (off or out of).* (łit' (stem), vi.); łet[']+p *to jump.* (łetp'); łét'+p+m+ncut *bound, jump, leap.* (łet'pmntsut. (lit. He caused himself to leap), vi.); s+łet'+p+m+ncut *capriole.* (słet'pmntsut (lit. leaping or jumping), n.); s+łét'+łt'+p'+m+n'cut *caper.* (słet'łt'p'm'ntsut (lit. leaping or frisking about), n.); § nukᵂ+ł+łt'+č'=ús+m-n-n *coincide.* (nukwłłt'ch'usmnn (lit. We tripped simultaneously), vi.) [?]

√łt'₂ † łit' *sprinkle (ceremonially).* (łit' (stem), vt.); ‡ łit'-nt-s *besprinkle, he sprinkled it with water.* (łit'nts, vt.) [see also √łt'q'ᵂ]

√łt'q'ᵂ₁ † łet'q'ᵂ *splash.* (łet'q'w (stem), vi.) [see also √łt'₂]

√ɫt'q'ʷ₂ † ∥ hn+ɫát'+ɫt'q'ʷ=cn *brusque, he is brusque.* (hnɫa̲t'ɫt'q'wtsn (lit. He is discourteously blunt), adj.)

√ɫw ∥ u+n+ɫ+ɫú?+m=us *acute.* (unɫɫu̲'mus (lit. It is sharp-pointed), adj.)

√ɫwč' † či?_ɫéwč' *deteriorate.* (chi'ɫe̲wch' (lit. I am deteriorating; I am growing worse physically), vi.)

√ɫws † ɫuwis+tn *uncle (foster...), uncle of a person with a deceased mother.* (ɫuwistn (lit. uncle of a person whose parent is dead), n.)

√ɫw'n † ɫuw'en *opposed, opposite.* (ɫu'wen); ɫuw'e[n] *that near third person or remote.* (ɫu'we, n.); § ɫuw'en ɫu? xes+t *that one is a good man, besides.* (ɫu'wenɫu̲'qhest, vi.)

√ɫxʷ † ɫexʷ *clothes, needle, draw (...together), put on, sew, slip on.* (ɫekhw (stem), n, vt.); ɫexʷ+m *sew.* (ɫekhum (lit. He sewed), vt.); ɫéxʷ+ɫuxʷ+m *They sewed.* (ɫekhwɫukhum, vt.); s+ɫéxʷ+m *baste (clothing), couture, crochet, needle work.* (sɫe̲khum (lit. sewing), n.); ɫ+ɫéxʷe? *blouse, bodice, cloth, clothes, clothing, dress, shirt, fabric.* (ɫɫe̲khwe' (lit. something sewed), n.); ɫuxʷ+mín+n *needle, sewing machine.* (ɫukhwmi̲nn (lit. a means of sewing), n.); ɫúxʷ+min+n *needle.* (ɫu̲khwminn, n.); ∥ s+ɫuxʷ=čt *glove, mitten.* (sɫukhwcht, n.); ni s+[ɫ]uxʷ=čt-s *Is it his glove?* (ni stu̲khwchts? (qu.).); s+ɫuxʷ+xʷ=íw'es *context, intertwining.* (sɫukhukhwi̲'wes (lit. weaving together), n.); § et+k'ʷul' hey+ɫéxʷ *brocade.* (etk'u'l heyɫekhw (lit. A woven thing of design), n.); ul sye+cuw'-n't-wíš he s+ɫúxʷ=čt *glove (boxing...).* (ul syetsu'w'ntwi̲sh he sɫu̲khwcht (lit. glove of a boxer), n.)

√ɫxʷp ∥ ɫéxʷ+xʷ+p=us *convict, culprit.* (ɫekhukhwpus. (lit. He became lassoed (by guilt)), vt, n.); s+ɫéxʷ+xʷ+p=us *conviction.* (sɫekhukhwpus (lit. becoming lassoed (by guilt), n.); § kʷl=u?s+ɫuxʷp+ú *Red Lasso.* (Kwlu'sɫukhwpu̲, n.) [xref √ɫx̌ʷp]

√ɫx̌ ∥ s+n+ɫax̌+p=ílgʷes *calamity.* (snɫaqhpilgwes (lit. cause of great distress), n.); can+ɫax̌+p=ílgʷes *commiserate, sympathized (he...).* (tsanɫaqhpilgwes (lit. he felt sorrow or pity), vi.); s+can+ɫáx̌+p=ilgʷes *concern, distress, dither, tribulation, worry.* (stsanɫa̲qhpilgwes, n.)

√ɫx̌ʷ₁ ∥ č+ɫe+ɫx̌ʷ=ál'qʷ *flute, cembalo, music.* (chɫeɫqhwa̲'lqw (lit. Holes bored on a hollow stick, log, etc.) piano, n.); č+ɫ+ɫx̌ʷ=ál'qʷ *harpsichord.* (chɫɫqhwa̲'lqw (lit. Holes bored on a hollow stick, log, etc, n.); sya+č+ɫ+ɫx̌ʷ=ál'qʷ *artist, flutist, musician, pianist.* (syachɫɫqhwa̲'lqw, n.); § sya·+q'éy'+n tgʷel' č+ɫ+ɫx̌ʷ=álqʷ *composer.* (syaaq'e̲'yn tgwe'l chɫɫqhwa̲lqw (lit. writer for the flute, piano, etc.), n.) [see also √lx̌ʷ]

√ɫx̌ʷ₂ † ɫáx̌ʷ+ɫx̌ʷ *cherry.* (ɫaqhwɫqhw, n.); ɫáx̌ʷ+lux̌ʷ *cherry, choke cherry, chokecherries.* (ɫaqhwɫuqhw (wild cherries, pl. form), n.); [also recorded as √lx̌ʷ] láx̌ʷ+lux̌ʷ *wild cherries, wild cherry.* (laqhwluqhw. cherry, choke cherry, n, pl n.)

√ɫx̌ʷp † ɫax̌ʷ *(?) momentum.* (ɫaqhw (stem), n.); ɫáx̌ʷ+p *escape, escaped (He...), away (to get...).* (ɫa̲qhwp, vi.); ∥ cen+ɫ+ɫux̌ʷp+m'=ín'č *crossed (He...the mountain pass), mountain pass (He crossed the...).* (Tsenɫɫukhwp'mi̲'nch (lit. name of a pass in the Clear Water Mountains), vt, n.); § ɫáx̌ʷp tel' hn+lč'+mín+n *prison (He escaped from...).* (ɫa̲qhwp te'l hnlch'mi̲nn, n.) [xref √lx̌ʷp, √ɫx̌ʷp']

√ɫx̌ʷp' † ɫax̌ʷp' *rush (to...out).* (ɫaqhwp' (stem), vi.); hn+ɫáx̌ʷp'+m *rush, dart, dash.* (hnɫaqhop'm. (lit. He rushed in), vt.) [xref √ɫx̌ʷp]

√łx̌ʷq' † łax̌ʷq' *slip*. (łaqhwq' (stem), vt.)

√ły † łay *marks (to make dirty...), scribble*. (łay (stem), v.); u· łáy *dingy, streaks (it has dirty...)*. (uułay, adj.); łe+łay' *spotted*. (łeła'y (stem), adj.); łáy+y *blot*. (łayy (lit. It became blotted), vt.); łáy+iy *contaminate*. (łayiy (lit. It became impure), vt.); s+ł'+ł'ay' *soil*. (sł'ła'y, n.); s+łi?+łay' *soil*. (słi'ła'y. one who is always soiled, n.); ∥ łáy+y=us *begrime, besmear, dirty, soil*. (łayyus. (lit. He became soiled as to the face), vt.); ł+łiy=ál'xʷ *pinto*. (łłiya'lkhw, n.); ł+łiy'=al'xʷ *horse (a spotted..., pinto), pinto*. (łłiy'al'khw (lit. one with a spotted or marked hide), n.); a·+łay'=elxʷ *brindled, streaked, striped*. (aała'yelkhw (It, animal's coat, is...), adj.); ‡ łáy-nt-m *dirtied (to be...), besmirch, besmirched (to be...)*. (łayntm (lit. H/s/i was dirtied), vi, vt.); łáy-nt-s *befoul, soil, sully*. (łaynts. (lit. He sullied it), vt.)

√łʕʷ † łaʕʷ *slippery*. (ła(w (stem), adj.); łeʕʷ *skate, slide (on ice)*. (łe(w (stem), vi.)

√łʔ₁ † łi? *border, edge (close to the...)*. (łi' (stem), vt, adj.); łe?+p *(?) bold, courageous, undaunted*. (łe'p (stem), adj.); č+łi?- *beside*. (chłi- (pref), adv.); č+łi? *beside*. (chłi', prep.); č+łí?+i? *adjacent, next to, Saturday*. (chłi̲'i' (lit. it came next to the wall/What comes next to Sunday), n.); ∥ s+łe?+p=us=šn *boundary, deadline, destination, destiny*. (słe'pusshn, (lit. end of the trail), n.); s+n+łá?+p=alq+s *end (dead...)*. (snła̲'palqs (lit. end of the trail), n.); § elu+s+łe?+p=ús=šn *boundless, limitless*. (elusłe'pu̲sshn (lit. It is w/o limit), adj.); lut'+hey'p+s+łe?+p=ús+ši+s *infinity*. (lut'he'ypsłe'pu̲sshis (lit. It has no limit), n.); xʷł+n+łá?p=alqs he

s+yuxʷm=ús+m=ul'umxʷ *arctic*. (khułnła̲'palqs he syukhwmu̲smu'lumkhw. (lit. the most cold land), n.); hn+łá?+p=alqs č'es+t *atrocious, evil*. (hnła̲'palqs ch'est. (lit. He is extremely evil), adj.); hn+łá[?]p=alqs he s+yuxʷm=ús+m= ul'umxʷ *North Pole*. (hnła̲palqs he syukhwmu̲smu'lumkhw. (lit. the most cold land), n.)

√łʔ₂ † łu? *near (a third person)*. (łu (stem), adj.); łu? *that which is over there (away from us)*. (łu', adv.); e n+łú? *attend, it is there (at a distance)*. (enłu̲'. (lit. He was present there), v, vi.); [also recorded as √łwʔn] teč+łuw' *there (over there)*. (techłu'w, adv.)

√łʔ₃ ∥ łu?+u?+um+n=us=us *fell (he...forward)*. (łu'u'umnusus, vi.) [?]

√mc † mec *dull*. (mets (stem), adj.); mec+mc+t *blunt (for objects only), dull*. (metsmtst (lit. It, e.g. the knife, is dull), adj, n.)

√mckʷ † mcukʷ *caps (wild black...), (berries)*. (mtsukw, n.)

√mcq † macq *asunder (fall) as a house, etc., shattered. (lit. it fell to pieces)*. (matsq, vt.); hn+mácq *caved (it...in), cave-in*. (hnma̲tsq, vi, n.)

√mc' ∥ mc'=ús+en *balm, oil, face cream*. (mts'u̲sen (lit. a means of oiling one's face), n.); mc'=us+n *balm*. (mt'susn (lit. means of oiling one's face), n.) [xref √mʔc]

√mc'łt † mác'ułt *pus*. (ma̲ts'ułt, n.); s+mc'c'áłt+m *infection*. (smts'ts'a̲łtm, n.); s+mc'c'ołt+m *abscess*. (smts'ts'ołtm, n.)

√mc'p † mac'p *bee, bumblebee, honeybee, Deborah*. (mats'p, n.); ?apł+mac'p *beekeeper*. (apłmats'p, n.); § ul mac'p he cétxʷ+s *apiary*. (ul mats'p he tse̲tkhws (lit. belonging to a bee's house), n.)

√mc'y' // t+mc'+mc'íy'=ełp *Round Top
(north of St. Maries, Idaho).*
(Tmts'mts'i̱'yełp (lit. a tree with shiny
bark and leaves from which bows and
arrows were made), n.)

√mč † u· méč *convex.* (uumech, n.)

√mh // múh=elxʷ *cowhide, rawhide.*
(mu̱helkhw (onom. mu-helkhw,
moo-hide), n.)

√mkʷʔ // s+múkʷeʔ=šn *sunflower.*
(smu̱kwe'shn, n.)

√mkʷ † mikʷ *snow.* (mik'w (stem), n.);
s+mikʷ+n *January.* (smik'wn (lit.
month of snows), n.); s+mikʷ+t *snow.*
(smik'wt, n.) [xref √mx̌ʷ]

√ml₁ † mul *dip.* (mul (stem), vt.);
cen+múl+emn *dipper.* (tsenmu̱lemn,
n.); hn+múl+m *fetched (He...water).*
(hnmu̱lm, vt.); s+čet+múl *butter,
cream.* (schetmu̱l. (lit. that which is
scrape off the surface of milk), n.);
hn+čet+múl+n *creamery.*
(hnchetmu̱ln. (lit. place where butter,
etc., are made), n.)

√ml₂ // mel+mel+t=ičt+m *dally, delay,
linger, played, passed time with his
hands.* (melmeltichtm (lit. he dallied),
v.); mel+mel+t=ícs+n *bauble.*
(melmeltichsn (lit. plaything, toy), n.);
s+mel+mel+t=íčt+m *dalliance,
toying, trifling.* (smelmeltichtm, n.);
s+mel+mel+t=íčt+mš *dalliance,
trifling, toying.* (smelmeltichtmsh, n.);
mel+mel=cn+mí+ncut *babble,
chatter.* (melmeltsnmintsut (lit. He
played himself with his mouth), vi.);
s+mel+mel+t=ičt+mn+n *desecration,
using as a toy (something sacred).*
(smelmeltichtmnn, n.); ‡ mel+mel+t=
íčt-m-nt-m *desecrate.*
(melmeltichtmntm (lit. It (sacred
object) was used as a toy), vi.)

√ml₃ † mul *dirty.* (mul (stem), adj.); //
ml'=ól'mxʷ *ground, soil.* (m'lo̱'lmkhw,
n.); ml=ól'mxʷ *earth (soil).*
(mlo̱'lmkhw, n.); ml=ol'umxʷ *ground,
soil.* (mlo̱'lumkhw, n.); § u+x̌ʷal'+á
ml=ól'umxʷ *unrefined, earthy.*
(uqhwa'la̱ mlo̱'lumkhw (lit. It
resembles the soil), adj.)

√ml₄ † ml=qn=úps *eagle.* (mlqnu̱ps
(etym. mlqn-dark, ups-tail), n.); ml=
qen=ups *Aquila, eagle.* (Mlqenups,
n.); § u+x̌ʷel'+é ml=qn=úps *aquiline.*
(uqhwe'le̱ mlqnu̱ps (lit. like an eagle),
n.)

√mlkʷ₁ † melkʷ *complete, intact,
whole.* (melk'w (stem), adj.);
ec+mélkʷ *absolute, aggregate, whole.*
(etsme̱lk'w, adj.); ec+mélkʷ+m
*all-encompassing, comprehensive,
entire.* (etsme̱lk'um (lit. It is totally
inclusive), vi.); // ec+mlkʷ+m=úl'mxʷ
cosmos, universe, world.
(etsmlk'umu̱'lmkhw (lit. Everywhere
on Earth), n.); ul ec+mlkʷ+m=úl'mxʷ
cosmopolitan, ecumenical. (ul
etsmlk'umu̱'lmkhw (lit. common to the
whole world), adj.) [xref √mlq'ʷ]

√mlkʷ₂ † melkʷ *curdle.* (melk'w
(stem), v.); mél·kʷ *coagulate.*
(me̱llk'w (lit. It thickened completely),
vi.); má l·kʷ+x̌ʷ *coagulate (lit. It
thickened completely).* (ma̱llk'qhw, vi.)
[for expected kʷ]; s+n+mél·kʷ
clabber, curd, crud. (snme̱llk'w. (lit.
coagulated part of milk), n, vi.);
hn+mél·kʷ *curdle.* (hnme̱llk'w (lit. it
became curdled), vi.) [xref √mlq'ʷ]

√mlq † s+malq+n *moss (cooked).*
(smalqn, n.)

√mlq'ʷ † malq'ʷ *rounded, spherical.*
(malq'w (stem), adj.); u· malq'ʷ
bulbous. (uumalq'w (lit. It is bulb
shaped), adj.); m'+m'(=)al'q'ʷ *bolus.*
('m'ma'lq'w. lump, n.); m'+m'alq'ʷ
sphere. (m'm'alq'w, dim.n.);
m'l'+m'el'q'ʷ *ammunition, bullets.*
('m'l'me'lq'w (lit. Little Spheres), n.);
m'l'+mel'q'ʷ *bullet, cartridge.*
('m'lme'lqw' (lit. Little Spheres), n.);
s+mál·q'ʷ *clot.* (sma̱llq'w (lit. a thick,

viscous or coagulated mass), n.); s+málq'ʷ+m+šeš *conglomeration.* (smalq'umshesh, n.); ac+mál'qʷ *convex (lit. It is in the form of a lump having a round top).* (atsmal'qw, vi.); ∥ mlq'ʷ=ečs+ncut *clench, determined.* (mlq'wechsntsut (lit. he brought together (hands) tightly), vt.); s+mlq'ʷ=ečs+ncút *determination.* (smlq'wechsntsut (lit. clenching one's fist as a sign of being firm in decisions), n.); s+can+ml'q[']ʷ=áp=qn' *chignon.* (stsanm'lqwapq'n (lit. A lump (of hair) at the back of the head), n.); ‡ málq'ʷ+m-s-n *conglomerate.* (malq'umsn (lit. I gathered it (them) into a round mass), vt.); málq'ʷ+m-stu-s *agglomerate.* (malq'umstus (lit. He formed it into a rounded mass), vi.); § u+n+málq'ʷ=qn he łp'+łp'+mín'+n' *pen (ball-point...).* (unmalq'wqn he łp'łp'mi'n'n, n.); [xref √mlk'ʷ]

√mlš † mulš *cottonwood.* (mulsh, n.); ∥ hn+múlš=enč *beaver, Rockford, Washington.* (Hnmulshench (lit. concave wall with concave facing the beholder), n.); čn‿tel'+hn+mulš=enč *Rock ford, Washington (lit. I am from Rockford, Washington).* (chntel'(h)nmulshench, v.) [Similar constr. (with tl fused to the stem) occurs in Ok]

√mlxʷ † milxʷ *naked.* (milkhw (stem), adj.)

√ml? † m'el'e? *bait.* ('me'le (stem), n.); ∥ m'l'y'=iy'e?+n' *bait.* ('m'l'yi'ye"n, n.); m'l'y'=i?y'e?+n' *decoy.* ('m'l'y'i'y'e'n (bait for fishing or trapping), n.)

√ml'₁ † mal' *boil (come to...), hot, stifling, warm.* (ma'l (stem), v, adj.); mal'+ml'+t *It causes uncomfortable warmth (like woolen clothes in hot summer).* (ma'lm'lt, vt.); s+mal'+p *warm (condition of being uncomfortably...).* (sma'lp, n.);

čn‿mál'+p *discomfort.* (chnma'lp (lit. I was made uncomfortable by the heat), n.); hn+mal'+m *boil.* (hnma'lm, v.); s+n+mal'+n *boiling.* (snma'ln, vt.); hn+mal'+p *kettle boiled.* (hnma'lp, vi.); hn+mal'+ml'+p *The kettles boiled.* (hnma'lm'lp, vi.); i c+mál'+p *H/s is being uncomfortably warm.* (itsma'lp, vi.); ∥ s+ml'=ól'mxʷ *dumplings.* (sm'lo'lmkhw (lit. bread boiled), n.); ‡ hn+mál'-n *boil.* (hnma'ln (lit. I boiled it), vt.)

√ml'₂ † mil' *aimless.* (mi'l (stem), adj.); mil' *await.* (mi'l (stem), vt.)

√ml'₃ † mil' *distribute, pass out (food), repair.* (mi'l (stem), vt.); s+mil'+m *digestion.* (smi'lm (lit. distributing), n.); ‡ mil'-n *digest.* (mi'ln (lit. I distributed it, I digested it (food for thoughts)), vt.); mil'-nt-s *distributed (He...it).* (mi'lnts, vt.); míl'-nt-m *allot (lit. it was distributed by lot).* (mi'lntm, v.)

√ml'₄ † mel' *addition (in...to), by, on, near, touching.* (me'l, prep, adv, adj.); ∥ c+m+mól'=qn *cumulate.* (tsmmo'lqn (lit. It became heaped up), vi.); s+co+mól'=qn *cumulus.* (stsomo'lqn (lit. putting in a heap or pile), n.); s+n+mel'=cín' *address, curtilage, home.* (snme'ltsi'n. (lit. place where one stays (lives), n.); § mel'+ci? *by that (place).* (me'ltsi', adv.); e+mel'+xʷí? *here (right...).* (eme'lkhwi', adv.); ac+mal'+máq'ʷ *composite.* (atsma'lmaq'w, n.); ac+mál+ maq'ʷ *convex lumps.* (atsmalmaq'w, v.); s+mal'+máq'ʷ+m *composition.* (sma'lmaq'um, n.); mel'+s+če+t'uk'ʷ+útn *bedside.* (me'lschet'uk'utn (lit. It is by the bed), n.); ?ep+s+n+mel'=cín' *denizen, inhabitant, resident.* (epsnme'ltsi'n (lit. H/s has a place to live in), n.); s+mel'+c'uq'ʷún+m *connotation.* (sme'lts'uqunm (lit. mentioning (or

inferring) something with what is
said), n.); mal'+t+pér'+per'qʷ=
alqʷ-nt-m *crucified (to be...), crucify.*
(ma'ltpe̲'rpe'rqwalqwntm (lit. He was
put to death by being nailed to crossed
poles), vi, vt.); s+mal'+t+pér'+per'qʷ=
alqʷ *crucifixion.*
(sma'ltpe̲'rpe'rqwalqw, n.);
mel'+čen'-nt-s *comprise.*
(me'lche'nnts, vt.) [Reichard
identifies √ml' as a prefix, see
§408]

√ml'xʷ † mil'xʷ *tobacco.* (mi'lkhw
(stem), n.); s+mil'xʷ *tobacco.*
(smi'lkhw, n.); s+n+míl'xʷ+n *pipe.*
(snmi̲'lkhwn, n.); čs+n+míl'xʷ+n
Grizzly Mountain. (Chsnmi̲'lkhwn (lit.
Name of mountain in the Clear Water
Mountains of Idaho where materials
for pipes were got), n.); ‡
ni+s+mil'xʷ-s *Is it his tobacco?* (ni
smi'lkhws? (qu.).); ni+i-s+n+míl'xʷ+n
Is it your pipe? (ni isnmi̲'lkhwn?
(qu.).); § kʷen+ł+s+míl'xʷ *took
(H/s...tobacco along).* (kwenłsmi̲'lkhw,
vt.)

√mł † mił *rest.* (mił, vi.); meł *lying
down (persons...).* (meł (stem));
s+mił+m *breather, rest (a
short...period).* (smiłm (lit. resting),
n.); u+m'+m'e?łí· *ease.* (u'm'me'ł̲iii
(lit. It remains free from pain,
exertion), n.); ∥ hn+míł=kʷe? *St. Joe
River.* (Hnmi̲łkwe', n.); §
s+nukʷ+méł+l+iš *bed-fellow.*
(snukwme̲łlish, n.);
hn+č'n'+n'+mełi·+t+s+pú?s *come.
(lit. his heart came to its own position).*
(hnch"n'nmełiitspu̲'s, vt.)

√młč † s+młič *salmon.* (smłich, n.);
ye+s+młíč *salmon (He got a...).*
(yesmłi̲ch, n.); ?ep+s+młič *salmon
waters.* (epsmłich (lit. It has salmon),
n.); § s+č+čáy'+p he s+młíč *dried
salmon.* (schcha̲'yp he smłich, n.);
čeł‿či‿?iłn e s+młíč *I am going to*

eat some salmon. (cheł chii' yiłn e
smłich.)

√młq † małq *heavy convex object
collapses.* (małq)

√mm ∥ s+mí+mem=elt *berceuse,
lullaby.* (smi̲memelt, putting one's
child to sleep, chanting or singing. n.);
‡ mum-šit *help (to...).* (mumshit
(stem), vt.)

√mn † mí+mn=ułt *white fish.*
(mi̲mnułt, n.)

√mnč ∥ mnáč=alqs *intelligence,
Raven.* (mna̲chalqs (metaph.
intelligence, one who observes/looks
over all); cf. also Shllchł Mnachalqs,
Circling Raven, a great Coeur d'Alene
chief of the 1700's, n.); §
šl+l+tš+ł+mnač=alqs *Circling Raven.*
(Shlltshłmnachalqs, n.)

√mnk † mo·nki *monkey.* (moonki (l.w.
from Engl.), n.); § xay'+xi?+t ha
mo·nkí *ape, gorilla.* (qha̲'yqhi't ha
moonki̲. (lit. big monkey), n.)

√mnkh † čs+mononkih+m
rheumatism, stiffness (body), arthritis.
(chsmononkihm, n.)

√mntw ∥ mntúw=il'š *punctual.*
(mntuwi'lsh (stem), adj.) [see vol. 1
for stress]

√mn? † míne? *apt (to be...), apt, likely
(to be...).* (mi̲ne, adj.); mine? *suitable.*
(mine', adj.)

√mn' † min' *paint, smear.* (mi'n (stem),
vt.); mín'+emn *brush, paintbrush.*
(mi̲'nemn (lit. a means of painting), vt,
n.); s+min'+m *rubbing.* (smi'nm, vt.);
ec+mín'+men'+iš *pacer.*
(etsmi̲'nme'nish, n.); ‡ mín'-nt-s
groom, paint, rub. (mi̲'nnts (lit. He
rubbed it), vt.)

√mps † m(=)ups *anal.* (mups, adj.)

√mqʷ † moq[ʷ] *aggressive, forward.*
(moq (stem), adj.); ∥
hn+móqʷ+moqʷ=cn *blunt, brusque,
(lit. He is outspoken).*
(hnmo̲qwmoqwtsn, adj.)

√mq'ʷ † maq'ʷ *pile, stack.* (maq'w (stem). vt.); s+máq'ʷ+m *compilation, heaping together.* (smaq'um, n.); a+n+máq'ʷ *contents.* (anmaq'w (lit. They were contained in something, imprisoned), n.); s+čat+máq'ʷ *cargo, load.* (schatmaq'w. (lit. something loaded on), n.); hn+móq'ʷ+min+n *depot.* (hnmoq'wminn (lit. warehouse for sacks of wheat, etc.), n.); čat+m'oq'ʷ+m'oq'ʷ+m'in+n *boxcar, (lit. that on which things are loaded repeatedly).* (chat'moq'w'moq'w'minn. truck, n.); **∥** s+maq'ʷ=qn *Medimont (between Harrison & Rose Lake, Idaho).* (Smaq'wqn, n.); hn+moq'ʷ=íčn'+n *cantle.* (hnmoq'wich'nn (lit. saddle), n.); hn+móq'ʷ=ičn'+n *saddle.* (hnmoq'wich'nn, n.); **‡** máq'ʷ-nt-s *compiled (he...them), objects (h/s put...down), he put them down like sacks of wheat.* (maq'wnts, n, v.); **§** ac+mal'+máq'ʷ *composite.* (atsma'lmaq'w, n.); ac+mál+ maq'ʷ *convex lumps.* (atsmalmaq'w, v.); s+mal'+máq'ʷ+m *composition.* (sma'lmaq'um, n.); elu+ł+n+muq'ʷ=íčn'+n *bareback.* (elułnmuq'wich'nn (lit. It, e.g. horse, is w/o a saddle), adj.)

√mr₁ ∥ mar=kʷeʔ *flavor, season.* (markwe' (stem), vt.)

√mr₂ § lim-t-š ma·rí *Ave Maria, Hail Mary!.* (Limtsh Maari! (lit. Rejoice, Mary!), excl.); sant ma·ri *Holy Mary, Virgin Mary, Mary, Saint Mary.* (Sant Maari (l.w. from French), n.)

√mrm₁ ∥ marare·m=íw'es *couple, marriage partners.* (marareemi'wes, n.); marare·m=íw'-lš *marry, wed.* (marareemi'wlsh (lit. They got married), vi, v.); **§** s+nukʷ+mararím+em *wife, husband, mate, spouse.* (snukwmararimem, n.); ul s+nukʷ+mararím+n *conjugal.* (ul snukwmararimn (lit. pertaining to a spouse), adj.)

√mrm₂ † marim *treatment.* (marim (stem), n.); marím+ncut+n *antiseptic, medicine.* (marimntsutn, n.); marim+ncut+n *antidote, medicine, cure, also used jokingly for "wife" because of initial pun: "mari..." "marry..." =My wife, my medicine!* (marimntsutn (orig. old medicinal herb cures), n.); sya+marím+n *doctor.* (syamarimn, n.); **∥** marim=ul'umxʷ+n *compost, fertilizer, that which treats (fertilizes) the land.* (marimu'lumkhwn, n.); t+marím=łp= ečt *medicine (...tree).* (tmarimłpecht (lit. a tree that has medicinal branches), n.); marám=łp=alqʷ *medicine fir tree.* (maramłpalqw, n.); marám+šp=alqʷ *medicine fir tree.* (maramshpalqw, n.); **‡** marím-nt-m *doctored (He was...up).* (marimntm, vi.); **§** ʔapł+n+marím+ncut+n *apothecary, pharmacist.* (apłnmarimntsutn (lit. One who has a place for medicines), n.)

√mr' ∥ mar'+ar'=áx̌n *disjointed, dislocate.* (ma'ra'raqhn (lit. He was disjointed as to the arm), vi, vt.)

√mr'kʷ ∥ s+mar'kʷ=ús *black tail deer.* (sma'rkus, n.)

√ms₁ † mas+ms *plant or root of disagreeable smell but good food.* (masms, n.)

√ms₂ † mus *feel about (to...), fumble, grope.* (mus (stem), vi.); **‡** mus-nt-s *felt (he...it with the hand).* (musnts, v.); **§** elu+ł+n+mús=elgʷesn *despair.* (elułnmuselgwesn (lit. H/s is w/o hope), n.)

√ms₃ † mus *four.* (mus, n.); t+mus *persons (four).* (tmus, n.); **∥** mós=q'it *four days.* (mosq'it, n.); mós=q'iʔt *Thursday.* (mosq'i't (lit. four days), n.); mós=qit *Thursday.* (Mosqit, n.); a uł mós=qit *Thursday (on...).* (a uł mosqit (lit. on the fourth day), adv.); mus=čt *four hands.* (muscht, n.); t+mús=elps

grizzlies (four...), pigs (four).
(tmu̱selps, n.); hn+mús=p *four
bottoms, four eggs.* (hnmu̱sp, n.); §
ʔupen uɫ mus *fourteen.* (upen uɫ mus,
n.); mos+aˑl+ʔopan+č=sqʼit *Lent.*
(Mosaaʼlopanchsqʼit (lit. 40 days), n.);
mus+eˑl+ʔupn *forty.* (museeʼlupn, n.);
tʼuʔ čn‿mus+eˑl [ʔ]úpan *Well, I am
forty.* (tʼuʼchn mus ee lu̱pan, v.)

√mš₁ † mi+mš *box, carton.* (mimsh,
n.); mʼ+mʼi+mʼš *box (small), cassette.*
(mʼmʼiʼmsh (lit. small box), n.)

√mš₂ † miš *dearth, destitute.* (mish, n.);
mš *destitution, need, scarcity, want.*
(msh (lit. He is without necessities),
n.); ut+míš *but, only.* (utmi̱sh, adv.); ∥
t+mš=qn+mí+ncut *acquiesce,
capitulate, comply.* (tmshqnmi̱ntsut
(lit. He made himself empty-headed),
vi.); s+t+mš=qn+mi+ncut
*compliance, a disposition to yield to
others.* (stmshqnmintsut, n.); a+t+mš=
qn+mí+ncut *compliant, agreeable.*
(atmshqnmi̱ntsut, vi. (lit. He
acquiesces), adj.)

√mš₃ † -iš *be in the act of.* (-ish);
čín+mš *What in the world are you
doing (here)?* (chi̱nmsh?, qu.)

√mšl † mšél *Michael.* (Mshe̱l (l.w.
from French), n.)

√mt † moʔt *smoke.* (moʼt (stem), v.);
s+moʔt *smoke.* (smoʼt, n.); ∥
hn+moʔt=áɫcʼe *smoked (It...inside).*
(hnmoʼta̱ɫtsʼe, vi.); s+mót=ɫcʼeʔ
bacon. (smo̱tɫtsʼe (lit. smoked flesh of
pigs), n.); hn+moʔt=qítxʷ *The
chimney smoked.* (hnmoʼtqi̱tkhw, vi.)

√mtʼ₁ ∥ mátʼ=us *kidney.* (ma̱tʼus, n.); §
čs+tʼiš+iš+ɫ+mátʼ=us *diabetes.*
(chstʼishishɫma̱tʼus (lit. supplying the
kidneys with sugar), n.)

√mtʼ₂ ∥ uˑ mótʼ=ulʼumxʷ *bumpy.*
(uumo̱tʼuʼlumkhw (lit. The ground is
bumpy), adj.)

√mtʼčʼ ∥ mítʼčʼ=edeʔ *blood.*
(mi̱tʼchʼede, n.); § eluɫ+mítʼčʼ=edeʔ

bloodless. (eluɫmi̱tʼchʼede (lit. It has no
blood), adj.); s+síxʷ+m xʷe mítʼčʼ=
edeʔ *bloodbath, bloodshed.* (ssi̱khum
khwe mi̱tʼchʼede (lit. spilling that w/c
is blood), n.); s+nukʷ+mítʼčʼ=edeʔ
consanguineous. (snukwmi̱tʼchʼede
(lit. fellow by blood), adj.)

√mtʼqʼʷ † i c+mátʼqʼʷ+mš *He is
pulling back the trigger.*
(itsma̱tʼqʼumsh, vt.)

√mxʷ₁ † mexʷ *laugh.* (mekhw (stem),
vi.); méxʷ+t *laugh.* (me̱khwt (lit. He
laughed), vi.); s+mexʷ+t *laugh (to...),
laughing.* (smekhwt, vi.); t+mʼéxʷ+nʼ
butt. (tʼme̱khwʼn (lit. a laughing stock),
[n.]); t+mʼ+mʼéxʷ+nʼ *butt (lit. a
laughing stock).* (tʼmʼme̱khwʼn, n.); ‡
t+mʼuxʷ+mʼuxʷ+nʼ+mʼí-nt-s *deride.*
(tʼmukhwʼmukhwʼnʼmi̱nts (lit. He
laughed at him, He mocked him), vt.)

√mxʷ₂ † mixʷ *hang (in bunches).*
(mikhw (stem), vt.)

√mx̌ ∥ s+max̌=íʔčnʼ *bear (grizzly...),
bear (polar...).* (smaqhi̱ʼchʼn, n.)

√mx̌ʷ₁ † max̌ʷ *snow-covered.* (maqhw
(stem), n.); máx̌ʷ+x̌ʷ *snow.* (ma̱qhuqh
(lit. It snowed), vi.); max̌ʷ+x̌ʷ *snowed.*
(maqhuqhw, vt.); icʼ+máx̌ʷ+x̌ʷ
snowing (It is...). (itsʼma̱qhuqh, vi.);
s+max̌ʷ+x̌ʷ *snowing.* (smaqhuqh, vi.);
‡ máx̌ʷ-nt-m-lš *snowed upon (They
were...).* (ma̱qhwntmlsh, vi.); §
nokʼʷ+oʔ=qín ha s+máx̌ʷ+x̌ʷ+s
centennial. (nokʼoʼqin ha smaqhuqhws
(lit. one hundred snowings), n.);
ʔax̌ál+ɫ a+ʔsálʼ=qnʼ ha s+máx̌ʷ+x̌ʷ+s
bicentennial. (adj. aqha̱ɫ aʼsa̱ʼlqʼn ha
smaqhuqhws (lit. at every two hundred
heads that it snows), n.) [xref √mkʼʷ]

√mx̌ʷ₂ † mex̌ʷ *agony, anguish, travail.*
(meqhw (stem), n.)

√mx̌ʷyʼl † mox̌ʷʔyʼal *Peone (Mrs.
Louie..., a tribal elder).* (Moqhwʼyʼal,
n.)

√my₁ † may *muddy.* (may (stem), adj.);
máy+ay *soiled (It became...with mud).*

(ma̱yay, vi.); ∥ may+y=us *H/h face became muddy.* (mayyus, vi.); máy+may+ay=šn *H/h feet (shoes) got muddy.* (ma̱ymayayshn, vi.); hn+máy+ay=qn+m *H/s got stuck in the mud.* (hnma̱yayqnm, vi.); s+may= qn *dirt, filth, mud.* (sma̱yqn, n.); miy= qn=íl'š *It (dirt) turned to mud.* (miyqni̱'lsh, vi.); ‡ may-nt-m *bespatter, he was soiled with mud.* (mayntm, vt.); § u+kʷar+éq ha s+máy=qn *clay.* (ukwaṟeq ha sma̱yqn (lit. *mud that it yellow*), n.)

√**my₂** † may *foresee, foretell, predict.* (may (stem), vt.); ∥ t+máy=qn *clairvoyance.* (tma̱yqn (lit. *knowing head*), n.); a+t+máy=qn *clairvoyant, seer, prophet.* (atma̱yqn (lit. *He has a knowing head; he sees the future*), n.) [xref √my₃,₄, √m'y']

√**my₃** † mey *apparent, evident.* (mey (stem), adj.); mi· *to be evident that not.* (mii); u· méy *clarity, definitive, plain (it is...), understandable (it is...), suppose (I...it is so).* (uumey, n, n, adj, adj. vt.); mey+p *coming to know, learn, learned (he...).* (meyp, v, vi.); s+mey+p *to learn, master.* (smeyp, v.); ec+mey+s *know.* (etsmeys, vt.); mey+miy+t *adroit, knowledgeable, proficient, skillful, he is adroit, he knows what to do.* (meymiyt, adj.); s+méy'+miy' *chronology.* (sme̱'ymi'y (lit. *the relating or narrating of an event or series of events*), n.); t'i?+ec+méy *decisive, it is already determined.* (t'i'etsmey, v.); ∥ s+n+méy=cn *commentary, exegesis, explanation (...of a text), interpretation (...of a text).* (snme̱ytsn (lit. *making words, statements, plain*), n.); mey+miy+p=šn *learned (he...to walk), walk (he learned to...).* (meymiypshn, v.); t+méy+miy=ečt *deft, dexterous.* (tme̱ymiyecht (lit. *He knows as to the hands, He is skillful with the hands*), adj.); s+t+mey+miy= ečt *dexterity, (lit. knowing as to the hands, skill with the hands).* (stmeymiyecht, n.); sye+n+méy=cn *commentator.* (syenme̱ytsn (lit. *One who interprets*), n.); ‡ ec+méy-s-n *I know it.* (etsme̱ysn, vt.); ec+méy-st-xʷ *you know it.* (etsme̱ystkhw, vt.); ni ec-méy-st-xʷ *Do you (sg.) know it?* (ni etsme̱ystkhw? (qu.).); ec+méy-st-me-t *We know it.* (etsme̱ystmet, vt.); te·+méy+m-stu-s *destine.* (teemeymstus (lit. *He resolved it beforehand*), v.); čs+may'=qn'-t-s *h/s proved it, h/s made it evident, h/s evidenced it.* (chsma'yq'nts, vt.); § lut hey'+c+méy+s *casual, unsorted.* (lut he'ytsmeys (lit. *It is uncertain, without design or premeditation*), adj.); x̌e+ec+méy+st+m *celebrated, famous, well-known, celebrity, star.* (qhe etsme̱ystm. adj, n.) [xref √my₂,₄, √mys, √m'y']

√**my₄** † mi· *discover, learn.* (mii (stem), vt.); s+miy+scút *awareness, consciousness, self-knowledge.* (smiystsut, n.); ec+miy+scút *aware, conscious.* (etsmiystsu̱t, vt. (lit. *He knows himself*), adj.); miy+p+nun+t- ew'eš *acquainted.* (miypnunte'wesh (lit. *they came to know each other*), vt.); ∥ s+miy+p=ngʷíln *learning.* (smiypngwi̱ln (lit. *it is the means of learning, of education*), n.); may+miy= i?qs *nose, gourmand, gourmet.* (maymiyi'qs (lit. *He has a discriminating nose for food*), n.); sye+mi[y]+p=ngʷíln *collegian.* (syemipngwi̱ln (lit. *a learner*), n.); ni+kʷu ⌣ miy+p=ngʷíln *Did you learn anything?* (nikumiypngwi̱ln? (qu.).); t+miy=ípele? *expounded, clarified.* (tmiyi̱pele' (lit. *H/s made plain concerning something*), vt.); s+t+my= ipele? *clarification.* (stmyipele', n.); s+t+miy=ípele? *description, revealing* *the background of something.* (stmiyi̱pele', n.); s+t+miy+iy=ípele? *caption, short legend or description, as of an illustration or photograph.* (stmiyiyi̱pele', n.); s+ti+miy+y=ípele?+s *anthropology.* (stimiyyi̱pele's (lit. exposition of the nature of man (human beings)), n.); hn+miy=ep+mí+ncut *confessed, confessional, avowed.* (hnmiyepmintsut (lit. He told on himself), vi.); s+n+miy=ep+mí+ncut *confession.* (snmiyepmi̱ntsut (lit. making known one's own experience), n.); sye+n+miy=ep+mí+ncut *confessor.* (syenmiyepmi̱ntsut (lit. One who makes known his sins), n.); t+miy+p=úl'mxʷ+n *compass.* (tmiypu̱'lmkhwn (lit. means of getting to known land), n.); t+miy=ílmxʷ+n *cairn, landmark, milestone.* (tmiyi̱lmkhwn (lit. a mound of stones erected as a landmark or memorial), n.); [also recorded as √m?] s+t+mi?=s+m *attention (paying...).* (stmi'sm, n.); s+t+mi?=s+mn *concentration.* (stmi'smn, n.); ‡ hn+miy+cín-n *clarified.* (hnmiytsi̱nn (lit. I made plain his words or statements, I interpreted his words), vt.); hn+miy=cín+t-s *construe, decode, cite, interpret.* (hnmiytsi̱nts (lit. He translated his words, he quoted him as an authority or example), vt.); miy+p+nun-t-s *ascertain.* (miyppnunts (lit. he succeeded in learning it), vt.); t+miy=ípele?-nt-s *characterize, describe.* (tmiyi̱pele'nts (lit. He described the qualities of it), vt.); t+mí?=s+m-nt-s *concentrate.* (tmi̱'smnts (lit. He produced a clear image of it, H/s paid close attention to it), vi.); § lut+u·+míy *chancy, conditional.* (lutuumiy (lit. It is uncertain), adj.); lut u·míh *ambiguous (lit. It is not certain).* (lutuumi̱h, adj.); lut un+míy=elgʷes *capricious, fickle.*

(lut unmi̱yelgwes (lit. He has no definite thoughts), adj.); s+t+miy+iy=ípele?+s xʷe t+č'm=ásq'it twe tmíxʷ=ulmxʷ *cosmography.* (stmiyiyi̱pele's khwe tch'ma̱sq'it twe tmi̱khulmkhw, n.); s+t+miy+iy=ipele?+s xʷe s+t+c[']éx̌ʷ+ncut *astronomy.* (stmiyiyipele's khwe sttseqhwntsut, n.); s+t+miy+y=ípele?+s xʷe s+q'es+p=ilgʷe?+s *archeology, (lit. exposition of ancient property).* (stmiyyipele's khwe sq'espilgwe's, n.); s+t+miy+y=ipele?+s łe tmíxʷ=l'umxʷ *earth (description of...), description (...of earth).* (stmiyyipele's łe tmikhw'lumkhw, n.); s+t+miy+y=ipele?+s xʷe tmixʷ=l'umxʷ *description of earth, geology, geography.* (stmiyyipele's khwe tmikhw'lumkhw, n.); s+t+my+y=ípele?+s xʷe n+xʷel+xʷl+n *biology. (lit.exposition of the origin of what is the means of life).* (stmyyipele's khwe nkhwelkhwln, n.); s+qil=tč he s+t+miy+iy=ípele?+s *anatomy.* (sqiltch he stmiyiyipele's (lit. science of the body), n.) [xref √my₂,₃]

√my₅ † miy *dignified.* (miy (stem), adj.) [xref √mys]

√mył † miyéł *blatant, much (too...).* (miye̱ł (lit. he is too loud) (stem), adj.); § miyeł+lút *extravagant, unreasonable, degenerate, person of low morals.* (miyełlu̱t, adj., n.); miyeł+x̌ʷp+t *inept (he is too...).* (miyełqhupt, adj.); miyeł+pí?+pe?+t *extravagant, deluxe.* (miyełpi̱'pet (lit. he is too generous), adj.); miyeł+léč'+lč'+t *belligerent.* (miyełle̱ch'lch't (lit. he is too (very) aggressive), n.); s+miyeł+díł+m+šeš *concussion.* (smiyełdi̱łmshesh (lit. more than ordinary jarring), n.); miyeł+t+x̌as=ic'e? *bedizen.* (miyełtqhasits'e' (lit. he is dressed too

well), n.); s+myał+n+laqʷ=ús *bubble
gum, extra gum.* (smyałnlaqu̱s, n.);
miyał+y'aˤ'+p=qin' *congest, crowded.*
(miyał'ya'(pqi'n (lit. *there are too many
heads*), vt.); miyał+yaˤ+p=qin'
*congest, crowded (lit. there are too
many heads).* (miyałya(pqi'n, vt.);
miy+miyał+sya+t+c'ux̌ʷ=ipele?
*judge (competent and critical),
connoisseur.* (miymiyałsyatts
uqhwipele', n.)

√**mys** § s+miyes+čínt *aristocracy,
aristocrat, baron, dignitary, bigwig,
blue blood, noble descent, nobleman.*
(smiyeschi̱nt (lit. *more than ordinary
human beings*), n.); lut s+miyes+čínt
commoner. (lut smiyeschi̱nt (lit. *He is
not a nobleman*), n.); hn+miyes=
čín+n *dignity.* (hnmiyeschi̱nn (lit.
*means of becoming worthy or
honorable*), n.); miyes+čínt-m-st-m
elevate, dignify, ennoble.
(miyeschi̱ntmstm (lit. *h/s was made
noble*), vi.); s+m'+m'iy'es+čín't
bourgeois. (sm"mi'yeschi̱nt (lit. *little
nobleman*), n.); s+meyes+x̌em=enč=
es=čínt *devotion.*
(smeyesqhemencheschi̱nt (lit. *having a
more ardent love for a person*), n.);
s+myes+n+piy+iy=ílgʷes *trance (a
kind of...), ecstasy, joy (excessive...).*
(smyesnpiyyi̱lgwes (lit. *more than
ordinary thrilling of the heart*), n.);
miyes+pu?s+mín-n *comtemplate,
meditate, ponder.* (miyespu'smi̱nn (lit.
I considered it more than ordinary),
vt.); miyes+péw+n *drummed
(He...loudly).* (miyespe̱wn, vi.);
ac+miyás+n+qʷi? *cave, cavern.*
(atsmiya̱snqwi' (lit. *A hollow that is
larger than usual*), n.);
hi?c+miyes+k'ʷin'+m *collate.*
(hi'tsmiyesk'wi'nm (lit. *I am testing/
taking it very carefully*), vt..);
ic+miyes+qʷ+qʷá?+qʷa·l' *commune.*
(itsmiyesquqwa̱'qwaa'l (lit. *They are

conversing intimately*), vi.);
s+miyas+qʷ+qʷá?+qʷe?el *commune.*
(smiyasquqwa̱'qwe'el (lit. *speaking at
length*), n.); s+miyes+gʷél+p
conflagration. (smiyesgwe̱lp (lit.
extraordinary fire), n.);
s+myes+taq+aq+n=us+čínt *coup,
deception (extraordinary...).*
(smyestaqaqnuschi̱nt, n.) [xref √my₃,₅]
√**myw** † s+miyíw *coyote.* (smiyi̱w, n.)
√**my'** ∥ hn+máy'+ay'=qn *noon.*
(hnma̱'ya'yqn (lit. *time when sun is
directly overhead*), n.);
s+n+máy'+ay'=qn+m *lunch, dinner.*
(snma̱'ya'yqnm. *midday meal*, n.); a
n+máy'+ay'=qn+m *to dine, eat, eat at
noon.* (anma̱'ya'yqnm, v.);
č'in‿máy'+ay'=qn+mš *dining (we
are...).* (ch'inma̱'ya'yqnmsh, vi.);
čn'‿n+may'+ay'=qn+m *dine.* ((cust)
ch'nnma̱'ya'yqnm, vi.);
č'+s+n+máy'+ay'=qn+m *dine.*
(ch'snma̱'ya'yqnm, vi.);
čiy'+n+máy'+ay'=qn+mš *dining,
eating.* (chi'ynma̱'ya'yqnmsh (lit. *I am
dining*), vt, vi.); čn‿n+máy'+ay'=
qn+m *dine (I...).* (cust)
(chnnma̱'ya'yqnm, vt.);
čn‿n+may'+áy'=qn+m *dined.*
(chnnma̱'ya'yqnm. (lit. *I dined*), vi.);
t'i? čn‿n+máy'+ay'=qn+m *dined (I
have...).* (t'i'chnnma̱'ya'yqnm, vi.); t'ixʷ
eh is-n+máy'+ay'=qn+m *I had dined,
had taken the midday meal.*
(t'ikhwehisnma̱'ya'yqnm, v.);
čeł‿či‿s+n+máy'+ay'=qn+mš
*lunch, (lit. I will have my mid-day
meal).* (chełchisnma̱'ya'yqnmsh, vi.);
k'ʷne? čn‿máy'+ay'=qn+m *dine (I
am going to...).* (k'wne'chnma̱'ya'yqnm,
vi.); kʷ‿n'+máy'+ay'=qn+m *dine
(you (sg.)...).* (ku'nma̱'ya'yqnm, vi.);
kʷu‿y'‿n+máy'+ay'=qn+mš *You
(sg) are dining.* (ku'ynma̱'ya'yqnmsh,
vi.); t'ixʷ e? is+n+máy'+ay'=qn+m <
in-s *You (s) had dined.*

(t'i'khwe'isnma'ya'yqnm, v.); t'iʔ kʷ‿n+máy'+ay'=qn+m *dined (You (sg.) have...)*. (t'i'kunma'ya'yqnm, vi.); čeł‿kʷup‿may'+ay'=qn+mš *(lit. You (sg) will dine)*. (chełkupsnma'ya'yqnmsh, vt.); k'ʷ neʔ kʷu‿n+may'+ay'=qn+m *You (sg.) are going to dine*. (k'wne'kunma'ya'yqnm, vi.); hn+máy'+ay'=qn+mš *You dine! (imp.)*. (hnma'ya'yqnmsh, vi.); hn+máy'+ay'=qn+m *H/s dined*. (hnma'ya'yqnm, vi.); an+máy'+ay'=qn+m *dine, eat*. (anma'ya'yqnm. *H/s dines at noon*, v.); in+may'+áy'=qn+mš *is dining (H/s...)*. (inma'ya'yqnmsh (lit. having mid-day meal), vi.); t'iʔ n+máy'+ay'=qn+m *dined (H/s has...)*. (t'i'nma'ya'yqnm, vi.); t'ixʷ es+n+máy'+ay'=qn+m-s *H/s had dined*. (t'i'khwesnma'ya'yqnms, v.); čas‿n+máy'+ay'=qn+mš *(lit. h/s will dine)*. (chasnma'ya'yqnmsh, vt.); k'ʷ neʔ n+máy'+ay'=qn+m *H/s is going to dine*. (k'wne'nma'ya'yqnm, vi.); č‿ʔi+n+máy'+ay'=qn+mš *We are dining, having our midday meal*. (ch'inma'ya'yqnmsh, vi.); č‿ʔa+n+máy'+ay'=qn+m *we dine*. (ch'anma'ya'yqnm, vi.); č‿n+máy'+ay'=qn+m *we dined*. (chnma'ya'yqnm, vt.); t'ixʷ es+n+máy'+ay'=qn+met *We had dined*. (t'i'khwesnma'ya'yqnmet, v.); t'iʔ čn‿máy'+ay'=qn+m *dined (We have...)*. (t'i'chnma'ya'yqnm, vi.); čał+čs+n+máy'+ay'=qn+mš *dine*. (chałchsnma'ya'yqnmsh (lit. we will dine), vi.); k'ʷ neʔ čn‿máy'+ay'=qn+m *We are going to dine*. (k'wne'chnma'ya'yqnm, vi.); kʷup‿ʔa‿n+máy'+ay'=qn+m *You (pl.) dine (lit. have your midday meal)*. (kup'anma'ya'yqnm, vi.); kʷ‿n+máy'+ay'=qn+m *dined (you*

(pl, sg.)...). (kunma'ya'yqnm, vi.); kʷ-u[p]‿n+máy'+ay'=qn+m *You (pl) dined*. (kunma'ya'yqnm, vi.); kʷup‿ʔi‿n+máy'+ay'=qn+mš *You are dining, eating your midday meal*. (kup'inma'ya'yqnmsh, v.); t'ixʷ es+n+máy'+ay'=qn+m-p *You (pl) had dined*. (t'i'khwesnma'ya'yqnmp, v.); tiʔ+kʷup‿n+máy'+ay'=qn+m *You (pl) have dined*. (ti'kupnma'ya'yqnm, v.); čeł‿kʷup‿s+n+máy'+ay'=qn+mš *(lit. you (pl) will dine)*. (chełkupsnma'ya'yqnmsh, vt.); k'ʷ neʔ kʷup‿máy'+ay=qn+m *You (pl.) are going to dine*. (k'wne'kupnma'ya'yqnm, vi.); hn+máy'+ay'=qn+m+ul *You (plural) dine! (imp.)*. (hnma'ya'yqnmul, vi.); a n+máy'+ay'=qn+m-lš *They dine, eat*. (anma'ya'yqnmlsh, vi.); hn+máy'+ay'=qn+m-lš *They dined*. (hnma'ya'yqnmlsh, vi.); in+máy'+ay'=qn+m-lš *are dining (they...)*. (inma'ya'yqnmlsh (lit. having mid-day meal), vi.); t'iʔ n+máy'+ay'=qn+m-lš *dined (They have...)*. (t'i'nma'ya'yqnmlsh, vi.); t'ixʷ es+n+máy'+ay'=qn+m-s-lš *They had dined*. (t'i'khwesnma'ya'yqnmslsh, v.); čas‿n+máy'+ay'=qn+m-lš *(lit. they will dine)*. (chasnma'ya'yqnmlsh, vt.); k'ʷ neʔ n+máy'+ay'=qn+m-lš *They are going to dine*. (k'wne'nma'ya'yqnmlsh, vi.)

√mʕʷ † meʕʷ *broken, ruined*. (me(w (stem), adj.); meʕʷ+t *bankrupt, broke*. (me(wt (lit. He became bankrupt), adj.); ac+meʕ['ʷ] *to be broken*. (atsme(, vi.); s+meʕʷ+t *break (to...), breakage*. (sme(wt, vi, n.); čn‿meʕʷ+t *broke, impoverished*. (chnme(wt (lit. I am out of funds), adj.); čn‿méʔʕʷ+t *broke*. (chnme('wt (lit. I went broke, I am out of funds), adj.); can+méʕʷ+t *break, (lit. They had a break out)*. (tsanme(wt (lit. a break), vt.); twiʔ+meʕʷ+t *He became* *poor, went broke.* (twi' me(wt, vi.); meʕʷ+ʕʷ+t+m *breakable, (lit. capable of being broken).* (me(u(utm, n.); s+can+méʕʷ+meʕʷ+t *debris.* (stsanme(wme)wt lit. parts broken off from a whole), n.); ‡ méʔʕʷ-n *demolish, destroy, I destroyed it.* (me'(wn, vt.); § s+meʕʷ+l+s+c'áx̌ʷ+m *promise (a...broken), promise (breach of...).* (sme(wlsts'aqhum, n.); hi+s+nukʷ+meʕʷ+l+nt+c'ux̌ʷ= ípleʔ+n *complicity.* (hisnukwme(wlntts'uqhwiple'n (lit. He is my partner in violating the law), n.)

√mʔ₁ † miʔ *annoy, bore.* (mi' (stem), vt.); miʔ+meʔ+t *he is bothersome, nuisance.* (mi'me't, n.); meʔ+mí+ncut *cockney, brat.* (me'mintsut (lit. He acted like a brat. He acted like a woman). single women, n.); s+meʔ+m+scút *bridge, card playing, game.* (sme"mstsut (lit. annoying oneself), n.); ∥ hn+meʔ+eʔ=ílgʷes *chafe.* (hnme'e'ilgwes (lit. He became annoyed), vi.); hn+meʔ+meʔ=ílgʷes *choleric, peevish, cranky.* (hnme'me'ilgwes (lit. He is irritable, ill-tempered, easily annoyed), adj.); s+n+meʔ+meʔ=ílgʷes *bile, ill humor.* (snme'me'ilgwes. irritability, n.); s+meʔ=íčt+m *annoyance.* (sme'ichtm, n.); s+meʔe+mín=łc'eʔ *brush-off.* (sme'eminłts'e', n.); ‡ meʔ=íčt+m-nt-s *bedevil, bother, harass, to annoy.* (me'ichtmnts (lit. He bothered (annoyed) him), vt.); meʔ= íčt+m-nt-m *besieged, harassed.* (me'ichtmntm. inconvenienced, vi.); § č'n'+č'n'eʔ=cin'+m'eʔ+tn-se-s *decry.* (ch"nch"ne'tsi'n'me'tnses, vi.)

√mʔ₂ † meʔ+eʔ *send away.* (me'e' (stem), v.); ‡ meʔ+eʔ+mí-nt-m *averted, dismissed, banish, he was sent away.* (me'e'mintm, vt.); meʔ+eʔ+mí-nt-s *discharge.*

(me'e'mints (lit. He/she sent him/her away), vi.)

√mʔc † meʔc *grease.* (me'ts (stem), n.) [xref √mc']

√mʔč † meʔč *well-shaped (as work horse).* (me'ch (stem), v.)

√mʔm † s+mí+mʔeʔem *women.* (smi'me'em, n.); s+mʔ+meʔíʔm *woman (little...).* (sm'me'i'm, n.); meʔmí+ncut *to pout, brat, cockney (lit. He acted like a woman).* (me'mintsut, vt.); ∥ maʔ+maʔám= al'qs *nun, sister.* (ma'ma'ama'lqs (lit. one who wears religious women's garb), n.); hn+maʔ+maʔám=al'qs+n *cloister.* (hnma'ma'amal'qs (lit. a place for those who wear women's habits), n.); ul maʔ+máʔam=al'qs *conventual.* (ul ma'ma'ama'lqs (lit. belonging to nuns), adj.); s+méʔm= ulumxʷ *man's younger sister.* (sme'mulumkhw, n.); § s+t'+t'íkʷ+s+m'eʔeʔm *crone, beldam, old maid.* (st't'ik'us'me'e'm, n.); cétxʷ+s xʷa maʔ+maʔám=al'qs *convent.* (tsetkhws khwa ma'ma'ama'lqs (lit. their house those who wear women's clothes (nuns)), n.); ec+meʔm+l+cégʷ+t *effeminate.* (etsme'mltsegwt (lit. He is delicate or unmanly), adj) [xref √mʔym]

√mʔt † miʔt *centered, middle (in the...).* (mi't (stem), adj, n.); ∥ míʔt= ew'es *dichotomy.* (mi'te'wes (lit. division into two equal parts), n.); ni?+míʔt=ew'es *among, between.* (ni'mi'te'wes, prep.); ni?+míʔt=ewes *amid, axis, center, middle, midpoint.* (ni'mi'tewes, adv, n.); e+ni?+míʔt= ew'es *among, between, in the middle, central.* (eni'mi'te'wes (lit. H/s is...), prep, vi, adv.); tel' niʔ+miʔt=ew'es *centrifugal.* (te'l ni'mi'te'wes (lit. moving or directed from the center), adj.); ʔepł s+niʔ+miʔt=ew'es *concentric.* (epł sni'mi'te'wes (lit. It has a common center), adj.); [also written as my't] hn+mey't+e?w+ał+[x̌]élexʷ *bucktooth (lit. middle tooth).* (hnme'yte'wałkhelekhw, n.)

√m?ym † s+mí?yem *bride, wife, woman.* (smi'yem, n.); s+miy+es+mí?yem *dame.* (smiyesmi'yem (lit. a noble woman), n.); ul s+mí?yem *bisexual.* (ul smi'yem, adj.); § ul s+qil'+tmxʷ, ul s+mí?yem *bisexual.* (ul sqi'ltmkhw, ul smi'yem, adj.); ul s+mi?yem ha can+gʷán+t=al'qs *camisole.* (ul smi'yem ha tsangwanta'lqs (lit. belonging to woman an undergarment), n.); s+mi?yem he s+nukʷ+n=úłxʷ *co-ed.* (smi'yem he snukw'nułkhw (a woman fellow-student), n.); at+p'át'+t' he s+mi?yem *coquette, flirt.* (atp'at't' he smi'yem (lit. A woman who clings to men), n.); č's+eł+cégʷ+t he s+mi?yem *cotquean.* (ch'seltsegwt he smi'yem (lit. woman of bad manners), n.); uw'+em'n'=ús he s+mí?yem *worthless (a woman who is...), woman (a...who is worthless).* (u'we'm'nus he smi'yem, adj, n.); ye·+mí?yem *He won a wife.* (yeemi'yem, vt.); tí?xʷe s+mí?yem *succeeded (He...in getting a wife).* (ti'khwe smi'yem, vi.); s+mí?yem ha sya·+q'ʷey'+m+ncut *ballerina.* (smi'yem ha syaaq'we'ymntsut (lit. woman who dances), n.) [xref √m?m]

√m'c § s+m'u+m'úc=šn' ha n+qʷo+q[']ʷos+m'i *bitch.* (sm'u'mutssh'n hanqoqos'mi (lit. a female dog), n.)

√m'n ∥ s+m'e·+m'ín=ep *toad.* (s'mee'minep, n.); s+m'e·+m'ín'=ep *toad.* (s'mee'mi'nep, n.)

√m'n's † ne?+m'n'us *maybe so.* (ne"m'nus, adv.)

√m'qʷl' † s+m'aqʷl' *Moscow.* (S'maqw'l, n.)

√m'y' † m'ey'+m'iy'+m' *communicate, communicated, report, story (he told a...).* ('me'y'mi'y'm, vi, v.); s+m'éy'+m'iy' *chronology (lit. the relating or narrating of an event or series of events).* (s'me'y'mi'y, n.); s+m'éy'+miy'+m' *communication.* (s'me'ymi'y'm (lit. the exchange of thought, messages), n.); s+m'+m'éy'+m'iy' *anecdote.* (s'm'me'y'mi'y, n.); m'iy'+m'iy'+m'+úl' *communicative, communitive, talkative.* ('mi'y'mi'y'mu'l (lit. He is...), adj.); sye·+m'éy'+m'iy'+m' *courier.* (syee'me'y'mi'y'm (lit. One who brings messages), n.); ic+m'iy'+m'iy'-šít-ew'es *converse, talk.* (its'mi'y'mi'yshite'wes. (lit. They are telling one another stories)., vi.); s+m'iy'+miy'-šít-ew'eš *conversation.* (s'mi'ymi'yshite'wesh (lit. telling one another stories (information), n.); ‡ m'ey'+miy'-nt-m *delate, publicized, reported, it was made public.* ('me'ymi'yntm, vt.); m'ey'+m'iy'-nt-m *delate.* ('me'ymi'yntm, vt.); m'iy'+m'iy'-šit-s *informed (he...him).* ('mi'y'mi'yshits, v.); čs+m'áy'=qi-łt-s *inform, apprize.* (chs'ma'yqiłts (lit. He caused him to know it for certain), vt.) [xref √my₂,₃]

√m'? ∥ hn+m'á+m'a?+m=cn *Canada goose.* (hn'ma'ma'mtsn, n.)

√nc † noc *pliable, soft (as meat, rubber), tender.* (nots (stem), adj.); u n'+n'ó·c *weak-willed.* (u'n'nooots (lit. He is very soft, He yields easily to pressure), adj.); ∥ u+n+n'+n'óc=us *docile.* (un'n'notsus (lit. The pony is soft-necked, He is easily managed), adj.)

√nč † nič *drive away, goad.* (nich (stem), vt.); s+cen+níč+m *defense.* (stsennichm (lit. driving off from under), n.); ul+s+cen+níč+m *defensive.* (ulstsennichm (lit. belonging to defense), adj.); cen+neč+ncút+n *body guard*. (tsennechntsu̲tn (lit. means of protecting oneself), n.); ‡ níč-nt-s *drive away*. (ni̲chnts (lit. He drove them away, put them to flight), vt.); § s+p'ú?xʷ e· níč=elt *son (...of light)*. (sp'u̲'khw ee ni̲chelt, n.)

√nč' † nič' *cut (with a blade)*. (nich' (stem), vt.); s+níč'+m *carving*. (sni̲ch'm (lit. cuttings), n.); níč'+emn *burin, cutter*. (ni̲ch'emn. saw, crosscut, n.); níč'+nič'+emn *cutlery*. (ni̲ch'nich'emn (lit. cutting instruments), n.); e+n'+n'íč'+n'ič' *cutlet, slice (of meat)*. (e'n'ni̲ch"nich' (lit. Thin slices of meat), n.); ∥ s+nič'=ɫxʷ *son-in-law*. (snich'ɫkhw (lit. one who divides the family by taking a member away), n.); č+níč'=čs+n *chip*. (chni̲ch'chsn (lit. a small piece cut off by hand), n.); níč'=ew'es+n *crosscut*. (ni̲ch'e'wesn (lit. He crosscut it (log, etc.)), vt.); hiy-níč'=ew'es *board*. (hiyni̲ch'e'wes, n.); hiy·-nič'=ew'es *board, lumber, wood (cut)*. (hiyyni̲ch'e'wes. It is my..., n.); níč'=ul'umxʷ+n *disc*. (nich'u'lumkhwn (lit. means of cutting the ground), n.); s+níč'=ul'umxʷ *allotment*. (sni̲ch'u'lumkhw (lit. land that is cut (allotted) and apportioned to individuals; also disking), n.); s+ni?č'+č'=én'e? *atom*. (sni'ch'ch'e̲'ne' (lit. the very smallest entity (in ancient times), n.); ni?č'+č'ar'=ál'qʷ *Sanders, Idaho*. (Ni'ch'ch'a'ra̲'lqw (lit. a cut in the woods), n.); ‡ níč'-nt-s *He cut it*. (ni̲ch'nts, vt.); cen+níč'-nt-s *amputate*. (tsenni̲ch'nts (lit. He cut it off), vi.); níč'=ew'es-n *'I ...' crosscut (lit. He crosscut it (log, etc.))*. (ni̲ch'e'wesn, vt.); níč'=ew'es-t-m *divide*. (nich'e'westm (lit. It was cut into (two or more) parts), vt.); hn+níč'=ew'es-nt-m *bisect, cut (...in two)*. (hnni̲ch'e'wesntm (lit. It was

bisected), v.); hn+níč'=us-nt-m *decapitate*. (hnni̲ch'usntm (lit. His head was cut off), v.)

√nǰr † naǰaró· *rascal, scoundrel*. (najarooo!, n.)

√nkʷ † s+nukʷ(-) *fellow, together, with*. (snukw-. (comb form), n, pref.); s+núkʷ+n *atavism*. (snu̲kwn (lit. the inheritance of a characteristic), n.); s+č+nukʷ *solitude, tranquility*. (schnukw (stem). (lit. feeling alone in the heart), n.); § s+nukʷ+síxʷ+xʷ *blood-brother, concourse*. (snukwsi̲khukhw (lit. fellow in issue of blood/ a moving or flowing together), n.); s+nukʷ+síxʷ+sixʷ+xʷ *brethren, fellow-bloods*. (snukwsi̲khwsikhukhw, n.); s+nukʷ+méɫ+l+iš *bed-fellow*. (snukwme̲llish, n.); nukʷ+ɫ+ɫt'+č'=ús+mn-n *coincide [I tripped with him.]*. (nukwɫlt'ch'usmnn (lit. We tripped simultaneously), vi.); s+nukʷ+šén+n *colleague*. (snukwshe̲nn (lit. fellow worker), n.); s+nukʷ+s+šén+n *cooperation*. (snukwsshe̲nn (lit. working together), n.); hi?-nukʷ+šn+mín+m *collaborate*. (hi'nukwshnmi̲nm (lit. I am employing him as my collaborator), vi.); hi-s+nukʷ+?íɫn *commensal*. (hisnuk'i̲ɫn (lit. He is my companion at table), n.); hi-s+nukʷ+?a·c+?áx̌l *contemporaneous*. (hisnukw'aats'a̲qhl (lit. He is my like (equal)), adj.); s+nukʷ+?a·c+?áx̌l *counterpart, colleague*. (snukw'aats'a̲qhl (lit. fellow worker of one's kind), n.); s+nukʷ+ǰéy'+m+ncut *correspondent*. (snukwje̲'ymntsut (lit. fellow evildoer), n.); s+nukʷ+c'uqʷ'+c'uqʷún'+m' *classmate (lit. fellow reader)*. (snukwts'uq'wts'uqu̲'n'm, n.); s+nukʷ+t'ík'ʷ+t'ik'ʷ+t *commensurate, one of the same old age*. (snukwt'i̲k'wt'ik'ut. grandparents, adj.); s+nukʷ+k'ʷúl' *associate, colleague,*

fellow worker, partner. (snukwk'u̱'l,
n.); s+nuk^w+k'^wúl'+l' *spouse,
component, mate, consort.*
(snukwk'u̱'lu'l, n.); tč+ʔsél+k^w
s+nuk^w+k'^wúl'+l' *two spouses.*
(tch'se̱lkw snukk'u̱'lu'l, n.);
s+nuk^w+q^wíl+n *collude.* (snukwqwi̱ln
(lit. one who is deceiving in
conjunction with another), vi.);
s+nuk^w+mararím+em *wife, husband,
mate, spouse.* (snukwmarari̱mem, n.);
ul s+nuk^w+mararím+n *conjugal.* (ul
snukwmarari̱mn (lit. pertaining to a
spouse), adj.); s+nuk^w+q'éy'+m
coauthor. (snukwq'e̱'ym, n.);
s+nuk^w+lím+t *congratulation,
felicitation (lit. rejoicing with).*
(snukwli̱mt, n.); s+nuk^w+x^wy+m+n
convection. (snukwkhuymn (lit.
carrying with or together), n.);
s+nuk^w+yilmíx^w+m *condominium (lit.
fellow chiefs).* (snukwyilmi̱khum, n.);
hi-s+nuk^w+n+g^wáy'=qn *concrescence.*
(hisnukwngwa̱'yqn (lit. He is my
fellow in growing up), n.);
s+nuk^w+púl=ułc'eʔ *accomplice.*
(snukwpu̱lułts'e' (lit. helper in killing),
n.); s+nuk^w+mít'č'=edeʔ
consanguineous. (snukwmi̱t'ch'ede'
(lit. fellow by blood), adj.);
s+nuk^w+n+x^wc+x^wc'+m=íl's
compassion. (snukwnkhwtskhwts'mi̱'ls
(lit. fellow sufferer), n.);
s+nuk^w+t'áp'-nt-w'eš+m'n'm' x^we
s+ník'^w=elumx^w *civil war.*
(snukwt'a̱p'nt'wesh'm'n'm khwe
sni̱k'welumkhw, n.);
hi+s+nuk^w+meʕ^w+ł+nt+c'ux̌^w=
ípleʔ+n *complicity.*
(hisnukwme(włntts'uqhwi̱ple'n (lit. He
is my partner in violating the law), n.);
nuk^w+x^wúy+m-n-ts *abduct, kidnap.*
(nukwkhu̱ymnts. (lit. He took her
along with him), vt.);
nuk^w+šen+n+mí-nt-s-es *cooperate.*
(nukwshennmi̱ntses (lit. She worked

with me), vi.); nuk^w+lím+t+m-n-n
congratulate. (nukwli̱mtmnn (lit. I
rejoiced with, or expressed
sympathetic pleasure to, him), vt.);
nuk^w+íʔcč+n+m-nt-s *played
(H/s...with h/h).* (nukwi̱'tschnmnts,
vi.); nuk^w+ʕíp=cn+m-nt-s *confide.*
(nukw(iptsnmnts (lit. He put a secret
into his trust). gossip, vi.);
s+nuk^w+q'ey'-šít-ew'eš
correspondent. (snukwq'e'yshi̱te'wesh
(lit. One with whom one corresponds),
n.); s+nuk^w+g^wáx̌+t=elt *one of the
same young age.* (snukwgwa̱qhtelt, n.);
s+nuk^w+s+k^wís+t *a name two persons
have in common.* (snukwskwi̱st, n.);
[xref √nk'^w]

√nk'^w † nek'^w *one, unit.* (nek'w (stem),
n.); nik'^w *tribe (of the same...),
tribesman.* (nik'w (stem), n.); nék'^weʔ
one, dollar. (ne̱k'we' (colloq.), n.); u·
nék'^weʔ *ace, quantity (a small...),
small (a...quantity).* (uune̱k'we' (lit.
only one), n, adj.); g^wł nék'^weʔ *apiece,
They are one or united.* (guł ne̱k'we'
(lit. one to each one), adv.); uł nek'^weʔ
another. (uł nek'we' (lit. and one), n.);
cenʔ+n'ék'^weʔ-s *dividend.*
(tsen"ne̱k'we's (lit. It is his/her little
sack or bag; it is his/her share), n.);
nék'^w+k'^w+em' *conciliate, They
became one.* (ne̱k'uk'we'm (lit. They
brought together. They united), vt.);
s+nek'^w+k'^w+ém' *combination,
consonance.* (snek'uk'we̱'m (lit.
becoming one), n.); s+nék'^w+k'^w+em'
*coalition, confederacy, corporation,
union.* (snek'uk'we'm (lit. becoming
one), n.); č+nék'^weʔ *person (it is
one...).* (chne̱k'we', n.); uł+č+nek'^weʔ
another. (ułchnek'we', adj.);
u+č+nék'^weʔ *one (we are...), person
(only one...).* (uchne̱k'we', n.);
s+č+nuk'^w *peace.* (schnuk'w (lit.
feeling alone in the heart), n.); u
č+nuk'^weʔ+mncút *desolate (lit. H/S is

alone, by himself). (uchnuk'we'm̲i̲ntsut,
vt.); uʔu+č+nuk'ʷeʔ+mí+ncut
desolate. (u'uchnuk'we'm̲i̲ntsut (lit.
H/S is alone, by himself), adj.); ∥
č+nékʷ'eʔ=us *cyclops.* (chn̲e̲k'we'us
(lit. one with one eye), n.); nékʷ'eʔ=cn
comment. (n̲e̲k'we'tsn (lit. a statement
of opinion), n.); nukʷ'eʔ=cín+m
*comment, remark, state, he made a
statement.* (nuk'we'tsinm, vi.); e
nukʷ'eʔ=cín+n *utter.* (enuk'we'tsinn
(lit. He speaks a word. He utters a brief
exclamation), v.); e+nukʷ'eʔ=cín+m
ejaculate. (enuk'we'tsinm (lit. He
speaks a word. He utters a brief
exclamation), v.); cen+nékʷ'eʔ=gʷl
carload. (tsenn̲e̲k'we'gul (lit. One load
on a car or wagon), n.); hn+nákʷ'=qn
monotone. (hnn̲a̲k'wqn (lit. one
howling sound), n.); u n+nákʷ'aʔ=qn
unanimous (They were....).
(unn̲a̲k'wa'qn (lit. They spoke with one
voice), adj.); hn+nukʷ'eʔ=íłc'eʔ
compartment, room, chamber.
(hnnuk'we'i̲łts'e', n.);
hn+nukʷ'+nukʷ'eʔ=íłc'eʔ *apartment,
suite.* (hnnuk'wnuk'we'i̲łts'e', n.);
nokʷ'óʔ=qin *one hundred.* (nok'o̲'qin
(lit. one head), n.); nukʷ'eʔ=ílmxʷ
people, tribe, community.
(nuk'we'i̲lmkhw, n.); ul nukʷ'eʔ=ílmxʷ
communal. (ul nuk'we'i̲lmkhw (lit.
belonging to a tribe or nation), adj.);
nékʷ'eʔ-lš *corps.* (n̲e̲k'we'lsh (lit. They
(persons) are under common direction,
they are one), n.); s+níkʷ'=elumxʷ
cognate, compatriot, tribesman.
(sni̲k'welumkhw (lit. a fellow
countryman), n.); § nukʷ'+ł+túm'
bevy, covey, brood, group, class.
(nuk'włtu̲'m, n.); ʔupen ul nékʷ'eʔ
eleven. (upen ul n̲e̲k'we' (lit. ten plus
one), n.); nokʷ'+oʔ=qín ha
s+máx̌ʷ+x̌ʷ+s *centennial.* (nok'o̲'qi̲n
ha sma̲qhuqhws (lit. one hundred
snowings), n.); nokʷ'+oʔ=qin+s+pín=

tč *centenarian.* (nok'o'qinspintch (lit. a
person of one hundred years), n.);
nukʷ'+s+pín=tč *one year.*
(nuk'wspintch, n.); s+nukʷ'+s+pín=tč
New Years. (Snuk'wspintch, n.);
sye+nukʷ'+s+pín=tč *anniversary.*
(syenuk'wspintch (lit. acquiring
another year), n.); ul s+nukʷ' s+pín=
tč *annual.* (ul snuk'w spintch, adj.) ;
nukʷ'+ł+p'n+mín+n *wood (one rick
of...).* (nuk'włp'nmi̲nn (lit. one means
of piling long objects), n.);
nukʷ'+ł+l'+l'pót *cupful.* (nuk'włl'l'po̲t
(lit. just one cup (of content)), n.);
nukʷ'+s+šél·č+m *cycle.*
(nuk'wsshe̲llchm (lit. one round), n.);
nukʷ'+ł+cétxʷ *caste.* (nuk'włtse̲tkhw
(lit. one house), n.); nukʷ'+ł+tum' ha
sóltes *battalion.* (nuk'włtu'm ha so̲ltes
(lit. a unit of soldiers), n.);
nukʷ'+ł+č+tel'q+mín+n *degree, rung.*
(nuk'włchte'lqmi̲nn. (lit. one bar of a
ladder), n.); u· nékʷ'eʔ-lš *one (they
are...).* (uun̲e̲k'we'lsh, adj.);
ʔax̌al+ł+č+nékʷ'+eʔ *every, each.*
(aqhełchn̲e̲kwe' (lit. every person of a
number), adj.); x̌al nekʷ'eʔ *another.*
(qhal nek'we' (lit. also one), n.);
ʔax̌el+ł+č+nékʷeʔ *each.*
(aqhełchn̲e̲kwe' (lit. every person of a
number), adj.); ʔax̌el+ł+č+nkʷeʔ
each. (aqhełchn̲e̲kwe' (lit. every
person of a number), adj.);
s+nukʷ'+s+kʷís+t *alias, one (another)
name.* (snuk'wskwi̲st, n.); s+miʔyem
he s+nukʷ'+n=úłxʷ *co-ed.* (smi'yem
he snukw'nu̲łkhw (a woman fellow--
student), n.); s+nukʷ'+c+wiš *co-exist,
fellow, inmate, roommate.*
(snuk'wtswish. in a house, n.);
nukʷ'+e+ʔełi+c+púʔs-lš *concordant.*
(nuk'we'ełitspu̲'slsh (lit. They are of
one heart), adj.);
s+nukʷ'+e+ʔłiy+c+púʔ[s]
concordance. ((lit. having one heart),
n, (snuk'we'łiytspu̲'.); tč+ʔséł

s+nuk'ʷ+k'ʷl'+l' *bigamy*. (tch'sel̲
snukk'u̲'lu'l, n.); hn+nák'ʷa?=alqs ha
s+gʷárp+m *daffodil*. (hnn̲ak'wa'alqs
ha sgwa̲rpm, n.); x̌al+hn+nak'ʷá?=
al·'qs ha s+gʷárp+m *daisy*.
(qhalhnnak'wa̲'al'lqs ha sgwarpm, n.)
[xref √nk̲ʷ]

√nɫmq † h+nɫámqe? *bear, bruin.*
(hnl̲amqe', n.); ya+nɫámqe? *bear (He
killed the...), He succeeded in his bear
hunt, He got a bear.* (yanl̲amqe', n,
vt.); ya+nɫámqe?+m *He killed the
bear.* (yanl̲amqe'm, v.); č'iy+nɫámqe?
cub. ch'iynl̲amqe' (lit. offspring of a
bear, n.); § x̌es=íɫce? x̌ʷa+nɫamqe?
bear meat (...is good). (qhesiɫtse'
khwanl̲amqe' (lit. It is good meat that
which is bear), n.)

√np † nep+t *enter, they went in.* (nept
(stem). several.., vt.)

√nq † naq *satiated (with food).* (naq
(stem), adj.)

√nq',₁ † naq' *rotten (organic matter).*
(naq' (stem), adj.); na?q' *became.*
(na'q' (lit. It became putrid, it rotted, it
decomposed), vi.); naq'+t *corrupt,
decayed, putrid.* (naq't, adj, vi.);
s+na?q' *carrion, corruption,
putrefaction.* (sna'q' (lit.
decomposition, dead and decaying
fish/flesh), n.); ∥ s+nq'+s=ól'umx̌ʷ
chresard. (snq'so̲'lumkhw (lit. wet
ground), n.)

√nq'₂ † neq' *sticky.* (neq' (stem), adj.);

√nq'ʷ † naq'ʷ *steal.* (naq'w (stem), vt.);
s+naq'ʷ *abduction, adultery, boodle,
kidnapping, stealing.* (snaq'w, n.);
čn‿náq'ʷ *steal, stole
(I...(something)).* (chnn̲aq'w, vt.); ‡
náq'ʷ-nt-s *stole.* (n̲aq'wnts (lit. He
stole it, He stole from him), vt.)

√nr † ner *paint.* (ner (stem), vt.);
s+nér+m *coloration, coloring.* (sn̲erm
(lit. painting), n.)

√nrs † nors *Fr orge barley.* (nors, n.)

√nr'y † nár'ye *great-great grandparent.*
(na̲'rye, n.)

√ns † nas *wet.* (nas (stem), adj.); na?s
wet. (na's (lit. It got wet), adj.); a· nás
watered, wet. (aan̲as (lit. It is in a wet
state), adj.); u· nás *wet (it's...).* (uun̲as,
adj.); ∥ s+na?s=ál'umx̌ʷ *chresard (lit.
wet ground).* (sna'sa̲'lumkhw, n.);

√nsx̌? † nasx̌á?+x̌ *father-in-law.*
(nasqha̲'qh, n.)

√nš † anš *angel, cherub.* (ansh (l.w.
from French), n.)

√nwl † h+nwél *Christmas, Noel.*
(Hnwel, n.)

√nw' † e·+niw'+t *the wind blows.*
(eeni'wt, vi.); i· níw'+t *wind (The...is
blowing), blowing (The wind is...).*
(iini̲'wt, n, vt.); i+n'+n'íw'+t *breeze,
breezy.* (i'n'ni̲'wt. (lit. The little wind is
blowing), n, adj.); s+niw'+t *wind.*
(sni'wt, n.); s+n'+n'íw'+t *breeze,
zephyr.* (s'n'ni̲'wt, n.); ?epɫ
s+n'+n'iw'+t *to be breezy.* (epɫ
s'n'ni'wt, v. (lit. There is a small wind),
adj.); § čn‿t+c'uk̲ʷen+ɫ+niw' *(lit. I
ran by the side of, i.e., moving car).*
(chntts'ukwenɫni̲'w, vt.)

√nx̌ʷ † nux̌ʷ *swim (ref to a frog).*
(nukhw (stem), vi.)

√nys † enyés *Agnes.* (Eny̲es (l.w. from
English), n.)

√nʕʷ ∥ s+n'éʕʷ=qn *command.*
(s'ne̲(wqn (lit. giving orders (to), n.);
sya+néʕʷ=qn *commander.*
(syane̲(wqn (lit. One who commands),
n.); ‡ n'éʕʷ=qn-t-s *command, order.*
('ne̲(wqnts. (lit. He gave orders to
him), vt.)

√n?₁ † ne? *maybe, perhaps.* (ne',)

√n?₂ † ni? *among, in the midst of.* (ni',)

√n?₃ † nú+ne? *mother.* (nu̲ne', n.);
hi·+nú+ne? *mother.* (hiinu̲ne' (lit. She
is my mother), n.)

√n'y' † n'+n'óy'e? *weak.* ('n'no̲'ye' (lit.
He is weak) (dim. stem), adj.);

s+n'+n'óy'+e‷ *muscular weakness.* (s'n'no͟'ye', n.)

√pc † s+poc+t *blain.* (spotst (lit. a skin sore), n.); ∥ s+t+poc=cn *cold sore.* (stpotstsn, n.)

√pcčl † pécčele *blade, broccoli, brussels sprout, leaf, cabbage.* (pe͟tschele, n.); pecčle *cabbage, leaf.* (petschle, n.); § hoy ɫe pecčl-es *defoliate.* (hoyɫe petschles (lit. Its leaves were no more), vi.)

√pcxʷ † picxʷ *disappointed, disgusted.* (pitskhw (stem), vt.); pícxʷ+t *disgust.* (pi͟tskhwt (lit. He became very disappointed), n.); píc+pecxʷ+t *disappointing (h/s/i is very...).* (pi͟tspetskhwt, v.); s+picxʷ+t *disappointment, becoming disgusted, disgust.* (spitskhwt, n.); čn⁔pícxʷ+t *disappoint, disappointed.* (chnpi͟tskhwt (lit. I was defeated of hope or expectation; I was disgusted), adv, vt.); t'i‷+pícxʷ+t *disgusted, disappointed (H/s has become...).* (t'i'pi͟tskhwt, adj.); ‡ pícxʷ+t+m-n-n *disappointed (I became...at h/h/i).* (pi͟tskhwtmnn, v.)

√pc‷ † pice‷ *root digger.* (pitse', n.); § kʷen+ɫ+píce‷ *She took a root digger.* (kwenɫpi͟tse', v.)

√pčl' ∥ pácal'=qn *bald eagle.* (pacha'lqn, n.); pacǎl'=qn *bald eagle.* (pacha͟'lqn, n.)

√pčɫ † s+picɫ+ená *birch.* (spichɫena͟, n.)

√pčs ∥ pícǎ(=)us *peaches, peach-face.* (pi͟chus, n.); s+pécǒs=alqʷ *peach tree.* (spe͟chosalqw, n.); s+pécǎs=alqʷ *peach tree.* (spe͟chasalqw, n.)

√pgʷ † pigʷ *breathe, whole.* (pigw (stem). swell, vi.); pigʷ+t *bulge, swelled.* (pigwt (lit. It swelled up or bulge͟d), vi.); s+pigʷ+t *inflate, swell.* (spigwt, vi.); s+n+pígʷ+n' *balloon, blimp.* (snpi͟gw'n (that which is blown inside), n.); s+pígʷ+ncut *breathe, breathing, inhale, inhaling.*

(spigwntsut (lit. swell oneself up), vi.); pígʷ+pegʷ+ncut *breathe.* (pigwpegwntsut (lit. He expanded himself repeatedly), vi.); s+pígʷ+pégʷ+ncut *breath, exhalation.* (spigwpegwntsut (lit. swelling oneself over and over), n.); hn+pígʷ+pegʷe+ncut+n *air, atmosphere, breathing.* (hnpigwpegwentsutn, n.); ec+pígʷ+pegʷ+ncut *H/s breathes while we are looking at him (ref. to person who might have been dead).* (etspigwpegwntsut, vi.); ∥ págʷ=ax̌n *arm (H/h...swelled up), swelled (H/h arm...up).* (pa͟gwaqhn, n, vt.); págʷ+pagʷ=ax̌n *arms (H/h...swelled up).* (pa͟gwpagwaqhn, pl.n.); s+can+págʷ=ax̌n *bubo.* (stsanpagwaqhn (lit. swollen (gland) in the armpit), n.); cen+pígʷ=cn *neck (H/h...swelled up), swelled (H/h neck...up).* (tsenpigwtsn, n, vi.); t+pígʷ=cn *swelled (H/h mouth or lips...up).* (tpigwtsn, vi.); cen+pígʷ=us *cheek (H/h...swelled up), swelled (H/h cheek...up).* (tsenpigus, n, vi.); cen+pígʷ+peg=us *cheeks (H/h...swelled up), swelled (H/h cheeks...up).* (tsenpigwpegus, n, vi.); hn+pígʷ=ul'umxʷ+n *baking powder.* (hnpigu'lumkhwn (lit. means of swelling something (ie. bread) in the ground), n.); ni‷+págʷ=e‷qs *swelled (H/s nose...up).* (ni'pagwe'qs, vi.); ni‷+págʷ=iqs *nose (H/h...swelled up).* (ni'pagwiqs, n.); pígʷ+pegʷ=šn *swelled.* (pigwpegwshn. His feet swelled up, vi.); s+t+pígʷ=gʷl *bloating.* (stpigwgul. swelling of the stomach, n.); § s+pígʷ+l'č' *belt, cincture.* (spigw'lch', n.)

√ph † pih *float, separate (as cream).* (pih (stem), vi.); cǒet+píh+ih *(lit. it rose to the surface and spread out like cream).* (chetpi͟hih, vt.); s+cǒet+píh+ih cream. (schetpi̠hih (lit. substance that gathers and spreads on the surface of milk), n.)

√pkʷ₁ † pékʷ+t buff, cuticle, -derm, hide, leather, skin. (pe̠kut, suf, n.); peʔkʷ+t hide, leather, pelt. (pe'kut, n.); ul+pékʷ+t dermal. (ulpe̠kut (lit. pertaining to or consisting of skin), adj.)

√pkʷ₂ † pekʷ lay (round objects). (pekw (stem), vt.); s+pekʷ crumbs. (spekw, n.); s+pekʷ+kʷ crumb, fragments (spherical). (spekukw, n.); pékʷ+kʷ+m breakdown, he collapsed from illness or exhaustion. (pe̠kukum, n.); e t+pékʷ+pukʷ They, e.g. apples, are on the tree(s) here and there. (etpe̠kwpukw, vi.); ec+pékʷ+m apart, crumbly. (etspe̠kum, vi. (lit. It is put apart), adv.); // s+pukʷ+kʷ=íln young good-for-nothing, descendants who do not amount to anything. (spukukwi̠ln, n.); pukʷ=ílt+m It (mammal) produced a litter. (pukwi̠ltm, vt.); s+pukʷ= úl'umxʷ seeding. (spuku'lumkhw, vt.); pukʷ=úl'umxʷ+n seeder. (puku̠'lumkhwn (lit. means of putting many round objects (plants, seeds) in the ground), n.); ic+pukʷ=úl'umxʷ seeding (he is...). (itspuku̠'lumkhw, vi.); ‡ hn+pékʷ-nt-s bin, crate, sack. (hnpe̠kwnts (lit. He put round objects in it), n.); § gʷl' t+pékʷ=gʷl xref gʷł people with bulging stomachs. (gu'l tpe̠kwgul, n.); [low vowel unexplained] ac+pákʷ+m apart. (atspa̠kum, vi. (lit. It is put apart; scattered), adj.)

√pkʷ₃ † s+píkʷ+pekʷ+m'+n'cut dog-trot. (spi̠kwpekw'm'ntsut (lit. causing oneself to make a slow run like that of a dog), n.)

√pl † pól+pol=qn thimbleberry. (po̠lpolqn, n.)

√pl(t) † púlut harm, injure. (pu̠lut (stem), vt.); // pólot=qn father of Paul

Polatkin. (Po̠lotqn, (lit. killing head), n.); ec+púl=ułc'eʔ kill, killer, murderer. (etspu̠lułts'e', vt. (lit. He kills people), n.); s+pul=úłceʔ murdering. (spulu̠łtse', vt.); pul+pul= ełc'eʔ+ul blood-thirsty. (pulpulełts'e'ul (lit. He is habitually murdering), adj.); pul+pul=ełceʔ+úl kills (he habitually...people), blood thirsty, murderer, people (he habitually kills...). (pulpulełtse'ul, vt, n.); púl= ułc'eʔ assassinate (to...). (pu̠lults'e' (lit. He killed (somebody), vi.); s+púl= elt abortion. (spu̠lelt (lit. killing baby (foetus) life beginning at conception), n.); ‡ púlu-s-n killed (I...him). (pu̠lusn, vt.); púlu-stu-s h/s beat h/h up, killed (h/s...h/h). (pu̠lustus, v.); púlu-st-mel-em beaten (I was...up). (pu̠lustmelem (lit. I was killed), vt.); § pul+uł+s+te·m=ilgʷes relative (he killed his...), killed (he...his relative). (pulułsteemilgwes, n, vt.); s+nukʷ+púl=ułc'eʔ accomplice. (snukwpulułts'e' (lit. helper in killing), n.); pul+uł+šemen' enemy (he killed his...), killed (he...his enemy). (pulułsheme'n, n, vt.); pulut+l'+s+čí+čeʔ He slaughtered livestock. (pulut'lschi̠che', vt.)

√płč § káltes pa·łáč bonus (Chinook jargon). (ka̠ltes paała̠ch, n.) [also written as √šlts] šáltes pa·lač bonus (Chinook jargon). (sha̠ltes paalach, n.)

√plm // s+pálm=alqs highest mountain between Plummer and Worley, Idaho. (Spa̠lmalqs, n.);

√plm' // s+plím'=cn lips. (spli̠'mtsn, n.)

√plms † plams plums. (plams, n.); // pláms=alq[ʷ] plum tree, prunes. (pla̠msalq, n.)

√ply₁ † s+pílye coyote (Spokane). (spi̠lye, n.)

√ply₂ † pul'ye mole, gopher. (pu'lye, n.); pul'ya·+hál' witch, coyote's wife.

(pu'lyaaha'l. mole, n.); pulya·+hál'
mole. (pulyaaha'l, n.)

√pl'₁ // s+pál'=aqł *yesterday.* (aspa'laqł,
adv.) [see also √pn]

√pl'₂ † u p+pl' *whisky.* (upp'l (lit. little
flat thing (refers to bottle)), n.)

√pł₁ † peł *thick-layered.* (peł (stem),
adj.); péł+ł+t *thick (It (shingle, board)
is...).* (pełłt, adj.); s+péł+ł+t *density,
thickness.* (spełłt, n.); // páł+ł=al'qs
clothes (H/s has thick...). (pałła'lqs,
pl.n.); t+péł+ł=cn *lips (H/s has
thick...).* (tpełłtsn, n.); t+péł+ł=elxʷ
hide (It (animal) has thick...).
(tpełłelkhw, n.); h+péł+pł=enč *It
(house) has thick walls.* (hpełpłench,
n.)

√pł₂ † pił *scattered, strewn.* (pił (stem),
vt, vi.); ec+píł+m *it is scattered,
scattered (to be...).* (etspiłm, vi.);
s+píł+m+šeš *diffusion.* (spiłmshesh
(lit. spreading), n.); // s+píł=elgʷes
*belongings (scattering one's...),
scattering (...one's belongings).*
(spiłelgwes, n, v.) [see also √pt]

√pł₃ † puł *foam.* (puł (stem), n.); pu·ł *It
went splash!* (puuuł, excl.);
is+puł+puł+iš *splashing (He made the
noise of...).* (ispułpułish, n.); //
čet+pu?ł=ítkʷe? *rough (water).*
(chetpu'łitkwe' (lit. the surface of the
water was in turmoil, as near a falls),
vi.)

√płn † pułn *Portland.* (Pułn, n.)

√pm₁ † pam *bang.* (pam, vt.);
is+pám+pam+iš *boom.* (ispampamish
(lit. He is making many deep resonant
sounds), vi.)

√pm₂ † s+pum *fur.* (spum, n.); //
s+pom=al'qs *coat (fur...).* (spoma'lqs,
n.)

√pn // pin=tč *always.* (pintch, adv.);
s+pin=tč *chron-, relating to time,
year.* (-spintch, suf.); pen=t=íče?
*astronomical, colossal, inconceivably
large, great distance (lit. extending to
no one knows where).* (pentiche', adj.);
§ pin+č'e? *when?.* (pinch'e'?, qu.);
sye+nukʷ+s+pín=tč *anniversary.*
(syenuk'wspintch (lit. acquiring
another year), n.); ul s+nuk'ʷ s+pín=
tč *annual.* (ul snuk'w spintch, adj.);
pst+e?e+s+pín=tč *semiannual.*
(pste'espintch, n.); pínč c'ar+t *remains
(It...cold or chilly).* (pinch ts'art, vi.);
pinč+cégʷ+t *customary, usual.*
(pinchtsegwt, adj.); pin'č'+ne?
kʷ‿č'ic+xʷúy *When are you coming
over?.* (pi'nch'ne' kuch'itskhuy, qu.);
nok'ʷ+o?=qin+s+pín=tč *centenarian.*
(nok'o'qinspintch (lit. a person of one
hundred years), n.); nuk'ʷ+s+pín=tč
one year. (nuk'wspintch, n.);
s+nuk'ʷ+s+pín=tč *New Years (lit.
reaching another year).*
(Snuk'wspintch, n.); ?áx̌al+s+pin=tč
yearly. (aqhalspintch (lit. every year),
adv.); ?ax̌el+ł ?ese+s+pin=tč
biennial, biyearly. (aqhełł esespintch
(lit. happening every two years), adv.);
?upen+čs+pín=tč *decade.*
(upenchspintch (lit. ten consecutive
years), n.); ul+n+púte?+n he s+pin=
tč+s *anno-Domini.* (ulnpute'n he
spintchs (lit. belonging to the Lord's
year), adv.);
k'ʷu‿s+k'ʷin+š+es+pín=tč *How old
are you?* (k'usk'winshespintch?, vi.)
[see also √pl'₁]

√pn? † s+póne? *disadvantage.* (spone'
(lit. state of being taken advantage of),
n.); sya·+pón'e? *bully.* (syaapo'ne' (lit.
One who takes advantage of weaker
people), n.); ‡ pon'é?+m'-nt'-m
browbeat. (po'ne'm'nt'm (lit. He was
bullied), vi.); pon'é?+m'-n't-se-s
advantage (to take...of). (po'ne'm'ntses
(lit. He took advantage of me (my
inability), vi.); §
ac+pon'e?+mi+s+čént *opportunist.*
(atspo'ne"mischent (lit. One who takes
advantage of others), n.)

√pn'₁ † pen' *bent, bend.* (pe'n (stem), adj, vt.); pen'+m *bend.* (pe'nm, v.); s+pén'+n' *angle, bend, crease, curve.* (spe'n'n. (lit. place where bend is made), n.); ec+pén'+pn' *crooked.* (etspe'np'n, vi. (lit. It has bends or curves), adj.); ‖ hn+pén'+n'=us *H/h head became bent.* (hnpe'n'nus, vi.); ‡ pén'-n *bent (I...it).* (pe'nn, vt.); pén'-nt-s *bow, arched, deflect, bent (He...it), piled (H/s...the long objects).* (pe'nnts, n, vi, vt.); § kʷan+ł+pn'+pn'=aqs *par flesche.* (kwanłp'np'naqs (h/s took along a case of dried hide bent up), n.)

√pn'₂ ‖ pén'=enč *liver.* (pe'nench, n.)

√pq † peq *white, bleached, silver.* (peq (stem), adj.); paq *Easter.* (paq, n.); u· péq *blank, white (it is...).* (uupeq, adj.); s+paq+t *gray hair.* (spaqt, n.); či+n+pá?q *sunrise, dawn.* (chinpa'q (lit. it became white from the east), vi.); s+č+n+pá?q *cockcrow, dawn, daybreak.* (schnpa'q, n.); ‖ t+péq=ce? *Caucasian, man (white...).* (tpeqtse', n.); pa+pq=łc'e? *Ermine (white).* (papqłts'e', n.); pe+pá+pq=łce? *little ermine.* (pepapqłtse', n.); s+poq=(q)ín=mš *Spokane Tribe.* (Spoqinmsh, n.); t+p+péq=qn *hair (He has white...or head).* (tppeqq'n, n.); ut+péq=qn *blonde (He is platinum...).* (utpeqqn, n.); péq=a[s]gʷel *halibut.* (peqsagwel, n.); § u· péq he čis *cottage cheese.* (uupeq he chis (lit. white cheese), n.); elu+s+pá?q *unbleachable.* (eluspa'q (lit. It does not whiten e.g. by exposure to the sun), vi.); ul paq ha ?úse? *egg (Easter...).* (ul Paq ha use' (lit. an egg that belongs to Easter (Pasch), n.) [see also √p'q and √p'k]

√pqʷ † puqʷ+ilš *spy.* (puqwilsh (stem), vi.); s+puqʷ+ílš+n *scouting.* (spuqwilshn, n.); ul+s+puqʷ+ílš+n *pertaining to scouting.* (ulspuqwilshn, n.); sye+puqʷ+ílš *scout dance, scout, spy.* (syepuqwilsh, n.); sya+puqʷ+ílš+m *scout.* (syapuqwilshm (lit. means of scouting), n.); § i[c]+tkʷal't+s+puqʷ+ilš+mš *H/s is going around scouting.* (itkwa'ltspuqwilshmsh, vi.)

√pr † par *to be white (with powder).* (par (stem), adj.); u· pár *fade, pale (it is...).* (uupar, adj.); ‖ pár=us *albino, pale, pallid (lit. person with very pale face).* (parus, n.)

√pr'kʷ † per'kw *nail.* (pe'rkw (stem), vt.); ‖ pér'kʷ=ełxʷ+n *brad, nail.* (pe'rkwełkhwn (lit. means of piercing house), n.); ‡ pár'kʷ-nt-s *pierced (He...it).* (pa'rkwnts, vt.); t+pér'kʷ-nt-s *nailed (He...it on something).* (tpe'rkwnts, vt.); t+pér'kʷ-n *annex.* (tpe'rkwn (lit. I nailed it to something else), vt.) [xref √pr'qʷ]

√pr'qʷ ‡ t+pár'qʷ-nt-s *clinch.* (tpa'rqwnts (lit. He fastened it securely with a nail), vt.); § mal'+t+pér'+per'qʷ=alqʷ-nt-m *crucified (to be...), crucify.* (ma'ltpe'rpe'rqwalqwntm (lit. He was put to death by being nailed to crossed poles), vi, vt.); s+mal'+t+pér'+per'qʷ=alqʷ *crucifixion.* (sma'ltpe'rpe'rqwalqw, n.) [xref √pr'kʷ]

√prsn † parsón *person, one person of the Blessed Trinity.* (parson, n.); § t+čí?łes parsón *Blessed Trinity.* (Tchi'łes Parson (lit. three persons), n.)

√ps₁ † pas *amazed, astonished, bewildered.* (pas (stem), adj.); pas+p *amazed, awe-stricken, surprised (He was...).* (pasp, vi.); s+pas+p *astonishment, awe.* (spasp, n.); pás+ps+t *It is appalling, astonishing, awesome, awful, blood-curdling, breathtaking, dire, frightening.* (paspst, adj.); ps+ps+té *breathtaking.* (pspste

√ps

(lit. It inspired awe), vi.);
hn-i?‿c+ps+p+nón+m *frighten.*
(hi'tspspnonm (lit. I am frightening
him/her), vt.); ‡ ps+p-nón-t-s
astonish. (pspnonts (lit. He filled him
with sudden wonder), vt.)

√ps₂ † pa?s *surface.* (pa's (stem). to
come to the surface of the water
(person or animal), vi.); po?s
effervesce. (po's (lit. It bubbled up),
vi.); pu?s *bubble, ferment.* (pu's
(stem), vi.); u?c+pó?s *bubbly (It is...).*
(u'tspo's, adj.); s+pa?s *surfacing,
coming to the surface of water after
diving.* (spa's, vt.); čic+pá?s *He
surfaced after diving.* (chitspa's, vt.);
pós+pos+t *He is full of pranks, he is
comical.* (pospost, vi.); ∥ pó?s=cn
joked (he...). (po'tsn, vi.); s+po?s=cn
joke, joking. (spo'tsn, n.); s+pós=cn
humor, joke. (spostsn, n.);
s+čet+pu?s=ítkʷe? *bubble.*
(schetpu'sitkwe', n.); čat+pos=átkʷe?
bubble. (chatpo-satkwe' (lit. It (water)
gave off bubbles), v.); s+pos+t=
étkʷe? *Santa (name of).* (Spostetkwe'
(lit. bubbling waters), n.); §
pos+pos+ł+cégʷ+t *He has comical
ways.* (posposłtsegwt, vi.)

√ps₃ † pus *cat.* (pus, n.); p+pús *kitten.*
(ppus, n.); pús+pus *cats.* (puspus, n.);
§ ul pus ha s+táx̌=anč+s *catgut.* (ul
pus ha staqhanchs (lit. of cat his gut),
n.)

√ps₄ † pus *digest.* (pus (stem), vt.)

√ps₅ † pus *nuisance, pest.* (pus (stem),
n.); pús+pus+t *He is a gadabout.*
(puspust, adj.); gʷł pús+pus+t *They
play and play, never work, to the point
of being a nuisance.* (guł puspust, vi.)

√ps(t') ∥ s+pist'=ey't *bigness (of
things).* (spist'e'yt, n.); ul+píst'=ey't
pertaining to big things, people.
(ulpist'e'yt, n.); cen+pís=cn *necks
(They have big...).* (tsenpistsn, n.);
cen+pís=cn=šn *ankles (H/s has*

big...). (tsenpistsnshn, n.); pís=šn *feet
(he has big...).* (pisshn, vt.); p+pís=šn'
big feet. (ppissh'n, n.); t+pés=i?qs
noses (They have large...). (tpesi'qs,
n.); t+pés=qn *heads (They have
large...).* (tpesqn, n.); t+pís=elps
*grizzlies (They are big hogs or...), hogs
(They are big...or grizzlies).* (tpiselps,
n.); t+p+pís=gʷl' *caricature, comics,
funnies.* (tppisgu'l (lit. little people
with big bellies), n.); t+pís=us *eyes
(H/s has large...).* (tpisus, n.)

√ps? † púse? *uncle (if father is living).*
(puse', n.)

√psš † pesíš *gather (...wood), fetch
wood.* (pesish (stem), vt.); s+psiš+m
*fetching (...twigs on one's back), twigs
(fetching...on one's back).* (spsishm, v,
n.); č‿y'c+psíš+mš *lit. I am fetching
wood (sticks) on my back.*
(chi'tspsishmsh, vt.);

√pst † pést+e? *half, demi-, one-sided,
half dollar, one side.* (peste' (stem), n,
adj.); ∥ s+pste?=íłc'e? *side (one...of
the body).* (spste'iłts'e', n.); hn+pste?=
íłc'e? *one side (half) of a room.*
(hnpste'iłts'e', n.); hn+péste?=us *on
the side, opposed.* (hnpeste'us, adv.); §
hn+péste?=us+s x̌ʷe čníl+emn
antidote. (hnpeste'uss khwe chnilemn
(lit. the opposite side of poison,
something that counteracts poison,
injury or contagion), n.);
teč+n+peste?=us ha yukʷkʷm=
ús+m=ul'umx̌ʷ *antarctic.*
(technpeste'us ha
yukkwmusmu'lumkhw, n.);
hn+pést+e?=us ha qʷilem'
anti-phone. (hnpeste'us ha qwile'm (lit.
It is on the other side of a song, it is a
responsive song), n.); pst+a? a s+qíl=
tč *cross-breed, half-breed.*
(p'sta'asqiltch, n.); pste?e+s+pín=tč
semiannual. (pste'espintch, n.)

√psy † psáye *foolish (He was...).*
(psaye, vi.)

119

√pš † púše *paternal grandfather*. (pushe (Yakima), n.); púša *paternal grandfather*. (pusha, n.)

√pt † pit+m *He moved residence or position*. (pitm, vt.); pet+pet+m'+ul' *moves (He habitually...around)*. (petpet'mu'l, v.); ‡ pít+m-st-m *diffuse*. (pitmstm (lit. It was moved, spread (out), adj.) [possibly √pł]

√ptp † s+pétep *gopher*. (spetep, n.)

√ptq † pa·táq *potato*. (paataq, n.); hn+pa·táq+n *cellar*. (hnpaataqn (lit. storage room for potatoes), n.)

√ptqʷ † petqʷ *race*. (petqw (stem), vi.); petqʷ+m *to race, he raced*. (petqwm); hn+pét+petqʷ+n' *race horse*. (hnpetpetqw'n, n.); hn+pet+pétqʷ+n' *race track*. (hnpetpetqw'n (lit. means of racing), n.); sya·+pétqʷ+m *jockey, racer*. (syaapetqwm. (lit. one whose function is to race), n.)

√ptr † a·+potar *apostle*. (aapotar, n.)

√ptwnxʷ † s+ptwínxʷ *hog (mother...)*. (sptwinkhw, n.)

√ptx̌ʷ † patx̌ʷ *burst (ref. to oil, water, pus)*. (patqhw (stem), vi.) [written as √płx̌ʷ in volume 1] pałx̌ʷ *to burst forth (as oil, water, pus)*. (pałqhw); s+patx̌ʷ *oozing, as a well after being dug*. (spatqhw, n.); čic+pátx̌ʷ *It (i.e. oil, water, blood) burst forth hither*. (chitspatqhw, vt.)

√pty' † p+pty'ú *little one, dime*. (ppt'yu, n.)

√pt? † pute? *honor, respect, worship*. (pute' (stem), vt.); puté?+m *adore, celebrate, esteem, revere, worship*. (pute'm (lit. He observed (a day or event) with ceremonies of respect or festivity), vi, vt.); s+púte?+m *deference, respect, reverence*. (spute'm, n.); pút+pute?+t *civil, devout*. (putpute't (lit. He is polite), adj.); s+put+pute?+t *courtesy*. (sputpute't (lit. polite gesture or remark), n.); pute?+utm *adorable, likeable*. (pute'utm, adj.); hn+púte?+n *cult*. (hnpute'n (lit. means of honoring, respecting, adoring), n.); s+pute?+ncút *amour-propre, self-esteem*. (spute'ntsut, n.); s+púte?+mš *worship (to...)*. (spute'msh, vi.); ‡ pute?-nt-s *honor, respect, he honored (respected) h/h*. (pute'nts, vt.); § s+pute?+s+čínt *curtsy, bow*. (spute'schint (lit. showing respect for a person), n.); ul+n+púte?+n he s+pin=tč+s *anno-Domini*. (ulnpute'n he spintchs (lit. belonging to the Lord's year), adv.)

√pw † paw *drum (on tin)*. (paw (stem), vi.); pew *drum (on a drum)*. (pew (stem), vi.); p+péw'+m' *drummed (he...softly), softly (he drummed...)*. (ppe'w'm, v, adv.); pu·w+mín+n *drum*. (puuwminn, n.); puw+min+n *cymbal*. (puwminn (lit. a drum), n.) [also written as √ph] puh+mín+n *cymbal (lit. a drum)*. (puhminn, n.); sye·+péw+m *drummer*. (syeepewm (lit. one whose function is to drum), n.); i s+péw+puw+iš *He is in the act of sounding a drum*. (ispewpuwis); // s+pow=ál'q+n *woodpecker*. (spowa'lqn, n.); ‡ péw-nt-s *beat (He...it (drum))*. (pewnts, vi.); puw-šít-s *drummed (h/s...for h/h)*. (puwshits, vt.); puw+šít-se-s *drummed (h/s...for me)*. (puwshitses, vt.); § miyes+péw+n *drummed (He...loudly)*. (miyespewn, vi.); miyes+péw+m *He drummed loudly*. (miyespewm, vi.); t'ax̌+s+péw+m *drummed (He...quickly, with fast tempo)*. (t'aqhspewm, vt.); t'ax̌+s+péw+n *He drummed quickly, with fast tempo*. (t'aqhspewn, vt.)

√pw'₁ † piw' *jerk*. (pi'w (stem), vi.)

√pw'₂ † piw' *light (in weight)*. (pi'w (stem), n.); u· píw' *He started out briskly, lightly, as though light weight.*

(uupi̱'w, vi.); u̱ p+pи́w' *weight (It is light in...), light (It is...in weight).* (uppi̱'w, n, adj.); u+p+pи́·w' *light (It is (very)...).* (uppiии'w!, adj.); pи́w'+pew'+t *active, agile, brisk (he is...), lively, nimble.* (pi̱'wpe'wt, adj, vi.); s+pи́w'+pew' *lungs.* (spi̱'wpe'w (lit. means of being lightweight), n.); s+pи́w'+pew'+t *vigor, vivacity.* (spi̱'wpe'wt, n.)

√pwy † pи́wye *camas from Nez Perce country.* (pi̱wye, n.)

√px^{w}₁ † pex^w *wind-blown.* (pekhw (stem), adj.); s+pex^w+n *chaff.* (spekhwn (grain husks separated from), n.); péx^w+t+n' *snow drift.* (pe̱khwt'n, n.) [xref √px^{w}₂]

√px^{w}₂ † e n+péx^w *to be contained (lit. Spherical objects are contained in something).* (enpe̱khw, vi.)

√px^{w}₃ † pux^w *blow (with mouth).* (pukhw (stem), vt.); pux^w+m *blow.* (pukhum, vt.); s+pux^w+m *blowing by medicine man in treatment of ailment.* (spu̱khum, vt.); púx^w+emn *blowpipe.* (pu̱khwemn (lit. means of blowing), n.); pux^w+mи́n+n *winnower.* (pukhwmi̱nn, n.); ∥ hn+púx^w=enč *H/s blew on the wall.* (hnpu̱khwench, vi.); hn+púx^w=ɬce?+n *alpenhorn, brass, horn, bugle.* (hnpu̱khwɬtse'n (lit. means of blowing), n.); g^{w}l sye+n+púx^w=ɬc'e *combo.* (gul syenpukhwɬt'se (lit. a group of in-blowers), n.); ‡ púx^w-nt-m *blown (It was...), treated (h/s was...by a medicine man).* (pu̱khwntm (lit. h/s was blown on as a technique of healing), n, v, vi.); hn+púx^w-n *blow-up (to...).* (hnpu̱khwn (lit. I filled it with air), vt.); t+púx^w-n *blow-out.* (tpu̱khwn (lit. I blew out), vt.) t+póx^w=qn-t-m *was (H/h head...blown on).* (tpo̱khwqntm (ref. to curing technique), vi.) [xref √px^{w}₁]

√px̌ † pax̌ *thoughtful, wise.* (paqh (stem), to rub on surface (as striking a match), adj.); pax̌ *rub (on a surface).* (paqh (stem), v.); u· páč *canny, crafty, cunning, prudent, shrewd (he is...).* (uupa̱qh, adj.); s+pa?x̌ *craft.* (spa'qh (lit. wisdom in evasion or deception), n.); s+páč+pax̌ *allegory, Indian philosophy, wisdom story.* (spa̱qhpaqh, n.); páč+pax̌+t *astute, clever, intelligent, wise (he is very...), judgement (he is keen in...), keen (he is...in judgement).* (pa̱qhpaqht, vi.); s+páč+pax̌+t *brightness, common sense, wisdom (intellectual), intelligence.* (spa̱qhpaqht, n.); s+t+pax̌+mи́n+n *matchbox (striking surface on a...), striking (...surface on a matchbox).* (stpaqhmi̱nn, n.); c'+an+pá?x̌+m *reasoned (He...).* (ts'anpa'qhm, vi.); s+can+pá?x̌+m *a posteriori, contemplative, meditative, reasoning (lit. seeking the wisdom of).* (stsanpa̱'qhm, adj.); ac+pax̌+pax̌+scút *charlatan, fool.* (atspaqhpaqhstsu̱t (lit. He makes himself as if wise), n.); can+pax̌a+mи́n+n *reasoning (...power or faculty).* (tsanpaqhami̱nn, n.); i can+pá?x̌+mš *He is reasoning or figuring, philosophizing.* (itsanpa'qhmsh, vi.); ic+pá?x̌-lš *avoid, dodge, evade.* (itspa̱'qhlsh. (lit. They are "wised up." They are slipping away from something), vt.); ∥ s+pax̌+pax̌=cn+mи́+ncut *bon mot.* (spaqhpaqhtsnmi̱ntsut (lit. making oneself speak wisely - a clever saying), n.); pax̌+pax̌+t=и́l'š *wise (He became...).* (paqhpaqhti̱'lsh, vi.); s+pax̌+pax̌+t=и́l'š *prudent, becoming wise.* (spaqhpaqhti̱'lsh, adj.); s+can+pa?a?x̌=ng^{w}и́ln *concept.* (stsanpa'a'qhngwi̱ln (lit. attaining a result of reasoning), n.); ‡ can+pá?x̌-nt-s *cogitate.* (tsanpa̱'qhnts (lit. He thought carefully about it), vi.); t+páč-nt-s *lit (H/s...the match), struck*

(H/s...the match). (tpa̲qhnts, vt.); § paǔ+paǔ+t he q'ey'+mín+n *Bible.* (paqhpaqht he q'e'ymi̲nn (lit. A book that is wise), n.); ul s+can+paʔaʔx̌= ngʷíl+n *conceptual.* (ul stsanpa'a'qhngwiln (lit. belonging to attainment of reasoning), adj.); ul a+yáˤ gʷɬ páx̌+pax̌+t *All Saints Day.* (Ul aya̲(Guɬ paqhpaqht (lit. belonging to all the wise), n.)

√px̌ʷ † pax̌ʷ *distribute (in order).* (paqhw (stem), vt.); páx̌ʷ+m+ncut *defer, disband.* (paqhwmntsut (lit. They dispersed (for the time being); They put it off), vi.); s+páx̌ʷ+m+ncut *break-up, disintegration, dispersion.* (spa̲qhwmntsut (lit. scattering selves), n.); s+páx̌ʷo+mncut *lit. dispersing of a group or people.* (spaqhwomntsut, v.); ac+páx̌ʷ+m+ncut-lš *disperse, diverge.* (atspaqhwmntsutlsh (lit. They scatter out from onepoint), vi.); s+pax̌ʷ+m+šeš *distribution (lit. distributing things).* (spaqhumshesh, n.); hiyc+páx̌ʷ+m+šeš *distribution.* (hiytspa̲qhumshesh (lit. It is something I dealt out), n.); ‡ páx̌ʷ-nt-s *scattered (H/s...it).* (paqhwnts, vt.); páx̌ʷ+m-s-n *deal, distributed (I...it).* (paqhumsn, vt.); páx̌ʷ+m-stu-s *broadcast, scattered.* (paqhumstus, vt.); ac+páx̌ʷ+m-st-x̌ʷ *allot, distribute, deal out.* (atspaqhumstkhw, vt.); § s+pox̌ʷ+m+eɬ+q'ey'+mínn *circular, bulletin.* (spoqhmeɬq'e'ymi̲nn, n.)

√px̌ʷ₂ † hn+t+péx̌ʷ+n *cuspidor, spittoon.* (hntpeqhwn, n.); čat+péx̌[ʷ]+m *H/S spat on floor.* (chatpe̲qhm, vi.); čat+péx̌ʷ+pex̌[ʷ]+m' *H/S spat on this and that, or here and there).* (chatpe̲qhwpeqh'm, vi.); [for expected √px̌ʷ]

√py † piy *happy, joyful.* (piy (stem), adj.); péy+piy+t *delightful, enjoyable.* (pe̲ypiyt (stem), adj.); péy+py+t

thrilling (of the heart or soul) must be pure, real, moral as a beautiful song, ecstatic. (pe̲ypyt, vt.); // ec+piy=íč *delight, pleasure.* (etspiyi̲ch. (stem), vt.); hn+péy=elgʷes *cheerful, chipper, contented.* (hnpeyelgwes (lit. He is thrilled at heart), adj.); hn+piy= ílgʷes+n *beatitude.* (hnpiyi̲lgwesn (lit. place of great delight), n.); hn+piy+iy= ílgʷes+n *darling, Eden.* (hnpiyyi̲lgwesn (lit. place of great delight), n.); hn+piy+piy=ílgʷes *bon vivant, dashing.* (hnpiypiyi̲lgwes (lit. one who is always thrilled at heart, a person who enjoys life fully), adj.); s+piy+piy+čs=níxʷ *admiration.* (spiypiychsni̲khw, n.); his+piy+piy+čs=níxʷ *admire (to...).* (hispiypiychsnikhw (lit. H/S fills me with intense happy emotion), vi.); kʷu‿iʔ-c+piy=íčt-m-n-m *I am delighting you(s).* (kwi'tspiyi̲chtmnm, v.); čeɬ‿kʷ‿is+piy=íčt-m-n-m *delight.* (chetkwispiyi̲chtmnm. (lit. I will delight you (sg.)), vt.); hn-iʔ‿c+piy=íč-m-n-m *I am delighting him/her.* (hi'tspiyi̲chmnm, vt.); čeɬ‿his+piy=íčt-m-n-m *delight.* (cheɬhispiyichtmnm (lit. I will delight h/h), vt.); čeɬ‿kʷup‿hi-s+piy=íčt- m-n-m *delight (lit. I will delight you (pl)).* (cheɬkuphispiyichtmnm, vi.); kʷp‿hiʔc+piy=íčt-m-n-m *delighting (I am..you (pl)).* (kuphi'tspiyichtmnm, vt.); hn-iʔ‿c+piy=íčt+mn+m-lš *I am delighting them.* (hi'tspiyi̲chtmnmlsh, vt.); čeɬ‿hi-s+piy=íčt+mn+m-lš *I will delight them.* (cheɬhispiyichtmnmlsh, vt.); čn‿y'c+piy=íčt+mn-n *you (s) are delighting me.* (chni'tspiyi̲chtmnm, vt.); čeɬ‿čn‿ʔi-s+piy=íčt+mn+m *you (s) will delight me.* (cheɬchn'ispiyi̲chtmnm, vt.); iʔ c+piy= íčt+mn+m *You (sg.) are delighting h/h.* (i'tspiyi̲chtmnm, vt.);

čeł‿ʔi-s+piy=íčt+mn *you (s) will delight him.* (cheł'ispiyichtmn, vt.); i? c+piy=íčt+mn+m-lš *You [sg.] are delighting them.* (i'tspiyichtmnmlsh, vt.); čeł‿ʔi-s+piy=íčt+mn+m-lš *you [sg.] will delight them.* (cheł'ispiyichtmnmlsh, vt.); č‿y'c+piy=íčt+mn+m-s *H/s is delighting me.* (chi'tspiyichtmnms, vt.); čeł‿či‿s+piy=íčt+mn+m-s *h/s will delight me.* (chełchispiyichtmnms, vt.); kʷu‿y'‿c+piy=íčt+mn-m-s *H/S is delighting you (sg).* (ku'ytspiyichtmnms, vt.); čeł‿kʷu‿s+piy=íčt+mn-m-s *(lit. h/s will delight you (sg.)).* (chełkuspiyichtmnms, vt.); i? c+piy=íčt+m[n]+m-s *H/s is delighting h/h.* (i'tspiyichtmms, vt.); čes‿piy=íčt+mn+m-s *(lit. h/s will delight h/h)* (chespiyichtmnms, vt.); čn‿y'c+piy=ič=íčt+mn+m-p *(lit. you (pl.) are delighting me).* (chni'tspiyichichtmnmp, vt.); čeł‿čn‿ʔi-s+piy=íčt+mn+m-p *you (pl) will delight me.* (chełchn'ispiyichtmnmp, vt.); kʷup‿ʔi‿c+piy=íčt+mn+m+šeš *You (pl) are delighting us (or them).* (kup'itspiyichtmnmshesh, vt.); č‿y'c+piy=íčt+mn+m-s-lš *They are delighting me.* (chi'tspiyichtmnmslsh, vt.); čeł‿či‿s+piy=íčt+mn+m-s-lš *they will delight me.* (chełchispiyichtmnmslsh, vt.); kʷup‿ʔi‿c+piy=íčt+mn+m-s-lš *They are delighting you (pl).* (kup'itspiyichtmnmslsh, vt.); čeł‿kʷup‿s+piy=íčt+mn+m-s-lš *(lit. they will delight you (pl)).* (chełkupspiyichtmnmslsh, vt.); i? c+piy=íčt+mn+m-s-lš *They are delighting them.* (i'tspiyichtmnmslsh, vt.); čes‿piy=íčt+mn+m-s-lš *(lit. they will delight them).* (chespiyichtmnmslsh, vt.); ‡ ec+piy= íč-st-m-n *I delight you.* (etspiyichstmn, vt.); piy=íčt+m-nt-s-n *I delighted you (sg.).* (piyichtmntsn, vt.); k'ʷ ne? piy=íčt+m-nt-s-n *I am going to delight you (sg.).* (k'wne'piyichtmntsn, vi.); ec+piy= íč-s-n *I delight h/h.* (etspiyichsn, vt.); piy=íčt+mn-n *I delighted h/h.* (piyichtmnn, v.); k'ʷ ne? piy= íčt+mn-n *I am going to delight h/h.* (k'wne'piyichtmnn, vt.); ec+piy= íčt+mi-st-ulm-n *I delight you (pl.).* (etspiyichtmistulmn, vt.); piy= íčt-m-nt-ulm-n *delighted (I...you (pl.)).* (piyichtmntulmn, vt.); k'ʷ ne? piy=íčt+m-nt-ulm-n *I am going to delight you (pl.).* (k'wne'piyichtmntulmn, vi.); ec+piy= íčt+mi-s-n-lš *I delight them.* (etspiyichtmisnlsh, vt.); piy= íčt+mn-n-lš *I delighted them.* (piyichtmnnlsh, v.); k'ʷ ne? piy= íčt+mn-n-lš *I am going to delight them.* (k'wne'piyichtmnnlsh, vt.); piy= íčt+m-nt-s *You(s) delight me.* (piyichtmnts, v.); ec+piy=íč-st-me-xʷ *You (sg.) delight me.* (etspiyichstmekhw, vt.); piy= íčt+m-nt-se-xʷ *You (sg.) delighted me, you elated me.* (piyichtmntsekhw, vt.); ec+piy=íčt+mi-st-me-xʷ *to thrill, astonish, electrify (lit. You (sg.) thrill me).* (etspiyichtmistmekhw, vt.); ne?+piy=íčt+m-nt-se-xʷ *You (sg.) are to delight me (imper.).* (ne'piyichtmntsekhw, v.); k'ʷ ne? piy= íčt+m-nt-se-xʷ *You (sg.) are going to delight me.* (k'wne'piyichtmntsekhw, vi.); piy=íčt+m-nt *You (s) delight h/h.* (piyichtmnt, v.); ec+piy= íč-st-mi-s[]-xʷ *You (sg.) delight h/h.* (etspiyichstmistkhw, vt.); piy=íč+m-nt-xʷ *You (sg.) delighted h/h.* (piyichmntkhw, vt.); ne?+piy= íčt+m-nt-xʷ *You (sg.) are to delight*

123

h/h (imper.). (ne'piyichtmntkhw, v.);
k'ᵂ ne? piy=íčt+m-nt-xᵂ *You (sg.) are
going to delight h/h.*
(k'wne'piyichtmntkhw, vi.); ec+piy=
íč-st-me-s *H/s delights me.*
(etspiyichstmes, vt.); piy=
íčt+m-nt-se-s *H/s delighted me.*
(piyichtmntses, v.); k'ᵂ ne? piy=
íčt+m-nt-se-s *H/s is going to delight
me.* (k'wne'piyichtmntses, vi.);
ec+piy=íč-st-mi-s *H/s delights you
(sg.).* (etspiyichstmis, vt.); piy=
íčt+m-nt-si-s *H/S delighted you.*
(piyichtmntsis, vt.); k'ᵂ ne? piy=
íčt+m-nt-si-s *H/s is going to delight
you (sg.).* (k'wne'piyichtmntsis, vi.);
ec+piy=íčt+mi-stu-s *H/s delights h/h.*
(etspiyichtmistus, vt.); piy=íč+m-nt-s
H/s delighted h/h. (piyichtmnts, v.); k'ᵂ
ne? piy=íčt+m-nt-s *H/s is going to
delight h/h.* (k'wne'piyichtmnts, vt.);
ec+piy=íčt+mi-st-me-lp *You (pl.)
delight me.* (etspiyichtmistmelp, vt.);
piy=íčt+m-nt-sel-p *You (pl) delighted
me.* (piyichtmntselp, v.); ne?+piy=
íčt+m-nt-sel-p *You (pl.) are to delight
me (imper.).* (ne'piyichtmntselp, v.);
k'ᵂ ne? piy=íčt+m-nt-sel-p *You (pl.)
are going to delight me.*
(k'wne'piyichtmntselp, vi.); piy=
íčt+m-nt-ul *You (pl.) delight h/h.*
(piyichtmntul, vt.); ne?+piy=
íčt+m-nt-xᵂ-lš *You (pl.) are to delight
h/h (imper.).* (ne'piyichtmntkhwlsh,
v.); ec+piy=íčt+mi-st-xᵂ-lš *You (pl.)
delight them.* (etspiyichtmistkhwlsh,
vt.); piy=íčt+m-nt-xᵂ-lš *You (pl.)
delighted them.* (piyichtmntkhwlsh,
vt.); k'ᵂ ne? piy=íčt+m-nt-xᵂ-lš *You
(pl.) are going to delight them.*
(k'wne'piyichtmntkhwlsh, vi.);
ec+piy=íčt+mis-st-me-s-lš *They
delight me.* (etspiyichtmistmeslsh, vt.);
piy=íčt+m-nt-se-s-lš *They delighted
me.* (piyichtmntseslsh, v.); k'ᵂ ne?
piy=íčt+m-nt-se-s-lš *They are going

to delight me.* (k'wne'piyichtmntseslsh,
vi.); k'ᵂ ne? piy=íčt+m-nt-s-lš *They
are going to delight h/h.*
(k'wne'piyichtmntslsh, vi.); ec+piy=
íčt-ulm-is-lš *They delight you (pl.).*
(etspiyichtulmislsh, vt.); piy=
íčt+m-nt-si-s-lš *They delighted you
(pl.).* (piyichtmntsislsh, vt.); k'ᵂ ne?
piy=íčt+m-n-si-s-lš *They are going to
delight you (pl.).*
(k'wne'piyichtmnsislsh, vi.); ec+piy=
íčt+mi-stu-s-lš *They delight them.*
(etspiyichtmistuslsh, vt.); piy=
íčt+m-nt-s-lš *They delighted them.*
(piyichtmntslsh, vt.); § na+?xíł
ec+piy=íčt-mi-st-m-n *delight (Maybe
I...you (sg.).* (na'qhił etspiyichtmistmn,
vt.); na+?xíł ec+piy=íčt+m-is-n
delight (Maybe I...h/h). (na'qhił
etspiyichtmisn, vt.); na+?xíł ec+piy=
íčt+mi-stu-l-m-n *delight (Maybe
I...you (pl.).* (na'qhił
etspiyichtmistulmn, vt.); na+?xíł
ec+piy=íčt+mi-s-n-lš *Maybe I delight
them.* (na'qhił etspiyichtmisnlsh, v.);
na+?xíł ec+piy=íčt+mi-st-me-xᵂ
delight (Maybe you (sg.)...me). (na'qhił
etspiyichtmistmekhw, vt.); na+?xíł
ec+piy=íčt+mi-st-xᵂ *delight (Maybe
you (sg.)...h/h).* (na'qhił
etspiyichtmistkhw, vt.); na+?xíł
ec+piy=íčt-mi-st-me-s[] *delights
(Maybe h/s...me).* (na'qhił
etspiyichtmistmesw, vt.); na+?xíł
ec+piy=íčt+mi-st-m-is *delights
(Maybe h/s...you (sg.).* (na'qhił
etspiyichtmistmis, vt.); na+?xíł
ec+piy=íčt+mi-stu-s *delights (Maybe
h/s...h/h).* (na'qhił etspiyichtmistus,
vt.); na+?xíł ec+piy=íčt+mi-st+mel-p
delight (Maybe you (pl.)...me). (na'qhił
etspiyichtmistmelp, vt.); na+?xíł
ec+piy=íčt+mi-st-xᵂ-lš *delight
(Maybe you (pl.)...them).* (na'qhił
etspiyichtmistkhwlsh, v.); na+?xíł
ec+piy=íčt+mi-st-me-s-lš *delight

(Maybe they...me). (na'qhiⱡ etspiyi̱chtmistmeslsh, vt.); na+ʔx̌íⱡ ec+piy=íčt+mi-stu-s-lš *delight (Maybe they...h/h).* (na'qhiⱡ etspiyi̱chtmistuslsh, vt.); na+ʔx̌íⱡ ec+piy=íčt+mi-st+ul+mi-s-lš *delight (Maybe they...you (pl.).* (na'qhiⱡ etspiyi̱chtmistulmislsh, vt.); x̌áy'+x̌iʔ+t he s+n+piy+y=ílgʷes *bliss, ecstasy.* (qha̱'yqhi't he snpiyyi̱lgwes. bliss (lit. great thrilling of the heart), n.); s+myes+n+piy+iy=ílgʷes *trance (a kind of...), ecstasy, joy (excessive...).* (smyesnpiyyi̱lgwes (lit. more than ordinary thrilling of the heart), n.)

√pyl ∥ s+pa·yól=mš *Spanish, Castilian, Mexican.* (Spaayo̱lmsh, n.); an+pa·yól=mš=cn *Spanish (to speak...).* (anpaayo̱lmshtsn, n.)

√py'₁ † piy' *squeeze.* (pi'y (stem), vt.) [xref √p'y']

√py'₂ ∥ t+puʔ+púy'=us *humor (His eyes came to show prankish...), eyes (His...came to show prankish humor).* (tpu'pu̱'yus, n.); t+puy'+púy=us *came (His eyes...to show prankish humor).* (tpuy'pu̱yus, vi.); uʔ+t+púʔ+puy'=us *humor (His eyes customarily show prankish...).* (u'tpu̱'pu'yus, n.)

√pˤ₁ † u· páˤ *gray (it is...).* (uupa̱), adj.); paˤ+aˤ *bleach, blench (lit. it became colorless).* (pa(a(, vt.); ∥ u· páˤ=us *face (his...is pale), pale (his face is...).* (uupa̱(us, n, adj.); páˤ+aˤ=us *blanch, name of a mountain.* (pa(a(us. he became pale...as to the face, n.); § lut as+paˤ+aˤ+út+m-s *colorfast.* (lutaspa(a(u̱tms (lit. It is incapable of fading), adj.); lut es+peˤ+eˤ+út+m-s *colorfast (lit. It is incapable of fading).* (lutespe(e(u̱tms, adj.)

√pˤ₂ † paˤ *excess.* (pa((stem). left over, n.); peˤ+peˤʷ *left over.* (pe(pe(w (stem). excess, adj.); hi-s+péˤʷ+ˤʷ *surplus (it is my...).* (hispe̱(wu(w (lit. It

is what I have left over), n.) [pharyngeal sometimes rounded]

√pˤʷ † paˤʷ *defecate.* (pa(w (stem), vi.)

√pʔ₁ ‡ t+peʔ=šín+t-s *deflate* (tpe'shints (lit. He released the air from the tire), vt.)

√pʔ₂ † pí+peʔ *father.* (pipe', n.)

√pʔ₃ † píʔ+peʔ+t *He is bounteous, bountiful, broadminded, charitable, generous, magnanimous.* (pi̱'pe't, adj.); s+píʔ+peʔ+t *bounty, catholicity, liberality, generosity.* (spi'pe't, n.); § miyeⱡ+píʔ+peʔ+t *deluxe, extravagant.* (miyeⱡpi'pe't (lit. he is too generous), adj.)

√pʔ₄ † puʔ *thump (as fist against person).* (pu', vt.)

√pʔ(s) † puʔs *heart, desire.* (...pu's E.g. hiitspu's. It is my heart, desire, will, n.); hi·c-puʔs *will.* (...pu's. E.g. hiitspu's. It is my heart, desire, will, n.); hiyc-púʔs *desire, heart.* (hiytspu̱'s, n.); hn+púʔs+n *conscience, idea, imagination, mind, thought.* (hnpu̱'sn (lit. the means of thinking, that which is thought of), n.); puʔs+mín+t *consider.* (pu'smi̱nt (lit. Fix your mind upon it, contemplate it), vt.); s+puʔs+mín+n *commemoration, consideration.* (spu'smi̱nn (lit. thinking about something), n.); ul+iyc+púʔs *cardiac, coronary.* (uliytspu̱'s (lit. pertaining to the heart), adj.); ∥ puʔ+puʔs=ínč *aggrieve.* (pu'pu'si̱nch (lit. He was distressed, afflicted, he felt sadness, he mourned, bemoan, dejected), vt.); s+puʔ+puʔs=ínč *dirge, elegy, mourning, sorrow.* (spu'pu'si̱nch, n.); s+puʔs+p'uʔs=ínč *grieve (to...), grieving.* (spu'sp'u'si̱nch, vi.); hn+pʔeʔs+m=íneʔ *idea.* (hnp'e'smi̱ne' (lit. He had an idea of the meaning of a statement), n.); s+puʔuʔs=ngʷíln *brainstorm, brainwave.* (spu'u'sngwi̱ln (lit. success in getting a thought, a sudden

inspiration), n.); ‡ puʔs+mín-n *commemorate, considered.* (pu'sminn (lit. I thought of it), vt.); puʔ+puʔs= ínč+m-st-m *disgruntle.* (pu'pu'sinchmstm (lit. H/S was made dissatisfied), vt.); ec+puʔ+puʔs= ínč+m-st-m-n *distress.* (etspu'pu'sinchmstmn (lit. I inflict pain or suffering on you (sg.)), vt.); puʔ+puʔs=ínč+m-stu-s *deject.* (pu'pu'sinchmstus (lit. He grieved him), vt.); t+puʔ+puʔs=ínč-m-n *deplore.* (tpu'pu'sinchmn (lit. I grieved on his account), vt.); §
u+x̌ʷel'+e+yc+púʔs *cordate.* (uqhwe'leytspu's (lit. It is like a heart), adj.); nukʷʷ+e+ʔełi+c+púʔs-lš *concordant.* (nuk'we'ełitspu'slsh (lit. They are of one heart), adj.); s+nukʷʷ+e+ʔłiy+c+púʔ[s] *concordance.* ((lit. having one heart), n, (snuk'we'łiytspu'.); x̌áy'+x̌i+t ic+puʔ+puʔs=ínč *brokenhearted, mournful.* (qha'yqhi't itspu'pu'sinch. (lit. He is grievously mourning), adj.); hn+čn'+n'+meł+i·c+púʔs *come.* (hnch'n'nmełiitspu's. (lit. his heart came back to its own position), vt.); hn+č'n'+n'+meł+i·c+púʔs *come. (lit. his heart came to its own position).* (hnch''n'nmełiitspu's, vt.); miyes+puʔs+min-n *comtemplate, meditate, ponder.* (miyespu'sminn (lit. I considered it more than ordinary), vt.); uw'e+n+púʔs+n *abstract.* (u'wenpu'sn (lit. only in imagination), n.)

√p'c [also recorded as √p'c'] † p'oc' *smash.* (p'ots' (stem). vi.); s+p'oc+m *damage (with heavy blows), pound (with heavy blows).* (sp'otsm. flatten, vt.); s+p'+p'óc+t *dent.* (sp'p'otst (lit. slight depression caused by a blow or pressure), n.); // a n+p'oc=qn *H/s is wearing a squashed hat.* (anp'otsqn, vt.); ‡ p'oc-n *bashed (I...it), crush.*

(p'otsn, vt.); p'óc-nt-s *smashed (h/s...it).* (p'otsnts, vt.)

√p'c'₁ † p'ac' *defecate, squirt.* (p'ats' (stem). vi, vt.); s+p'ac' *dung.* (sp'ats', n.); p'ác'+m *threw off (H/s...dung).* (p'ats'm, vt.); hn+p'c'+mén+n *privy.* (hnp'ts'menn, n.)

√p'c'₂ † p'ic' *push.* (p'i'ts (stem), adv.); p'íc'+pec'+t *pressing, urgent (lit. it is naturally pushing).* (p'its'pets't, adj.); s+p'íc'+n *pushing, shoving.* (sp'its'n, vt.); sye+n+p[']íc'+p *one who pushes from the back.* (syenpits'p, n.); //
s+n+p'íc'=cn+n *accent (stress).* (snp'its'tsnn, n.); ‡ p'íc'-nt-se-s *pushed (h/s...me).* (p'its'ntses, v.); te·+p'íc['] -nt-s *counteract.* (teep'itsnts (lit. He counteracted him by pushing him back), v.); hn+p'ic'+p-nt-s *H/s gave the vehicle a push from the rear.* (hnp'its'pnts); hn+p'íc'=eč-n't-se-s *pushed (He...(urged) me on the back).* (hnp'its'ech'ntses. He pushed my back, vt.)

√p'č † p'ač *blooper.* (p'ach (lit. sound of a weakly hit baseball), n.)

√p'č' † p'[e]č' *glitter.* (p'ch' (stem), vi.); p'eč['] *shine.* (p'c'ch (stem), vi.); u· p'[e]č' *burnish, shiny, chrome.* (uup'ch' (lit. It is shiny (as by rubbing), vi, adj, n.)

√p'č'n' † p'éč'n' *bob-cat, lynx.* (p'ech'n', n.)

√p'gʷ // p'ugʷ=ílmxʷ *echo.* (p'ugwilmkhw (lit. sound on the earth), n.); § lut hey'p+s+p'ugʷ=ílumxʷ+s *anechoic.* (lut he'ypsp'ugwilumkhws (lit. It has no echoes), adj.)

√p'gʷn † p'ígʷne *barbarian, gentile, pagan.* (p'igwne, n.)

√p'k // t+p'ók=qn *blonde.* (tp'okqn (lit. one with grayish hair), n.) [xref √pq]

√p'kʷlʔ † p'ekʷleʔ *ball, baseball, basketball.* (p'ekwle', n.); s+p'ekʷleʔ *baseball, playing ball.* (sp'ekwle', n.); sye·+p'ékʷleʔ *baseball player.*

√p'l

√p'l

(syeep'ekwle', n.); // s+p'ákʷla?=alqs *suit, uniform (baseball...).* (sp'akwla'alqs, n.)

√**p'l** † p'il *flicker (e.g. eyelid).* (p'il (stem), vi.)

√**p'lč'** † p'elč' *turn (a flat object), to turn flat thing over.* (p'elch (stem), vt.); p'ilč' *turn (to...round objects), to turn eyes inward with pain.* (p'ilch' (stem), vt.); p'íl·č' *turned (they (flat objects)...over).* (p'illch', v.); p'élč'+mncut *H/s turned h/h self over.* (p'elch'mntsut, vt.); s+p'elč'+m+ncut *turning (...oneself over).* (sp'elch'mntsut, v.); // t+p'íl+p'il·č'=us *turned (H/s eyes...over (figuratively) from fear, astonishment, etc.).* (tp'ilp'illch'us, [v.]); ‡ p'élč'+m-stu-s *capsize, overturn, he overturned it or caused it to turn over, H/s turned flat thing over (as disc).* (p'elch'mstus, vt, v.)

√**p'lkʷ** † p'ulkʷ *fold.* (p'ulk'w (stem). (e.g. cloth), vt.); // a t+p'[l]k'ʷ=ałn *his arm is wrapped around.* (atp'łk'waqhn, vi.); et+p'+p'úl'+p'ul'k'ʷ=ece? *cigarettes.* (etp'p'u'lp'u'lk'wetse', n.); ‡ p'úlkʷ-nt-s *folded, H/s folded it up (as sheet, blanket).* (p'ulkwnts, vt.)

√**p'ł₁** † p'ił *sit (persons).* (p'ił (stem), vi.); kʷup‿?e‿c+p'í·ł *You are remaining seated, or at home, You are still seated!* (kup'etsp'i··ł!, vi.); ne?+kʷp‿?ec+p'í·ł *seated.* (ne'kup'etsp'iiiłł! (lit. Please remain seated), vi.); // s+t+p'íł=liš=w'es *cavalcade, riding on horses (lit. getting to sit on horseback).* (stp'iłlish'wes, n.)

√**p'ł₂** † p'uł *poison ivy.* (p'uł (stem), n.); // p'úł+p'uł+t=úmš *poison ivy.* (p'ułp'ułtumsh (lit. kind of poisonous plant), n.)

√**p'łq** † p'ałq *pack, put away.* (p'ałq (stem), vt.); // s+p'+p'łq=il'gʷes *belongings (small...).* (sp'p'łqi'lgwes.

storing away, n.); hi-s+p'łq=ílgʷes *possession (it is my...).* (hisp'łqilgwes, n.); č‿y'c+p'ałq=ílgʷes *I am putting away my belongings.* (chi'tsp'ałqilgwes, vi.); ‡ p'áł=qn-t-s *H/s put it away.* (p'ałqnts, vt.); t'i? p'áł=qn-(n)t *Put it away.* (t'i'p'ałqnt, v. imper.)

√**p'm₁** † p'em *mouse-colored.* (p'em (stem), adj.); // s+n+p'óm=qn *hides (smoking...).* (snp'omqn, n.); hn+p'ó[m]=qn *smoked (hides).* (hnp'onqn, vt.) [see v. 1]; ‡ p'úm-nt-s *smoked (h/s...it) (i.e. hide).* (p'umnts (lit. h/s made it mouse-color), v.)

√**p'm₂** † s+p'u?um *belching.* (sp'u'um, vi.)

√**p'm'** // p'em'=iw'es+n *compact, compress.* (p'e'mi'wesn, vt.); ec+p[']em'=íw'es *compact, compressed.* (etspe'mi'wes, vi. (lit. It is closely and firmly packed), adj.); s+p'em'=íw'es *compaction, compression, condensation.* (sp'e'mi'wes. (lit. pressing together), n.); siye+p'em'=íw'es *compressor.* (siyep'e'mi'wes (lit. that which presses together), n.); ‡ p'em'=íw'es-n *compact, compress, I pressed it closely together.* (p'e'mi'wesn, vt.); p'em'= íw'es-tu-s *compress, constrict.* (p'e'mi'westus. (lit. He pressed them together), vi.)

√**p'n** † p'en *lie (long objects).* (p'en (stem), vi.); ec+p'én *the long objects are in a lying position.* (etsp'en, vi.); // ac+p'n+p'n=áłn *H/h arms are in a lying position.* (atsp'np'naqhn, vi.); ec+p'én+p'n=šn *H/h legs are in a lying position.* (etsp'enp'nshn, vi.); § nukʷ+ł+p'n+mín+n *wood (one rick of...).* (nuk'włp'nminn (lit. one means of piling long objects), n.); ac+p'n+p'n'+as+c'am' *H/h bones are in a lying position.* (atsp'np'nasts'a'm, vi.)

127

√p'nl' † p'nal' *at least*. (p'na'l, adv.);
ča?+p'nal' *least (at...)*. (cha'p'na'l,
adv.); ča?+p'ná·l' *least (at...)*.
(cha'p'naa'l (lit. no matter how little),
adj.)

√p'n'x̌ † s+p'án'x̌ *bag (beaded), bag,
sack*. (sp'a̱'nqh, n.); § kʷan+ɬ+s+p'án'x̌
bag (she took a...), took (she...a bag).
(kwanɬsp'a̱'nqh, n, vt.);
s+kʷan+s+p'án'+p'an'x̌ *baggage*.
(skwansp'a̱'np'a'nqh (lit. bags carried
while travelling), n.)

√p'q † u+t+p'óq=qn *hair (He has
sandy...)*. (utp'o̱qqn, n.) [xref √pq]

√p'q' † is+p'áq'+p'aq'+iš *crackle*.
(isp'a̱q'p'aq'ish (lit. It going crackle,
crackle), vi.)

√p'qʷ † p'eqʷ *henpeck, nag, pick on*.
(p'eqw (stem), vt.)

√p'q'ʷ₁ † p'aq'ʷ *powder*. (p'aq'w
(stem), n.); hn+p'uq'ʷ+mín+m
granary. (hnp'uq'wmi̱nm, n.);
hn+p'oq'ʷ+mín+m *granary*.
(hnp'oq'wmi̱nm, n.); ∥ p'uq'ʷ=ús+n
cosmetic, face powder. (p'uq'u̱sn, n.);
p'uq'ʷ=us+ncút+n *face powder*.
(p'uq'usntsu̱tn (lit. means of putting
pulverized matter on one's face), n);
s+n+p'uq'ʷ=ítkʷe? *cornmeal*.
(snp'uq'wi̱tkwe' (lit. any coarsely
ground edible grain that is put into
water), n.); ‡ hn+p'áq'ʷ-nt-s *put
(He...powder in the gun)*. (hnp'a̱q'wnts,
vt); p'áq'ʷ+p'uq'ʷ-nt-s *H/s spilled
powder here and there or again and
again*. (p'a̱q'wp'uq'wnts, vt.)

√p'q'ʷ₂ † s+p'aq'ʷ+t *leprosy*. (sp'aq'wt,
n.); s+p'+p'áq'ʷ+t *leprosy, small pox*.
(sp'p'a̱q'wt, n.)

√p'r † p'er *excess, flood, overflow*. (p'er
(stem), n.); p'er+t *flooded*. (p'ert, vt.) ;
p['']er+t *flooded (It...)*. (pert, vi.);
s+p'er+t *cataclysm, deluge, flood,
inundation*. (sp'ert, n.); hn+p'ér+t
flooded (it...inside). (hnp'ert, vi.);
p'ér+er *buckle, warp*. (p'e̱rer, vt.);

čat+p'ér+t *flooded*. (chatp'ert. (lit. the
floor was flooded), vt.); ‡ p'ér-nt-n
awash. (p'e̱rntn (lit. It was flooded),
vi.)

√p'rk'ʷ ∥ s+p'árk'ʷ=alqs *turtle*.
(sp'a̱rk'walqs. apparel turned inside
out, n.); s+p'+p'ar'k'ʷ=al'qs *capstan*.
(sp'p'a'rk'wa'lqs (lit. a small turtle), n.);
§ t+č'lxʷ=íc'e?+is xʷa s+p'árk'ʷ=alqs
crust. (tch'lkhwi̱ts'e'is khwa
sp'ark'walqs (lit. covering (crust of
turtle), n.) [xref √p'rq']

√p'rq' † p'arq' *curved (upwards),
warped*. (p'arq' (stem), adj.); ∥
hn+p'árq'=qn *hat (turned-up...)*.
(hnp'arq'qn (lit. old-time lady's hat.),
n.); hn+p'ar+arq'=ús+m *inside out (to
turn...)*. (hnp'ararq'u̱sm (lit. It e.g. the
jacket was turned inside out), v.);
s+n+p'árq'=qn *Dolly Varden*.
(snp'a̱rq'qn (lit. large twisted hat).
(large hat for women with one side
bent down and trimmed with numerous
flowers), n.) [xref √p'rk'ʷ]

√p'sq'ʷ † p'asq'ʷ *collapse, crumble*.
(p'asq'w (stem), vi.); p'esaq'ʷ
bone-breaking, sound of bonebreaking.
(p'esaq'w (stem), adj.); p'sa·q'ʷ *crack
(as a bone breaking)*. (p'saaaq'w!,
excl.)

√p'st † p'ésta *magpie, nighthawk*.
(p'esta, n.)

√p't † p'et *fall (to ground of own weight
as grain)*. (p'et (stem), vi.); [for
expected p'ɬ] p'it *to sit (e.g. persons)*.
(p'it); s+p'ét+t+m *ripening (the falling
of wheat to the ground on its own
weight)*. (sp'e̱ttm, v.); ‡ p'ít-liš *sat
(They...down)*. (p'i̱tlish, vi.)

√p't'₁ † p'at' *dream, [mushy stuff (see
below)]*. (p'at' (stem), vi.); p'át'+t'
debilitate, weaken. (p'a̱t't (lit. It (mud)
fell on the ground), vt.); ac+p'át' *blob*.
(atsp'a̱t', n.); t+p'at'+t' *a sticky
substance clinging to something,
Metaph, term of ridicule for*

exaggerated affection, puppy love.
(tp'at't', n.); **//** ac+p'át'+p't'=ečt
butterfingered. (atsp'at'p't'echt, vi. (lit.
His fingers are soft and pulpy), adj.);
can+p't'=šén· *cemented.*
(tsanp't'shenn, vt.); can+p't'=icén=šn
concrete. (tsanp't'itsenshn (lit. cement
conglomerate material put under the
foot), n.); čat+p't'+t'=áne? *lava,*
magma. (chatp't't'ane' (lit. covering by
lava), n.); hn+p't'+p't'=os+ncót *He*
dreamed. (hnp't'p't'osntsot (lit. He put
mushy stuff in his eyes), vi.);
s+n+p't'+p't'=os+ncót *daydream,*
dream. (snp't'p't'osntsot (lit. putting
mushy stuff in one's own eyes), n.); **‡**
p'át'-nt-s *He put down soft yielding*
stuff, like mush. (p'at'nts, vt.); **§**
at+p'át'+t' he s+mi?yem *coquette,*
flirt. (atp'at't' he smi'yem (lit. A woman
who clings to men), n.); can+p't'=
šén+n *cemented.* (tsanp't'shenn, vt.)

√p't'₂ **†** p'et' *dislodge, slip (out of*
place), smooth. (p'et' (stem). vt, vi,
adj.); u· p'ét' *level, smooth (it is...).*
(uup'et', adj.); p't'+min+n *smoother.*
(p't'minn, n.); hn+p'et'+p *H/s slipped*
out of h/h clothes. (hnp'et'p, vi.); **//**
hn+p'át'=alqs+n *means of smoothing*
the road. (hnp'at'alqsn, n.); p't'+m=
úl'umxʷ+n *smoothing (means of...the*
ground). (p't'mu'lumkhwn, v.); p't'=
áswel *trout, brook trout.* (p't'aswel,
n.); **‡** p'ét'+m-stu-s *smoothed*
(H/s...it). (p'et'mstus, vt.)

√p't'₃ **†** p'ut' *end.* (p'ut' (stem). to end
(as river, road, woods), vi.);
č‿p'út'+m *finished, We came to an*
end, we finished. (chp'ut'm, vi.); **//**
čet+p'út'+m=kʷe? *beach, coast.*
(chetp'ut'mkwe' (lit. end of water), n.);
§ lut hey's+p'út'+m+s *abyss.* (lut
he'ysp'ut'ms (lit. It has no bottom, it
has no end.), n.)

√p't'₄ [also recorded as √p't and
√pt'] **†** p'u?t *greasy (It got...).* (p'u't,

vi.); pu?t' *greasy, oily.* (pu't' (stem),
adj.); p'ut'+p'ut'+t *greasy, oily, it*
gives greasiness. (p'ut'p'ut't, adj.);
s+p'u?t' *becoming greasy.* (sp'u't', vt.);
// po?t'=áp=aw'as=qn *greasy (h/h*
chin got...). (po't'ap'awasqn, adj.);
hn+p'ut'=íps+n *He got greasy on the*
corners of the mouth. (hnp'ut'ipsn, vi.);
‡ p'út'-nt-s *greasy (he got it...).*
(p'ut'nts, v.)

√p't'₅ **†** p'út'=c'e? *Of what could h/s*
be? Of what good is that? It's not
worth it. (p'ut'ts'e'! excl.)

√p't'm **†** s+p'ít'em *bitterroot, rockrose.*
(sp'it'em, n.); ?ep+s+p'ítem *prairie*
west of Coeur d'Alene country (lit. It
has bitterroots or rockroses).
(epsp'item, n.); **§** tíxʷ+m e s+p'ít'em
bitterroots (He went out to gather...),
gather (He went out to...bitterroots).
(tikhum e sp'it'em, n, vt.)

√p'xʷ₁ **†** p'exʷ+p[']uxʷ *camas (bulbs).*
(p'ekhwpukhw, n.)

√p'xʷ₂ **†** p'íxʷ *agleam, flashed, glow,*
glowed (it...), radiate. (p'ikhw, adj,
vi.); u· p'íxʷ *bright (it is...).* (uup'ikhw,
adj.); ec+p'íxʷ *brilliant, shiny.*
(etsp'ikhw (lit. It gives light), adj.);
s+p'í?xʷ *brilliance, light.* (sp'i'khw,
n.); p'xʷ+mín+n *candle.* (p'khwminn
(lit. lighter), n.); p'uxʷ+p'uxʷ+mín+n
chandelier. (p'ukhwp'ukhwminn (lit.
lights or means of lights), n.); i
s+p'íxʷ+p'exʷ+iš *He is flashing and*
flashing. (isp'ikhwp'ekhwish, v.); **//**
hn+p'e?xʷ+t+l=íw'es *aglow.*
(hnp'e'khwtli'wes (lit. It was all aglow
with light), adj.); hn+p'í?+p'e?xʷ=us
bedazzle, dazzle. (hnp'i'p'e'khus. (lit.
Light got in his eyes), vt.); s+p'éxʷ=
enč *yellow root.* (sp'ekhwench, n.);
s+t+p'a?xʷ=ásq'it *aurora borealis (lit.*
light in the sky (on high)).
(stp'a'khwasq'it, n.); **‡** p'íxʷ-nt-s *He lit*
it up. ('pikhwnts, vi.); p[']íxʷ+m-stu-s
brighten. (pikhumstus (lit. He made it

bright), vt.); § elu+s+p[']í?xʷ *to be w/o light, aphotic, dark.* (eluspi'khw (lit. It has no light), adj.); s+p'ú?xʷ e· níč=elt *son (...of light).* (sp'u'khw ee nichelt, n.)

√p'x̌₁ † p'a?x̌ *to heal, become well.* (p'a'qh (stem), vi.); s+p'a?x̌ *healed (becoming...).* (sp'a'qh, vi.); i c+p[']áx̌ *It (wound) is becoming healed.* (itspa'qh, vi.); čn‿p'a?x̌ *cure, cured, heal, healed.* (chnp'a'qh. (lit. I became healed, cured), vi.); § s+ta·m'+ł+p'áx̌ *healed (The wound was finally...), wound (The...was finally healed).* (staaa'młp'aqh, vt, n.); lut+as+p'á?x̌+s *wound (the...did not heal).* (lutasp'a'qhs, n.)

√p'x̌₂ ∥ hn+p'ex̌+p'éx̌=cn *cacophony.* (hnp'eqhp'eqhtsn (lit. He makes jarring, discordant sounds), n.)

√p'x̌ʷ † p'ax̌ʷi?+t *cough.* (p'aqhwi't (stem), vi.); hn+p'ax̌ʷi?+t *cough.* (hnp'aqhwi't (lit. He expelled air from the lungs suddenly and noisily), vt.); s+n+p'áx̌ʷi?+t *coughing, hacking.* (snp'aqhwi't, vi.); kʷu‿n+p'áx̌ʷi?+t *You (sg.) coughed.* (kunp'aqhwi't, vi.); č?in‿p'áx̌ʷ+p'ux̌ʷi+t *coughing (we are...).* (ch'inp'aqhwp'uqhwit, vi.)

√p'y † p'uy *crinkled, wrinkled.* ('puy (stem), adj.); u· p'úy *wrinkled (it is...).* (uup'uy, adj.); ∥ u· p'úy=us *face (he has a wrinkled...), wrinkled (he has a...face).* (uup'uyus, n, adj.); cen+p'+p'úy'=us *dimple.* (tsenp'p'u'yus (lit. small wrinkle on the cheek), n.); p'uy+p'uy=šn *automobile, car.* (p'uyp'uyshn (lit. wrinkled feet), n.); t+p'uy+p'uy=šn *automobile.* (tp'uyp'uyshn (lit. wrinkled feet), n.); hn+t+p'uy+p'uy=šn+n *carport, garage, showroom.* (hntp'uyp'uyshnn. carport, garage. (lit. place for cars), n.); p'ú+p'u?uy=šn *His feet became wrinkled.* ('pu'p'u'uyshn, vi.); u· p'uy+p'úy=čt *hands (he has wrinkled...).* (uup'uyp'uycht, n.); s+n+p'úy=ul'umxʷ *blintz.* (snp'uyu'lumkhw (lit. wrinkled bread), n.); ‡ p'óy-nt-m *crumple.* (p'oyntm (lit. It was crushed together into wrinkles), vi.); p'óy-nt-s *scribbled, wrinkled (h/s...it).* (p'oynts (lit. h/s wrinkled it), vt.); p'úy+m-st-m *corrugate, crinkle.* (p'uymstm (lit. It was made full of wrinkles), vi.); § p'oy-n xʷe hi+s+kʷís+t *scribbled.* (p'oyn khwe hiskwist (lit. I scribbled my name), vt.)

√p'y' † p'iy' *press.* (p'i'y (stem), vt.); p'ey' *milk.* (p'e'y (stem), vt.); s+cen+p'éy'+p'iy' *milk.* (stsenp'e'yp'i'y (lit. that which was pressed from under), n.); cen+p'éy'+p'iy'+m *milked (H/s...a cow).* (tsenp'e'yp'i'ym (lit. H/s pressed under again and again), vt.); cen+p'iy'+p'iy'+mín+n *milker.* (tsenp'i'yp'i'yminn (lit. means pressing under), n.); sye+cen+p'ey'+p'iy'+m *One whose function is to milk.* (syetsenp'e'yp'i'ym, n.); ‡ p'éy'-n *pressed (I...it).* (p'e'yn, vt.); p'éy'+p'iy'-nt-s *pressed (h/s...it here and there or again and again).* (p'e'yp'i'ynts, v.); t+p'iy'=álqʷ-nt-s *squeezed (H/s...h/h throat), throat (H/s squeezed h/h...).* (tp'i'yalqwnts, vt, n.) [see also √py']

√p'ʕʷ † s+p'aʕʷ *apathy.* (sp'a(w, n.); p'áʕʷ+p'aʕʷ+t *banal, commonplace, dull, uninteresting.* (p'a(wp'a(wt (lit. It is completely ordinary), adj.); s+p'áʕʷ+p'aʕʷ+t *dullness.* (sp'a(wp'a(wt, n.)

√p'? † p'e? *To squeeze in orgasm.* (p'e')

√qc † qec *dwindle, shrink (in quantity).* (qets (stem), vi.) [written as √qłs in volume 1] qełs *dwindle, shrink (in quantity).* (qełs)

√qcč † qicč *brother (a man's older...).* (qitsch, n.)

√qg^w † s+qíg^w+t+s *water potatoes.* (sqigwts, n.); qeg^w+g^w+n+útm *smellable.* (qegugwnutm. (lit. It was capable of being smelled), adj.); ic-qíg^w+nun+m+s *He is smelling it.* (itsqigwnunms, vt.); ‡ qíg^w-nun-t-s *He smelled it.* (qigwnunts, vt.); [xref √qx^w₁]

√qh † s+qéh+qeh *hawk.* (sqehqeh, n.); qeh+qeh+iš *cackle (lit. it cackled).* (qehqehish, vi.); is+qéh+qeh+iš *caw.* (isqehqehish (lit. The crow is cawing), vi.) [xref √q'h]

√ql₁ † qél+p=iye *swan (black).* (qelpiye, n.)

√ql₂ † qel *meat (raw...).* (qel (stem), n.); ∥ s+qil=tč *beef, body (human), corpus, flesh, meat.* (sqiltch, n.); hn+qíl=tč+n *butcher shop.* (hnqiltchn (lit. place of one who sell meat), n.); ul s+qil=tč *bodily, corporal.* (ul sqiltch (lit. belonging to the body), adj.); § s+qil=tč he s+t+miy+iy=ípele?+s *anatomy.* (sqiltch he stmiyiyipele's (lit. science of the body), n.); xay'+xi?+s+qíl=tč *chubby, buxom.* (qha'yqhi'sqilch. (lit. She has a big body), adj.); ?as+as+qíl=tč *bicorporal.* (asasqiltch (lit. two bodies), adj.); u+x^wal'á s+qil=tč *carnation.* (uqhwa'la sqiltch (lit. like the body in color), n.); i c+?łn+s+qíl=tč *to eat meat.* (its'łsqiltch, vt.); ?ił+s+qíl=tč *eat (meat).* (iłsqiltch, vt.); k'^w[n]e? čn ᴗ ?íłn a s+qil=tč *I am going to eat some meat.* (k'we' chn' iłn a sqiltch); ni čeł ᴗ k^wu ᴗ ?íłn a s+qil=tč *Are you going to eat some meat?* (ni cheł kuu'yiłn a sqiltch? (qu.).); ec+?ił+s+qil+[t]č *carnivorous.* (ets'łsqitlch (lit. He eats flesh), vi.); sya+?ił+s+qil=tč *carnivore.* (sya'łsqiltch (lit. who eats meat), n.); sye+?ił+s+qíl=[t]č *carnivore (lit. One who eats meat).* (sye'łsqilch, n.); pst+a? a s+qíl=tč *cross-breed, half-breed.* (psta'asqiltch, n.);

hiyc+xéq'^w ha s+qil+tč *burger.* (hiytsqheq'w ha sqiltch (lit. meat that is ground), n.)

√ql₃ ∥ qil=tč *land-bound, landlocked.* (qiltch (stem), adj.); čat+qál=tč=al'qs *cloak, coat, overcoat.* (chatqaltcha'lqs (lit. outer garment), n.); § k^wan+ł+čat+qál=tč=al'qs *overcoat (h/s took along a...), coat (h/s took along a...).* (kwanłchatqaltcha'lqs, n.)

√ql'₁ ∥ s+qil'=tmx^w *husband, male, man, a male human being.* (sqi'ltmkhw, n.); s+qíl'=tmx^w- *husband, groom, male, man.* (sqi'ltmkhw-, pref.); qel'=tmx^w+mí+ncut *bachelor, celibate.* (qe'ltmkhwmintsut. (lit. one who is a man by himself), n.); pan'+s+qíl'=tmx^w *bride-groom.* (pa'nsqi'ltmkhw (lit. a spouse man), n.); i n+qel'=tmx^w+nunt [possibly for -numt] *She wants to get married, to become one with a man.* (inqe'ltmkhwnunt, vi.); § ul s+qil'=tmx^w, ul s+mí?yem *bisexual.* (ul sqi'ltmkhw, ul smi'yem, adj.); qal'=tm+ł+qíx^w *prevailing wind. (lit. man wind).* (qa'ltmłqikhw, n.); qel'=tmx^w+loko·só *boar. (lit. male pig).* (qe'ltmkhwlokooso, n.); qel'=tmx^w+ł+wárč *bullfrog. (lit. male frog).* (qe'ltmkhwłwarch, n.)

√ql'₂ † qel'+is+píl+em *Kalispel Tribe.* (Qe'lispilem, n.); qel'+s+pil+em *Kalispel Tribe.* (Qe'lspilem, n.)

√ql'₃ ∥ s+qel'=éps *collar, necklace.* (sqe'leps, n.)

√ql'x ∥ qál'x=ełp *bramble, briar.* (qa'lqhełp. (lit. a rose bush), n.)

√qł † qeł *awake, overcome, succeed.* (qeł (stem). adj, vt, vi.); qił *rouse, wake up.* (qił (stem), vt.); qił+n *arouse, waken.* (qiłn, vt.); s+qił+t *awaken.* (sqiłt, vi.); ‡ qíł-nt-m *arouse (to...).* (qiłntm (lit. He was awakened from sleep), vi.); qíł-nt-s *awoke (he...him).* (qiłnts, vt.); §

131

čs+m'áy'+qiɫ-t-s *inform, apprize.* (chs'ma'yqiɫts (lit. He caused him to know it for certain), vt.)

√qm † qem *home (to be at...), unconcerned, uninterested, he is at home!* (qem (stem), n, adj.); u· qé·m *calm.* (uuqeeem (lit. He is quiet), n.); qem+p *He became serene.* (qemp, vi.); i+can+qém+mš *athirst.* (itsanqemmsh (lit. He is eager for something), adj.); ∥ s+n+qém=elgʷes *complacence.* (snqemelgwes, n.); s+n+qem=ílgʷes+m *calm, composure, presence, self-possession.* (snqemilgwesm, n.); u+n+qém= elgʷes *carefree, complacent.* (unqemelgwes (lit. He is calm in heart, He is confident), adj.); u+n+qé·m= elgʷes *composed.* (unqeeemelgwes (lit. He is calm. He is serene), adj.)

√qm' ∥ s+qím'=us *wood tick.* (sqi'mus, n.)

√qm's † qém'es *camas (baked...).* (qe'mes. (Nez Perce word), n.)

√qn? † qíne? *grandmother (paternal...).* (qine', n.)

√qp † qep *pad.* (qep (stem), vt.); ∥ qep=íɫc'e? *plate.* (qepiɫts'e', n.); hn+qep=íčn'+n *saddle blanket, saddle pad.* (hnqepich'nn, n.); hn+qap=qín= ups+n *saddle, seat cushion.* (hnqapqinupsn, n.); ‡ qép-nt-s *cushioned (he...it).* (qepnts, vt.); § s+n+c[']aw'+ɫ+qap=íɫc'e? *dish washing.* (sntsa'w'ɫqapiɫts'e', n.) [see also √kp]

√qpl' ∥ qap+qapl'=y'úy'e? *butterfly.* (qapqap'l'yu'ye', n.); č'iy+c+qap+qap'l=y'uy'e? *chrysalis.* (ch'iytsqapqap'l'yu'ye' (lit. the pupa of a butterfly enclosed in a firm case or cocoon), n.); § u+x̌ʷal'+á qap+qapl'= y'úy'e? *desultory.* (uqhwa'la qapqap'l'yu'ye'. (lit. He is like a butterfly; he is aimless, unsettled), adj.)

√qp? † qa+qépe? *bag (corn husk...), burlap (...bag).* (qaqepe', n.)

√qq † qeq *cackle.* (qeq (stem), vi.); is+qeq+éq+iš *cackle.* (isqeqeqish (lit. The hen is cackling), vi.); i s+qéq+qeq+iš *caw (lit. The crow is cawing).* (isqeqqeqish, vi.); § uw'i+c+qoq+há·?+qʷe?el' *lit. He kept on talking and talking.* (u'witsqoqhaaa'qwe'e'l, vt.)

√qqʷ₁ † qiqʷ *root, unearth.* (qiqw (stem). to root, vi, vt.)

√qqʷ₂ † qoqʷ *moldy.* (qoqw (stem), adj.); s+qoqʷ+t *molding.* (sqoqwt, n.)

√qs₁ † qa+qs *serenade, sing, chant.* (qaqs (stem), vt.)

√qs₂ † qes *scrape, scratch.* (qes (stem), vt.); i s+qás+qas+iš *H/s is scratching away audibly.* (isqasqasish, vi.)

√qxʷ₁ † qi?xʷ *smell, stink.* (qi'khw (stem), vi.); s+qí?xʷ *odor, scent, smell.* (sqi'khw, n.); qi?xʷ+qí?xʷ *Sprague, Washington.* (Qi'khwqi'khw (lit. smell smell), n.); ∥ qíxʷ=ilš *carp, fish.* (qikhwilsh, n.); qexʷ+qexʷ+lš=íye? *cabbage (skunk...).* (qekhwqekhwlshiye', n.); § qal'+tm+ɫ+qíxʷ *prevailing wind. (lit. man wind).* (qa'ltmɫqikhw, n.); se?+šáɫ+qixʷ *deodorize.* (se'shaɫqikhw (lit. it became deprived of odor), vt.); x̌as+aɫ+qixʷ *aroma, scent, fragrance.* (qhasaɫqikhw. (lit. good odor), n.); t'ax̌+aɫ+qi·xʷ=íl'š *wind (The...became strong), strong (The wind became...).* (t'aqhaɫqiikhwi'lsh, n, adj.); ǰiy'+ǰiy'+áɫ+[q]ixʷ *smells (it...bad).* (ji'yji'yaɫqhikhw, vi.); [see also √qgʷ]

√qxʷ₂ † qixʷ *forbid, prevent, prohibit.* (qikhw (stem), vt.)

√qx̌ † qax̌ *to make the "qh" sound.* (qaqh); qax̌+n *cleared (he...his throat).* (qaqhn, vt.); ‡ qax̌-nt-s *He cleared his throat.* (qaqhnts, vt.)

√qyp ∥ s+qayp=áqn *wild rose bush.* (sqaypaqn, n.) s+x̌ʷá·yap=a?qn *wild*

rose bush. (skhwa<u>a</u>yapa'qn, n.)
[written as √xʷyp in volume 1];
s+qáyap=q' *rose hip.* (sq<u>a</u>yapq', n.)

√q?s † qi?s *He had a dream,
nightmare, vision.* (qi's, n.); s+qi?s
*apocalypse, revelation (prophetic),
vision guest, vision.* (sqi's, n.)

√q'c † q'ec' *(?) braid, intertwine, knit,
weave.* (q'e<u>t</u>s' (stem), vt.); at+q'éc'
basket, weaving. (atq'<u>e</u>ts' (lit. That
which is interwoven), n.); at+q'ec
basket. (atq'ets, n.); s+q'éc'+m *weave,
to weave a basket, basketweaving.*
(sq'<u>e</u>ts'm, n, vt, v.); ∥ a<u>t</u>+q'íc'=enč
serpent, snake. (a<u>t</u>q'<u>i</u>ts'ench, n.);
a+n+q'ac+q'ac=íne? *Italian, braids
(to have...), having braided hair.*
(anq'atsq'ats<u>i</u>ne', n.); ‡ q'éc'-nt-s
braid. (q'<u>e</u>ts'nts (lit. He braided it), vt.)

√q'c' † q'ic' *grow, sprout.* (qi'ts'.
burgeon, vi.); q'i?c' *burgeon, to be
lush, verdant.* (q'i'ts' (stem), vi, adj.); ∥
s+n+q'e?c'=ít[k]ʷe? *aquatic flora.*
(snq'e'ts'<u>i</u>twe' (lit. grass or weeds in the
water)., n.); s+n+q'i?c'=ítkʷe?
spinach. (snq'i'ts'<u>i</u>tkwe' (lit. grass or
weeds in the water), n.);
s+can+q[']íc'=šn *undergrowth.*
(stsanq)<u>i</u>"tsshn, n.); s+q'i?c'=úl'mxʷ
crabgrass, grass. (sq'i'ts'<u>u</u>'lmkhw, n.);
s+q'i?c'=úl'umxʷ *grass*
(sq'i'ts'<u>u</u>'lumkhw, n.);

√q'd † q'ed+m *balky, stubborn.* (q'edm
(stem), adj.)

√q'h † s+q'éh+q'eh (Brinkman 2003)
hawk. (sq<u>e</u>hqeh, n.) (sq'ehq'eh). [xref
√qh]

√q'l₁ † čat+q'éle? *lake, Lake Chatcolet
(lit. a lake); a section of Coeur
d'Alene.* (chatq'<u>e</u>le', n.); ∥ q'ele?=i?p
lagoon. (q'ele'i'p (lit. source of lake, or
origin of lake), n.); q'ele?=íp *bayou,
bog, cove, lagoon, marsh, swamp.*
(q'ele'<u>i</u>p, n.)

√q'l₂ † q'el *swing.* (q'el (stem), vi.); ∥
sya+n+q'ele·=yúye? *acrobat.*

(syanq'eleey<u>u</u>ye' (lit. One who swings
on trapeze), n.)

√q'lw ∥ s+q'eliwe?=šn *snowshoes.*
(sq'eliwe'shn, n.)

√q'lxʷ † q'el'xʷ *to hook, snag.* (q'e'lkhw
(stem), vt.); ∥ q'el'xʷ=šn=íw'es *chain
(lit. one foot linked to another or a
series of things joined together).*
(q'e'lkhwshn<u>i</u>'wes, n.); ‡ q'él'xʷ-nt-s
He clapsed it, he hooked it.
(q'<u>e</u>'lkhwnts, vt.); t+q'élxʷ-n *affix.*
(tq<u>e</u>lkhwn (lit. I fastened it to
something), vt.); q'el'xʷ=šn=
íw'es-nt-m *catenate.*
(q'e'lkhwshn<u>i</u>'wesntm (lit. The feet
were linked together), vt.)

√q'ły' ∥ q'eły'=ílumxʷ *angleworm,
earthworm.* (q'e<u>t</u>'y<u>i</u>lumkhw, n.)

√q'm † q'em *covet, desire, long for,
swallow.* (q'em (stem), vt.);
a+can+q'ém+n *covet.* (atsanq'<u>e</u>mn
(lit. He desired things unlawfully), vt.);
s+can+q'ém+mš *avid.* (stsanq'<u>e</u>mmsh
(lit. desiring from below), n.);
s+can+q'ém+n *demand, to desire.*
(stsanq'<u>e</u>mn, vi.); s+n+q'ém+m
swallowing. (snq'<u>e</u>mm, v.); ∥ q'em=íln
Post Falls, Idaho. (Q'em<u>i</u>ln (lit.
throat), n.); s+q'em=íln *throat.*
(sq'emi<u>l</u>n, n.); s+č+q'am=íln
abstaining, fasting. (schq'amiln (lit.
making oneself hungry), vi.);
s+čs+q'em=íln *continence,
contraception, fasting, self-restraint.*
(schsq'emiln (lit. making oneself
hungry/becoming hungry), n.);
čs+q'em=iln *hungry (get).* (chsq'emiln
(lit. he became hungry), vi.);
čn‿čs+q'am=iln *I got hungry.*
(chnchsq'amiln, adj.); čn‿čs+q'em=
íln *famished, hungry (to get...).*
(chnchsq'emiln, adj, vi.); i+čs+q'am=
íln *hungry, He is hungry.* (ichsq'amiln,
adj.); ‡ hn+q'ém-nt *swallow
(you...it!).* (hnq'<u>e</u>mnt, vt.);
hn+q'ém-nt-s *swallowed (He...it).*

(hnq'e̲mnts, vt.); can+q'ém-nt-s *coveted, craved, desired, required, wished, demanded (He...it).* (tsanq'e̲mnts. *inwardly,* vt, vi.)

√q'm' // q'a+q'am'=iy'e? *to fish.* (q'aq'a'mi'ye (stem), vi.); q'a+q'm'=íy'e? *fished (he...).* (q'aq"mi'ye', vi.); hn+q'a+q'm'=íy'e?+n *fishing place.* (hnq'aq"mi'ye'n, n.); ic+q'a+q'm'=íye? *fishing (He is...).* (itsq'aq"miye', vi.); s+q'a+q'em'=íy'e? *fishing.* (sq'aq'e̲'mi'ye', vi.); s+q'a+q'am=íy'e? *fishing.* (sq'aq'ami'ye', v.)

√q'n ‡ q'an-t-siš *struggle (for one's life, as in a fire).* (q'antsish (stem), vi.) [?]

√q'p † q'ap+q'ap+í *delta, Sandpoint, Idaho.* (q'apq'api, n.); // s+q'ep+q'e·p=ín'e? *sand.* (sq'epq'eepi'ne', n.)

√q'pqʷ † q'epqʷ *snare.* (q'epqw (stem), vt.)

√q'p'xʷ † q'íp'xʷe? *walnut.* (q'i̲p'khwe', n.)

√q's₁ † q'es+p *ancient, chronic, long ago.* (q'esp (lit. It is a long time), adj, adv.); q'as+íp *It is a long time (Spokane).* (q'asi̲p, v.); s+q'es+p *antique.* (sq'esp, n.); // s+q'es+p=ílgʷes *artifact.* (sq'espi̲lgwes (lit. ancient property), n.); hn+q'es+p=ílgʷes+n *antique store, museum, second-hand store.* (hnq'espilgwesn, n.); ?epł n+q'es+p=ílgʷes+n *antiquary.* (epł nq'espi̲l gwesn (lit. One who has a place of antiquities, one who has a second-hand store), n.); § k'ʷay'+q'és+p *long-ago, past.* (k'wa'yq'e̲sp, adj.); ul k'ʷay+q'és+p *archaic, antique.* (ul k'wayq'e̲sp (lit. belonging to ancient time), adj.); s+t+miy+y=ipele?+s xʷe s+q'es+p=ilgʷe?s *archeology, (lit. exposition of ancient property).* (stmiyyipele's khwe sq'espilgwe's, n.)

√q's₂ † q'es+t *bad (it is...).* (q'est, vi.) [for expected √č's]

√q't'₁ † q'et'+p *climb (a hill), to reach the top of a hill.* (q'et'p (stem), vt.); q'et'+iš *mountain (He climbed the...), climbed (He...the mountain).* (q'et'ish, n, vt.); q'a+q'ét'+p *He finished climbing (a hill).* (q'aq'et'p, vt.); s+q'a+q'et'+p *hill top.* (sq'aq'et'p (lit. place for finishing climbing), n.); kʷp‿q'ét'+iš *climbed (you...the mountains).* (kupq'et'ish, vt.); // s+t+q'et+p=íčn' *culmination.* (stq'etpich'n (lit. reaching the ridge of the mountain)., n.); čn‿t+q'et'+p=íčn' *culminate.* (chntq'et'pi̲ch'n. (lit. I reached the ridge of the mountain), vi.)

√q't'₂ † ac+q'ít'+m *blemish, flaw.* (atsq'i̲t'm (lit. It has a flaw or disfigurement), n.)

√q'w † q'iw *bewitch.* (q'iw (stem), vt.); // s+q'íw=łc'e? *animal magnetism, charisma, charm.* (sq'i̲wts'e', n.); ‡ q'íw-nt-s *bewitched, cast spell, charmed.* (q'i̲wnts, vt.)

√q'w' † q'ew *to break, shatter, smash.* (q'e'w (stem), vt.); q'áw'+p *broke, cracked (it...).* (q'a̲'wp, vi.); q'éw'+p *it cracked, it broke.* (q'e̲'wp)

√q'x † q'ex *treasure, wealth.* (q'ckh (stem), n.) [xref √q'x̌]

√q'xʷ † q'exʷ *covetous, desire, longing, proud.* (q'ekhw (stem), n, adj.); u· q'éxʷ *classy.* (uuq'e̲khw (lit. He is sort of particular), adj.); q'éxʷ+xʷ *captivate.* (q'e̲khukhw (lit. He was fascinated by special charm or beauty), vi.); s+q'éxʷ+xʷ *courtship.* (sq'e̲khukhw (lit. the desire to possess), n.); q'axʷ+q'éxʷ+t *chic, modish, sophisticated.* (q'akhwq'e̲khwt (lit. He is particular, choosy, conceited, vain, dandy), adj.); s+q'axʷ+q'éxʷ+t *conceit, egotism.* (sq'akhwq'e̲khwt. *particularity,* n.); s+q'axʷ+q'axʷ+m'scút *conceit.* (sq'akhwq'akhu'mstsut (lit. having too high an opinion of oneself, n.);

√q'xʷ

q'exʷ+xʷ+m+útn *desirable.*
(q'ekhukhwmu̱tn (lit. H/S is desirable),
vi.); ac+q'exʷ+x[ʷ]-em+is *desire.*
(atsq'ekhukhemis (stem), vt.);
kʷu‿i?-c+q'exʷ+xʷ+mín+m *I am
desiring to have you (sg).*
(kwi'tsq'ekhukhwmi̱nm, vi.);
čeł‿kʷ‿is+q'exʷ+xʷ+mín+m *desire.*
(chełkwisq'ekhukhwmi̱nm. (lit. I will
desire to have you (sg.)), vt.);
hn-i?‿c+q'exʷ+xʷ+mín+m *I am
desiring to have him/her.*
(hi'tsq'ekhukhwmi̱nm, vt.);
čeł‿hi-s+q'exʷ+xʷ+mín+m *I will
desire to have h/h.*
(chełhisq'ekhukhwmi̱nm, vt.);
kʷp‿hi?c+q'exʷ+xʷ+mín+m *desiring
(I am...to have you (pl.).*
(kuphi'tsq'ekhukhwmi̱nm, vi.);
čeł‿kʷup‿hi-s+q'exʷ+xʷ+mín+m
*desire (lit. I will desire to have you,
(pl)).* (chełkuphisq'ekhukhwmi̱nm,
vi.); hn-i?‿c+q'exʷ+xʷ+[m]ín+m-lš *I
am desiring to have them.*
(hi'tsq'ekhukhwi̱nmlsh, vt.);
čeł‿hi-s+q'exʷ+xʷ+mín+m-lš *I will
desire to have them.*
(chełhisq'ekhukhwmi̱nmlsh, vt.);
čn‿y'c+q'exʷ+xʷ+mín+m *(lit. you
(sg.) are desiring to have me).*
(chni'tsq'ekhukhwmi̱nm, vt.);
čeł‿čn‿?i-s+t+q'exʷ+xʷ+mín+m
you (s) will desire to have me.
(chełchn'istq'ekhukhwmi̱nm, vt.); i?
c+q'exʷ+xʷ+mín+m *You (sg.) are
desiring to have h/h.*
(i'tsq'ekhukhwmi̱nm, vt.);
čeł‿?i-s+q'exʷ+xʷ+mín+m *you (s)
will desire to have h/h.*
(cheł'isq'ekhukhwmi̱nm, vt.); i?
c+q'exʷ+xʷ+mín+m-lš *You [sg.] are
desiring to have them.*
(i'tsq'ekhukhwmi̱nmlsh, vt.);
č‿y'c+q'exʷ+xʷ+mín+m-s *H/S is
desiring to have me.*
(chi'tsq'ekhukhwmi̱nms, vt.);

čeł‿či‿s+q'exʷ+xʷ+mín+m-s *h/s
will desire to have me.*
(chełchisq'ekhukhwmi̱nms, vt.);
kʷu‿y'c+q'exʷ+xʷ+mín+m-s *H/S is
desiring to have you (sg).*
(ku'ytsq'ekhukhwmi̱nms, vi.);
čeł‿kʷu‿s+q'exʷ+xʷ+mín+m-s *(lit.
h/s will desire to have you(sg.)).*
(chełkusq'ekhukhwmi̱nms, vt.);
čn‿i?c+q'exʷ+xʷ+min+m-p *desire.*
(chni'tsq'ekhukhwminmp. (lit. You (pl)
are desiring to have me), vi.);
čeł‿čn‿?i-s+q'exʷ+xʷ+mín+m-p
you (pl) will desire to have me.
(chełchn'isq'ekhukhwmi̱nmp, vt.);
čeł‿?i-s+q'exʷ+xʷ+mín+m-lš *you
(pl) will desire to have them.*
(cheł'isq'ekhukhwmi̱nmlsh, vt.);
č‿y'c+q'exʷ+xʷ+mín+m-s-lš *They
are desiring to have me.*
(chi'tsq'ekhukhwmi̱nmslsh, vt.);
čeł‿či‿s+q'exʷ+xʷ+mín+m-s-lš
they will desire to have me.
(chełchisq'ekhukhwmi̱nmslsh, vt.);
kʷup‿?i‿c+q'exʷ+xʷ+mín+m-s-lš
They are desiring to have you (pl).
(kup'itsq'ekhukhwmi̱nmslsh, vi.);
čeł‿kʷup‿s+q'exʷ+xʷ+mín+m-s-lš
(lit. they will desire to have you (pl)).
(chełkupsq'ekhukhwmi̱nmslsh, vt.); ‡
ac+q'exʷ+xʷ+mí-st-m-n *I desire to
have you (sg.).* (atsq'ekhukhwmi̱stmn,
vt.); q'exʷ+xʷ+mí-nt-s-n *desired (I...to
have you (sg.).* (q'ekhukhwmi̱ntsn, vi.);
ac+q'exʷ+xʷ+mí-s-n *I desire to have
h/h.* (atsq'ekhukhwmi̱sn, vt.);
q'exʷ+xʷ+mín-n *desired (I...to have
h/h).* (q'ekhukhwmi̱nn, vi.);
ac+q'exʷ+xʷ+mí-st-ulm-n *I desire to
have you (pl.).*
(atsq'ekhukhwmi̱stulmn, vt.);
q'exʷ+xʷ+mí-nt-ulm-n *desired (I...to
have you (pl.).* (q'ekhukhwmi̱ntulmn,
vi.); ac+q'exʷ+xʷ+mí-s-n-lš *I desire
to have them.* (atsq'ekhukhwmi̱snlsh,
vt.); q'exʷ+xʷ+mín-n-lš *desired (I...to*

have them). (q'ekhukhwm̲innlsh, vi.);
ac+q'exʷ+xʷ+mí-st-me-xʷ *You (sg.)
desire to have me.*
(atsq'ekhukhwm̲istmekhw, vt.);
q'exʷ+xʷ+mí-nt-se-xʷ *You (sg.)
desired to have me.*
(q'ekhukhwm̲intsekhw, vi.);
ac+q'exʷ+xʷ+mí-st-xʷ *You (sg.) desire
to have h/h.* (atsq'ekhukhwm̲istkhw,
vt.); q'exʷ+xʷ+mí-nt-xʷ *You (sg.)
desired to have h/h.*
(q'ekhukhwm̲intkhw, vi.);
ac+q'exʷ+xʷ+mí-st-me-s *H/s desires
to have me.* (atsq'ekhukhwm̲istmes,
vt.); q'exʷ+xʷ+mí-nt-se-s *H/S desired
to have me.* (q'ekhukhwm̲intses, vi.);
ac+q'exʷ+xʷ+mí-st-mi-s *H/s desires
to have you (sg.).*
(atsq'ekhukhwm̲istmis, vt.);
q'exʷ+xʷ+mí-nt-si-s *H/S desired to
have you (sg.).* (q'ekhukhwm̲intsis,
vi.); ac+q'exʷ+xʷ+mí-st-mel-p *You
(pl.) desire to have me.*
(atsq'ekhukhwm̲istmelp, vt.);
q'exʷ+xʷ+mí-nt-sel-p *You (pl.)
desired to have me.*
(q'ekhukhwm̲intselp, vi.);
ac+q'exʷ+xʷ+mí-st-xʷ-lš *You (pl.)
desire to have them.*
(atsq'ekhukhwm̲istkhwlsh, vt.);
q'exʷ+xʷ+mí-nt-xʷ-lš *You (pl.) desired
to have them.* (q'ekhukhwm̲intkhwlsh,
vi.); ac+q'exʷ+xʷ+mí-st-me-s-lš *They
desire to have me.*
(atsq'ekhukhwm̲istmeslsh, vt.);
q'exʷ+xʷ+mí-nt-se-s-lš *They desired
to have me.* (q'ekhukhwm̲intseslsh,
vi.); ac+q'exʷ+xʷ+mí-st-ulmi-s-lš
They desire to have you (pl.).
(atsq'ekhukhwm̲istulmislsh, vt.);
q'exʷ+xʷ+mí-nt-si-s-lš *They desired
to have you (pl.).*
(q'ekhukhwm̲intsislsh, vi.)

√q'xʷʔ † q'+q'í[x]ʷeʔ *few.* (q'q'ik̲we',
adj.)

√q'x̌ § s+q'éx̌+q'ex̌+t he n+ʔuk̲ʷún+n
dictionary. (sq'e̲qhq'eqht he 'nuk̲unn
(lit. sayings that are a treasure), n.)
[xref √q'x̌]

√q'y₁ ‡ q'ey=úʔs-nt-m *disbelieved (he
was...), possibly Spokane word.*
(q'eyu'snt, vi.); § s+q'eyuʔ+ɬ+xʷc̓+út
*Lawrence Nicodemus (Indian name
of).* (Sq'eyu'ɬkhwts'u̲t (lit. Disbelieved
Rocky Mountain), n.)

√q'y₂ † q'iy' *cleft, split.* (q'i'y (stem),
adj.); ∥ an+q'e·y=íw'es *pitchfork,
bifurcate.* (anq'eeyi'wes (lit. It is
divided into two branches), n, adj.);
q'a+q'ay'+q'ey'=íl'xʷ *perch.*
(q'aq'a'yq'e'yi'lkhw, n.) [?]

√q'y' † q'ey' *design, graphics, writing.*
(q'e'y (stem), n.); q'ey' *spotted,
variegated.* (q'e'y (stem), adj.);
s+q'éy'+m *writing.* (sq'e̲'ym, n.);
q'ey'+mín+n *book, correspondence,
document, epistle, letter, manuscript,
message, paper, text, treaty, writing.*
(q'e'ym̲inn (lit. That which is written),
n.); q'+q'ey'+mín+n *brochure.*
(q'q'e'y'm̲inn, n.); q'e+q'ey'+m'ín'+n'
booklet. (q'eq'e'y'mi'n'n (lit. a little
paper (book)), n.); čat+q'ey'+mín+n
desk, writing. (chatq'e'ym̲inn, n.);
t+q'[']ey'+mín+n *blackboard.*
(tqe'ym̲inn (lit. that on which one
writes), n.); q'éy'+ncut *registered
(he...), checked (he...in).* (q'e̲'yntsut (lit.
He wrote himself), vt, vi.);
s+can+q'éy'+iy' *chart, croquis, map,
outline, sketch.* (stsanq'e'yi'y (lit. A
thing traced), n.); s+can+q'éy'+m
design, draw, paint, sketching.
(stsanq'e̲'ym, vt.); s+can+q'ey'+ncút
close-up. (stsanq'e'yntsut (lit. making
outlines of oneself), n.);
s+can+q'ey'+ncút+n *drawing,
painting, picture.* (stsanq'e'yntsu̲tn (lit.
means of marking oneself or one's
outline), n.); sya+q'éy'+m *author,
clerk, secretary, columnist.* (syaq'e̲'ym

(lit. One who writes for another), n.);
q'ey'-šít-ew'eš *correspond*.
(q'e'yshite'wesh (lit. They
communicated by letter), vi.);
s+q[']ey'-šít-ew'eš *communication
(by letter), correspondence*.
(sqe'yshite'wesh, n.); ∥ s+can+q'ey=
úl'mxʷ *cartography, the making of
maps (lit. writing of land)*.
(stsanq'e'yu'lmkhw, n.); q'ey'+m=
utyeʔ *bill (five dollar...)*. (q'e'ymutye'.
paper money, n.); s+q'ey'=íčt+m
*calligraphy, handwriting (the art of
fine...), penmanship*. (sq'e'yichtm, n.);
‡ can+q'éy[']-nt-s *circumscribe*.
(tsanq'eynts (lit. He drew a line around
it), vt.); can+q'éy-n *depict*.
(tsanq'e'yn (lit. I painted him (around);
I portrayed him), vt.); q'ey'-šít-m
written (he was...to). (q'e'yshitm, vi.);
q'ay'+q'ay'=íč-st-n [?] *He occupied
himself with writing*. (q'a'yq'a'yichstn,
vt.); § sya·+q'éy'+n tgʷel' č+ł+łẍʷ=
álqʷ *composer*. (syaaq'e'yn tgwe'l
chłłqhwalqw (lit. writer for the flute,
piano, etc.), n.); s+q'ey'+al'+s+čí+čeʔ
brand. (sq'e'ya'lschiche' (lit. act of
marking animals), n.);
s+can+q'ey'+iy'+s xʷe s+čint
demography. (stsanq'e'yi'ys khwe
schint (lit. writing concerning people),
n.); ẍem=enč+eł+q'ey'+mín+n
*bibliophile, bookish, bookworm,
scholar, studious*.
(qhemenchełq'e'ymínn. (lit. He is fond
of books), adj.);
sye+k'ʷul'+ł+q'ey'+mín+n *bookie,
bookmaker*. (syek'u'lłq'e'yminn (lit.
One who accepts and pays off
bets/One who makes paper (books)),
n.); s+poẍʷm+eł+q'ey'+mín+n
circular, bulletin. (spoqhmełq'e'yminn,
n.); niʔ+q'eʔ=iw'es+na q'ey'+mín+n
bookmark. (ni'q'e'i'wesna q'e'yminn
(lit. a marker placed between the pages
of a book), n.); s+t+q'ey'+y'=ípeleʔ+s

he+n+xʷél+xʷl+n *biography*.
(stq'e'y'yipele's henkhwelkhwln (lit. a
written account of the origin of one's
life), n.); hn+ẍem=ínč+n ha
q'ey'+mín+n *billet-doux, love-letter*.
(hnqheminchn ha q'e'yminn (lit. a letter
that is the means of loving), n.);
qʷam+qʷam+t ha ic+q'ey' *belle
lettres*. (qwamqwamt ha itsq'e'y (lit.
writings that are beautiful), pl.n.);
y+ʔac'ẍa+ł+q'ey'+mín· *to read*.
('yats'qhałq'e'yminn, vt.); t'uʔ
čeł‿čiy‿ʔac'ẍ+al q'ey'+mín+n
*read (Well, I am going to...a book),
book (Well, I am going to read a...)*.
(t'u'cheł chi'yats'qhal q'e'yminn, vt, n.);
paẍ+paẍ+t he q'ey'+mín+n *Bible*.
(paqhpaqht he q'e'yminn (lit. A book
that is wise), n.); s+nukʷ+q'éy'+m
coauthor. (snukwq'e'ym, n.);
s+nukʷ+q'ey'-šít-ew'eš
correspondent. (snukwq'e'yshite'wesh
(lit. One with whom one corresponds),
n.); n+ʔílk'ʷ=elgʷes+n a q'ey'+mín+n
bookshelf, library. ('nilk'welgwesn a
q'e'yminn, n.); kʷen+ł+q[']ey'+mín+n
H/s took a book along.
(kwenłqe'yminn, v.)

√**q'ʔ₁** † q'iʔ *clasp, grasp, penetrate*. (q'i'
(stem), vt.); q'á̲ʔ+q'a̲ʔ+t *bugaboo*.
(q'a̲'q'a't (lit. a steady source of
annoyance or concern; stuck stuck or
stick stick), n.); ∥ s+n+q'íʔ=cn
*Blessed Sacrament, communion,
Consecrated Host, eucharist*.
(Snq'i'tsn. (lit. that which is put into
the mouth, between the lips), n.); q'aʔ=
qín+n *bung, cork*. (q'a'qinn (lit.
something stuck on the head, a stopper
for a bunghole), n.); s+q'íʔ=šn
brogan, shoe. (sq'i'shn. (lit. something
stuck on the foot), n.); § niʔ+q'eʔ=
iw'es+na q'ey'+mín+n *bookmark*.
(ni'q'e'i'wesna q'e'yminn (lit. a marker
placed between the pages of a book),
n.)

√q'ʔ₂ // s+n+q'eʔ+eʔ=ílgʷes *business, commerce, industry, occupation, profession.* (snq'e'e'ilgwes. commercial, industrial, or professional dealings (lit. sticking things in one's heart), n.); in+q'eʔ+eʔ=ílgʷes *busy.* (inq'e'e'ilgwes (lit. He is occupied), adj.); sya+n+q'eʔ+eʔ=ílgʷes *agent, broker, deputy.* (syanq'e'e'ilgwes (lit. One whose business is to occupy one's heart for another), n.); sya+n+q'eʔ+eʔ=íl[g]ʷes *committee.* (syanq'e'e'ilgwes, n.)

√qʷc † qʷic *warm.* (qwits (stem), adj.); [q]ʷic+t *warm.* (gwitst, adj.); qʷic+t *It is warm. (can refer to weather, usually to house, clothing, etc.).* (qwitst, vi.); qʷíc+m+ncut *bundle up, he dressed warmly.* (qwitsmntsut, vi.); s+qʷíc+mš *bunny, rabbit.* (sqwitsmsh, n.); ic+qʷíc+mš *warming (he is...himself).* (itsqwitsmsh, vt.); // qʷác=qn *chapeau, hat.* (qwatsqn (lit. head warmer), n.); hn-qʷác=qn *hat (It is my...).* (hnqwatsqn, n.); in-qʷác=qn *hat (It is your (sg.)...).* (inqwatsqn (lit. head warmer), n.); qʷác+qʷac=qn+m-p *They are your (sg.) hats.* (qwatsqwatsqnmp, vt.); qʷác=qi-s *It is h/h hat.* (qwatsqis, vt.); qʷác=qn-et *It is our hat.* (qwatsqnet, vt.); qʷac+qʷac=qn-et *They are our hats.* (qwatsqwatsqnet, vt.); qʷác=qn+m-p *It is your (pl.) hat.* (qwatsqnmp, vt.); qʷác=qi-s-lš *It is their hat.* (qwatsqislsh, vt.); s+qʷíc=ul'umxʷ *California, south (a warm country (the...)).* (sqwitsu'lumkhw, n.); § ul s+qʷíc=úl'mxʷ he s+čint *Apache.* (ul sqwitsu'lmkhw he schint (lit. Indian of a warm country), n.)

√qʷh † uˑ qʷíh *rich.* (uuqwih. He is well-to-do, wealthy, upper class, adj.); uˑ [qʷ]íh *upper class, wealthy, well-to-do.* (uuqhih. He is wealthy, rich, upper class, adj.)

√qʷl₁ † qʷaʔ+qʷel' *speak.* (qwa'qwe'l (stem). talk, vi.); qʷáʔ+qʷal' *talk.* (qwa'qwa'l (stem). speak, vi.); qʷaʔ+qʷeʔl'+úl *communicable.* (qwa'qwe'lul (lit. He is talkative), adj.); qʷ+qʷáʔ+qʷeʔel *conferred, chatted, consulted.* (quqwa'qwe'el, vi.); s+qʷáʔ+qʷeʔel *directive, order.* (sqwa'qwe'el, n.); s+qʷ+qʷáʔ+qʷeʔel' *conference, counsel.* (squqwa'qwe'e'l. conference (lit. meeting for discussion), n.); č'+ac+qʷaʔ+qʷeʔel *converse, speak, talk.* (ch'atsqwa'qwe'el, vi.); s+t+qʷaʔ+qʷeʔel'+m'ín' *chitchat.* (stqwa'qwe'e'lm'in' (lit. one who is the subject of gossip), n.); s+t+qʷaʔ+qʷeʔel'+mín *discussion.* (stqwa'qwe'e'lmin (lit. talking about something), n.); syaˑ+qʷáʔ+qʷeʔel *dictator.* (syaaqwa'qwe'el (lit. One who talks, one who gives commands), n.); sya+qʷ+qʷáʔ+qʷeʔel' *attorney, barrister, councilman, lawyer.* (syaqqwa'qwe'e'l (lit. One whose business is to talk for other people), n.); sya+qʷ+qʷáʔ+qʷeʔeʔl *lawyer.* (syaquqwa'qwe'e'l (lit. little speaker), n.); hiˑc+qʷáʔ+qʷeʔel *behest.* (hiitsqwa'qwe'el (lit. that which is spoken (commanded)), n.); hiyc+qʷáʔ+qʷeʔel *dictate, order, precept.* (hiytsqwa'qwe'el (lit. that which is spoken), n.); hn+qʷáʔ+qʷel'+n *language.* (hnqwa'qwe'ln, n.); hn+qʷ+qʷáʔ+qʷeʔl'+n' *basilica, court, courthouse, courtroom.* (hnqoqwa'qwe''l'n (lit. a room for talking), n.); ul s+qʷ+qʷaʔ+qʷeʔel' *colloquial.* (ul squqwa'qwe'e'l (lit. pertaining to conversation), adj.); hayc+qʷáʔ+qʷeʔel *covenant, decree, proclamation, commandment.* (haytsqwa'qwe'el. (lit. that which is proclaimed), n.); ic+qʷ+qʷáʔ+qʷeˑl

council. (itsqqwa'qweel (lit. An
important person is speaking), n.);
ʔapł+n+qʷaʔ+qʷeʔl+n *articulate,
verbal.* (apłnqwa'qwe'ln, vi. (lit. He
has the power of speech), vi.);
čeł‿kʷp‿hi-s+qʷaʔ+qʷel+m' *speak.*
(chełkuphisqwa'qwe'lm, vi.);
č‿y'c+qʷáʔ+qʷeʔel *speaking (I
am...), we are speaking.*
(chi'tsqwa'qwe'el, vi.);
k'ʷnaʔ+čn‿qʷáʔ+qʷeʔel *speak.*
(k'wna'chnqwa'qwe'el (lit. I am going
to speak), vi.);
čeł‿či‿s+qʷaʔ+qʷeʔel *speak.*
(chełchisqwa'qwe'el (lit. I will speak),
vi.); k'ʷ neʔ čn‿qʷaʔ+qʷeʔel *I am
going to speak.* (k'wne'chnqwa'qwe'el,
vi.); č‿y'c+qʷáʔ+qʷel'+m *spoken (I
am being...to).* (chi'tsqwa'que'lm, vi.);
čn'‿c+qʷáʔ+qʷeʔel *speak.*
(ch'ntsqwa'qwe'el. (lit. I customarily
speak), vt.); čn‿qʷáʔ+qʷeʔel *spoke
(I...).* (chnqwa'qwe'el, vi.);
hn-n+qʷáʔ+qʷel'-n *It is my language.*
(hnnqwa'qwe'ln, vi.); qʷáʔ+qʷeʔel-š
You (sg.) speak (imper.). address.
(qwa'qwe'elsh, vt.);
k'ʷu‿qʷáʔ+qʷeʔel *spoke (you (sg.)...).*
(kuuqwa'qwe'el, vi.);
k'ʷ‿c+qʷáʔ+qʷeʔel *speak (you
(sg.)...).* (ku'tsqwa'qwe'el, vi.);
k'ʷu‿y'‿c+qʷáʔ+qʷeʔel *You (sg) are
speaking.* (ku'ytsqwa'qwe'el, vi.);
čeł‿k'ʷu‿s+qʷáʔ+qʷel' *(lit. you (sg.)
will speak).* (chełkusqwa'qw'el, vt.); k'ʷ
neʔ k'ʷu·‿qʷáʔ+qʷe·l *You (sg.) are
going to speak.* (k'wne'kuuqwa'qweel,
vi.); k'ʷu‿y'‿c+qʷáʔ+qʷeʔel-m *You
(sg) are being spoken to.*
(ku'ytsqwa'qwe'lm, vi.);
in-n+qʷáʔ+qʷel'+n *It is your (sg.)
language.* (innqwa'qwe'ln, vi.);
qʷáʔ+qʷeʔel *H/s spoke. addressed.*
(qwa'qwe'el, vt.); ac+qʷáʔ+qʷeʔel *h/s
speaks.* (atsqwa'qwe'el, vi.);
ic+qʷáʔ+qʷeʔel *speaking (H/s is...).*

(itsqwa'qwe'el, vi.);
čas‿qʷáʔ+qʷeʔel *(lit. h/s will
speak).* (chasqwa'qwe'el, vt.); i
c+qʷaʔ+qʷeʔel+m *H/s is being
spoken to.* (itsqwa'qwe'lm, v.);
hn+qʷáʔ+qʷel'+is *language (It is
h/h...).* (hnqwa'qwe'lis, n.);
č‿qʷáʔ+qʷeʔel *spoke (we...).*
(chqwa'qwe'el, vi.);
č‿y'c+qʷáʔ+qʷeʔel *speaking (we
are...).* (chi'tsqwa'qwe'el, vi.);
čał‿č‿s+qʷáʔ+qʷeʔel *speak (lit. we
will speak).* (chałchsqwa'qwe'el, vi.);
čał‿č‿s+qʷ+qʷáʔ+qʷeʔel *we are
going to speak.* (chałchsquqwa'qwe'el,
vi.); k'ʷ neʔ č+qʷáʔ+qʷeʔel *We are
going to speak.* (k'wne'chqwa'qwe'el,
vi.); č‿y'c+qʷáʔ+qʷel'+m *We are
being spoken to.* (chi'tsqwa'qwe'lm,
vi.); hn-qʷáʔ+qʷel'+n-et *It is our
language.* (hnqwa'qwe'lnet, vi.);
qʷáʔ+qʷeʔel-ul *You (pl.) speak
(imper.). address.* (qwa'qwe'lul, vt.);
k'ʷp‿qʷáʔ+qʷeʔel *spoke (you (pl.)...).*
(kupqwa'qwe'el, vi.);
k'ʷp'‿ac+qʷáʔ+qʷeʔel *speak (you
(pl.)...).* (kup'atsqwa'qwe'el, vi.);
k'ʷup‿iʔ-c+qʷáʔ+qʷel'+m *You (pl)
are speaking.* (kupi'tsqwa'qwe'el, vi.);
čeł‿k'ʷup‿s+qʷáʔ+qʷeʔel *(lit. you
(pl) will speak).* (chełkupsqwa'qwe'el,
vt.); k'ʷup‿ʔi‿c+qʷáʔ+qʷel'+m *You
(pl) are being spoken to.*
(kup'i'tsqwa'qwe'lm, vi.);
hn-qʷáʔ+qʷel'+n+m-p *It is your (pl.)
language.* (hnqwa'qwe'lnmp, vi.);
qʷáʔ+qʷeʔel-lš *They spoke.
addressed.* (qwa'qwe'llsh, vt.);
ac+qʷáʔ+qʷeʔel-lš *They speak.*
(atsqwa'qwe'llsh, vi.); i
c+qʷaʔ+qʷeʔel-lš *They are speaking.*
(itsqwa'qwe'llsh, v.);
čas‿qʷáʔ+qʷeʔel-lš *(lit. they will
speak).* (chasqwa'qwe'llsh, vt.);
k'ʷ[n]aʔ qʷáʔ+qʷeʔ-lš *They are going
to speak.* (k'wa'qwa'qwe'lsh, v.); i

139

c+qʷaʔ+qʷeʔel+m-lš *They are being spoken to.* (itsqwa'qwe'lmlsh, v.); hn-qʷá?+qʷel'-is-lš *It is their language.* (hnqwa'qwe'lislsh, vi.); s+qʷaʔ+qʷeʔel'-st-w'íš *contention, controversy, debate.* (sqwa'qwe'e'lst'wish. contention (lit. talking against one another), n.); kʷu‿i?-c+qʷá?+qʷel'+m *I am speaking to you (s).* (kwi'tsqwa'qwe'lm, v.); če[ł]‿kʷ‿is+qʷá?+qʷel'+m *speak.* (chetkwisqwa'qwe'lm. (lit. I will speak to you (sg.)), vt.); hn-i?‿c+qʷá?+qʷel'+m *I am speaking to him/her.* (hi'tsqwa'qwe'lm, vt.); čeł‿hi-s+qʷá?+qʷel'+m *I will speak to h/h).* (chełhisqwa'qwe'lm, vt.); kʷup‿hi?-c+qʷá?+qʷel'+m *I am speaking to you (pl).* (kuphi'tsqwa'qwe'lm, vi.); čeł‿kʷup‿hi-s+qʷa?+qʷel'+m *speak (lit. I will speak to you (pl)).* (chełkuphisqwa'qwe'lm, vi.); hn-i?‿c+qʷá?+qʷel'+mš *I am speaking to them.* (hi'tsqwa'qwe'lmsh, vt.); čeł‿hi-s+qʷá?+qʷel'+m-lš *I will speak to them.* (chełhisqwa'qwe'lmlsh, vt.); čn‿?i+?+čs+qʷá?+qʷel'+m *(lit. you(sg.) are speaking to me).* (chn'i'tsqwa'qwe'lm, vt.); čeł‿čn‿?i-s+qʷá?+qʷel'+m *you (s) will speak to me.* (chełchn'isqwa'qwe'lm, vt.); qʷá?+qʷeʔel-eč *You (sg.) speak to h/h (imper.). address.* (qwa'qwe'lech, vt.) [analysis unclear, -eč possibly an imperative marker]; ic'+qʷá?+qʷel'+m *speaking (You (sg.) are...to h/h).* (i'tsqwa'qwe'lm, vi.); čeł‿?i-s+qʷá?+qʷel'+m *you(s) will speak to h/h.* (cheł'isqwa'qwe'lm, vi.); c‿y'c+qʷa?+qʷel'+m-s *H/s is speaking to me.* (chi'tsqwa'qwe'lms, vt.); čeł‿či‿s+qʷá?+qʷeʔel+m-s *h/s will speak to me.*

(chełchisqwa'qwe'lms, vi.); kʷu‿y'c+qʷá'+qʷeʔel-m-s *H/S is speaking to you (sg).* (ku'ytsqwa'qwe'lms, vi.); čeł‿kʷu‿s+qʷá?+qʷel'+m-s *(lit. h/s will speak to you (sg.)).* (chełkusqwa'qwe'lms, vt.); ic+qʷá?+qʷel'+m-s *speaking (H/s is...to h/h).* (itsqwa'qwe'lms, vi.); čas‿qʷá?+qʷel'+m-s *(lit. h/s will speak to h/h).* (chasqwa'qwe'lms, vt.); kʷu‿y'c+qʷá'+qʷeʔel+m-s *H/S is speaking to you (pl).* (ku'ytsqwa'qwe'lms, vi.); čn‿?i+?c+qʷá?+qʷel'+m-p *(lit. you (pl.) are speaking to me).* (chn'i'tsqwa'qwe'lmp, vt.); čeł‿čn‿?i-s+qʷá?+qʷel'+m-p *you (pl) will speak to me.* (chełchn'isqwa'qwe'lmp, vt.); ic'+qʷá?+qʷel'+m-lš *speaking (You (pl.) are...to them).* (i'tsqwa'qwe'lmlsh, vi.); čeł‿?i-s+qʷá?+qʷel'+m-lš *you (pl) will speak to them.* (cheł'isqwa'qwe'lmlsh, vi.); ic+qʷá?+qʷel'-lš *speaking (They are...).* (itsqwa'qwe'llsh, vi.); ic+qʷá?+qʷel'+m-lš *spoken (They are being...to).* (itsqwa'qwe'lmlsh, vi.); č‿y'c+qʷá?+qʷel'+m-s-lš *They are speaking to me.* (chi'tsqwa'qwe'lmslsh, vt.); čeł‿či‿s+qʷá?+qʷeʔel+m-s-lš *they will speak to me.* (chełchisqwa'qwe'lmslsh, vt.); ic+qʷá?+qʷel'+m-s-lš *speaking (They are...to h/h).* (itsqwa'qwe'lmslsh, vi.); čas‿qʷá?+qʷel'+m-s-lš *(lit. they will speak to h/h).* (chasqwa'qwe'lmslsh, vt.); kʷup‿?i‿c+qʷá'+qʷel'+m-s-lš *They are speaking to you (pl).* (kup'itsqwa'qwe'lmslsh, vi.); čeł‿kʷup‿s+qʷa?+qʷál'+m-s-lš *(lit. they will speak to you (pl)).* (chełkupsqwa'qwa'lmslsh, vt.); ‖ hn+t+qʷa?+qʷel'=íw'es+n *telephone.* (hntqwa'qwe'li'wesn. (lit. means of

talking by wire), n.); ‡
qʷá?+qʷe?el-st-mel-em *I was spoken to. addressed.* (qwa'qwe'elstmelem, vt.); ac+qʷá?+qʷe?el-st-me-le-m *I am spoken to.* (atsqwa'qwe'elstmelem, vi.); t'i?+qʷá?+qʷe?el-st-melem *spoken (I have been...to).* (t'i'qwa'qwe'elstmelem, vi.); t'ixʷ as+qʷá?+qʷe?el-st-mel-em *I had been spoken to.* (t'i'khwasqwa'qwe'e'elstmelem, v.); qʷá?+qʷe?el-st-m-n *I spoke to you (sg.). addressed.* (qwa'qwe'elstmn, vt.); ac+qʷá?+qʷe?el-st-m-n *I speak to you (sg.).* (atsqwa'qwe'elstmn, vi.); t'i?+qʷá?+qʷe?el-st-m-n *spoken (I have...to you (sg.)).* (t'i'qwa'qwe'elstmn, vi.); t'ixʷ as+qʷá?+qʷe?el-st-m-n *I had spoken to you (s).* (t'i'khwasqwa'qwe'elstmn, v.); k'ʷ na? qʷá?+qʷe?el-st-m-n *I am going to speak to you (sg.).* (k'wna'qwa'qwe'elstmn, vi.); qʷá?+qʷe?el-s-n *addressed, spoke (I...to h/h).* (qwa'qwe'elsn, vt.); ac+qʷá?+qʷe?el-s-n *I speak to h/h.* (atsqwa'qwe'elsn, vi.); t'i? qʷá?+qʷe?el-s-n *I have spoken to h/h.* (t'i'qwa'qwe'elsn, v.); t'ixʷ as+qʷá?+qʷe?el-s-n *I had spoken to h/h.* (t'i'khwasqwa'qwe'elsn, v.); k'ʷ na? qʷá?+qʷe?el-s-n *I am going to speak to h/h.* (k'wna'qwa'qwe'elsn, vi.); qʷá?+qʷe?el-st-ulm-n *I spoke to you (pl.). addressed.* (qwa'qwe'elstulmn, vt.); ac+qʷá?+qʷe?el-st-ulm-n *I speak to you (pl.).* (atsqwa'qwe'elstulmn, vi.); t'i?+qʷá?+qʷe?el-st-ulm-n *spoken (I have...to you (pl.)).* (t'i'qwa'qwe'elstulmn, vi.); t'ixʷ as+qʷá?+qʷe?el-st-ulm-n *I had spoken to you.* (t'i'khwasqwa'qwe'elstulmn, v.); k'ʷ na? qʷá?+qʷe?el-st-ulm-n *I am going to speak to you (pl.).*

(k'wna'qwa'qwe'elstulmn, vi.); qʷá?+qʷe?el-s-n-lš *I spoke to them. addressed.* (qwa'qwe'elsnlsh, vt.); ac+qʷá?+qʷe?el-s-n-lš *I speak to them.* (atsqwa'qwe'elsnlsh, vi.); t'i? qʷá?+qʷe?el-s-n-lš *I have spoken to them.* (t'i'qwa'qwe'elsnlsh, v.); t'ixʷ as+qʷá?+qʷe?el-s-n-lš *I had spoken to them.* (t'i'khwasqwa'qwe'elsnlsh, v.); k'ʷ na? qʷá?+qʷe?el-s-n-lš *I am going to speak to them.* (k'wna'qwa'qwe'lsnlsh, vi.); qʷá?+qʷe?el-st-mi-t *You (sg.) were spoken to. addressed.* (qwa'qwe'elstmit, vt.); t'i?+qʷá?+qʷe?el-st-mi-t *spoken (You (sg.) have been...to).* (t'i'qwa'qwe'elstmit, vi.); t'ixʷ as+qʷá?+qʷe?el-st-mi-t *You (s) had been spoken to.* (t'i'khwasqwa'qwe'elstmit, v.); qʷá?+qʷe?el-st-m-exʷ *You (sg.) spoke to me, addressed.* (qwa'qwe'elstmekhw, vt.); ac+qʷá?+qʷe?el-st-me-xʷ *You (sg.) speak to me.* (atsqwa'qwe'elstmekhw, vi.); t'i?+qʷá?+qʷe?el-st-me-xʷ *spoken (you (sg.) have...to me).* (t'i'qwa'qwe'elstmekhw, vi.); t'ixʷ as+qʷá?+qʷe?el-st-me-xʷ *You (s) had spoken to me.* (t'i'khwasqwa'qwe'elstmekhw, v.); k'ʷ na? qʷá?+qʷe?el-st-me-xʷ *You (sg.) are going to speak to me.* (k'wna'qwa'qwe'elstmekhw, vi.); qʷá?+qʷe?el-st-xʷ *You (sg.) spoke to h/h. addressed.* (qwa'qwe'elstkhw, vt.); ac+qʷá?+qʷe?el-st-xʷ *You (sg.) speak to h/h.* (atsqwa'qwe'elstkhw, vi.); na?+qʷá?+qʷe?el-st-xʷ *are (You (sg.)...to speak to h/h).* (na'qwa'qwe'elstkhw, vi.); t'i?+qʷá?+qʷe?el-st-xʷ *spoken (You (sg.) have...to h/h).* (t'i'qwa'qwe'elstkhw, vi.); t'ixʷ as+qʷá?+qʷe?el-st-xʷ *You (s) had*

spoken to h/h.
(t'i'khwasqwa̱'qwe'elstkhw, v.); kʼʷ naʔ
qʷáʔ+qʷeʔel-st-xʷ *You (sg.) are going
to speak to h/h.*
(k'wna'qwa̱'qwe'elstkhw, vi.);
qʷáʔ+qʷeʔel-st-m *H/s was spoken to.
addressed.* (qwa̱'qwe'elstm, vt.);
ac+qʷáʔ+qʷeʔel-st-m *H/s is spoken
to.* (atsqwa̱'qwe'elstm, vi.);
t'iʔ+qʷáʔ+qʷeʔel-st-m *spoken (H/s
has been...to).* (t'i'qwa̱'qwe'elstm, vi.);
t'ixʷ as+qʷáʔ+qʷeʔel-st-m *H/s had
been spoken to.*
(t'i'khwasqwa̱'qwe'elstm, v.);
qʷáʔ+qʷeʔel-st-m-es *H/s spoke to me.
addressed.* (qwa̱'qwe'elstmes, vt.);
ac+qʷáʔ+qʷeʔel-st-me-s *H/s (cust.)
speaks to me.* (atsqwa̱'qwe'elstmes,
vi.); t'iʔ+qʷáʔ+qʷeʔel-st-me-s *spoken
(H/s has...to me).* (t'i'qwa̱'qwe'elstmes,
vi.); t'ixʷ as+qʷáʔ+qʷeʔel-st-me-s
H/s had spoken to me.
(t'i'khwasqwa̱'qwe'elstmes, v.); kʼʷ naʔ
qʷáʔ+qʷeʔel-st-me-s *H/s is going to
speak to me.* (k'wna'qwa̱'qwe'elstmes,
vi.); qʷáʔ+qʷeʔel-st-m-is *H/s spoke to
you (sg.). addressed.* (qwa̱'qwe'elstmis,
vt.); ac+qʷáʔ+qʷeʔel-st-mi-s *H/s
speaks to you (sg.).*
(atsqwa̱'qwe'elstmis, vi.);
t'iʔ+qʷáʔ+qʷeʔel-st-mi-s *spoken (H/s
has...to you (sg.)).* (t'i'qwa̱'qwe'elstmis,
vi.); t'ixʷ as+qʷáʔ+qʷeʔel+st+mi-s
H/s had spoken to you (s).
(t'i'khwasqwa̱'qwe'elstmis, v.); kʼʷ naʔ
qʷáʔ+qʷeʔel-st-mi-s *H/s is going to
speak to you (sg.).*
(k'wna'qwa̱'qwe'elstmis, vi.);
qʷáʔ+qʷeʔel-stu-s *He spoke to h/h.
addressed.* (qwa̱'qwe'elstus, vt.);
ac+qʷáʔ+qʷeʔel-stu-s *H/s speaks to
h/h.* (atsqwa̱'qwe'elstus, vi.);
t'iʔ+qʷáʔ+qʷeʔel-stu-s *spoken (H/s
has...to h/h).* (t'i'qwa̱'qwe'elstus, vi.);
t'ixʷ as+qʷáʔ+qʷeʔel-stu-s *H/s had
spoken to h/h.*

(t'i'khwasqwa̱'qwe'elstus, v.); kʼʷ naʔ
qʷáʔ+qʷeʔel-stu-s *H/s is going to
speak to h/h.* (k'wna'qwa̱'qwe'elstus,
vi.); t+qʷáʔ+qʷeʔel+mí-nt-me-t
discuss. (tqwa'qwe'elmi'ntmet (lit. We
talked about it, We reasoned upon it),
v.); qʷáʔ+qʷeʔel-st-elit *We were
spoken to. addressed.*
(qwa̱'qwe'elstelit, vt.);
ac+qʷáʔ+qʷeʔel-st-m-eli-t *We are
spoken to.* (atsqwa̱'qwe'elstmelit, vi.);
t'iʔ qʷáʔ+qʷeʔel-st-eli-t *We have been
spoken to.* (t'i'qwa̱'qwe'elstelit, v.); t'ixʷ
as+qʷáʔ+qʷeʔel-st-eli-t *We had been
spoken to.* (t'i'khwasqwa̱'qwe'elstelit,
v.); qʷáʔ+qʷeʔel-st-ulmi-t *You (pl.)
were spoken to. addressed.*
(qwa̱'qwe'elstulmit, vt.);
ac+qʷáʔ+qʷeʔel-st-ulmi-t *You (pl.)
are spoken to.* (atsqwa̱'qwe'elstulmit,
vi.); t'iʔ+qʷáʔ+qʷeʔel-st-ulmi-t
spoken (You (pl.) have been...to).
(t'i'qwa̱'qwe'elstulmit, vi.); t'ixʷ
as+qʷáʔ+qʷeʔel-st-ulmi-t *You (pl)
had been spoken to.*
(t'i'khwasqwa̱'qwe'elstulmit, v.);
qʷáʔ+qʷeʔel-st-mel-p *You (pl.) spoke
to me, addressed.* (qwa̱'qwe'elstmelp,
vt.); ac+qʷáʔ+qʷeʔel-st-mel-p *You
(pl.) speak to me.*
(atsqwa̱'qwe'elstmelp, vi.);
t'iʔ+qʷáʔ+qʷeʔel-st-me-lp *spoken
(You (pl.) have...to me).*
(t'i'qwa̱'qwe'elstmelp, vi.); t'ixʷ
as+qʷáʔ+qʷeʔel-st-mel-p *You (pl)
had spoken to me.*
(t'i'khwasqwa̱'qwe'elstmelp, v.); kʼʷ
naʔ qʷáʔ+qʷeʔel-st-mel-p *You (pl.)
are going to speak to me.*
(k'wna'qwa̱'qwe'elstmelp, vi.);
qʷáʔ+qʷeʔel-nt-lš *You (pl.) speak to
h/h (imper.). address.* (qwa̱'qwe'lntlsh,
vt.); qʷáʔ+qʷeʔel-st-xʷ-lš *You (pl.)
spoke to them. addressed.*
(qwa̱'qwe'elstkhwlsh, vt.);
ac+qʷáʔ+qʷeʔel-st-xʷ-lš *You (pl.)*

speak to them. (atsqwa'qwe'elstkhwlsh, vi.); t'iʔ+qʷá?+qʷeʔel-st-xʷ-lš *spoken (You (pl.) have...to them)*. (t'i'qwa'qwe'elstkhwlsh, vi.); t'ixʷ as+qʷá?+qʷeʔel-st-xʷ-lš *You (pl) had spoken to them.* (t'i'khwasqwa'qwe'elstkhwlsh, v.); naʔ+qʷá?+qʷeʔel-st-xʷ-lš *are (You (pl.)...to speak to them).* (na'qwa'qwe'elstkhwlsh, vi.); kʷ naʔ qʷá?+qʷeʔel-s-p-lš *You (pl.) are going to speak to them.* (k'wna'qwa'qwe'elsplsh, vi.); qʷá?+qʷeʔel-st-m-lš *They were spoken to. addressed.* (qwa'qwe'elstmlsh, vt.); t'iʔ+qʷá?+qʷeʔel-st-m-lš *spoken (They have been...to).* (ti'qwa'qwe'elstmlsh, vi.); t'ixʷ as+qʷá?+qʷeʔel-st-m-lš *They had been spoken to.* (t'i'khwasqwa'qwe'elstmlsh, v.); qʷá?+qʷeʔel-st-me-s-lš *They spoke to me. addressed.* (qwa'qwe'elstmeslsh, vt.); ac+qʷá?+qʷeʔel-st-me-s-lš *They speak to me.* (atsqwa'qwe'elstmeslsh, vi.); t'iʔ+qʷá?+qʷeʔel-st-me-s-lš *spoken (They have...to me).* (t'i'qwa'qwe'elstmeslsh, vi.); t'ixʷ as+qʷá?+qʷeʔel-st-me-s-lš *They had spoken to me.* (t'i'khwasqwa'qwe'elstmeslsh, v.); kʷ naʔ qʷá?+qʷeʔel-st-me-s-lš *They are going to speak to me.* (k'wna'qwa'qwe'elstmeslsh, vi.); qʷá?+qʷeʔel-stu-s-lš *They spoke to h/h.* (qwa'qwe'elstuslsh, vt.); ac+qʷá?+qʷeʔel-stu-s-lš *They speak to h/h.* (atsqwa'qwe'elstuslsh, vi.); t'iʔ+qʷá?+qʷeʔel-stu-s-lš *spoken (They have...to h/h).* (t'i'qwa'qwe'elstuslsh, vi.); t'ixʷ as+qʷá?+qʷeʔel-stu-s-lš *They had spoken to h/h.* (t'i'khwasqwa'qwe'elstuslsh, v.); k'ʷ naʔ qʷá?+qʷeʔel-stu-s-lš *They are*

going to speak to h/h. (k'wna'qwa'qwe'elstuslsh, vi.); qʷá?+qʷeʔel-st-m-is-lš *They spoke to you (pl.). addressed.* (qwa'qwe'elstmislsh, vt.); ac+qʷá?+qʷeʔel-st-mi-s-lš *They speak to you (pl.).* (atsqwa'qwe'elstmislsh, vi.); t'iʔ+qʷá?+qʷeʔel-st-mi-s-lš *spoken (They have...to you (pl.)).* (t'i'qwa'qwe'elstmislsh, vi.); t'ixʷ as+qʷá?+qʷeʔel-st-ulmi-s-lš *They had spoken to you (pl).* (t'i'khwasqwa'qwe'elstulmislsh, v.); k'ʷ naʔ qʷá?+qʷeʔel-st-ulmi-s-lš *They are going to speak to you (pl.).* (k'wna'qwa'qwe'elstulmislsh, vi.); § na+ʔx̌íɫ qʷá?+qʷeʔel-st-m-n *speak (I may...to you (sg.)).* (na'qhiɫ qwa'qweelstmn, vi.); na+ʔx̌íɫ qʷá?+qʷéʔel-s-n *speak (I may...to h/h).* (na'qhiɫ qwa'qwe'elsn, vi.); na+ʔx̌íɫ qʷá?+qʷeʔel-st-ulm-n *speak (I may...to you (pl.)).* (na'qhiɫ qwa'qwe'elstulmn, vi.); na+ʔx̌íɫ qʷá?+qʷeʔel-s-n *speak (Maybe I...to them).* (na'qhiɫ qwa'qwe'elsn, vi.); na+ʔx̌íɫ qʷá?+qʷeʔel-st-xʷ *speak (you (sg.) may...to h/h).* (na'qhiɫ qwa'qwe'elstkhw, vi.); na+ʔx̌íɫ qʷá?+qʷeʔel-st-me-s *speak (h/s may...to me).* (na'qhiɫ qwa'qwe'elstmes, vi.); na+ʔx̌íɫ qʷá+qʷeʔel-st-mi-s *Maybe h/s will speak to you (s).* (na'qhiɫ qwa'qwe'elstmis, v.); na+ʔx̌íɫ qʷá?+qʷeʔel-stu-s *speak (H/s may...to h/h).* (na'qhiɫ qwa'qwe'elstus, vi.); na+ʔx̌íɫ qʷá+qʷeʔel-stu-s-lš *H/s may speak to h/h.* (na'quiɫ qwa qwe'estuslsh, v.); na+ʔx̌íɫ qʷá?qʷeʔel-st-mel-p *speak (Maybe you (pl.)...to me).* (na'qhiɫ qwa'qwe'elstmelp, vi.); na+ʔx̌íɫ qʷá?+qʷeʔel-st-xʷ-lš *speak (You (pl.) may...to them).* (na'qhiɫ qwa'qwe'elstkhwlsh, vi.); na+ʔx̌íɫ qʷá?+qʷe?el-st-me-s-lš *speak (They may...to me)*. (na'qhiɫ qwa'qwe'elstmeslsh, vi.); na+?x̌íɫ qʷá?+qʷe?e[l]-stu-s-lš *speak (They may...to h/h)*. (na'qhiɫ qwa'qwe'estuslsh, vi.); na+[?]x̌íɫ qʷá?+qʷe?el-st-mi-s-lš *speak (They may...to you (pl.))*. (naqhiɫ qwa'qwe'elstmislsh, vi.); ic+miyes+qʷ+qʷá?+qʷa·'l *commune*. (itsmiyesququwa'qwaa'l (lit. They are conversing intimately), vi.); s+miyas+qʷ+qʷá?+qʷe?el *commune*. (smiyasququwa'qwe'el (lit. speaking at length), n.); ul soltes han+qʷ+qʷá?+qʷe?l'+n' *court-martial*. (ul soltes hanququwa'qwe'l'n' (lit. courthouse of soldiers), n.); uw'+ic+qox̌á·?+qʷ?el' *buttonhole*. (u'witsqoqhaaa'qw'e'l (lit. He kept on talking and talking), vt.); uw'i+c+qoq+há·?+qʷe?el' *lit. He kept on talking and talking*. (u'witsqoqhaaa'qwe'el, vt.)

√qʷl₂ † qʷil *cheat, swindle*. (qwil (stem). cheat, vt.); s+qʷíl+n *deceit*. (sqwiln (lit. cheating), n.); qʷel+qʷel+n+úl *bilker, cheater, chiseler, defrauder, swindler*. (qwelqwelnul. (lit. He cheats habitually), n.); qʷel+nun+cút *He cheated himself. bilked, defrauded, chiseled, swindled*. (qwelnuntsut, vt.); kʷu‿i?-c+qʷíl+m *I am cheating you (s)*. (kwi'tsqwilm, v.); čeɫ‿kʷ‿is+qʷíl+m *cheat*. (cheɫkwisqwilm. (lit. I will cheat you (sg.)), vt.); hn-i?‿c+qʷíl+m *I am cheating him/her*. (hi'tsqwilm, vt.); čeɫ‿hi-s+qʷil+m *cheat*. (cheɫhisqwilm (lit. I will cheat h/h), vi.); kʷp‿hi?c+qʷíl+m *cheating (I am...you (pl))*. (kuphi'tsqwilm, vt.); čeɫ‿kʷup‿hi-s+qʷíl+m *cheat (lit. I will cheat you (pl)*. (cheɫkuphisqwilm, vi.); hn-i?‿c+qʷíl+m-lš *I am cheating them*. (hi'tsqwilmlsh, vt.);

čeɫ‿hi-s+qwil+m-lš *I will cheat them*. (cheɫhisqwilmlsh, vt.); čn‿?i+?c+qʷíl+m *You (sg.) are cheating me*. (chn'itsqwilm, vt.); čeɫ‿čn‿?i-s+qʷíl+m *you (s) will cheat me*. (cheɫchn'isqwilm, vt.); ic'+qʷíl+m *cheating (you(s) are...h/h)*. (i'tsqwilm, vt.); čeɫ‿?i-s+qʷíl+m *you (s) will cheat h/h*. (cheɫ'isqwilm, vi.); čeɫ‿?i-s+qʷíl+m-lš *cheat (lit. you (sg.) will cheat them)*. (cheɫ'isqwilmlsh, vi.); č‿y'c+qʷíl+m-s *H/s is cheating me*. (chi'tsqwilms, vt.); čeɫ‿či‿s+qʷíl+m-s *h/s will cheat me*. (cheɫchisqwilms, vi.); kʷu‿y'‿c+qʷíl+m-s *H/S is cheating you*. (ku'ytsqwilms, vt.); čeɫ‿kʷu‿s+qʷíl+m-s *(lit. h/s will cheat you (sg))*. (cheɫkusqwilms, vt.); čn‿?i+?c+qʷíl+m-p *You (pl.) are cheating me*. (chn'itsqwilmp, vt.); čeɫ‿či‿s+qʷíle+m-p *you (pl) will cheat me*. (cheɫchisqwilmp, vi.); ic'+qʷíl+m-lš *cheating (you (pl) are...them)*. (i'tsqwilmlsh, vt.); č‿y'c+qʷíl+m-s-lš *They are cheating me*. (chi'tsqwilmslsh, vt.); kʷup‿?i‿c+qʷíl+m-s-lš *They are cheating you [pl.]*. (kup'itsqwilmslsh, vt.); čeɫ‿kʷup‿s+qʷíl+m-s-lš *(lit. they will cheat you (pl))*. (cheɫkupsqwilmslsh, vt.); ‡ ac+qʷíl-st-m-n *I cheat you (sg.)*. (atsqwilstmn, vt.); qʷil-nt-s-n *I cheated you (sg.)*. (qwilntsn, vt.); kʷ na? qʷíl-nt-s-n *I am going to cheat you (sg.)*. (k'wna'qwilntsn, vi.); qʷíl-n *bilked, cheated, chiseled, defrauded (I...h/h)*. (qwiln, vt.); ac+qʷíl-s-n *I cheat h/h*. (atsqwilsn, vt.); kʷ'na?+qʷíl-n *I am going to cheat h/h*. (k'wna'qwiln, vi.); ac+qʷíl-st-ulm-n *I cheat you (pl.)*. (atsqwilstulmn, vt.); qʷíl-nt-ulm-n *I cheated you (pl.)*. (qwilntulmn, vt.); ac+qʷíl-s-n-lš *I*

cheat them. (atsqwilsnlsh, vt.);
qʷil-n-lš *I cheated them.* (qwilnlsh,
vt.); ac+qʷíl-st-me-xʷ *You (sg.) cheat
me.* (atsqwilstmekhw, vt.);
qʷíl-nt-se-xʷ *You (sg.) cheated me.*
(qwilntsekhw, vt.); kʼʷ naʔ
qʷíl-nt-se-xʷ *You (sg.) are going to
cheat me.* (k'wna'qwilntsekhw, vi.);
ac+qʷíl-st-xʷ *You (sg.) cheat h/h.*
(atsqwilstkhw, vt.); qʷil-nt *You (sg.)
cheat h/h (imper.).* (qwilnt, vt.);
qʷil-nt-xʷ *You (sg.) cheated h/h.*
(qwilntkhw, vt.); kʼʷ naʔ qʷíl-nt-xʷ
You (sg.) are going to cheat h/h.
(k'wna'qwilntkhw, vi.); qʷil-nt-lš *You
(sg.) cheat them (imper.).* (qwilntlsh,
vt.); ac+qʷíl-st-me-s *H/s cheats me.*
(atsquilstmes, vt.); qʷíl-nt-se-s *H/s
cheated me.* (qwilntses, vt.); kʼʷ naʔ
qʷíl-se-s *H/s is going to [cheat me].*
(k'wna'qwilntses, vi.); ac+qʷíl-st-mi-s
H/s cheats you (sg.). (atsqwilstmis,
vt.); qʷíl-nt-si-s *H/s cheated you (sg.).*
(qwilntsis, vt.); kʼʷ naʔ qʷíl-nt-si-s
H/s is going to cheat you (sg.).
(k'wna'qwilntsis, vi.); qʷil-nt-s *He
cheated him.* (qwilnts, vt.);
ac+qʷíl-st-mel-p *You (pl) cheat me.*
(atsqwilstmelp, vt.); qʷíl-nt-sel-p *You
(pl.) cheated me.* (qwilntselp, vt.);
ac+qʷíl-st-xʷ-lš *You (pl.) cheat them.*
(atsqwilstkhwlsh, vt.); qʷil-nt-xʷ-lš
You (pl.) cheated them. (qwilntkhwlsh,
vt.); ac+qʷíl-st-me-s-lš *They cheat
me.* (atsqwilstmeslsh, vt.);
qʷíl-nt-se-s-lš *They cheated me.*
(qwilntseslsh, vt.);
ac+qʷíl-st-ulmi-s-lš *They cheat you
(pl.).* (atsqwilstulmislsh, vt.);
qʷíl-nt-si-s-lš *They cheated you (pl.).*
(qwilntsislsh, vt.); § s+nukʷ+qʷíl+n
collude. (snukwqwiln (lit. one who is
deceiving in conjunction with another),
vi.)

√qʷl₃ // s+n+qʷúl=enč *cotton, denim,
wool.* (snqulench, n.); § u+x̌ʷel'+é

s+n+qʷúl=enč he s+t'+t'ús *cotton
candy.* (uqhe'le snqulench he st't'us (lit.
candy that resembles cotton), n.)

√qʷl'₁ † qʷel' *kindle, light.* (qwe'l
(stem), vt.); qʷil' *start a fire, kindle.*
(qwi'l); // hn+t+qʷíl'=kʷp+n *oven,
stove.* (hntqwi'lkupn (lit. place for
kindling), n.) [xref √gʷl]

√qʷl'₂ † qʷel' *angry, enraged, livid.*
(qwe'l (stem). black and blue wound,
adj.); u· qʷél' *black and blue, dark,
purple.* (uuqwe'l, adj.); // un+qʷél'=us
black-eye. (unqwe'lus (lit. He was
discolored as to the eye), n.); qʷ+qʷl'=
ít *black pine.* (qoqo'lit, n.);
qʷl'+qʷl'+m+n=íłp *sagebrush.*
(qw'lqw'lmniłp (lit. dark dark plant),
n.); t+qʷál'=sq'it *cloudy (It is dark
or...).* (tqwa'lsq'it, adj.); ut+qʷál'=sq'it
*cloud (The sky has a) dark...), dark
(The sky has a...cloud).* (utqwa'lsq'it,
adj, n.)

√qʷl'₃ † qʷil' *starve.* (qwi'l (stem), vt.)

√qʷlm' † qʷílem' *anthem, aria, ballad,
canticle, canto, carol, chanson, song.*
(qwile'm, n.); qʷ+qʷíl'em'-et *ditty.*
(ququi'le'met (lit. It is our little song),
n.); § hn+pést+e?=us ha qʷilem'
anti-phone. (hnpeste'us ha qwile'm (lit.
It is on the other side of a song, it is a
responsive song), n.);

√qʷlw † qʷlíw+l'š *bulb, wild onion,
onion.* (qwliw'lsh, n.)

√qʷł₁ † qʷéł+qʷeł+t *stamina,
endurance.* (qwełqwełt, vi.) [xref
√qʷł]

√qʷł₂ † qʷuł *dusty.* (quł (stem), adj.);
s+qʷuʔł *dirt, dust.* (squ'ł. dirt, n.)

√qʷm † qʷam *attractive, pleasant,
pleasing.* (qwam (stem), adj.);
qʷám+qʷam+t *attractive, beautiful,
choice, cute, dainty, delectable,
delicious, elegant, pleasing.*
(qwamqwamt, adj.); s+qʷám+qʷam+t
*delicacy, elegance, refinement,
sensibility.* (sqwamqwamt. (lit.

agreeableness), n.); ul qʷám+qʷam+t *aesthetic.* (ul qwamqwamt, adj.); ∥ hn+qʷám+qʷam=cn *good speaker.* (hnqwamqwamtsn (lit. He's a speaker of beautiful things), n.); kʷ‿n+qʷám+qʷam=cn *eloquent.* (kunqwamqwamtsn (lit. You (sg.) express yourself in vivid and appropriate speech), adj.); § qʷam+qʷam+t ha ic+q'ey' *belle lettres.* (qwamqwamt ha itsq'e'y (lit. writings that are beautiful), pl.n.); x̌am=anč+ɬ+qʷám+qʷam *aesthete.* (qhamanchɬqwamqwam (lit. He loves beautiful things), n.); x̌am= anč+ɬ+qʷám+qʷam+t *aesthete (lit. He loves beautiful things).* (qhamanchɬqwamqwamt, n.);

√qʷm' † qʷum' *dim, gray, lacklustre.* (qu'm (stem) adj.); qʷem' *ignore, oblivious, overlook.* (qwe'm (stem), vt.); qʷem'+p *bemuse.* (qwe'mp (lit. He became preoccupied), vt.); can+qʷém'+p *blacked out (He...), unconscious (He became...).* (tsanqwe'mp, vi, adj.); a+can+qʷém'+p *comatose (become...), faint, pass out.* (atsanqwe'mp (lit. He blacks out), vi.); s+can+qʷém'+p *apoplexy, blackout, blacking out, coma, unconscious, fainting.* (stsanqwe'mp, n.); ∥ hn+qʷm'+p=ílgʷes *amnesia, forgetfulness.* (hnqu'mpilgwes, (lit. He went gray as to memory), n.); hn+qʷm'+qʷm'=ílgʷes *forgetful.* (hnqu'mqu'milgwes (lit. He is habitually forgetful), adj.); s+qʷúm'=c'e? *blanket (gray...).* (squ'mts'e', n.); ‡ cen+qʷm'+p+nú-nt-m *desensitize.* (tsenqu'mpnuntm (lit. He was rendered insensitive), vt.); § qʷm'=íl'kʷ+p *benighted, crass, ignorant, inane, asinine, silly, stupid.* (qu'mi'lkup. a stupid silly person (lit. dark ashes), adj.)

√qʷn † qʷn *blue.* (qwn, n.); qʷen *blue, green, celadon.* (qwen. (stem) (lit. pale to very pale blue), n.); qʷin *blue.* (qwin (stem), adj.); u· qʷn *blue, green.* (uuqwn. It is blue/green, adj.); qʷín+emn *bluing.* (qwinemn (lit. means of making blue), n.); ∥ s+qʷn= íɬkʷp *ashes, clinker.* (sqwniɬkup. (lit. grayish-blue to white to black residue of combustion), n.); u· qʷn=ul'umxʷ *ground (The...is green).* (uuqwnu'lumkhw, n.); t+qʷn+qʷén=us *blue-eyed.* (tqwnqwenus (lit. He has eyes with bright blue iris), adj.); t+qʷn=sq'it *blue (...sky).* (tqwnsq'it, n.); ut+qʷn=sq'it *cerulean.* (utqwnsq'it (lit. The sky is blue, It is azure), adj.); ‡ u· qʷn-lš *green (They are...).* (uuqwnlsh, adj.)

√qʷr † qʷ+qʷár'e?+t *gold.* (qoqwa're't, n.); ∥ t+qʷar+éq=qn *blonde.* (tqwareqqn (lit. one with pale or yellowish hair), n.) [for expected √kʷr]

√qʷs₁ † qʷes *blurred, confused.* (qwes (stem), adj.); qʷés+s *dim.* (qwess (lit. It became indistinct), vt.); u· qʷés *blurred (it is...), blurred (mentally), callow, childish, dense, dim, immature, inexperienced.* (uuqwes. He is..., adj.); s+qʷés+s *blur.* (sqwess (lit. becoming blurred), vt.); qʷés+s+m *befog.* (qwessm (lit. It became obscure), vt.); as+qʷ+qʷés+e? *boy, chiquito.* (asqqwese' (lit. Little blurred son), n.); s+qʷás+qʷs+e? *child.* (sqwasqwse', n.); ∥ qʷás=qn' *blue jay.* (qwasq'n (lit. blurred head), n.); qʷás+s=qn' *crazy, entranced, possessed.* (qwassq'n (lit. He is crazy), adj.); t+qʷás+qʷs+s=us *blear.* (tqwasqwssus (lit. He became blurred as to the eyes), adj.); s+t+qʷás+qʷas+s=us *visual indistinctness.* (stqwasqwassus, n.); [xref √?sqʷ]

√qʷs₂ ‡ hn+qʷs+t=íl'š-stu-s *deepen.* (hnqwsti̱'lshstus (lit. He deepened the well, etc.), vt.)

√qʷy₁ † qʷay *joke.* (qway (stem). (lit. to talk backwards), vi.)

√qʷy₂ ∥ s+qʷá·y=apaʔ *rose hip.* (sqwa̱ayapa', n.)

√qʷy₃ † qʷiy *to abound, He is affluent, wealthy.* (qwiy, adj.); u· qʷíy *abundant.* (uuqwi̱y (lit. He has abundance), n.); ∥ qʷe·y=úl'mxʷ *capitalist.* (qweeyu̱'lmkhw (lit. He has plenty of land), n.); qʷe·y=úl'umxʷ *rich.* (qweeyu̱'lumkhw (lit. He is well-to-do as to land), vi.); l+qʷe·y=úl'mxʷ+n *bonanza.* (lqweeyu̱'lmkhwn. (lit. means of becoming wealthy), vi.) [see also √qʷh]

√qʷy₄ ∥ qʷiy=ós *Negro.* (qwiyo̱s, n.) [xref √qʷh]

√qʷy'₁ † qʷay' *impoverished, pitiable, poor.* (qwa'y (stem), adj.); qʷiy' *to pity.* (qwi'y (stem), vt.); qʷáy'+qʷiʔ+t *He is indigent, pitiful, poor.* (qwa̱'yqwi't, adj.); s+n+qʷéy'+t *alms, alms-giving, benevolence, clemency, compassion, consolation, mercy-giving, pitying.* (snqwe̱'yt, n.); s+qʷáy'+qʷiʔ+t *beggary.* (sqwa̱'yqwi't, n.); qʷiy'+qʷiy'+scút *He made himself humble.* (qwi'yqwi'ystsu̱t, vt.); s+qʷiʔ+qʷiʔ+scút *humility.* (sqwi'qwi'stsut (lit. the act of making oneself poor, of lowering oneself), n.); s+qʷiy'+qʷiy'+scút *humble (be).* (sqwi'yqwi'ystsu̱t, vt.); sya+n+qʷéy'+t *benefactor.* (syanqwe̱'yt, n.); hn+qʷáy'+qʷiy'+n *alms-house, poor-house, poverty.* (hnqwa̱'yqwi'yn, n.); ∥ qʷiʔ=cín+m *conjure, implore.* (qwi'tsi̱nm, vt.); qʷiy'+qʷiy'=cín+m *beseech.* (qwi'y qwi'ytsi̱nm (lit. Make oneself as poor), v.); qʷiʔ+qʷiʔ=cín+m *beseech, implore.* (qwi'qwi'tsi̱nm, vt.); qʷiy'=ús+m *blench.* (qwi'yusm. quail (lit. he made his face pitiful, winced by

closing his eyes), vi.); s+n+qʷiy'+qʷiy'=ílgʷes *gentleness, sympathy.* (snqwi'yqwi'yi̱lgwes, n.); hn+qʷiʔ+qʷiy'=ílgʷes *pity, sympathy.* (hnqwi'qwi'yi̱lgwes. fellow feeling.(lit. He has a sympathetic heart), n.); hn+qʷiy'+qʷiy'=ílgʷes *clement, compassionate, merciful.* (hnqwi'yqwi'yi̱lgwes. (lit. He is merciful), adj.); ‡ hn+qʷiʔ+t+mí-nt-s *console.* (hnqwi'tmi̱nts. (lit. He offered him sympathy), vt.) § elu+s+n+qʷéy'+t *cold-blooded, ruthless, merciless.* (elusnqwe̱'yt (lit. He has no mercy), adj.); qʷy'+qʷi+ł+cegʷ+t *He has a poor personality. (lit. He is poor as to his nature).* (qwu'yqwiłtsegwt, vi.)

√qʷy'₂ ∥ hn+qʷiy'=ítkʷeʔ *wash.* (hnqwi'yi̱tkwe'. (lit. She washed clothes), vt.)

√qʷyʔ † s+qʷéyuʔ *grapes, Oregon grapes.* (sqwe̱yu', pl.n.)

√qʷʕʷ † qʷeʕʷ *drunk, insane.* (qwe(w (stem). irresponsible, adj.); qʷeʕʷ *boob, booby.* (qwe(w (lit. a stupid person), n.); u· qʷéʕʷ *He is absurd, batty, brainless, cuckoo, daft, dull, ignorant, stupid.* (uuqwe(w (lit. He has absurd ideas), adj.); qʷéʕʷ+ʕʷ *besot.* (qwe̱(w(w (lit. He became intoxicated), vt.); qʷeʕʷ+qʷeʕʷ+t *feebleminded, foolish, silly.* (qwe(wqwe(wt (lit. H/s is a foolish person), adj.); hn+qʷéʕʷ+ʕʷ+n *alcohol, intoxication.* (hnqwe(w(wn (lit. means of getting silly), n.); hn+qʷéʕ'ʷ+qʷéʕ'ʷ+ʕʷ+n *asylum (lit. place for mentally ill).* (hnqwe'(wqwe'(w'(w'n, n.); ic+qʷéʕʷ+ʕʷ *drunk (he is being...).* (itsqwe(w(w, vi.); ic+qʷéʕʷ+qʷeʕʷ+ʕʷ *binge.* (itsqwe̱(wqwe(w(w (lit. people having a carousal), n.); ic+qʷeʕ'ʷ+qʷeʕ'ʷ+ʕ'ʷ *crazy.* (itsqwe'(wqwe'(w'(w (lit. He is insane),

adj.); [also recorded as √kʷˤʷ]
ic+kʷeˤ'ʷ+kʷeˤ'ʷ+ˤ'ʷ *demented.*
(itskwe'(wkwe'('(w (lit. He is going
crazy), adj.); s+qʷéˤ'ʷ+kʷeˤ'ʷ+ˤ'ʷ
insanity. (skwe'(wkwe(u'(, n.);
s+qʷéˤʷ+qʷeˤʷ+ˤʷ *carousal.*
(sqwe(wqwe(u(w (lit. people
becoming intoxicated), n.);
s+qʷéˤʷ+m+ncut *blunder, bungle.*
(sqwe(wmntsut. (lit. making oneself
silly), n.); s+qʷéˤʷ+m+šeš *craze,*
delirium, fad. (sqwe(umshesh. (lit.
becoming insane), n.); ʔus+niʔ+qʷéˤʷ
black sheep. (usni'qwe(w (lit. most
inane among family), n.);
čs+qʷeˤʷ+eˤʷ+míncut *He got carried*
away. (chsqwe(we(wmintsut, vi.); //
qʷeˤʷ=cn+mí+[n]cut *blather.*
(qwe(wtsnmimtsut (lit. He spoke
foolishly or nonsensically), vi.);
s+qʷeˤʷ=cn+mí+ncut *bilge.*
(sqwe(wtsnmintsut (lit. making oneself
talk nonsense), n.); ‡ qʷéˤʷ+m-st-m
berserk (he went...), *delirious,*
deranged (he was...). (qwe(wumstm
(lit. He became phrenetic, frantic), adj,
vt.)

√qʷʔ₁ // s+n+qʷáʔ=alq=šn *angle,*
corner. (snqwa'alqshn, n.); hn+qʷáʔ=
alq=šn *alcove.* (hnqwa'alqshn (lit. a
space at the foot of a corner or wall),
n.); ʔap+s+n+qʷáʔ=alq=šn *angular.*
(apsnqwa'alqshn (lit. It has an angle or
corner), adj.)

√qʷʔ₂ † qʷeʔ *to continue.* (qwe' (stem),
vt.)

√qʷʔ₃ † qʷiʔ *hollow.* (qwi' (stem), adj.);
s+n+qʷíʔ *cavity.* (snqwi', n.); an+qʷíʔ
cave. (anqwi' (lit. That which is
hollow), n.); § ac+miyás+n+qʷiʔ
cave, cavern. (atsmiyasnqwi' (lit. A
hollow that is larger than usual), n.)

√qʷʔ₄ † qʷiʔ *accustomed.* (qwi' (stem),
adj.)

√qʷc₁ † qʷec *durable, firm, lasting,*
solid. (q'wets (stem), adj.)

√qʷc₂ † qʷuc *fat, obese.* (q'uts (stem).
to be fat, adj.); qʷuc+t *H/s is*
corpulent, fat. (q'utst, adj.); s+qʷuc+t
blubber, corpulence, diesel fuel, fat
(excessive body...), fatness, gasoline,
obesity, oil. (sq'utst, n.)

√qʷc' † qʷic' *full, replete.* (q'wits'
(stem), adj.); qʷic'+t *brim-full,*
chock-full. (q'wits't, adj.); ac+qʷic'
full (to be...). (atsq'wit's (lit. It is...),
vi.) ‡ qʷíc'+s-n *filled (I...it up).*
(q'wits'sn, vt.)

√qʷc'w' // qʷc'w=íyeʔ *chipmunk.*
(q'wts'wiye', n.); qʷ+qʷc'w'=íy'eʔ
chipmunk. (q'q'wts"wi'ye', n.)

√qʷd † qʷid *blacken.* (q'wid (stem),
vt.); qʷed *black (ref. to horse), black.*
(q'wed (stem), n.); u· qʷéd *black,*
dingy (It is...). (uuq'wed, adj.);
qʷ+qʷd *horse (little black).* (q'wq'wd,
n.); qʷd+qʷéd *bison.* (q'wdq'wed (lit.
black black), n.); // s+qʷéd=ups
grouse. (sq'wedups (lit. black tail), n.);
qʷád=al'qs *black robe, clergy, cleric,*
divine, minister, priest. (q'wada'lqs,
(lit. One dressed in black), adj, n.);
t+qʷed=c'eʔ *black (...of skin), Negro.*
(tq'wedts'e' (lit. Black of skin), n.);
t+qʷed=elps *horse (black).*
(tq'wedelps, n.); t+qʷéd=elxʷ *horse*
(black...). (tq'wedelkhw, n.);
ut+qʷád=qn *black, dark (He*
has...hair). (utq'wadqn, adj.);
ni+s+qʷíde=gʷeł=mš *dark race.*
(nisq'widegwełmsh, n.); ‡
qʷéd+p+m-stu-s *to blacken it.*
(q'wedpmstus, vt.); § u· qʷéd he
šét'+ut *basalt.* (uuq'wed he shet'ut (lit.
rock that is black), n.)

√qʷh † qʷih *black (ref. to a person).*
(q'wih (stem), adj.); // s+t+qʷíh=šn=
mš *Blackfoot.* (Stq'wihshnmsh (lit. one
of the Blackfoot Tribe), n.) [xref
√qʷy₄]

√qʷl₁ † qʷal *char, singe.* (q'wal (stem),
vt.); qʷel' *burn, cook.* (q'we'l (stem),

vt.); s+q'ʷel+t *burn, cooked (being).* (sq'welt, n, vt.); ∥ q'ʷl=íln *His food became cooked.* (q'wliln, vt.); s+q'ʷl= íln *delicatessen.* (sq'wliln (lit. cooked foods), n.); s+n+q'ʷl=úl'umxʷ *bread, croutons, toast.* (snq'wlu'lumkhw (that which is baked in the ground), n.); s+n+q'ʷ+q'ʷl'=úl'm'xʷ *brioche.* (snq'uq"lu'l'mkhw (lit. little bread (loaf)), n.); hn+q'ʷl=úl'umxʷ+n *bakery.* (hnq'ulu'lumkhwn (lit. place for baking bread), n.); sya+n+q'ʷl= úl'mxʷ *baker.* (syanq'ulu'lmkhw (lit. One whose occupation is to bake (bread) in the ground), n.); s+t+q'ʷíl'= kʷp *match(es).* (stq'wi'lkup (lit. means of starting a fire), n.); ‡ q'ʷel-n *braise, cook.* (q'weln. (lit. I cooked it (meat)), vt.); § q'ʷl+x̌ʷí? *Burnt Mountain.* (Q'wlqhwi', n.)

√q'ʷl₂ † s+q'ʷel+t *ripe (to be...).* (sq'welt, vi.); ∥ s+q'ʷl=ál[q]ʷ=astq *fruit.* (sq'wlalgwastq (lit. ripened crops), n.)

√q'ʷlpš † q'ʷelpš *Good for him! It serves him right!* (q'welpsh! interj.)

√q'ʷls ∥ q'ʷóls=alqʷ *pussy willow (used for baskets).* (q'olsalqw, n.)

√q'ʷlw' † q'ʷelíw' *bear eats berries.* (q'weli'w)

√q'ʷl' † q'ʷul' *produce.* (q'u'l (stem), vt.) [xref? √kʷl']

√q'ʷɫ † q'ʷeɫ *endurance (to have...).* (q'weł (stem), v.); q'ʷiɫ *enduring, persevering.* (q'wił (stem), adj, vi.) [xref √qʷɫ]

√q'ʷm † q'ʷem+p *cramp, spasm (to have a muscle...).* (q'wemp (stem), v.); ∥ s+can+q'ʷém+p=cn *crick.* (stsanq'wemptsn (lit. cramp in the neck, note: similarity between q'wamp and cramp), n.); s+n+q'ʷém+p=šn *charley horse, cramp (getting a...).* (snq'wempshn (lit. cramp of the leg), n, vt.)

√q'ʷnp' † q'ʷenp' *disappear below horizon, go out of sight behind hill, evening.* (q'wenp', n.); s+q'ʷénp'+n *sunset, west.* (sq'wenp'n, n.); § ul s+čen[t]+cóc ha s+q'ʷenp' *sunset (Canadian...).* (ul schentsots ha sq'wenp', n.); s+can+q'ʷenp'+eɫ+?aɫ+dár=enč *eclipse.* (stsanq'wenp'eł'ałdarench (lit. sun/moon going behind something), n.)

√q'ʷn' † q'ʷín'+t *burped (h/s).* (q'wi'nt. belched, blurted, vi.); q'ʷí?n'+t *belched (h/s), blurted (h/s).* (q'wi"nt. burped, vi.)

√q'ʷp' † q'ʷup' *rain.* (q'up' (stem), n.); q'ʷup[']+t *rained.* (q'upt, vi.); s+q'ʷp'+t *rain.* (sq'up't, n.); ic+q'ʷp[']+t *raining (It is...).* (itsq'upt, v.)

√q'ʷs † q'ʷes *pleated, shrivelled, wrinkled.* (q'wes (stem), adj.); q'ʷus *to be pleated.* (q'us); ac+q'ʷés+m' *pleated.* (atsq'wes'm (lit. It is...), adj.); ∥ s+q'ʷús+p=ugʷl *skirt.* (sq'uspugul. pleated, n.); hn+q'ʷ+q'ʷos+m'=íčn'= šn' *dog.* (hnq'oq'os'mich'nsh'n (lit. with pleated soles), n.); hn+q'ʷ+q'ʷs+m'=íčn'+š[n]=tkʷe? *walrus, seal.* (hnq'oq'os'mich'nshtkwe' (lit. water dog), n.); sya+čeɫ+n+q'ʷ+q'ʷos+m=íčn=šn' *dog catcher.* (syachełnq'oq'osmich'nsh'n (lit. One who goes after dogs), n.); § u+x̌ʷal'+a+n+q'ʷ+q'ʷs+m'í *canine.* (uqhwa'lanq'oq'os'mi. (lit. It is doglike), n.); s+m'u+m'úc=šn' ha n+q'ʷo+q[']ʷos+m'i *bitch.* (sm'u'mutssh'n hanqoqos'mi (lit. a female dog), n.)

√q'ʷt ∥ hn+q'ʷt+út=mš=kʷe? *Coeur d'Alene River.* (Hnq'wtutmshkwe', n.) [xref √q'ʷt'₂]

√q'ʷt'₁ † q'ʷut' *knitted, woven (to be...).* (q'ut' (stem), vt.); ∥ hn+q'ʷt'=šn *sock(s), stockings.* (hnq'ut'shn, n.);

149

√q'ʷ't'

hn+q'ʷ+q'ʷút'=šn' *bootie.*
(hnq'uq'ut'sh'n (lit. little sock), n.)

√q'ʷ't'₂ † ał+q'ʷét'+ut *Plummer Butte,*
Plummer. (Ałq'we't'ut, n.); s+q'ʷt'ú
Cataldo, Idaho, Old Mission, Old
Sacred Heart Mission. (Sq'wt'u, n.)
[xref √q'ʷ't]

√q'ʷy'₁ † q'ʷey' *dance, bounce.* (q'we'y
(stem), vi.); s+q'ʷéy'+m+ncut
cotillion, ballet. (sq'we'ymntsut. (lit.
squeezing oneself), n.);
č'at+s+q'ʷey'+m+ncut *dance.*
(ch'atsq'we'ymntsut, vi.); gʷł
sya·+q'ʷéy'+m+ncut *chorus.* (guł
syaaq'we'ymntsut (lit. a group of
dancers in a musical comedy, revue,
etc.), n.); hn+q'ʷiy'+m+ncút+n
dancing place, ballroom.
(hnq'wi'ymntsutn. (lit. place for
squeezing oneself rhythmically), n.);
čn'‿c+q'ʷéy'+m+ncut *dance.*
(ch'ntsq'we'ymntsut. (lit. I,
customarily, dance), vt.);
čn‿q'ʷéy'+m+nc[u]t *danced (I...).*
(chnq'we'ymntsnt, vi.);
č‿y'c+q'ʷéy'+m+ncut *I am dancing.*
(chi'tsq'we'ymntsut, v.);
k'ʷne?+čn‿q'ʷéy'+m+ncut *dance (I*
will...), (lit. I am going to dance)
(k'wne'chnq'we'ymntsut, vi.);
q'ʷéy'+m+ncut-š *dance (imper.).*
(q'we'ymntsutsh, vi.);
kʷu‿q'ʷéy'+m+ncut *You (sg.)*
danced. (kuuq'we'ymntsut, vi.);
kʷ?‿c+q'ʷéy'+m+ncut *dance (you*
(sg.)...). (ku'tsq'we'ymntsut, vi.);
kʷu‿y'c+q'ʷéy'+m-nt-s-n-t *You (sg)*
are dancing. (ku'ytsq'we'ymntsnt, vi.);
k'ʷ ne? kʷu·‿q'ʷéy'+mncut *You (sg.)*
will dance. (k'wne'kuuq'we'ymntsut,
vi.); q'ʷéy'+mncut *H/S danced.*
(q'we'ymntsut, vi.); ac+q'ʷéy'+mncut
H/s dances. (atsq'we'ymntsut, vi.);
ic+q'ʷéy'+m+ncut *dancing (h/s is...).*
(itsq'we'ymntsut, vi.);
čas‿q'ʷáy'+mncut *dance (lit. h/s is*

going to dance). (chasq'wa'ymntsut,
vt.); k'ʷ na? q'ʷéy+mncut *H/s is*
going to dance. (k'wna'q'we'ymntsut,
vi.); č‿q'ʷéy'+m+ncut *danced*
(we...). (chq'we'ymntsut, vi.);
č‿?a+c+q'ʷey'+m+ncut *dance (lit.*
we dance). (ch'atsq'we'ymntsut, vi.);
čat+čs+q'ʷéy'+m+ncut *dance.*
(chatchsq'we'ymntsut (lit. we are going
dance), vi.); k'ʷ ne?
č‿q'ʷáy'+m+ncut *We will dance.*
(k'wne'chq'wa'ymntsut, vi.);
č‿y'c+q'ʷé[y]'+m+ncut *dancing (I*
am...), dancing (we are...).
(chi'tsq'we'umntsut, vi.);
q'ʷéy'+mncut-ul *You (pl.) dance*
(imper.). (q'we'ymntsutul, vi.);
kʷp'‿ac+q'ʷéy'+m+ncut *dance (you*
(pl.)...). (kup'atsq'we'ymntsut, vi.);
kʷp‿q'ʷéy'+m+ncut *danced (you*
(pl.)...). (kupq'we'ymntsut, vi.);
kʷup‿?i‿c+q'ʷéy'+m+ncut *You*
(pl.) are dancing. (kup'itsq'we'ymntsut,
vi.); k'ʷ ne? kʷup‿q'ʷéy'+m+ncut
You (pl.) will dance.
(k'wne'kupq'we'ymntsut, vi.);
q'ʷéy'+m+ncut-lš *They danced.*
(q'we'ymntsutlsh, vi.);
ac+q'ʷéy'+mcut-lš *They dance.*
(atsq'wey'mntsutlsh, vi.);
ic+q'ʷéy'+m+ncut-lš *dancing (they*
are...). (itsq'we'ymntsutlsh, vi.);
čas‿q'ʷáy'+m+ncut-lš *dance (lit.*
they are going to dance).
(chasq'wa'ymntsutlsh, vt.);
k'ʷna?+q'ʷéy'+m+ncut-lš *dance (they*
will...). (k'wna'q'we'ymntsutlsh, vi.); §
s+mí?yem ha sya·+q'ʷéy'+m+ncut
ballerina. (smi'yem ha
syaaq'we'ymntsut (lit. woman who
dances), n.)

√q'ʷy'₂ † q'ʷey' *strangle, wring, choke.*
(q'we'y (stem), vt.); ‡ q'ʷey'-nt-s *He*
squeezed it, he wringed it (wet
clothes), rinse. (q'we'ynts, vt.);
can+q'ʷi?=cín-t-s *choke.*

150

√q'ʷyʔ

(tsanq'wi'tsints (lit. He constricted him as to the neck), vt.); ł+q'ʷiy'=álpqʷ-nt-s *choke.* (ɪq'wi'yalpqwnts, vi.); ł+q'ʷey'=álpqʷ-nt-s *to choke.* (tq'we'yalpqwnts, vi.)

√q'ʷyʔ † q'ʷúyeʔ *name of coyote's powers.* (q'uye', n.)

√q'ʷʕ † q'ʷeʕ+p *slid (it...), he slid involuntarily.* (q'we(p, [v].); ‖ s+q'ʷaʕ+eʕ+p=líyeʔ *sledding, coasting.* (sq'wa(e(pliye'. (lit. sliding down an inclined slope on a sled), vi.) [xref √k'ʷʕ]

√q'ʷʔ ‖ [one entry recorded as √q'ʷʔ] an+qʷaʔ+qʷaʔ=ep=eʔs+t *castrate, geld.* (anqwa'qwa'epe'st (lit. He, e.g. bull, is castrated), vt, n.); hn+q'ʷaʔ+q'ʷeʔ=ép=eʔst *castrated.* (hnq'wa'q'we'epe'st, vi.); ‡ hn+q'ʷaʔ+q'ʷeʔ=ép=eʔs-nt-s *castrated.* (hnq'wa'q'we'epe'snts (lit. he castrated the bull), vt.)

√q'ʷʔł † q'ʷiʔł *camp (to move...), decamp, migrate.* (q'wi'ł, vt, vi.)

√sc₁ † sic *new, new (It is...).* (sits (stem), adj.)

√sc₂ ‖ síc=i[t]kʷ *winter.* (sitsikw, n.); s+síc=itkʷ+m *hibernate.* (ssitsitkum (lit. passing the winter), vi.)

√sc' † sic' *blanket, blanketed.* (si'ts (stem), n, adj.); sic'+m *blanket, cover.* (sits'm, n.); sic'+síc'+m *bedding.* (sits'sits'm (lit. blankets), n.)

√sč₁ † sič *squirrel.* (sich, n.) [v. 1 has √sč']

√sč₂ † si+sč *onion (species of wild...).* (sisch, n.)

√sč'₁ ‖ séč'=ečt *moss on a tree.* (sech'echt, n.)

√sč'₂ † hn+séč'+ntis *channel, river.* (hnsech'ntis, n.); ‖ sč'=łwís *dead salmon.* (sch'lwis, n.); ʔep+sč=l'wís *It, e.g., the river, has dead salmon.* (epsch'lwis, vt.)

√sds † sídis+t *during (...the night).* (sidist, adv.); sidis+t *overnight (to...).*

(sidist (stem), vi.); et+sids+t *night.* (etsidst, n.); sds+tíł+mš *travelled (He...by night).* (sdstiłmsh, v.) [see also √ds]

√sgʷ † sigʷ *ask for, inquire, question (to...), request.* (sigw (stem), vi, vt.); sigʷ+n *ask, question.* (sigwn, vt.); s+sígʷ+n *ask, inquiry, question.* (ssigwn, vt, n.); segʷ+et *who?.* (segwet (stem), inter.); kʷu‿ségʷ+et *are (who...you?).* (kuusegwet?, vi.); neʔ+ségʷet *I wonder who it is?* (ne'segwet, qu.); s+segʷ+segʷ+n+úl *curiosity, inquisitiveness.* (ssegwsegwnul, n.); ‡ hn+sígʷ=cn-n *consult.* (hnsigwtsnn. (lit. I asked his permission, took counsel with him), vt.);

√skʷ₁ † u· sí·kʷ *voice (His...was rather hoarse).* (uusiiikw, n.); u+n+sí·kʷ *hoarse (His voice was rather...).* (unsiiikw, adj.)

√skʷ₂ ‖ s(=)íkʷeʔ *alcohol, aqua, booze, bourbon, cordial, liquor, water.* (sikwe', n.); s(=)ikʷeʔ tel' kolón *cologne.* (sikwe' te'l Cologne (lit. water from Cologne), n.); čs+s(=)íkʷe=kʷeʔ *alcoholic.* (chssikwekwe' (lit. one who became enslaved by water (liquor)), adj.); hn+s(=)íkʷeʔ+n *barroom, buttery, aquarium.* (hnsikwe'n. liquor store. (lit. a place for water), n.); s+čs+n+s(=)íkʷeʔ=kʷeʔ *alcoholism.* (schsnsikwekwe, n.); s+n+s(=)íkʷeʔ=mš *aquanaut, dipper.* (snsikwe'msh (lit. aquatic animal or water tribesman), n.); ʔepł n+s(=) íkʷeʔ+n *barkeeper, bartender.* (epł n sikwe'n (lit. One who has a liquor place), n.); s+s(=)ákʷaʔ=q'n *lost lake.* (ssakwa'q'n (lit. water on the head (mountain), n.); [also recorded as √sqʷ] s+s(=)áqʷaʔ=qn *lake (little crater...).* (ssaqwa'qn (lit. water on the head (mountain), n.); § elu+ł+s(=)íkʷeʔ *waterless, parched, anhydrous.*

151

(eluɫsikwe' (lit. It has no water), adj.); ul s(=)ikʷe? ha sóltes *blue-jacket.* (ul sikwe'ha soltes (lit. soldier of the sea), n.) [xref √sxʷ₁]

√sk'ʷ † suk'ʷ *float (...with current).* (suk'w (stem), vi.); ‡ súk'ʷ-nt-m *afloat.* (suk'wntm (lit. He was set adrift), adj.)

√sl₁ † sel *turn (to...), rotate.* (sel (stem), vi.); sel+p *spin.* (selp (stem), vi.); sel+úp *to spin.* (selup,); ∥ hn+sél+sl+p=us *drunk, tipsy.* (hnselslpus. (lit. His eyes spun), adj.); s+n+sél+p=us *daze.* (snselpus (lit. turning of eye), n.); s+n+sél+sl+p=us *daze (lit. turning of eye).* (snselslpus, n.); čiy'+n+sél+sl+p=us *dizzy, giddy.* (chi'ynselslpus (lit. I am having a whirling sensation in my head), adj.); s+n+sl+p=ítkʷe? *eddy.* (snslpitkwe' (lit. a turning of water), n.); sl'+pst'=úlixʷ *earth (twisted...), earth (whirling...).* (s'lpst'ulikhw (name of Circling Raven's eldest son), n.)

√sl₂ † sel *hazy, obscure.* (sel (stem), adj.); sel' *indistinct, obscure.* (se'l (stem), adj.); u· sél' *complex, complicated, confused, intricate (It is...).* (uuse'l, adj.); sl'e·+séle *unknown ancestor.* (s'leesele, n.); ni?+sél+l+m *clutter.* (ni'sellm (lit. It was piled in a disordered state), n.); e ni?+sél+m *assorted, mixed.* (eni'selm, vt. (lit. It is a mixture), adj.); s+sél'+m+ncut *error, mistake.* (sse'lmntsut, n.); če·+síl+el *oversleep.* (cheesilel (lit. he overslept), vi.); ∥ e t+sél'=šn *clubfoot.* (et se'lshn (lit. H/h foot has an uncertain shape), n.); t+sél'+sl'=ečt *awkard, clumsy.* (t-se'ls'lecht (lit. He is unsure by hand), vi.); s+t+sél+sl'=ečt *clumsiness.* (stsels'lecht (lit. He is ignorant in hand), n.); e n+sl+m=ítkʷe? *cocktail, drink (cocktail).* (enslmitkwe' (lit. mixed water, drink), n.); s+n+sl+p=ílgʷes *amnesty,*

forgetting. (snslpilgwes, n.); ‡ ni?+sél+m-s-n *concoct, mix.* (ni'selmsn. compound, (lit. I mixed it), vt.); ni?+sél+m-st-m *blend.* (ni'selmstm (lit. It was mixed (with other entities)), vt.); § sl'+sl'+eɫ+cégʷ+t *block-head, chump.* (s'ls'leɫtsegwt (lit. A person who is uncertain in his ways), n.); ni?+sél+m-st-m e lut šiɫ *adulterate.* (ni'selmstm e lut shiɫ (lit. It was mixed with something not just right, it was made impure by mixing in a foreign or poorer substance), vt.)

√sl₃ † sul *cold, refrigerated, to be cold.* (sul (stem), adj.); sul+t *cold (he got...).* (sult, vi.); čn‿súl+t *cold (I got...).* (chnsult, vi.); ∥ súl=ul'umxʷ *froze (The ground was frozen...).* (sulu'lumkhw, vt, adj, n.); § sul+sul+ɫ+cégʷ+t *bleak.* (sulsulɫtsegwt (lit. He has a somber and gloomy manner (nature)), n.)

√slkʷ † hn+séluk[ʷ] *a place on the Coeur d'Alene river where canoes mysteriously stop and many were killed, a place of superstition.* (Hnseluk, n.)

√slp' † slip' *woody.* (slip (stem), adj.); sl'l'ip' *baton.* (s'l'lip' (lit. little wooden stick), n.); slip'+t *wood.* (slip't, n.)

√sls † sils+us *blow down (e.g. houses).* (silsus (stem), vt.) [?]

√slts † sóltes *armed forces.* (soltes, n.); gʷɫ sóltes *army, brigade, soldiers.* (guɫ soltes, n.); § lut sóltes *civilian.* (lut soltes (lit. He is not a soldier); soltes=l.w. from English), n.); ul soltes ha n+qʷ+qʷǎ?+qʷe?l'+n' *court-martial.* (ul soltes hanquqwa'qwe'l'n' (lit. courthouse of soldiers), n.); nukʷ'+ɫ+tum' ha sóltes *battalion.* (nuk'wɫtu'm ha soltes (lit. a unit of soldiers), n.); ul s(=)ikʷe? ha sóltes *blue-jacket.* (ul sikwe'ha soltes (lit. soldier of the sea), n.)

√sl? † sile? *maternal grandfather.*
(silc', n.); síle?e *lake (small...near
Cheney).* (sile. pat, grandfather, n.)

√słq † sła[q] *sarvice berry.* (słag, n.)

√smš † su·méš *power (Spokane).*
(suumesh, n.)

√smx † su·míx *power (San Poil).*
(suumikh, n.)

√sm' † sum' *smell (to...), sniff.* (su'm
(stem), vt.); ‡ súm'-nt-s *sniffed
(he...at it).* (su'mnts, vi.)

√sn₁ † san *drowsy, sleepy.* (san (stem),
adj.)

√sn₂ ∥ sn=íne? *owl.* (snine', n.)

√sn₃ ∥ č+sún=kʷe? *island.* (chsunkwe',
n.); č+s+sún'=kʷe? *cay, island (a
small...), key, islet.* (chssu'nkwe', n.);
?epł+č+sún+sun=kʷe? *archipelago.*
(epłchsunsunkwe' (lit. It has islands),
n.)

√snc? † since? *deacon, kid brother.*
(sintse', n.); s+sín'ce? *cadet.* (ssi'ntse'
(lit. younger brother), n.)

√sns † s+sén'+sn's? *cents, pennies,
copper.* (sse'ns'n, n.); § ?upen e·séns
dime. (upeneesens (lit. ten cents), n.)

√snt † sant ma·ri *Virgin Mary, Mary,
Saint Mary, Holy Mary.* (Sant Maari
(l.w. from French), n.)

√sn'₁ † sen' *tame (to...).* (sen' (stem),
vt.); s+sán'+sn'+ł *It is a broken,
tamed horse.* (ssa'ns'nt, vi); ‡
s+sn'+sn'+ł+él'š-stu-s *tamed (he
caused it to be...), caused (he...it to be
tamed).* (ss'ns'nte'lshstus, adj, vt.)

√sn'₂ † se·+sín'+n'cut'+n *perfume.*
(seesi'n'ntsut'n, n.)

√sn'₃ † sú+sn' *spoon.* (sus'n, n.); §
č+łuk'ʷ+łuk'ʷ+p+sín'+n *fork.*
(chłuk'włuk'wpsi'nn., n.)

√sp † sip *sheep.* (sip, n.); ∥ síp=elxʷ
cape-skin. (sipelkhw. sheepskin, n.);
sp=íłc'e? *elk.* (spiłts'e' , n.)

√spn † sipn *daughter-in-law.* (sipn, n.)

√sps † s+čs(=)úps+n *tail.* (schsupsn,
n.); ul s+čs(=)úps+n *caudal.* (ul

schsupsn (lit. pertaining to the tail or
hind parts), adj.); § ?ep+s+čs+s=
úps+n' *Fernwood, Idaho (lit. It has a
little tail).* (Epschssups'n, n.)

√sp'y' † sip'ey' *buckskin.* (sip'e'y
(stem), n.); síp'ey' *leather; finished
hide.* (si'pe'y, n.); sip[']ay' *leather.*
(sipa'y, n.); ∥ se?p'y=al'qs *buckskin
(jacket), leather (coat).* (se'p'ya'lqs, n.);
sép'y=al'qs *buckskin suit, leather
coat.* (sep"ya'lqs, n.); síp'+sip'ay'=šn
mocasins. (sip'sip'a'yshn, n.);
č+sep'+sep'y'=alq=šn *leather pants,
leggings, pants (leather...).*
(chsep'sep"yalqshn, n.); t+sep+sep'y=
alq=šn *breeches.* (tsepsep'yalqshn, n.)

√sq'₁ † saq' *split (...in two).* (saq'
(stem), vi.); s+sáq'+m *cleavage.*
(ssaq'm (lit. splitting), n.); s+sáq'+p
*cleft, chink, crack, cranny, fissure
(narrow).* (ssaq'p, n.); ‡ sáq'-nt-s *split.*
(saq'nts. cleave (lit. He split (the
blocks of wood)), vt.)

√sq'₂ † hn+séq'+m *criminal, digress,
perverted, strayed, wandered.*
(hnseq'm. (lit. He erred, turned aside,
went off the path/He went astray/He
was perverted), n, vi, adj.);
an+séq'+m *devious.* (anseq'm, vi. (lit.
He strays from the way of right and
duty), adj.); s+n+séq'+mš *anomaly,
crime, deviation.* (snseqmsh. go astray
(lit. erring (from the path of life), n.);
in+séq'+mš *aberrant.* (inseq'msh (lit.
H/s is going astray), adj.);
čeł‿čin‿séq[']+mš *I am going
astray, deviate (I am going to...).* (cheł
chi nseqmsh, vi.);
čeł‿čis+n+séq[']+mš *astray (I am
going...).* (cheł chisnseqmsh, vi.)

√sr † sar *cricket.* (sar, n.)

√srqʷs † sarqʷs *pine squirrel.* (sarqws,
n.)

√stč₁ † setč *twist.* (setch (stem), vt.);
e·+setč *amiss, awry.* (eesetch (lit. It is
twisted toward one side), adj.); ∥

ni?+sátč=i?qs+n *crank*. (ni'satchi'qsn (lit. nose twister), n. and vt.); ‡ sétč+m-st-m *distort*. (setchmstm (lit. It was twisted from the natural shape), v.); stč=íčs-t-m *awry*. (stchichstm (lit. He put his hand in a twisted manner), adv.)

√stč₂ † sítč *bladder, stomach*. (sitch (stem), n.)

√stq † sétq=aps *April*. (setqaps, n.)

√st' † su?t' *stretched*. (su't' (stem), adj.); sut'e·+sút'e *accordian, rubber*. (sut'eesut'e (lit. that which is stretchable), n.); u+s+sút' *elastic*. (ussut' (lit. It is having the power of returning to its original form), adj, n.); ∥ sót'=al'qs *cardigan, sweater or colorless jacket opening down the front (lit. elastic clothes)*. (sot'a'lqs, n.); sót'=i?qs *nickname (...of an Indian), stretch nose*. (Sot'i'qs, n.); ‡ e· sút'+m-s-n *stretch, elongate (lit. I stretch (cust.) it out)*. (eesut'msn, vt.)

√st'q ∥ ac+sé[t]=q'it *date, day, time*. (atsseq'it (lit. day), n.); a+č+sét'=q'it *day, daytime*. (achset'q'it, n.); hn+?ač+set'=qit *My time*. (hn'achset'qit.); § xes+t ha c+sét'q+it *day (It is good...)*. (qhest ha' tsset'qit, n.) [see =sq'it in Appendix D]

√sw' † s+séw'+suw'+iš *whisper*. (sse'wsu'wish, n.)

√sw's † síw's *ground hog*. (si'ws, n.); § čn‿gʷíč e siw's *groundhog (lit. I saw a groundhog)*. (chngwich e si'ws, n.); čn‿gʷič e· siw's *groundhog*. (chngwich ee si'ws (lit. I saw a groundhog), n.)

√sxʷ₁ † sixʷ *pour*. (sikhw (stem), vt.); s+síxʷ+xʷ *effluence*. (ssikhukhw (lit. a flowing out), n.); ‡ síxʷ-nt-s *spilled (He...it)*. (sikhwnts, v.); síxʷ-nt-xʷ *effuse, spill*. (sikhwntkhw (lit. you(s) poured it out), v.); č+síxʷ+ɬ+p-nt-s *decant*. (chsikhwɬpnts (lit. He poured (the water) out of doors outside; he

poured it forth), vt.); § s+síxʷ+m xʷe mít'č'=ede? *bloodbath, bloodshed*. (ssikhum khwe mit'ch'ede' (lit. spilling that w/c is blood), n.); s+nukʷ+síxʷ+síxʷ+xʷ *brethren, fellow-bloods* (snukwsikhwsikhukhw, n.); s+nukʷ+síxʷ+xʷ *blood-brother, concourse*. (snukwsikhukhw (lit. fellow in issue of blood/a flowing or moving together), n.) [xref √skʷ₂]

√sxʷ₂ † sexʷ *carry (on back)*. (sekhw (stem), vt.); sexʷ+m *bear, carry*. (sekhwm (lit. Carry on the back), vt.); sye·+séxʷ+m *carrier*. (syeesekhum (lit. One who carries or conveys), n.); ∥ s+suxʷ=ílgʷes *burden*. (ssukhwilgwes (lit. something that is carried on the back), n.); s+suxʷ+suxʷ=íl'gʷes *chapman*. (ssukhwsukhwi'lgwes (lit. one who packs around goods to sell). peddler, n.); ‡ sexʷ-t-s *convey, bear, packed (He...him (it) on his back)*. (sekhwts, he carried him, vt.); sexʷ-nt-s *carried (He...him)*. (sekhwnts. He packed him (it) on his back. to bear, convey, vt.); e·+séxʷ-stu-s *carry, lug, piggyback*. (eesekhwstus (lit. He is carrying it/him on his back), vt, adv.)

√sxʷ₃ † suxʷ *acquainted (with), know (be acquainted with)*. (sukhw (stem), adj, vt.); ∥ hn+súxʷ=ene? *comprehended, understood*. (hnsukhwene'. (lit. He recognized with his ear, he came to understand (a new language)), vt.); s+n+súxʷ=ene? *comprehension*. (snsukhwene', n.); čn‿n+súxʷ=ene? *recognized, understand, understood*. (chnnsukhwene'. (lit. I recognized him with my ear), v, vi.); ni kʷu‿n+súxʷ=ene? *Did you understand?* (nikunsukhwene'? (qu.).); ni kʷup‿n+súxʷ=ene? *Did you (pl.) understand?* (nikupnsukhwene'? (qu.).); can+sóxʷ+p=qn' *head (He *recognized the back of his...), back (He recognized the...of a head).* (tsansokhwpq'n, n.); č+súxʷ=meʔ+n *barometer, criterion, indicator, sign.* (chsukhwme'n (lit. A means of recognizing standard landmark), n.); č+súxʷ=meʔ+n *gauge.* (chsukhwme'n (lit. a means of recognizing), [v].); łš+súxʷ+meʔ+n *barometer, guide (lit. something to go by).* (łshsukhwme'n, n.); s+n+súxʷ=meʔ=cn+mš *a means of the weather.* (snsukhwme'tsnmsh, n.); ‡ súxʷ-n *recognized (I...him).* (sukhwn, vt.); súxʷ-s-n *recognized (I...his voice).* (sukhusn, vt.); súxʷ=us-n *I recognized his face.* (sukhusn, vt.); suxʷ-t-s *acquainted (He got...with him), recognized (He...him).* (sukhwts, vi, vt.); hn+súxʷ=ečn'-n *I recognized his back.* (hnsukhwech'nn, vt.); hn+súxʷ=eneʔ+mn-n *I understood h/h.* (hnsukhwene'mnn, vt.); e·+súxʷ-s-n *know, aquainted.* (eesukhwsn (lit. I know/recognize him), vt, vi.); e· súxʷ-s-n-lš *I know, recognize, am acquainted with them.* (eesukhwsnlsh, vt.); hn+súxʷ=eneʔ+m-nt-se-s *He understood me.* (hnsukhwene'mntses, vt.); e· súxʷ-st-me-s *H/s knows, recognizes, is acquainted with me.* (eesukhwstmes, vt.); suxʷ+xʷ+nú-nt-s *acquainted (he got...with him).* (sukhukhwnunts, vi.); can+sóxʷ+p=qn'-t-s *recognized (He...the back of his head).* (tsansokhwpq'nts, vt.); e· súxʷ-st-eli-s *H/s knows, recognizes, is acquainted with us.* (eesukhwstelis, vt.); § suxʷ+s+čínt *recognized (He...a human being).* (sukhwschint, vt.); sye+č+súxʷ=eneʔ tel' s+t+c'éx̌ʷ+ncut *astrologer, one who understands the stars.* (syechsukhwene' te'l stts'eqhwntsut, n.); č+súxʷ=meʔ+n ha s+t+c'exʷ+ncut *astrology.* (chsukhwme'n ha stts'ekhwntsut (lit.

self illuminating body that is a guide), n.); lut hey'p+súxʷ=meʔ+is *anesthesia.* (lut he'ypsukhwme'is (lit. He has no feeling), n.); lut he y'+suxʷ=meʔ+m+s *analgesia.* (lut he'ysukhwme'ms (lit. He does not feel), n.)

√sxʷ₄ † súxʷ+xʷ *empty, vacated (it became...).* (sukhukhw, n.)

√sxʷ₅ ∥ suxʷ=elš *jump (ref. to a fish).* (sukhwelsh (stem), vi.); súxʷ=lš *jumped (it (fish)...).* (sukhwlsh, vi.); s+suxʷ=elš *to jump (ref. to a fish).* (ssukhwelsh, [vi.])

√sxʷq † sexʷq *splash (to...).* (sekhwq (stem), vi.)

√sx̌ † sax̌ *carve, hew, whittle.* (saqh (stem), vt.)

√sx̌ʷ₁ † saʔx̌ʷ *dissolve, melt.* (sa'qhw (stem). thaw, v.); seʔx̌ʷ *to dissolve, melt.* (se'qhw)

√sx̌ʷ₂ ∥ sáx̌ʷ=[t]kʷeʔ *aorta, arteries, blood vessels, veins.* (saqhwłkwe', n)

√sx̌ʷ₃ † sex̌ʷ *cracking (ref. to wood).* (seqhw (stem), v.); s+séx̌ʷ+t *crevasse, crevice.* (sseqhwt. (lit. a split), n.); ‡ séx̌ʷ-nt-s *cleave.* (seqhwnts. split (lit. He split (the blocks of wood)), vt.)

√sy₁ † siy *cedarbark.* (siy (stem), n.)

√sy₂ † siy *exert.* (siy (stem), v.); siy+m+scút *act, contended, strove, vied.* (siymstsut (lit. make an effort), vi.); s+siy+m+scút *ambition, attempt.* (ssiymstsut (lit. doing one's best to succeed, making an effort), n, vt.); s+č+siy+m+scút *ambition.* (schsiymstsut (lit. doing one's best to reach a goal), n.); s+č+siy+m+cút+m *crusade.* (schsiymtsutm (lit. any zealous movement for a cause), n.); k'ʷnéʔ+čn‿siy+m+scút *do (I am going to...my best).* (k'wne'chnsiymstsut, vt.); i+siy+m+scút *ambitious.* (isiymstsut (lit. He is doing his best.), adj.); ∥ siy+siy=ús *astute, capable, clever,*

intelligent (He is...), shrewd. (siysiyus
(stem), adj.); s+si+siy=us *capability.*
(ssisiyus. the little one is.., n.);
s+siy+siy=ús *ability, aptitude, skill,
talent.* (ssiysiyus, n.); s+síy+siy=us
skill, talent, ability, aptitude.
(ssiysiyus, n.); si+siy=us *able (to be).*
(sisiyus, vi.); s+niʔ+siy+siy=ús
champ. (sni'siysiyus (lit. one who is
most capable), n.)

√sˤʷ † saˤʷ *flow, pour, leak (to...).*
(sa(w (stem), vi.); saˤʷ+p *dripped,
overflowed.* (sa(wp. It
dripped/overflowed, vi.); ∥ sˤʷ=íl'š
*vomiting, botulism, regurgitating,
throwing up.* (s(wi'lsh, n, vt.);
s+č+sáˤʷ+sˤʷ+p=us *aqueous humor.*
(schsa(s(wpus (lit. tears), n.)

√sʔ † s+sí? *maternal uncle.* (ssi', n.);
ul+s+si? *avuncular.* (ulssi' (lit.
pertaining to a maternal uncle), adj.);
si?+st+m *woman's brother-in-law.*
(si'stm, n.)

√sʔq' ‡ t+sé?+se?q'+m'-s-n' *punned
(I...on it).* (t-se'se'q"ms'n (lit. I took it
(word) off the beaten path repeatedly; I
played with words), vi.);
t+sé?+se?q'+m'-st-xʷ *punned (you
(sg.)...on it).* (t-se'se'q"mstkhw, vi.);
t+sé?+se?q'+m-stu-[s] *H/S punned
on it.* (t-se'se'q"mstun, vi.);
t+sé?+se?q'+m-st-m'et *We punned
on it.* (t-se'se'q"mst'met, vi.);
t+sé?+se?q'+m-st-p *You (pl.) punned
on it.* (t-se'se'q"mstp. vi.);
t+sé?+se?q'+m'-stu-s-lš *punned
(they...on it).* (t-se'se'q"mstuslsh, vi.)

√sc † šec *dig.* (shets (stem), vi.);
šec+m *dig, dug (He...something).*
(shetsm, vi, vt.); hn+šéc+m *delve,
dig.* (hnshetsm. (lit. He dug a hole),
vt.); s+n+šéc+m *digging (...a hole),
hole (digging a...).* (snshetsm, vt, n.); ∥
hn+šc=úl'umxʷ *He dug a hole in the
ground.* (hnshtsu'lumkhw.); hn+šc=
úl'umxʷ+n *excavator.*

(hnshtsu'lumkhwn. (lit. means of
digging in the earth), n.); s+n+šc=
úl'umxʷ *a hollow cavity or hole
formed by cutting or digging out earth.*
(snshtsu'lumkhw, n.); čn‿n+šc=
ul'úmxʷ *dig (in the ground), excavate,
I excavated land.* (chnnshtsulumkhw.
(lit. I dug in the ground), vt.); ‡
hn+šc=ul'umxʷ-nt-xʷ *dug (you...it
up).* (hnshtsu'lumkhwntkhw, vt.); šc=
ítš-st-m *pawed (the horse...).*
(shtsitshstm, vi.)

√šc', † šec' *firm, permanent, solid.*
(shets' (stem), adj.); šec'+šc'+t
consistent. (shets'shts't, adj.);
šec[']+šc'+t *solid (It is...).* (shet'ssh'tst,
vi.); s+šéc'+šc'+t *firmness, solidity.*
(sshets'shts't, n.); ∥ hn+šč'+šc'=ílgʷes
stout-hearted. (hnshch'shts'ilgwes (lit.
He is stout-hearted, emotionally stable,
toughened, adj.); ‡ šc'+šc'+t=íl'š-st-n
corroborate. (shts'shts'ti'lshstn (lit. It
was strengthened, it was made sturdy),
vi.); § šét'+s+šic'=e?st *diamond.*
(shet'sshits'e'st (lit. hard stone), n.)

√šc'₂ † šec' *wait.* (shets' (stem), vi.); ‡
cen+šéc'-n *waited (I...for him).*
(tsenshets'n, vi.) [xref √šč']

√šct † š(=)ečt *thumb, any finger.*
(shecht, n.)

√šč'₁ ∥ a+šč'=qín+m *eavesdrop,
overhear.* (ashch'qinm (lit. H/s
customarily listens), vi.); hn+šč'=
qín+emn *auditorium.*
(hnshch'qinemn. (lit. a place for
listening), n.); ‡ šč'+mí-nt-s *heard
(He...it).* (shch'mints, vt.)

√šč'₂ † šeč' *wait.* (shech' (stem), vi.);
cen+šé[]č'-n *I waited for him.*
(tsenshetch'n, vi.) [xref √šc']

√šč'₃ † šič' *miss (the target).* (shi'ch
(stem), vt.); ∥ šíč'=e?st *missed
(he...the target), target (he missed
the...).* (shich'e'st, vt, n.); t+šéč'=alqʷ
derail. (tshech'alqw (lit. It (train) ran
off the rails), vt.); ‡ šíč'+nun-n *missed*

156

(I...my target), target (I missed my...). (sh<u>i</u>ch'nunn, vt, n.); šíč'+nun-t-s missed (he...it). (sh<u>i</u>ch'nunts, vt.)

√šgʷ † ša+šagʷ sharp. (shashagw (stem), adj.); šá+šagʷ+t sharp (It is...). (shashagwt, vi.); **∥** hn+šá+šagʷ=ens H/s/i has sharp tooth or teeth. The saw has sharp teeth. (hnsh<u>a</u>shagwens, vi.)

√šgʷl † hn+šégʷel trail, path, road. (hnsh<u>e</u>gwel. the path of life, n.); **§** ac+ʕep+el+šugʷíl+m elope. (ats(epelshugw<u>i</u>lm (lit. H/s goes away by a secret road), vi.); ic+ʕepé+ł+šegʷel+mš He is going (away) through a secret path. (its(ep<u>e</u>łshegwelmsh, vi.); hn+xʷuy+ł+šugʷíl He went on his last trip. (hnkhuyłshugw<u>i</u>l, vi.)

√šl † šel chop, split. (shel (stem), vt.); šél+men adze. (sh<u>e</u>lmen, n.); šél+mn cleaver, axe, tomahawk. (shelmn, n.); **∥** šl=ítkʷp split (He...wood for the fire). (shl<u>i</u>tkup, vt.); s+šl=ítkʷp block. (sshl<u>i</u>tkup (lit. wood split into pieces), n.); š+šl'=ús battle-axe, enemy, hostile, hostility, tomahawk. (shsh'l<u>u</u>s (lit. chop face), n, adj.); **‡** šél-nt-s chop. (sh<u>e</u>lnts (lit. He cut it by striking with a heavy sharp tool), vt.)

√šlč [also recorded as √šlč'] † šelč' circle. (shelch' (stem), vt.); šelč circled (h/i...). (shelch (lit. He went around, in a circle), vi.); s+šélč+m+ncut cortege. (sshelchmntsut (lit. making a circle in ceremonial procession), n.); [recorded once as √šl'c'] šl'+šl'c'+m+n'cút turning (...and...in a war dance). (sh'lsh'lts'm'nts<u>u</u>t, vi.); s+šél'+šl'č+m'+n'cut carrousel, merry-go-round. (ssh<u>e</u>'lsh'lch'mntsut. (lit. going round and round), n.); s+t+šelč detour. (stshelch (lit. going a roundabout way), n.); **‡** t+šélč-n compass. (tsh<u>e</u>lchn (lit. I circled it; I

went around it), vt.); t+šélč-nt-m around, beleaguer, beset, surrounded (he was...). (tsh<u>e</u>lchntm (lit. He was encircled, crowded around), adv, vt.); t+šélč-nt-s circle. (tsh<u>e</u>lchnts (lit. He circled it; h/s went around h/h/i), vt.); **§** šl+l+tš+ł+mnač=alqs Circling Raven. (Shlltshłmnachalqs, n.); nukʷ+s+šél·č+m cycle. (nuk'wsshellchm (lit. one round), n.)

√šl'₁ **∥** eł+šél'=ečt sucker (fish). (ełsh<u>e</u>'lecht, n.)

√šl'₂ † ši+šil' fine, precise. (shishi'l (stem), adj.); u š+šl' fine (It is very...), formed (nicely), shapely. (ushsh'l, adj.)

√šł † šił correct, exact, fitting. (shił (stem), adj.); o· šił accu[]rate. (ooshił (lit. It is accurate), adj.); ši+ši?ł precise. (shishi'ł (stem), adj.); ne?+šił about, approximately, circa, roughly (approximately). (ne'shił, adv.); u+n+šił appropriate, apropos, cozy (becoming...). (unshił (lit. It is accurate), adj.); **‡** šíł-nt-s adjust (to...). (shi<u>l</u>nts (lit. He made it accurate), vi.); u·+šíł-stu-s befit, beseem. (uushi<u>l</u>stus (lit. It is suitable or appropriate for him), vt.); **§** na+?x̌íł šił circa, about, Maybe or just about. (na'qhił shił (used before approximate dates or figures), prep.); šił t'+t'áx̌+t cruise. (shił t't'<u>a</u>qht (lit. He speeded just right), vi.) (na'qhi); ni?+sel+m-st-m e lut šił adulterate. (ni'selmstm e lut shił (lit. It was mixed with something not just right, it was made impure by mixing in a foreign or poorer substance), vt.)

√šm₁ † šam between (to be...). (sham (stem), adv.); **∥** e šm=íw'es two-sided, bilateral. (eshm<u>i</u>'wes (lit. both sides), adj.); **‡** hn+šem-nt-s H/s put it (a long thing) between (in a bag). (hnsh<u>e</u>mnts, vt.)

√šm₂ † s+šém+p+mš fog. (ssh<u>e</u>mpmsh, n.)

√šmn' † šemen' *enemy, foe, opponent.* (sheme'n, n.); s+šm[n]+ín'+en' *antagonism, hostility.* (sshmmi̱'ne'n, n.); § pul+uɫ+šemen' *enemy (he killed his...), killed (he...his enemy).* (puluɫsheme'n, n, vt.); ylmíxʷ+m he šémen' *devil, archenemy, Satan.* (ylmi̱khum he she̱me'n. (lit. enemy who is chief), n.)

√šm', † šim' *benefit (to...).* (shi'm (stem), vt.); t+ším' *benefited (H/s...from something).* (tshi̱'m, vi.); s+t+ším'+n *benefitting (from something), profitting.* (stshi̱'mn, vt.); ‡ t+ším'-n *benefit (I...from h/h).* (tshi̱'mn, vi.); t+šim'-nt-s *benefited (H/s...from h/h).* (tshi̱'mnts, vi.)

√šm'š † šim'íš *all-a-round, any, anybody, anything, anytime.* (shi'mi̱sh, adj, adv, pron.); u šim'íš *ad-lib, anything, anyway.* (ushi'mi̱sh (lit. to one's liking), n.); § u šim'íš tel' tč+ʔésel *either (lit. one or the other of two persons).* (ushi'mi̱sh te'l tch'e̱sel, n.)

√šn † šen *labor, work (to...).* (shen (stem), vi.); šén+n *worked (H/s...).* (she̱nn, vi.); e· šén+n *labor, work.* (eeshe̱nn (lit. H/s/i works), vi.); s+šén+n *labor, work.* (sshe̱nn, vi.); s+šén+n+s *earnings, pay, wages.* (sshe̱nns. (lit. They are things h/s worked for), n.); šén+šn+t *diligent, earnest, industrious (H/s is industrious), zealous.* (she̱hshnt (lit. H/s loves to work), adj.); s+šén+šn+t *diligence, industry.* (sshe̱nshnt, n.); šén+n+ul *work (pl.).* (she̱nnul!, imper.); šen+n-š *work (pl.).* (she̱nnsh, imper.); hiyc+šén+n+s *deserving.* (hiytsshe̱nns (lit. something he worked for, he is deserving of it), vt.); čes‿šen+n *labor, work.* (chesshe̱nn, vi.); ul sye·+šén+n *blue-collar.* (ul syeeshe̱nn (lit. of worker), adj.); čn‿šén+n *worked.* (chnshe̱nn. (lit. I

worked), vt.); čn'‿š'en+n *I work (cust).* (ch'nsh'e̱nn, v.); či ʔ‿šén+n *working.* (chi'she̱nn (lit. I am working), vt.); t'iʔ+čn‿šén+n *worked (I have...).* (t'i'chnshe̱nn, vi.); t'ixʷ hi+s+šén· *I had worked.* (t'i'khwehisshe̱nn, v.); čeɫ‿či‿s+šén+n *work.* (cheɫchisshe̱nn (lit. I will work), vi.); kʷne ʔ+čn‿šén+n *work (I am going to...).* (k'wne'chnshe̱nn, vi.); kʷʔ‿šén+n *work (you (sg.)...).* (ku'she̱nn, vi.); kʷu‿šén+n *You (sg.) worked.* (kuushe̱nn, vi.); kʷu‿y'‿šén+n *You (sg) are working.* (ku'yshe̱nn, vi.); t'iʔ kʷu‿šén· *You (s) have worked.* (t'i'kuushe̱nn, v.); t'ixʷ eʔ i-s+šén· *You (s) had worked.* (t'i'khwe'isshe̱nn, v.); čeɫ‿kʷu‿s+šén+n *(lit. you(sg.) will work).* (cheɫkusshe̱nn, vt.); neʔ+kʷu‿šén+n *work (You (sg.) shall...).* (ne'kuushe̱nn (imper.), vi.); kʷ neʔ kʷu·‿šén+n *You (sg.) are going to work.* (k'wne'kuushe̱nn, vi.); i· šén+n *H/s is working.* (iishe̱nn, vi.); t'iʔ+šén+n *worked (H/s has...).* (t'i'she̱nn, vi.); t'ixʷ es+šén·-s *H/s had worked.* (t'i'khwesshe̱nns, v.); čes‿šén-n *he/she will work.* (chesshe̱nn, vi.); kʷeʔ n+šén+n *H/s is going to work.* (k'wen'she̱nn, v.); č‿šén+n *worked (we...).* (chshe̱nn, vt.); čʔe·‿šen+n *work.* (ch'eeshe̱nn (lit. we work), vi.); č‿ʔi+šén+n *lit. we are working.* (ch'iishe̱nn, vt.); t'iʔ+č‿šén+n *worked (We have...).* (t'i'chshe̱nn, vi.); t'ixʷ es+šén·-et *We had worked.* (t'i'khwesshe̱nnet, v.); č‿šen+n *We will work.* (chshe̱nn, vt.); čet+čs+šén+n *work.* (chetchsshe̱nn (lit. we will work), vi.); ceɫ‿č‿s+šén+n *work (lit. we will work).* (cheɫchsshe̱nn, vi.); kʷne[ʔ]+č+šén+n *We are going to work.* (k'wnechshe̱nn, v.);

kʷp'‿e·+šén+n *work (you (pl.)...).* (kup'eeshenn, vi.); kʷp‿šén+n *worked (you (pl.)...).* (kupshenn, vi.); kʷup‿ʔi·‿šén+n *You (pl) are working.* (kup'iishenn, vi.); t'iʔ kʷup‿šén· *You (pl) have worked.* (t'i'kupshenn, v.); t'ixʷ es+šén·+m-p *You (pl.) had worked.* (t'i'khwesshennmp, v.); čeł‿kʷup‿s+šén+n *(lit. you will work).* (chełkupsshenn, vi.); neʔ kʷup‿šén+n *You (pl.) shall work (imper.).* (ne'kupshenn, v.); k'ʷ neʔ kʷup‿šén+n *You (pl.) are going to work.* (k'wne'kupshenn, vi.); šén+n-lš *worked (They...).* (shennlsh, vi.); e· šén+n-lš *They work, labor.* (eeshennlsh, vi.); i· šén+n-lš *They are working.* (iishennlsh, vi.); t'iʔ+šén+n-lš *worked (They have...).* (t'i'shennlsh, vi.); t'ixʷ es+šén·-s-lš *They had worked.* (t'i'khwesshennslsh, v.); čes‿šén+n-lš *they will work.* (chesshennlsh, vi.); k'ʷ neʔ šén+n-lš *They are going to work.* (k'wne'shennlsh, vi.); ‡ šen+n-šít-s *worked (He...for him).* (shennshits, vi.); šn+n+mí-nt-s *used (He...him for work).* (shnnmints, vt.); § s+nukʷ+šén+n *colleague.* (snukwshenn (lit. fellow worker), n.); s+nukʷ+s+šén+n *cooperation.* (snukwsshenn (lit. working together), n.); hiʔ+nukʷ+šn+mín+m *collaborate.* (hi'nukwshnminm (lit. I am employing him as my collaborator), vi.); nukʷ+šen+n+mí-nt-s-es *cooperate.* (nukwshennmintses (lit. She worked with me), vi.); čen'+uʔš+čn‿šén+n *desire I work.* (che'nu'shchnshenn, vt.); čen'+uʔš+kʷu·‿šén+n *desire you (s) works.* (che'nu'shkuushenn, vt.); čen'+uʔš+šén+n *desire h/s works.* (che'nu'shshenn, vt.); čen'+uʔš+č‿šén+n *desire we work.* (che'nu'shchshenn, vt.); čen'+uʔš+kʷup‿šén+n *desire you (pl) work.* (che'nu'shkupshenn, vt.); čen'+uʔš+šen+n-lš *desire they work.* (che'nu'shshennlsh, vt.);

√šn' † šen' *lie (ref. to a flat object).* (she'n (stem), vi.); ∥ a+n+šén'+šn'=us *bespectacled, glasses (to wear...).* (anshe'nsh'nus, adj, vi.); hn+šén'+šn'=us *glasses (for the eyes).* (hnshe'nsh'nus, n.); šn'=aqs+n *breastplate.* (sh'naqsn (lit. a plate lying on the chest), n.); s+cen+šn'=ílgʷes *badge.* (stsensh'nilgwes (lit. flat object on the chest), n.); t+šan'=alqʷ *billboard.* (tsha'nalqw, n.); t+šn'=álqʷ+n *cardboard.* (tsh'nalqwn (lit. flat object that is put on a post), n.)

√šp₁ † šep *chew, eat off bone.* (shep (stem), vt.); s+šép+m *corrosion, rot.* (sshepm. (lit. gnawing), n.); t+šép+m *lit. h/s chewed meat from bone.* (t-shepm, vt.); s+t+šép+m *chewing (meat from bone), gnawing.* (stshepm, vt.); ‡ šép-nt-m *corrode.* (shepntm (lit. It was gnawed to pieces), vi.); šép-nt-s *chewed (h/s...it).* (shepnts, vt.)

√šp₂ † šep *select, sift, sort, discriminate.* (shep (stem), vt, vi.)

√šp₃ † šip *deliberate.* (ship (stem), adj.); šip *complete, finish, own (to...).* (ship (stem), vt.); šíp+ep *accomplish, complete, it became finished (He...).* (shipep, vt, vi.); e·+šip+ep *consummated, complete, done, finished, perfect.* (eeshipep (lit. It is complete, finished), adj.); s+šíp+ep *completion, finishing.* (sshipep. completion, n.); s+šíp+ep+n *complement, supplement.* (sshipepn. (lit. something that completes, perfects or makes up a whole), n.); ∥ šep+ep=cín *conclude.* (shepeptsin (lit. His speech came to an end), vi.); s+šep+ep=cín *conclusion.*

(sshepeptsin (lit. finishing one's speech), n.); ‡ šíp+ep+s-n *complete, finished (I...it).* (shipepsn, vt.); šíp+ep-stu-s *consummate.* (shipepstus (lit. He completed or achieved it. H/s fulfilled (a marriage) with the first act of sexual intercourse), vt.); i·+šíp+ep+m-s *finishing (He is...it).* (iishipepms, vt.); § tel' t'i?s šíp+ep *a priori.* (te'l t'i's shipep (lit. from what is finished), conj.)

√šp₄ † šip *slow.* (ship (stem), adj.); šip+t *belated, slow (He is...), sluggish.* (shipt, adj.); ∥ šep+t=íl'š *decelerate.* (shepti'lsh (lit. It became slow, less speedy), vi.)

√šp₅ † č+šíp *chase.* (chship (stem), vt.); ‡ č+šip-nt-s *He chased him.* (chshipnts, vt.); č+[š]íp-nt-se-s *chase.* (chschipntses (lit. He chased me), vt.)

√šr₁ † šar *annoying, difficult, disobedient, indolent, lazy, steep, unruly.* (shar (stem), adj.); u· ša·r *to be indolent, lazy.* (uushaaar (lit. he seems in a lazy state), v.); šár+šar+t *arduous, difficult, steep (It is...).* (sharshart, adj.); šar+šar+t+úl *lazy (He is habitually...).* (sharshartul, adj.); hn+šár+n *indolence, laziness.* (hnsharn, n.); u čn‿šár *lazy (I feel...).* (uchnshar, vt, adj.); ∥ hn+šár+šar=cn *bull-headed, headstrong.* (hnsharshartsn. (lit. he is steep (difficult) for the mouth (of the speaker)/great difficulty is felt by parents whose disobedient children fail to respond to verbal discipline), adj.); ‡ šar=čt+m-nt-se-s *He caused me to feel lazy by his detaining me.* (sharchtmntses, vt.) [see also √šrč]

√šr₂ † šar *hang (to...a person).* (shar (stem), vt.); a+t+šár *addition, appendage.* (atshar (lit. It is appended), vi.); ∥ a+n+šár=enč *hang (on the wall).* (ansharench, vi, vi.); s+ni?+šár=us *boiled beef, broiling*

meat. (sni'sharus (lit. hanging over fire), n.); t+šar=íčs+n *bail.* (tsharichsn (lit. means of carrying (hanging on hand), n.); t+šar=íčt+m *hung (H/s...something on h/h hand).* (tsharichtm, vt.); u? t+šar=qn *H/s just hangs on.* (u'tsharqn, vi.); t+šar= qn+cút *suspended (He...himself by hanging on to it).* (tsharqntsut, vt.); ni?+šár+m=i?qs *Thanksgiving Day, turkey, elephant.* (ni'sharmi'qs, n.); ni?+šar=usi?+útm *squash.* (ni'sharusi'utm, n.); § kʷan+ɫ+sc+šár= čt *H/S took (along) a valise, lantern, etc.* (kwanɫstsharcht, vt.). [xref √šr']

√šr₃ † šar *Charles.* (Shar, n.)

√šrč † šarč *troublesome.* (sharch (stem), adj.) [see also √šr]

√šrš † s+n+šáriš *going upstream, downstream.* (snsharish, n.); ∥ an+šari·š+íɫ *upstream.* (anshariishiɫ, adv.) [?]

√šr' † hn+šar'+ar'=ípm *He fell to his knees.* (hnsha'ra'ripm, vt.). [xref √šr₂]

√šs₁ † šes *unbelieving, doubtful.* (shes (stem), adj.); ∥ hn+šés+p=cn *disbelieve.* (hnshesptsn. (lit. He disbelieved), vt.); ‡ hn+šs+p=cín-t-m *disbelieve.* (hnshsptsintm. (lit. He was refused belief), vt.); e+n+šs+p= cí-stu-s *distrust.* (enshsptsistus (lit. H/s (cust.) doubts h/h), vt.)

√šs₂ ∥ e+šús+t=us *command, bid, order.* (eshustus, vt.)

√št † šet *tease.* (shet (stem), vt.); s+št+št-n't-w'íš *teasing (one another).* (sshtsht'nt'wish, vt.); ∥ št+št=íɫc'e? *teased (he...someone).* (shtshtiɫts'e', vt.); s+št+št=íɫc'e? *banter.* (sshtshtiɫts'e' (lit. teasing another), n.); ‡ šét+št-n't-s *aggravate (to...), chaff, teased (h/s...h/h).* (shetsht'nts (lit. He teased him), vi, vt.)

√št'₁ † šet' *beat (to...in a contest), win.* (shet' (stem), vt.); šet' *encircled,* *surrounded*. (shet' (stem). standby, adj.); šét'+t' *also-ran*. (she't't (lit. He was defeated in a competition), n.); s+šét'+t' *defeat, defeated*. (sshet't. becoming defeated, n, vt.); s+št'+t'+nu+ncút *defeatism, self-defeat*. (ssht't'nuntsut, n.); ∥ št'+t'= ástq *checkmate*. (sht't'astq (lit. He defeated others completely), vt.); s+št'+t'=ástq *conquest*. (ssht't'astq (lit. subduing), n.); čn'‿šit'+et'=ástq *beat (I...my opponent), won (I...the contest)*. (ch'nshit'et'astq, vt.); čn‿št'+t'=astq *beat (an opponent), vanquish, win (a contest)*. (chnsht't'astq, vt.); sya+št'+t'=ás[t]q *victor*. (syasht't'asq, n.); sya+št'+t'=[a]stq *conqueror*. (syasht't'stq, n.); ‡ št'+t'+nún-t-s *conquer, overcame (He...him)*. (sht't'nunts, vt.)

√**š t'₂** † šet' *extend, project (e.g. a long object)*. (shet' (stem), vi.); e·šét' *upright*. (eeshet' (lit. It, e.g. a tree, stands upright), adj.); u·šét' *It is level (as ground)*. (uushet', vi.); ∥ t+št'= íw'es *boiler, kettle*. (tsht'i'wes (lit. spout jutting from another object), n.); t+š+št'=iw'es *caldron*. (tshsht'i'wes (lit. vessel with a projection from the body), n.); č+šet[']=íw'es *kettle*. (chshe'ti'wes (lit. vessel with a projection from the body), n.); č+šet'= íw'es *caldron, kettle (lit. vessel with a projection from the body)*. (chshe'ti'wes, n.); e+ni?+št'=íw'es *conspicuous, outstanding*. (eni'sht'i'wes, vi. (lit. H/s/i towers above the rest), adj.); et+š?t'=íne? *attentive*. (etsh't'ine' (lit. He pays attention by ear), vi.); t+šét'=ečt *branch*. (tshet'echt (lit. projection from a tree), n.); u+n+šát'=qn *egalitarianism, equality*. (unshat'qn (lit. of equal heights on top of the head), n.); u·+šét'=ul'umxʷ *ground (The...is level), level (The ground is...)*.

(uushet'u'lumkhw, n, adj.); ‡ hn+št'= ičn'-t-m *He was constrained. (lit. something (ie gun) was set up on his back)*. (hnsht'ich'ntm, vi.)

√**š t'₃** † šet' *care (take...of)*. (shet' (stem), n.); s+č+šet[']+m *custody*. (schshe'tm (lit. act of guarding), n.); e+t+št'+ncút *fastidious*. (etsht'ntsut (lit. He takes care of himself), vi.); e+t+št'+ncút-š *to be fastidious, choosy*. (etsht'ntsutsh (lit. He takes care of himself), vi.); č+št'+ncút+n *confident (lit. he has the means of taking care of oneself)*. (chsht'ntsutn, n.); t+št'+ncút+n *amulet*. (tsht'ntsutn (lit. means of taking care of oneself), n.); kʷ‿in+t+št'+ncút+n *depend*. (kwintsht'ntsutn (lit. you are my means of taking care of myself), vi.); sye+č+šét'+m *caretaker, chaperone, curator, custodian*. (syechshet'm, n.); ∥ t+št'=ílt *babysit (to...)*. (tsht'ilt (lit. He cared for his own or other's children), vi.); hi+[š]t'=ílt *apprentice*. (hischt'ilt (lit. He is (my) child under my charge), n.); ‡ č+šet'-nt-s *He took care of him*. (chshet'nts, vi.); §
sye+č+št'+el'+s+čí+če? *cowboy*. (syechsht'e'lschiche' (lit. One who tends horses, (livestock, or cattle) for another), n.); ul sye+č+št'+el'+s+čí+če? *bucolic*. (ul syechsht'e'lschiche' (lit. belonging to a cattle herder), adj.)

√**š t'₄** † šét'+ut *rock*. (shet'ut, n.); š+št'+ut *little rock, pebble*. (shsht'ut, n.); š+[š]t'+út *calculus*. (shst'ut (lit. small rock), n.); šet+št'+ut *stone*. (shetsht'ut. (lit. pebble), n.); cen+šét'+ut *bedrock*. (tsenshet'ut, n.); § šét'+s+šic'=e?st *diamond*. (shet'sshits'e'st (lit. hard stone), n.); x̌em x̌ʷe šét'+ut *rock (The...is heavy), heavy (The rock is...)*. (qhem khwe shetut, n, adj.); u· qʷéd he šét'+ut *basalt.* (uuq'w<u>e</u>d he sh<u>e</u>t'ut (lit. rock that is black), n.)

√**šw'** † šiw' *female, feminine.* (shi'w (stem), adj.); šiw'+t+m *girl (adolescent...(12)13-21).* (shi'wtm, n.); šíw'+šew'+t+m *girls.* (sh<u>i</u>'wshe'wtm, n.); š+šíw'+t+m' *girl (a very young...).* (shshi'wt'm, n.); ∥ s+šíw'+t+m=elt *daughter.* (sshi'wtmelt (lit. girl offspring), n.); § s+wi?+núm+t+mš he šíw'+t+m *Diana, belle.* (swi'n<u>u</u>mtmsh he shi'wtm (lit. a girl who is beautiful), n.)

√**šw't** † šiw't *rat.* (shi'wt, n.); § ul šiw't he čníl+emn *rat poison.* (ul shi'wt he chn<u>i</u>lemn, n.)

√**šx̌** ∥ šáx̌+šax̌+t=ałp *spruce.* (sh<u>a</u>qhshaqhtałp, n.)

√**šy'** † hn+ší+šey'+t *He was famished.* (hnsh<u>i</u>she'yt)

√**š?₁** † ši? *respect (to...), revere.* (shi' (stem), vt.); ∥ hn+še?+še?=ílgʷes *chivalrous, considerate, courteous.* (hnshe'she'<u>i</u>lgwes. (lit. He is respectful at heart), adj.); ‡ e·+ší?-stu-s *respect, revere.* (eeshi'stus (lit. H/s treats h/h with respect, reverence.), vt.); § lut ší?+še?+t *cheeky.* (lut shi'she't (lit. He is disrespectful), adj.)

√**š?₂** ‡ hn+še?+še?=íne?-nt-se-xʷ *You rebuked me, you scolded me.* (hnshe'she'<u>i</u>ne'ntsekhw, vt.); hn+še?+še?=íne?-nt-s *rebuke, remonstrate.* (hnshe'she'<u>i</u>ne'nts. call down, chew out. (lit. He rebuked him in the ears), vt.)

√**š?(t)** † ši?(t) *firstborn.* (shi' (stem), adj.); ši?t *firstborn, oldest.* (shi't (stem), adj.); č+ši?t *alpha.* (chshi't (lit. first), n.); e+t+ší?t *first (he is).* (etshi't, vi.); e+t+ši+ší?t *best, foremost.* (etshish<u>i</u>'t. (He is first), adj.); e+c+š+ší?t *element.* (etsshshi't (lit. that which comes first), n.); e+c+še+ší?t *element, a main principal.* (etsshesh<u>i</u>'t (lit. that w/c

comes first), n.); e+č+ší?t *capital, distinguished, first, foremost, prime.* (echshi't (lit. that w/c or he who is...), adj.); e+č+š+ší?t *cardinal, important, primary.* (echshshi't (lit. It is of foremost importance), adj.); ul eč+š+ší?t *classical.* (ul echshshi't (lit. belonging to the first rank), adj.); sye+c+ší[?]t *bell-wether.* (sye'tsshit (lit. One who acts as leader), n.); sya+c+ší?t *bell-wether (lit. One who acts as leader).* (sya'tsshi't, n.); sya+cen+ši?+m *conductor.* (syatsenshi'm (lit. One who leads or guides), n.); ∥ hn+ši?[t]=cn+m+scút *boast.* (hnshi'tsnmsts<u>u</u>t. (lit. He placed himself first verbally). pride, vi.); hn+ši?t=cn+[c]út+n *ancestor.* (hnshi'tsnsutn. (lit. one who goes before oneself), n.); ‡ cen+ší?-nt-s *convoy, lead away.* (tsenshi'nts (lit. He escorted h/h for protection; he went ahead of him), n.); te+cen+ší?-nt-s *conduct.* (tetsenshi'nts (lit. He led or guided him), vi.)

√**tc** † tuc *well-fed.* (tuts (stem), adj.)

√**tččxʷ** † s+tíččxʷ *snow berries.* (n. st<u>i</u>chtskhw, pl.n.); ∥ s+tiččxʷ=élp *red willow.* (stichtskhw<u>e</u>lp. (bitter berries), n.)

√**tčy'** † i+čs+tččíy'+ey' *diuretic.* (ichstchch<u>i</u>'ye'y (lit. H/s is disturbed with too much urine), adj.); § elu+s+tčíy'+m *anuresis.* (elustch<u>i</u>'ym (lit. It does not urinate), n.); lut hey'+n+tččiy'+n=gʷílis *urinate (unable to...).* (lut he'yntchchi'yngw<u>i</u>lis, vi.)

√**tdš** † tédiš *crawl, crawled, creep, crept.* (t<u>e</u>dish (stem), vi.)

√**tgʷ₁** † tagʷ *buy.* (tagw (stem), vt.); tegʷ *buy, sell.* (tegw (stem), vt.); tegʷ+mí+ncut *bought (He...for himself).* (tegwmintsut, vi.); s+tegʷ+mí+ncut *commerce, commercialism, buy, purchase,*

shopping (go...for oneself).
(stegwmintsut, n, vt, vi.);
hn+tegʷ+mí+ncut+n *marketplace.*
(hntegwmintsutn, n.);
hn+t+tegʷ+m'í+n'cut+n' *shop,*
boutique, store. (hnttegw'mi'ntsutn'.
(lit. little place for buying for oneself),
n.); č‿y'+tegʷ+mí+ncut *buy.*
(chi'tegwmintsut (lit. I am buying for
myself), vi.); sye+tegʷ+mí+ncut
buyer, consumer, customer.
(syetegwmintsut (lit. One who buys for
himself), n.); ‖ tagʷ=álpqʷ *food (He*
bought...), bought (He...food).
(tagwalpqw, n, vt.); hi·+tágʷ=alpqʷ
cate, food (boughten...). (hiitagwalpqw
(lit. something bought for the mouth),
n.); hn+tágʷ=alpqʷ+n *commissary,*
market, store. (hntagwalpqwn (lit.
place to buy food), n.); tágʷ=alqs
bought (He...clothing), clothing (He
bought...). (tagwalqs, vt, n.); ‡
tegʷ+mín-šit-se-s *bought*
(He...(things) for me).
(tegwminshitses, vt.)

√tgʷ₂ † tegʷ *fail (to reach).* (tegw
(stem), v.); can+tégʷe?+n *reach (He*
failed to...). (tsantegwe'n, vi.);
cen+tégʷe?+n *failed (He...to reach).*
(tsentegwe'n, vi.); e+cen+tégʷe?+n
neophyte, novice, amateur.
(etsentegwe'n (lit. One who has not
quite reached (a requisite goal)), n.)

√tgʷm' † tígʷem' *belly button, navel.*
(tigwe'm, n.)

√tkʷ₁ † tikʷ *smell out, suspect.* (tikw
(stem), vt.); s+tíkʷ+tekʷ+n *clue,*
implication, indication, inference.
(stikwtekwn. (lit. means of arousing
suspicion), n.); ‖ tekʷ=e·ní? *heard*
(He...). (tekweeni', vt.); čn‿tekʷ=
e·ní? *I heard (something) about*
(something). (chntekweeni' (lit. I
detected with the ear), vt.)

√tkʷ₂ † tukʷ *chug (e.g. a motor).* (tukw
(stem), vi.); u· túkʷ+tukʷ+tukʷ *chug.*

(uutukwtukwtukw (lit. It (engine)
chugged on), vi.)

√tkʷ? † tikʷe? *paternal aunt (if father*
is living). (tikwe', n.)

√tk'ʷ₁ † tek'ʷ *choke, smother.* (tek'w
(stem), vt.); [also written as √tkʷ]
ni?+tékʷ *brake, brushwood, thicket.*
(ni'tekw. (lit. a woods whose interior is
suffocating, n.); ni?+tákʷ *brushy.*
(ni'takw (lit. It is brushy), adj.);
s+tékʷ+tuk+p+t *angina, asthma.*
(stekwtukwpt. angina (lit. becoming
suffocated periodically, impairing the
respiration again and again), n.)

√tk'ʷ₂ † tí?k'ʷ+t *Tekoa.* (ti'k'ut, n.); ‖
[also recorded as √tkʷ] s+tikʷ=mš
Tekoa people. (Stikwmsh, n.)

√tl † tel *break off (ref. to a soft object).*
(tel (stem), vi.); tel+p *break-up,*
crumble (ref. to a single object). (telp
(stem), vi.); til+til+p *break-up,*
disintegrate. (tiltilp (stem), vi.);
hn+tél+ncut *diarrhea (to have...).*
(hntelntsut (lit. he had diarrhea), n.)

√tl'q † tal'q *touch with foot, kick, step*
on, tread. (tal'q (stem), vt, v, vi.);
č+tl'+tl'q+mín+n *steps.* (cht'lt'lqminn,
n.); i·+tál'q+m-s *He is square*
dancing, round dancing. (iita'lqms, n.);
‖ č+tl'+tl'q=íčn' *bicycle, bike.*
(cht'lt'lqich'n, n.); sya+č+tl'+t[l]'q=
íčn' *cyclist.* (syacht'lt'qich'n, n.); ‡
tál'q-nt-s *kicked (He...it).* (ta'lqnts,
vt.); § nuk'ʷ+ł+č+tel'q+mín+n
degree, rung. (nuk'włchte'lqminn. (lit.
one bar of a ladder), n.)

√tł₁ † teł *straight.* (teł (stem), adj.); u·
téł *aright, correct, direct, straight (it*
is...). (uuteł, adj.); u· teł+t *go directly,*
beeline. (uutełt (stem), vi.); tł+ł+útm
corrigible. (tłłutm (lit. He is capable of
being straightened), adj.);
s+téł+m+ncut *discipline, training.*
(stełmntsut. (lit. straightening oneself),
n.); s+téł+m+šeš *correction.*
(stełmshesh. aligning, n.);

sye·+téł+m+šeš *administrator.* (syeetełmshesh (lit. One who settles on estate), n.); ∥ cen+téł+t=cn *cut off, short cut.* (tsentełttsn, vt.); ‡ teł+m-s-n *amend, rectified (I...it).* (tełmsn, v.); § uc+ʔaẍił s+tł+t=cín+m *catachresis.* (uts'aqhił stłttsịnm (lit. for no reason directing one's speech or discourse), n.); uc+ʔaẍíł e+tł+t= cín+m *blabber.* (uts'aqhił etłttsịnm (lit. For nothing he talks straight. He talks rapidly, incessantly and inanely), vi.)

√tł₂ † tił *brushy objects sprawl.* (tił); ∥ tíł+teł=l'mxʷ *blackberries (vine of the...).* (tịłteł'lmkhw, n.); § s+n+gʷár'= us xʷe· tíł+teł=l'mxʷ *boysenberry.* (sngwa'rus khwee tịłteł'lmkhw (lit. descendant of blackberry vine), n.)

√tł₃ ∥ s+tół=łxʷ *adobe.* (stołłkhw, n.); hn+toł=álqs+n *black-top.* (hntołalqsn. asphalt. (lit. means of paving roads), n.)

√tłm † s+téłm *boat, skiff, ship, vessel.* (stełm, n.)

√tm₁ † tam *scorch, singe, toast.* (tam (stem), vt.); u· tám *hot, scorching (It remains...).* (uutam, adj.); tam+p *scorched (It was...).* (tamp, adj.); s+tam+p *cinder.* (stamp (lit. a partly charred substance that can burn further, but without flame), n.); ‡ tam-nt-m *char.* (tamntm (lit. It was scorched), v.)

√tm₂ † tem+tem+n+úl *sociable (He is...).* (temtemnul, adj.); tam+tam+n+úl *He is sociable.* (tamtamnul, adj.); ∥ s+te·m= ílgʷes *relation (blood...), relative (collateral...).* (steemilgwes (lit. a companion at heart), n.); gʷł s+ta·m= ílgʷes *clan.* (guł staamilgwes (lit. relatives), n.); čn‿is+te·m=ílgʷes *related (to be a relative to). relative (to be a relative to).* (chnisteemilgwes (lit. I am your relative), vi.); či‿s+te·m=

ílgʷes-s *I am h/h relative.* (chisteemilgwess, adj.); čn‿is+te·m= ílgʷes+m-p *relative.* (chnisteemilgwesmp. (lit. I am your (pl) relative), n.); čis‿s+te·m= ilgʷes-s-lš *relative.* (chissteemilgwesslsh (lit. I am their relative), adj.); kʷ‿i-s+te·m=ílgʷes *You (sg.) are my relative.* (kwisteemilgwes, vi.); kʷu‿s+teem= ílgʷes-s *You (sg.) are his/her relative.* (kusteemilgwess, vi.); hi-s+te·m= ílgʷes *H/S is my relative.* (histeemilgwes, vt.); is+te·m=ílgʷes *relative (H/s is your (sg.)...).* (isteemilgwes, n.); s+te·m=ílgʷes-s *is (H/s...h/h relative).* (steemilgwess, vi.); s+te·m=ílgʷes-et *is (H/s...our relative).* (steemilgweset, vi.); s+te·m=ílgʷes+m-p *is (H/s...your (pl.) relative).* (steemilgwesmp, vi.); kʷup‿hn-s+te·m=ílgʷes *You (pl) are my relatives.* (kuphisteemilgwes, n.); kʷup‿s+te·m=ílgʷes-s *You (pl.) are his/her relatives.* (kupsteemilgwess, vi.); hi-s+s+te·m=ílgʷes-lš *They are my relatives.* (histeemilgweslsh, vt.); s+te·m=ílgʷes-s-lš *are (They...h/h relatives).* (steemilgwesslsh, vi.); § e+tem+n+es=čínt *convivial, kind.* (etemneschint, vt. (lit. He treats others sociably), adj.); s+tem+n+es+čint *entertain, host.* (stemneschint, vt.); elu+s+tem+n+es+čínt *cantankerous, perverse (disposition), unfriendly, unsociable.* (elustemneschint (lit. One who is not sociable), adj.); pul+uł+s+te·m=ílgʷes *relative (he killed his...), killed (he...his relative).* (pulułsteemilgwes, n, vt.); ẍes+t he s+te·m=ílgʷes *boon.* (qhest he steemilgwes (lit. He is good who is a relative), adj.); s+t+kʷel'+tem+n= elwís *visiting (He is going about...people).* (stkwe'ltemnelwịs, vt.); t+kʷeł+tem+n=elwís *visiting (He went about...people, treating them sociably).* (tkwełtemnelwi̲s, vt, vi.); nuk'ʷ+ł+túm' *bevy, covey, brood, group, class.* (nuk'włtu̲'m, n.); nuk'ʷ+ł+tum' ha sóltes *battalion.* (nuk'włtu'm ha so̲ltes (lit. a unit of soldiers), n.); [xref √tmn₂,₃]

√tm₃ // eč+tm=ílxʷ *bare (to be...).* (echtmi̲lkhw, vi.); č+tm=elxʷ+ncút *divest.* (chtmelkhwntsu̲t (lit. H/S make h/h self bare), vt.)

√tm₄ // en+tém+tm=ens *cavity (teeth), decayed.* (entemtmens, vt. (lit. To have decayed teeth), n, adj.); s+n+tém+p=ens *caries.* (sntempens (lit. decaying of a tooth), n.)

√tm₅ † tum *pump, suck (e.g. through a tube).* (tum (stem), vt.) [xref √t'm'₃]

√tm₆ † u n+tó·m *dirty (It is...), unclean (The water is...).* (untoooom, adj.); u n+tó·m *water (The...is unclean).* (untoooom, n.)

√tmds † tmídus *tomato.* (tmi̲dus, n.)

√tmh // s+ni?+tm+tmi·h=ús+mš *blizzard.* (sni'tmtmiihu̲smsh, n.)

√tmn₁ † tm+tmní? *body, cadaver, carcass, corpse, defunct.* (tmtmni̲' (lit. He is a dead body), n.); hn+tm+tmn+in *grave, tomb.* (hntmtmnin, n.); hn+tm+tmní?+n *mausoleum, cemetery, tomb.* (hntmtmni̲'n, n.); s+n+tm+tmní?+n *cemetery, catacomb.* (sntmtmni̲'n (lit. a burying place for the dead), n.); § u+x̌ʷel'+e+tm+tmní? *cadaverous, corpselike.* (uqhwe'letmtmni̲' (lit. He looks like a dead body), adj.)

√tmn₂ † s+timn *amusement, entertainment.* (stimn, n.); ‡ tímn-t-m *amused (He was...).* (ti̲mntm, vi.); § e+temn+es=čínt *convivial, kind.* (etemneschi̲nt, vt. (lit. He treats others sociably), adj.); s+temn+es+čint *entertain, host.* (stemneschint, vt.); elu+s+temn+es+čínt *cantankerous, perverse (disposition), unfriendly,*

unsociable. (elustemneschi̲nt (lit. One who is not sociable), adj.) [xref √tm₂]

√tmn₃ † tímn+n *chattel, commodity, utility.* (ti̲mnn (lit. a useful thing), n.); č+tímn+n *caliber, quality, usefulness, worth.* (chti̲mnn, adj, n.) [xref √tm₂]

√tmrs † tmer'us *ketchup.* (tme'rus (l.w. from Engl. tomatoes), n.) ; tmérus *catsup, ketchup.* (tme̲rus (lit. tomatoes. Note the sound of the word), n.)

√tmš † u tmíš *only, but.* (utmi̲sh, adv.)

√tmt † timu·tí *Timothy.* (Timuuti̲, n.)

√tmxʷ₁ † temxʷ *rotten (ref. to a tree).* (temkhw (stem), adj.)

√tmxʷ₂ † t+tm'íxʷ *animal, beast, bird, cattle.* (tt'mi̲khw, n.); hn+t+tm'íxʷ+n' *aviary, birdcage.* (hntt'mi̲khwn'. (lit. a place for birds), n.); ?epł+t+tm'íxʷ *livestock (to have...).* (epłtt'mi̲khw (lit. H/s has livestock, commonly ref. to animals or birds), vt.); // t+tm'i·xʷ=íl'š *dehumanize.* (tt'miikhwi̲'lsh (lit. He became a mere animal), v.); tmíxʷ=ul'mxʷ *country, earth, soil, territory.* (tmi̲khu'lmkhw, n.); t+tm'íxʷ=ul'um'xʷ *acre.* (tt'mi̲khu'lum'khw (lit. a small field), n.); in-tmíxʷ=lumxʷ *district.* (intmi̲khwlumkhw (lit. It is your land, territory, province, etc.), n.); e+tmíxʷ=ul'umxʷ *earth (to be on...).* (etmi̲khu'lumkhw, vi.); § ul xʷi?+ye+tmixʷ=lmxʷ *American, earthly.* (ul khwi'yetmi̲khw'lmkhw (lit. belonging to this land (country), adj.); ul li·béč he tmíxʷ=ul'm[xʷ] *diocese.* (ul liibe̲ch he tmi̲khu'lms (lit. It is a land or district in which a bishop has authority), n.); s+t+miy+iy=ípele?+s x̌ʷe t+č'm=ásq'it twe tmíxʷ=ulmxʷ *cosmography, science of what is in the sky and earth.* (stmiyiyi̲pele's khwe tch'ma̲sq'it twe tmi̲khulmkhw, n.); s+t+miy+y=ipele?+s łe tmíxʷ=l'umxʷ *earth (description of...), description (...of earth).* (stmiyyi̲pele's łe tmi̲khw'lumkhw, n.); s+t+miy+y=

ipele?-s xʷe tmixʷ=l'umxʷ
*description of earth, geology,
geography.* (stmiyyipele's khwe
tmikhw'lumkhw, n.);
s+cen+k[']ʷúl'+l'+s xʷe tmíxʷ=l'umxʷ
map. (stsenku̱'l'ls khwe
tmi̱khw'lumkhw (lit. means of making
a description of land), n.); s+č'm=
álpqʷ+s he t+tm'íxʷ *craw.*
(sch'ma̱lpqws he tt'mi̱khw (lit.
esophagus of a bird), n.); s+c'uwe·ní
he t+tm'íxʷ *dinosaur.* (sts'uweeni̱ he
tt'mi̱khw (lit. It is a giant one who is an
animal), n.); qel'+tmxʷ+loko·so *boar.*
(qe'ltmkhwlokooso. (lit. male pig), n.);
qel'+tmxʷ+ł+wárč *bullfrog.*
(qe'ltmkhwłwa̱rch. (lit. a male frog),
n.); u+x̌ʷel'+é t+tm'íxʷ *bestial,
birdlike.* (uqhwe'le̱ tt'mi̱khw (lit. It is
like an animal), n.);
qel'+tmxʷ+mí+ncut *bachelor,
celibate.* (qe'ltmkhwmi̱ntsut. (lit. one
who is a man by himself), n.); ul
s+qil'+tmxʷ *bisexual.* (ul sqi'ltmkhw,
adj.); s+gʷl'=tmxʷ *flirt.* (sg'ltmkhw, n.)

√tm? † tímu? *fern.* (ti̱mu', n.)

√tm'₁ † s+č+tem'+p *cloud.* (schte'mp,
n.); ?ep+s+č+tém'+p *cloudy, dim,
dull (...day), overcast.* (epschte̱'mp (lit.
It has clouds), adj.); §
elu+s+č+tém'+p *clear (sky),
cloudless.* (eluschte̱'mp (lit. It has no
cloud), adj.)

√tm'₂ † tim' *ground is clear of snow.*
(ti'm)

√tm'₃ † tim' *to use.* (ti'm (stem), vt.);
s+tim' *device.* (sti'm. appliance, tool
(lit. something that is used), n.);
s+tim'+n *appliance, tool.* (sti'mn.
device (lit. something that is used), n.);
sye·+tím'+n *applicator.* (syeeti̱'mn
(lit. an instrument for applying
something), n.); § łoqʷ+s+tim['] *what
else.* (łoqwstim, adv.); lut s+tim'
cipher, nothing, zero. (lut sti'm, n.);
s+č+tuxʷ+s+tim' *by-product.*

(schtukhwsti'm (lit. something added
to a thing in the making), n.);
s+ta·m'+ł+p'áx̌ *healed (The wound
was finally...), wound (The...was
finally healed).* (staaa'młp'a̱qh, vt, n.);
tgʷel'+s+tím' *Why?, why.* (tgwe'lsti'm,
qu, adv.); tgʷel' s+tim'+ł
kʷ‿čic+xʷy? *come (Why did you...?).*
(tgwe'l sti'mł ku chitskhuy?, vi.);
s+tim' xʷe s+kʷes+t=ílumxʷ-s *What
is the name of the place?* (sti'm khwe
skwesti̱lumkhws? (qu.).) [xref √t?]

√tn † ten *pull (rope), tight.* (ten (stem),
vt, adj.); ten+tn+t *fit tightly (clothes).*
(tentnt (stem), vi.)

√tnš † tunš *nephew.* (tunsh, n.); ∥
tunš=íw'es *uncle and nephew [or vice
versa].* (tunshi̱'wes, n.)

√tn' † ten' *arranged in a line, lined up.*
(te'n (stem), v.); s+tén'+m+šeš
classification, echelon. (ste̱'nmshesh.
(lit. arranging in a line), n.); ‡
tén'+m-s-n *arrange.* (te̱'nmsn (lit. I
put them in a deliberate order or
relation), v.); tén'+m-stu-s *classify.*
(te̱'nmstus (lit. He lined (them)
according to category), v.); §
s+ten[']+kʷl'+l' *structure.* (stenk'u'lu'l
(lit. a model formed under), n.)

√tp₁ ∥ s+tp=čín *tin.* (stpchin, n.) [?]

√tp₂ † tup *cool.* (tup (stem), vt.)

√tp₃ § tap+s+x̌es+t *is (It...not good).*
(tapsqhest (Spokane), vi.);
s+tep+kʷín+m *detention (lit.
witholding something from things
taken away).* (stepkwinm, n.)

√tpłq † s+tapałqi *Liberty Butte (near
Tensed and DeSmet).* (Stapałqi̱ (about
three miles SW of Tensed, Idaho), n.)

√tpn' † tupen' *black widow, daddy
longlegs, spider.* (tupe'n, n.)

√tq₁ † taq *cover (with hand), deceive,
fool, touch.* (taq (stem), vt.); teq *cheat,
outwit.* (teq (stem), vt.); té+teq+t
cagey (He is...). (te̱teqt, adj.);
téq+teq+t *artful, crafty, cagey,*

calculating, coy, crafty, deceitful, sly, wily, shrewd (He is...). (teqteqt, adj.); s+téq+teq+t *cunning.* (steqteqt (lit. skill in deception), n.); a+ča·+táq *blind.* (achaataq (lit. He is covered over, touched), adj.); taq+aq+útm *concrete, corporeal, tangible.* (taqaqutm (lit. It is capable of being touched (physically), n.); taq+taq+i·ʔ+útm *cable-gram, telegraph, typewriter.* (taqtaqii'utm (lit. that which is operated by the touch), n.); taq+taq+taq+i·ʔ+útm *telegraph, typewriter.* (taqtaqtaqii'utm (lit. that which is operated by the touch), n.); s+taq+aq+nún+m *artifice.* (staqaqnunm (lit. suceeding in making subtle deception), n.); // táq=čt+m *wave.* (taqchtm (lit. He put his hand in a touching attitude), vi.); [t]áq+[t=č]t+m *waved.* (łaqłshtm (lit. He put his hand in a touching attitude), vi.); an+taq+taq=íneʔ *deaf (to be...).* (antaqtaqine', vi. (lit. Touched in both ears), vi.); s+taq+aq+n=úłc'eʔ *barratry.* (staqaqnułts'e' (lit. deceiving other people), n.); ‡ táq-n *touched (I...him).* (taqn, vt.); táq-šit-s *bespeak.* (taqshits (lit. He gave a sign to him with his hand), v.); taq+aq+nún-n *deceive, fooled (I...him), touching (I succeeded in...him).* (taqaqnunn, vi, vt.); taq+aq+nún+t-se-s *beguile, deceived (He...me).* (taqaqnuntses, vt.); § s+taq+aq+nu+s+čínt *chicanery, deception.* (staqaqnuschint. (lit. deceiving people), n.); s+myes+taq+aq+n=us+čínt *coup, deception (extraordinary...).* (smyestaqaqnuschint, n.)

√tq₂ † [t]a+tq *hang (strips of smoked fat).* (łatq (stem), vt.) [for expected √łq^w₁]

√tq₃ // taq=il'p-nt-m *clog.* (taqi'lpntm (lit. It (stream) was clogged (dammed up), v.)

√tq₄ † // čat+teq=eg^weł *bluebird.* (chatteqegweł, n.)

√tqw' † taqáw' *deaf-mute, dumb (He is a...(mute) person).* (taqa'w, n, adj.) [see also √tq]

√tq' † taq'+taq'+mí *Chilco Mountain.* (Taq'taq'm, n.); taq'+taq'+n+mí *Chilco Mountain.* (Taq'taq'nmi', n.)

√tq^w // an+tuq^w=úlm'x^w *crypt.* (antuqul'mkhw (lit. Hole in the ground), n.); an+tuq^w=úll'mx^w *grave.* (antuqul'lmkhw (lit. Hole in the ground), n.); s+n+tuq^w+q^w=úl'mx^w *crater.* (sntuququ'lmkhw (lit. a depression in the ground caused by a volcano, meteor, etc.), n.)

√tq'^wsm' † s+tuq'^wsúm' *weasel.* (stuq'wsu'm, n.)

√tr₁ † tar *loosen, stretch out, extend, untie.* (tar (stem), vt.); s+tár+m *absolve, compurgation.* (starm. (lit. untying), n.) [xref √tr']

√tr₂ † tor *tough (as meat, leather).* (tor (stem), adj.)

√tr₃ // tor=s *beckon (with the eye).* (tor...s (stem), vt.)

√trq // s+taréq=šn *mud hen.* (stareqshn, n.)

√tr' † tar' *trail (to be laid out in trails), have trails.* (tar' (stem), n.); // tar'=ítk^weʔ *canalize.* (ta'ritkwe' (lit. He provided an outlet for water), vi.); s+tar'=ítk^weʔ *canal, ditch.* (sta'ritkwe'. canal (lit. a man-made stream), n.); s+niʔ+tar'=íłx^w *avenue, boulevard.* (sni'ta'riłkhw (lit. road among houses), n.); s+niʔ+ta+tar'=íłx^w *alley.* (sni'tata'riłkhw, n.) [xref √tr₁]

√ts † tes *bulge.* (tes (stem), vi.); tes+p *bloat.* (tesp (lit. It became swollen), vi.); // s+niʔ+tés+ts+p=enč *bulkage, swelling (...up of the intestines).* (sni'testspench (lit. swellings among the intestines, any substance that stimulates peristalsis by increasing the

bulk of material in the intestines), n,
v.)

√tt § ʕʷa+ʕʷe+ł+t+tót+ot *H/s has many pets.* (a(wełttotot, vt.)

√twn ∥ tíwn=łc'eʔ *doe.* (tiwnłts'e', n.)

√twp' † twip' *step over.* (twip' (stem), vi.); ‡ twíp'=šn-t-s *bestride, stepped (He...over it).* (twip'shnts, v.)

√twš † tewš *cross (country or prairie), traversed.* (tewsh. (lit. he traversed a plain), vt.); s+tewš *diameter.* (stewsh (lit. going across, traversing, measure thereof), n.); ∥ téwš=ečt *six.* (tewshecht (lit. H/h finger went across), n.); tuwš=íčt=us *cube.* (tuwshichtus (lit. It has six faces), n.); hn+tuwš=íč=łceʔ *cylinder, six-shooter, revolver.* (hntuwshichłtse', n.); s+tuwš=íl'=kʷeʔ *to swim.* (stuwshi'lkwe', vi.); § ʔupen uł téwš=ect *sixteen.* (upen uł tewshect, n.); tuwš+ačl+ʔúpen *sixty, six times ten.* (tuwshach'lupen, n.); tuwš+ačl+ʔúpen *sixty.* (tuwshach'lupen, n.)

√twʔ † tiweʔ *indulge.* (tiwe' (stem), vi.); ‡ tíweʔ-nt-s *coddle.* (tiwe'nts (lit. She babied h/h), v.) [xref √tw't]

√tw' † tuw' *crowd, stuff, swarm.* (tu'w (stem), vi, vt.); ‡ hn+túw'-nt-m *cram.* (hntu'wntm (lit. It was stuffed), vi.)

√tw't † t+tw'ít *adolescent boy, young man.* (tt'wit, n.); peł+t+tuw'it *adolescents.* (pełttu'wit, n.); ∥ s+t+tw'i·t=íl'š *adolescence.* (stt'wiiti'lsh (lit. becoming youth), n.); § t+tw'ít ha s+l'aẋ+t *boyfriend.* (tt'wit ha sl'aqht, n.) [xref √twʔ]

√txʷ † tíxʷ+m *obtain (He looked to...necessities).* (tikhum, vi, n, vt.); s+č+téxʷ+m *addiction.* (schtekhum, n.); s+č+téxʷ+xʷ *accretion, addition.* (schtekhukhw, n.); hiyč+téxʷ *appendix, appurtenance.* (hiychtekhw (lit. something added to another, more important, thing), n.); i· tíxʷ+mš *She is*

gathering something. (iitikhumsh, vt.); ∥ č+tuxʷ=cín+n *condiments, relishes.* (chtukhwtsinn (lit. something added to food eaten), n.); ‡ č+téxʷ-nt-s *add (to...), aggrandize, increased (he...it).* (chtekhwnts (lit. he added it to something else), vt.); č+téxʷ+tuxʷ-n't-s *exaggerated (h/s...it).* (chtekhwtukhw'nts (lit. h/s colored it highly), vt.); § uẋʷel'é č+tuxʷ+mín+n *complementary.* (uqhwe'le chtukhwminn (lit. like an addition), n.); tíxʷ+m e s+p'ít'em *gather (He went out to...bitterroots).* (tikhum e sp'it'em, n, vt.); s+č+tuxʷ+s+tim' *by-product.* (schtukhwsti'm (lit. something added to a thing in the making), n.); his+tiʔxʷa+s+l'áẋ+t *acqua[i]ntance.* (histi'khwas'laqht (lit. He is one who became a friend), n.); tíʔxʷe s+mí'yem *succeeded (He...in getting a wife).* (ti'khwe smi'yem, vi.); tiʔiʔxʷ+as+hoy+s *afterwards, later.* (ti'i'khwashoys, adv.); tiʔxʷ+eł+cégʷ+t *acquire (to...).* (ti'khwełtsegwt (lit. He acquired a way (habit), vt.); tuxʷ+ł+s+kʷís-nt-s *named (He...him).* (tukhwłskwisnts, vt.); tiʔxʷ+eł+n+dol+dolq'ʷ+t=íl'š-n *confirmed.* (ti'khwełndoldolq'wti'lshn (lit. He gained strength, he received the rite of confirmation), vi.)

√txʷcč † tixʷcč *tongue.* (tikhwtsch, n.); s+n+m+n+ʔepł+tíxʷcč *dagger (small).* (snmnepłtikhwtsch (lit. blade in form of tongue), n.)

√tẋ₁ † taẋ *bitter (taste), piquant, sharp (taste).* (taqh (stem), adj.); taẋ+t *acid, acidic, bitter.* (taqht (lit. having a taste that is sharp and unpleasant), n, adj.); taẋ+táẋ *pepper, spice.* (taqhtaqh (lit. bitter bitter), n.); hn+taẋ+táẋ+n *pepper shaker.* (hntaqhtaqhn, n.); x+taẋ+taẋ+n *pepper shaker.* (khtaqhtaqhn, n.) [?]; taẋ+t-š

unbearable. (taqht...sh (stem), adj.)
[written as √t'x̌ in volume 1]
t'ax̌+t-š unbearable. (t'aqht...sh); //
tax̌+tax̌=iłp birch (black...).
(taqhtaqhiłp, n.); tax̌+tax̌+q=iłp black
birch. (taqhtaqhqiłp, n.); in+ta?x̌=
ílg^wes anxious. (inta'qhilgwes (lit. H/s
felt a sting of pain in h/h heart), adj.);
hn+ta?x̌=ilg^wes agitate, disturb, upset
(lit. His heart was concerned. He was
disturbed). (hnta'qhilgwes (lit. His
heart was made bitter), v.); s+n+ta?x̌=
ílg^wes anxiety, apprehension, care,
uneasiness. (snta'qhilgwes, n.);
s+n+tax̌=ílg^wes angst. (sntaqhilgwes,
n.); § tax̌+t ha n+x̌^wús=k^we? ale.
(taqht hanqhuskwe' (lit. (more) bitter
beer), n.); u+x̌^wal'+á tax̌+táx̌ all-spice.
(uqhwa'la taqhtaqh (lit. It is like
pepper), n.)

√tx̌₂ // s+táx̌=enč bowel, colon,
intestine. (staqhench, n.);
ni?+s+táx̌+tax̌=enč intestines.
(ni'staqhtaqhench, pl.n.); § ul pus ha
s+táx̌=anč+s catgut. (ul pus ha
staqhanchs (lit. of cat his gut), n.);
[probably the same as √tx̌₁]

√tx̌₃ † s+tax̌+tex̌=él'č doll.
(staqhteqhe'lch, n.); s+t+tax̌+téx̌=el'č
doll. (sttaqhteqhe'lch, n.); s+t+ta+téx̌=
el'č [d]olly. (sttateqhe'lch (lit. a little
doll), n.)

√tx̌^w † tax̌^w stop (to...). (taqhw (stem),
vi.); táx̌^w+x̌^w died (He...). (taqhuqhw,
vi.); u· táx̌^w rest (He is at...), still.
(uutaqhw, n, adj.); s+táx̌^w+x̌^w dead,
death, decease. (staqhuqhw (lit.
coming to a stop), adj, n, vi.);
ul+s+táx̌^w+x^w deleterious.
(ulstaqhukhw (lit. It belongs to death),
adj.); hn+táx̌^w+x̌^w+n deadly, death.
(hntaqhuqhwn (stem), n.);
ul+n+táx̌^w+x̌^w+n deathly, mortal.
(ulntaqhuqhwn (lit. belonging to
death), adj.); s+táx̌^w+m+šeš barrier,
blockade, delay, dam. (staqhumshesh.

(lit. stopping something), n.);
s+táx̌^w+n+šeš check. (staqhunshesh.
(lit. an abrupt or stop), n.);
t+tx̌^w+x̌^w+í·? found (He was...dead).
(ttqhoqhwiii, vi.); t+tux̌^w+x̌^w+í· He was
found dead. (ttuqhoqhwiii, vi.);
u+ci·+táx̌^w+ax̌^w caesura.
(utsiitaqhwaqhw (lit. He made a pause
in phrasing a metrical line), n.);
pan'+táx̌^w+x̌^w widow, widower, H/h
spouse died. (pa'ntaqhuqhw. She/He
became a widow/widower, n.); //
u+č+táx̌^w=us bug-eyed, excited,
expectant. (uchtaqhus (lit. He is
looking with a still eye), adj.); ‡
táx̌^w+m-stu-s delay. (taqhumstus (lit.
He detained (stopped) him), v.);
tux̌^w+x̌^w+m-nú-nt-s deactivate.
(tuqhuqhumnunts (lit. He secceeded in
stopping him), v.); tux̌^w+x̌^w+nú-nt-s
devitalize. (tuqhuqhwnunts (lit. He
succeeded in bringing him to a
standstill), v.); uł+[c]i·+táx̌^w+m-st-m
deferred. (ułsiitaqhumstm (lit. It is
stopped for now), vi.)

√ty' † tuy'+m+ncut bend down, bend,
bow, crouch. (tu'ymntsut (lit. He
bowed), vi, v.)

√ty'q^w † tiy'eq^w fight. (ti'yeqw (stem),
vt.); s+tiy'éq^w+t bout, combat, fight.
(sti'yeqwt. (lit. fighting), n.);
hn+t'+tey'éq^w+n arena. (hnt'te'yeqwn.
(lit. a place for fighting), n.);
hn+tiy'+tiy'eq^w+n' Armageddon.
(hnti'yti'yeqwn', the scene of a final
battle between the forces of good and
evil, n.); čeł‿n+tiy'+tiy'éq^w+n'
Armageddon. (chełnti'yti'yeqw'n (lit.
the scene of a final battle between
good and evil), n.);
a+n+tiy'eq^w+t+núm+t combative.
(anti'yeqwtnumt, vi. (lit. He is eager to
fight), adj.); tiy'+tiy'eq^w+t+úl
bellicose, pugnacious (He is...).
(ti'yti'yeqwtul, adj.); siya+tiy'éq^w+t
champion. (siyati'yeqwt (lit. One who

defends a cause or another person), n.);
‡ čs+tiy'éqʷ-nt-s *champion, support.*
(chsti'yeqwnts (lit. He fought as
champion of i/h/etc.), vi.);
tiy'+tiy'éqʷ-t-lš *conflict.*
(ti'yti'yeqwtlsh (lit. They fought with
each other), n.)

√tˁ † taˁ *extend.* (ta((stem), vt.)

√tˁl ∥ sya+tˁél=qn *barber.* (syat(elqn
(lit. One who trims another head), n.)
[?]

√tˁn † s+tˁin *antelope.* (st(in, n.); §
xʷis+t ha s+tˁin *Louie Antelope.*
(Khwist Ha St(in. name of my
maternal grandfather (lit. antelope that
walked), n.)

√tʔ₁ † tiʔ *hit, pound.* (ti' (stem), vt.);
tiʔ+iʔ *bump.* (ti'i' (stem), vt.); s+tiʔ+m
baste (food), beating (dried meat).
(sti'm, vt.); č+teʔ+eʔ+mín'-t-ew'eš
clash. (chte"emi̱'nte'wesh (lit. they
collided), vi.); ∥ s+n+taʔ=qín
confirmation, credential. (snta'qi̱n (lit.
hitting on top of head), n.);
s+č+teʔe+m'i·n=íw'es *collision.*
(schte'e'mii̱ni'wes, n.); §
č+teʔ+eł+wl+wlím+n *anvil.*
(chte'ełwlwli̱mn, n.);
hn+teʔ+eł+wl+wlím+n *blacksmith
shop, forge, smithy.* (hnte'ełwlwli̱mn
(lit. place for shaping metals by
hammering), n.);
sye+teʔ+eł+wl+wlím *blacksmith,
coppersmith.* (syete'ełwlwli̱m (lit. One
who shapes metals by hammering), n.)

√tʔ₂ † s+tiʔ *article, belonging,
possession (personal).* (sti', n.);
hi+s+tíʔ *mine (It is...).* (histi̱', vi.);
s+tiʔ-s *It is his.* (sti's, vi.) [xref √tm']

√tʔ₃ † e n+túʔ *there (at a distance).*
(entu̱', vi.)

√tʔ₄ † e+n+t+tuʔ+tuʔ *bologna, lunch
meat.* (enttu'tu' (lit. stuffed stuffed). hot
dogs, weiners, n.)

√tʔł † tiʔ[ł] *fly.* (ti'l (stem), vi.); tiʔł *to
fly.* (ti'ł,); s+tiʔł *aviation, flying.* (sti'ł,)

n.); e·+tiʔ+teʔł *airplane.* (eeti'te'ł
(flying machine), n.); [also recorded
as √tł] e·+ti+teł *machine.* (eetiteł
(flying machine, airplane), n.);
teʔ+teʔłi·ʔ+útm *airplane.* (te'te'łii'utm
(lit. that which flies by itself), n.)

√t'c'₁ † t'ic' *smooth (by rubbing).* (t'its'
(stem), vt.); s+t'ic'+m *to stroke,
caress, iron (clothes).* (st'i̱ts'm, v.);
t'íc'+emn *iron (for pressing clothes).
from to stroke, caress.* (t'i̱ts'emn, n.
st'i̱ts'm,); ∥ t'éc'=alqs *pressed
(He...(ironed) his clothes).* (t'e̱ts'alqs,
vt.); s+t'íc'+t'ec'=šn *rubbers.*
(st'i̱ts't'ets'shn, n.); sye·+t'íc'+t[']ec'=
[š]n *boot-black.* (syeet'i̱tste'tschn, n.);
§ yuqʷ+eʔ+ł+t'íc'+m *pretended
(She...to iron).* (yuqwe'łt'i̱ts'm, vi.);
yuqʷ+eʔ+s+t'íc'+m *She pretended to
iron.* (yuqwe'st'i̱ts'm, v.)

√t'c'₂ † s+t'úc'+t=ew'es *Mission Point;
due NW of St. Maries, Idaho.*
(St'u̱ts'te'wes, n.)

√t'č † t'ič *protrude.* (t'ich (stem), vi.); ∥
t'íʔč=cn+m *stuck (He...his tongue
out), tongue (He stuck his...out).*
(t'i̱'chtsnm, vt, n.)

√t'č'₁ † če+t'č'+et *blackbird.*
(chet'ch'et', n.); t'eč'+t'č' *blackbird.*
(t'ech't'ch', n.); t'éʔč'+tč *blackbird.*
(t'e̱'ch'tch, n.) [see also √č't'₃]

√t'č'₂ † t'ič' *provide (food for travel),
stock up (as food for travel).* (t'ich'
(stem), vt, vi.); t'ič'+t+m *took
(He...along provisions).* (t'ich'tm, vt.);
[xref √t'č'l]

√t'č'₃ † sye·+t'íč'+t *boatman, bowman.*
(syeet'i̱ch't (lit. One who rows a boat
or paddles a canoe), n.); §
xes+es+t'íč+t *He rowed without
trouble or difficulty.* (qhesest'i̱cht, v.)

√t'č'l † s+t'íč'l *provisions (travelling...).*
(st'ich'l, pl.n.); t'ič'l+m *provisions (He
took along...).* (t'ich'lm, n.) [xref √t'č'₂]

√t'd₁ † t'éde? *ship, canoe.* (t'ede', n.); §
xáy'+xiʔ+t he t'éde *argosy.*

(qh̲a̲y'qhi't he t'e̲de (lit. a big canoe),
n.)

√t'd₂ † t'é?+td+t *difficult (It is...)*.
(t'e̲tdt, adj.); t'é+t'd+t *crucial, crux.*
(t'e̲t'dt, adj.); t'+t'éd+d+t *crucial, crux,
it is difficult, trying.* (t't'e̲ddt, adj.);
t'éd+d+t *difficult (It is...), trying (It is
trying).* (t'e̲ddt, adj.); **//** s+t'd+m=éstq
difficulty. (st'dme̲stq (lit. having a hard
time), n.); **§** lut t'é+t'd+t' *effortless.*
(lut t'e̲t'dt' (lit. It is not too difficult),
adj.)

√t'd₃ † t'id+m' *fragile, frail.* (t'id'm
(stem), adj.); u+t'+t'íd+m *brittle,
crisp.* (ut't'i̲dm (lit. It is fragile), adj.);
§ u+t'+t'íd+m' ha n+x̌em=ínč+n *false
love.* (ut't'i̲d'm hanqhemi̲nchn (lit. love
that is brittle (term of old-time Coeur
d'Alenes'), n.)

√t'd? † s+t'éde? *alfalfa, clover, fodder,
grass, hay.* (st'e̲de', n.); ni?+t[']éd+iš
*It crept in the grass. He acted
foolishly.* (ni't̲edish, v.); **//** s+t'áda?=
qn *wheat.* (st'a̲da'qn (lit. hay head), n.);
[see vol. I] t'áda?=alqʷ *white pine.*
(t̲adalqw, n.); **§** l+č'is+t'éde?e *very
slick grass on hills.* (lch'ist'e̲de'e, n.)

√t'ǰ † t'eǰ *pour.* (t'ej (stem), vt.);
t'ǰ+mín+n *carafe.* (t'jmi̲nn (lit. Bottle
for pouring wine or water at the table),
n.); hn+t'ǰ+mín+n *barrel (for holding
liquids), cask, decanter, demijohn.*
(hnt'jmi̲nn (lit. a large container for
holding liquids), n.)

√t'kʷ₁ † t'ekʷ *cry out, whinny.* (t'ekw
(stem), vi.); t'+t'ék̲ʷ+t'uk̲ʷ *colt, foal.*
(t't'e̲kwt'ukw, n.)

√t'kʷ₂ † t'ekʷ *watertight.* (t'ekw (stem),
adj.); [written as √tkʷ in volume 1]
tekʷ *watertight.* (tekw); t'ék̲ʷ+s *burst.*
(t'e̲kws (stem), vi.); **//** s+t'ík̲ʷ+s=us
sap of a tree used as an eye medicine.
(st'i̲kwsus, n.); **‡** hn+t'uk̲ʷ+s=ús-nt-s
He burst his eye. (hnt'ukwsu̲snts, vt.)

√t'kʷ₃ † t'ikʷ *old.* (t'ikw (stem), adj.)
[for expected √t'k'ʷ₃]

√t'k'ʷ₄ **//** s+t'ok̲ʷ=alpqʷ *bow tie.*
(st'okwalpqw, n.)

√t'k'ʷ₅ **//** s+n+t'uk̲ʷ=u·s=íw'es
argument. (snt'ukuusi'wes (lit. crossing
a statement), n.); ul+s+n+t'uk̲ʷ=u·s=
íw'es *argumentative.* (ulsnt'ukuusi'wes
(lit. pertaining to argument), adj.); **‡**
hn+t'uk̲ʷ=u·s=íw'es-nt-s *argue (to...).*
(hnt'ukuusi'wesnts (lit. He contradicted
him, he crossed his statement), vi.)

√t'k'ʷ₁ † u+t'ék'ʷ *bedridden.* (ut'e̲k'w
(lit. He just lies down all the time),
adj.); e t'úk'ʷ+i? *There he is lying
down.* (et'u̲k'wi', vi.); t'ék'ʷ+m *chip in,
contributed (He...money).* (t'e̲k'um, v.);
t'ek'ʷ+k'ʷ *collapse, fell (He...down).*
(t'ek'uk'w, v.); s+t'ék'ʷ+m
appointment. (st'e̲k'um, n.);
s+t'uk'ʷ+útn *bed.* (st'uk'u̲tn, n.);
s+t'+t'k'ʷ+útn' *cradle, crib.* (st't'k'u̲t'n.
(lit. small bed), n.); s+n+t'uk'ʷ+útn
casket, coffin. (snt'uk'u̲tn, n.);
s+n+t'ék'ʷ+m *confinement.* (snt'e̲k'um
(lit. being put in), n.); s+č+t'ék'ʷ+n
application. (scht'e̲k'wn, n.);
s+č+t'ék'ʷ+m *application.*
(scht'e̲k'wm, n.); s+če+t'uk'ʷ+útn *bed,
berth, bunk.* (schet'uk'u̲tn (lit. a means
for lying), n.); s+čet'+t'k'ʷ+útn' *cot.*
(schet't'k'u̲t'n (lit. narrow bed), n.);
cen+t'uk'ʷ+mín+n *chock, support,
brace.* (tsent'uk'wmi̲nn, n.);
s+t'uk'ʷ+ncut *sleeping bag.*
(st'uk'wntsut, n.); s+t'uk'ʷ+ncút+n
sleeping bag, spot for laying down.
(st'uk'wntsutn, n.);
u+t'+t'uk'ʷ+m'+n'cút *dilatory.*
(ut't'uk'w'm'ntsu̲t (lit. He establishes or
situates himself, He lingers or loiters),
adj.); s+t'+t'uk'ʷ+m'+ncút *andante.*
(st't'uk'w'mntsu̲t (lit. making oneself go
slowly), adj.); x̌ʷey+t[']ék'ʷ *appointee.*
(khweytek'w (lit. one who put down
(set)), n.); **//** hn+t'ák'ʷ=alqs *beeline,
shortcut.* (hnt'a̲k'walqs (lit. that which
is put on a fast, straight course), n.);

h[n]+t'ák'ʷ+k'ʷ=alqs *brunt.*
(hmt'ak'uk'walqs (lit. He fell in the
middle of the road), n.); s+n+t'ak'ʷ=
alqs+ncút *constancy, loyalty,*
perseverance, stability, steadfastness.
(snt'ak'walqsntsut (lit. establishing
oneself on the road (of life)), n.);
ča·+t'ák'ʷ+m=alqs *Tensed.*
(Chaat'ak'wmalqs (lit. object laid on
spur), n.); čn‿č+t'uk'ʷ+k'ʷ=ipele?
charge, duty, responsibility, I was
entrusted with a duty or responsibility.
(chncht'uk'uk'wipele' (lit. Something
fell to my charge), n.); t'uk'ʷ=ílt+m
child (She gave birth to one...), gave
birth (She...to one child). (t'uk'wiltm,
n, vi.); s+t'uk'ʷ=ílt+m *childbirth,*
parturition (lit. laying down an
offspring). (st'uk'wiltm, n.); t'u·k'ʷ=ip
begin. (t'uuk'wip (stem), vt.); t'uk'ʷ=
íp+m *began, commenced, started*
(He...). (t'uk'wipm, vi.); s+t'uk'ʷ=
íp+mš *beginning, commencement,*
creation, origination, to begin, debut.
(st'uk'wipmsh, adj, n, v.); s+t'uk'ʷ+k'ʷ=
íp+m *beginning, conception, origin,*
start. (st'uk'uk'wipm, n.);
ul+s+t'uk'ʷ+k'ʷ=íp+m *elementary.*
(ulst'uk'uk'wipm (lit. belonging to the
begining or first principle(s)), adj.);
s+cen+t'uk'ʷ=íp=ce? *backfire, to*
ignite. (stsent'uk'wiptse', n.);
xʷey'+t'uk'ʷ=íp=mš *debutante.*
(khwe'yt'uk'wipmsh (lit. one who
makes a start (a first appearance in
society), n.); č+t'uk'ʷ=łc'e?=íp *purse*
(beaded belt...), beaded belt purse on
the hip. (cht'uk'włts'e'ip, n.); ‡
t'ék'ʷ-nt-m *to appoint.* (t'ek'wntm (lit.
He was fixed or set by authority), v.);
t[']ék'ʷ-nt-s *deposit.* (tek'wnts (lit. He
put it down), v.); č+t'ék'ʷ-nt-s *apply*
(to...). (cht'ek'wnts (lit. he put it on
something), vt.); hn+t'ék'ʷ-nt-m
confine, enclose. (hnt'ek'wntm (lit. He
was put into something), v.);

hn+t'ék'ʷ-nt-s *deposit.* (hnt'ek'wnts
(lit. He put it in a bank), v.); t'uk'ʷ=
íp+m-st-eli-t *create.* (t'uk'wipmstelit
(lit. We were originated (by God), v.);
t'uk'ʷ=íp+m-stu-s *concoct.*
(t'uk'wipmstus (lit. He invented it, originated it), v.); t'uk'ʷ+ep=
(c)ín+m-nt-s *broach.*
(t'uk'wepsinmnts (lit. He began to talk
about it (the subject), v.); t'uk'ʷ+p=
íw'es-nt-s *athwart.* (t'uk'wpi'wesnts
(lit. He went contrary to it. He
interfered with another's act), adj.); §
mel'+s+če+t'uk'ʷ+útn *bedside.*
(me'lschet'uk'utn (lit. It is by the bed),
n.); t'uk'ʷ=ilt+m xʷa s+t'm'á *calve.*
(t'uk'wiltm khwa st"ma (lit. the cow
gave birth to a calf), n.); s+t'uk'ʷ+k'ʷ=
íp+ms ha?ł+dar=enč *calends, the*
first day of the month (lit. its beginning
what is a moon). (st'uk'uk'wipms
ha'łdarench, n.)

√t'k'ʷ₂ † t'ek'ʷ+ílš *conjurer, medicine*
man, shaman, psychic master.
(t'ek'wilsh, n.); s+t'ek[']+lš+scút
conjuration, sorcery. (st'e'kwlshstsut.
(lit. the practice of magic), n.)

√t'k'ʷ₃ † t'ík'ʷ+ut *elder.* (ti'k'ut, n.);
t'ík'ʷ+t'k'ʷ+t *old (H/s is...), ancient.*
(t'ik'wt'k'ut, adj.); t'ik'ʷ+u·t+út+m
elderly. (t'ik'uututm (lit. H/s looks or is
somewhat old), adj.);
hn+t'ík'ʷ+tik'ʷ+tn *old people's home.*
(hnt'ik'wtik'utn, n.);
s+ni?+t'ík'ʷ+t'ík'ʷ+t *eldest.*
(sni't'ik'wt'ik'ut (lit. H/s is the oldest
person in group), n.); ∥ s+t'ek'ʷ+ót=
qn *allegory.* (st'ek'otqn. fairy tale,
parable (lit. older head), n.);
s+t'ihk'ʷ+ót=qn *parable.* (st'ihk'otqn.
fairy tale, allegory (lit. older head), n.);
s+t'i·k'ʷ+ót=qn *fairy tale.* (st'iik'otqn.
parable, allegory (lit. older head), n.);
§ s+nukʷ+t'ík'ʷ+t'ik'ʷ+t
commensurate, one of the same old
age. (snukwt'ik'wt'ik'ut. grandparents,

adj.); ylmuxʷ+s+t'i·k'ʷ+ót=qn *son (oldest)*. (ylmukhwst'iik'otqn, n.); s+t'+t'ík'ʷ+s+m'e?e?m *crone, beldam, old maid*. (st't'ik'us'me'e'm, n.); eluɫ+ɫ+t'ík'ʷ+t *bastard, illegitimate*. (eluɫt'ik'ut (lit. H/s is w/o legitimate elders), n, adj.)

√t'k'ʷ₄ † t'uk'ʷ *uneven (roots on the ground)*. (t'uk'w (stem), adj.); s+t'úk'ʷ+m *carrot (wild)*. (st'uk'um, n.); ∥ hn+t'uk'ʷ=í?sn *acorn, bur (burr), seed*. (hnt'uk'wi'sn, n.)

√t'l₁ † t'el' *rip, tear*. (t'e'l (stem), vt.); ∥ s+č+t'l=íw'es *surgery*. (scht'li'wes, n.); č+t'l'+t'l=íw'es *burst*. (cht"lt"li'wes (lit. It was torn apart from internal pressure), vi.); s+č+t'l'+t'l'=íw'es *air burst, blow-up, cloudburst, downpour, explosion*. (scht"lt"li'wes (lit. becoming torn up on the surface), n.) ; s+č+t'él'+p=šn *blow-out, bursting (a sudden...)*. (scht'e'lpshn (lit. tearing of the foot; flat tire), n.); t'l'=úl'mxʷ *cultivate, plowed (He...)*. (t"lu'lmkhw (lit. He tore the earth), vt.); s+t'l'=úl'mxʷ *plowing, cultivation*. (st"lulmkhw. (lit. tearing up the earth), n.); t'il'=lumxʷ+útm *arable*. (t'i'llumkhutm (lit. capable of being plowed), n.); ‡ t'él-nt-s *tore (He...it)*. (t'elnts, vt.)

√t'l₂ ‡ e+čs+t'lú·-stu-s *bystander (to be a...)*. (echst'luuustus, vi.) [?]

√t'l'₁ † t'ul' *approachable, civilized, decent, humane, poised, refined, sympathetic, well-bred*. (t'u'l (stem), adj.)

√t'l'₂ † hn+t'l'=áne? *wolf*. (hnt"lane', n.)

√t'lq' † t'alq' *scoop, to scoop ice cream*. (t'alq' (stem), vt.); hn+t'álq'+m *gulp, to scoop (lit. He scooped, food)*. (hnt'alq'm (lit. He gulped), v.)

√t'lqʷ ‡ hn+t'lqʷ=ups-nt-m *He was hit in the buttocks (to be kicked)*. (hn't'lqupsntm, v.)

√t'ɫ₁ † e·+t'éɫ+t'ɫ *blotched*. (eet'eɫt'ɫ (lit. H/s is caked with damp blotches of mud, dust), adj.); s+t'éɫ+ɫ *blotch*. (st'eɫɫ, n.); ∥ s+t'+t'ɫ=úl'e?xʷ *brick, earthenware*. (st't'ɫu'le'khw. ceramic, china, n.); s+t'+t'ɫ=úl'exʷ *ceramic, china*. (st't'ɫu'lekhw. earthenware, brick, n.); ‡ t'eɫ-nt-s *daub*. (t'eɫnts (lit. He smeared it), v.); t'eɫ-nt-m *besmirch*. (t'eɫntm, v.); [xref √t'ɫ₂]

√t'ɫ₂ † t'oɫ *lumpy, sticky*. (t'oɫ (stem), adj.); ∥ can+t'óɫ=šn+n *cement*. (tsant'oɫshnn (lit. An adhesive put under the feet), n.); ‡ t'óɫ-nt-s *bedaub*. (t'oɫnts, vt.); č+t'óɫ=c'e?-nt-m *besmeared (it was body...)*. (cht'oɫts'e'ntm, vi.) [xref √t'ɫ₁]

√t'm₁ † t'em *scissors (to cut with...)*. (t'em (stem), v) [written as √t'm' in volume 1] t'em' *to cut with scissors*. (t'e'm)

√t'm₂ † t'em *damp*. (t'em (stem), adj.); t'am' *damp*. (t'a'm (stem), adj.); u·t'ém *dank*. (uut'em (lit. It is uncomfortably damp), adj.); t'em+p *damp*. (t'emp (lit. It became moistened), adj.); ‡ t'ém+p+m-s-n *dampen*. (t'empmsn (lit. I dampened it), vt.)

√t'm₃ † t'im *shake hands*. (t'im (stem), vi.); ∥ t'im=čt *hands (He shook...), shook (He...hands)*. (t'imcht, n, vt.); t'em+t'em=čs+ncút *He pressed his hands together (as in prayer)*. (t'emt'emchsntsut, vt.); t'ím=čs-n't-ew'eš *hands (They shook each other's...), shook (They...each other's hands)*. (t'imchs'nte'wesh, n, vt.)

√t'm₄ † s+t'úm+um *breast, milk*. (st'umum, n.); s+t'úm+t'um+um *breasts*. (st'umt'umum (lit. Name of 2 hills between Tekoa and Farmington Washington which look like breasts), n.); hn+t'úm+um+n *dairy*. (hnt'umumn (lit. an establishment that processes and/or sells milk and milk

products), n.); // s+t'm=qen=íɬxʷ
tepee. (st'mqeniɬkhw (lit. cone-shaped
dwelling), n.); § u+x̌ʷel'+é s+t'm=qn=
íɬxʷ *conical.* (uqhwe'le st'mqniɬkhw
(lit. It is shaped like a tepee), n.)

√t'm₅ † t'um *smirk.* (t'um (stem), vi.)

√t'm₆ † s+t'm'a *buffalo, cow.* (st"ma,
sg.n.); ha s+t'má *mammal (bovine...).*
(hast'ma, n.); čn‿ʔp+s+t'má *cattle (I
have...).* (ch'npst'ma, n.);
čn‿ʔp+s+t'ma *cattle (to own).*
(ch'npst'ma (lit. I have cattle), vt.);
ya+s+t'm'á *He got a buffalo.*
(yast"ma, v.); // s+t'm'=ált=mš *cattle
(herd of), bison (herd of), (lit. licking
tribe).* (st"maltmsh. buffalo, n.);
s+t'+t'm=alt=mš *buffalo (herd of).*
(st"tmaltmsh. bison, cow, n.);
ʔap+s+t'm=ált=mš *buffalo country.*
(apst'maltmsh (lit. It has a herd, bison),
n.); ya+s+t'm=ált=mš *buffalo (He
killed the...).* (yast'maltmsh, n.); §
t'm'+m+čí· *caravan.* (t'm'mchiii! (lit.
There goes a single file of many
vehicles or pack animals), n.);
u+x̌ʷal'á+ s+t'm'=ált+mš *bovine.*
(uqhwa'la st"maltmsh (lit. It resembles
a cow), n.); t'uk'ʷ=ilt+m x̌ʷa s+t'm'á
calve. (t'uk'wiltm khwa st"ma (lit. the
cow gave birth to a calf), n.);
s+n+ɬaqʷ=ús+s ha s+t'm'=ált=mš
cud. (snlaquss ha st"maltmsh (lit. a
cow's chewing gum), n.)

√t'mč † s+t'ímč'e? *daughter.*
(st'imch'e', n.); s+t'ím+t'emče?
daughters. (st'imt'emche', pl.n.)

√t'ml'x̌ † t'omól'x̌ *hailstone.*
(t'omo'lqh, n.)

√t'm'₁ † t'am' *kiss, lick.* (t'a'm (stem),
vt.); t'am'+um'+ótm *tasted, licked (It
is capable of being...).* (t'a'mu'mot, vi.);
// s+n+t'ám[']=cn *kiss.* (snt'amtsn, n.);
s+n+t'am'=cn *kissing.* (snt'a'mtsn, n.);
t'am'+tam'=yóye? *blood-sucker,
snail.* (t'a'mta'myoye', n.); t'm'=
algʷás=cen+m *licked (He...his lips).*

(t"malgwastsenm, vt.); ‡ t'am'-nt-s
lick. (t'a'mnts (lit. He licked it), vt.);
[gloss?] t'ám'-nt-s *licked (I...it).*
(t'a'mnts, vt.)

√t'm'₂ // hn+t'í+t'm'=el'ps *gooseberry.*
(hnt'it"me'lps, n.)

√t'm'₃ † t'um' *pipelike, tubelike.* (t'u'm
(stem), adj.); t'úm'+pn *chimney,
conduit, pipe, tube.* (t'u'mpn (lit.
stovepipe), n.) [xref √tm]

√t'n₁ // s+t'én+t'en=ax̌n *name of arm
ornaments in form of fringes (lit. wing
dress).* (st'ent'enaqhn, n.)

√t'n₂ // s+t'ún=ɬc'e? *ass, mule deer.*
(st'unɬts'e', n.); s+t'+t'ún'=ɬc'e? *burro.*
(st't'u'nɬts'e' (lit. a small donkey), n.); §
s+n+ʔukʷún=cn+is xʷe s+t'ún=ɬc'e?
bray. (s'nukuntsnis khwe st'unɬts'e' (lit.
the cry of a donkey), n.)

√t'n? † t'(=)íne? *ear.* (t'ine', n.); t'ín+t'
(=)ene? *ears.* (t'int'ene', n.)

√t'p₁ † t'ap *shoot.* (t'ap (stem), vt.);
t'áp+emn *arrow, arrowhead, bomb,
exploder.* (t'apemn, n.); sya·+t'áp+m
archer, bombardier. (syaat'apm (lit.
One who shoots with a bow and
arrow), n.); s+t'áp-n't-w'eš *battle,
war.* (st'ap'nt'wesh. (lit. shooting one
another), n.); i·+t'áp-n't-w'eš
belligerency. (iit'ap'nt'wesh (lit. They
are in the state of being at war), n.);
sya·+t'áp-n't-w'eš *brave, warrior
(note: old timers preferred the term
"warrior" to "brave").*
(syaat'ap'nt'wesh, n.); h[n]+t'ap-n't-
w'eš+n' *field (battle...).* ((lit. place of
battle), ht'ap'nt'wesh, n.); // t'ap=
šn+cót *shot (He...himself on the foot).*
(t'apshntsot, n, vt.); a·+t'áp=ɬc'e?
*desperado, gangster, maverick,
outlaw.* (aat'apɬts'e' (lit. H/s shoots
people), n.); hn+t'ap=ɬc'e?+ncót+n
pineapple. (hnt'apɬt'se'ntsotn (lit.
"shooting oneself in the stomach",
referring to acid reaction in the
stomach), n.); s+t'a+t'a·p=áčs+n'

archery. (st'at'aapac͟hs'n (lit. shooting target), n.); hn+t'áp=ul'mx^w *He blasted the earth.* (hnt'apu'lmkhw, v.); ‡ t'ap-n *shot (I...it).* (t'apn, vt.); t'áp-nt-s *shot (He...him).* (t'a͟pnts, vt.); t'áp=šn-t-s *shot (He...him on the foot).* (t'a͟pshnts, n, vt.); § s+nuk^w+t'áp-n't-w'eš+m'n'm' x͡ʷe s+ník'ʼʷ=elumx^w *civil war.* (snukwt'a͟pnt'wesh'm'n'm khwe snik'welumkhw, n.)

√t'p₂ † t'ep *to stand up, stop.* (t'ep (stem), vi.); s+t'ép+p *arrival (of more than one person).* (st'epp, n.); t'ép-liš *stood (They...up).* (t'eplish, vi.);

√t'p₃ // s+t'op=qs *spool, thread.* (st'opqs, n.); s+č+t'op=qs *bobbin, spool.* (scht'opqs, n.)

√t'pq † t'aqp *puncture, perforate.* (t'apq (stem), vt.)

√t'px̌ʷ † u t'póx̌ʷ *It made sound of flat stone falling vertically into water (onomatopoeia).* (ut'po͟qhw!)

√t'py? † t'upye? *great grandfather.* (t'upye', n.)

√t'q₁ † t'aq *lie (bushy objects).* (t'aq (stem), vi.); // t'aq+ap=w'as=qn *beard.* (t'aqa͟p'wasqn, n.); s+t'aq+áp=w'as=qn *beard.* (st'aqa͟p'wasqn. bushy, n.)

√t'q₂ † t'aq+t *return (birds from migration), migrate.* (t'aqt (stem). (lit. The birds have come back from the south), vi.) [also written as √tq in volume 1] taq+t *Bird returns in the spring.* (taqt, v.); // t'aq+t=íčn' *to succeed in killing game, hunt (successfully), killed (He...game).* (t'aqtich'n, vi, vt, n.); čn‿t'aq+t=íčn' *hunt (I was successful in my...), successful (I was...in my hunt).* (chnt'aqtich'n, n, adj.)

√t'q₃ // t'áq=ney' *cyst.* (t'a͟qne'y (lit. a sack), n.); s+w'i?+p+ł+t'áq=ney' *flour sack.* (s'wi'płt'a͟qne'y, n.)

√t'q₄ // s+t'eq=?łn' *huckleberries (a species of...found in the woods).*

(st'eq'łn, n.) [written as √tq in volume 1] s+teq=łn *(a species of) huckleberries (found in the woods).* (steqłn, n.)

√t'q' † hn+t'áq'+n *Hayden Lake.* (hnt'a͟q'n, n.); ?apł t'+t'áq'+n *Worley, saddle-shaped mountain S.E. of Worley.* (Apł t't'a͟q'n, n.)

√t'qʷ₁ † t'aqʷ *slap.* (t'aqw (stem), vt.); s+t'áqʷ+m *buffet, slap.* (st'a͟qum. (lit. slapping with the hand), vt.); s+t'+t'áqʷ+n' *dab.* (st't'a͟qw'n (lit. a quick light pat), n.); // t'uqʷ+t'uqʷ=ačs+ncút *clap.* (t'uqwt'uqwachsnts͟ut (lit. He clapped himself as to the hands), v.); s+t'uqʷ+t'uqʷ=čs+n'cút *acclaim (lit. clapping one's hands).* (st'uqwt'uqwchs'ntsut, n.); ‡ t'áqʷ-nt-s *cuff, he slapped him.* (t'aqwnts, v.); t'+t'áqʷ+t'uqʷ-nt-s *dab.* (t't'a͟qwt'uqwnts (lit. He struck or hit him lightly repeatedly with the palms of the hands), v.); t'uqʷ=u?s=ús-nt-s *slapped. (He...him in the face),* (t'uqu's͟usnts, v.)

√t'qʷ₂ † t'eqʷ *explode, burst.* (t'eqw (stem)., vi.) [xref √t'q'ʼʷ]

√t'qʷ₃ † t'oqʷ *to have power, succeed in everything.* (t'oqw)

√t'qʷ₄ † t'u·qʷ *partners (make...with), marry, team up.* (t'uuqw (stem), n, vi.); t'oqʷ *marry.* (t'oqw (stem), vt.); // an+t'oqʷ+m=íw'es *conjoin, conjunct, join together, united (to be...).* (ant'oqmi'wes, vi. (lit. They are united/joined together), vi.); hn+t'oqʷ+qʷ+m=íw'es *coalesce.* (hnt'oqoqwmi'wes. (lit. They became grown together), vi.); s+n+t'oqʷ+m=íw'es *contraction, drawing together.* (snt'oqmi'wes, n.); ‡ hn+t'oqʷ+m=íw'es-nt-m *combine, merge.* (hnt'oqwmi'wesntm. (lit. It was merged), vi.); hn+t'oqʷ+m=íw'es+m-st-m-lš *contract.*

(hnt'oqmi'wesmstmlsh. (lit. They were drawn together), vi.);

√t'qʷ₅ s+n+t'uqʷ+úmn *sheath (for arrows), quiver.* (snt'uqumn, n.) [v. 1 has √t'gʷ, analysis unclear]

√t'q'ʷ † t'u·q'ʷ *extinguish, put out (e.g. light).* (t'uuq'w (stem), vt.); ∥ t'aq'ʷ=s *burst (ref. to egg or eye).* (t'aq'w...s (stem), vi.); ɫ+t'q'ʷ=cin+m *blurt, (lit. he uttered impulsively).* (ɫt'q'wtsinm., vt.) [xref √t'qʷ]

√t'rk'ʷ † s+t'ark'ʷ *flee, fleeing.* (st'ark'w. vi, n.)

√t'rm' † s+t'ar+t'arím' *thunder.* (st'art'ari'm, n.)

√t's₁ † t'as *skinny, thin.* (t'as (stem), adj.); s+č+t'ás+s *atrophy.* (scht'ass (lit. becoming emaciated), n.)

√t's₂ † s+t'us *marrow.* (st'us, n.); s+t'+t'ús *bonbon, candy, confection.* (st't'us. (lit. little marrow), n.); s+t'+t'ús+t'us *bonbons, confetti, confiture, sweetmeats.* (st't'ust'us, pl.n.); hn+t'+t'ús+n' *candy store, confection, confectionary.* (hnt't'usn'. candy, n.); § u+x̌ʷel'+é s+n+qʷúl=enč he s+t'+t'ús *cotton candy.* (uqhe'le snqulench he st't'us (lit. candy that resembles cotton), n.)

√t'sq'ʷ † t'asq'ʷ *weary (with waiting).* (t'asq'w (stem), adj.)

√t'š † t'eš *sweet.* (t'esh (stem), adj.); t'eš+t *delicate, sweet, sweetened (It is...or very sweet, delicate).* (t'esht, adj.); t'iš *sugar, sweetened.* (t'ish (stem), n, adj.); u· t'íš *It is sweet.* (uut'ish, adj.); hn+t'iš+n *bowl.* (hnt'ishn. (lit. sugar container), n.); s+t'šá *huckleberries.* (st'sha, pl.n.); ʔepɫ+t'íš *Waverly, Washington.* (Epɫt'ish (lit. It has sugar), n.); ∥ s+t'š=ástq *huckleberries.* (st'shastq (lit. sweet crop), pl.n.); hn+t'íš=ul'mxʷ *eclair.* (hnt'ishu'lmkhw. (lit. sweet bread, that which is baked in the ground), n.); hn+t'iš+t'íš=ulmxʷ

cookie. (hnt'isht'ishulmkhw. (lit. sweet little loaves of bread), n.); § s+cil'+eɫ+s+t'š=ástq *blueberry (lit. a huckleberry substitute).* (stsi'leɫst'shastq, n.); u· hén he t'iš *brown sugar.* (uuhen he t'ish (lit. sugar that is more or less tan), n.); čs+t'iš+iš+ɫ+mát'=us *diabetes.* (chst'ishishɫmat'us (lit. supplying the kidneys with sugar), n.)

√t'šʔ † t'išsoʔ *sneeze.* (t'ishso' (stem), vi.)

√t'xʷ₁ † t'exʷ *to die (people only), kill (people).* (t'ekhw (stem), vi, vt.); s+t'exʷ+p *corpses, carnage.* (st'ekhwp. dead people, people who are slaughtered, n.)

√t'xʷ₂ † t'oxʷ *superstition.* (t'okhw (stem), n.)

√t'xʷ₃ † t'uxʷ *to wade.* (t'ukhw (stem), vi.); ∥ t'uxʷ=ilš *jump off.* (t'ukhwilsh (stem), vt.); t'uʔúxʷ=l'š *cavort.* (t'u'ukhw'lsh (lit. He jumped around), v.); hn+t'úxʷ=lš=kʷeʔ *dip.* (hnt'ukhwlshkwe' (lit. He plunged in, as into water), vt.)

√t'xʷl † t'ixʷl *abnormal, different.* (t'ikhwl (stem), adj.); t'íxʷl+m *alien, foreigner.* (t'ikhwlm (lit. A person of a different family), n.); e· t'íxʷl+m *unlike, diverse, bizarre, different, stranger (lit. It is...).* (eet'ikhwlm (lit. H/s is different), adj, n.); e· t'íxʷl+m-lš *pl. cf. sg. eet'ikhwlm.* (eet'ikhwlmlsh, adj.); s+t'íxʷl+m *difference, diversity, variety.* (st'ikhwlm, n.); t'ixʷx["]l+m *different, alienated (He became different or alienated).* (t'ikhukhlm, adj.); t'ixʷ+xʷl+m+útm *convertible.* (t'ikhukhwlmutm (lit. It is transformable), adj.); ∥ en+t'ʔíxʷl+m=elgʷes *differ, disagree.* (ent"ikhwlmelgwes (lit. H/s is different in heart or thought), vi.); e+n+t'íʔxʷl+m=cn *language (to speak a different...).* (ent'i khwlmtsn, vt.);

t'íxʷxʷl+m=us *discolor.*
(t'ikhwkhwlmus (lit. He was change as
to his face), v.); ‡ t'íxʷl+m-s-n *change,*
convert, differentiate, transform.
(t'ikhwlmsn (lit. I caused it to become
different (as by modification), v.);
t'íxʷl+m-stu-s *alter, different (He*
made it...). (t'ikhwlmstus, adv.); §
e+t'íxʷl+m+ɫ+cégʷ+t *eccentric, odd,*
queer, strange. (et'ikhwlmɫtsegwt, vi.
(lit. H/s has different ways), adj.);
s+t'íxʷl+m+ɫ+cégʷ+t *eccentricity,*
idiosyncrasy, peculiarity.
(st'ikhwlmɫtsegwt. (lit. differences of a
person's ways), n.);
t'íxʷl+m+ɫ+cégʷ-nt-m *denature.*
(t'ikhwlmɫtsegwntm (lit. He was
changed as to his nature), v.)

√t'xʷp † t'u·xʷp *to win, to earn.*
(t'uukhup (stem), vt.); t'uxʷúp *to*
attain, earn. (t'ukhup (lit. He gained or
accomplished), v, vt.); s+t'uxʷúp
attainment, breakthrough,
compendium, convert. (st'ukhup (lit.
winning), n.); kʷʔ‿t'uxʷúp *earn.*
(ku'tukhup (lit. You (sg.) gain a just
pay for your labor, services, etc.), vt.)

√t'x̌ † [also recorded as √tx̌] tax̌
swift. (taqh (stem), adj.); s+t'áx̌+m
accelerate. (st'aqhm (lit. speeding a
thing up), vt.); t'ax̌+t *fast (It is..., He is*
a...runner). (t'aqht, adj. n.); s+t'áx̌+t
alacrity, celerity, speed, swiftness.
(st'aqht, n.); ∥ t'ax̌=ítkʷeʔ *swiftly (The*
stream runs...). (t'aqhitkwe', vi, n,
adv.); s+t'ax̌=ítkʷeʔ *rapids.*
(st'aqhitkwe', n.); i+č+t'áx̌=šn *apace.*
(icht'aqhshn (lit. He is going at a rapid
pace), adj.); i č+t'áx̌=šin+mš *apace.*
(lit. He is going at a rapid pace).
(icht'aqhshinmsh, adj.); t'ax̌=ísč'ey't
long-winded (He is ...). (t'aqhisch'e'yt
(lit. He has fast breath), adj.); hn+t'áx̌=
cn *bold, brazen, loud, loud-mouthed.*
(hnt'aqhtsn (lit. He is
loud/loud-mouthed), adj.); ‡ hn+t'ax̌=

cín+m-nt-s *blare, deafen.*
(hnt'aqhtsinmnts (lit. H/s/i sounded
loudly to him), v.); § t'ax̌+aɫ+q·ixʷ=
íl'š *strong (The wind became...).*
(t'aqhaɫqiikhwi'lsh, n, adj.); šiɫ
t'+t'áx̌+t *cruise.* (shiɫ t't'aqht (lit. He
speeded just right), vi.);
t'ax̌+s+péw+m *drummed*
(He...quickly, with fast tempo).
(t'aqhspewm, vt.); t'ax̌+s+péw+n *He*
drummed quickly, with fast tempo.
(t'aqhspewn, vt.) [for expected +m]

√t'x̌ʷč' † s+n+t'áx̌ʷč' *arroyo, coulee,*
couloir. (snt'aqhwch' (lit. gully), n.)

√t'yč † s+t'iyč+míš *virgin.*
(st'iychmish, n.)

√t'ʔ₁ † t'iʔ *after.* (t'i', prep.)

√t'ʔ₂ † t'uʔ *well.* (t'u', adv.); t'iʔ+ciʔ
adequate, sufficient. (t'i'tsi' (lit. That is
enough), adj.); t'uʔ+láʔx̌ʷ *Well,*
tomorrow I am coming. (t'u'la'qhw, v.);
t'uʔ u+čn x̌é·s *Well, I'm fine.* (t'u'
uchnqheees, v.)

√wh † wih *bark.* (wih (stem), v.);
wíh+m *bark, barked (he (the dog)...).*
(wihm, vi.); s+wíh+m *bark (dog's...),*
bow-wow. (swihm, n.); wíh+weh+m
barked (the dogs...), dogs
(the...barked). (wihwehm, vi, n.);
ec+wih+m *The dog (cust.) barks.*
(etswihm, vi.); ec+wih+weh+m *The*
dogs (cust.) bark. (etswihwehm, vi.);
ic+wíh+mš *The dog is barking.*
(itswihmsh, vi.); ic+wíh+weh+mš
barking (the dogs are...).
(itswihwehmsh, vi.); t'iʔ+wíh+m *The*
dog has barked. (t'i'wihm, v.);
t'iʔ+wíh+weh+m *dogs (The...have*
barked). (t'i'wihwehm, n.);
t'iʔ+wí+weh+m *barked (The dogs*
have...). (t'i'wiwehm, vi.);
t'iʔxʷe+s+wíh+m+s *barked (The dog*
had...). (t'i'khhweswihms, vi.);
t'iʔxʷe+s+wíh+weh+m+s *barked*
(The dogs had...). (t'i'khweswihwehms,
vi.); čes‿wíh+m *h/s will be barked*

at, the dog will bark. (cheswi̲hm, vt.); čes‿wíh+weh+mš *bark.* (cheswi̲hwehmsh. (lit. the dogs will bark), vi.); k'ʷ neʔ wíh+m *The dog is going to bark.* (k'wne'wi̲hm, vi.); k'ʷ neʔ wíh+weh+m *The dogs are going to bark.* (k'wne'wi̲hwehm, vi.); wih+m-š *(You-sg.) bark! (imper.).* (wi̲hmsh, vi.); wíh+weh+m-ul *(You dogs) bark! (imper.).* (wi̲hwehmul, vi.); č‿y'c+wíh+m *I am being barked at.* (chi'tswi̲hm, vt.); čeł‿či‿s+wíh+m *barked.* (chełchiswi̲hm (lit. I will be barked at), vi.); k'ʷu‿y'‿c+wíh+m *You (sg.) are being barked at.* (ku'ytswi̲hm, v.); čeł‿k'ʷu‿s+wíh+m *You (sg.) will be barked at.* (chełkuswi̲hm, vi.); i c+wíh+m *H/s is being barked at.* (itswi̲hm, vi.); č‿y'c+wíh+m *We are being barked at.* (chi'tswi̲hm, vt.); čeł‿č‿s+wíh+m *bark.* (chełchswi̲hm (lit. we will be barked at), vi.); k'ʷup‿ʔi‿c+wíh+m *You (pl.) are being barked at.* (kup'itswi̲hm, vi.); čeł‿k'ʷup‿s+wíh+m *(lit. you will be barked at).* (chełkupswi̲hm, vt.); i c+wíh+m-lš *They are being barked at.* (itswi̲hmlsh, vi.); čes‿wíh+m-lš *they will be barked at.* (cheswi̲hmlsh, vi.); ‡ wíh-nt-sel-em *barked (I was...at).* (wi̲hntselem, vi.); ec+wih-st-mel-em *I am barked at (by a dog).* (etswi̲hstmelem, v.); t'iʔ+wíh-nt-sel-em *I have been barked at.* (t'i'wi̲hntselem, v.); t'iʔxʷe+s+wíh-nt-sel-em *barked (I had been...at).* (t'i'khweswi̲hntselem, vi.); k'ʷ neʔ wíh-nt-sel-em *I am going to be barked at.* (k'wne'wi̲hntselem, vi.); wíh-nt-si-t *You (sg.) were barked at.* (wi̲hntsit, vi.); ec+wih-st-mi-t *You (sg.) are barked at.* (etswi̲hstmit, v.); t'iʔ+wíh-nt-si-t *You (s) have been barked at.* (t'i'wi̲hntsit, v.); t'iʔxʷe+s+wíh-nt-si-t *barked (You (sg.) had been...at).* (t'i'khweswi̲hntsit, vi.); k'ʷ neʔ wíh-nt-si-t *You (sg.) are going to be barked at.* (k'wne'wi̲hntsit, vi.); wih-nt-m *H/S was barked at.* (wi̲hntm, vi.); ec+wih-st-m *H/s/i is barked at.* (etswi̲hstm, vi.); t'iʔ+wíh-nt-m *H/s had been barked at.* (t'i'wi̲hntm, v.); t'iʔxʷe+s+wíh-nt-m *barked (H/s had been...at).* (t'i'khweswi̲hntm, vi.); k'ʷ neʔ wíh-nt-m *H/s is going to be barked at.* (k'wne'wi̲hntm, vi.); wíh-nt-eli-t *We were barked at.* (wi̲hntelit, vi.); ec+wih-st-eli-t *We are barked at.* (etswi̲hstelit, vi.); t'iʔ+wíh-nt-eli-t *We have been barked at.* (t'i'wi̲hntelit, v.); t'iʔxʷe+s+wíh-nt-eli-t *barked (We had been...at).* (t'i'khweswi̲hntelit, vi.); k'ʷ neʔ wíh-nt-eli-t *We are going to be barked at.* (k'wne'wi̲hntelit, vi.); wíh-nt-ulmi-t *You (pl.) were barked at.* (wi̲hntulmit, vi.); ec+wíh-st-ulmi-t *bark at.* (etswi̲hstulmit (lit. You (pl.) are barked at), vi.); t'iʔ+wíh-nt-ulmi-t *You (pl) have been barked at.* (t'i'wi̲hntulmit, v.); t'iʔxʷe+s+wíh-nt-ulmi-t *barked (You (pl.) had been...at).* (t'i'khweswi̲hntulmit, vi.); k'ʷ neʔ wíh-nt-ulmi-t *You (pl.) are going to be barked at.* (k'wne'wi̲hntulmit, vi.); wih-nt-m-lš *They were barked at.* (wi̲hntmlsh, vi.); ec+wih-st-m-lš *They are barked at.* (etswi̲hstmlsh, vi.); t'iʔ+wíh-nt-m-lš *They have been barked at.* (t'i'wi̲hntmlsh, v.); t'iʔxʷe+s+wíh-nt-m-lš *barked (They had been...at).* (t'i'khweswi̲hntmlsh, vi.); k'ʷ neʔ wíh-nt-m-lš *They are going to be barked at.* (k'wne'wi̲hntmlsh, vi.)

√wlč' † welč' *roll, rolled (it (sphere)...), thrown (he was...off horse).* (welch' (stem) (e.g. a solid object), v, vi.);

wíl·č' *thrown (they were...off horse), walked (they (plump people)...around).* (wi̲llch', vi.); s+čet+w'él'+w'l'č'+m'š *bowling.* (schet'we̲'l'w'lch"msh (lit. rolling on repeatedly), n.); ‡ e+čet+w'el+w'l'č+t'+m'-st'-m *ball (bowling).* (echet'we'lw'lcht"mst'm (lit. That w/c is rolled in bowling), n.); e+čet+w'el'+wl'č'+m'-st-m' *bowling ball.* (echet'we'lw'lch"mst'm (lit. That w/c is rolled in bowling), n.)

√**wlm** † wl+wlím *aluminum, argent, capital, coin, metal, money, silver.* (wlwli̲m, n.); w'l'+w'l'im' *knife.* ('w'l'w'li'm. (lit. little iron), n.); w'l'+wl'ím' *knife.* ('w'lw'li̲'m, n.); s+n+wl+wlím+n *bank, billfold.* (snwlwli̲mn (lit. something to contain paper money), n.); ʔepł+wl+wlím *money (to have...), he has money.* (epłwlwlim, vt.); ʔep+s+n+wlím+n *banker.* (epsnwli̲mn (lit. One who has a place for metal money), n.); ʔep+s+n+wl+wlím+n *cashier, teller.* (epsnwlwli̲mn (lit. One who has a place for metal money), n.); cmiʔ epł+wl+wlím *money (he used to have...).* (tsmi'epł wlwli̲m, n.); ∥ s+wl+wlm=ín'č *gun, rifle.* (swlwlmi̲'nch (lit. metal weapon), n.); s+w'+w'l'+w'l'm'=ín'č *carbine.* (s'w'w'l'w'l'mi̲'nch (lit. a small rifle), n.); s+n+wl+wlm=ín'č+n *arsenal.* (snwlwlmi̲'nchn (lit. place for weapons (guns), n.); § ʔaʕʷ+eł+wl+wlím *well-to-do, rich, wealthy (to be...).* (a(wełwlwli̲m (lit. H/s has much money), adj.); wl+wlím ha ʕec+el'+s+čí+če?+n *cable.* (wlwli̲m ha (etse'lschi̲che'n (lit. metal what is a rope), n.); a+ʕʷ+eł+wl+wlím *rich (to be...).* (a(wełwlwli̲m (lit. H/s has much money), vi.); kʷenł+w'l'+w'l'ím' *knife (h/s took a...).* (kwenł'w'l'w'li̲'m, n.); kʷenł+wl+wlím *money (h/s took some...).* (kwenłwlwli̲m, n.);

č+te?+eł+wl+wlím+n *anvil.* (chte'ełwlwli̲mn, n.); hn+te?+eł+wl+wlím+n *blacksmith shop, forge, smithy.* (hnte'ełwlwli̲mn (lit. place for shaping metals by hammering), n.); sye+te?+eł+wl+wlím *blacksmith, coppersmith.* (syete'ełwlwli̲m (lit. One who shapes metals by hammering), n.); s+k'ʷul'+ł wl+wlím *coinage.* (sk'u'lł wlwli̲m (lit. making money), n.); č'+č'en'e? he wl+wlim *chicken feed (lit. small money, trifling amount of money).* (ch'ch'e'ne' he wlwli̲m, n.)

√**wlms** † wlums+mú *Williams (name of).* (Wlumsmu, n.)

√**wl?** ∥ s+wé+wla?=qn *sound (...of wind on tree tops etc.), wind (sound of...on tree tops etc.).* (swe̲wla'qn, n.)

√**wnm** † s+wánem' *economizing, economy, thrift.* (swa̲ne'm, n.)

√**wnš** † winš *wardance.* (winsh (stem), vi.); s+winš *dancing (war...), war (to...dance).* (swinsh, vi, n.)

√**wr** ∥ s+wár=ep *skunk's organ for spraying.* (swa̲rep, n.); t+wár=gʷl *stomach (Person with a well-rounded...).* (twa̲rgul, n.)

√**wrč** † warč *frog.* (warch, n.); is+wár+warč+iš *croak.* (iswa̲rwarchish (lit. It (frog) is making croaking sounds), vi.); § qel'+tmxʷ+ł+wárč *bullfrog.* (qe'ltmkhwłwa̲rch. (lit. a male frog), n.)

√**wsx̌** † wésx̌+ax̌ *robin.* (we̲sqhaqh, n.)

√**wš** † wiš *build, raise poles.* (wish (stem), v.); ec+wíš *stand.* (etswi̲sh (lit. The house stands), vi.); hiyc+wíš *structure.* (hiytswish (lit. that which is built up), n.); ∥ wíš=łxʷ *built, construct.* (wishłkhw (lit. He built a house), vt.); s+wíš=łxʷ *building (...a house), construction.* (swi̲shłkhw, vt, n.); ic+wíš=łxʷ *build.* (itswi̲shłkhw (lit. He is building a house), vt.); §

s+nuk'ʷ+c+wiš *co-exist, fellow, inmate, roommate.* (snuk'wtswish. in a house, n.)

√wšn † wašn *administration, bureaucracy, Washington, D.C..* (Washn, n.); § lut ul wášn *apolitical.* (lut ul Washn (lit. not belonging to Wash., D.C.), adj.)

√wš? † wíšu?+s *white tail deer.* (wishu's, n.)

√wt₁ † wit *maggoty, worm-ridden.* (wit (stem), adj.); u· wí·t *expression of a person when he swarm of maggots.* (uuwi··t, excl.)

√wt₂ ∥ wt=cn+mé+ncut *always finding fault, carp, complain.* (wttsnmentsut (lit. He found fault and complained constantly/He expressed feelings of dissatisfaction), vt, vi.); s+wt= cn+mé+ncut *complaint, fretting.* (swttsnmentsut, n.)

√wt'č ∥ s+wít'č=alqʷ *type of pine on top of Mt. Grizzly, has edible cones once every seven years.* (swit'chalqw, n.)

√ww † u+wí·w *chatterbox, mumble, prattle (He made a continuous mumble or...).* (uwiiiw!. He is a chatterbox, n.)

√wxʷ † wuxʷ *draft.* (wukhw (stem), n.) [xref √wx̌ʷ]

√wx̌₁ † wax̌ *murm[u]r (e.g. a brook).* (waqh (stem), v.); ∥ wáx̌=i?łp *dog-wood, wild maple.* (waqhi'łp, n.)

√wx̌₂ † wex̌ *chapped.* (weqh (stem), adj.) [see also √w?x̌]

√wx̌ʷ † wu·x̌ʷ *draft, wind.* (wuuqhw (stem), n.) [xref √wxʷ]

√wy † wa·y *babel.* (waaay! (lit. a confused sound of voices), n.); way· *babel (lit. a confused sound of voices).* (wayyy !, n.); u· wá·y *babel.* (uuwaaay! (lit. They made a confused sound of voices), excl.)

√wyč † we·+wyíč *wee owl, whip-poor-will, figuratively: cannibal or assimilation.* (weewyich, n.)

√wyp ∥ s+wiyép+mš=mš *acculturation, civilization.* (swiyepmshmsh (lit. becoming non-Indian), n.); ic+wiyép+mš=mš *Anglicize, civilize.* (itswiyepmshmsh (lit. He is becoming English idiom or character/as Caucasian race; h/s is being civilized), vi.); s+n+wyép+mš= cn *English language.* (snwyepmshtsn, n.); s+n+wyép+mš=cn=mš *English language.* (snwyepmshtsnmsh, n.)

√wyq † wayq *bother.* (wayq (stem), vi.); ‡ wáyq-nt-s *aggravate.* (wayqnts (lit. He bothered him), vt.)

√wy' † s+wi? *goodlooking, handsome, (ref to persons only).* (swi' (stem), adj.); s+wi?+núm+t+mš *beautiful (She is...), beauty, beautiful girl, handsome (He is...), comely, curvaceous.* (swi'numtmsh, vi, adj.); s+w'i?+w'i?+n'úm'+t'+mš *young people (usually good looking).* (s'wi"wi"nu'mt'msh, n.); § s+wi?+núm+t+mš he šíw'+tm *Diana, belle.* (swi'numtmsh he shi'wtm (lit. a girl who is beautiful), n.); čn‿x̌e[m]=[en]č [ł] s+wi?+núm+t= mš *aesthete, connoisseur.* (chnqhencht swi'numtmsh (lit. I love beautiful persons), n.)

√w? † wi? *announced, annunciated, cry out, shout, shouted (he...).* (wi' (lit. town crier in Indian village), vi, vt.); wi·? *shouting (Kept on...).* (wiii', vt.); s+wi? *announcement (public...), shouting.* (swi', n.); ec+wi?+s+t *call (...aloud).* (etswi'st. (stem), vt.); ec+wí?+š *call aloud.* (etswi'sh...); is+wí?+we?+iš *bluster.* (iswi'we'ish (lit. He is speaking again and again noisily and boastfully), vi.); is+wí?+we?+wiš *shouting, chatter.* (iswi'we'wish (lit. He is uttering inarticulate speechlike sounds), vi.); sye·+wi? *announcer, barker, emcee, herald, town crier.* (syeewi', n.);

√w?

č‿y'c+wí?+m *I am being called aloud.* (chi'tswi'm, vt.); čeł‿či‿s+wí?+m *I will be called aloud.* (chełchiswi'm, v.); kʷu‿i?-c+wí?+n *I am calling you(s) aloud.* (kwitswi'n, v.); čeł‿kʷ‿i-s+wí?+m *call.* (chełkwiswi'm. (lit. I will call you (sg.)), vt.); hi?c+wí?+m *am calling (I...h/h).* (hi'tswi'm, vt.); čeł‿hi-s+wí?+m *I will call h/h aloud.* (chełhiswi'm, v.); kʷp‿hi?c+wí?+m *calling (I am...you (pl) aloud).* (kuphi'tswi'm, vt.); hi?c+wí?+m-lš *am calling (I...them aloud).* (hi'tswi'mlsh, vt.); čeł‿hi-s+wí?+m-lš *I will call them aloud.* (cheł hiswi'mlsh, v.); kʷu‿y'‿c+wí?+m *You (sg.) are being called aloud.* (ku'ytswi'm, v.); čeł‿kʷu‿s+wí?+m *(lit. you(sg.) will be called aloud).* (chełkuswi'm, vt.); čn'‿y'c+wi?+m *you (s) are calling me aloud.* (chn'i'tswi'm, v.); čeł‿čn‿?i-s+wí?+m *you (s) will call me aloud.* (chełchn'iswi'm, v.); i? c+wí?+m *You(s) are calling h/h aloud.* (i'tswi'm, vt.); čeł‿?i-s+wí?+m *you (s) will call h/h aloud.* (cheł'iswi'm, v.); i? c+wí?+m-lš *You [sg] are calling them aloud.* (i'tswi'mlsh, vt.); čeł‿?i-s+wí?+m-lš *you [sg] will call them aloud.* (cheł'iswi'mlsh, v.); i c+wí?+m *H/s is being called aloud.* (itswi'm, vt.); čes‿wi?+m *he/she will be called aloud.* (cheswi'm, vt.); č‿y'c+wí?+m *h/s is calling me aloud.* (chi'tswi'ms, vt.); čeł‿či‿s+wí?+m-s *h/s will call me aloud.* (chełchiswi'ms, v.); kʷu‿y'‿c+wí?+m-s *H/s is calling you (sg.) aloud.* (ku'ytswi'ms, v.); čeł‿kʷu‿s+wí?+m *(lit. h/s will call you(sg.) aloud).* (chełkuswi'ms, vt.); i c+wí?+m-s *H/s is calling h/h aloud.* (itswi'ms, vt.); čes‿wi?+m-s *h/s will call h/h aloud.* (cheswi'ms, v.);

č‿y'c+wí?+m *We are being called aloud.* (chi'tswi'm, vi.); kʷup‿?i‿c+wí?+m *You (pl.) are being called aloud.* (kup'itswi'm, vi.); čeł‿kʷup‿s+wí?+m *(lit. you (pl) will be called aloud).* (chełkupswi'm, vi.); čn'‿y'c+wí?-m-p *You (pl.) are calling me aloud.* (chn'i'tswi'mp, vt.); čeł‿či‿s+wí?-m-p *you (pl) will call me aloud.* (chełchiswi'mp, v.); i c+wí?+m-lš *They are being called aloud.* (itswi'mlsh, vt.); čes‿wé?+m-lš *they will be called aloud.* (cheswe'mlsh, v.); č‿y'c+wí?+m-s-lš *They are calling me aloud.* (chi'tswi'mslsh, vt.); čeł‿č‿hi-s+wí?+m-s-lš *they will call me aloud.* (chełchiswi'mslsh, v.); i c+wí?+m-s-lš *They are calling h/h aloud.* (itswi'mslsh, vt.); čes‿wi?+m-s-lš *they will call h/h aloud.* (cheswi'mslsh, v.); kʷu‿y'c+wí?+m-s-lš *They are calling you (pl.) aloud.* (ku'ytswi'mslsh, v.); čeł‿kʷup‿s+wí?+m-s-lš *(lit. they will call you (pl.) aloud).* (chełkupswi'mslsh, vt.); ‡ wí?-nt-sel-em *called (I was...aloud).* (wi'ntselem, vt.); ec+wí?-st-mel-em *I am called aloud.* (etswi'stmelem, vt.); t'ixʷ es+wí?-nt-sel-em *I had been called aloud.* (t'i'khweswi'ntselem, v.); t'i?+wí?-nt-sel-em *I have been called aloud.* (t'i'wi'ntselem, v.); kʷ ne? wí?-nt-sel-em *I am going to be called aloud.* (k'wne'wi'ntselem, vi.); wí?-nt-s-n *called (I...you (sg.) aloud).* (wi'ntsn, vt.); ec+wí?-st-m-n *I call you (sg.) aloud.* (etswi'stmn, vt.); t'ixʷ es+wí?-nt-s-n *I had called you (s) aloud.* (t'i'khweswi'ntsn, v.); t'i?+wí?-nt-s-n *I have called you (s) aloud.* (t'i'wi'ntsn, v.); kʷ ne? wí?-nt-s-n *I am going to call you (sg.) aloud.* (k'wne'wi'ntsn, vi.); wí?-n

181

called (I...h/h aloud). (wi̱'n, vt.);
ec+wíʔ-s-n I call h/h aloud. (etswi̱'sn,
v.); t'ixʷ es+wíʔ-n I had called h/h
aloud. (t'i'khweswi̱'n, v.); t'i?+wíʔ-n I
have called h/h aloud. (t'i'wi̱'n, v.); k'ʷ
neʔ wíʔ-n I am going to call h/h
aloud. (k'wne'wi̱'n, vi.); wíʔ-nt-ulm-n
called (I...you (p1.) aloud). (wi̱'ntulmn,
vt.); ec+wíʔ-st-ulm-n I call you (pl.)
aloud. (etswi̱'stulmn, vt.); t'ixʷ
es+wíʔ-nt-ulm-n I had called you (pl)
aloud. (t'i'khweswi̱'ntulmn, v.);
t'i?+wíʔ-nt-ulm-n I have called you
(pl) aloud. (t'i'wi̱'ntulmn, v.); k'ʷ neʔ
wíʔ-nt-ulm-n I am going to call you
(pl.) aloud. (k'wne'wi̱'ntulmn, vi.);
wíʔ-n-lš called (I...them aloud).
(wi̱'nlsh, vt.); ec+wíʔ-s-n-lš I call
them aloud. (etswi̱'snlsh, vt.); t'ixʷ
es+wíʔ-n-lš I had called them aloud.
(t'i'khweswi̱'nlsh, v.); t'i?+wíʔ-n-lš I
have called them aloud. (t'i'wi̱'nlsh,
v.); k'ʷ neʔ wíʔ-n-lš I am going to call
them aloud. (k'wne'wi̱'nlsh, vi.);
wíʔ-nt-si-t You (sg.) were called
aloud. (wi̱'ntsit, vt.); ec+wíʔ-st-mi-t
you (sg.) are called aloud. (etswi̱'stmit,
vt.); t'ixʷ es+wíʔ-nt-si-t you (s) had
been called aloud. (t'i'khweswi̱'ntsit,
v.); t'i?+wíʔ-nt-si-t You (s) have been
called aloud. (t'i'wi̱'ntsit, v.); k'ʷ neʔ
wíʔ-nt-si-t You (sg.) are going to be
called aloud. (k'wne'wi̱'ntsit, vi.);
wíʔ-nt-se-xʷ You (sg.) called me
aloud. (wi̱'ntsekhw, vt.);
ec+wíʔ-st-me-xʷ you (sg.) call me
aloud. (etswi̱'stmekhw, vt.); t'ixʷ
es+wíʔ-nt-se-xʷ you (s) had called me
aloud. (t'i'khweswi̱'ntsekhw, v.);
t'i?+wíʔ-nt-se-xʷ You (s) have called
me aloud. (t'i'wi̱'ntsekhw, v.); k'ʷ neʔ
wíʔ-nt-se-xʷ You (sg.) are going to
call me aloud. (k'wne'wi̱'ntsekhw, vi.);
wiʔ-nt-s (You sg.) call me aloud!
(imper.). (wi̱'nts, vt.); wíʔ-nt-sel Call

me aloud! (wi̱'ntsel, v. (Imp. sg.));
neʔ+wíʔi-nt-se-xʷ call (You (sg.)
shall...me aloud!). (ne'wi̱'ntsekhw
(imp.), vt.); wíʔ-nt-xʷ You (sg.) called
h/h aloud. (wi̱'ntkhw, v.);
ec+wíʔ-st-xʷ you (sg.) call h/h aloud.
(etswi̱'stkhw, vt.); t'ixʷ es+wíʔ-nt-xʷ
you (s) had called h/h aloud.
(t'i'khweswi̱'ntkhw, v.); t'i?+wíʔ-nt-xʷ
You (s) have called h/h aloud.
(t'i'wi̱'ntkhw, v.); k'ʷ neʔ wíʔ-nt-xʷ
You (sg.) are going to call h/h aloud.
(k'wne'wi̱'ntkhw, vi.); neʔ+wíʔi-nt-xʷ
call (You (sg.) shall...h/h aloud!).
(ne'wi̱'intkhw (imp.), vt.); neʔ+wíʔi-
nt-xʷ-lš call (You (sg.) shall...them
aloud!). (ne'wi̱'intkhwlsh (imp.), vt.);
wiʔ-nt-m H/S was called aloud.
(wi̱'ntm, vt.); ec+wíʔ-st-m h/s is
called aloud. (etswi̱'stm, vt.); t'ixʷ
es+wíʔ-nt-m h/s had been called
aloud. (t'i'khweswi̱'ntm, v.);
t'i?+wíʔ-nt-m h/s has been called
aloud. (t'i'wi̱'ntm, v.); k'ʷ neʔ
wíʔ-nt-m H/s is going to be called
aloud. (k'wne'wi̱'ntm, vi.); wíʔ-nt Call
h/h aloud! (wi̱'nt, v. (Imp. sg.));
wíʔ-nt-se-s H/S called me aloud.
(wi̱'ntses, vt.); ec+wíʔ-st-me-s h/s
calls me aloud. (etswi̱'stmes, vt.); t'ixʷ
es+wíʔ-nt-se-s h/s had called me
aloud. (t'i'khweswi̱'ntses, v.);
t'i?+wíʔ-nt-se-s h/s has called me
aloud. (t'i'wi̱'ntses, v.); k'ʷ neʔ
wíʔ-nt-se-s H/s is going to call me
aloud. (k'wne'wi̱'ntses, vi.);
wíʔ-nt-si-s H/S called you (sg.) aloud.
(wi̱'ntsis, vt.); ec+wíʔ-st-mi-s h/s calls
you (sg.) aloud. (etswi̱'stmis, vt.); t'ixʷ
es+wíʔ-nt-si-s h/s had called you (s)
aloud. (t'i'khweswi̱'ntsis, v.);
t'i?+wíʔ-nt-si-s h/s has called you (s)
aloud. (t'i'wi̱'ntsis, v.); k'ʷ neʔ
wíʔ-nt-si-s H/s is going to call you
(sg.) aloud. (k'wne'wi̱'ntsis, vi.);
wiʔ-nt-s H/s called h/h aloud. (wi̱'nts,

vt.); ec+wíʔ-stu-s *h/s calls h/h aloud.*
(etswi̲'stus, vt.); t'ixʷ es+wíʔ-nt-s *h/s
had called h/h aloud.* (t'i'khweswi̲'nts,
v.); t'iʔ+wíʔ-nt-s *h/s has called h/h
aloud.* (t'i'wi̲'nts, v.); k'ʷ neʔ wíʔ-nt-s
H/s is going to call h/h aloud.
(k'wne'wi̲'nts, vi.); wíʔ-nt-eli-t *We
were called aloud.* (wi̲'ntelit, vt.);
ec+wíʔ-st-eli-t *we are called aloud.*
(etswi'stelit, vt.); t'ixʷ es+wíʔ-nt-eli-t
We had been called aloud.
(t'i'khweswi̲'ntelit, v.); t'iʔ+wíʔ-nt-eli-t
We have been called aloud.
(t'i'wi̲'ntelit, v.); k'ʷ neʔ wíʔ-nt-eli-t
We are going to be called aloud.
(k'wne'wi̲'ntelit, vi.); wíʔ-nt-ulmi-t
You (pl.) were called aloud.
(wi̲'ntulmit, v.); ec+wíʔ-st-ulmi-t *you
(pl.) are called aloud.* (etswi̲'stulmit,
vt.); t'ixʷ es+wíʔ-nt-ulmi-t *you (pl)
had been called aloud.*
(t'i'khweswi̲'ntulmit, v.);
t'iʔ+wíʔ-nt-ulmi-t *You (pl) have been
called aloud.* (t'i'wi̲'ntulmit, v.); k'ʷ
neʔ wíʔ-nt-ulmi-t *You (pl.) are going
to be called aloud.* (k'wne'wi̲'ntulmit,
vi.); wíʔ-nt-sel-p *You (pl.) called me
aloud.* (wi̲'ntselp, vt.);
ec+wíʔ-st-me-lp *you (pl.) call me
aloud.* (etswi̲'stmelp, vt.); t'ixʷ
es+wíʔ-nt-sel-p *you (pl) had called
me aloud.* (t'i'khweswi̲'ntselp, v.);
t'iʔ+wíʔ-nt-sel-p *you (pl) have called
me aloud.* (t'i'wi̲'ntselp, v.); k'ʷ neʔ
wíʔ-nt-sel-p *You (pl.) are going to
call me aloud.* (k'wne'wi̲'ntselp, vi.);
neʔ+wíʔi-nt-sel-p *call (You (pl.) are
to...me aloud!).* (ne'wi̲'intselp (imp.),
vt.); wíʔ-nt-ul *(You pl.) call h/h aloud!
(imper).* (wi̲'ntul, vt.); neʔ+wíʔi-nt-p
call (You (pl.) shall...h/h aloud!).
(ne'wi̲'intp (imp.), vt.); wiʔ-nt-p-lš
You (pl.) called them aloud. (wi̲'ntplsh,
v.); ec+wíʔ-st-xʷ-lš *you (pl.) call them
aloud.* (etswi̲'stkhwlsh, vt.); t'ixʷ
es+wíʔ-nt-p-lš *you (pl) had called

them aloud. (t'i'khweswi̲'ntplsh, v.);
t'iʔ+wíʔ-nt-xʷ-lš *You (pl) have called
them aloud.* (t'i'wi̲'ntkhwlsh, v.); k'ʷ
neʔ wíʔ-nt-p-lš *You (pl.) are going to
call them aloud.* (k'wne'wi̲'ntplsh, vi.);
neʔ+wíʔi-nt-p-lš *call (You (pl.) are
to...them aloud!).* (ne'wi̲'intplsh (imp.),
vt.); wiʔ-nt-m-lš *They were called
aloud.* (wi̲'ntmlsh, vt.);
ec+wíʔ-st-m-lš *they are called aloud.*
(etswi̲'stmlsh, vt.); t'ixʷ
es+wíʔ-nt-m-lš *they had been called
aloud.* (t'i'khweswi̲'ntmlsh, v.);
t'iʔ+wíʔ-nt-m-lš *They have been
called aloud.* (t'i'wi̲'ntmlsh, v.); k'ʷ neʔ
wíʔ-nt-m-lš *They are going to be
called aloud.* (k'wne'wi̲'ntmlsh, vi.);
wíʔ-nt-lš *Call them aloud!* (wi̲'ntlsh,
v. (Imp. [pl.])); wíʔ-nt-se-s-lš *They
called me aloud.* (wi̲'ntseslsh, vt.);
ec+wíʔ-st-me-s-lš *they call me aloud.*
(etswi̲'stmeslsh, vt.); t'ixʷ
es+wíʔ-nt-se-s-lš *they had called me
aloud.* (t'i'khweswi̲'ntseslsh, v.);
t'iʔ+wíʔ-nt-se-s-lš *They have called
me aloud.* (t'i'wi̲'ntseslsh, v.); k'ʷ neʔ
wíʔ-nt-se-s-lš *They are going to call
me aloud.* (k'wne'wi̲'ntseslsh, vi.);
wiʔ-nt-s-lš *They called h/h aloud.*
(wi̲'ntslsh, vt.); ec+wíʔ-stu-s-lš *they
call h/h aloud.* (etswi'stuslsh, vt.); t'ixʷ
es+wíʔ-nt-s-lš *they had called h/h
aloud.* (t'i'khweswi̲'ntslsh, v.);
t'iʔ+wíʔ-nt-s-lš *They have called h/h
aloud.* (t'i'wi̲'ntslsh, v.); k'ʷ neʔ
wíʔ-nt-s-lš *They are going to call h/h
aloud.* (k'wne'wi̲'ntslsh, vi.);
wíʔ-nt-ulmi-lš *They called you (pl.)
aloud.* (wi̲'ntulmislsh, vt.);
ec+wíʔ-st-mi-s-lš *they call you (pl.)
aloud.* (etswi̲'stmislsh, vt.); t'ixʷ
es+wíʔ-nt-ulmi-s-lš *they had called
you (pl) aloud.* (t'i'khweswi̲'ntulmislsh,
v.); t'iʔ+wíʔ-nt-si-s-lš *They have
called you (pl) aloud.* (t'i'wi̲'ntsislsh,
v.); k'ʷ neʔ wíʔ-nt-ulmi-s-lš *They are*

going to call you (pl.) aloud.
(k'wne'wi̱'ntulmislsh, vi.)

√w?p § s+w'i?p+ɬ+t'a̱q=ney' *flour
sack.* (s'wi'pɬt'a̱qne'y, n.) [possibly
related to √wyp]

√w?t' † s+we?ít'+n *spring, well.*
(swe'i̱t'n, n.)

√w?x̌ † wa?x̌ *sting, smart (to...).* (wa'qh
(stem), vi.) [probable inchoative of
√wx̌₂]

√w' † uw'e?+n+t *low (to be very...).*
(u'we'nt (stem), v.); ∥ uw'e+m'n'=ús
coistrel, knave, bogus, rascal.
(u'we'm'nu̱s (lit. He is good for
nothing), n.); § uw'+em'n'=ús he
s+mí?yem *worthless (a woman who
is...).* (u'we'm'nu̱s he smi'yem, adj, n.);
úw'e k'ʷ+k'ʷn=iy'e? *awhile.* (u'we
k'uk'w'ni̱'ye' (lit. for a short time only),
adv.); uw'+ic+qox̌á·?+qʷ?el'
buttonhole. (u'witsqoqha̱aa'qw'e'l (lit.
He kept on talking and talking), vt.);
uw'e+n+pú?s+n *abstract (lit. only in
imagination).* (u'wenpu̱'sn, n.) [see
appendix C]

√w'l' † w'el' *clownish, silly, unnatural.*
('we'l (stem), adj.)

√w't † w'et *to roll (e.g. a solid object),
to be just outside door.* ('wet)

√w'? † s+w'a? *cougar, tiger.* (s'wa', n.)

√xʷc₁ † xʷec *to suffer.* (khwets (stem),
vi.); ∥ s+n+xʷc+xʷc+m=?íl's *agony,
anguish.* (snkhwtskhwts'mi̱'ls (lit.
suffering with great anguish), n.);
hn+xʷc+xʷc+m=íl's *suffered (he...).*
(hnkhwtskhwtsmi̱'ls, vi.); §
s+nukʷ+n+xʷc+xʷc+m'=íl's
compassion. (snukwnkhwtskhwts'mi̱'ls
(lit. fellow sufferer), n.)

√xʷc₂ † xʷ+xʷic *short.* (khukhwits
(stem), adj.); xʷ+xʷíc+e? *concise,
brief, curt, short, terse.* (khukhwi̱tse'.
(lit. It goes only here, not there), adj.);
čs+xʷ+xʷíc+e? *bob-tail.*
(chskhukhwi̱tse' (lit. a short tail), n.); ∥
xʷ+xʷéc=al'qʷ *short (He is...).*

(khukhwe̱tsa'lqw, adj.);
s+can+[x]ʷ+xʷic=cn' *bob.*
(stsanqhukhwitsts'n (a short haircut on
a woman or child), n.); [xref √x̌ʷc₂]

√xʷc'₁ † xʷc'+út *crag, Rocky
Mountains, Clear Water Mountains (in
Idaho).* (Khwts'ut (lit. rocky
mountain), n.); § s+q'eyu?+ɬ+xʷc'+út
*Lawrence Nicodemus (Indian name
of).* (Sq'eyu'ɬkhwts'ut (lit. Disbelieved
Rocky Mountain), n.)

√xʷc'₂ † xʷic' *amuse, befriend,
companion (be a...to), entertain.*
(khwits' (stem). whistle, vt, n.)
[written as √xʷc in volume 1] xʷic
to entertain, amuse. (khwits); ‡
xʷíc'+e?-nt-s *consort.* (khwi̱ts'e'nts
(lit. He kept him company), vt.)

√xʷc'₃ † xʷic' *indicate, point out.*
(khwit's (stem), vt.)

√xʷd † xʷed *to itch.* (khwed (stem),
vi.); xʷed+p *It itched.* (khwedp, vi.); ∥
xʷád=alqʷ *grub worm, wood worm.*
(khwa̱dalqw. (lit. tickling of pole), n.);
s+t+xʷd+p=íc'e? *eczema.*
(stkhwdpi̱ts'e' (lit. intense itching of
the skin), n.)

√xʷdnt † s+xʷúdent *ice cream, ice.*
(skhu̱dent, n.); ∥ xʷdent=íl'š *congeal,
freeze.* (khudenti̱'lsh. conceal (lit. It
(water) was turned into ice by cold),
vt.) [xref √x̌ʷdnt]

√xʷk'ʷ₁ † xʷek'ʷ *clean, sweep.*
(khwek'w (stem), vt.); u· xʷék'ʷ
*candid, chaste, clean, decent, pure,
sincere (it is...).* (uukhwe̱k'w, adj.); u·
xʷúk'ʷ+xʷk'ʷ *cleans (she...habitually).*
(uukhu̱k'wkhuk'w, vi.); u·
xʷúk'ʷ+xʷk'ʷ+xʷk'ʷ *habitually (she
cleans...).* (uukhu̱k'wkhuk'wkhuk'w,
adv.); s+xʷék'ʷ+m *clean (to make...).*
(skhwe̱k'um, vi.); sye·+xʷék'ʷ+m
cleaning person. (syeekhwe̱k'um (lit.
One who is hired to do cleaning), n.);
∥ hn+xʷk'ʷ=íɫc'e+n' *cathartic.*
(hnkhuk'wi̱ɫts'e'n (lit. cleaning inside),

n.); hn+xʷkʼʷ=íns+n *dentifrice.*
(hnkhuk'winsn (lit. means of cleaning
the teeth), n.); hn+xʷukʼʷ+xʷukʼʷ=
íns+m *He brushed his teeth.*
(hnkhuk'wkhuk'winsm, vt.);
s+t+xʷkʼʷ+p=ílgʷes *catharsis.*
(stkhuk'wpilgwes (lit. the heart
becoming clean, a purifying or
figurative cleansing of the emotions),
n.); sye+xʷkʼʷ=íɫxʷ *charwoman.*
(syekhuk'wiɫkhw. (lit. One who cleans
house(s)), n.); xʷkʼʷ=ílup+n *broom.*
(khuk'wilupn (lit. instrument for
cleaning floors, mattress, etc.), n.);
s+[x]ʷukʼʷ=ílup *to sweep.*
(sqhuk'wilup, vt.); ‡ t+xʷékʼʷ-nt-s
efface, delete. (tkhwek'wnts (lit. He
cleaned it off, he erased it), v.) [xref
√x̌ʷkʼʷ]

√xʷkʼʷ₂ † s+xʷíkʼʷ+t *frost.* (skhwik'wt,
n.); ∥ t+xʷ+xʷíkʼʷ+xʷakʼʷ=ečen'=us
frosty eyebrows.
(tkhukhwik'wkhwak'weche'nus, n.)

√xʷl₁ † xʷel *alive, live.* (khwel (stem),
adj.); xʷél+xʷl+t *debt.* (khwelkhwlt (lit.
It came back to life, that which is due
from one person to another), n.) ;
ec+xʷél+xʷl+t *alive (to be...), living
(be).* (etskhwelkhwlt, v, vi.);
s+xʷel+xʷl+m *conservation (lit.
preserving in life from destruction).*
(skhwelkhwlm, n.); hn+xʷél+xʷl+n
*culture, electro-chemistry, life, life
(way of...), lifestyle, vital capacity.*
(hnkhwelkhwln, n.); ul hn+xʷél+xʷl+n
cultural. (ul hnkhwelkhwln (lit.
belonging to a way of living), adj.);
hn+xʷl+xʷl+scút+n *Christ, Savior.*
(Hnkhwlkhwlstsutn (lit. means of
resurrecting oneself), n.);
ʔepɫ+xʷé[l]+xʷl+t *debtor*
(epɫkhwekhwlt (lit. One who owes
something to another), n.);
ʔapɫ+n+xʷél+xʷl+n *animated (to
be...).* (apɫnkhwelkhwln (lit. What has
life), vi.); ‡ xʷél+[x]ʷl+s-n *conserve,*

preserve, save. (khwelkwlsn. (lit. I
preserved (saved) his life), vt.); §
s+t+my+y=ípeleʔ+s xʷe
n+xʷel+xʷl+n *biology (lit.exposition of
the origin of what is the means of life).*
(stmyyipele's khwe nkhwelkhwln, n.);
s+t+qʼey'+y'=ípeleʔ+s he
n+xʷél+xʷl+n *biography.*
(stq'e'y'yipele's henkhwelkhwln (lit. a
written account of the origin of one's
life), n.); can+x̌i[ɫ]+ɫ+xʷél+xʷl+t
condone. (tsanqhilɫkhwelkhwlt (lit. He
abandoned another's debt to himself),
vt.)

√xʷl₂ † xʷel *clean material like moss,
cotton, a swab.* (khwel (stem), n.)

√xʷl₃ † i+xʷu·l *be (some).* (ikhwuul.
(stem), vi.)

√xʷl₄ † xʷul *bore (a hole).* (khul (stem),
vt.); xʷúl+emn *auger, bit.* (khulemn.
(lit. means of drilling a hole), n.); ∥
l'+l'+xʷil'=us *DeSmet, Idaho.*
(L'l'khwil'us (lit. a little hole in the
forehead, referring to a spring on the
north side of DeSmet hill), n.);
en+xʷúl=ul'mxʷ *burrow, cave.*
(enkhulu'lmkhw (lit. a hold dug in the
ground), n.); [?] čn‿yá+s+xʷl'+ót=qn
I finally got a jack rabbit.
(chnyaskhw'lotqn, vt.) [xref √lxʷ]

√xʷlʔ † xʷéleʔ *lark, meadowlark.*
(khwele', n.)

√xʷl' † xʷel' *spin (as a top).* (khwe'l
(stem), vt.)

√xʷlkʷ † s+xʷlíkʷ *cyclone, whirlwind.*
(skhwlikw, n.)

√xʷɫ₁ † xʷuɫ *proceed.* (khuɫ (stem). as
far as, vi.)

√xʷɫ₂ † s+xʷuʔɫ *mist.* (skhu'ɫ. (stem).
smog, n.) [xref √x̌ʷɫ]

√xʷm † xʷam *roan-colored.* (khwam
(stem), adj.); ∥ xʷám=qn *roan horse.*
(khwamqn, n.); xʷém=ečt
woodpecker. (khwemecht, n.)

√xʷm'₁ † xʷum' *homesick, lonely.*
(khu'm (stem), adj.)

√xʷm'₂ † xʷum'+út *of course*. (khu'mut, adv.)

√xʷny' † s+xʷú+xʷney' *ant, rice (from resemblance of a swarm of ants).* (skhu̱khwne'y, n.) [xref √x̌ʷny']

√xʷn' // an+xʷan'=áx̌n *point (at this...), now.* (ankhwa'na̱qhn. *from now on,* adv.); xʷa tal' an+xʷan'=áx̌n *anymore.* (khwa ta'l ankhwa'na̱qhn. *from now on* (lit. *from this arm over*), adv.); č[i]+n+xʷen'=ítkʷe? *America(n).* (chnkhwe'ni̱tkwe' (lit. *on this side of the water*), n.)

√xʷp₁ † xʷep *flatten out, spread.* (khwep (stem). *to flatten out blanket,* vt.); s+xʷép+m+šeš *development, unfolding, unrolling.* (skhwe̱pmshesh, n.); ‡ xʷép+m-st-m *develop, grow, mature, unfold.* (khwe̱pmstm, vt.)

√xʷp₂ † xʷu·p *show-off, ostentatious.* (khuup (stem). *intentional or vain display of wealth,* adj.)

√xʷps † xʷ(=)ups *to slap (with tail).* (khups (stem), vt.)

√xʷq'ʷ // t+xʷéq'ʷ=ečn' *calliope, cello.* (tkhwe̱q'wech'n (lit. *An organlike musical instrument*), n.); § x̌áy'+x̌i?+t ha t+xʷéq'ʷ=ečn' *bass viol* (lit. *It is big big what is a viol (means of pulverizing)).* (qha̱'yqhi't ha tkhwe̱q'wech'n, n.) [see also √x̌ʷq'ʷ]

√xʷr₁ † xʷar *time (a very long...).* (khwar (stem), n.);

√xʷr₂ † xʷar *to quiver, tremble.* (khwar (stem), vi.); xʷar+p *convulse, quake, trembled.* (khwarp, vi.); s+xʷar+p *convulsion, to shake as with fear, cold, or weakness, vibrate.* (skhwarp, n, vt.); // t+xʷar+p=ílgʷes *shook (He...in his heart from effects of fat.).* (tkhwarpilgwes, vi.); xʷar+p=úl'umxʷ *earth (The...quaked), earthquake, tremor.* (khwarpu̱'lumkhw, n.)

√xʷs₁ † xʷis *to travel.* (khwis (stem). *to go about,* vi.); s+xʷis+t *departure, going away, walking.* (skhwist, n, vi.);

čn‿xʷís+t *walked (I...).* (chnkhwist (lit. *I went away*), vi.); č‿y'c+xʷís+t *walking (I am...).* (chi'tskhwist, adj.); čn'‿c+xʷis+t *(lit. I, customarily, walk).* (ch'ntskhwist, vt.); čeł‿či‿s+xʷis+t *walk.* (chełchiskhwist (lit. *I will walk*), vi.); k'ʷne? čn‿xʷís+t *walk (I am going to...).* (k'wne'chnkhwist, vi.); kʷu‿xʷís+t *You (sg) walked.* (kuukhwist, vi.); kʷ?‿c+xʷís+t *walk (you (sg.)...).* (ku'tskhwist (lit. *go places*), vi.); kʷu‿y'‿c+xʷís+t *You (sg.) are walking.* (ku'ytskhwist, v.); čeł‿kʷ‿s+xʷís+t *You (sg.) will walk.* (chełkuskhwist, vi.); k'ʷ ne? kʷu·‿xʷís+t *You (sg.) are going to walk.* (k'wne'kuukhwist, vi.); xʷis+t-š *(You sg.) walk (imper).* (khwistsh, vi.); xʷis+t *H/S walked; h/s departed.* (khwist, vi.); ec+xʷís+t *H/s walks.* (etskhwist, vi.); ic+xʷís+t *walking (h/s is...).* (itskhwist, vi.); čas‿xʷís+t *he/she will walk.* (chaskhwist, vi.); k'ʷ ne? xʷís+t *He/she is going to walk.* (k'wne'khwist, vi.); // xʷis+t=áx̌n *along-side.* (Khwista̱qhn (lit. *one who walked by the side of a crowd; name of a Coeur d'Alene Indian*), adv.); xʷis+s+t=úl'umxʷ *He came to a walking status (lit. forced by circumstances to go on foot).* (khwi̱sstu'lumkhw, v.); § xʷis+t ha s+tˁin *Louie Antelope.* (Khwist Ha St(in. *name of my maternal grandfather* (lit. *antelope that walked*), n.); n+?ed+xʷu·s=íw'es *alternate.* ('nedkhuusi'wes (lit. *It alternated, It changed places, that which occurs in successive turns*), vi.);

√xʷs₂ † e? xʷ(=)ús *hunt, look for.* (e'khus... (stem). vt, vi.); ‡ e? xʷús-n' *I looked for h/h/i.* (e'khus'n, vi.); a?+xʷós=qn'+t-s *H/s looked for lice, etc. on h/h head.* (a'khosq'nts, vt.)

√xʷs₃ † xʷ+xʷs+ós *rebellious, resistant, defiant, opposed.* (khukhwsos. (lit. He is full of, or expressing, resistance or opposition), adj.)

√xʷt₁ † xʷet *depleted.* (khwet (stem), adj.); in+xʷét+p *breathless.* (inkhwetp (lit. He is panting), adj.); hn+xʷet+p *He was out of wind, he or she got exhausted.* (hnkhwetp, vi.); s+n+xʷét+p *exhaustion.* (snkhwetp (lit. being out of breath), vi.); hn+xʷt+p+útm *exhaustible (h/s/i is...).* (hnkhwtputm, vi.); // ac+xʷt=áx̌n *amputee.* (ats khwtaqhn (lit. He is amputated as to the arm), n.); hn+xʷt= ús *Cree, Dakota, Sioux.* (Hnkhwtus, n.); s+n+xʷát+p=alqs *climax.* (snkhwatpalqs (lit. the road, story coming to an end), n.); ul+s+n+xʷát+p=alqs *climatic.* (ulsnkhwatpalqs (lit. pertaining to the end of a story), adj.) [xref √xʷt'₂ and √x̌ʷt]

√xʷt₂ † i+c+xʷít *whistling (he is...).* (itskhwit, vi.); s+xʷe·+xʷít *bobwhite (lit. whistle whistle).* (skhweekhwit, n.)

√xʷt'₁ // s+xʷét'=ečt *shoulder blade.* (skhwet'echt, n.); s+xʷét'+xʷt'=ečt *shoulder blades.* (skhwet'khwt'echt, n.)

√xʷt'₂ † xʷet'+p *He ran off, away.* (khwet'p, vi.); s+teč+s+xʷét'+p+n *counterattack.* (stechskhwet'pn (lit. counterattack by running), n.); ‡ xʷét'+p+m-stu-s *[run] cause.* (khwet'pmstus (lit. He caused it to run, as a car), vt.); čs+xʷét'+p-nt-s *dash.* (chskhwet'pnts (lit. He ran against (towards) him), vi.); [xref √xʷt₁ and √x̌ʷt]

√xʷtk'ʷ † xʷé?tk'ʷ *rise (suddenly) (like hair).* (khwe̲tk'w (stem), vi.)

√xʷy † xʷuy *go (over there), over there (He went...).* (khuy, vi, adv.); s+xʷuy *journey.* (skhuy, n.); uɬ+xʷúy *went (He...over there again).* (uɬkhuy, vi.); uln'+xʷúy+iy+m *dilatory.*

(ul'nkhuyiym (lit. He often becomes behind in work), adj.); hn+xʷúy+n *passageway.* (hnkhuyn (lit. means of passage), n.); sye·+xʷúy *delegate.* (syeekhuy (lit. One who goes to a place for another or others), n.); [also recorded as √x̌ʷy] sye·+x̌ʷúy *ambassador, consul.* (syeeqhuy (lit. One who goes to a place for another or others), n.); čn‿xʷúy *I went over there.* (chnkhuy, vt.); k'ʷne?+čn‿xʷúy *over there (I am going...).* (k'wne'chnkhuy, adv.); kʷu‿xʷúy *You went over there.* (kuukhuy, vi.); kʷ‿čic+xʷy? *come (Why did you...?).* (tgwe'l sti'mɬ ku chitskhuy?, vi.); č‿xʷúy+š *command, sg. come over here.* (chkhuysh); čic+xʷúy *came (he....over here).* (chitskhuy, vt.); či+te·+xʷúy *He came to meet me on my way over there.* (chiteekhuy, vi.); te·+xʷúy *went (He...to meet him),* (teekhuy, vi, vt.); č‿xúy *we went over there.* (chkhuy); kʷup‿xʷúy *You went over there.* (kupkhuy, vi.); // s+xʷy=elwís *travel, trip.* (skhuyelwis, n.); ‡ čs+xʷúy-n *went (I...to see him).* (chskhuyn, vi.); čs+xʷuy-nt-s *He went to see him.* (chskhuynts, vi.); čic+xʷúy-stu-s *brought.* (chitskhuystus (lit. He brought him/her/it over here), vt.); čič+s+xʷúy-nt-sel-p *lit. you (pl) came after me.* (chichskhuyntselp, vt.); § a·+yaʕ čic+xʷúy *came (they all...).* (aaya) chitskhuy (lit. They all came), vi.); pin'č'+ne? kʷ‿č'ic+xʷúy *When are you coming over?.* (pi'nch'ne' kuch'itskhuy, qu.); tgʷel s+tim'+ɬ kʷ‿čic+xʷy? *come (Why did you...?).* (tgwe'l sti'mɬ ku chitskhuy?, vi.); xʷay'+t+x̌es=ípele? *beneficiary.* (khwa'ytqhesipele' (lit. one who is the recipient of a benefit), n.); t+kʷeɬ+xʷy= elwís *circulate.* (tkweɬkhuyelwis (lit. He moved around from place to place), vi.); s+t+kʷel'+čs+xʷy+s+čínt *people (He is going about visiting...), gathering (He is going about...people).* (stkwe'lchskhuyschint, n, vt.); s+nukʷ+xʷúy+m+n *convection.* (snukwkhuymn (lit. carrying with or together), n.); nukʷ+xʷúy+m-n-ts *abduct, kidnap.* (nukwkhuymnts. kidnap (lit. He took her along with him), vt.); čn‿xʷuy hił čn‿gʷič e c'i? *lit. I went over there and I saw a deer.* (chnkhuy hił chngwich e ts'i', vt.); kʷup‿xʷuy teč+e·+líš *You went to the mountain.* (kupkhuy tech eelish, vi.); hn-xʷuy+ł+šugʷíl *He went on his last trip.* (hnkhuyłshugwil, vi.); yuqʷ+e?+s+xʷúy *He feigned to go there.* (yuqwe'skhuy, vt.)

√xʷy' † xʷ+xʷéy'+e? *narrow (it is...).* (khukhwe'ye (stem), adj, n.); ‖ hn+xʷ+xʷáy'+a?=al'qs *bottleneck.* (hnkhukhwa'ya'a'lqs (lit. The road is narrow), n.); hn+xʷ+xʷey'=íłc'e? *(?) cell.* (hnkhukhwe'yiłts'e' (lit. a narrow confining room, a room that is only (so large), n.); hn+xʷ+xʷiy'=íłc'e? *The room is narrow.* (hnkhwkhwi'ya'iłts'e', vi.); xʷxʷ=iy'e?=il'š *It lessened in breadth, reduced, diminished.* (khukhwi'ye'i'lsh, vt.); ‡ xʷ+xʷiy'+e?=íl'š-s-n' *diminish, reduce.* (khukhwi'ye'i'lshs'n. (lit. I lessened it in breadth), vt.)

√xʷ§ † xʷé§+iš *to step over a person ceremonially.* (khwe(ish)

√xʷ? † xʷi? *direction (this...), moment (at this...), here, this.* (khwi' (stem), n, adv, adj.); xʷí?+in *to go along here.* (khwi'in, stem); e+n+t+xʷí? *here (it is...).* (entkhwi', vi.); § e+mel'+xʷí? *here (It is right...).* (eme'lkhwi', adv.); ul xʷi?+ye+tmíxʷ=l'mxʷ *American, earthly.* (ul khwi'yetmikhw'lmkhw (lit. belonging to this land (country/world), adj.)

√xʷ?s † xʷu?s *awake (He became wide...), awake (wide...).* (khu's (stem), adj.) [written in volume 1 as √ph?s] phu?s *He became wide awake.* (phu's, vi.)

√xʷ?t₁ † xʷe?+t *run away.* (khwe't)

√xʷ?t₂ † xʷi?t *abuse, attack, berate.* (khwi't (stem) (abuse with words or acts), vt.)

√x̌c₁ † x̌ac *to bet.* (qhats (stem), vi.); x̌ác+x̌ac+m' *bet, wager.* (qhatsqhats'm. bet (lit. He made a bet), vt.); s+x̌ác+x̌ac+m' *dice, gamble.* (sqhatsqhats'm, n, vt.); ul s+x̌ac+x̌ác+m' *aleatory.* (ul sqhatsqhats'm (lit. belonging to gambling, chance), adj.); hn+x̌ac+x̌ac+m'ín'+n' *casino, house (gambling...).* (hnqhatsqhats'mi'n'n, n.)

√x̌c₂ † x̌ec *clothed, dressed, ready.* (qhets (stem), adj.); ac+x̌éc+m *prepared, conditioned.* (atsqhetsm (lit. He is prepared for something in particular), adj.); x̌ec+út *companion.* (qhetsut (stem), n.); s+x̌éc+ut *attendant, companion, companionship, one who accompanies another.* (sqhetsut, n.); hi-s+x̌éc+ut *companion.* (hisqhetsut (lit. He is my companion along the way), n.); s+x̌ác+x̌ac+ut *crew, those who accompany oneself.* (sqhatsqhatsut, n.); twas+x̌éc+ut *concomitant.* (twasqhetsut (lit. He is with a companion), n.); s+x̌éc+m+šeš *edition (lit. preparing for something).* (sqhetsmshesh, n.); i? c+x̌éc+m+šeš *edit (lit. You(s) are preparing it (for something).* (i'tsqhetsmshesh, vt.); sya·+x̌éc+m+šeš *editor (lit. One whose business is to prepare (for something)).* (syaaqhetsmshesh, n.); ac+x̌ec+núm'+t *to be clothed, dressed.* (atsqhetsnu'mt (lit. He is clothed), adj.); x̌ec+núm'+n *attire, clothing, costume, dress.* (qhetsnu'mn,

n.); ʔapɬ+n+x̌ec+núm'+n *clothier.*
(apɬnqhetsnu'mn (lit. One who has a
clothing store), n.); // x̌ec+u·t=íw'es
They went together. (qhetsuuti'wes,
vi.); s+n+x̌éc+t=us *advocate, ally.*
(snqhetstus, n.); ‡ hn+x̌ec+t=
ús-nt-se-s *behalf.* (hnqhetstusntses
(lit. He acted in my behalf), n.); §
kʷan+ɬ+x̌ec+núm'+n *clothes (h/s took
along...), took (h/s...along clothes).*
(kwanɬqhetsnu'mn, n, vt.)

√x̌c₃ † x̌ic *raise (one's hand), threaten.*
(qhits (stem), vt.); s+n+x̌íc+m *bluff.*
(snqhitsm (lit. a feint), n.); ‡
hn+x̌íc-nt-s *bluff.* (hnqhitsnts (lit. He
intimidated him by a pretended motion
to hit him), vt.)

√x̌c'₁ † x̌ac' *extraordinary, outstanding.*
(qhats' (stem), adj.); x̌ec' *curiosity (to
arouse...), outstanding.* (qhe'ts (stem),
adj.); x̌ác'+x̌ac'+t *admiration (object
of), appealing, dilly, exciting,
extraordinary, fascinating, interesting,
outstanding.* (qhats'qhats't, adj.); //
s+t+x̌ec'+p=us *belvedere.* (stqhets'pus
(lit. viewing something beautiful,
loose- getting an eyeful), n.)

√x̌c'₂ // s+x̌íc'=ul'mxʷ *deforestation,
cutting down trees or slashing of
thickets.* (sqhits'u'lmkhw. grass, n.)

√x̌l₁ † x̌el *bright, clear, light, redhot.*
(qhel (stem), adj.); x̌al *redhot.* (qhal);
u· x̌él *crystal, It is clear (air).* (uuqhel
(lit. transparent), n, vi.); u n+x̌él *clear
(It is...water).* (unqhel, adj, n.); //
s+x̌el'=ús+m *diagnosis.* (sqhe'lusm
(lit. quickly detecting the symptoms of
disease), n.); u y'+t+x̌al+p=ásq'it
clearing (it (sky) is...up again).
(u'ytqhalpasq'it, vi.); ‡ x̌el=ú·s-tu-s
*recognized, spotted (He...him
immediately).* (qheluuustus, vt.); § x̌al
s+gʷarp+m *dandelion.* (qhal
sgwarpm, n.); x̌al+hn+nak'ʷá?=all'qs
ha s+gʷárp+m *daisy.*
(qhalhnnak'wa'al'lqs ha sgwarpm, n.)

√x̌l₂ † x̌el *lay (side by side as lumber).*
(qhel (stem), vt.); // hn+x̌el=íw'es
bridge, deck, trestle. (hnqheli'wes (lit.
boards set side by side over waterway
or other obstacle), n.); hn+x̌el=
íw'es+n *bridge.* (hnqheli'wesn (lit.
means of making a bridge), n.);
čat+x̌el=ílup+n *floor.* (chatqhelilupn,
n.)

√x̌lxʷ † x̌élexʷ *tooth, cog.* (qhelekhw,
n.); ul+x̌élexʷ *dental.* (ulqhelekhw (lit.
pertaining to the teeth), adj.);
x̌ál+x̌alexʷ *teeth.* (qhalqhalekhw,
pl.n.); hn+x̌elíxʷ+n *dentistry, office
(dentist's...).* (hnqhelikhn, n.);
ʔepɬ+n+x̌elíxʷ+n *dentist.*
(epɬnqhelikhwn (lit. One who has a
place for dental surgery), n.); §
s+cil'+eɬ+x̌élexʷ *denture.*
(stsi'leɬqhelekhw (lit. substitute for
teeth), n.); čam'+ʔelu+ɬ+x̌al+x̌elexʷ
toothless. (cha'm'eluɬqhalqhelekhw (lit.
he no longer has his teeth), adj.); č'am'
a+lut x̌ál+x̌alexʷ *toothless, he no
longer has his teeth.* (ch'a'm alut
qhalqhalekhw, adj.);
hn+mey't+e?w+aɬ+[x̌]élexʷ
bucktooth (lit. middle tooth).
(hnme'yte'waɬkhelekhw, n.)

√x̌ɬ₁ † x̌aɬ *to frighten, scare.* (qhaɬ
(stem), vt.); hn+x̌iɬ *be afraid, fear.*
(hnqhiɬ (lit. feel alone inside), v.);
hn+x̌áɬ+x̌a[ɬ]+n' *deterrent.*
(hnqhaɬqhal'n (lit. means of
discouraging by fear), n.);
hn+x̌aɬ+x̌e·ɬ+úl *caitiff,
chicken-hearted, coward, craven,
dastard(ly), pusillanimous.*
(hnqhaɬqheeɬul (lit. He is given to
fear), n.); hn+x̌eɬ+x̌e·ɬ+ul *afraid,
cowardly, fearful (habitually).*
(hnqheɬqheeɬul, adj.); in+x̌íɬ *afraid,
chicken, frightened.* (inqhiɬ, adj.);
s+n+x̌íɬ *fear (to...), fear, fearing,
fright, phobia.* (snqhiɬ, vt, n.);
s+n+x̌eɬ+x̌e·ɬ+úl *cowardice.*

(snqhełqheeḻul (lit. lack of courage, fearfulness), n.); s+n+x̌áł+x̌ał+m' *bug-bear*. (snqhaḻqhaľm (lit. an object of obsessive dread; the act of scaring), n.); ‡ hn+x̌áł+x̌ał-n't-m' *deter, hindered, daunt*. (hnqhaḻqhaľnt'm (lit. He was thoroughly frightened), vt.); hn+x̌íł+m-nt-s *feared (he...him)*. (hnqhiḻmnts, vt.); § elu+s+n+x̌íł *brave, daring, dauntless, courageous*. (elusnqhiḻ (lit. He has no fear), adj.); x̌eł+s+čs+n+ˤél'+l'=ep *claustrophobia*. (qhełschsn(ḙľlep (lit. fear of being confined), n.); lut hey'+s+n+x̌íł+s *courage*. (lut he'ysnqhiḻs (lit. He has no fear), n.); lut hay'+[s]+n+x̌íł+s *bravery*. (lut ha'ynqhiḻs (lit. He has no fear), n.); lut hay'p+s+n+x̌íł-s *to be brave, courageous, fearless (lit. He has no fear)*. (lut ha'ypsnqhiḻs, vi.)

√x̌ł₂ † x̌íł *to abandon, desert, leave*. (qhił (stem), vt.); x̌eł+t *whipped (He was...)*. (qhełt, vt.); s+x̌íł+n *damnation*. (sqhiłn, n.); s+x̌i[ł]+n *abandonment*. (sqhiln, n.); a+can+x̌íł *destroyed (to be...)*. (atsanqhiḻ (lit. It is abandoned from under), vi.); s+x̌íł+emn *devil*. (sqhiłemn (lit. one who is abandoned), n.); ul+s+x̌íł+emn *demoniac, demonial*. (ulsqhiłemn (lit. one belonging to the devil), adj.); hn+x̌íł+en+n *place for abandoned things or junk*. (hnqhiḻenn, n.); x̌eł+eł+útm *damnable*. (qhełełḙtm (lit. He is [deserving] to be eternally punished), adj.); x̌íł+el+ncút *abandoned (He...his offspring)*. (qhiḻelntsḙt, vt, n.); s+can+x̌íł+ł *blight*. (stsanqhiḻł (lit. becoming abandoned beneath the surface), n.); s+can+x̌íł+m *abolish, annihilation, destruction*. (stsanqhiḻm (lit. to abandon from under), n.); s+can+x̌íł+n *condemnation*. (stsanqhiḻn, n.); čas‿can+x̌íł+m-s *abolish, wipe out, destroy, eliminate*. (chastsanqhiḻms. (lit. he is going to destroy it), vt.); ∥ s+x̌íł=s+m *frown, scowl (lit. leaving face)*. (sqhiłsm, vi.); s+x̌íł=č+mn *(?)cession, surrendering (lit. letting go with the hand)*. (sqhiłchmn, n); ‡ x̌íł-t-s *He abandoned him*. (qhiłts, vt.); cen+x̌íł-t-s *annihilate, destroy (lit. he abandoned it from under; he destroyed it completely)*. (tsenqhiḻts, vt.); can+x̌íł-t-s *decimate, destroy, annihilate*. (tsenqhiḻts (lit. He abandoned/deserted it from under; he destroyed it completely), vt.); can+x̌íł-t-m *condemn*. (tsanqhiłtm (lit. He was forsaken from under), vi.); x̌íł=čt+m-nt-s *relinquish, cede*. (qhiłchtmnts. (lit. He ceased his hold on it), vt.); § can+x̌i[ł]+ł+xʷél+xʷl+t *condone*. (tsanqhiłłkhwelkhwlt (lit. He abandoned another's debt to himself), vt.); u+x̌ʷal'+a s+x̌íł+emn *diabolic*. (uqhwa'lasqhiłemn (lit. He is like the devil; he is outrageously wicked), adj.); s+x̌íł+ł+yʔíłn *feast*. (sqhiłł'yiḻn (lit. throwing food away), n.); s+x̌íł+s+yʔíłn *potlatch*. (sqhiłs'yiḻn. giving away food, n.)

√x̌ł₃ † s+x̌ʔoł+alyóʔ *Smoke Mountain (located west of DeSmet)*.(Sqh'ołalyọ, n.)

√x̌m₁ † x̌em *cumbersome, important, heavy*. (qhem (lit. It is heavy/cumbersome), adj.); s+x̌em *avoirdupois, heaviness, importance, weight*. (sqhem, n.); ∥ x̌em=íčn' *weighed down (He was...)*. (qhemich'n, vt.); § x̌amá+[c]'am' *heavy-boned*. (qhamast'a'm (lit. He is heavy as to the bone), adj.); x̌ama+[c]'am' ł dol+dólqʼʷ+t *burly, husky*. (qhamats'a'm ł doldọlq'wt. (lit. He is heavy-boned and strong), adj.); x̌em xʷe šét'+ut *rock (The...is heavy)*,

heavy (The rock is...). (qhem khwe shet̲ut, n, adj.)

√x̌m₂ ‖ x̌em=inč *to like, love.* (qheminch (stem), vt.); x̌em=ínč-s *He loves her, she loves him, love is large in extent, quality, powerful.* (qhem̲inchs, vt.); ac+x̌em=ínč *love, h/s loves.* (atsqheminch. (stem), vt.); s+x̌am=inč *affection, esteem.* (sqhaminch (lit. an attitude to one who has value), n.); s+x̌em=ínč+m *love.* (sqheminchm, n.); s+x̌em=ínč+n *love.* (sqheminchn, n.); hn+x̌am=ínč *like (I...it).* (hnqham̲inch, vt.); hn+x̌em=ínč *love (I...h/h).* (hnqheminch, vt.); hn+x̌em=ínč-lš *love (I...them).* (hnqheminchlsh, vt.); hn+x̌em=í·nč *beloved.* (hnqhemíiinch! (lit. She is my beloved; I love her very much), n.); hn+x̌em=ínč+n *affection, beneficence, love.* (hnqheminchn (lit. means of loving (God), means of attachment), n.); x̌em=enč=íw'es *They loved mutually.* (qhemenchi'wes, vt.); hn+x̌em=enč=íw'es+n *charity.* (hnqhemenchi'wesn (lit. love of one another), n.); x̌am=énč=qi-s *He likes her voice.* (hnqham̲enchqis, vt.); gʷł+n+x̌em=ínč *love (I...them).* (gułnqhem̲inch, vt.); čn‿x̌em=inč *loved.* (chnqheminch (lit. I am loved), vt.); x̌em=ínč-s *love (powerful, large in extent or quality).* (qheminchs. He loves her, she loves him, n.); kʷu‿i-n+x̌em=ínč *I love you (sg.).* (kwnqhem̲inch, vt.); kʷu‿i?-c+x̌em=ínč+m *I am loving you (s).* (kwi'tsqhem̲inchm, v.); hi?c+x̌em=ínč+m *loving (I am...h/h).* (hi'tsqhem̲inchm, vt.); kʷp‿hn+x̌em=ínč *love (I...you (pl)).* (kuphnqhem̲inch, vt.); kʷp‿hi?c+x̌em=ínč+m *loving (I am...you(pl)).* (kuphi'tsqhem̲inchm, vt.); hn-i?‿c+x̌em=ínč+m-lš *I am loving them.* (hi'tsqheminchmlsh, v.);

kʷu‿x̌em=ínč *You (sg) are loved.* (kuqheminch, vi.); čn'‿in+[x̌]em=ínč *love.* (chn'ingheminch. (lit. you (sg.) love me), vt.); čn'‿y'c+x̌em=ínč+m *You (sg.) are loving me.* (chn'i'tsqhem̲inchm, vt.); in-x̌em=ínč *You (sg.) love h/h.* (inqheminch, vt.); hn-i?c+x̌em=ínč+m *You(s) are loving h/h.* (i'tsqheminchm, vt.); i?c+x̌em=ínč+m-lš *You(s) are loving them.* (i'tsqhem̲inchmlsh, vt.); čn‿x̌em=ínč-s *lit. H/s loves me.* (chnqhem̲inchs, vt.); č‿y'c+x̌em=ínč+m-s *H/S is loving me.* (chi'tsqhem̲inchms, vt.); kʷu‿x̌em=ínč-s *H/S loves you (sg).* (kuqhem̲inchs, vt.); kʷu‿y'‿c+x̌em=ínč+m-s *H/s is loving you (sg.).* (ku'ytsqhem̲inchms, v.); i c+x̌em=ínč+m-s *H/s is loving h/h.* (itsqhem̲inchms, vt.); č‿x̌em=ínč *loved.* (chqhem̲inch. We are loved, adj.); kʷup‿x̌em=ínč *You (pl.) are loved.* (kupqheminch, vi.); čn‿x̌em=ínč+m-p *lit. You (pl) love me.* (chnqhem̲inchmp, vt.); čn'‿y'c+x̌em=ínč+m-p *You (pl.) are loving me.* (chn'i'tsqhem̲inchmp, vt.); in-x̌em=ínč-lš *You (pl) love them.* (inqheminchlsh, vt.); x̌em=ínč-lš *They are loved.* (qheminchlsh, vt.); čn‿x̌em=ínč-s-lš *lit. They love me.* (chnqheminchslsh, vt.); č‿y'c+x̌em=ínč+m-s-lš *loving (they are...me).* (chi'tsqhem̲inchmslsh, vt.); x̌em=ínč-s-lš *They love h/h.* (qheminchslsh, vt.); i c+x̌em=ínč+m-s-lš *They are loving h/h.* (itsqhem̲inchmslsh, vt.); kʷup‿x̌em=ínč-s-lš *They love you (pl).* (kupqheminchslsh, vt.); kʷu‿y'c+x̌em=ínč+m-s-lš *They are loving you (pl.).* (ku'ytsqheminchmslsh, v.); ‡ x̌em=ínč-st-m-n *I loved you (sg.).* (qhem̲inchstmn, vt.); ac+x̌em=ínč-st-m-n *I customarily love you*

(sg.). (atsqheminchstmn, vt.); k'ʷ naʔ
x̌em=ínč-st-m-n *I am going to love
you (sg.).* (k'wna'qheminchstmn, vi.);
x̌em=ínč-s-n *I loved h/h.*
(qheminchsn, vt.); ac+x̌em=ínč-s-n *I
love h/h.* (atsqheminchsn, vt.); x̌em=
ínč-s-n *loved (I...h/h).* (qheminchsn,
vt.); k'ʷ naʔ x̌em=ínč-s-n *I am going
to love h/h.* (k'wna'qheminchsn, vi.);
x̌em=ínč-st-ulm-n *I loved you (pl.).*
(qheminchstulmn, vt.); ac+x̌em=
ínč-st-ulm-n *I love you (pl.).*
(atsqheminchstulmn, vt.); k'ʷ naʔ
x̌em=ínč-st-ulm-n *I am going to love
you (pl.).* (k'wna'qheminchstulmn, vi.);
x̌em=ínč-s-n-lš *I loved them.*
(qheminchsnlsh, vt.); ac+x̌em=
ínč-s-n-lš *I love them.*
(atsqheminchsnlsh, vt.); k'ʷ naʔ x̌em=
ínč-s-n-lš *I am going to love them.*
(k'wna'qheminchsnlsh, vi.); x̌em=
ínč-st-me-x̌ʷ *You (sg.) loved me.*
(qheminchstmekhw, vt.); ac+x̌em=
ínč-st-me-x̌ʷ *you (sg.) love me.*
(atsqheminchstmekhw, vt.); k'ʷ naʔ
x̌em=ínč+č-st-me-x̌ʷ *You (sg.) are
going to love me.*
(k'wna'qheminchchstmekhw, vi.);
x̌em=ínč-st-x̌ʷ *You (sg.) loved h/h.*
(qheminchstkhw, vt.); ac+x̌em=
ínč-st-x̌ʷ *you (sg.) love h/h.*
(atsqheminchstkhw, vt.); k'ʷ naʔ
x̌em=ínč-st-x̌ʷ *You (sg.) are going to
love him/her.* (k'wna'qheminchstkhw,
vi.); x̌em=ín-t *H/s is loved.* (qhemint,
vt.); x̌em=ínč-st-me-s *H/s loved me.*
(qheminchstmes , vt.); ac+x̌em=
ínč-st-me-s *H/s customarily loves me.*
(atsqheminchstmes, vt.); k'ʷ naʔ x̌em=
ínč-st-me-s *H/s is going to love me.*
(k'wna'qheminchstmes, vi.); x̌em=
ínč-st-mi-s *H/s loved you (sg.).*
(qheminchstmis, vt.); ac+x̌em=
ínč-st-mi-s *h/s loves you (sg.).*
(atsqheminchstmis, vt.); k'ʷ naʔ x̌em=

ínč-st-mi-s *He/she is going to love
you (sg.).* (k'wna'qheminchstmis, vi.);
x̌em=ínč-stu-s *H/s loved h/h.*
(qheminchstus, vt.); k'ʷ naʔ x̌em=
ínč-stu-s *He/she is going to love him/
her.* (k'wna'qheminchstus, vi.); x̌em=
ínč-st-mel-p *You (pl.) loved me.*
(qheminchstmelp, vt.); ac+x̌em=
ínč-s-mel-p *you (pl.) love me.*
(atsqheminchsmelp, vt.); k'ʷ naʔ
x̌em=ínč-st-mel-p *You (pl.) are going
to love me.* (k'wna'qheminchstmelp,
vi.); x̌em=ínč-st-x̌ʷ-lš *You (pl.) loved
them.* (qheminchstkhwlsh, vt..);
ac+x̌em=ínč-st-x̌ʷ-lš *you (pl.) love
them.* (atsqheminchstkhwlsh, vt.); k'ʷ
naʔ x̌em=ínč-st-x̌ʷ-lš *You (pl.) are
going to love them.*
(k'wna'qheminchstkhwlsh, vi.); x̌em=
ínč-st-me-s-lš *They loved me.*
(qheminchstmeslsh, vt.); ac+x̌em=
ínč-st-me-s-lš *they love me.*
(atsqheminchstmeslsh, vt.); k'ʷnaʔ
x̌em=ínč-st-me-s-lš *They are going to
love me.* (k'wna'qheminchstmeslsh,
vi.); x̌em=ínč-stu-s-lš *They loved h/h.*
(qheminchstuslsh, vt.); ac+x̌em=
ínč-stu-s-lš *they love h/h.*
(atsqheminchstuslsh, vt.); k'ʷ naʔ
x̌em=ínč-stu-s-lš *They are going to
love him/her.* (k'wna'qheminchstuslsh,
vi.); x̌em=ínč-st-m-s-lš *They loved
you (pl.).* (qheminchstmslsh, vt.);
ac+x̌em=ínč-st-ulmi-s *they love you
(pl.).* (atsqheminchstulmis, vt.); k'ʷ
naʔ x̌em=ínč-st-ulmi-s-lš *They are
going to love you (pl.).*
(k'wna'qheminchstulmislsh, vi.); §
[naʔ]x̌íɫ meʔ k'ʷu‿n+x̌m=ínč *I may
love you (sg.).* (qhiɫme'kwnqheminch,
vt.); na+[ʔ]x̌íɫ hn+x̌em=ínč *love
(Maybe I...h/h).* (naqhiɫ hnqheminch,
vt.); na+ʔx̌íɫ k'ʷp‿hn+x̌em=ínč *love
(Maybe I...you (pl.).* (na'qhiɫ
kuphnqheminch, vt.); na+ʔx̌íɫ

hn+x̌em=ínč-lš *love (Maybe I...them)*. (na'qhił hnqheminchlsh, vt.); na+ʔx̌íł čn'‿in+x̌em=ínč *love (You (sg.) maybe...me)*. (na'qhił chn'inqheminch, vt.); na+ʔx̌íł in+x̌em=ínč *love (Maybe you (sg.)...h/h)*. (na'qhił inqheminch, vt.); na+ʔx̌íł in+x̌em=ínč-lš *love (Maybe you (sg.)...them)*. (na'qhił inqheminchlsh, vt.); na+ʔx̌íł čn‿x̌em=ínč-s *love (H/s maybe...me)*. (na'qhił chnqheminchs, vt.); na+ʔx̌íł x̌em=ínč-s *loves (maybe h/s...h/h)*. (na'qhił qheminchs, vt.); na+ʔx̌íł čn‿x̌em=inč+m-p *love (You (pl.) maybe...me)*. (na'qhił chnqheminchmp, vt.); na+ʔx̌íł čn‿x̌em=ínč-s-lš *love (They may...me)*. (na'qhił chnqheminchslsh, vt.); na+ʔx̌íł x̌em=ínč-s-lš *love (Maybe they...h/h)*. (na'qhił qheminchslsh, vt.); x̌em=enč+es+čínt *Indian-lover*. (qhemencheschint (lit. one who loves Indians), n.); x̌em=enč+eł+q'ey'+mín+n *bibliophile, bookish, bookworm, scholar, studious*. (qhemenchełq'e'yminn. (lit. He is fond of books), adj.); hn+x̌em=ínč+n ha q'ey'+mín+n *billet-doux, love-letter*. (hnqheminchn ha q'e'yminn (lit. a letter that is the means of loving), n.); x̌am=anč+ł+qʷám+qʷam+t *aesthete*. (qhamanchłqwamqwamt (lit. He loves beautiful things), n.); čn‿x̌e[m]=[en]č [ł] s+wiʔ+núm+t=mš *aesthete, connoisseur*. (chnqhencht swi'numtmsh (lit. I love beautiful persons), n.); u+t'+t'íd+m' ha n+x̌em=ínč+n *false love*. (ut't'id'm hanqheminchn (lit. love that is brittle (term of old-time Coeur d'Alenes'), n.); elu+s+x̌em=ínč e s+čin[t]+coc *Anglophobe*. (elusqheminch e Schntsots, n.); s+meyes+x̌em=enč+es+čínt *devotion*. (smeyesqhemencheschint (lit. having a more ardent love for a person), n.)

√x̌m₃ † x̌eme+ncot+n *to leave one's own people, go to live with in-laws*. (qhementsotn, vi.)

√x̌mc † x̌emc *shave*. (qhemts (stem), v.); // x̌emc=us+ncút *He shaved*. (qhemtsusntsut, vt.)

√x̌m'₁ † x̌am' *monster, ghoul*. (qha'm (stem), n.); x̌em' *monster*. (qhe'm (stem), n.)

√x̌m'₂ † x̌em' *bite (to...)*. (qhe'm (stem). animal bite, vt.)

√x̌n' † x̌a+x̌an'+út *nine*. (qhaqha'nut, n.); // x̌a+x̌n'=ósq'it *novena*. (qhaqh'nosq'it (lit. nine days), n.); § ʔupen uł x̌a+x̌an'+út *nineteen*. (upen uł qhaqha'nut, n.); x̌ax̌n'+u·l+ʔúpen' *ninety*. (qhaqh'nuu'lupe'n, n.)

√x̌nwt † s+x̌e·níwt *Chief Moctelme (great, great-grandfather of...)*. (Sqheeniwt, n.)

√x̌p₁ † x̌ep *pile (flat objects)*. (qhep (stem), n.); x̌a+x̌ép *book, tome, volume*. (qhaqhep, n.); x̌á+x̌ep *breviary*. (qhaqhep (lit. little pile of plates (sheets) of paper), n.); s+x̌a+x̌ep *entrails (game animals), the entrails of a deer or other game, near the stomach*. (sqhaqhep, n.); ac+x̌ép *to be accumulated, stacked, placed over another*. (atsqhep, adj.); // čat+x̌ep=iłxʷ+n *roofing, shingle, shingles*. (chatqhepiłkhwn, n.); čat+x̌ep=ilxʷ+n *thatch*. (chatqhepilkhwn, n.)

√x̌p₂ † s+x̌ep=íw'es *a person's double, soul, spirit, energy, second self*. (sqhepi'wes, n.); s+n+x̌ep=íw'es *double (a person's...), soul, spirit*. (snqhepi'wes, n.); § elu+s+n+x̌ep=íw'es *dead, dead (to be...)*. (elusnqhepi'wes (lit. It has no second self, soul), adj.)

√x̌p₃ † x̌ip *to gnaw*. (qhip (stem), vt.)

√x̌pʔ † x̌ípeʔ *grandfather (paternal)*. (qhipe', n.)

√x̌p' † x̌ep' *button, fasten, sew*. (qhep' (stem), vt.); ‡ x̌ép'-nt-s *He buckled,*

fastened, latched, buttoned it.
(qhep'nts, vt.)

√x̌q' † x̌aq' *pay, reward.* (qhaq' (stem),
n.); s+x̌áq'+aq' *award, prize.*
(sqhaq'aq', n.); s+x̌aq'+ncút *tax.*
(sqhaq'ntsut (lit. *paying oneself*), n.);
čas‿x̌áq'+aq' *coupon (lit. pay to be
made).* (chasqhaq'aq', n.);
čas‿x̌aq'+aq'+q *coupon.*
(chasqhaq'aq'q, n.); ∥ x̌aq'=kʷeʔ
*paying in the water. Refers to same
place as Hnseluk: meaning place of
confusion.* (Qha'qkwe'); x̌áq'=kʷeʔ
paying with water. (qhaq'kwe', vt.);
s+x̌áq'=ul'umxʷ *demise.*
(sqhaq'u'lumkhw (lit. *pay for use of
land*), n.); ‡ x̌áq'-nt-s *defray, paid,
supplied.* (qhaq'nts. *He defrayed it,
paid it,* vt.); § s+lu+s+x̌áq'+n
decompensation. (slusqhaq'n (lit.
reversal of recompense), n.)

√x̌s † x̌es *to be good, well.* (qhes
(stem), adj, adv.); u· x̌és *well, fine (he
is...).* (uuqhes, adj.); x̌és+x̌es *good
good.* (qhesqhes, adj.); x̌ás+x̌as *good
good.* (qhasqhas, adj.); x̌es+t *It is
good!.* (qhest!, excl.); x̌es+t *beneficial,
bon voyage, clean-cut, good evening,
good morning, good, goodbye, hello,
wholesome.* (qhest, adj.); x̌e+x̌és+t
benignant. (qheqhest, adj.); hn+x̌és+n
benefit, blessing, boon. (hnqhesn (lit.
condition of being good), n.);
s+x̌eʔs+mín+n *appreciation.*
(sqhe'sminn, n.); x̌és+m+ncut *behave,
deport.* (qhesmntsut. (lit. *He behaved
himself well*), vi.); x̌es+m+ncút+n
bricabrac, ornaments. (qhesmntsutn.
(lit. *means of making oneself good*),
pl.n.); s+x̌es+m+ncút *cleanliness.*
(sqhesmntsut (lit. *habitually dressing
oneself neat and clean*), n.);
s+x̌és+m+ncut *behavior (good...),
demeanor.* (sqhesmntsut, n.);
čn‿x̌es+t *good (lit. I am good).*
(chnqhest, adj.); ni x̌es+t *Is it good?*

(ni qhest? (qu.).); s+niʔ+x̌és+t *H/s is
the best in the crowd, best, elite.*
(sni'qhest. (*he is the...of them*), adj, n.);
cmiʔ+u+čn‿x̌é·s *fine (I was...).*
(tsmi'uchnqheees (lit. *I used to be
fine*), adj.); t'uʔ u+čn‿x̌é·s *fine
(Well, I'm...).* (t'u' uchnqheees, adj.); ∥
x̌as=ál'qs *dapper.* (qhasa'lqs. *He has
neat clothes, he is neatly dressed,* adj.);
x̌ás=iʔqs *moose.* (qhasi'qs (lit. *a good
nose*), n.); t+x̌ás=iʔqs *meal (He had a
good...).* (tqhasi'qs (lit. *He enjoyed
something good with his nose*), n.);
x̌as=ílup *bed (He has a comfortable...)*
(lit. good bedding). (qhasilup, n.);
čat+x̌es=íw'es *plain.* (chatqhesi'wes
(lit. *good middle of surface*), n.);
x̌as+x̌as+t=cin+m *extoll.*
(qhasqhasttsinm (lit. *Say good about*),
vt.); s+x̌as+x̌as+t=cín+m *extolling,
praise (to...), praising.*
(sqhasqhasttsinm, vt.); s+x̌as+x̌as+t=
cín+mn *praising, commendation.*
(sqhasqhasttsinmn, n.); x̌es+x̌es+t=
cn+mí+ncut *boast, brag.*
(qhesqhesttsnmintsut. (lit. *He talked
about himself*), vi.); x̌es=íɬxʷ *house
(He has a good...).* (qhesiɬkhw, n.);
hn+x̌es=ílgʷes *to be amiable, kind,
sociable.* (hnqhesilgwes, adj.);
kʷu‿n+x̌es=ílgʷes *You are
kind-hearted.* (kunqhesilgwes, vi.);
s+n+x̌és=elgʷes *contentment.*
(snqheselgwes (lit. *state of being
contented*), n.); s+n+x̌es=ílgʷes
benevolence. (snqhesilgwes, n.);
s+x̌as+x̌as=ílgʷes *art.*
(sqhasqhasilgwes (lit. *having beautiful
ways of doing things*), n.); un+x̌és=
elgʷes *blithe, content.* (unqheselgwes
(lit. *He is cheerful, etc.*), adj.); x̌es+t=
il'š *cured, recovered.* (qhesti'lsh. (lit.
He became good), vt.); x̌es+t=íl'š *Get
well!.* (qhesti'lsh, (excl.)); x̌es+t=íl'š-s
Get well! (qhesti'lshs (excl.).);
s+x̌es+t=íl'š+m *detoxification.*

(sqhesti̱'lshm (lit. curing of poison or toxins, removing venom by the mere touch of the medicine man), n.); x̌es+t=il'š+útm *healable, curable.* (qhesti'lshu̱tm. It is healable, adj.); x̌es=ul'úmx^w *fertile (land), land (good, fertile, productive), open country, plain, productive (land).* (qhesu'lu̱mkhw, adj.); ec+x̌es+m= íčt+m+n *decorated, ornate, elaborate.* (etsqhesmi̱chtmn, adj.); s+x̌es= íčt+m+n *benefit, treating (...well).* (sqhesi̱chtmn, vi.); k^wu‿n+x̌es= ísč'eyt *You have a beautiful, good voice.* (kunqhesi̱sch'eyt, vt.); s+x̌es= ítk^we? *bouillon, broth, consomme.* (sqhesi̱tkwe' (lit. good water), n.); hn+x̌es=ítk^we? *water (it is good...).* (hnqhesi̱tkwe', n.); s+x̌es+e·y=?íɫn *diet.* (sqhesee'yi̱ɫn (lit. eating correctly), n.); t+x̌as=ásq'it *beautiful, clear, good (The vault of the sky is...).* (tqhasa̱sq'it, adj.); s+t+x̌e?s=ús *belvedere (lit. viewing something beautiful. loose- getting an eyeful).* (stqhe'su̱s, n.); ‡ x̌e?s+mín-n *appreciate, esteem, value.* (qhe'sminn. (lit. I realized the good in something), vt.); x̌és-stu-s *approve.* (qhe̱sstus (lit. He made it good), vt.); x̌es+t=íl'š-s-n *I healed him, I put him into proper condition.* (qhesti̱'lshsn, vt.); x̌as+x̌as+t=cin+mn-n *commend.* (qhasqhasttsinmnn (lit. I represented it as worthy), vt.); na?+x̌es+m= íčt+m-nt-x^w *elaborate.* (na'qhesmi̱chtmntkhw (lit. You manipulate it carefully), v.); § lut+x̌es+t *amoral, immoral.* (lutqhest (lit. It is not good), adj.); lut ha s-x̌es+t-s *It is not good.* (lut ha sqhe̱sts, vi.); x̌as+aɫ+qix^w *aroma, fragrance, scent.* (qhasa̱ɫqikhw. (lit. good odor), n.); tel'+ci?+x̌es+t *better.* (te'ltsi'qhest (lit. Good from that point on), adj.); x̌es+t he s+te·m=ílg^wes

boon. (qhest he steemi̱lgwes (lit. He is good who is a relative), adj.); x̌es= íɫce? x^wa+nɫamqe? *bear meat (...is good).* (qhesi̱ɫtse' khwanɫamqe' (lit. It is good meat that which is bear), n.); x^way'+t+x̌es=ípele? *beneficiary.* (khwa'ytqhesi̱pele' (lit. one who is the recipient of a benefit), n.); č's= cin+m-nt-s x^wa x̌es+t *blasphemy, profanity.* (ch'tsinmnts khwa qhest, n.); ul+ápel(s) ha s+can+x̌as= ítk^we?+s *apple brandy, apple-jack.* (ula̱pel ha stsanqhasi̱tkwe's (lit. good juice from the apple), n.); miyeɫ+t+x̌as=ic'e? *bedizen.* (miyeɫtqhasits'e' (lit. he is dressed too well), n.); tap+s+x̌es+t *is (It...not good).* (tapsqhest (Spokane), vi.); ta?+s+x̌es+t *It is not good (Spokane).* (ta'sqhest, v.); x̌es+t ha c+sét'q+it *day (It is good...).* (qhest ha' tsse̱t'qit, n.); his+k'^wl'+ɫ+x̌ést *deign.* (hisku'lɫqhest (lit. I deem it worthy), vt.); s+k'^wl'+ɫ x̌es+t *deem.* (sk'u'lɫ qhest (lit. It is something considered good), n.); x̌e+ec+méy+stm *celebrated, famous, well-known, celebrity, star.* (qhe etsme̱ystm, adj, n.); čn‿x̌es+e·y+ítš *slept.* (chnqhesee'yi̱tsh (lit. I slept well), vt.); x̌es+eɫ+c'ég^w+t *courtly, refined.* (qheseɫts'e̱gwt. He has nice manners, he is courtly. adj.); x̌es+es+t'íč+t *He rowed without trouble or difficulty.* (qhesest'i̱cht, v.)

√x̌t † x̌et *club.* (qhet (stem), n.); x̌et *to punish.* (qhet (stem), vt.); x̌et+m *beat.* (qhetm, vt.); s+x̌ét+t *chance, disaster, luck (hard...), penalty.* (sqhett (lit. a whipping), n.); x̌at+mín+n *bat.* (qhatmi̱nn (lit. means of clubbing), n.); x̌et+x̌et+m'+úl' *caterpillar.* (qhetqhet'mu̱l (lit. one given to whip whip), n.); x̌at+ncút *ascetic.* (qhatntsu̱t (lit. He whipped himself), n.); s+x̌ét-t-s *punishment (It is his...).*

195

(sqhe̲tts, n.); s+x̌ét+t-et *punishment (It is our...).* (sqhe̲ttet, n.); ∥ x̌at=áp= qn+n *club, black-jack.* (qhatapqnn. (lit. that with which one clubs another), n.); x̌a+x̌t=áp=qn'+n' *club, bludgeon, billy, cudgel.* (qhaqhtapq'n'n. small club, n.); x̌at= qín+n *thrashing machine.* (qhatqinn (lit. means of clubbing the head), n.); s+t+x̌at=qín+n *straw.* (stqhatqinn (lit. what is left after flailing grain), n.); can+x̌ét=cn *batting (He is...).* (tsanqhe̲ttsn, vi.); sya+can+x̌et=cn *batter (baseball).* (syatsanqhettsn (lit. One who hits (the ball), n.); ‡ x̌ét-n *beat (I...him).* (qhe̲tn, vt.); x̌ét-nt-m *castigated, corrected, punished.* (qhe̲tntm. He was castigated, punished (lit. He was whipped), vt.); x̌ét-nt-s *beat, belabor, chastise, whip.* (qhe̲tnts, vt.); x̌at=qín-t-s *belabor, thrash.* (qhatqints. (lit. He beat the head. He thrashed it (grain)), vt.); t+x̌at+x̌at= úps-nt-s *spanked (He...him).* (tqhatqhatupsnts, v.); x̌at=áp=qn-t-s *He clubbed him.* (qhatapqnts, vt.); x̌at+x̌at=[a]p=qn-t-s-lš *clubbed (He...several persons).* (qhatqhatqpqnts, vt.); § gʷiy'+a+s+x̌át=qn *harvest (after...).* (gwi'yasqha̲tqn, n.)

√x̌t'₁ † x̌et' *to gnaw, graze.* (qhet' (stem), vi, vt.); s+x̌ét'+m *corrosion, rot.* (sqhe̲t'm. (lit. gnawing), n.); ∥ x̌at'=úl'mxʷ *He grazed.* (qhat'u̲'lmkhw (lit. He munched on the ground), vi.); ic+x̌et'=úl'umxʷ *browse.* (itsqhet'u̲'lumkhw (lit. It (horse) is grazing), vi.)

√x̌t'₂ [also recorded as √x̌t] † x̌it *corrugated.* (qhit (stem). marked, adj.); x̌it' *marked.* (qhit' (stem). corrugated, adj.); ∥ s+x̌it'+m=šn *breeches, chinos, corduroy, pants, trousers.* (sqhit'mshn, n.)

√x̌w † x̌iw *ashamed, embarrassed, shy, timid.* (qhiw (stem), adj.); x̌íw+t *ashamed (be), blushed, confound, embarrassed (be).* (qhi̲wt. (lit. He was ashamed), vt.); x̌éw+x̌ew+t *derogatory, disparaging, shameful.* (qhewqhewt, adj.); x̌ew+x̌ew+t+úl *bashful, shy, withdrawn.* (qhewqhewtu̲l. (lit. He is habitually ashamed), adj.); s+x̌iw+t *chagrin, decency, embarrassment, humiliation, modesty, shyness.* (sqhiwt, n.); hn+x̌íw+n *disgrace, ignominy.* (hnqhi̲wn (lit. It is a cause of shame), n.); hn+x̌íw+m *disgrace, ignominy (lit. It is a cause of shame).* (hnqhi̲wm, n.); ic+x̌íw+t *ashamed.* (itsqhi̲wt (lit. He is being ashamed), vi.); x̌ew+um+scút *shame, disgrace, dishonor.* (qhewumstsu̲t. (lit. He brought reproach upon himself), vt.); s+x̌ew+um+scút *degradation, disgrace (...oneself).* (sqhewumstsu̲t, n, vt.); s+n+x̌ew+p+ší+cut *compunction.* (snqhewpshi̲tsut (lit. feeling shame of one's experience), n.)

√x̌wt † x̌ewit+x̌awít *swan (white).* (qhewitqhawit, n.)

√x̌w' † x̌iw' *raw (uncooked).* (qhi'w); ac+x̌íw' *crude, raw.* (ats qhi̲'w, vt. (lit. It is raw), adj.); § s+x̌aw'+lu+tx̌ʷe? *camas (raw...).* (sqha'wlutqhwe', n.)

√x̌w'ł † a· x̌íw'ł *today, now, presently.* (aaqhi̲'wł, adv.); ul a· x̌íw'ł *current.* (ul aaqhi̲'wł (lit. belonging to the time now passing), adj.)

√x̌x̌ † ał+x̌áx̌+ax̌ *crow.* (ałqha̲qhaqh, n.)

√x̌y † x̌iy *gray (horse).* (qhiy (stem), adj.); ∥ t+x̌íy=elps *gray horse.* (tqhi̲yelps, n.); § s+x̌ey+l'+s+čí+če? *horse (worn out...), plug.* (sqhey'lschi̲che'. old horse, n.)

√x̌yš † x̌eyiš *revenge.* (qheyish (stem), n.)

√x̌y'₁ † x̌áy'+x̌iy' *large.* (qha̲'yqhi'y (stem), adj.); x̌áy'+x̌i?+t *It is ample,*

big, bulky, gross, huge, large.
(qha̱'yqhi't, adj.); s+x̌ay'+x̌iʔ+t
amplitude, bulk, capacity, volume.
(sqha̱'yqhi't, n.); s+x̌áy'+x̌iy'+m
apotheosis. (sqha̱'yqhi'ym (lit. making
one great), n.); ∥ hn+x̌áy'+x̌iy'=alqs
considerable, costly, dear, road (It is a
wide...), valuable. (hnqha̱'yqhi'yalqs
(lit. It is a wide road), adj.);
s+n+x̌áy'+x̌iy'=alqs costliness, high
price(s). (snqha̱'yqhi'yalqs (lit. bigness
of road), n.); x̌ay'+x̌iʔ+t=ílš It became
enlarged or extended or dilated.
(qha̱'yqhi'ti̱lsh, vt.); s+x̌ay'+x̌iʔ+t=
íl'š+m dilation. (sqha̱'yqhi'ti̱'lshm, n.);
hn+x̌áy'+x̌iʔ=łc'eʔ cannon.
(hnqha̱'yqhi'łts'e' (lit. a gun with a large
interior), n.); x̌ay'+x̌í?=łx̌ʷ building
(big), chateau. (qha̱'yqhi̱'łkhw, n.);
t+x̌áy'+x̌iy'=eʔst big rock, boulder.
(tqha̱'yqhi'ye'st, n.); x̌ay'+x̌í=q[n]' He
has a big head. (qha̱'yqhi̱q'm, vi.);
t+x̌áy'+x̌iy'=us eye (He has a large...),
large flame. (tqha̱'yqhi'yus, n.); ‡
x̌ay'+x̌iʔ+t=íl'š-s-n dilate.
(qha̱'yqhi'ti̱'lshsn. (lit. I enlarged or
widened it in all directions), vt.);
x̌ay'+x̌iy'+t=íl'š-st-m amplify,
augment, enlarge. (qha̱'yqhi'yti̱'lshstm,
vt.); x̌ay'+x̌iy'+t=íl'š-stu-s amplified,
enlarging (He succeeded in...it).
(qha̱'yqhi'yti̱'lshstus, vt.); § x̌áy'+x̌iʔ+t
he t'éde argosy. (qha̱y'qhi't he t'e̱de
(lit. a big canoe), n.); x̌áy'+x̌iʔ+t ha
gʷar=úl'mx̌ʷ+n bulldozer. (qha̱'yqhi't
ha gwaru̱'lmkhwn (lit. big ground
scraper), n.); x̌ay'+x̌iʔ+t ha mo·nkí
ape, gorilla. (qha̱'yqhi't ha moonki̱.
(lit. big monkey), n.); x̌áy'+x̌iʔ+t ha
t+x̌ʷéq'ʷ=ečn' bass viol. (qha̱'yqhi't ha
tqhweq'wech'n. (lit. It is big big what
is a viol (means of pulverizing)), n.);
x̌áy'+x̌iʔ+t ha t+x̌ʷéq'ʷ=ečn' bass viol
(lit. It is big big what is a viol (means
of pulverizing)). (qha̱'yqhi't ha
tkhweq'wech'n, n.); x̌ay'+x̌iʔ+t

ic+puʔ+puʔs=ínč brokenhearted,
mournful. (qha̱'yqhi't itspu'pu'si̱nch.
(lit. He is grievously mourning), adj.);
x̌áy'+x̌iʔ+t hen+cún=meʔ+n school
(It is a big...). (qha̱'yqhi't hentsu̱nme'n,
n.); x̌áy'+x̌iʔ+t he s+n+piy+y=ílgʷes
bliss, ecstasy. (qha̱'yqhi't he
snpiyyi̱lgwes. (lit. great thrilling of the
heart), n.); x̌ay'+x̌iʔ+s+qíl=tč chubby,
buxom. (qha̱'yqhi'sqi̱lch. (lit. She has a
big body), adj.)

√x̌y'₂ † x̌ey' leftovers (food). (qhe'y
(stem), n.)

√x̌ˤ † x̌a[ˤ] fan (to...). (qha (stem), vt.);
s+x̌aˤ+p breeze. (sqha(p, n.);
s+x̌áˤ+ncut air conditioning
(oneself). (sqha(ntsut, vt.)

√x̌ˤgʷ † x̌eˤigʷ perforated. (qhe(igw
(stem), adj.)

√x̌ʔ₁ † hn+x̌áʔ+x̌aʔ+mn sturgeon,
whale. (hnqha̱'qha'mn, n.)

√x̌ʔ₂ ∥ x̌eʔ=úl'mx̌ʷ rattler.
(qhe'u̱'lmkhw, n.)

√x̌ʷc₁ † t+x̌ʷéc+t by-gone, past.
(tqhwe̱tst, adj, n.); ‡ t+x̌ʷéc-nt-s
beyond (He went...him), bypassed
(He...it). (tqhwe̱tsnts, adv.)

√x̌ʷc₂ † s+x̌ʷ+x̌ʷic+eʔ brevity,
concision, shortness. (sqhuqhwitse',
n.); ∥ s+can+x̌ʷ+[x̌]ʷic=cn' bob, a
short haircut on a woman or child.
(stsanqhukhwitsts'n, n.) [xref √xʷc]

√x̌ʷd † x̌ʷad comical, funny, humorous.
(qhwad (stem), adj.); x̌ʷád+x̌ʷad+t He
is comical, funny, humorous.
(qhwa̱dqhwadt, adj.);
s+x̌ʷad+x̌ʷad+m'+scút comedy, to be
humorous, funny.
(sqhwadqhwad'mstsu̱t, adj.);
sya+x̌ʷad+x̌ʷad'+m+scút clown,
buffoon. (syaqhwadqhwad'mstsu̱t (lit.
One who makes himself funny), n.);
sya+x̌ʷa+x̌ʷad+m'+scút comedian.
(syaqhwaqhwad'mstsu̱t (lit. one whose
profession is to make himself
comical), n.); ∥ hn+x̌ʷád+x̌ʷad=cn He

is funny as to the mouth.
(hnqhwadqhwadtsn, vi.); s+x̌ʷa+x̌ʷad=
cn'+m'i+n'cut *funny, humorous,
comical.* (sqhwaqhwadts'n'mi'ntsut (lit.
continually telling jokes), adj.)

√x̌ʷdnt † s+x̌ʷdent *ice cream, ice.*
(sqhudent, n.) [xref √xʷdnt]

√x̌ʷkʼʷ † s+x̌ʷkʼʷ=ilup *sweep.*
(sqhuk'wilup, vt.) [xref √xʷkʼʷ]

√x̌ʷl † s+x̌ʷúʔul *awl, bodkin.* (sqhu'ul,
n.) [for expected √xʷl]

√x̌ʷlʼ † u+x̌ʷel'+e *resembling.*
(uqhwe'le, n.); **§** ux̌ʷel'+é s+n+qʷúl=
enč he s+t'+t'ús *cotton candy.*
(uqhe'le snqulench he st't'us (lit. candy
that resembles cotton), n.); ux̌ʷel'é
č+tuxʷ+mín+n *complementary.*
(uqhwe'le chtukhwminn (lit. like an
addition), n.); u+x̌ʷal'+a č'n'p'=qín'=
čt *annular.* (uqhwa'la ch"np'qi'ncht
(lit. It is like a ring), n.); u+x̌ʷal'+á
čp=qínn *capillary.* (uqhwa'la chpqinn
(lit. It resembles hair), n.); u+x̌ʷal'+a
s+x̌íł+emn *diabolic.*
(uqhwa'lasqhiłemn (lit. He is like the
devil; he is outrageously wicked),
adj.); u+x̌ʷal'+a· gʷáx̌+t=elt *childlike,
humble, innocent (he is...).*
(uqhwa'laagwaqhtelt, adj.);
u+x̌ʷel'+eʔ+líš *like (it is...a mountain).*
(uqhwe'le'lish, vi); u+x̌ʷel'+e+l'íš
mountain (it is like a...). (uqhwe'le'lish,
n.); u+x̌ʷal'+á ml=ól'umxʷ *unrefined,
earthy.* (uqhwa'la mlo'lumkhw (lit. It
resembles the soil), adj.); u+x̌ʷel'+é
ml=qn=úps *aquiline.* (uqhwe'le
mlqnups (lit. like an eagle), n.);
u+x̌ʷel'+e+yc+púʔs *cordate.*
(uqhwe'leytspu's (lit. It is like a heart),
adj.); u+x̌ʷal'+a+n+qʼʷ+qʼʷs+m'í
canine. (uqhwa'lanq'oq'os'mi. (lit. It is
doglike), n.); u+x̌ʷal'+á s+qil=tč
carnation. (uqhwa'la sqiltch (lit. like
the body in color), n.); u+x̌ʷal'+á
qap+qapl'=y'úy'eʔ *desultory.*
(uqhwa'la qapqap'l'yu'ye'. (lit. He is

like a butterfly; he is aimless,
unsettled), adj.); u+x̌ʷal'+á tax̌+táx̌
all-spice. (uqhwa'la taqhtaqh (lit. It is
like pepper), n.);
u+x̌ʷel'+e+tm+tmníʔ *cadaverous,
corpselike.* (uqhwe'letmtmni' (lit. He
looks like a dead body), adj.);
u+x̌ʷel'+é t+tm'íxʷ *bestial, birdlike.*
(uqhwe'le tt'mikhw (lit. It is like an
animal), n.); u+x̌ʷel'+á s+yól=alqʷ
arboreal. (uqhwe'la syolalqw (lit.
resembling a tree), n.); u+x̌ʷal'+á
s+c'am' *bony.* (uqhwa'la sts'a'm (lit. It
is like a bone), adj.); ul s+c'éx̌ʷ+ncut
or u+x̌ʷel'+e *astral.* (ul sts'eqhwntsut
or uqhwe'le (lit. It is like a star), adj.);
u+x̌ʷel'+e kʷ‿kʼʷl'+ncút+n *divine.*
(uqhwe'le kuk'u'lntsutn (lit. You (sg.)
are godlike), adj.); u+x̌ʷal'+á s+t'm'=
ált+mš *bovine.* (uqhwa'la st"maltmsh
(lit. It resembles a cow), n.); u+x̌ʷel'+é
s+t'm=qn=íłxʷ *conical.* (uqhwe'le
st'mqniłkhw (lit. It is shaped like a
tepee), n.)

√x̌ʷl'qʼʷ // hn+čat+x̌ʷl'+x̌ʷl'qʼʷ=íčn
billiards, pool table.
(hnchatqho'lqho'lq'wichn. (lit. place for
rolling things), n.)

√x̌ʷł₁ † x̌ʷał *dart.* (qhwał (stem), n.);
x̌ʷił *dart, to hurry (at something).*
(qhwił (stem), vi.); [see also √x̌ʷt']
x̌ʷł+x̌ʷáł *billy goat.* (qhwłqhwał, n.); **//**
x̌ʷíł=cn *cursory, meal (he had a
quick...).* (qhwiłtsn (lit. He made a
hasty reading (talk), n.)

√x̌ʷł₂ † s+x̌ʷuʔł *mist, smog.* (sqhu'ł, n.)
[xref √xʷł]

√x̌ʷn † x̌ʷen' *to hurry.* (qhwe'n (stem),
vi.); x̌ʷén+t-š *Hurry up!.* (qhwentsh,
(excl.)); čn‿x̌ʷen+t *hurried (I...).*
(chnqhwent, vi.); **//** s+x̌ʷen=itkʷeʔ
rapids, hurrying water. (sqhwenitkwe',
n.); s+x̌ʷe+x̌ʷn'=itkʷeʔ *small brook,
streamlet.* (sqhweqhw'nitkwe', n.
(dim.)); s+x̌ʷ+x̌ʷn'=ítkʷeʔ *brook (lit.
little fresh water stream).*

(sqhuqhw'nitkwe', n.); s+can+x̌ʷen=
ítkʷeʔ *aqueduct*. (stsanqhwenitkwe'
(lit. underground stream), n.)

√x̌ʷny' † s+x̌ʷ+x̌ʷeney' *rice*.
(sqhuqhwene'y, n.) [xref √xʷny']

√x̌ʷn' ‖ s+x̌ʷún'=ič *thornberry*.
(sqhu'nich, n.); s+x̌ʷún'=eč
thornberry. (sqhu'nech, n.);
s+x̌ʷʔ+x̌ʷn'=íč=ełp *thornberry bush*.
(sqhu'qhu'nichełp, n.)

√x̌ʷp † x̌ʷup *careless, inefficient*. (qhup
(stem), adj.); x̌ʷup+t *incapable, unable
(to be), unable*. (qhupt. He is
incapable, adj, vi.); s+x̌ʷup+t
disability, state of being incapable.
(sqhupt, n.); **§** miyeł+x̌ʷp+t *inept (he
is too...)*. (miyełqhupt, adj.)

√x̌ʷq'ʷ₁ † x̌ʷaq'ʷ *ground meal, meal
(ground like corn)*. (qhwaq'w (stem),
n.); x̌ʷáq'ʷ+p *detached, disconnected,
separated (It became...)*. (qhwaq'wp,
vt.); hi·c+x̌ʷéq'ʷ *flour*. (hiitsqhweq'w
(lit. that which is milled), n.);
hiyc+x̌ʷéq'ʷ *bread-stuff*.
(hiytsqhweq'w (lit. that which is
pulverized), n.); **‖** s+x̌ʷq'ʷ+p=iw'es
divorce, separation. (sqhuq'wpi'wes,
n.); t+x̌ʷéq'ʷ=ečn' *calliope (lit. An
organlike musical instrument)*.
(tqhweq'wech'n, n.); **‡** x̌ʷéq'ʷ-nt-s
grate, ground, pulverize. (qhweq'wnts.
He ground it, vt.); x̌ʷáq'ʷ+p+m-stu-s
to analyze. (qhwaq'wpmstus (lit. He
separated it), vt.); **§** x̌áy'+x̌iʔ+t ha
t+x̌ʷéq'ʷ=ečn' *bass viol*. (qha'yqhi't ha
tqhweq'wech'n. (lit. It is big big what
is a viol (means of pulverizing)), n.);
hiyc+x̌ʷéq'ʷ ha s+qil+tč *burger*.
(hiytsqheq'w ha sqiltch (lit. meat that
is ground), n.)

√x̌ʷq'ʷ₂ † i s+x̌[ʷ]óq'ʷ+x̌ʷoq'ʷ+iš *He
was grunting*. (isqhoq'qhoqwish, vi.)

√x̌ʷs † x̌ʷus *to foam (water, beer)*.
(qhus (stem), vi.); x̌ʷus *Rose*. (Qhus
(proper name), n.); s+x̌ʷús+m *foam
berries*. (sqhusm, n.); **‖** hn+x̌ʷús=kʷeʔ

beer, brew, water (foamy...)..
(hnqhuskwe'. (lit. Foaming water), n.);
hn+x̌ʷús=kʷeʔ+n *brewery*.
(hnqhuskwe'n, n.); **§** tax̌+t ha
n+x̌ʷús=kʷeʔ *ale*. (taqht hanqhuskwe'
(lit. (more) bitter beer), n.)

√x̌ʷt₁ † x̌ʷat *to cut (in two)*. (qhwat
(stem), vt.); **‡** can+x̌ʷét-nt-s *curtail*.
(tsanqhwetnts (lit. He cut it off; he cut
it short), vt.); hn+x̌ʷt=ús-nt-m *behead*.
(hnqhwtusntm (lit. He was beheaded),
vi.) [xref √xʷt'₂ and xʷt₁]

√x̌ʷt₂ † x̌ʷát+x̌ʷat *duck*. (qhwatqhwat
(lit. quack quack), n.)

√x̌ʷt' † s+[x̌]ʷt'iʔ *billy goat*. (sqwt'i', n.);
§ ul s+x̌ʷt'+íʔ he č'ím'-is
Capricornus. (ul sqhwt'i'he ch'i'mis
(lit. a horn that belongs to the goat),
n.); t+gʷép=elxʷ ha s+x̌ʷet'+iʔ
Angora. (tgwepelkhw ha sqhwet'i' (lit.
He (the goat) has long hair), n.)

√x̌ʷy₁ ‖ [also recorded as √xʷy and
√x̌y] t+x̌ʷáy=ap *cape, promontory*.
(tqhwayap (lit. A point or head of land
projecting into a sea or other body of
water), n.); t+x̌áy=ap *cape,
promontory (lit. A point or head of
land projecting into a sea or other
body of water)*. (tqhayap, n.); t+xʷéy=
ep *peninsula*. (tkhweyep, n.);
s+t+x̌ʷéy+iy=ep *Lewiston, Idaho*.
(Stqhweyiyep (lit. becoming a
peninsula), n.); s+t+x̌ʷey+y=ep
Lewiston (Idaho). (stqhweyyep (lit.
Becoming a peninsula), n.)

√x̌ʷy₂ ‖ s+x̌ʷiy=iʔłp=mš *Colville Tribe*.
(Sqhwiyi'łpmsh, n.)

√x̌ʷʕʷ † s+x̌ʷéʕʷ+x̌ʷeʕʷ *fox*.
(sqhwe(wqhwe(w, n.)

√yc'₁ † yec' *tight (e.g. a belt or rope)*.
(yet's (stem), adj.); yoc' *tight (e.g. belt
or rope)*. (yots'); yác'+yic'+t *tight (It is
very..., like a nut on a bolt)*. (yats'yits't,
adj.); yóc'+yec'+t *It is very tight, like
a nut on a bolt*. (yots'yets't, v.); yac'+p
clam up. (yats'p (lit. It became

tightened up), vt.); yec[']+óp *tighten (to...suddenly)*. (yetsop (stem), vt.); u yc'+óp *tightened (it suddenly became...)*. (uyts'op, adj.); s+yác'+p *clutch*. (syats'p (lit. that which is tightened), n.); yac'+mn *clamp*. (yats'mn (lit. tightener), n.); yc'+mén· *clamp (lit. tightener)*. (yts'menn, n.); č+yác'+p *fond*. (chyats'p. (lit. H/s became very attached to someone--a home, occupation, etc.), adj.); **//** yc'+p=áw'es *connect*. (yts'pa'wes (lit. They were tightened together), vt.); s+yc'+p=áw'es *connection, tightening together*. (syts'pa'wes, n.); č+yec'+m=šén+n *brake*. (chyets'mshenn. (lit. means of tightening feet (wheels)), vi.); sya+či+yac'+m=šn *brake-man*. (syachiyats'mshn (lit. One who tightens the feet (wheels), n.); ‡ yác'+m-s-n *belay, secured (I...it)*. (yats'msn, vt.)

√yc'₂ † yec'+p *wore (it (metal)...out)*. (yets'p, vi.); s+yéc'+p *attrition, detrition, abrasion*. (syets'p (lit. what is worn out), n.)

√yc'₃ † yuc' *cosmetics (Indian...)*. (yuts' (stem), n.) [also written as √yc in volume 1] yuc *Indian cosmetics*. (yuts)

√yc'p † yic'p+yíc'p *Cheney*. (Yits'pyits'p, n.); t'uʔ+yic'p+iyícp *Cheney (Well, it's...)*. (t'u'yits'piyitsp, n.)

√yh † yih *calm, quiet*. (yih (stem), adj.); s+yíh+ih *March, mild weather*. (syihih, n.); če·+yíh+ih *spring (lit. the beginning of spring again)*. (cheeyihih (lit. the beginning of spring), n.); y'+y'ehe *serene, peaceful*. ('y'yehe, adj.); y'eh+ehí· *quiet*. ('yehehiii! (lit. to remain quiet; said of weather), excl.); yehe+hí·· *quiet (lit. to remain quiet; said of weather)*. (yehehÍ··, excl.); y'+y'eh+ehí· *peaceful, serene*. ('y'yehehiii, adj.); y'i+y'eh+ahí· *allay,*

bland, moderate. ('yi'yehahiii. (lit. It (weather) is in a pacified state), vt, adj.); **//** yeh+m'=stwéxʷ *demobilize*. (yeh'mstwekhw (lit. They made peace), vt.); s+yéh+m'=stwexʷ *appease, armistice, peace treaty*. (syeh'mstwekhw (lit. making peace with others), vi, n.); **§** s+c'ip'al+yóh+m *dole*. (sts'ip'alyohm (lit. dealing out something sparingly), vt.)

√yl₁ **//** s+yól=alqʷ *log, stick, tree*. (syolalqw, n.); niʔ+s+yól=alqʷ *forest*. (ni'syolalqw, n.); s+niʔ+s+yól=alqʷ *backwoods*. (sni'syolalqw (lit. among trees), n.); **§** u+x̌ʷel'+á s+yól=alqʷ *arboreal*. (uqhwe'la syolalqw (lit. resembling a tree), n.)

√yl₂ **//** ec+če·+yéluʔ=cn *bearded, mustached*. (etscheeyelu'tsn, vi. (lit. He has a mustache), adj.)

√ylmxʷ † yilmíxʷ+m *king, leader, potentate, ruler*. (yilmikhum, n.); ylmíxʷ+m *chief, czar, king, leader, president*. (ylmikhum, n.); yl+ylmíxʷ+m *cadre*. (ylylmikhum (lit. group of chiefs, a group of trained personnel forming the nucleus of an organization (tribe)), n.); y'+y'l'm'íxʷ+m' *boss, basilisk, chief's right hand man*. ('y'y'l'mikhum'. (lit. little chief), n.); ul ylmíxʷ+m *kingly, royal*. (ul ylmikhm (lit. belonging to a chief), adj.); s+ylmíxʷ+m *allegiance, authority (of a chief)*. (sylmikhwm, n.); pen'+yilmíxʷ+m *first lady, queen*. (pe'nyilmikhum. (lit. She is the wife of the chief), n.); **§** s+čint+eł+ylmíxʷ+m *bureaucrat, chief (indian...), superintendent*. (schintełylmikhum, n.); s+čint+eł+yilmixʷ+m *Indian chief, agency, agent (Indian), superintendent*. (schintełyilmikhm (lit. Indian chief), n.); ylmíxʷ+m he šémen' *devil, archenemy, Satan*. (ylmikhum he sheme'n. (lit. enemy who is chief), n.); s+nukʷ+yilmíxʷ+m *condominium (lit. fellow chiefs).* (snukwyilmikhum, n.); ylmuxʷ+s+t'i·kʷ+ót=qn *son (oldest).* (ylmukhwst'iik'otqn, n.); ylmixʷ+m a+n+gʷís+ł *the chief who dwells on high.* (ylmikhumangwist, n.)

√yl'xʷ † yél'xʷ *cover (to...with cloth).* (ye'lkhw (stem), vt.); yl'xʷ+mín+n *arras, hanging, tapestry.* (y'lkhuminn, n.); ∥ yl'xʷ=áqs+n *dickey.* (y'lkhwaqsn (lit. a detached shirt front), n.); yl'+yl'xʷ=áqs+n *brassiere.* (y'ly'lkhwaqsn, n.); če+yl'xʷ=iłxʷ+n *awning.* (chey'lkhwiłkhwn, n.); č+yél'+ye[l]'xʷ=al'q=šn *chaps.* (chye'lye'khwa'lqshn. (lit. covering for the legs), n.); č+yél'+yel'xʷ=alq=šn *chaps. (lit. covering for the legs).* (chye'lye'lkhwalqshn, n.); en+yél'+yl'xʷ=us *blindfolded.* (enye'lyl'khus (lit. He was covered as to the eyes), vi.); hn+yl'xʷ=ús+n *curtain (window).* (hny'lkhusn, n.); ni?+yl'xʷ=ús=šn *apron.* (ni'y'lkhusshn (lit. a covering for the lap), n.); č+yl'+yl'xʷ=ós=ax̌n *cape.* (chy'ly'lkhosaqhn. (lit. covering on the shoulders), n.); cen+yl'xʷ=cín+n *bib, dickey.* (tseny'lkhwtsinn (lit. cloth placed under the chin, especially of a child to protect the clothes), n.); s+cen+y'+y'l'[x]ʷ=íl'gʷes *bib, bibs.* (stsen'y'y'lkwi'lgwes, n.); s+če+yl'xʷ= ílup *bedspread, rug.* (schey'lkhwilup (lit. oversheet), n.); hn+y'lxʷ=ínč+n *a wall hanging.* (hny'lkhwinchn, n.); yl'xʷ=ílup+n *carpet, rug.* (y'lkhwilupn, n.) [see also √ʕl'xʷ]

√ym yem *silent, speechless.* (yem (stem), adj.); y'am'+s *close-mouthed, reticent.* ('ya'ms. close-mouthed/ reticent person, adj.); yem-š *shut up!.* (yemsh!, excl.); ∥ s+cen+ym+p+e?s= cín *cold shoulder, cold war, silent treatment.* (stsenympe'tsin, n.);

e+n+yém=ep *eternity, forever.* (enyemep (lit. He left forever. Refers to the hereafter with implication of seeing a new, thrilling aspect of God through all time), adv.)

√ymtt? † s+ymtíte? *butte, Steptoe Butte.* (Symtite', n.)

√ymx̌ʷ? † yámx̌ʷe? *corn husk hat.* (yamqhwe' (used also for picking berries), n.)

√ym' † yim' *encircle, surround.* (yi'm (stem), vt.); s+yím'+m+šeš *con[j]uncture.* (syi'mmshesh (lit. critical time), n.)

√ynp' † yenp' *clamp (to...).* (yenp' (stem), vt.); ∥ hn+ynp'=óps+n *diaper.* (hnynp'opsn (lit. piece of cloth put around a baby's buttocks), n.)

√ynqʷ † yanúqʷ *coil (to...suddenly, e.g. a snake).* (yanuq'w (stem), vi.); yenúqʷ *to coil suddenly (e.g. a snake).* (yenuq'w); a· yánqʷ *coiled, coils.* (aayanq'w (lit. It, e.g. the snake, is in coils), adj, n.); ‡ yánqʷ-nt-m *convolute, encoiled (He was...by a snake).* (yanq'wntm, vi, vt.)

√yp ∥ gʷł yóp+yop=ene? *sorceresses, witches.* (guł yopyopene', n.)

√yp' † yep' *rock, sway (to...).* (yep' (stem), vi.); yép'+yp+iš *rocked, rocking chair.* (yep'ypish. He rocked, vt, n.); y'i+y'ép'+yp'+iš *rocking chair (small).* ('yi'yep'yp'ish, n.)

√yq'₁ † yaq' *to file, sharpen, whet.* (yaq' (stem), vt.)

√yq'₂ † is+yáq'+yaq'+iš *creak.* (isyaq'yaq'ish (lit. He is making rasping sounds), vi.)

√yqʷ † yoqʷ *busy (to...oneself).* (yoqw (stem). to pretend to..., vt.); y'oqʷ *to lie.* ('yoqw (stem), vi.); yuqʷ *to pretend.* (yuqw); yuqʷ+e? *pretend.* (yuqwe' (stem), vi.); s+č'+yóqʷ+n' *calumny, gossip, an object of slander.* (sch'yoqw'n. telling lies about others, n.); y'oqʷ+n'cút *lie.* ('yoqw'ntsut (lit.

He lied), vi.); s+y'óqʷ+ncut *telling a lie*. (s'yoqwntsut, n.);
y'oqʷ+y'oqʷ+n'cu·t+úl' *liar (He is a habitual...)*. ('yoqw'yoqw'ntsuutu'l, n.);
y'oqʷ-š *lying*. ('yoqwsh. You are telling a lie. I don't believe you, vi.); ∥
y'óqʷ=cn *belie*. ('yoqtsn, vt.);
hn+y'oqʷ=cn *H/S misrepresented the words of somebody else, belie*. (hn'yoqwtsn, vt.); hn+y'óq[ʷ]+p=al'qs *He told a false story*. (hn'yoqpa'lqs, vt.); s+n+y'óqʷ+p=al'qs *canard*. (sn'yoqwpa'lqs (lit. telling a false or unfound story), n.); ‡ hn+y'oqʷ=cn'-n' *distort*. (hn'yoqwts'n'n (lit. I turned his words from their true meaning), vt.); č+y'óqʷ-n't-s *calumniate, lie, slander*. (ch'yoqw'nts. (lit. He spoke falsely and maliciously of him, he told lies to him, he slandered him), vt.); č+y'óqʷ+p-n't-m' *defame, slander*. (ch'yoqwp'nt'm. defame. (lit. False things were said about h/h), vt.); §
yuqʷ+e?+y+?íłn *pretended (H/s...to eat)*. (yuqwe''yiłn, vi.); yuqʷ+e?+y+?ítš *pretended (H/s...to sleep)*. (yuqwe''yitsh, vi.); yoqʷ+e?+s+k'ʷúl' *counterfeit, fake, pretend*. (yoqwe'sk'u'l, (lit. He pretended to work), vt.); yuqʷ+e?+ł+t'íc'+m *pretended (She...to iron)*. (yuqwe'łt'its'm, vi.); yuqʷ+e?+s+t'íc'+m *She pretended to iron*. (yuqwe'st'its'm, v.); yuqʷ+e?+s+čá(=)stq *She pretended (to go) digging roots*. (yuqwe'schastq, v.); yuqʷ+e?+s+xʷúy *He feigned to go there*. (yuqwe'skhuy, vt.)

√yr₁ † yar *roll (to...a hooplike object)*. (yar (stem), vt.); u· yár *circle, circular (it is...)*. (uuyar, n, adj.); yár+ncut *moon (full...)*. (yarntsut (lit. It made itself round), n.); s+yar+ncut *full moon*. (syarntsut, n.); y'i+y'ér+y'ey+s *wagon (small)*. ('yi'yer'yeys. cart, n.) [see also √yrp, √yrp']

√yr₂ § ul a·yár ha y+ne+?kʷún+am-is *will (it is the...of all)*. (ulaayar hayne' kunamis, n.) [xref √yˤ₁]

√yrk'ʷ † yark'ʷ *crooked, curved*. (yark'w (stem), adj.); a·+yárk'ʷ *crook, curve, deviator, shyster*. (aayark'w (lit. that which (he who) deviates from straightness in a continuous fashion), n.); s+yárk'ʷ+m *curving*. (syark'um, adj.); s+yár+ark'ʷ *curvature*. (syarark'w (lit. Measure of curving), n.); ∥ yar+yark'ʷ=íčt+m *bent (He...his fingers)* (yaryark'wichtm, vt, n.); yer+yerk'ʷ=á?x̌n+m *bent (He...his arms)*. (yeryerk'wa'qhnm, n, vt.); č+yér+yerk'ʷ=alq=šn *bowlegged*. (chyeryerk'walqshn. (lit. legs that curve outward at the knees), adj.); č+yér+yerk'ʷ=alq=šn+m *He bent his legs outward*. (chyeryerk'walqshnm); ‡ yárk'ʷ+m-s-n *crook*. (yark'umsn (lit. I bent it), n.); yárk'ʷ+m-st-m *bent, curved*. (yark'umstm. It was bent/curved, adj.)

√yrp † yarp *rolled (It (circle)...), wheeled*. (yarp. h/s went away by wagon, car, etc, vi, vt.); yér+yerp *carriage, wagon*. (yeryerp. (lit. wheel wheel), n.); y'i+y'ér+y'erp *cart*. ('yi'yer'yerp. small wagon, n.); č+yárp+n *axis, axle*. (chyarpn. (lit. something on which something turns (wheels)), n.); ul č+yárp+n *axial*. (ul chyarpn, n.); i· yárp *travelling (He is in the act of...in a wagon), wagon (He is in the act of travelling in a...)*. (iiyarp, vi, n.); ∥ č+yarp=šn *cartwheel*. (chyarpshn, n.); [see also √yr, √yrp']

√yrp' † yarp' *hoop*. (yarp'. circle, n.); yarp' *to lie (e.g. a hoop)*. (yarp' (stem), vi.); a· yárp' *tire, arc, arch, hoop*. (aayarp' (lying on the ground), n.); yearp' *circle*. (yearp'. hoop, n.); y'+y'ar'p' *circlet*. ('y'ya'rp', n.); ∥ yarp'=qin+m *coronation*. (yarp'qinm

(lit. putting a crown on the head), n.);
si+yarp'=qín+m *coronation (lit.
putting a crown on the head)*.
(siyarp'qinm, n.); can+yarp'=áx̌n
cirro-stratus. (tsanyarp'a̱qhn (lit. It (the
moon) has a circle around its armpits),
n.); ‡ yarp'=qín-t-m *crown, he was
crowned*. (yarp'qintm, n. and vt.); [see
also √yr, √yrp]

√ytkʷ † yetkʷ *decay, decompose,
putrify, rot*. (yetkw (stem), vt, vi.);
s+yétkʷ *decadence, growing rotten*.
(sye̱tkw, n.); i·+yétkʷ *decadent*.
(iiye̱tkw (lit. It is decaying), adj.)

√yt' † yit' *stir (as mush)*. (yit', n, vt.); ‡
hn+yít'-n *stirred (I...the coffee, tea,
etc.)*. (hnyi̱t'n, vt.)

√yw † s+yéw+n *compliment*. (sye̱wn
(lit. praising, admiration), n.); ∥
i·+yew=ł[w]c'e? *complimentary*.
(iiyewłwts'e' (lit. He is praising), adj.)

√yx̌ʷm ∥ yuxʷm=ús *cold, freezing,
frigid (It is very...)*. (yukhumu̱s, adj.);
[also recorded as √yk̓ʷm]
s+yukʷk̓ʷm=ús+m=ul'mx̌ʷ *Aleut*.
(syukkwmu̱smu'lmkhw. (lit. One who
lives in a cold country), n.); s+yuxʷm=
ús+m=ul'umx̌ʷ *North, cold land
(Alaska)*. (syukhwmu̱smu'lumkhw, n.);
ul s+yuxʷm=ús+m=ul'mx̌ʷ *boreal*. (ul
syukhwmu̱smu'lmkhw (lit. pertaining
to a cold country), adj.); § hn+łáp=
alqs he s+yuxʷm=ús+m=ul'umx̌ʷ
North Pole, arctic. (hnła̱palqs he
syukhwmu̱smu'lumkhw. (lit. the most
cold land), n.); x̌ʷł+n+łá?p=alqs he
s+yuxʷm=ús+m=ul'umx̌ʷ *arctic*.
(khułnła̱'palqs he
syukhwmu̱smu'lumkhw. (lit. the most
cold land), n.); ul s+yuxʷm=ús+m=
ul'mx̌ʷ he c'i? *caribou*. (ul
syukhmu̱smu'lmkhw he ts'i' (lit. deer
of a cold country), n.); teč+n+peste?=
us ha yukʷk̓ʷm=ús+m=ul'umx̌ʷ
antarctic. (technpeste'us ha
yukkwmu̱smu'lumkhw, n.)

√yx̌ ∥ yax̌+yax̌+út=šn *badger (lit.
sound of scratching feet)*.
(yaqhyaqhu̱tshn, n.)

√yˤ₁ † yaˤ *assemble, crowd, gather*.
(ya̱((stem), vi.); a· yáˤ *all, everyone,
sum, total*. (aaya̱) (lit. all of them), n.);
a· yaˤ' *all*. (aaya'), adj.); a y'áˤ
collective. (a'ya̱((lit. by all, adj.);
yáˤ+aˤ *assemble, congregate*. (ya̱)a).
(lit. They gathered together in a
group), vt.); yáˤ'+aˤ' *assemble,
congregate*. (ya̱')a'). (lit. They gathered
together in a group), vt.); yáˤ+aˤ+m
convene, gather, meet. (ya̱)a)m. (lit.
They came together), vt.); ul a· yaˤ
worldwide, catholic, cosmic, universal.
(ul aaya̱) (lit. It belongs to all,
common, ecuminical), adj.); a· yáˤ ul
a· yáˤ *communism*. (aaya̱) ul aaya) (lit.
all for all), n.); s+yáˤ+aˤ *banquet,
convocation, getting together,
memorial dinner, potlatch dinner*.
(sya̱(a(, n.); s+yáˤ+aˤ+m *to amass,
collection, gathering together*.
(sya̱(a(m, v, n.); s+n+yáˤ+aˤ *getting
together indoors; an appointed
meeting for discussing some topic*.
(snya̱)a), v.); ∥ yáˤ'+p=qin' *to abound*.
('ya̱(pqi'n (stem), vi.); y'aˤ'+p=qín'
canaille, masses (the...). ('ya̱(pqi'n.
(lit. They are many), pl.n.); y'aˤ'+p=
qín'+m' *crowd, mob*. ('ya̱(pqi̱'n'm. (lit.
They gathered in numbers to
celebrate), vi.); s+y'aˤ'+p=qín'+m'
celebration, big crowd. (s'ya̱(pqi̱'n'm,
n.); ‡ yáˤ+m-s-n *collected (I...them),
gather*. (ya̱)msn, vt.); yaˤ'+m-stu-s
assemble, gather, meet. (ya̱('mstus,
vi.); § miyał+y'aˤ'+p=qin' *congest,
crowded*. (miyał'ya̱('pqi'n (lit. there are
too many heads), vt.); miyał+yaˤ+p=
qin' *congest, crowded (lit. there are
too many heads)*. (miyałya̱(pqi'n, vt.);
ul a+yáˤ gʷł páx̌+pax̌+t *All Saints
Day*. (Ul aya̱(Guł pa̱qhpaqht (lit. belonging to all the wise), n.); a·+yaˤ

čic+xʷúy *came (they all...)*. (aaya) chitskhuy (lit. They all came), vi.); a·+yaˤ'+ec+k'ʷl'-stu-s *almighty, omnipotent*. (aaya')etsk'u'lstus (lit. one who makes all things), adj.) [see also √yr₂]

√yˤ₂ † yaˤ *hesitant, shy, timid, uncertain*. (ya((stem), adj.); yaˤ *lack, need*. (ya((stem), vt.); s+yaˤ+t *deficiency, necessity, need*. (sya(t, n.); yaˤ'+yaˤ'+aʔ+úl *bashful, shy*. (ya')ya')a'ul. (lit. He is habitually shy), adj.); ‡ yaˤ'+t+mí-nt-s *needed, required*. (ya'(tmints. He needed/required it, vt.)

√yˤgʷ † yeˤʷpiy'ígʷ+t *able, capable, dependable, virtuous*. (ye(wpi'yigwt (stem), adj.); yˤʷ+piy'ígʷ+t *He is competent, qualified*. (y(wpi'yigwt, adj.); yuˤʷpiy'ígʷ+t *conscientious, virtuous*. (yu(wpi'yigwt. (lit. He is influenced or regulated by conscience), adj.); s+yˤʷpiy'ígʷ+t *ability, capability, competence, efficiency, virtue, quality of being competent*. (sy(wpi'yigwt, n.); kʷ‿yˤʷpiy'ígʷ+t *efficient*. (kuy(wpi'yigwt (lit. You (sg) are able to produce desired effects or results), adj.)

√yʔ † ye·ʔ *to procure game supplies*. (yee')

√yʔqmʔ † yaʔáqmeʔ *Yakima*. (Ya'aqme', n.)

√yžp † eyžíp *Egypt*. (Eyzhip, n.)

√y'd ∥ y'id=čt *to avenge*. ('yidcht, vt.); y'id=cn *antonym, comeback, retort*. ('yidtsn. (lit. presenting a counter-argument, using words of a sense opposite to that of other words), n.) [xref √ʔd]

√y'kʷʔ † y'ukʷeʔ *sister (a woman's older...)*. ('yukwe', n.); č'+y'úkʷeʔ *brother*. (ch"yukwe' (lit. a woman's younger brother), n.)

√y'l ∥ y'al=stq *summer*. ('yalstq, n.)

√y'lns † y'élens *wood pitch, asphalt*. ('yelens, n.)

√y'r' ∥ hn+y'arˤ=íp *back yard, house (rear of...)*. (hn'ya'rip, n.)

√y'x̌ † ay'x̌ *crab, oyster, bluepoint (a type of oyster)*. (a'yqh, n.)

√ˤc † ˤec *to tie*. ((ets); ac+ˤéc *He is tied*. (ats(ets, vi.); ˤec+mín+n *chord, cord, string*. ((etsminn (lit. that which ties), n.); ∥ ˤec=íčn *bow, bowstring*. ((etsichn (lit. something tied in the rear), n.); ˤec=ičn' *bow*. ((etsich'n (lit. that which is tied in back), n.); hn+ˤac=álpqʷ+n *bridle*. (hn(atsalpqwn. (lit. mouth tier, means of tying inner mouth), n.); hn+ˤac+ˤac=ineʔ *earrings (to wear...), an Italian, Italians, Pend Oreille, Idaho (lit. H/s is wearing earrings)*. (hn(ats(atsine' (lit. people with earrings), n.); hn+ˤec+ˤac=íneʔ *Italians*. (Hn(ats(atsine', n.); s+ˤec=íw'es+m *astringent*. (s(etsi'wesm (lit. tying together), n.); t+ˤec=íw'es *Sunday (lit. flag day)*. (T(etsi'wes, n.); s+t+ˤec=íw'es *bunting, flag, banner, Sunday flag*. (st(etsi'wes (lit. tied on a pole). Sunday, n.); čat+ˤac=ilxʷ *tie*. (chat(atsilkhw, v.); čat+ˤac=ilxʷ+n *bind, tie*. (chat(atsilkhwn, v.); ˤac=alp'q+n *curb*. ((atsalp'qn (lit. a strap serving in conjunction with the bit to restrain a horse), n.); ˤac=áplaʔ=qn *curb (lit. a strap serving in conjunction with the bit to restrain the horse)*. ((atsapla'qn, n.); ˤac+áp=al'qs+n *cincture, girdle*. ((atsapa'lqsn (lit. a cord for tying clothes around the body), n.); ‡ ˤec-nt-s *He tied him up; he lassoed the horse*. ((etsnts, vi.); § ˤec+el'+s+čí+čeʔ+n *rope*. ((etse'lschiche'n (lit. the means of lassoing a horse), n.); hn+ˤac+ˤac+el'+s+čí+čeʔ+n *corral*. (hn(ats(atse'lschiche'n. (lit. enclosure for lassoing horses), n.);

hn+ˤec+el'+s+čí+čeʔ+n *hitching post.* (hn(etse'lschiche"n, n.); wl+wlím ha ˤec+el'+s+čí+čeʔ+n *cable.* (wlwlim ha (etse'lschiche'n (lit. metal what is a rope), n.);

√ˤc'₁ † ˤe[c]' *exhausted, worn out.* ((eɬs' (stem), adj.)

√ˤc'₂ † ˤic' *persistent, tenacious.* ((it's (stem), adj.)

√ˤc'xʷ † ˤéc'xʷ *to be hungry (...for meat), tired.* ((ets'khw (stem), adj.); ‖ hn+t+ˤec'xʷ=ílgʷes+n *antipasto, appetizer, hors d'oeuvres.* (hnt(et'skhwilgwesn (lit. means of stimulating the appetite), n.)

√ˤd † ˤid *glowing, redhot.* ((id (stem), adj.)

√ˤgʷ † ˤigʷ *to throw (...many objects).* ((igw (stem), vt.); ‡ ˤígʷ-nt-s *bestrew.* ((igwnts (lit. He threw them about), vt.)

√ˤhm † t+ˤehím *to give a warhoop, yell.* (t(ehim (stem), vi.) [see also √ˤʷh]

√ˤhn † s+ˤíhn+t *goose.* (s(ihnt, n.)

√ˤl † s+ˤel+p *demerit.* (s(elp (lit. loss (of merit)), n.); ‡ ˤel+p+mí-nt-s *confiscate.* ((elpmints (lit. He forfeited it (to public use)), vt.)

√ˤl' † ˤel' *block, obstruct, fence, curtain.* ((e'l (stem), vt.); a+can+ˤél' *booth, gazebo, stand.* (atsan(e'l (lit. That which is closed in), n.); can+ˤel'+mín+n *fence, bulwark.* (tsan(e'lminn (lit. means of fencing in), n.); ‖ an+ˤél'=us *closed (the window is...).* (an(e'lus, vi.); a+čat+ˤel'=íneʔ *cover.* (achat(e'line'. (stem), vt.); an+ˤel'=íw'es *divided, partitioned.* (an'(e'li'wes, adj.); hn+ˤel'=íw'es+n *diaphragm.* (hn(e'li'wesn. (lit. partition or septum), n.); čat+ˤel'=íneʔ+n *disguise, cover, something that conceals or disguises.* (chat(e'line'n, n.); čs+n+ˤél'+l'=ep *closed.* (chsn(e'l'lep (lit. It (door) was

(became) closed), adj.); a+čs+n+ˤél'= ep *closed.* (achsn(e'lep (lit. The door, gate is closed), adj.); s+čs+n+ˤél'=ep *closure.* (schsn(e'lep (lit. act of closing door), n.); čat+ˤel'=eneʔ+ncút+š *cover yourself.* (chat(e'lene'ntsutsh, imper.); čat+ˤel'=eneʔ+encut+ul *cover yourselves.* (chat(e'lene'entsutul, imper.); čn‿čet'+ˤel'=eneʔ+ncut *covered.* (chnchet'(el'ene'ntsut (lit. I covered myself), vi.); kʷ‿čat'+ˤel'= eneʔ+ncút *covered (you (sg.)...yourself.* (kuchat'(e'lene'ntsut, vt.); čat+ˤel'=eneʔ+ncút *cover (oneself), he/she covered himself/herself.* (chat(e'lene'ntsut, vt.); č‿čet+ˤel'=eneʔ+ncút *We covered ourselves.* (chchet(e'lene'ntsut, vt.); kʷp‿čat+ˤel'=eneʔ+ncút *covered (you (pl.)...yourselves).* (kupchat(e'lene'ntsut, vt.); čat ˤel'= eneʔ+ncút-lš *they covered themselves.* (chat (e'lene'ntsutlsh, imper.); ‡ a čat+ˤel'=íneʔ-st-m-n *I cover (cust.) you (sg.).* (achat(e'line'stmn, vt.); a čat+ˤel'= íneʔ-s-n *I cover h/h/i.* (achat(e'line'sn, vt.); a čat+ˤel'=íneʔ-st-ulm-n *I cover you (pl.).* (achat(e'line'stulmn, vt.); a čat+ˤel'=íneʔe-s-en-elš [?] *I cover them.* (achat(e'linesenelsh, vt.); a čat+ˤel'=íneʔ-st-me-xʷ *You (sg.) cover me.* (achat(e'line'stmekhw, vt.); a čat+ˤel'=íneʔ-st-xʷ *You (sg.) cover h/h/i.* (achat(e'line'stkhw, vt.); a čat+ˤel'=íneʔ-st-me-s *H/s covers me.* (achat(e'line'stmes, vt.); a čat+ˤel'= íneʔ-st-mi-s *H/s covers you (sg.).* (achat(e'line'stmis, vt.); ˤél-nt-s *He covered it.* ((e'lnts, vt.); a čat+ˤel'= íneʔ-st-me-lp *You (pl.) cover me.* (achat(e'line'stmelp, vt.); a čat+ˤel'= íneʔ-st-xʷ-lš *You (pl.) cover them.* (achat(e'line'stkhwlsh, vt.); a čat+ˤel'= íneʔ-st-me-s-lš *They cover me.* (achat(e'line'stmeslsh, vt.);

(achat(e'line'stmeslsh, vt.); a čat+ʕel'=
íneʔ-st-ulmi-s-lš *They cover you (pl.).*
(achat(e'line'stulmislsh, vt.);
čs+n+ʕel'=íp-nt-m *contain.*
(chsn(e'lipntm (lit. It was shut up, it
was contained), vi.); čs+n+ʕel'=
íp-nt-s *He closed it (the door).*
(chsn(e'lipnts, st.); §
x̌eł+s+čs+n+ʕél'+l'=ep
claustrophobia. (qhełschsn(e'l'lep (lit.
fear of being confined), n.)

√ʕl'xʷ // ʕal'x̌ʷ=alqs+n *coverall.*
((a'lkhwalqsn (lit. a covering for
clothes), n.) [xref √yl'xʷ]

√ʕłs † ʕełs *tie.* ((ełs (stem), vt.)

√ʕm₁ † ʕem *dissolve, melt, waste away.*
((em (stem), vi.); ʕem+t *melt
(...away).* ((emt (lit. It melted away),
vi.); ‡ ʕém-nt-s *defrost.* ((emnts (lit.
He removed ice or frost (from it), vt.)

√ʕm₂ † s+ʕém+ʕem *bete noir.*
(s(em(em (lit. one who is often picked
on), n.); § s+ʕem+ʕem+s+čínt
animosity, animus, hate, hostility.
(s(em(emschint. (lit. feeling hostility
toward a human being), n.)

√ʕp † ac+ʕíp *arcane, clandestine,
concealed, hidden, secret.* (ats(ip (lit. It
is hidden), adj.); ʕíp+lš *He hid
himself.* ((iplsh, vt.); ʕip+ilš *to hide.*
((ipilsh (stem), vi.); ʕáp+ʕ'ap-lš *hid
(they...).* ((ap'(aplsh, vi.); s+ʕíp+lš *to
abscend, abscond, bolt, hide, hiding,
flee.* (s(iplsh, vi, vt.); hn+ʕíp+lš+n
lair. (hn(iplshn. den. (lit. hiding place),
n.); hiʔc+ʕíp+m *conceal.* (hi'ts(ipm
(lit. I am keeping it from discovery or
understanding), vt.); hn+ʕíp+emn
cache. (hn(ipemn. (lit. hiding place
used for storage), n.); hn+ʕip+mn
hiding place. (hn(ipmn. (lit. a secret
storage place), n.); hn+ʕip+[e]mn *a
secret hiding place.* (hn(iplmn, n.); //
ʕíp=čt+m *connive.* ((ipchtm (lit. He
aided secretly by sleight of hand), vi.);
s+ʕíp=čt+m *connivance,*

cryptography. (s(ipchtm. conspiracy,
n.); ʕíp=cn *backbite, confabulate.*
((iptsn (lit. He concealed his words
about another), vi.); ul s+ʕip=cn
confidential. (ul s(iptsn (lit. pertaining
to something spoken as a secret), adj.);
ʕap=elwís *He hid himself for a time.*
((apelwis, vt.); ʕap+ʕ'ap+lš=íyeʔ *He
played hide and seek.* ((ap'(aplshiye',
vt.); § ac+ʕep+el+šugʷíl+m *to elope.*
(ats(epelshugwilm (lit. H/s goes away
by a secret road), vi.);
ic+ʕepé+ł+šegʷel+mš *He is going
(away) through a secret path.*
(its(epełshegwelmsh, vi.);
ʔepł+ʕep+s+kʷís+t *anonymous,
nameless.* (epł(epskwist, v. (lit. He has
a hidden name), adj.); nukʷ+ʕíp=
cn+m-nt-s *confide.* (nukw(iptsnmnts
(lit. He put a secret into his trust).
gossip, vi.)

√ʕw † ʕaw *drop, to drop as water.* ((aw
(stem), vt.); ʕ'ew+p *dripped (it...).*
('(ewp, vi.)

√ʕx̌₁ † ʕax̌ *wind.* ((aqh (stem). to wrap
string evenly, vt.)

√ʕx̌₂ // t+ʕa+ʕáx̌=c'eʔ *cantaloupe.*
(t(a(aqhts'e' (lit. a melon ribbed
around), n.)

√ʕx̌ʷ // hn+ʕux̌ʷ+ʕux̌ʷ=ełníw'+n
harness. (hn(uqhw(uqhwełni'w, n.)

√ʕy † ʕey *embittered.* ((ey (stem), adj.);
ʕey' *angry.* ((e'y (stem), adj.); ʕey+y
He felt angry. ((eyy, vi.); s+ʕéy+y
anger, to be angry, peeved. (s(eyy.
being irked, irritated, n, adj.);
ʕey+ʕey+iy+úl *He habitually gets
angry.* ((ey(eyiyul, vi.); // ʕey+y=
ús+m *frowned (he...).* ((eyyusm (lit.
He showed anger in his face), vi.);
hn+ʕay+iy=ílgʷes *angry (be).*
(hn(ayiyilgwes, vi.); in+ʕey+y=ílgʷes
angry. (in(eyyilgwes (lit. He is being
angry in the heart), adj.); s+n+ʕey+iy=
ílgʷes *despite.* (sn(eyiyilgwes (lit.
becoming angry in heart), n.); ‡

206

ʕey+mín-n *I got angry with him.* ((eyminn, vi.); ʕey+y+mín-n *angry (I got...with him).* ((eyyminn, vi.); ʕey+mí-nt-se-s *He got angry with me.* ((eymintses, vi.)

√ʕʷ † aʕʷ *abundant, ample, copious, many things, much.* (a(w- (pref.), adj.); ∥ aʕʷ+aʕʷ=ílt *H/s has many children.* (a(w'a(wilt, vt.); áʕʷ=gʷul *H/s has many vehicles.* (a(wgul, vt.); § aʕʷ+eł+cetxʷ *H/s has many houses.* (a(wełtsetkhw, vt.); aʕʷ+eł+wl+wlím *to be rich, well-to-do, wealthy (to be...).* (a(wełwlwlim (lit. H/s has much money), adj, vi.); ʕʷa+ʕʷ+s+c'ám' *bony.* ((a(wsts'a'm (lit. it has many bones), adj.); ʕʷa+ʕʷe+ł+t+tót+ot *H/s has many pets.* (a(wełttotot, vt.) [analysis unclear, possibly a prefix]

√ʕʷc' † ał+ʕʷéc' *magpie.* (ał(wets', n.); ∥ hn+ʕʷéc'+ʕʷec'=cn *boisterous.* (hn(wets'(wets'tsn. (lit. He is noisy as to the mouth). shrill, adj.)

√ʕʷh † t+ʕʷeh+ím *shout.* (t(wehim (lit. He uttered a loud and sudden cry), vi.); s+t+ʕʷeh+ím *clamor.* (st(wehim (lit. shouting), n.); [see also √ʕhm]

√ʕʷl † hn+ʕʷéle?+n *beach, shore.* (hn(wele'n, n.); ∥ ʕʷél=e?el *shore.* ((wele'el, n.); tač+s+ʕʷél=e?el *coastward, toward seashore.* (tachs(wele'el, adv.)

√ʕʷł ∥ s+ʕʷéł=enč *greasy intestine.* (s(wełench, n.)

√ʕʷm † ʕʷim+iš *hurried, rushed (He...).* ((wimish, vi.); ic+ʕʷím+iš *hurrying (he is...).* (its(wimish, vi.)

√ʕʷs † ʕʷus *astray, lost.* ((us (stem). to be lost, adj.); u· ʕʷús *to disappear.* (uu(us, vi.); ʕʷus+t *He got lost.* ((ust, vi.); s+ʕʷus+t *cost, loss, lost, penalty, price.* (s(ust. to be lost, n.); ʕʷus+t-š *lost (get...).* ((ustsh, vi.); ∥ s+ʕʷús=elgʷes *damage, detriment.* (s(uselgwes. (lit. loss of property), n.);

hn+ʕʷó+ʕʷs=kʷe? *a stream west of DeSmet and southwest of Tensed (lit. lost waters).* (Hn(os(oskwe', n.)

√ʕʷš † s+ʕʷáš+ʕʷš+š *battle cry.* (s(wash(wshsh, n.)

√ʕʷt' † s+ʕʷet'+ʕʷet'+s+m *to smile, smiling.* (s(wet'(wet'sm, vi, adj.)

√ʕʷx̌ʷ † ʕʷux̌ʷ+mín+n *barbed wire.* ((wuqhwminn. barb, n.); ∥ hn+ʕʷ+ʕʷox̌ʷ=íčn' *streetcar.* (hn(wo(woqhwich'n. (lit. reins on the back), n.)

√ʕʷy † ʕʷuy *to cajole, coax, urge, waste.* ((uy (stem), vt.); ∥ ʕʷuy=čt *to mistreat (the old or helpless).* ((uycht (stem), vt.) [xref √hy']

√ʕʷ? † s+t+ʕʷe?=łc'e?=íp *hip pocket.* (st(we'łts'e'ip, n.); [also recorded as √ʕ'ʷ?] s+t+ʕ'ʷe?=łc'e?=ip *pocket (hip).* (st'(we'łts'e'ip, n.)

√?cč † ?icč *play.* (itsch (stem), vi.); n+?ícč+n+n *playground.* ('nitschnn (lit. means of playing, place for playing), n.); si+yícč+n *play.* (siyitschn, n.); s+y+?ícč+n *drama.* (s'yitschn, n.); s+y+?icč+nn *drama, play.* (s'yitschnn, n.); y+?ícč+n *antic, gambol, playing.* ('yitschn, vi, n.); [also recorded as √?c'č] y+?íc'eč+č+n *diversion, pastime, recreation.* ('yits'echchn. (lit. playing of several people), n.); či‿?cícč+n *playing (I am...).* (chi'tsitschn, vi.); i n+?ecč+númt *H/s wants to play.* (i'netschnumt, vi.); ‡ n+?ícč+n+m-nt-s *used (H/s...it for a playground, with reference to place or thing not intended for play).* ('nitschnmnts, vt.); § nukʷ+[?]ícč+n+m-nt-s *played (H/s...with h/h).* (nukwi'tschnmnts, vi.)

√?ckʷ † ?úckʷ+m *bath (He took a..., He went swimming).* (utskum, n, vi.); y+?úckʷ+m *bath, to bathe, swim.* ('yutskum (lit. H/s swam), n, vi.); n+?úckʷ+emn *bathroom, bathtub,* *shower.* ('n̲utskwemn. (lit. bathing place/bathing area), n.); i·c+ʔúckʷ+mš *H/s is bathing or swimming.* (iits'u̲tskumsh, vi.)

√**ʔcqʔ** † ʔácqeʔ *exit, go out, he went out.* (atsqe', vi.); y+ʔácqeʔ *going out.* ('y̲atsqe', vi.); ʔác+ʔcqeʔ *exit (to), go out.* (a̲ts'tsqe' (lit. They went out), vi.); n+ʔácqéʔ+n *place for going out, lavatory, etc.* ('n̲atsqe̲'n, n.); ‡ čs+ʔácqeʔ-nt-s *h/s went out to meet h/h.* (chs'a̲tsqe'nts, vi.)

√**ʔc'x̌** † ʔac'x̌ *behold, to look (at), he looked, observe, view.* (ats'qh. he beheld, vt.); ʔac'x̌-š *look (at).* (ats'qhsh, vt.); ʔác'x̌+emn *binoculars, telescope.* (a̲ts'qhemn (lit. Means of looking), n.); n+ʔác'x̌+n *cinema, coliseum, motion-picture theatre.* ('n̲ats'qhn (lit. a place for looking at pictures), n.); y+ʔác'c'áʔx̌ *color, perspective.* ('y̲ats'ts'a̲'qh. (lit. a way of looking at something, an appearance to the eye, especially from a specific view), n.); can+ʔac'x̌+ncút *caution.* (tsa'na'tsqhntsu̲t (lit. He looked under himself), n.); a+can+ʔac'x̌+ncút *circumspect, discreet, prudent.* (atsa'nats'qhntsu̲t, vi. (lit. He looks around himself. He is heedful of circumstances), adj.); can+ʔac'x̌a+mí+ncut-š *be cautious (of), beware.* (tsa'na'tsqhami̲ntsutsh, vt.); can+ʔac'x̌+ncut-š *beware!, look out!, watch out!.* (tsa'nats'qhntsutsh!, imper.); ʔac'+ʔac'x̌+m'+scut *showoff, sycophant, fop.* (ats"ats'qh'mstsut (lit. He showed himself off), n.); ča+č'y+ác'x̌ *we are going to a movie (lit. We are going to look).* (chach'y̲ats'qh, vt.); // ʔac'x̌=us+n'cút+n' *mirror.* (ats'qhus'ntsu̲t'n (lit. Means of seeing one's own face), n.); ‡ ʔác'x̌-nt *look (at).* (ats'khnt (lit. H/s/i looked at h/h), vt.); ʔác'x̌-nt-s *H/s looked at me.* (ats'qhnts es, vt.); §

y+ʔac'x̌a+ɬ+q'ey'+mín· *to read.* ('yats'qhaɬq'e'ymi̲nn, vt.); t'uʔ+čeɬ‿čiy+ʔac'x̌+al+q'ey'+mín+n *read (Well, I am going to...a book).* (t'u'cheɬ chi'yats'qhaɬ q'e'ymi̲nn, vt, n.); ʔac'ax̌+ʔax̌íl' *related (to be...).* (ats'aqh'aqhi̲'l (lit. They are related by similarity), vi.)

√**ʔčn** † n+ʔčín+n *cabinet, case, closet, container, crate, receptacle, storage box, trunk.* ('nchi̲nn. (lit. instrument for putting things in), n.); e·+n+ʔéčen' *contained.* (ee'n̲eche'n (lit. It is contained in a receptacle, bag, sock), adj.); ‡ n+ʔčí-s-n *bag, sack (I put it in a...).* ('nchi̲sn, n.)

√**ʔd** † n+ʔid *exchange.* ('nid (stem), stem.); s+ce·n+ʔíd+m *alteration.* (stsee'ni̲dm, n.); s+ce·n+ʔíd+mš *adapt, change (to...).* (stsee'ni̲dmsh, vi.); // hiy+n+ʔíd=us *bought.* (hiy'ni̲dus (lit. something I bought), vt.); n+ʔed=u·s=íw'es *trade, barter.* ('neduusi̲'wes (lit. He traded, v.); s+n+ʔed=u·s=íw'es *deal, trade, bargain, barter, exchanging, sell.* (s'neduusi̲'wes, vi, n, vt.); ul s+n+ʔed=u·s=íw'es *commercial.* (ul s'neduusi̲'wes, adj.); s+ca·n+ʔád=al'qs *change.* (stsaa'n̲ada'lqs (lit. a fresh set of clothing), n.); ‡ ce·n+ʔíd-n *exchange.* (tsee'ni̲dn (lit. I exchanged it or replaced it by another), vt.); n+ʔid=us-nt-s *bought (h/s...it), traded.* ('nidusnts, v.); § e+lus+ce·n+ʔíd+ed *enduring, lasting.* (elustsee'ni̲ded, adj.); e+lus+ce·n+ʔíd+et *to be changeless, durable, enduring, lasting.* (elustsee'ni̲det, adj.); n+ʔed+xʷu·s=íw'es *alternate.* ('nedkhuusi̲'wes (lit. It alternated, It changed places, that which occurs in successive turns), vi.); n+ʔed=us=el'+s+čí+čeʔ *H/S traded horses with another person (sg.).*

('neduse'lschiche', vt.); [see also
√y'd]

√ʔgʷ † [ʔ]igʷ- *set out for.* (igw-)

√ʔh † ʔih+ʔi *turtledove.* (ih'i, n.);
is+ʔúh+ʔuh+iš *coo.* (is'uh'uhish (lit. It
(pigeon) uttered its murmuring sound),
vi.); § hn+kʷar+ar+ʔóh+m *crow
(to...).* (hnkwarar'ohm, vi.)

√ʔhʔ † ʔohiʔ+t *cold (to have a...),
caught (he...cold).* (ohi't (stem), n, vi.);
y+ʔohiʔ+t *cold, flu.* ('yohi't. (lit.
catching cold), n.); kʷ‿y'c+ʔóhiʔ+t.
cold (You(s) are having a...).
(ku'yts'ohi't, v.)

√ʔkʷ₁ † ʔukʷ+t *crawled (He...).* (ukwt,
vi.); ec+ʔe+ʔúkʷ+t *children, insect.*
(ets'e'ukwt (lit. Little creature that
crawls about), n.); e·c+ʔúkʷ+kʷ+t
creepers, crawlers. (eets'uk'ukwt (lit.
That which creeps or crawls about),
n.); ec+ʔe+ʔúkʷ+ʔukʷ+t *arthropod,
bug, insect.* (ets'e'uk'ukwt (lit. Little
creature that crawls about), n.); [also
recorded as √ʔk'ʷ]
ec+ʔe+ʔúk'ʷ+ukʷ+t *bug.*
(ets'e'uk'ukwt (lit. Little creature that
crawls about), n.);
t'iʔ+ec+ʔe+ʔúkʷ+kʷ+t *crawls (The
baby already...).* (t'i'ets'e'uk'ukwt, vi.);
∥ n+ʔúkʷ+t=enč *crawled (It...on the
inside of the wall).* ('nukwtench, vi.);
ʔúkʷ+t=ul'umxʷ *H/s crawled on the
ground.* (ukwtu'lumkhw, vi.);
n+ʔúkʷ+t=ul'umxʷ *crawled (H/s...in
the ditch, trench).* ('nukwtu'lumkhw,
vt, n.); n+ʔókʷ+t=alqs *crawled
(H/s...on the road, path).* ('nokwtalqs,
vi, n.); t+č+ʔókʷ+t=alqʷ *crawled
(H/s...on a log, stick).* (tch'okwtalqw,
vi, n.); i tč+ʔúkʷ+t=ičn *H/S is
crawling on the ridge of a mountain.*
(itch'ukwtichn, vi.); i· n+ʔúkʷ+t=ečn'
It is crawling on the back of a person.
(ii'nukwtech'n, vi.)

√ʔkʷ₂ † y+ʔúkʷ+m *to move something
yonder.* ('yukum, vt.); y+ʔúkʷ+mš

carrying, transporting. ('yukumsh,
vt.); n+ʔúkʷ+emn *truck.* ('nukwemn
(lit. means of carrying over there), n.);
s+či·c+ʔúkʷ+m *bringing (...here).*
(schiits'ukum, vi.); ∥ ʔúkʷ=elgʷes
*belongings (H/s took h/h...over there),
thither (H/s took h/h belongings over
there).* (ukwelgwes, pl.n., adv.); ‡
či·c+ʔúkʷ-nt-s *h/s brought it over
here.* (chiits'ukwnts, vt.); §
n+ʔukʷ+s+čín+n *cab, bus, coach,
taxicab.* ('nukwschinn. (lit. vehicle for
carrying passengers), n.)

√ʔkʷn † ʔékʷn *to claim, say, state (lit.
he stated it to be true).* (ekwn (lit. He
said), vt.); y+ʔékʷn *claim, saying.*
('yekwn (lit. statement of something as
a fact), n.); y+ʔukʷún *claim.* ('yukun
(lit. a statement of something as a
fact), n.); ne+ʔkʷun *think.* (ne'kun
(stem), vi.); ne+ʔkʷún+m *agreed,
thought.* (ne'kunm (lit. He thought, he
agreed), vi.); n+ʔukʷún+n *adage,
aphorism, apothegm, byword, clause,
diction, proverb, saying.* ('nukunn.
aphorism, n.); ʔu+n+ʔukʷún+n
aphorism. ('unukunn. apothegm,
byword, proverb, saying, adage,
diction, clause, n.); ic+ʔukʷún+m
denote. (its'ukunm (lit. It is being said;
h/s is being told), vt.);
hiy+n+[ʔ]ekʷún+mn *desire.*
(hiynekunmn (lit. means of willing,
n.); cen+ʔukʷ+ʔukʷún'+em'n'
allurement, temptation.
(tse'nuk'uku'ne'm'n (lit. undermining
verbally), n.); t'uʔ+č‿y'c+ʔukʷún *am
saying (Well, I...).* (t'u'chi'ts'ukun, vi.);
kʷu‿y'c+ʔukʷún *You are saying.*
(ku'yts'ukun, vi.); ∥ y+ʔukʷún=ciʔ
applause. ('yukuntsi' (lit. saying it's all
right), n.); y+ʔekʷn=ciʔ *applause (lit.
saying it's all right).* ('yekwntsi', n.);
u+ʔn+ʔukʷún=cn *brogue, aphasia.*
(u"nukuntsn (lit. He does not speak
distinctly or normally), n.); ‡

cen+ʔukʷ+ʔukʷún'-t-s *allure, entice, tempt.* (tse'nuk'uku̱nts (lit. He allured h/h), vt.); § s+n+ʔukʷún=cn+is xʷe s+t'ún=ɫc'eʔ *bray.* (s'nuku̱ntsnis khwe st'únts'e' (lit. the cry of a donkey), n.); s+q'éx̌+q'ex̌+t he n+ʔukʷún+n *dictionary.* (sq'eqhq'eqht he 'nuku̱nn (lit. sayings that are a treasure), n.); ul a·yár ha y+ne+ʔkʷún+am-is *will (it is the...of all).* (ulaayar hayne' ku̱namis, n.) [possibly related to √ʔk'ʷn, see also √ʔkʷs]

√ʔkʷs † ʔekʷus *tell.* (ekus, vt.); ‖ ʔakʷós=tq *accost, tell (to tell someone).* (akostq (lit. He told someone/ He spoke to a person first), vt.); ʔekʷós=tq *accost.* (ekostq (lit. He spoke to a person first), vt.); ʔekʷús+t=us *bid, order.* (ekustus. (stem), vt.); ‡ ʔekʷús-t-m-n *I told you (sg.).* (ekustmn, vt.); ʔekʷús-n *I told him.* (ekusn, vi.); ʔekʷ?s-t-ulm-n *tell, to tell someone (lit. I told you).* (eku'stulmn, vt.); ʔekʷús-t-[u]lm-n *I told you (pl.).* (ekustlmn, vt.); ʔekʷús-n-lš *I told them.* (ekusnlsh, vi.); ʔekʷús-t-me-xʷ *you told me.* (ekustmekhw, vt.); ʔekʷús-t-ali-s *He told us.* (ekustalis, vt.); ʔekʷús-t-me-t *We told him.* (ekustmet, vi.); ʔekʷus-t-mel-p *You (pl.) told me.* (ekustmelp, vt.); § ʔekʷus+t=us huy *allow, permit.* (ekustus "huy" (lit. say all right), v.); [see also √ʔk'ʷn]

√ʔk'ʷl † ʔík'ʷl *salmon eggs.* (ik'wl, n.)

√ʔk'ʷn † cen+ʔukʷ+kʷún'+em'n' *temptation.* (tse'nuk'uku̱ne'm'n (lit. undermining verbally), n.); ‡ cen+ʔuk'ʷ+k'ʷún-t-s *tempt.* (tse'nuk'uku̱nts (lit. He allured h/h), vt.) [possibly related to √ʔkʷn]

√ʔl † ʔél+m+ncut *automobile, betake (to...).* (elmntsut (lit. H/s/i caused h/h/i to move), n, v.); ʔé·l+m+ncut *H/s finally stirred.* (eeelmntsut, vi.); y+ʔél+m+ncut *action, kinema, self motion.* ('yelmntsut. Move oneself, n.); sye·+ʔél+m+ncut *actor.* (syee'elmntsut (lit. one whose business is to move himself), n.); ‖ ʔel+m=íčt+m *H/s moved h/h hand.* (elmichtm, vt.); ʔél+m=šín+m *H/s moved or stirred h/h foot.* (elmshinm, vt.); ‡ ʔél+m-s-n *to move, stir, rouse.* (elmsn (lit. I moved it), vt.); ʔél+m-st-m *bestir, rouse, stir.* (elmstm (lit. It was moved), vi.); ʔél+m-stu-s *activate, motion (to set in...).* (elmstus, vt.); § n+ʔm+iš ʔe·l=úp-nt-s *commute.* ('nmisheelu̱pnts (lit. He sat in his (another's) place), vi.); lut he· y+ʔel+mncut+s *H/S did not move h/h self, h/s did not go anywhere.* (luthee'yelmntsu̱ts, vt.)

√ʔlč † ʔilč *knick-knick berries, red berries, wild cranberry.* (ilch, n.); ‖ ʔálč=aɫp=alqʷ *cranberry (wild), wild cranberry bush.* (alchaɫpalqw, n.)

√ʔlk'ʷ † ʔilk'ʷ *to cache, store, especially new acquisitions.* (ilk'w (stem), vt.); y+ʔil'k'ʷ+emn *keepsake (to put away as a...).* ('yi'lk'wemn, v.); y+ʔílk[']ʷ+emn *heirloom.* ('yilkwemn, n.); hi·y+ʔílk'ʷ+emn *cherish.* (hii'yi̱lk'wemn (lit. It is something I hold dear), vt.); ‖ y'il'k'ʷ=élgʷes *to store away belongings.* ('yi'lk'welgwes, v.); n+ʔílk'ʷ=elgʷes+n *briefcase, bureau, ark, bin, chest of drawers.* ('nilkwelgwesn. (lit. box for storing things, belongings), n.); č‿y'c+ʔílk'ʷ=elgʷes *I am storing my last property or belongings.* (chi'ts'i̱lk'welgwes, vt.); ʔálk'ʷ=alqs+m *put away (clothes).* (a̱lk'walqsm (lit. H/s put away h/h clothes), vt.); § n+ʔílk'ʷ=elgʷes+n a s+n+č'n'=íčnʔ *caisson.* ('nilk'welgwesn a snch'n'i̱chn' (lit. storage (box) for ammunition), n.); n+ʔílk'ʷ=elgʷes+n a q'ey'+mín+n *bookshelf, library.* ('nilk'welgwesn a q'e'ymi̱nn, n.)

√ʔɬn † ʔiɬ *eat*. (iɬ, (stem), [v].); ʔíɬn *to eat*. (iɬn (lit. He ate), v.); y+ʔiɬn *aliment, chow, to eat, food, nutriment, victuals*. ('yiɬn, n, vt.); ʔiɬ+ɬ+útm *comestible*. (iɬɬutm (lit. It is edible), adj.); n+ʔíɬn+n *cafe, dining room, eating place, restaurant*. ('niɬnn, n.); n+ʔíɬ+p+n *dessert*. ('niɬpn, n.); n'e+ʔíɬn'+n' *cabaret, bistro, restaurant (little...)*. ('ne'iɬ'n'n, n.); s+n+ʔiɬn+úmt *appetite*. (s'niɬnumt (lit. desiring to eat), n.); če·t+ʔíɬn+n *buffet, sideboard, table*. (cheet'iɬnn. (lit. that on which one eats), n.); čet+ʔi[ɬ]n+n *table (lit. place on which to eat)*. (chet'itnn, n.); kʷn'e?+kʷu·‿ʔíɬn *eat*. (k'ne'kuu'iɬn (lit. You (sg.) are going to eat), vi.); ‡ ʔíɬn-t-s *assimilation*. (iɬnts (lit. He ate it), n.); § s+x̌ese·+ʔíɬn *diet (lit. eating correctly)*. (sqhesee'yiɬn, n.); n+[ʔ]iɬ+s+čín+n *cannibalism*. (niɬschinn, n.); n+ʔíɬn+n ɬ n+ʔítš+n *boarding house*. ('niɬnn ɬ 'nitshn (lit. place for eating and sleeping), n.); ʔiɬ+s+qíl=tč *eat (meat)*. (iɬsqiltch, vt.); i c+ʔn+s+qíl=tč *to eat meat*. (its'ɬsqiltch, vt.); ec+ʔiɬ+s+qí[l=t]č *carnivorous*. (ets'iɬsqitlch (lit. He eats flesh), vi.); sya+ʔiɬ+s+qil=tč *carnivore*. (sya'iɬsqiltch (lit. who eats meat), n.); sye+ʔiɬ+s+qíl=[t]č *carnivore (lit. One who eats meat)*. (sye'iɬsqilch, n.); tep+ʔíɬn *eat (He stopped on the way to...)*. (tep'iɬn, vi.); tap+ʔiɬn *He stopped on the way to eat*. (tap'iɬn, v.); yuqʷ+e?+y+ʔíɬn *eat (H/s pretended to...)*. (yuqwe''yiɬn, vi.); hi+s+nukʷ+ʔíɬn *commensal*. (hisnuk'iɬn (lit. He is my companion at table), n.); s+x̌iɬ+ɬ+y'íɬn *feast (after a wake)*. (sqhiɬɬ'yiɬn (lit. throwing food away), n.); s+x̌iɬ+s+y'íɬn *potlatch*. (sqhiɬs'yiɬn. giving away food, n.); kʷen+ɬ+y'íɬn *food (h/s took along...)*. (kwenɬ'yiɬn, n.); s+[n]+yaɬn+laqʷ=ús

gum (extra...). (smyaɬnlaqus, n.); k'ʷ[n]e? čn‿ʔiɬn a s+qil=tč *I am going to eat some meat*. (k'we' chn' iɬn a sqiltch); ni?+čeɬ‿kʷu‿ʔíɬn a s+qil=tč *Are you going to eat some meat?* (ni cheɬ kuu'yiɬn a sqiltch? (qu.).); čeɬ‿či‿ʔíɬn e s+mɬíč *I am going to eat some salmon*. (cheɬ chii' yiɬn e smɬich.)

√ʔɬxʷ † n+ʔuɬxʷ *to enter, entered, went (He...to school)*. ('nuɬkhw, vt, vi.); čn‿n+ʔúɬxʷ *go in, enter, enroll, enrolled (I...in school), entered (I...), went (I...in)*. (chn'nuɬkhw, vi, vt.); ‡ n+ʔuɬxʷ-s-n *admit*. ('nuɬkhwsn (lit. I permitted him to enter), vt.)

√ʔm₁ † y+ʔém+n *alms-giving, alimony*. ('yemn. (lit. feeding), n.); ʔem+ʔem+n+úl *to be charitable, generous, hospitable*. (em'emnul (lit. H/s habitually feeds others), adj.); ∥ ʔem+n=ílt *feed, H/s fed h/h offspring*. (emnilt (children), vt.); ‡ ʔem-t-s *feed, he fed h/h/i*. (emts, vt.); § ʔem+n+el'+s+čí+če? *feed*. (emne'lschiche' livestock, vt.)

√ʔm₂ ʔém+m *to alight, land*. (emm, vi.); ʔém+iš *sit down*. (emish (lit. He sat down), vi.); n+ʔém+iš *sat*. ('nemish (lit. He sat within), vi.); ʔem+m+íš+iš *He came to a sitting position*. (emmishish, vi.); ∥ ʔem+íš= ul'umxʷ *sit (on the ground), H/s sat on the ground*. (emishu'lumkhw, vi.); n+ʔm+íš=kʷe? *sat (h/s...in shallow water)*. ('nmishkwe', v.); sye+t+č+ʔm+íš=ew'es *chevalier*. (syetch'mishe'wes (lit. One who rides (horseback), n.); ‡ ce·n+ʔím-nt-s *await (to...)*. (tsee'nimnts (lit. He waited for him), vi.); § n+ʔm+iš ʔe·l= úp-nt-s *commute*. ('nmisheelupnts (lit. He sat in his (another's) place), vi.) [xref √ʔmt]

√ʔmč † ʔimč *to pick up*. (imch (stem), vt.); ʔímč+t+m *H/s picked up a* handful of small objects (peanuts, berries, etc.). (imchtm, vt.)

√ʔmt † eˑc+ʔémut *at home, seated.* (eets'emut (lit. H/s is seated or home), adj, adv.); ec+ʔmúˑt *there he is, sitting down.* (ets'muuut, vi.); eče·+t+ʔémut *He is seated on (a chair).* (echeet'emut); hi-yumút+n *sitting-place, residence.* (hi-yumutn (lit. It is my residence, it is my sitting-place), n.); s+čet+ʔumút+n *bench, chair, couch.* (schet'umutn (lit. piece of furniture on which one may sit or recline), n.); ∥ ʔamót=qn *president, chairman, executive, head (lit. one who sits at the head).* (amotqn, n.); t+č+ʔmút=ew'es *horseback (on...).* (tch'mute'wes, adv.); s+t+č+ʔumút= ew'es+n *cow pony, saddle pony.* (stch'umute'wesn, n.); t+č+ʔmút+p= kʷeʔ *Mt. Baldy (in Idaho, near the St. Joe River).* (Tch'mutpkwe' (lit. one who sits by the water), n.) [xref √ʔm]

√ʔngʷt † ʔingʷet *what say, be who.* (-ingwet); ʔíngʷet *What did h/s say?* (ingwet? (qu.).); čn‿[ʔ]íngʷe[t] *say.* ((lit. What did I say?), chningwe, vt.); č‿y'c+ʔíngʷet *What am I saying?* (chi'ts'ingwet, qu.); čn‿ʔéngʷet *I.* (chn'engwet (lit. it is I, I am I), pro.); čn ʔéngʷet *I am he or she.* (chn'engwet, vi.); čn‿ʔuˑl=ʔengʷet *mine.* (chn'uu'lengwet (lit. it is mine), vi.); kʷu‿w+ʔéngʷet *It is you (sg).* (kuu'wengwet, vt.); kʷu‿ʔuˑl+ʔéngʷet *It is yours (sg).* (ku'uu'lengwet, vt.); iˑ c+ʔíngʷet *What is h/h saying?* (iits'ingwet? (qu.).); iˑ c+ʔíngʷet-lš *What are they saying?* (iits'ingwetlsh? (qu.).); ∥ i c+ʔingʷe(t)=cn+míncut *What is h/s saying to himself of herself? (reference to excessive repetition to which others pay no attention).* (its'ingwetsnmintsut, qu.);

√ʔns † ʔenís *depart, leave, go away.* (enis, vi.); ʔeníˑs *there he goes.* (eniˑs, vi.); tel' ci+ʔenís *continue.* (te'l tsi'enis (lit. from there he went on), v.); čs+ʔenes+mí+ncut *h/s set h/h self out on a gallivanting spree.* (chs'enesmintsut, vi.)

√ʔpls † ʔepls *apple.* (epls (l.w. from English), n.); ∥ s+ʔápls=alqʷ *apple (tree).* (s'aplsalqw, n.); § ul+ápel ha s+can+x̌as=ítkʷeʔ+s *apple brandy, apple-jack.* (ulapel ha stsanqhasitkwe's (lit. good juice from the apple), n.)

√ʔpn † ʔúpen *ten.* (upen, n.); tč+ʔúpen *ten persons.* (tch'upen, n.); ∥ ʔo+ʔópan'=čt=qn' *thousand (one...).* (o'opa'nchtq'n, n.); ʔupen=čt=élxʷ *dicker.* (upenchtelkhw (lit. ten hides or ten skins), n.); tč+ʔúpen=čt=elps *There are ten hogs or grizzlies.* (tch'upenchtelps, v.); § ʔupen+čs+pín=tč *decade.* (upenchspintch (lit. ten consecutive years), n.); ʔupen eˑséns *dime.* (upeneesens (lit. ten cents), n.); ʔupen ul nékʷeʔ *eleven.* (upen ul nek'we' (lit. ten plus one), n.); ʔeseˑl+ʔúpen *twenty.* (esee'lupen (lit. ten times ten), n.); ʔupen uɫ ʔésel *twelve.* (upen uɫ esel, n.); čeʔɫeˑl+ʔúpen *thirty.* (che'ɫee'lupen, n.); čeʔɫeˑl+ʔupn *thirty.* (che'ɫee'lupn (lit. three times ten), n.); ʔupen uɫ číʔɫes *thirteen.* (upen uɫ chi'ɫes, n.); ʔupen uɫ mus *fourteen.* (upen uɫ mus, n.); mos+aˑl+ʔopan+č=sq'it *Lent.* (Mosaa'lopanchsq'it (lit. 40 days), n.); mus+eˑl+ʔupn *forty.* (musee'lupn, n.); t'uʔ čn‿mus eˑl ʔúpan *forty (Well, I am...).* (t'u'chn mus ee lupan, adj.); ʔupen uɫ cil *fifteen.* (upen uɫ tsil, n.); cil+čl+ʔúpen *fifty.* (tsilch'lupen (lit. 5 times 10), n.); ʔupen uɫ téwš=ect *sixteen.* (upen uɫ tewshect, n.); tuwš+ačl+ʔúpen *six times ten, sixty.* (tuwshach'lupen, n.); ʔupen uɫ cun=

čt+m *seventeen.* (upen uł tsunchtm, n.); cun=čt+m+e·l+ʔúpen *seventy.* (tsunchtmee'lupen (lit. 7 times 10), n.); heʔen'+m+e·l+ʔúpen *eighty.* (he'e'nmee'lupen (lit. eight times ten), n.); ʔupen uł haʔín'+m *eighteen.* (upen uł ha'i'nm, n.); ʔupen uł x̌a+x̌an'+út *nineteen.* (upen uł qhaqha'nut, n.); x̌a+x̌n'+u·l+ʔúpen' *ninety.* (qhaqh'nuu'lupe'n, n.)

√ʔp' † ʔip' *wipe (stem).* (ip', [v].); ʔíp'+emn *buffer, dust-cloth, towel.* (ip'emn (lit. a wiping cloth), n.); n+ʔíp'+emn *wiping (means of...inside something).* ('nip'emn, vi.); če·t+ʔíp'+emn *cloth (wiping...), mop, wiping cloth for top (of floor, table, etc.).* (cheet'ip'emn, n.); // ʔíp'+ʔep'=čt+m *hands (H/s wiped h/h...).* (ip"ep'chtm, pl.n.); ʔíp'+ʔap'=čs+n *napkin.* (ip"ap'chsn (lit. means of wiping the hands), n.); ʔíp'+ʔep'=čs+n *napkin (lit. means of wiping the hands).* (ip"ep'chsn, n.); ʔíp'=us+n *face-towel.* ('ip'usn. See Coeur d'Alene, n.); in-ʔíp'=us+n *It is your face-towel, it is your means of wiping your face.* (in'ip'usn); ʔíp'+ʔep'=šn+m *feet (H/s wiped h/h...).* (ip"ep'shnm, pl.n.); ʔíp'+ʔep'=šn+n *doormat, H/s wiped h/h feet.* (ip"ep'shnn (lit. means of wiping one's feet), n.); e· n+ʔíp'=ečn'+m *dry off, wipe.* (ee'nip'ech'nm (lit. H/s wipes, dries off h/h back), vt.); ni+ʔáp'=iʔqs+n *handkerchief.* (ni'ap'i'qsn (lit. means of wiping one's nose), n.); n+ʔíp'=łc'eʔ+n *dish cloth.* ('nip'łts'e'n (lit. means of wiping inside the dishes), n.); n+ʔíp'=ens+m *wiped (H/s...h/h tooth or teeth).* ('nip'ensm, vt.); čn‿ʔap'+p=ow'as=qn+m *wipe.* (chn'ap'po'wasqnm (lit. I wiped my chin and mouth after a meal), vt.); čn‿ʔap+p=ow'as=qn'+m' *I wiped my chin and mouth, after a meal.*

(chn'ap'po'wasq'n'm, vi.); ‡ ʔíp'-n *blot (out).* (ip'n (lit. I wiped it), vt.)

√ʔqʷs † ʔóqʷs *drink, he drank.* (oqws (stem), v.); yoqʷs *to drink.* (yoqws, vt.); y+ʔoqʷs *drink, drinking.* ('yoqws, n, vt.); ʔoqʷ+ʔoqʷs+úl *He drinks habitually, bibulous.* (oq'oqsul (lit. given to drinking), adj.); hiyc+ʔóqʷs *beverage.* (hiyts'oqws (lit. that (not water) which is drunk), n.); n+ʔóqʷs+n *bumper, tavern.* ('noqwsn. (lit. a drinking vessel), n.); n+ʔóqʷs+p+n *coffee, tea.* ('noqwspn (lit. that which is drunk after a meal to wash down food), n.); n+ʔoqʷs+p+m *He washed it down.* ('noqwspm, vt.); tap+ʔoqʷs *drank (He...water on the way).* (tap'oqs, vt, n.); ʔoqʷ+ʔóqʷs-lš *drank (They...).* (oq'oqslsh, vi.); ‡ ʔóqʷs-nt-s *drank (lit. He drank it), vt.)

√ʔr † ʔor *frozen.* (or (stem), adj.); ʔor+t *froze.* (ort (lit. It froze), vi.); y+ʔor+t *frozen, e.g. meat.* ('yort, adj.); čn‿ʔor+t *to be very cold, frozen.* (chn'ort (lit. I am frozen stiff), adj.)

√ʔs † ʔús+lš *dive, dove (He...).* (uslsh, vi.); i+ʔus *Benewah Lake.* (I'us, n.); kʷp'‿e·c+ʔús+lš *dive.* (kup'eets'uslsh (lit. You (pl.) plunge headfirst into the water), vi.); y+ʔus+lš *to dive (lit. H/s dove).* ('yuslsh, v.); č‿gʷł sye·+ʔús+lš *diver.* (chguł syee'uslsh (lit. we are divers), n.); u ʔus+lš *They dove, each one of them dove.* (u'uslsh, vi.); ‡ čs+ʔus+lš-nt-s *h/s dove after it.* (chs'uslshnts, vt.)

√ʔsl † ʔésel *two.* (esel, n.); ʔeséł *twice.* (eseł, adv.); c+ʔsil+m *both.* (ts'silm, adj.); ec+ʔsíl+m *both (on both sides).* (ets'silm (amph...pref.), adv.); ʔesel+scút *dimorphic.* (eselstsut (lit. It has two forms or selves), adj.); tč+ʔésel *persons (They are two...).* (tch'esel, n.); gʷl' tč+ʔesel *binary.* (gu'l tch'esel, adj.); gʷl' c+ʔésel *binary, conjugate, two by two.* (gu'l t'sesel, adj); t'č+ʔsíl+m *both (persons).* (t'ch'silm, n.); e+tč+ʔsíl+m *both (of them).* (etch'silm, adj.); ∥ ʔasál=alqs *H/s has two items of clothing of the same kind.* (asalalqs, vt.); a ʔsal'=qn' *two hundred.* (a'sa'lq'n (lit. two little heads), n.); en+ʔsíl=cn *bilingual (to be...).* (e'nsiltsn (lit. He speaks two languages), vt.); et+č+ʔsíl=tč *ambidextrous.* (etch'siltch, vi. (lit. With both hands), adj.); ec+ʔsíl=čt+m *H/s (still) has both hands.* (ets'silchtm, vi.); n+ʔsil=łc'e? *bicameral.* ('nsiłts'e' (lit. two rooms or chambers), adj.); e+tč+ʔsíl+m=us *binocular.* (etch'silmus, vi. (lit. With both eyes), n.); tč+ʔsíl=šn *biped.* (tch'silshn (lit. One having 2 feet), n.); n+ʔsíl=ens *bicuspid.* ('nsilens (lit. two teeth), n.); ul+n+ʔsíl=us+m *bipartisan.* (ul'nsilusm (lit. pertaining to two sides), adj.); [ʔ]as(=)ásq'it *days (two...).* (asasq'it, n.); uł [ʔ]as=ásq'it *Tuesday.* (Ułasasq'it, n.); ʔes=íłxʷ *H/s has two houses.* (esiłkhw, vt.); ‡ ni+ʔsél+m-s-n *compound.* (ni'selmsn. mix, concoct (lit. I mixed it), vt.); t+č+ʔsíl+m-st-m *taken (They were both...).* (tch'silmstm, vi.); tč+ʔsíl=ene?+m-nt-m *binaural.* (tch'silene'mntm (lit. He was heard by 2 ears), n.); § ʔese·l+ʔúpen *twenty.* (esee'lupen (lit. two times ten), n.); ʔupen uł ʔésel *twelve.* (upen uł esel, n.); tč+ʔsél+kʷ s+nukʷ+kʷúl'+l' *two spouses, bigamy.* (tch'sel snukk'u'lu'l, n.); u+šim'íš tel' tč+ʔésel *either.* (ushi'mish te'l tch'esel (lit. one or the other of two persons), n.); ʔax̌el+ł ʔesel ha?+ł+dár=enč *bimonthly.* (aqhełł esel ha'łdarench (lit. happening every two months), adj.); ʔax̌ál+ł a+ʔsál'=qn' ha s+máx̌ʷ+x̌ʷ+s *bicentennial.* (adj. aqhałł a'sa'lq'n ha

smaqhuqhws (lit. at every two hundred heads that it snows), n.); ʔax̌el+ł ʔesel+ł he ni?+t+il=iw'es *biweekly.* (aqhełł eseł he ni'tili'wes (lit. happening every two weeks), adj.); ʔesel'+s+čí+če? *H/s has two horses.* (ese'lschiche', vt.); ul+n+ʔesl+s+kʷíst *exp It belongs to him who has 2 names.* (ul 'nselskwist, v.); ʔax̌el+ł ʔese+s+pin=tč *biennial, biyearly, every two years.* (aqhełł esespintch (lit. happening every two years), adj.); ʔas+as+qíl=tč *bicorporal.* (asasqiltch (lit. two bodies), adj.)

√ʔsqʷ † ʔasqʷ *son.* (asqw, n.); hn-i?‿n+ásqʷ *son (he is my...).* (hi'nasqw, n.); i·n+ʔásqʷ *son (He is your...).* (ii'nasqw, n.); § s+kʷl'+ł ʔasqʷ *to adopt.* (sk'u'łł asqw (lit. making one a son), vt.); p+[ʔ]asqʷ+qʷése? *small boys.* (pasquqwese', n.); [ʔ]asq[ʷ]+qʷ=ése? *small boy, chiquito, boy (lit. Little blurred son).* (asqqwese', n.) [xref √qʷs]

√ʔs? † ʔúse? *eggs.* (use', n.); n+ʔúse?+n *bird's nest.* ('nuse'n, n.); § us+ʔúse?+m+úl *is laying (The hen habitually...eggs).* (us'use'mul, vt.); ul paq ha ʔúse? *egg (Easter...).* (ul Paq ha use' (lit. an egg that belongs to Easter (Pasch), n.)

√ʔtqʷ ∥ y?átqʷ=ełp *conifer, pine tree.* ('yatqwełp, n.)

√ʔtš † ʔitš *He slept.* (itsh, vi.); y?ítš *to sleep.* ('yitsh, vi.); i·c+ʔítš *asleep, sleeping (He is...).* (iits'itsh, adj, vi.); n+ʔítš+n *bedchamber, bedroom, bunkhouse (lit. little hotel), caravansary, cubicle, hotel, inn, motel,* ('nitshn (lit. a place for sleeping), n.); n'e+ʔítš+n' *bunkhouse.* ('ne'itsh'n (lit. little hotel), n.); t+ʔyítš+n *curfew.* (t'yitshn (lit. time of evening for retiring), n.); tu?+y+ʔítsš *sleep ((You) go over there to...).* (tu"yitssh, vi.); ∥

tč+ʔít(=)šn *bedtime, numb*. (tch'itshn
(lit. His leg went to sleep), n.); §
yuqʷ+eʔ+y+ʔítš *sleep (H/s pretended
to...)*. (yuqwe"yitsh, vi.);
čn‿x̌es+e·y+ʔítš *slept*.
(chnqhese'yitsh (lit. I slept well), vt.);
n+ʔíłn+n ł n+ʔítš+n *boarding house*.
('niłnn ł 'nitshn (lit. place for eating
and sleeping), n.); hn+cun'+cún'=
m'eʔ+n ł n+ʔítš+n *boarding school*.
(hntsu'ntsu'n'me'n ł 'nitshn (lit. place
for teaching and sleeping), n.)

√ʔtx̌ʷ † ʔétx̌ʷeʔ *camas (baked...)*.
(etqhwe', n.); [also recorded as
√ʔtx̌ʷ] ʔapł+ʔétx̌ʷeʔ *to have baked
camas (a sweet, edible bulb)*.
(apł'etkhwe', n.); § s+x̌aw'+lu+tx̌ʷeʔ
camas (raw...). (sqha'wlutqhwe', n.)

√ʔw † ʔew *adverse (to be...to),
confront, contravene, oppose*. (ew...
(stem), vt.); ∥ ʔew+t=ús *antagonism,
competition, contestant, opposition,
rival, rivalry*. (ewtus (stem), n.);
y?ew+t=ús *aversion, dislike*. ('yewtus.
(lit. going against another), n.);
sye+ʔéw+t=us *competitor*. (sye'ewtus
(lit. One who rivals), n.); y?uw+t=
ús+m'-n't-ew'eš *competition,
opposing one another*.
('yuwtus'm'nte'wesh (lit. a vying with
others), n.); ic+ʔuw+t=ús+m'-n't-
ew'eš *compete*. (its'uwtus'm'nte'wesh
(lit. They are contending with one
another), vi.); ‡ ʔew+t=ús+m-nt-se-s
*adverse (to be...to), confront,
contravene, oppose*. (ewtusmntses (lit.
He was adverse to me), vi.); § ʔew+t=
us+s xʷa ǰisukrí *antichrist*. (ewtuss
khwa jisukri (lit. opponent of Jesus
Christ), n.)

√ʔws † ʔews *absorbed (to be...),
soaked, drenched (to get...), get wet*.
(ews (lit. It got...), (stem), adj, v, vi.)

√ʔxʷl † ʔíxʷel *sometime, some*. (ikhwel,
adj.); ʔíxʷl *some (...of them)*. (ikhwl,
adv.); ʔixʷu·l *to be (some)*. (ikhwuul)

√ʔxʷʔ † e+ʔíxʷeʔ *maternal aunt*.
(e'ikhwe', n.)

√ʔx̌l † ʔax̌el *thus (to do...)*. (aqhel... (v.
stem), vi.); a·c+ʔáx̌l *alike, as, similar*.
(aats'aqhl (lit. It is similar), adj, conj.);
ac+ʔax̌í·l *constant (to be)*, *ditto, stay
(the same)*. (ats'aqhiiil (lit. H/s/i stays
the same), vi, n.); ac+ʔax̌+ʔax̌íl'
*related, correlated, same, similar (to
be...)*. (ats'aqh'aqhi'l (lit. They are
related by similarity), vi.);
ʔax̌al+m+útm *able, capable, He
seems capable*. (aqhalmutm (lit. He is
capable of doing this or that), adj.);
čn‿ʔax̌el *thus (I did...)*. (chn'aqhel,
[vi.]); ∥ ʔax̌él=sq'it *daily, everyday*.
(aqhelsq'it, adv.); ul ʔax̌él=sq'it
diurnal. (ul aqhelsq'it (lit. pertaining to
a day), adj.); gʷl'+n+ʔax̌íl=elgʷes
compatible, concur. (gu'lnaqhilelgwes
(lit. They have the same heart), adj,
v.); s+n+ʔax̌íl=elgʷes *compatibility*.
(s'naqhilelgwes (lit. sharing the same
tastes), n.); ʔax̌íl=čt+m *H/s did thus
with h/h hand*. (aqhilchtm, vt.); ʔax̌il=
us+m *to change one's facial
expression (lit. H/s made h/h face
thus)*. (aqhilsm, vt.); ac+ʔax̌íl=us *to
have a face similar to (lit. H/s has a
face that looks like that of...)*.
(ats'aqhilus e, vi.); ‡ gʷl'+n+ʔax̌íl=
elgʷes-lš *congenial*.
(gu'lnaqhilelgweslsh (lit. They have
the same heart), adj.); § čáw'n'+š
a·c+ʔáx̌al *amen (lit. would that it be
so)*. (cha'w'nsh aats'aqhal, interj.);
ʔax̌el+ł ʔesel ha?+ł+dár=enč
bimonthly. (aqhelł esel ha'łdarench (lit.
happening every two months), adj.);
ʔax̌ál+ł a+ʔsál'=qn' ha s+máx̌ʷ+x̌ʷ+s
bicentennial. (adj. aqhałł a'sa'lq'n ha
smaqhuqhws (lit. at every two hundred
heads that it snows), n.); ʔax̌el+ł
ʔesel+ł he niʔ+t+il=iw'es *biweekly*.
(aqhelł eselł he ni'tili'wes (lit.
happening every two weeks), adj.);

ʔáx̌al+s+pin=tč *yearly.* (aqhalspintch (lit. every year), adv.); ʔax̌el+ɫ ʔese+s+pin=tč *biennial, biyearly.* (aqhelɫ esespintch (lit. happening every two years), adj.); ʔax̌al+ɫ+č+nék̕ʷ+eʔ *every, each.* (aqhelɫchnekwe' (lit. every person of a number), adj.); ʔax̌el+tč+nék̕ʷ+eʔ *each, every (lit. every person of a number).* (aqheltchnekwe', n.); hi+s+nuk̕ʷ+ʔa·c+ʔáx̌l *contemporaneous.* (hisnukw'aats'aqhl (lit. He is my like (equal), adj.); s+nuk̕ʷ+ʔa·c+ʔáx̌l *counterpart, colleague.* (snukw'aats'aqhl (lit. fellow worker of one's kind), n.); [xref √ʔx̌ɫ]

√ʔx̌l' † aʔx̌i·l'=il'š *codger.* (a'qhii'li'lsh (lit. an old man), n.)

√ʔx̌ɫ † na+ʔx̌íɫ *maybe, possibly.* (na'qhiɫ, adv.); § na+ʔx̌íɫ šiɫ *circa, about, Maybe or just about.* (na'qhiɫ shiɫ (used before approximate dates or figures), prep.); na+ʔx̌íɫ ec+piy=íčt+m-is-n *delight (Maybe I...h/h).* (na'qhiɫ etspiyichtmisn, vt.); na+ʔx̌íɫ ec+piy=íčt+mi-st-me-s-lš *delight (Maybe they...me).* (na'qhiɫ etspiyichtmistmeslsh, vt.); na+ʔx̌íɫ q̕ʷá+q̕ʷeʔe[l]-stu-s-lš *speak (They may...to h/h).* (na'qhiɫ qwa'qwe'estuslsh, vi.); na+ʔx̌íɫ q̕ʷá+q̕ʷéʔel-s-n *speak (I may...to h/h).* (na'qhiɫ qwa'qwe'elsn, vi.); na+x̌íɫ q̕ʷaʔ+q̕ʷeʔel-st-mi-s-lš *speak (They may...to you (pl.)).* (naqhiɫ qwa'qwe'elstmislsh, vi.); na+ʔx̌íɫ čn'‿in+x̌em=ínč *love (You (sg.) maybe...me).* (na'qhiɫ chn'inqheminch,

vt.); na+ʔx̌íɫ čn‿x̌em=ínč+m-p *You (pl.) maybe love me.* (na qhiɫ chnqheminchmp, v.); uc+ʔax̌iɫ s+tɫ+t=cín+m *catachresis.* (uts'aqhiɫ stɫttsinm (lit. for no reason directing one's speech or discourse), n.); u+c+ʔax̌íɫ e+tɫ+t=cín+m *blabber.* (uts'aqhiɫ etɫttsinm (lit. For nothing he talks straight. He talks rapidly, incessantly and inanely), vi.) [xref √ʔx̌l]

√ʔx̌ʷ † n+ʔax̌ʷ *downstream.* ('naqhw (stem), adv.); in+ʔax̌[ʷ]+tíɫ *catadromous.* (i'naqhtiɫ) (lit. The fish is going back to the sea to spawn), adj.)

√ʔynɫ † e+ʔyníɫ *because.* (e'yniɫ, conj.)

√ʔyx̌ʷ † ʔayx̌ʷ *fatigued, tired.* (ayqhw... (v. stem), adj.); ʔayx̌ʷ+t *he became tired.* (ayqhwt.. v.); ʔay+ʔáyx̌ʷ+t *bore, They became tired.* (ay'ayqhwt (lit. He arouses boredom), n.); ʔáy+ʔayx̌ʷ+t *boredom.* (ay'ayqhwt. bore, n.); i·c+ʔáyx̌ʷ+t *aweary.* (iits'ayqhwt (lit. He is tired), adj.); n+ʔáyx̌ʷ+n *tiredness.* ('nayqhwn, n.); y̕ʔáyx̌ʷ+t *to be exhausted, fatigue, tired.* ('yayqhwt, adj, n, vt.); ∥ n+ʔay+ʔayx̌ʷ=cn *belabor (lit. He talks tediously on, he belabors a point).* ('nay'ayqhwtsn, v.); ‡ čs+ʔayx̌ʷ-n *I got tired going after it; I put much effort to attain it.* (chs'ayqhwn, vt.); n+ʔáy+ʔayx̌ʷ-t-s-n *belabor.* ('nay'ayqhwtsn (lit. He talks tediously on, he belabors a point), vt.)

√ʔʕʷ † s+t+ʔáʕʷ+ʔaʕʷ+p=us *teardrops.* (st'a(w'a(wpus, pl.n.) [?]

APPENDIX A: PREFIXES

This appendix lists all morphemes which Nicodemus identifies as grammatical prefixes, and which we have removed from the main body of the dictionary. It also includes other morphemes which we think may be prefixes, but which are not identified as such by Nicodemus. We have included a bracketed question mark [?] after entries with no corresponding information in Reichard 1938. We follow Reichard in organizing these morphemes as follows: Nominal prefixes (section 1), prefixes denoting aspect, state and plural (section 2), locative prefixes (section 3), and directional prefixes (section 4). After each paragraph header, we have included Reichard's gloss in italics followed by the section in her grammar where it is found. This is not an exhaustive list of Coeur d'Alene prefixes.

Section 1: Nominal Prefixes

č'iy- probably an allomorph of *tc'it, offspring, child of:* (§377a)
    č'iy+nłámqe? *cub.* ch'iynḻamqe' (lit. offspring of a bear, n.)

hiy- *hii-, that which, the one who:* (§375)
    hiy+ni?+k'ʷín' *eclectic.* (hiyni'k'wi̱'n (lit. that which is picked out), adj.); hiy+t+c'áx̌ʷ *deliberate.* (hiytts'a̱qhw (lit. It was done deliberately), vt.)

ul- *u̱l-, belonging to:* (§377)
    ul *belonging to.* (ul. -an, adj.)

nukʷ- *nukʷ-, companion, fellow, one of same kind:* (§378)[26]
    s+nukʷ(-) *fellow, together, with.* (snukw-. (comb form), n, pref.);
    s+nukʷ+síxʷ+sixʷ+xʷ *brethren, fellow-bloods.* (snukwsi̱khwsikhukhw, n.);
    s+nukʷ+méł+l+iš *bed-fellow.* (snukwme̱łlish, n.)

pan'- *pän'-, spouse:* (§379)
    pan' *husband, mate, spouse, wife.* (pa'n (stem), n.); § pan'+táx̌ʷ+x̌ʷ *widow, widower.* (pa'nta̱qhuqhw. She/He became a widow/widower, n.); pen'+yilmíxʷ+m *first lady, queen.* (pe'nyilmi̱khum. (lit. She is the wife of the chief), n.); pan'+s+qíl'=tmxʷ *bride-groom.* (pa'nsqi̱'ltmkhw (lit. a spouse man), n.)

sya- (sye-) *syä- (sya-), the one whose business is...:* (§374)
    sya+dax̌+él'+s+či+če? *cattle herder.* (syadaqhe̱'lschiche', n.); sya·+kʷán=ax̌n *captor.* (syaakwa̱naqhn (lit. One who takes (another) by the arm), n.); sye·+k'ʷúl' *creator, dean, originator, servant.* (syeek'u̱'l (lit. One who produces), n.)

aʕʷ- *copious.* (a(w...(pref.), adj.) [?]

---

[26] We have analyzed both *nukʷ* and *nukʷ* as lexical roots, and have left them within the main body of the dictionary.

Section 2: Prefixes Denoting Aspect, State and Plural

ac- (ec-) *äts- (ats-), customary* (§382)
  ac+q'ʷés+m' *pleated.* (atsq'wes̲'m (lit. It is...), adj.); ec+pén'+pn' *crooked.*
  (etspe̲'np'n, vi. (lit. It has bends or curves), adj.)

peł- *pał-, a prefix meaning plural,we have found only with words meaning "boys".*
It seems to be borrowed from Kal. pał, *folk, where it is common (Giorda):* (§390)
  peł+t+tuw'it *adolescents.* (pełttu'wit, n.)

Section 3: Locative Prefixes

ce- ce *is (There it...).* (tse, vi.) [?]

č- *tc- on, attached to but not part of, at a point:* (§395)
  č- *on (...the surface).* (ch- (stem), adv.); eče· *top (on top of), atop, on.* (echee... pref,
  prep.); etč- *at or on, in the sense of clinging or grasping.* (etch... pref.)

čłi?- *beside.* (chłi'- (pref.), adv.) [?]

čs- *tcs- (tss-) after, behind, in pursuit of, for a purpose:* (§399)
  čs *course, goal.* (chs- (pref), n.)

čet- *tcät-, on a surface or object broader than subject, above, over:* (§398)
  čet *above, top (on top of).* (chet, prep.)

gʷl'- *gul', under ledge or inclined plane, "almost touching"[27]:* (§407)
  s+gʷl'=tmxʷ *flirt.* (sg'ltmkhw, n.); gʷl'+t=méš *clique.* (gu'ltme̲sh (lit. They are an
  exclusive group of people), n.)

ni?- ni? *among.* (ni' (stem). in the midst of, adv.) [?]

ep- *base, bottom.* (ep... (pref.), n.) [?]

tč(')- *ttc-, This prefix is used with numerals in counting persons; it means*
"astraddle" or "straddling object"; or that the object on top is larger than the one it
is on: (§396)
  tč'- *bi-, bin-.* (tch'-, pref.); tč+?úpen *ten persons.* (tch'upen, n.); gʷl' tč+?esel
  binary. (gu'l tch'esel, adj.); tč+?ésel *are (They...two persons).* (tch'e̲sel, vi.);
  e+tč'+?síl+m=us *binocular.* (etch'si̲lmus, vi. (lit. With both eyes), n.); tč'+?síl=šn
  biped. (tch'si̲lshn (lit. One having 2 feet), n.); tč+?síl=ene?+m-nt-m *binaural.*
  (tch'silene'mntm (lit. He was heard by 2 ears), n.); tč+?síl+m-st-m *were (They...both*
  taken). (tch'si̲lmstm, vi.); u+ši?+míš tel' tč+?ésel *either.* (ushi'mi̲sh te'l tch'e̲sel (lit.
  one or the other of two persons), n.)

---

[27] The following 2 examples consist solely of affixes, with no apparent root. We usually identify *tmxʷ* as a lexical root, but it may
also be analyzed as a lexical suffix.

tee- *beforehand.* (tee- (pref.)) [?]

tpen- *below (comb. form).* (tpen-. (pref.), circum-.) [?]

Section 4: Directional Prefixes (§409-431)

čic- *tcits- hither, i.e., toward speaker.* (§412)
s+či·c+ʔúkʷ+m *bringing (...here).* (schiits'ukum, vi.); čic+xʷúy *came (he....over here).* (chitskhuy, vt.); čic+xʷúy-stu-s *brought.* (chitskhuystus (lit. He brought it over here), vt.); pin'č'+neʔ kʷ+č'ic+xʷúy *When are you coming over?.* (pi'nch'ne' kuch'itskhuy, qu.); s+čic+en+déxʷ+xʷ+t+m *come (...down).* (schitsendekhukhtm (lit. a decline this way in status), vi.); tgʷel' s+tim'+ɬ kʷ‿čic+xʷy? *come (Why did you...?).* (tgwe'l sti'mɬ ku chitskhuy?, vi.); [also recorded as √čʔc] čiʔc= ʔegʷeɬ+cétxʷ=mš *bound.* (chi'ts'egweɬtsetkhumsh (lit. I am headed for home), adj.)

tč- teč *to, towards.* (tech, adv.); teč+ciʔ *direction (in your...), yonder, there (over there).* (techtsi', adv.); teč+ɬuw' *there (over there).* (techɬu'w, adv.); teč+ciʔ-š *begone!, get (...away!), go ((You)...in that direction!).* (techtsi'sh, vi.); tač+s+ˤʷél=eʔel *coastward, toward seashore.* (tachs(wele'el, adv.); teč+n+gʷís+t *above, aloft, overhead, upstairs, in heaven, into a high place, toward the sky.* (techngwist, adv.); tač s+t+c'íkʷeʔ *apart.* (tach stts'ikwe' (lit. toward the left hand), n.); teč s+či·t'+íʔ+čn *Eastern.* (tech schiit'i'chn (lit. situated toward the part of the earth which is toward the sunrise (rising this way), adj.); ɬe kʷ'ey' teč+ciʔ *before.* (ɬe k'we'y techtsi'. in former days, adv.); s+teč+s+xʷét'+p+n *counterattack.* (stechskhwet'pn (lit. counterattack by running), n.); tč+n+kʷín+peleʔ *carol.* (tchnkwinpele' (lit. He celebrated or praised in song), v.); tč+čmín+p=ɬxʷ-nt-m *degrade, eject.* (tchchminpɬkhwntm (lit. He was thrown out of the house, He was deprived of dignity, He was ousted), vi.) [?]

APPENDIX B: LEXICAL SUFFIXES

This appendix lists the lexical suffixes we found in *Snchitsu'umshtsn* volume 1 and 2, grouped into three sections[28]. The suffixes are arranged alphabetically by consonant.

Section 1 includes the suffixes we could match with those listed in Reichard (1938). Each entry consists of a phonemic transcription of the suffix, Reichard's transcription and gloss, and the section number where found, all in italics. Sub-entries list the allomorphs of each suffix, and examples of these allomorphs taken from *Snchitsu'umshtsn* volume 1 and 2. We have also included the number of occurences of each morph in square brackets.

Section 2 includes 32 forms for which we could not find matches in Reichard, but which we believe to be suffixes.

Section 3 lists entries consisting of a single segment and a lexical suffix. Examples for each suffix are taken from the dictionary.

Section 1: Matches with Reichard (1938).

=cin *-tsin (-tsän, -tsEn) edge, mouth, shore §475*
    =cn(') t+caq=cn *phonograph.* (ttsaqtsn (lit. that which is put by the mouth with concave side up (refers to megaphone), n.); s+n+čícu?u=mš=cn. *Coeur d'Alene.* (snchitsu'umshtsn, (to speak...).) [118]
    =cin ł+t'q'ʷ=cin+m *blurt.* (łt'q'wtsinm., vt.); x̌as+x̌as+t=cin+mn-n *commend.* (qhasqhasttsinmnn (lit. I represented it as worthy), vt.) [57]
    =ci·n ci·n'+útm *abominable, accursed, outrageous.* (ch'stsii'nutm (lit. it is accursed), adj.); č's+č's=ci·n'=íye? *dispute.* (ch'sch'stsii'niye' (lit. He exchanged mean words with another), n.) [4]

=ic'e? *-its'äˈä all around, all over §533*
    =ce? t+péq=ce? *Caucasian, man (white...).* (tpeqtse', n.); s+cen+t'uk'ʷ=íp=ce? *backfire.* (stsent'uk'wiptse', n.); hn+hala·=cé? *raspberry.* (hnhalaatse', n.) [4]
    =c'e? č+l'+l'pot=c'e? *can, jar.* (ch'l'lpotts'e', n.); t+q'ʷed=c'e? *black (...of skin), Negro.* (tq'wedts'e' (lit. Black of skin), n.); [10]
    =ic'e? s+t+kʷ'l'+l'=ic'e? *aura.* (stkw'l'lits'e', n.); miyeł+t+x̌as=ic'e? *bedizen.* (miyełtqhasits'e' (lit. he is dressed too well), n.); s+can+cuˤʷ=íc'e? *shawl.* (stsantsu(wits'e', n.); c+c'm=íc'e? *midgets, pygmies.* (tsts'mits'e', n.) [11]

=ičn' *-itcn' (-ätcn', -Etcn') back §459*
    =ečen' t+xʷ+xʷík'ʷ+xʷak'ʷ=ečen'=us *frosty eyebrows.* (tkhukhwik'wkhwak'weche'nus, n.) [1]

=ičn' ˤec=ičn' *bow*. ((etsich'n (lit. that which is tied in back), n.); hn+č'+č'el'xʷ=ičn' *roof (a car...)*. (hnch'ch'e'lkhwichn' (lit. concave form as one's back), n.) [26]

=íʔčn(') s+či·t'=íʔčn *east*. (schiit'i'chn, n.); s+maǎ=íʔčn' *bear (grizzly...), bear (polar...)*. (smaqhi'ch'n, n.) [4]

=ičs *-itcs , hand entire §488*

    =čs č+níč'=čs+n *chip*. (chnich'chsn (lit. a small piece cut off by hand), n.); ʔíp'+ʔap'=čs+n *napkin*. (ip"ap'chsn (lit. means of wiping the hands), n.) [9]

    =áčs s+t'a+t'a·p=áčs+n' *archery*. (st'at'aapachs'n (lit. shooting target), n.) [2]

    =ečs mlq'ʷ=ečs+ncut *clench, determined*. (mlq'wechsntsut (lit. he brought together (hands) tightly), vt.) [2]

    =íčs c'ukʷ=íčs+n *cane*. (ts'uk'wichsn (lit. walking stick), n.); li·béč he c'ukʷ=íčs+is *crosier*. (liibech he ts'uk'wichsis (lit. a bishop's staff (cane), n.); t+šar=íčs+n *bail*. (tsharichsn (lit. means of carrying (hanging on hand), n.) [6]

=ičt *-itct , hand, finger §487*

    =čt taq=čt+m *wave*. (taqchtm (lit. He put his hand in a touching attitude), vi.); ǎíł=čt+m-nt-s *relinquish, cede*. (qhiłchtmnts. (lit. He ceased his hold on it), vt.) [48]

    =ečt s+c'íʔ+c'eʔ=ečt *hands*. (sts'i'ts'e'echt, n.); čn‿gʷíw'+ew'=ečt *became (my hand (glove)...worn out)*. (chngwi'we'wecht, vi.) [21]

    =íčt cuw'=íčt+m *boxing (he feinted in...), feinted (he...in boxing)*. (tsu'wichtm, n, vi.); c'l=íčt+m *bungle*. (ts'lichtm (lit. He acted ineptly or inefficiently), vi.) [106]

=čeʔ *-tcä⁷ä ? §527*

    =čeʔ s+k'ʷus+ús=čeʔ *apparition, ghost*. (sk'ususche', n.); k'ʷs=čeʔ *haunted, spook, ghost*. (k'usche' (stem). adj, n.) [5, only with √k'ʷs]

=gʷl *-gwil, hollow object, abdomen, wagon, canoe §492*

    =gʷl s+t+c'áʔar=gʷl *bellyache, colic, stomach ache*. (stts'a'argul, n.); s+t+č'ém=gʷl *abdomen, belly*. (stch'emgul, n.) [13]

    =gʷl' t+p+pís=gʷl' *caricature, comics, funnies*. (tppisgu'l (lit. little people with big bellies), n.) [1]

=kʷp *-kup, fire, fuel §480*

    =kʷp † hn+t+qʷil'=kʷp+n *oven, stove*. (hntqwi'lkupn (lit. place for kindling), n.); šl=ítkʷp *split (He...wood for the fire)*. (shlitkup, vt.); gʷíč'+s=kʷp+n *kindling*. (gwich'skupn, n.); s+šl+ít=kʷp *block*. (sshlitkup (lit. wood split into pieces), n.) [6]

    =íl'kʷp qʷm'=íl'kʷp *benighted, crass, ignorant, inane, asinine, silly, stupid*. (qu'mi'lkup. a stupid silly person (lit. dark ashes), adj.) [1]

    =íłkʷp s+qʷn=íłkʷp *ashes, clinker*. (sqwniłkup. (lit. grayish-blue to white to black residue of combustion), n.) [1]

=kʷeʔ *-kʷä⁷ä , water, liquid §519*

    =kʷeʔ s+caq+aq=cín=kʷeʔ+n *dock*. (stsaqaqtsinkwe'n, n.); a+n+c'ór=kʷeʔ *salt water*. (ants'orkwe', n.) [34]

=atkʷeʔ čat+pos=atkʷeʔ *bubble*. (chatpo-satkwe' (lit. It (water) gave off bubbles), v.) [1]

=ítkʷeʔ hn+č's=ítkʷeʔ *stagnant*. (hnch'sitkwe'. (lit. bad water, bitter water), adj.); hn+ɫen'=ítkʷeʔ *Europe, overseas, the Continent*. (hnɫe'nitkwe'. (lit. on the other side of the water), n.) [25]

=ilgʷes -ilgwäs (-älgwäs), *property, §508* and *heart, stomach §490*

=elgʷes s+n+lím=elgʷes *cheer, heartiness, rejoicing*. (snlimelgwes, n.); lut un+míy=elgʷes *capricious, fickle*. (lut unmiyelgwes (lit. He has no definite thoughts), adj.) [28]

=ilgʷes s+t+c'ar'=ilgʷes *ailing, ill*. (stts'a'rilgwes, vt, n.); hn+šč'+šc'=ilgʷes *stout-hearted*. (hnshch'shts'ilgwes (lit. He is stout-hearted, emotionally). toughened, adj.); s+n+duxʷ+p=ílgʷes *dolor, grief, sorrow*. (sndukhwpilgwes (lit. lowering of the heart), n.); hn+ɫoqʷ=ílgʷes+n *cabinet, closet*. (hnɫoqwilgwesn. (lit. place for hanging (storing) things), n.) [79]

=ílmxʷ -ilumxʷ (-älumxʷ, -alumxʷ), *person, man §504*

=lmxʷ xʷiʔ+ye+tmixʷ=lmxʷ *American*. (ul khwi'yetmikhw'lmkhw (lit. belonging to this land (world), adj.) [1]

=ílmxʷ t+miy=ílmxʷ+n *cairn, landmark*. (tmiyilmkhwn (lit. a mound of stones erected as a landmark or memorial), n.); nukʷʼeʔ=ílmxʷ *people*. (nuk'we'ilmkhw. community, tribe, n.) [4]

=ilup -ilup (-älup), *foundation §485*

=ílup xʷkʼʷ=ílup+n *broom*. (khuk'wilupn (lit. instrument for cleaning floors, mattress, etc.), n.); čat+x̌el=ílup+n *floor*. (chatqhelilupn, n.) [6]

=alpqʷ -alpqʷ, *mouth inside, oral cavity §499*

=alpqʷ hi·+tágʷ=alpqʷ *cate, food (boughten...)*. (hiitagwalpqw (lit. something bought for the mouth), n.); s+tʼokʷ=alpqʷ *bow tie*. (st'okwalpqw, n.); s+čʼm=álpqʷ+s he t+tmʼíxʷ *craw*. (sch'malpqws he tt'mikhw (lit. esophagus of a bird), n.); s+č'n'=álpqʷ *cowbell*. (sch''nalpqw (lit. that (ball that strikes a bell) which is hung to the (anterior portion of the) neck), n.) [12]

=elps -ilps (älps), *throat of person, back of animal's neck §514*

=elps t+čeʔɫís=elps *bears (three grizzly...), pigs (three...)*. (tche'liselps, n.); t+mús=elps *grizzlies (four...), pigs (four)*. (tmuselps, n.) [8]

=alqs -alqs, *end §477* and *road §509*

=alqs hn+x̌áy'+x̌iy'=alqs *considerable, costly, dear, road (It is a wide...), valuable*. (hnqha'yqhi'yalqs (lit. It is a wide road), adj.); s+cas=alqs *mosquito*. (stsasalqs, n.); hn+toɫ=álqs+n *black-top*. (hntoɫalqsn. asphalt. (lit. means of paving roads), n.) [42]

=alqʷ -alqʷ (-alq) *long object §498*

=alqʷ kʼʷay's=alqʷ *cedar (tree)*. (k'wa'ysalqw, n.); marám=ɫp=alqʷ *medicine fir tree*. (maramɫpalqw, n.) [40]

=al'qʷ č+ł+łx̌ʷ=ál'qʷ *harpsichord.* (chłłqhwa'lqw (lit. Holes bored on a hollow stick, log, etc, n.); x̌ʷx̌ʷ+éc=al'qʷ *short (He is...).* (khukhwetsa'lqw, adj.) [11]

=ilt *-ilt (-ält, -äl't) offspring, child §502*
>   **=elt** s+kʷ'ét'=elt *fawn.* (sk'wet'elt, n.); s+mí+mem=elt *berceuse, lullaby.* (smimemelt, putting one's child to sleep. chanting or singing, n.) [16]
>   **=ált** s+t'm'=ált=mš *cattle (herd of), bison (herd of).* (st"maltmsh. buffalo, n.); s+t'+t'm=alt=mš *buffalo (herd of).* (st"tmaltmsh. bison, cow, n.) [7]
>   **=ilt** s+t'ukʷ'=ilt+m *childbirth, parturition.* (st'uk'wiltm, n.); ʔem+n=ílt *feed.* (emnilt (children), vt.) [14]
>   **=íl't** s+c+c'm=íl't *children, offspring.* (ststs'mi'lt, n.); gʷ+gʷax̌i+t=íl't *cradleboard (for doll).* (gugwaqhiti'lt, n.); gʷ+gʷax̌+t=il't *baby.* (gugwaqhti'lt, n.) [5]

=elwis *-älwis , about to indefinite places §532*
>   **=elwís** s+t+kʷel'+tem+n=elwís *visiting (He is going about...people).* (stkwe'ltemnelwis, vt.); tkʷ+eł+x̌ʷy=elwís *circulate.* (tkwełkhuyelwis (lit. He moved around from place to place), vi.); s+x̌ʷy=elwis *travel, trip.* (skhuyelwis, n.) [8]
>   **=lwís** sč'=lwís *dead salmon.* (sch'lwis, n.) [1]
>   **=l'wís** sč'=lwís ʔep+sč=l'wís *It, e.g., the river, has dead salmon.* (epsch'lwis, vt.) [1]

=ilxʷ *-ilxʷ (älxʷ, -lxʷ) hide, skin, mat, covering, §491*
>   **=elxʷ** síp=elxʷ *cape-skin.* (sipelkhw. sheepskin, n.); č+tm=elxʷ+ncut *divest.* (chtmelkhwntsut (lit. H/S make h/h self bare), vt.); t+č't'=élxʷ *brown.* (tch't'elkhw (lit. A horse with brown fur (hide)), adj.); ʔupen=čt=élxʷ *dicker.* (upenchtelkhw (lit. ten hides or ten skins), n.) [10]
>   **=íl'xʷ** t+kʷl'+kʷl'=íl'xʷ *calf.* (tkw'lkw'li'lkhw (lit. red red hide), n.); q'a+q'ay'+q'ey'=íl'xʷ *perch.* (q'aq'a'yq'e'yi'lkhw, n.) [2]
>   **=al'xʷ** ł+łiy'=al'xʷ *horse (a spotted..., pinto), pinto.* (łłiy'al'khw (lit. one with a spotted or marked hide), n.) [1]
>   **=elxʷeʔ** s+t+gʷiš=elxʷeʔ+ł+s+čí+čeʔ *curry.* (stgwishelkhwe'lschiche' (lit. rubbing down and cleaning a horse), vt.) [2]

=ul'umxʷ *-ul'umxʷ (-əl'umxʷ), ground §486*
>   **=ul'umxʷ** s+x̌áq'=ul'umxʷ *demise.* (sqhaq'u'lumkhw (lit. pay for use of land), n.); s+yuxʷm=ús+m=ul'umxʷ *North.* (syukhwmusmu'lumkhw, n.); hn-n+č'ar=úl'umxʷ *ditch, trench.* (hnnch'aru'lumkhw. (lit. It is my trench cut in the earth), n.); č'uw+č'uw=úl'umxʷ *eeri[e], weird.* (ch'uwch'uwu'lumkhw. eerie. (lit. It is a territory that is usually without people, a lonely, weird, mysterious place), adj.); x̌es=ul'úmxʷ *fertile (land), land (good, fertile, productive), open country, plain, productive (land).* (qhesu'lumkhw. good land, fertile land, plain, open country, adj.) [49]
>   **=l'úmxʷ** luxʷ=l'úmxʷ *cave.* (lukhu'lumkhw, n.); s+t+miy+y=ipeleʔ+s łe tmíxʷ=l'umxʷ *earth (description of...), description (...of earth).* (stmiyyipele's łe

tmikhw'lumkhw, n.); s+cen+k[']ʷúl'+l'+s xʷe tmíxʷ=l'umxʷ *map*. (stsenku̱'l'ls khwe tmi̱khw'lumkhw (lit. means of making a description of land), n.) [6]

=ul'mxʷ s+n+tuqʷ+qʷ=ul'mxʷ *crater*. (sntuququ̱'lmkhw (lit. a depression in the ground caused by a volcano, meteor, etc.), n.); s+yukʷkʷm=ús+m=ul'mxʷ *Aleut*. (syukkwmu̱smu'lmkhw. (lit. One who lives in a cold country), n.); hn+c's+p= úl'mxʷ-st-m *devastate*. (hnts'spu̱'lmkhwstm (lit. The land was deprived of inhabitants), vi.) [35]

=ól'mxʷ ml'=ól'mxʷ *ground, soil*. (m'lo̱'lmkhw, n.); ml=ól'mxʷ *earth (soil)*. (mlo̱'lmkhw, n.); s+ml'=ól'mxʷ *dumplings*. (sm'lo̱'lmkhw (lit. bread boiled), n.) [3]

=ól'umxʷ s+nq'+s=ól'umxʷ *chresard*. (snq'so̱'lumkhw (lit. wet ground), n.); u+x̌ʷal'+á ml=ól'umxʷ *unrefined, earthy*. (uqhwa'la̱ mlo̱'lumkhw (lit. It resembles the soil), adj.) [3]

=ulmxʷ s+t+miy+iy=ípele?+s xʷe t+č'm=ásq'it twe tmíxʷ=ulmxʷ *cosmography*. (stmiyiyi̱pele's khwe tch'ma̱sq'it twe tmi̱khulmkhw, n.); hn+t'iš+t'íš=ulmxʷ *cookie*. (hnt'isht'i̱shulmkhw. (lit. sweet little loaves of bread), n.) [4]

=ulumxʷ s+bi·nwáh=ulumxʷ *Benewah County*. (Sbiinwa̱hulumkhw (lit. Benewah land, named after a Coeur d'Alene), n.); s+mé?m=ulumxʷ *man's younger sister*. (sme̱'mulumkhw, n.) [2]

=al'qs *-al'qs, clothes §471*

=al'qs hn+c+cám'=al'qs+n' *roads (small...), vegetables*. (hntstsa̱'ma'lqsn', n.); cétxʷ+s xʷa ma?+ma?+ám=al'qs *convent*. (tse̱tkhws khwa ma'ma'a̱ma'lqs (lit. their house those who wear women's clothes (nuns)), n.); x̌as=ál'qs *dapper*. (qhasa̱'lqs. He has neat clothes, he is neatly dressed, adj.) [27]

=il'š *-il'c , grow, become through growth §442*

=il'š č'+č'n'e?=il'š-s-n *diminish*. (ch'ch"ne'i'lshsn, vt.); s+pax̌+pax̌+t=il'š *prudent*. (spaqhpaqhti'lsh, adj.) [44]

=ilš č'+č'n'e?=ilš *decrease, grow small*. (ch'ch"ne'ilsh (lit. it became small or smaller), v.); qíxʷ=ilš *carp, fish*. (qi̱khwilsh, n.) [4]

=ełp *-ä̱łp (-ałp, Ełp) bush, plant §469*

=ałp šáx̌ʷ+šax̌ʷ+t=ałp *spruce*. (sha̱qhshaqhtałp, n.); ?álč=ałp=alqʷ *cranberry (wild)*. (a̱lchałpalqw, n.) [3]

=ełp s+x̌ʷ?+x̌ʷn'=ič=ełp *thornberry bush*. (sqhu'qhu'nichełp, n.); y?átqʷ=ełp *conifer, pine tree*. ('ya̱tqwełp, n.) [5]

=iłp tax̌+tax̌=iłp *birch (black...)*. (taqhtaqhiłp, n.); qʷl'+qʷl'+m+n=iłp *sagebrush*. (qw'lqw'lmni̱łp (lit. dark dark plant), n.) [2]

=i?łp wáx̌=i?łp *dog-wood, wild maple*. (wa̱qhi'łp, n.); s+x̌ʷiy=i?łp=mš *Colville Tribe*. (Sqhwiyi'łpmsh, n.) [2]

=łp marám=łp=alqʷ *medicine fir tree*. (mara̱młpalqw, n.); t+marím=łp=ečt *medicine (...tree)*. (tmari̱młpecht (lit. a tree that has medicinal branches), n.) [2]

=iłxʷ *-iłxʷ (-łxʷ) house §496*

224

=łxʷ s+cóm'=łxʷ *longhouse.* (stsó̲młkhw (lit. house of mats), n.); tč+čmín+p=łxʷ-nt-m *degrade, eject.* (tchchmi̲npłkhwntm (lit. He was thrown out of the house, He was deprived of dignity, He was ousted), vi.) [14]

=iłxʷ hn+čm'=iłxʷ *burglarize, robbed.* (hnch'mi̲łkhw (lit. One who takes from a house), vi.); s+č'+č'l'xʷ=iłxʷ *tent.* (sch'ch"lkhwiłkhw (lit. House turned upside down), n.); čet+č'm+c=iłxʷ *awning, porch, eaves.* (chetch'mtsi̲łkhw, n.); čat+x̌ep=iłxʷ+n *roofing, shingle, shingles.* (chatqhepiłkhwn, n.) [22]

=mš *-ųmc (-Emc) people §506*

=mš gʷl'+t=méš *clique.* (gu'ltme̲sh (lit. They are an exclusive group of people), n.)[29]; čiy'+n+máy'+ay'=qn=mš *dining, eating.* (chi'ynma̲'ya'yqnmsh (lit. I am dining), vt, vi.); s+pa·yól=mš *Spanish.* (Spaayo̲lmsh, n.); s+qʷíc=mš *bunny, rabbit.* (sqwi̲tsmsh, n.); ic+qʷíc=mš *warming (he is...himself).* (itsqwi̲tsmsh, vt.)[30] [28]

=emš sí+dl=emš *Indians (Jocko Valley...of Montana).* (Si̲dlemsh, n.) [1]

=inč *-intc (-äntc) hollow, belly §493*

=anč ul pus ha s+táx̌=anč+s *catgut.* (ul pus ha sta̲qhanchs (lit. of cat his gut), n.); x̌am=anč+ł+qʷám+qʷam *aesthete.* (qhamanchłqwa̲mqwam (lit. He loves beautiful things), n.) [5]

=enč n+ʔúkʷ+t=enč *crawled (It...on the inside of the wall).* ('nu̲kwtench, vi.); s+niʔ+c'áʔ+c'ar'=enč *pains (intestinal...).* (sni'ts'a̲'ts'a'rench, n.) [37]

=inč x̌em=inč *like, love.* (qheminch (stem), vt.); s+x̌am=inč *affection, esteem.* (sqhaminch (lit. an attitude to one who has value), n.); ac+x̌em=ínč *love.* (atsqheminch. (stem), vt.); s+x̌em=ínč+m *love.* (sqheminchm, n.) [117]

=ín'č ʔał+d+dar'=ín'č *clock, sundial, timepiece, watch, chronometer.* (ałdda'ri̲'nc, n.); čn‿kʷ+kʷel'=ín'č+m' *bask, sunbathe.* (chnkukw'li̲'nch'm. (lit. I sunbathed my entrails, belly, etc.), vi.); ł+łq'=ín'č *brisling, sardine.* (łłq'i̲'nch. (lit. little wide intestine), n.) [8]

=ngʷiln *-ingwilEn (-EngwilEn), something §512*

=ngʷíln s+miy+p=ngʷíln *learning.* (smiypngwi̲ln (lit. it is the means of learning, of education), n.); s+can+paʔaʔx̌=ngʷíln *concept.* (stsanpa'a'qhngwi̲ln (lit. attaining a result of reasoning), n.) [7]

=ins *-ins (-äns) tooth §516*

=ens n+ʔíp'=ens+m *wiped (H/s...h/h tooth or teeth).* ('nip'ensm, vt.); n+ʔsíl=ens *bicuspid.* ('nsi̲lens (lit. two teeth), n.) [8]

---

[29] This particular entry consists entirely of lexical affixes. There is no clear lexical root, and so this entry occurs only in this appendix.

[30] There are two homophonous /+mš/ suffixes. One is a grammatical suffix and functions to indicate continuity, the other is a lexical suffix meaning *tribe.* Consider the following entry:

√hmłt hamáłt=mš *fly.* (hama̲łtmsh (lit. swarming tribe), n.)

Based on this entry, one could analyze the entry s+qʷíc=mš as meaning literally "warming tribe". In the following entry, ic+qʷíc=mš it seems the suffix would be better analyzed as a continuative. This is an example of the problem in isolating one homophonous suffix from the other. See Reichard §506

=íns hn+xʷk'ʷ=íns+n *dentifrice.* (hnkhuk'wi̱nsn (lit. means of cleaning the teeth), n.) [3]

=ine -inä*ˈä* (-änä*ˈä*), *ear §473* and *over, on top of §541*
 =ane čat+p't'+t'=ane *lava, magma.* (chatp't't'ane' (lit. covering by lava), n.); hn+t'l'=áne *wolf.* (hnt"la̱ne', n.) [2]
 =ene gʷł yóp+yop=ene *sorceresses, witches.* (guł yo̱pyopene', n.); čat+ʕel'=ene+ncut *cover (oneself).* (chat(e'lene'ntsut, vt.) [28]
 =e·ní tekʷ=e·ní *heard (He...).* (tekweeni̱', vt.); čn‿tekʷ=e·ní *heard (I...something).* (chntekweeni̱' (lit. I detected with the ear), vt.) [2]
 =íne hn+t+caq=íne+n *acoustics.* (hnttsaqi̱ne'n (lit. means of hearing sounds), n.); t=caq=íne+m-nt-s *heeded, heard, obeyed (He...him).* (ttsaqi̱ne'mnts, vt.); et+š*ʔ*t'=ine *attentive.* (etsh't'ine' (lit. He pays attention by ear), vi.); hn+ʕac+ʕac=ine *earrings (to wear...), Italian, Italians.* (hn(ats(atsine' (lit. people with earrings), n.) [33]

=ip -ip (-ap, -äp, -p) *bottom, behind, after §463-466*
 =ap s+can+č'm'=ap=qn' *head (back of...).* (stsanch"mapq'n, n.); po*ʔ*t'=ap=w'as=qn *greasy (h/h chin got...).* (po't'ap'wasqn, adj.); s+can+č'lxʷ=áp=qn *canope.* (stsanch'lkhwapqn (lit. vault covering with the concave side over the head), n.); hn+č'uxʷ+č'uxʷ=áp=en'e*ʔ*+m' *retired, slept.* (hnch'ukhwch'ukhwa̱pe'ne"m. (lit. H/s laid his head against (something)), vt.) [10]
 =ip =ip *back, bottom.* (stem) (N); caq=ip *follow.* (tsaqip (stem), vt.); hn+č'm=ip *bottom.* (hnch'mip, n.) [6]
 =aps sétq=aps *April.* (se̱tqaps, n.) [1]
 =apa s+qʷá·y=apa *rose hip.* (sqwa̱ayapa', n.) [1]

=iple -iplä*ˈä* (-aplä*ˈä*, -äplä*ˈä*), *attachment, handle, connection §458*
 =ple t+č'éʕʷ=ple-nt-s *dedicate.* (tch'e(wple'nts (lit. He prayed for its special use), v.) [1]
 =pele s+t+č'éʕʷ=pele *benediction, benison, blessing, consecration, dedication.* (stch'e(wpele'. (lit. praying for the origin of one), n.); at+č'éʕʷ=pele *blessed, consecrated.* (atch'e(wpele', vi. (lit. Divine favor was invoked upon h/h/i), adj.) [3]
 =ápala s+t+čn'=ápala=qn *steering (a horse).* (stch'na̱pala'qn, vt.) [1]
 =ípele =ípele *concerning.* (-ipele', (suff.)) (N); č+leč'+m=ípele *commandeer.* (chle-chmi̱pele (lit. he seized arbitrarily), v.); t+miy=ípele *expounded.* (tmiyi̱pele' (lit. H/s made plain concerning something), vt.); s+t+c'ox̌ʷ=ipele *decision.* (stts'oqhwipele', n.); s+t+c'ux̌ʷ=ipele *judgement.* (stts'uqhwipele', n.) [41]
 =iple sya+t+c'ux̌ʷ=iple *arbiter.* (syatts'uqhwiple', n.); hi+s+nukʷ+meʕʷ+ł+nt+c'ux̌ʷ=íple+n *complicity.* (hisnukwme(włntts'uqhwiple'n (lit. He is my partner in violating the law), n.); hn+t+c'ux̌ʷ=íple+n *edict, equity, law.* (hntts'uqhwi̱ple'n (lit. promise made by one for others, public announcement having the force of a law, means of judging), n.) [5]

=ups -ups, anus, anal region §456

    =up hn+č'em=up *buttocks.* (hnch'emup, n.); hn+č'em=up *buttocks.* (hnch'emup, n.); n+ʔm+iš ʔeˑl=úp-nt-s *commute.* ('nmisheelupnts (lit. He sat in his (another's) place), vi.) [5]

    =úps =ups *tail, anal.* (-ups, (pertaining to the anus), suf.) (N); ul s+čs=úps+n *caudal.* (ul schsupsn (lit. pertaining to the tail or hind parts), adj.); ml=qn=úps *eagle.* (mlqnups (etym. mlqn-dark, ups-tail), n.); hn+qap=qín=ups+n *saddle, seat cushion.* (hnqapqinupsn, n.); s+q'ʷéd=ups *grouse.* (sq'wedups (lit. black tail), n.) [10]

=qin -qin (-qEn) voice §518 and *head, tip, top §489*

    =qn(') =qn *head, skull.* ((aff), relating to the head or skull. n.) (N); s+niʔ+cl=áw'as=qn *quill (porcupine...over head).* (sni'tsla'wasqn, n.); c+cółm'=qn' *Little Bull Head.* (Tstsoł'mq'n (name of a Flathead Indian), n.) [195]

    =qin(') t+coʔ=qin-t-m *clobber (slang).* (ttso'qintm (lit. He was batted with fists as to the head), v.); čp=qin+n *hair.* (chpqinn (lit. head softener), n.); yarp'=qín+tm *crown.* (yarp'qintm, n. and vt.); y'aʔˤ+p=qín' *canaille, masses (the...).* ('ya'(pqi'n. (lit. They are many), pl.n.) [64]

    =qínn u+x̌ʷal'+á čp=qínn *capillary.* (uqhwa'la chpqinn (lit. It resembles hair), n.) [1]

    =qn =ečt -s=qen=e[č]t *toe, digit.* (-sqeneht, suf.) [1]

=aqs -aqs breast §467

    =aqs šn'=aqs+n *breastplate.* (sh'naqsn (lit. a plate lying on the chest), n.); kʷan+ł+pn'+pn'=aqs *par flesche.* (kwanłp'np'naqs (h/s took along a case of dried hide bent up), n.) [4]

    =qs s+t'op=qs *spool, thread.* (st'opqs, n.); s+č+t'op=qs *bobbin.* (scht'opqs, n.); a+can+c'áw'+c'aw'=qs+t+m *bureau, chest (of drawers), dresser.* (atsants'a'wts'a'wqstm, n.) [3]

=us -us eye, face, orifice through which light shines, fire §478

    =us uˑ cáp=us *blink.* (uutsapus (lit. His eye blinked), vi.); hn+c'éč=us *accounted, ciphered, computed, counted.* (hnts'echus, v.); hn+c'č=ús+n *calculator.* (hnts'chusn (lit. keyboard machine for the automatic performance of arithmetic operations), n.); s+mar'kʷ=ús *black tail deer.* (sma'rkus, n.) [200]

    =s hn+c'ór=s+m *winked (he...).* (hnts'orsm, vi.); tor=s *beckon (with the eye).* (tor...s (stem), vt.) [14]

=isč'ey't -istc'äy't pharynx §507 (see also 3.11.2h)

    =isč'ey't is+hel'=íščey't *deathbed.* (ishe'lishche'yt (lit. He is near his last breath), n.); t'ax̌=ísč'ey't *long-winded (He is ...).* (t'aqhisch'e'yt (lit. He has fast breath), adj.) [2]

=isgʷel -isgwäl (-asgwäl, -sgwäl) fish §481

    =ísgʷel lĵ=ísgʷel *fish (He speared...), harpoon, spear.* (ljisgwel (lit. He speared fish, usually salmon), n, vt.) [1]

    =asgʷel péq=a[s]gʷel *halibut.* (peqsagwel, n.) [1]

=asq'it *-asq'it (-sq'it) day, sky, atmosphere §472* [see also √st'q]
    =sq'it cél+č=sq'it *Friday*. (Tsel̲chsq'it (lit. five days), n.); u+t+gʷár'=sq'it *sky (The...is clear)*. (utgwa̲'rsq'it, n.) [11]
    =ásq'it t ɪ x̌as=ásq'it *sky (The vault of the...is clear, good, beautiful)*. (tqhasa̲sq'it, n.); t+x̌as=ásq'it *vault (The...of the sky is clear, good, beautiful)*. (tqhasa̲sq'it, n.); t+č'm=asq'it *firmamanet, heaven, sky*. (tch'masq'it (lit. vault of the sky), n.); s+t+p'a?xʷ=asq'it *aurora borealis*. (stp'a'khwasq'i, n.) [12]

=astq *-stq vegetation, crops §517 and -astq (-stq) in opposition to §542*
    =stq y'al=stq *summer*. ('yalstq, n.); k'ʷol'=stq *colonize*. (k'o'lstq (lit. He farmed or settled), vt.) [8]
    =astq =astq *harvest*. (astq. (stem), n.); s+q'ʷl=ál[q]ʷ=astq *fruit*. (sq'wla̲lgwastq (lit. ripened crops), n.); s+t'š=astq *huckleberries*. (st'shastq (lit. sweet crop), n.); s+št'+t'=ástq *conquest*. (ssht't'a̲stq (lit. subduing), n.); s+t'š=ástq *huckleberries*. (st'sha̲stq. sweet crop, pl.n.) [11]
    =astq' *crop*, (astq', n.) (N.) [1]

=šn *-cin (-cän, -cEn) foot, leg §482*
    =šn ec+búc+buc=šn *boots (to be wearing...)*. (etsbu̲tsbutsshn (lit. He is wearing boots), n.); s+t+č'ám+č'm=alq=šn *legs*. (stch'amch'malqshn, pl.n.) [85]
    =šn' s+č'a?=qin'=šn' *knee cap, knee joint, knee*. (sch'a'qi'nsh'n, n.); k'ʷax̌=qin'=šn' *toe nail*. (k'waqhqi'nsh'n, n.) [11]

=ut *-ut, possibility, be in position, state of §447-448* [31]

=iw'es *-iw'äs (-aw'äs, -äw'äs) between, together, be in contact §537*
    =w'es č+ɫec+ɫec=w'es+cútn' *boutonniere*. (chɫetsɫets'westsu̲t'n (lit. buttons), n.); s+t+p'iɫ=liš=w'es *cavalcade*. (stp'iɫlish'wes, n.) [2]
    =áw'as s+ni?+cl=áw'as=qn *quill (porcupine...over head)*. (sni'tsla̲'wasqn, n.); s+ni?+č'm=áw'as=qn *chest*. (sni'ch'ma̲'wasqn (lit. The top of the head), n.); ni?+ɫóq'ʷ=aw'as=qn *bald*. (ni'ɫo̲q'wa'wasqn (lit. one lacking hair on the top of the head), adj.) [4]
    =ew'es mí?t=ew'es *dichotomy*. (mi̲'te'wes (lit. division into two equal parts), n.); níč'=ew'es+n *crosscut*. (ni̲ch'e'wesn (lit. He crosscut it (log, etc.)), vt.) [21]
    =iw'es =iw'es *mutually*, (-i'wes, (suf) adv.) (N); t+št'=iw'es *kettle*. (tsht'iw'es, n.); čm=iw'es *Chatcolet (Lake)*. (chmi'wes (lit. midsection), n.); a+caq=e·p=íw'es *consecutive*. (atsaqeepi̲'wes (lit. They follow one another), n.); s+c'p'q'=íw'es *cohesion*. (sts'p'q'i̲'wes (lit. sticking together), n.) [84]

=ax̌n *-ax̌En, arm §457*
    =áx̌n(') s+čugʷ=áx̌n *arm, limb (body)*. (schugwaqhn (lit. that which extends into space from the body), n.); s+č'm=áx̌n *edge*. (sch'ma̲qhn (lit. extreme border; outer side of arm), n.); ul s+čogʷ=ax̌n *brachial*. (ul schogwaqhn (lit. of the arm), adj.); s+t+č'm+č'm=ós=ax̌n *shoulders*. (stch'mch'mo̲saqhn, pl.n.) [27]

---

[31] It may be possible to analyze this as a lexical suffix, although we have not done so. We have parsed it as a derivational affix.

=áʔx̌n yer+yerk'ʷ=áʔx̌n+m *arms (He bent his...), bent (He...his arms).* (yeryerk'wa̱'qhnm, n, vt.) [1]

=yuyeʔ *-yuyä^{rä}, back and forth §536*

=yúyeʔ sya+n+q'eleˑ=yúyeʔ *acrobat.* (syanq'eleeyu̱ye' (lit. One who swings on trapeze), n.) [1]

=y'úy'eʔ qap+qapl'=y'úy'eʔ *butterfly.* (qapqap'l'yu̱'ye', n.); u+x̌ʷal'+á qap+qapl'= y'úy'eʔ *desultory.* (uqhwa'la̱ qapqap'l'yu̱'ye'. (lit. He is like a butterfly; he is aimless, unsettled), adj.); č'iy+c+qap+qap'l=y'uy'eʔ *chrysalis.* (ch'iytsqapqap'l'yu'ye' (lit. the pupa of a butterfly enclosed in a firm case or cocoon), n.) [3]

=iyeʔ *-iyä^{rä} playingly, §446*

=íyeʔ ic+q'a+q'm'=íyeʔ *fishing (He is...).* (itsq'aq"miye', vi.); q'ʷc'w=íyeʔ *chipmunk.* (q'wts'wi̱ye', n.); č's+č's=ciˑn'=íyeʔ *dispute.* (ch'sch'stsii'ni̱ye' (lit. He exchanged mean words with another), n.); qexʷ+qexʷ+lš=íyeʔ *cabbage (skunk...).* (qekhwqekhwlshi̱ye'. n.) [5]

=íy'eʔ q'a+q'm'=íy'eʔ *fished (he...).* (q'aq"mi̱'ye', vi.); q'ʷ+q'ʷc'w'=íy'eʔ *chipmunk.* (q'q'wts"wi̱'ye', n.); s+č's+č's=ciˑn'=íy'eʔ *argue, bicker, brawl, quarrel, debate.* (sch'sch'stsii'ni̱'ye' (lit. exchanging mean/angry words), vi.); úw'e k'ʷ+k'ʷn=iy'eʔ *awhile.* (u̱'we k'uk'w'ni̱'ye' (lit. for a short time only), adv.); x̌ʷx̌ʷ=iy'eʔ=íl'š-s-n' *diminish, reduce.* (khukhwi'ye'i̱'lshs'n. (lit. I lessened it in breadth), vt.) [14]

=iʔqs *-i^{ri}qs (-a^{rä}qs), nose, beak; oral and nasal cavity, seat of taste §501*

=eʔqs niʔ+págʷ=eʔqs *swelled (H/s nose...up).* (ni'pa̱gwe'qs, vi.) [1]

=iʔqs s+niʔ+č'ám=iʔqs *nose (surface of the).* (sni'ch'a̱mi'qs, n.); e+niʔ+gʷáp+[g]ʷp=iʔqs *hairy (nostrils).* (eni'gwa̱pqupi'qs, vt. (lit. He has hair in his nostrils), adj.); s+har=íʔqs=mš *snore (to...).* (s-hari̱'qsmsh, vi.) [12]

=iqs niʔ+págʷ=iqs *nose (H/h...swelled up).* (ni'pa̱gwiqs, n.) [1]

=uʔs *-u'us, directly, "spang" §538*

=uʔs t'uqʷ=uʔs=ús-nt-s *slapped.* (He...him in the face), t'uqu'su̱snts, v.); kʷl= uʔs+łuxʷp+ú *Red Lasso.* (Kwlu'słukhwpu̱, n.) [4]

=iʔst *-i^{ri}st (-a^{rä}st, ä^{rä}st), surface of round object, rock §513*

=áʔst gʷeč=qan=áʔst *Wenatchee.* (gwechqana'st (lit. he saw over a rock, cliff, precipice), n.); a+t+k'ʷet'=áʔst=qn *bare-headed.* ((lit. His head is uncovered), adj. atk'wet'a̱'stqn, vi.) [2]

=eʔst č'c'=us=eʔst *brink, cliff, bluff.* (ch'ts'use'st, n.); t+kʷar+kʷar+éq=eʔst *orange.* (tkwarkwareqe'st (lit. yellow yellow on the outside), adj.); šét'+s+šic'=eʔst *diamond.* (she̱t'sshits'e'st (lit. hard stone), n.) [9]

=íʔst s+c'+c'x̌=íʔst *gravel.* (sts'ts'qhi̱'st, n.) [1]

Section 2: Lexical Suffixes Without Matches in Reichard

=icén can+p't'=icén=šn *concrete.* (tsanp't'itsᴇnshn (lit. cement conglomerate material put under the foot), n.) [1]

=ece? et+p'+p'úl'+p'ul'k'ʷ=ece? *cigarettes.* (etp'p'u̱'lp'u'lk'wetse', n.) [1]

=ič s+x̌ʷn'=ič *thornberry.* (sqhu'nich, n.); s+x̌ʷ?+x̌ʷn'=ič=ełp *thornberry bush.* (sqhu'qhu'nichełp, n.) [3]

=ede? elu+ł+mít'č'=ede? *bloodless.* (elułmi̱t'ch'ede' (lit. It has no blood), adj.) [7]

=ílčs ǰm=ílčs+n *brooch.* (jmi̱lchsn (lit. safety pin), n.) [1]

=(e)lš suxʷ=elš *jump (ref. to a fish).* (sukhwelsh (stem), vi.); súxʷ=lš *jumped (it (fish)...).* (su̱khwlsh, vi.) [8]

=líye? s+q'ʷaˤ+eˤ+p=líye? *sledding, coasting.* (sq'wa(e(pli̱ye'. sledding (lit. sliding down an inclined slope on a sled), vi.) [1] maybe *-iyä̍ᵃ playingly, §446*

=el'č s+t+tax̌+téx̌=el'č *doll.* (sttaqhtᴇqhe'lch, n.); s+t+ta+téx̌=el'č *[d]olly.* (sttatᴇqhe'lch (lit. a little doll), n.) [2] maybe *-El'tc' ? §526*

=ál'n hn+c'+c'm=ál'n *arrowhead.* (hntsts'ma̱'ln (lit. piece of bone on end of an arrow), n.) [1]

=l'ip caq+caq+aq=l'íp+m *backwards (He fell...), fell (He...backwards).* (tsaqtsaqaq'li̱pm, adv, vi.) [1] [related to =ip ?]

=il's s+nukʷ+n+xʷc+xʷc'+m=íl's *compassion.* (snukwnkhwtskhwts'mi̱'ls (lit. fellow sufferer), n.); hn+xʷc+xʷc+m=íl's *suffered (he...).* (hnkhwtskhwtsmi̱'ls, vi.) [3]

=úl'exʷ s+t'+t'ł=úl'exʷ *ceramic, china.* (st't'łu̱'lekhw. earthenware, brick, n.) [1][32]

=il'ey' gʷ+gʷax̌+t=il'ey' *cradleboard (for doll).* (gugwaqhti'le'y, n.); gʷ+gʷax̌+t=íl'ey' *doll.* (gugwaqhti̱'le'y, n.) [2]

=łc'e? s+mót=łc'e? *bacon.* (smo̱tłts'e' (lit. smoked flesh of pigs), n.); pa+pq=łc'e? *Ermine (white).* (papqłts'e', n.) [21][33]

=ełc(')e? pul+pul=ełc'e?+ul *blood-thirsty.* (pulpuletts'e'ul (lit. He is habitually murdering), adj.); pul+pul=ełce?+ul *kills (he habitually...people), people (he habitually kills...).* (pulpulełtse'ul, vt, n.); pul+pul=ełce?+ul *murderer.* (pulpulełtse'ul, n.) [2]

---

[32] Possibly related to *ulixʷ* in *st'ulixʷ*, the name of Circling Raven's son. See √st'lxʷ.

[33] Possibly the same as =c'e?

=iłc'e? hn+č+čaˁ=iłc'e? *tube, narrow.* (hnchcha(iłt'se'. tube. (lit. It has a very small
internal diameter), adj.); s+t+gʷp+gʷp=iłc'e?=us *eyelashes.* (stgupgupiłts'e'us,
pl.n.); s+caq=iłc'e? *smoking process.* (stsaqiłts'e', n.); s+caq=í?łc'e? *Indian
barbecue.* (stsaqi'łts'e', n.); s+cuw'=iłc'e? *clout.* (stsu'wiłts'e' (lit. hitting a person
with the fist), vt.) [21]

=ułc'e? s+nukʷ+púl=ułc'e? *accomplice.* (snukwpulułts'e' (lit. helper in killing), n.);
ec+púl=ułc'e? *kill, killer, murderer.* (etspulułts'e', vt. (lit. He kills people), n.);
[3]

=ełníw' s+cen+łp'=ełníw' *definition.* (stsenłp'ełni'w, n.); hn+ˁux̌ʷ+ˁux̌ʷ=ełníw'+n
harness. (hn(uqhw(uqhwełni'w, n.) [3]

=ułt mí+mn=ułt *white fish.* (mimnułt, n.) [1]

=m'e? łs+łs=m'e?+ncut+n' *barbell.* (łsłs'me'ntsut'n, n.) [8]

=íneč s+le·w'=íneč *cricket.* (slee'winech. locust, n.) [1] maybe =inč

=nixʷ čis+s+č's+č's+čs=nixʷ *detest.* (chissch'sch'schsnikhw (lit. I am customarily
hated), vt.); s+piy+piy+čs=níxʷ *admiration.* (spiypiychsnikhw, n.) [8]

=pu?s =pu?s *cardio, relating to the heart.* (-pu's, suf.) (N) [analyzed as a root]

=aqł s+pál'=aqł *yesterday.* (aspa'laqł, adv.) [1]

=stwéxʷ yeh+m'=stwéxʷ *demobilize.* (yeh'mstwekhw (lit. They made peace), vt.);
s+yéh+m'=stwexʷ *appease, armistice, peace treaty.* (syeh'mstwekhw (lit. making
peace with others), vi, n.) [2]

=úse? s+c'sl'=úse? *hail.* (sts's'luse', n.) [1]

=tč nok'ʷ+o?=qin+s+pín=tč *centenarian.* (nok'o'qinspintch (lit. a person of one hundred
years), n.); pst+a? a s+qil=tč *cross-breed.* (psta'asqiltch, n.) [56]

=tmxʷ pan'+s+qíl'=tmxʷ *bride-groom.* (pa'nsqi'ltmkhw (lit. a spouse man), n.); s+qil'=
tmxʷ *husband, male, man.* (sqi'ltmkhw, n.) [9] [usually analyzed as a root]

=ítš šc=ítš-st-m *pawed (the horse...).* (shtsitshstm, vi.) [1]

=tq ?akʷós=tq *tell (to tell someone).* (akostq (lit. He told someone), vt.); ?akʷos=tq
accost. (akostq (lit. He spoke to a person first), vt.) [3]

=utye? q'ey'+m=utye? *bill (five dollar...).* (q'e'ymutye'. paper money, n.) [1]

=e?el ˁʷél=e?el *shore.* ((wele'el, n.); § tač+s+ˁʷél=e?el *coastward, toward seashore.*
(tachs(wele'el, adv.) [2]

=oʔp hn+lǰ=oʔp=stq *copulate.* (hnljo'pstq. (lit. He engaged in coitus), vi.) [1]

=íʔsn hn+t'uk'ʷ=íʔsn *acorn, bur (burr), seed.* (hnt'uk'wi'sn, n.); s+t+cugʷ+cugʷ=íʔsn
 feather(s). (sttsugwtsugwi'sn, n.) [2]

Section 3: Lexical Suffixes with a Single Preceding Segment[34]

√cɫxʷ c(=)eɫxʷ *house.* (tseɫkhw (stem), n.) [xref ctxʷ]
√skʷ₂ s(=)íkʷeʔ *alcohol, aqua, booze, bourbon, cordial, liquor, water.* (sikwe', n.);
√čstq č(=)astq *dig (roots, camas).* (chastq, vi.)
√sps s+čs(=)úps+n *tail.* (schsupsn, n.); ul s+čs(=)úps+n *caudal.* (ul schsupsn (lit.
 pertaining to the tail or hind parts), adj.)
√ščt † š(=)ečt *thumb, any finger.* (shecht, n.)
√mps m(=)ups *anal.* (mups, adj.)
√t'nʔ t'(=)íneʔ *ear.* (t'ine', n.); t'ín+t'(=)eneʔ *ears.* (t'int'ene', n.)
√xʷps xʷ(=)ups *slap (with tail).* (khups (stem), vt.)
√xʷs₂ eʔ xʷ(=)ús *hunt, look for.* (e'khus... (stem). vt, vi.)

---

[34] We have included these entries in the dictionary proper, where we have listed the root as consisting of all segments. By definition they are lexical roots.

APPENDIX C: OTHER AFFIXES AND MORPHEMES

This appendix consists of miscellaneous affixes and morphemes which Nicodemus includes in *Snchitsu'umshtsn*, but which are not lexical roots. We have followed Reichard's classification of exclamations (section 1), nominal and verbal compounds (section 2), and finally other elements and clausal connectives (section 3), and have included Reichard's gloss where possible. We have also included a section on child's speak in Coeur d'Alene (section 4). This appendix is not an exhaustive list, but is instead my attempt to account for entries which do not neatly fit into the main body of the dictionary or the other appendices.

Section 1: Exclamations

The following is a list of exclamations which we have determined are not lexical roots. There are a number of entries which Nicodemus marks with *(excl.)* which do contain lexical roots, and which we have left within the dictionary proper.

ci? ci? *bravo.* (tsi'! (lit. expression of approval), excl.)
c'um' c'um' *cheep.* (ts'u'm! (lit. a faint, shrill chirp, as of a young bird; of a mouse), excl.)
e e *oh my!.* (e!, excl.)
e eyé *boo.* (eye! (expression of contempt or disapproval) the ugly thing, excl.)
el el· *yikes!.* (ellll! (lit. expression of a cold sensation, as a person who falls in ice cold water), excl.)
m'ew m'ew *cat call, meow, meow!.* ('mew!, n, excl.)
twi? twi? *alas!.* (twi'!, excl.)
yo· yo· *Oh, my!.* (yooo!, excl.)
?en ?en· *ouch!.* (ennnn! (expression of pain), excl.); ?ené? *ouch!.* (ene'! (expression of pain), excl.)

Section 2: Nominal Incorporation and Verbal Compounding (see §627)

From Reichard:
The following verbs have occurred in compounded forms, but it is likely that many others have the potentiality of being used in the same way:

ya *yä̞ᵃ, secure game* (§632)
  ya+s+t'mál+t+m-š *killed (He...the buffalo).* (yast'maltmsh, vt.);
  s+m+ya+s+taq+aq+nu=sčínt *coup.* (smyastaqaqnuschint, n.); ya+n+łámqe? *bear (He killed the...), killed (He...the bear).* (yanłamqe', n, vt.); ye+s+młíč *salmon (He got a...).* (yesmlich, n.); ya+s+t'm+ált=mš *buffalo (He killed the...).* (yast'maltmsh, n.)

?epł *äpł, have* (§627)

233

ʔepł *have, own, possess.* (epł, vt.); čn‿ʔpł *have (I...).* (ch'npł, vt.); ʔapł+ʔał+dar=enč *clear, sunny (to be...).* (apł'ałdarench (lit. It has sun), vi.); ʔepł n+q'es+p=ílgʷes+n *antiquary.* (epł nq'espil gwesn (lit. One who has a place of antiquities, one who has a second-hand store), n.); ʔepł+wl+wlím *money (to have...).* (epłwlwlim, vt.); c+mi? ʔepł wl+wlím *used (he...to have money).* (tsmi' epł wlwlim, vi.); ʔapł t'+t'áq'+n *Worley.* (Apł t't'aq'n, n.); ʔepł+t'íš *Waverly, Washington.* (Epłt'ish (lit. It has sugar), n.); ʔep+s+čs+s=úps+n' *Fernwood, Idaho.* (Epschssups'n (lit. It has a little tail), n.); ʔapł+n+qʷa?+qʷel'+n *articulate, verbal.* (apłnqwa'qwe'ln, vi. (lit. He has the power of speech), vi.); ʔapł+n+xec+num'+n *clothier.* (apłnqhetsnu'mn (lit. One who has a clothing store), n.); ʔepł+t+tm'íxʷ *livestock (to have...).* (epłtt'mikhw (lit. H/s has livestock, commonly ref. to animals or birds), vt.); ʔapł+mac'p *beekeeper.* (apłmats'p, n.); ʔapł+ʔétxʷe? *camas (a sweet, edible bulb).* (apł'etkhwe'. baked, n.); ʔepł+n+xelíxʷ+n *dentist.* (epłnqhelikhwn (lit. One who has a place for dental surgery), n.); ʔapł+n+marím+ncut+n *apothecary, pharmacist.* (apłnmarimntsutn (lit. One who has a place for medicines), n.); ʔepł s+ni?+mi?+t=ew'es *concentric.* (epł sni'mi'te'wes (lit. It has a common center), adj.); ʔepł s+n'+n'iw'+t *breezy.* (epł s'n'ni'wt, v. (lit. There is a small wind), adj.); ʔepł n s(=)íkʷe?+n *barkeeper, bartender.* (epł n si kwe'n (lit. One who has a liquor place), n.); ʔepł+č+sún+sun=kʷe? *archipelago.* (epłchsunsunkwe' (lit. It has islands), n.); ʔapł+n+xʷél+xʷl+n *animated (to be...).* (apłnkhwelkhwln (lit. What has life), vi.); ʔepł+xʷé[l]+xʷl+t *debtor* (epłkhwekhwlt (lit. One who owes something to another), n.)

Section 3: Other Elements and Clausal Connectives (see 769-801)

cmí? tsmi'' *used to...., but is not now; had the intention but did not carry it out:* (§787)

cmí? *used (it...to be), was (it...to be).* (tsmi', vi.); cmi? ʔepł wl+wlím *used (he...to have money).* (tsmi' epł wlwlim, vi.); cmi?+u·+čn+xé·s *was (I...fine).* (tsmi'uuchnqheees (lit. I used to be healthy), vi.); cmi? epł+wl+wlím *money (he used to have...).* (tsmi'epł wlwlim, n.)

tel' *literally "from", but taking on idiomatic connotations* (§789)

tel' *from (...the).* (te'l, adv.); tel' t'i?s šíp+ep *a priori.* (te'l t'i's shipep (lit. from what is finished), conj.); tel' hn+gʷis+t *high (from on...).* (te'l hngwist, adv.); tel' n+gʷis+t *above (from...).* (te'l ngwist, adv.); tel' lékʷ+t *afar (from...).* (te'l lekut, adv.); tel' ni?+mi?+t=ew'es *centrifugal.* (te'l ni'mi'te'wes (lit. moving or directed from the center), adj.); łáxʷp tel' hn+lč'+mín+n *prison (He escaped from...).* (łaqhwp te'l hnlch'minn, n.); tel' ci+ʔenís *continue.* (te'l tsi'enis (lit. from there he went on), v.); tel'+ci?+xes+t *better.* (te'ltsi'qhest (lit. Good from that point on), adj.); tel' s+k'ʷ+k'ʷúl'+l' *congenital.* (te'l sk'uk'u'lu'l (lit. It exists from birth), adj.); te[l]' s+gʷel+p *igneous.* (te' sgwelp, adj.); tel' s+en+k'ʷde?=ú(s)=šn *derivative.* (te'l senk'wde'ushn (lit. from the source), n.)

l' † ul' *again.* (u'l, adv.) [?]

uł, hił *There are several connectives,* hił *and* ł, *which at times are interchangeable...Both have the function of emphasizing what follows because the verbs themselves may be used without them.* (§799)
    uł *and, again.* (uł, conj, adv.)
    hił *and.* (hił, conj.)

ne? *nä'ᵃ is a word (element, particle) which performs a great many functions which lend subtlety to a language. Primarily it expresses doubt.* (see §777)
    ne? *maybe, perhaps.* (ne' (stem), adv.); ne?+gʷníxʷ *maybe, perhaps.* (ne'gwnịkhw. it's true, adv.); ne?+m'n'us *maybe so.* (ne"m'nus, adv.)

šum' šum' *then.* (shu'm, conj.) [?]

syuqʷe?ł syuqʷe?ł *as if.* (syuqwe'ł, conj.) [?]

tgʷel' *Cause is expressed in two ways: by tgwäl', that is the reason, with a purposive construction (one of the s- constructions) to express the dependent clause, then ł with the independent clause.* (§802)
    tgʷel' *because, for, since.* (tgwe'l, prep, conj.); tgʷel'+s+tím' *Why?, why.* (tgwe'lsti'm, qu, adv.); tgʷel' s+tim'+ł kʷ+čic+xʷy? *come (Why did you...?).* (tgwe'l sti'mł ku chitskhuy?, vi.)

t'i? *ti", already, surely, absolutely, quite. An emphatic particle used frequently:* (§782)
    t'i? *after.* (t'i', prep.); t'i?+ec+méy *decisive.* (t'i'etsmey, v.); t'i?+ci? *adequate, sufficient.* (t'i'tsi' (lit. That is enough), adj.)

t'u? t'u? *well.* (t'u', adv.) [?]

x̌al x̌al *also, too.* (qhal, adv.); x̌al nek'ʷe? *another.* (qhal nek'we' (lit. also one), n.) [?]

uw' The meaning of this form is unclear, and may actually be a root. We have left it within the normal context of the dictionary under √w'.[35]
    uw'e?+n+t *low (to be very...).* (u'we'nt (stem), v.); uw'e+m'n'=ús *coistrel, knave, bogus, rascal.* (u'we'm'nus (lit. He is good for nothing), n.); uw'+em'n'=ús *he s+mí?+yem worthless (a woman who is...), woman (a...who is worthless).* (u'we'm'nus he smị'yem, adj, n.); úw'e k'ʷ+k'ʷn=iy'e? *awhile.* (ụ'we k'uk'w'nị'ye' (lit. for a short time only), adv.); uw'+ic+qox̌á·?+qʷ?el' *buttonhole.* (u'witsqoqhaaa'qw'e'l (lit. He kept on talking and talking), vt.)

---
[35] See Reichard §387 for possible connection.

Section 4: Child's Speak

√b † bé·beʔ *father (child's word).* (b<u>ee</u>be', n.); bi·+bíʔ *milk bottle.* (biib<u>i</u>' (lit. A child's word for milk), n.)

√d † de·+déʔ *food (a child's word), eating (baby's term for).* (deed<u>e</u>, n, vi.); du·+dú *bug, insect.* (duud<u>u</u> (a child's word), n.)

√hm † s+hem *animal (a child's name for a fierce..., even bug, spider, etc.).* (s-hem, n.)

√m₁ † me+mé· *mama, mother (child's word for...).* (mem<u>ee,</u> n.)

√m₂ † mu *cow.* (mu (children's word), n.)

√nn † ne·né *a child's word for hurt.* (neen<u>e</u>, n.)

√w₁ † we·+wé *water (a child's word for...).* (weew<u>e</u>, n.); we·+wéʔ *drink (a child's word for...).* (weew<u>e</u>, n.)

√w₂ † wa·wáʔ *baby (a child's word for...).* (waaw<u>a</u>', n.)

√y † ye·+yéʔ *grandmother (child's word for maternal...).* (yeey<u>e</u>', n.)

APPENDIX D: LEXICAL BORROWINGS

To cultural anthropologists and linguists alike, borrowings are important in identifying points of contact between two cultures. Word meanings may give clues about the direction of semantic shift as well as identify the originating language. Lexical borrowings also imply that a given item was not present in a culture prior to contact.

We have listed in this appendix a total of 134 lexical borrowings, arranged by donor language. Some borrowings have become a part of the Coeur d'Alene lexicon, and also take inflection and derivation. By our reckoning, the proportion of borrowings from other Salish languages in *Snchitsu'umshtsn* volume I and II is very small (5.2%), compared to borrowings from English and French (93%). Because of the influence of early Francophone trappers and missionaries, French has donated many items, a large percentage of which pertain to the Catholic religion. Spokane-Kalispel-Flathead has donated six entries. Other donor languages include Okanagan (San Poil), the Sahaptin languages Nez Perce and Yakama, and Chinook Jargon, each with one entry. Nicodemus sometimes identifies the donor languages and we have followed his analysis in these cases.

Section 1: English (74 entries/38 words)

√**bc** buc *boots.* (buts, n); ec+búc+buc=šn *boots (to be wearing...).* (etsbutsbutsshn (lit. He is wearing boots), n); s+búc+buc=šn *boot.* (sbutsbutsshn (lit. a borrowed root), n.); s+búc+buc=šn=mš *putting (...on rubber boots).* (sbutsbutsshnmsh, vt.); s+búc+buc=šn=mš *rubber boots (putting on...).* (sbutsbutsshnms, pl.n.)

√**bl** bu·lí *bull.* (buuli, n.)

√**bn** benéne *banana.* (benene, n.)

√**bns** bins *bean.* (bins (l.w. from Engl.), n.)

√**btlym** be·tlyém *Bethlehem.* (beetlyem, n.)

√**cc** s+čn[t]+coc *British, Canada.* (Schntsots. Canada (lit. Indian (or people) of George), adj.); gʷł s+čin[t]+cóc *Angles.* (guł schintsots (lit. King George men, n.); ul s+čin[t]+cóc *Anglican.* (ul schintsots (lit. pertaining to King George's men)., n.); ul s+čen[t]+cóc ha s+qʷʼenpʼ *sunset (Canadian...).* (ul schentsots ha sq'wenp', n.); elu+s+x̌em=ínč e s+čin[t]+coc *Anglophobe.* (elusqheminch e Schntsots, n.)

√**cnmn** cánmn *chinese.* (Tsanmn, n.)

√**csp** ni kʷu꞊cósep *Are you Joseph?* (ni ku Tsosep? (qu.).)

√**cry** √**jly** co·ray/ǰuulay *July.* (tsooray/Juulay, n.)

√**čs** čis *cheese.* (chis, n.); √**pq** u·+péq he čis *cottage cheese.* (uupeq he chis (lit. white cheese), n.)

√**dn** De·nyél *Daniel.* (Deenyel, n.); den *Dan (prop name).* (Den, n.); Di·ní *Denny.* (Diini, n.)

√**dpt** Da·pít *David.* (Daapit, n.)

√**dw** A·+dwa *Edward.* (Aadwa. A Coeur d'Alene chief in the 1800's, n.); pan' a·dwá *She is Mrs. Edward.* (pa'n Aadwa, vi.)

237

√ǰly ǰso·ráy *July.* (Jsooray, n.); s+ǰu·lay=mš *Fourth of July, Independence Day.* (sjuulaymsh, n.); i ǰuláy+[m]š *Independence Day (celebration of).* (Ijulaynsh, n.)

√ǰm mi ǰim *Jim (I am...).* (mi Jim, n); kʷu ǰim *Are you Jim?* (ni ku Jim?(qu.))

√ǰpn ǰe·pni *Japanese.* (jeepni (l.w. from Engl.), n.); ǰe·pní *Japanese.* (Jeepni, n.); ǰ+ǰe·pn'í *little Japanese.* (Jjeep'ni, n.)

√ǰs ǰi·sú. *Jesus.* (Jiisu, n.); **√ʔw** ʔew+t=us+s xʷa ǰisukrí *antichrist.* (ewtuss khwa jisukri (lit. opponent of Jesus Christ), n.)

√ǰssp ǰsúsep *Joseph.* (Jsusep (lit. Chief of Nez Perce). Suusep, n.)

√kml ke·mél *camel.* (keemel, n.)

√kr Kri *Christ.* (Kri, n.); ul Jiso· Krí *Christian.* (ul Jisoo Kri (lit. pertaining to Christ), n.)

√lt hn+li·tíh+n *caddy.* (hnliitihn (lit. a small box-like container for tea), n.)

√mh múh=elxʷ *cowhide.* (muhelkhw (onom. mu-helkhw, moo-jide), n.)

√mnk mo·nki *monkey.* (moonki (l.w. from Engl.), n.); **√x̌y'** x̌ay'+x̌iʔ+t ha mo·nkí *ape, gorilla.* (qha'yqhi't ha moonki. lit. big monkey), n.)

√nys enyés *Agnes.* (Enyes (l.w. from English), n.)

√pčs píčus *peaches.* (pichus, n.); píč=us *peach-face.* (pichus, n.); s+péčos=alqʷ *peach tree.* (spechosalqw, n.); s+péčas=alqʷ *peach tree.* (spechasalqw, n.)

√plms plams *plums.* (plams, n.); pláms=alq[ʷ] *plum tree, prunes.* (plamsalq, n.)

√ps pus *cat.* (pus, n.); p+pus *kitten.* (ppus, n.); p+pús *kitten.* (ppus, n.); pús+pus *cats.* (puspus, n.)

√ptq pa·táq *potato.* (paataq, n.) [?][36]

√ptr a·+potar *apostle.* (aapotar, n.)

√pyl s+paayól=mš *Spanish.* (Spaayolmsh, n.); s+paayol=mš *Mexican.* (Spaayolmsh, n.); a+n+paayól=mš=cn *Spanish (to speak...).* (anpaayolmshtsn, n.)

√slts soltes *armed forces.* (soltes, n.); gʷł soltes *army, brigade, soldiers.* (guł soltes, n.); **√lt** lut soltes *civilian.* (lut soltes (lit. He is not a soldier); soltes=l.w. from English), n.); **√skʷ** ul s(=)ikʷeʔ ha soltes.*blue-jacket.* (ul sikwe'ha soltes (lit. soldier of the sea), n.); **√nk'ʷ** nuk'ʷ+ł+tum' ha sóltes *battalion.* (nuk'włtu'm ha soltes (lit. a unit of soldiers), n.)

√sns s+sén'+sn's *cents, pennies.* (sse'ns'ns, n.); **√ʔpn** ʔu+pen e·sén *dime.* (upeneesen (lit. ten cents), n.)

√sp sip *sheep.* (sip, n.); síp=elx *cape-skin.* (sipelkh. sheepskin, n.); sp=łc'e *elk.* (spiłts'e, n.)

√tmds tmídus *tomato.* (tmidus, n.)

√tmrs tmer'us *ketchup.* (tme'rus (l.w. from Engl. tomatoes), n.); tmérus *catsup, ketchup.* (tmerus (lit. tomatoes. Note the sound of the word), n.)

√tmt timu·tí *Timothy.* (Timuut, n.)

√wlms wlums+mú *Williams (name of).* (Wlumsmu, n.)

√wšn Wašn *administration, bureaucracy, Washington, D.C..* (Washn, n.); lut ul Wášn *apolitical.* (lut ul Washn (lit. not belonging to Wash, D.C.), adj.)

√yž̌p Eyžhíp *Egypt.* (Eyzhip, n)

---

[36] The stress pattern is French, but the article consonant /l/ has not been borrowed with the noun.

√ʔpls ʔepls *apple*. (epls (l.w. from English), n.); s+ʔápls=alqʷ *apple (tree)*. (s'a̱plsalqw, n.); ul+ápel ha s+can+x̌as=ítkʷeʔ+s *apple brandy, apple-jack*. (ula̱pel ha stsanqhasi̱tkwe's (lit. good juice from the apple), n.)

Section 2: French (50 entries/22 words)[37]

√lbč li·béč *bishop*. (liibe̱ch (l.w. from French), n.); **√c'k'ʷ** li·béč he c'uk'ʷ=íčs+is *crosier*. (liibe̱ch he ts'uk'wi̱chsis (lit. a bishop's staff (cane), n.); **√tmxʷ** ul li·béč he tmíxʷ=ul'ms *diocese*. (ul liibe̱ch he tmi̱khu'lms (lit. It is a land or district in which a bishop has authority), n.)

√lbtm₁ lebe·tém-nt-m *baptize, christen*. (lebeetemntm, vt.); lebe·tém+m *baptize, (he...)*. (lebeete̱mm (l.w. from French), v.); s+lebeetém+n *christening*. (slebeete̱mn (lit. The Christian sacrament of baptism), n.)

√lbtm₂ lebu·tem *bottle, can, flask*. (lebuutem (from French, le bouteile), n.); leb+lebu·tém *bottles*. (leblebuute̱m, pl.n.); **√kʷn** kʷan+ł+lebu·tém *bottle (h/s took a...)*. (kwanłlebuutem, n.)

√lčm lče·mí *maize*. (lcheemi̱. Indian corn, n.)

√lkp lka·pí *coffee*. (lkaapi (l.w. from French), n.); hn+lka·pí+hn *coffeepot*. (hnlkaapi̱hn. (lit. a pot for brewing or serving coffee), n.)

√lks loko·só *pig*. (lokooso̱ (l.w. from French), n.); luko·só *bristle*. (lukooso̱ (lit. hair of a pig), n.); **√tmxʷ** qel'+tmxʷ+lokooso *boar*. (qe'ltmkhwlokooso. (lit. male pig), n.)

√lmn la·mná *syrup, honey*. (laamn̠a, n)

√lpl li·púl *chicken, hen*. (liipu̱l (l.w. from French, used mostly by the Kalispel), n.)

√lpp ul la pap *apostolic*. (ul la Pap (lit. belonging to the Pope), adj.)

√lpt † l'+l'pót *chalice, cup, dipper, glass*. (l'l'po̱t. (cup, chalice), n.); ∥ č'+l'+l'pót=c'eʔ *pickled, preserved, canned*. (ch'l'l'po̱tts'e' (lit. It is preserved in a container), adj.); č+l'+l'pót=c'eʔ *amphora*. (ch'l'lpo̱tts'e', n.); č+l'+l'pot=c'eʔ *can, jar*. (ch'l'lpotts'e', n.); č+l'+l'pót=ceʔ+eʔ *jar*. (ch'l'lpottse'e', n.); hn+č+l'+l'pót=c'eʔ+n *cannery*. (hnch'l'lpotts'e'n. (lit. cupping around; place where food is canned), n.); hn+l'+l'póteʔ+n *cupboard*. (hn'l'lpoten'. (lit. a closet for holding cups), n.); § kʷan+ł+l'+l'pot *cup (h/s took a...)*. (kwanł'l'lpot, n.); nuk'ʷ+ł+l'+l'pót *cupful*. (nuk'wł'l'lpo̱t (lit. just one cup (of content)), n.)

√lpw li·pwé *pea(s)*. (liipwe̱ (l.w. from French), n.)

√lswp le·swíp *Jew*. (Leeswi̱p, n.); **√č's** **√tmn** č's+č's+tmen+ł le·swíp *anti-Semite*. (ch'sch'stmen leeswi̱p, n.)

√lt li·tí *tea*. (liiti̱ (l.w. from French), n.); hn+li·tíh+n *caddy*. (hnliiti̱hn (lit. a small box-like container for tea), n.)

√łčp łčíp *bucket*. (łchi̱p, n.)

√mr₂ § lim-t-š ma·rí *Ave Maria, Hail Mary!*. (Limtsh Maari! (lit. Rejoice, Mary!), excl.); sant ma·ri *Holy Mary, Virgin Mary, Mary, Saint Mary.* (Sant Maari (l.w. from French), n.)

√mšl † mšél *Michael.* (Mshel (l.w. from French), n.)

√nrs nors *barley.* (nors, n.)

√nš anš *angel, cherub.* (ansh (l.w. from French), n.)

√prsn † parsón *person.* (parson, n.); § t+čí?łes parsón *Blessed Trinity.* (Tchi'łes Parson (lit. three persons), n.)

√skʷ sikʷe? tel' kəlón *cologne.* (sikwe' te'l Cologne (lit. water from Cologne, n.)

√snt † sant ma·ri *Virgin Mary, Mary, Saint Mary, Holy Mary.* (Sant Maari (l.w. from French), n.)

√šr šar *Charles.* (Shar, n.)

Section 3: Flathead-Kalispel-Spokane (6 entries)

√č'l' hn+č'el'e? *coyote.* (hnch'e'le (Kalispel), n.); hn+č'+č'a·l'í *Little Coyote, a medicine man.* (Hnch'ch'aa'li, n.)

√l? lo?+lo?+ótm *valley.* (lo'lo'otm (a Spokane word), n.)

√ply s+pílye *coyote (Spokane).* (spilye, n.)

√q's₁ q'as+íp *It is a long time (Spokane).* (q'asip, v.)

√q'y q'ey=ú?s-nt-m *disbelieved (he was...).* (q'eyu'snt, vi.)

√smš su·méš *power (Spokane).* (suumesh, n.)

√tp √x̌s tap+s+x̌es+t *is (It...not good).* (tapsqhest (Spokane), vi.)

Section 4: Other Languages

San Poil (Okanagan)
√smš su·míx *power (San Poil).* (suumikh, n.)

Nez Perce
√qm's qem'es *camas (baked...).* (qe'mes. (Nez Perce word), n.)

Yakama
√pš púše *paternal grandfather.* (pushe (Yakima), n.)

Chinook Jargon
√kl √plč káltes pa·láč *bonus (Chinook jargon).* (kaltes paałach, n.)

REFERENCES

Czaykowska-Higgins and Kinkade, M. Dale, eds. 1998. *Salish Languages and Linguistics: Theoretical and Descriptive Perspectives*. Berlin: Morton De Gruyter.

Doak, Ivy 1997. *Coeur d'Alene Grammatical Relations*. Ph.D. dissertation, University of Texas at Austin.

Greene-Wood, Becky 2004. *An Edition of Snchitsu'umshtsn: Volume I: A Root Dictionary*. MA thesis, University of Montana.

Kuipers, Aert H. 2002. *Salish Etymological Dictionary. University of Montana Occasional Papers in Linguistics* No. 16. Missoula.

Lyon, John 2005. *An Edition of Snchitsu'umshtsn: Volume II: A Root Dictionary*. MA thesis, University of Montana.

Mattina, Anthony 2005. "Okanagan and Salishan Languages." *Encyclopedia of Linguistics*. Ed. Philipp Strazny. New York: Routledge. Pp. 767-771.

Nicodemus, Lawrence 1975. *Snchitsu'umshtsn: Coeur d'Alene-English Dictionary: Volumes I and II*. Spokane: University Press.

Noonan, Michael 1997. "Inverted Roots in Salish." *International Journal of American Linguistics* 63:475-515. University of Chicago Press.

Reichard, Gladys A. 1938. "Coeur d'Alene." In Franz Boas (ed.), *Handbook of American Indian Languages vol 3*. Glückstadt, Germany. J.J. Augustin, Inc. and New York: Columbia University Press. Pp. 517-707.

Teit, James.1930. *Salishan tribes of the Western Plateau*. 45th Annual Report of the Bureau of American Ethnology, 1927-1928, pp.23-396. Franz Boas, ed. US Govt Printing Office.

PUBLICATIONS LISTING LAWRENCE NICODEMUS AS A MAJOR CONTRIBUTOR

Brinkman, Raymond. 2003. *Etsmeystkhw khwe Snwiyepmshtsn,* 'You know how to talk like a Whiteman.' Ph.D. dissertation. The University of Chicago.

Doak, Ivy G. 1997. Coeur d'Alene grammatical relations. Unpublished Ph.D. dissertation. University of Texas at Austin.

Johnson, Robert Erik. 1975. The role of phonetic detail in Coeur d' Alene phonology. Ph.D. dissertation. Washington State University.

Nicodemus, Lawrence. 1975. *Snchitsu'umshtsn: the Coeur d'Alene language.* Textbook (Albuquerque, NM: Southwest Research Associates, Inc.) 2 vol. dictionary (Spokane, WA: University Press), and 6 audio cassettes.

Nicodemus, Lawrence, Reva Hess, Jill Maria Wagner, Wanda Matt, Gary Sobbing, and Dianne Allen. 2000. *Snchitsu'umshtsn.* Workbooks in two volumes and a Reference book. Curriculum developed for high school classes in the *Coeur d'Alene* language. Printed by Omni Graphics Center, Coeur d'Alene, ID. Coeur d'Alene Tribe.

Palmer, Gary B. 1988. The language and culture approach in the Coeur d' Alene language preservation project. *Human Organization.* 47(4):307-317.

Palmer, Gary B., and Lawrence Nicodemus. 1985. "Coeur d' Alene Exceptions to Proposed Universals of Anatomical Nomenclature. *American Ethnologist.* 12(2):341-359.

Palmer, Gary B., Lawrence Nicodemus, and Thomas E. Connolly, S.J. 1987a. *Khwi' Khwe Guł Schitsu' umsh, These are the Coeur d' Alene People: A book of Coeur d' Alene Personal Names.* Department of Anthropology and Ethnic Studies. University of Nevada, Las Vegas.

Palmer, Gary B., Lawrence Nicodemus, and Lavina Felsman. 1987b. *Khwi' Khwe Hntmikhw 'lumkhw: This is my Land: A Workbook in Coeur d' Alene Indian Geography.* Department of Anthropology and Ethnic Studies. University of Nevada, Las Vegas.

Reichard, Gladys A. circa 1935. *Coeur d'Alene.* Unidentified informant [Lawrence Nicodemus] Audiotape 85-550-F. Copy of EC 10" 4200. Indiana University Archives of Traditional Music. [Includes three texts and a song fragment]

— 1938. "Coeur d'Alene." In Franz Boas (ed.), *Handbook of American Indian Languages vol 3.* Gliickstadt, Germany. J.J. Augustin, Inc. and New York: Columbia University Press. Pp. 517-707.

— 1939. Stem-list of the Coeur d' Alene language. *International Journal of American Linguistics* 10:92-108.

— 1947. *An analysis of Coeur d' Alene Indian myths.* Memoirs of the American Folklore Society, no. 41. (Reprinted: Krauss Reprint Co., New York, 1969.) Note: this volume is dedicated, "To Julia and Lawrence."

Sloat, Clarence. 1966. *Phonological redundancy rules in Coeur d' Alene.* Ph. D. dissertation. University of Washington.

Wagner, Jill Maria. 1997. *Language, power, and ethnicity on the Coeur d'Alene Reservation.* Ph.D. Dissertation. Washington State University.